My Last Last Name Is
GRACE

A Novel Based on My Memoir

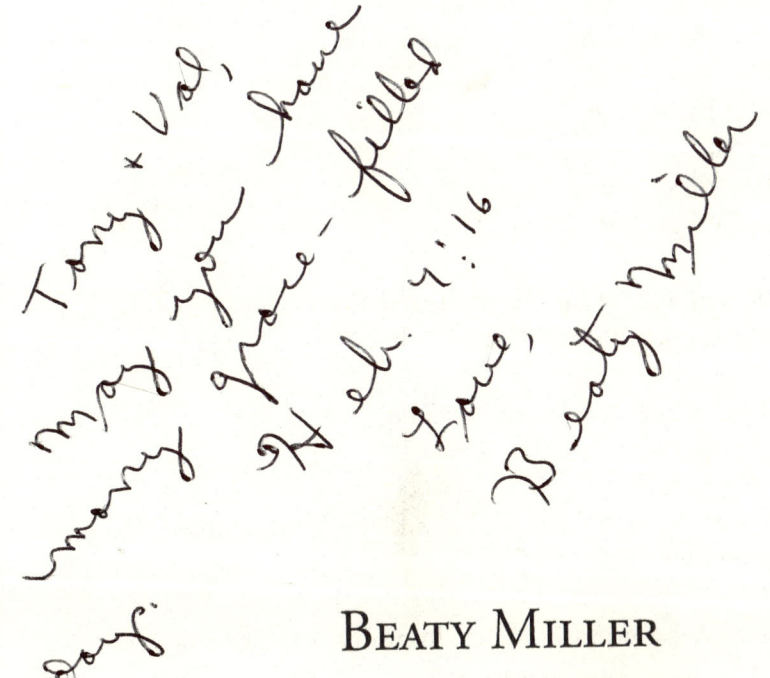

Beaty Miller

ISBN 978-1-64114-837-5 (paperback)
ISBN 978-1-64114-838-2 (digital)

Copyright © 2018 by Beaty Miller

All rights reserved. No part of this publication may be reproduced, distributed, or transmitted in any form or by any means, including photocopying, recording, or other electronic or mechanical methods without the prior written permission of the publisher. For permission requests, solicit the publisher via the address below.

Christian Faith Publishing, Inc.
832 Park Avenue
Meadville, PA 16335
www.christianfaithpublishing.com

All Scripture quoted from New International Version (NIV) (Zondervan Corporation, 1990) unless otherwise indicated

A few Scriptures are quoted from King James Version (KJV) (Zondervan Corporation, 1987)

A few Scriptures are quoted from New Living Translation (NLT) (Tyndale House Publishers, 2007)

Some names, places, addresses, dates, locations and timelines have been changed to fictionalize into a novel

Printed in the United States of America

This book is dedicated to my wonderful, loving husband, Mike, and my three awesome children, Steph, Darrin and Rochelle and my fantastic seven grandchildren. May you know the heights of God's love and grace, the depths of His mercy and the scope of His salvation. I pray God's purpose in your life exceeds your expectations.

Acknowledgments

Thanks to all my supportive friends and neighbors, Bible study members, BSF class members, and family who have heard about this book in progress for over three years.... yes, it has finally birthed! Many thanks go out to Lee Miller, my Creative Writing teacher, who advised me on many points and kept encouraging me along the way. Kay Carver's insight and help has proven beneficial. May other Creative Writing participants experience the thrill of writing their memoirs and keep plugging away until their final page is written.

Contents

Chapter 1	My Forgotten Seventh Birthday	9
Chapter 2	My Memorable Horse and Buggy Ride	19
Chapter 3	The Luxury of Cars and Radios	31
Chapter 4	Folklore, Witchcraft, and Satan	40
Chapter 5	Rumspringa and Shunning	50
Chapter 6	Aunt Lucy's Life-Changing Decision	64
Chapter 7	"Where You See, I Have Done Good…"	77
Chapter 8	Bugsy and Aunt Joyce	91
Chapter 9	Learning to Sing Alto in Second Grade	100
Chapter 10	My Mennonite Heritage	107
Chapter 11	My Reoccurring Frightful Dream	130
Chapter 12	From Country Living to In-Town Living	140
Chapter 13	*Mauh De Dara Ztu!* (Make the Door Shut!)	156
Chapter 14	Cousin Rachel Stricken with Polio	169
Chapter 15	Moving to Noodle Doosie	176
Chapter 16	Joining Church and Wearing a Head Covering	189
Chapter 17	Baptism, Council Meeting, Communion, and Foot Washing	202
Chapter 18	My 1967 Brag Book	211
Chapter 19	Needle and Thread and Cutout Letters	221
Chapter 20	Have T-shirts Gone Out of Style Yet?	237
Chapter 21	First to Graduate in My Family	241
Chapter 22	"Boys Have Needs"	262
Chapter 23	Planning a Wedding at Eighteen	277
Chapter 24	Teaching in a Two-Room Parochial School	290
Chapter 25	A Replica of Me Running Around in Heaven?	307
Chapter 26	One of My Most Sacred Moments	312
Chapter 27	My Only Son, the Army Officer	325

Chapter 28	My Best Ever Christmas Present	344
Chapter 29	Ironing with a Twist	352
Chapter 30	If She Can Wear Mary Kay	355
Chapter 31	Leanne's Bargain Boutique	364
Chapter 32	From Dairy Farm to Poultry Farm	369
Chapter 33	The Agony of Being Destoned	374
Chapter 34	"Must It Be a Cruise?"	383
Chapter 35	My Dirty Laundry Flapping in the Wind	391
Chapter 36	Against Marriage to Your Father	395
Chapter 37	"Grandpa Said I Should Hate You"	403
Chapter 38	Sea of Black	412
Chapter 39	Heart-to-Heart Letters	421
Chapter 40	I Said "I Do" But Then I Don't	432
Chapter 41	Turning Forty During Nursing School	443
Chapter 42	"Summr" Meets "Pa_Great Guy"	453
Chapter 43	Divorce Number Two	461
Chapter 44	I Do Love You, But I Will Not Remarry	469
Chapter 45	Our Sedona Wedding	477
Chapter 46	One Church Hurt Me, Another Healed Me	489
Chapter 47	Miracle of the Portable Potty	502
Chapter 48	How September 11 Affected Me	521
Chapter 49	Having My Wild Eyelashes Pulled	532
Chapter 50	The Cost of Unhappy Marriages	536
Chapter 51	Steph and Eric's Journey	550
Chapter 52	Rochelle and Carl's Journey	570
Chapter 53	Semper Fi Power Wash Inc.	593
Chapter 54	"Dearest Daddy"	600
Chapter 55	Daddy's Death	608
Chapter 56	Unconditional Love from Grandchildren	629
Chapter 57	What the Locusts Have Destroyed Has Been Redeemed	656
Chapter 58	Our First Mission Trip to Mexico	666
Chapter 59	A Vacation That Changed Our Lives	675
Chapter 60	It Is Only Stuff	690
Chapter 61	Bald Eagles Flying Overhead	701
Chapter 62	Touching the Hem of His Garment	721
Chapter 63	The Best, Mature Me Dancing with Jesus	734

Chapter 1

My Forgotten Seventh Birthday

My favorite verse: "Let us then approach the throne of grace with confidence, so that we may receive mercy and find grace to help us in our time of need"
—Hebrews 4:16

The author, as the baby, and her six older siblings

FACING THE CLEAN BLACKBOARD, SWEET Mrs. Weinhold, with white chalk in hand, was poised ready to write the date and short weather

report. Her small-rose brown print cotton dress hung slightly higher in front exposing half of her knees, as a thin dark-brown belt rested slightly above her rotund waist.
Monday, November 8, 1959, partly cloudy

Wait! November 8? My seventh birthday was yesterday, and nobody in my family, including me, remembered it?

After glancing at the blackboard and mumbling "Good morning, Mrs. Weinhold," I slowly strolled back to my desk and sat down, slumping in a reflection of my disappointment. My mind was still numb as I opened up my wooden desk lid and pulled out my second-grade book *Sally Finds Friends…Fun with Dick and Jane* to prepare for my reading class.

The school bell rang, as it always did, loud and expected, signaling students to be seated and ready for Bible reading, a short prayer, and a pledge of allegiance to the flag. Glancing over at my friend, Martha, with tears welling up inside me, I managed to blurt out, "My birthday was yesterday. I turned seven, but nobody said happy birthday to me. I didn't know it was the seventh."

"Well, I am saying happy birthday to you now, Leanne," Martha said with big blue eyes the same hue as her buttoned-down sweater. "Then at recess, I'll even sing 'Happy Birthday' to you." Confident she cured my sadness, Martha also got her reading book from her desk.

With a broken heart that made for heaviness in my chest, I gave a weak smile and my attention to Mrs. Weinhold, who was pulling out the small devotional and roll call log out of her top desk drawer, preparing to start the day. "Good Morning, class." She smiled as she put on up her black reading glasses and glanced around the room. "Let's take roll call."

Mrs. Weinhold's familiar voice echoed in the back of my brain as she called out each of my classmates' names, while my mind wandered back to yesterday's events in my Mennonite, Lancaster County, Pennsylvania, home. Mom is always so busy cooking and taking care of us kids. She didn't realize the date while bustling to get us all out the door to go to church and all. Surely, she would have said "Happy

Birthday" to me? But Daddy or none of my seven brothers and sisters remembered either?

But, I'll start from the beginning to give some background.

My birth was needed to secure a fourth player for my frequent card-playing family. At any given point, including Daddy as one of the four players, either one or two card tables of four were now filled. With no television, playing cards was our entertainment, and we loved a good competition. Following behind five brothers and one sister, I was child number seven born into a Mennonite family of Anabaptist roots to Aaron and Elizabeth (Fisher) Martin. Anabaptist is a Protestant sect that arose in the sixteenth century advocating for the baptism and church membership of adult believers only, nonresistance, and the separation of church and state.

On the outskirts of New Holland, Pennsylvania, GreenBank is a small rural area in the Garden Spot school district in Northern Lancaster County, where I was born. In 1727, my ancestors stepped on Philadelphia soil after disembarking off the ship *Molly*. The Queen had given her blessing for my relatives to leave Europe. The village founders, a mixture of German, English, and Welsh Quakers, Episcopalians, a few Swiss-German Mennonites, and some Scotch-Irish Presbyterians, were fleeing religious persecution.

A German, John Diffenderfer of Heidelberg, settled New Holland. A distant grandfather, David Martin, purchased eighty-nine acres of farming land in the area. Grasping the same life-and-death urgency, he toiled the land with the intention to savor his farming livelihood from the Old World. Two sons each inherited a farm and raised wheat, barley, oats, and rye. In the 1880s, one barn tragically burned down. Great-grandpa Joseph Martin rebuilt it and later sold his farm when he retired. My ancestors' hard work paid off. Today, the area is appropriately named "Garden Spot" defined as "a well-cultivated or an especially fertile region." Philadelphia is sixty miles to the east, while Baltimore is ninety miles to the south, and Harrisburg is forty miles to the northwest. According to the Lancaster County's

Visitor Bureau in 2014, more than eight million tourists visited beautiful Lancaster County!

One of several rural locations, GreenBank, true to its name, consists of many picturesque neighboring patchwork Amish farms dotting the landscape for miles. Today, radio and TV stations, the tourist industry and realtors promote and advertise for one and all to visit or relocate to this beautiful, productive agricultural Garden Spot area. There is still an elementary school named GreenBank.

Typical of Mom, she gave birth to me at home with the assistance of Dr. Martin, a physician who continued to make house calls. I was born on November 7, 1952, sharing the same birthday with Billy Graham, in the late fall when local farm fields were plentiful with baled, square-shaped corn fodder (silage-type feed for livestock). I had dark hair, and eventually as I grew up, became dark-complexioned, resembling relatives on both Daddy's and Mom's sides of the family. I remember asking my mother the typical questions—what time of day I was born, my weight and height, but Mom didn't remember.

In total, my parents, Aaron and Elizabeth, had nine kids; my baby brother, Douglas (Doug), was born as an early menopausal baby when Mom was forty-two, ten years behind my youngest sister, Lorna. By age thirty-two, my mom had given birth to eight children and had two miscarriages.

Plenty of information has been written about birth order of a "middle" child in the pecking order of a family. Prior to my youngest brother's birth (child number nine), I always thought of our family as two units of four kids: the first set consisting of my four older brothers, and the second set of four kids consisting of the three girls, with my brother sandwiched in-between my sister and me.

Years later, psychologist Dr. Kevin Leman was a guest speaker at my former church. I learned through his lecture that a middle child may receive less attention, feels left out, is less of a perfectionist, but more of a people-pleaser, somewhat rebellious, thrives on friendships, has a large social circle, is a peacemaker, and a fixer, which was confirmed many times later during my annual job reviews. One expert has gone to the extent to say, "When you (middle child) actually accomplish something, nobody cares."

My personality was pretty much scripted, as experts predicted. Out of the brood of nine, no one had any exceptional gifts, a reason to stand out, or deep individuality. If asked, except perhaps for the youngest, Doug, I am sure any of the other eight would answer: "We were just another cookie in the cookie jar." As nondescript as a plain Amish doll, which is faceless and without curves, we were simply the sum of the whole of "us kids."

You can imagine how spoiled my older sister Lenora was after being born behind four brothers. Mom was so happy when my older sister was born that she kept her beside her in bed all night long the night of her birth. She wouldn't let anyone take the baby from her. By the time I came along, another baby sister wasn't so novel.

Daddy suggested they name me after a friend, and Mom agreed. Thus, my official name became Leanne Rose Martin. As it played out, the three girls' names all start with the letter L: Lenora Arlene, Leanne Rose, and Lorna Sue.

When Mom called me by my full name, she was agitated and usually at her wit's end. Realizing a calm request or simply yelling at me to do something was ineffective, Mom resorted to her use-of-full-name yell. To get my attention as a last-ditch effort and to give me the third chance to obey, she yelled louder, "*Leanne Rose*, get in here *now* and do the dishes!" That got my attention, as I knew the use of the belt to my backside followed her using my full name if I didn't obey and comply with her command.

My brother Matthew (Matt), one and a half years older than me and my sister Lenora, who was about three years older, engaged in some pretty harrowing childhood fights. I can only imagine the ugly early childhood fights that ensued amongst my four older brothers. Perhaps due to my younger sister being the baby of the family for ten years and realizing punishments could be more severe, I don't recall having as many squabbles with her as I did with Lenora and Matt.

Typical childhood noise and fights were expected, but there was one house rule—we were not allowed to hit each other. We overcompensated by using our weapon of choice: a mouth. Our parents tried to make it clear that they were the parents, and they doled out punishments, including hitting and spanking. Besides using the belt, a snap from a dishcloth, a twig or switch from a tree in the yard was as a good belt substitute (especially if the disobedience occurred outside), or simply a hand slap was used with purpose and expected behavior improvement. That didn't stop us from punching and slapping each other when our parents weren't around. The frequent flying of rude, hurtful words was our most-used assault. Teasing of some kind was a nearly daily occurrence as we each wanted to be heard and gave our two cents in this noisy family of eleven. Hurts came and went as they were passed around. Sometimes, I was the giver; other times the recipient. Come to think of it, I don't remember ever my parents teaching me to say "I'm sorry" to my siblings.

Teasing topics included references to a sibling being adopted "because you are just too weird to be a part of the Martin clan" or a facial feature, ears or nose would do. Somehow, it proved in our feeble minds, he or she could not possibly be an actual blood relative. When feeling like queen over the siblings for the day, or at least for that hour, I sometimes questioned Mom, "Since he (or she) is 'adopted', you love me the most, right?" Or I'd question her about the local bum's involvement, "Maynard is their dad, right?" On the days I was not winning too many fights, I recall asking Mom, "Why did you have to have so many kids? Couldn't you have done without some of us?"

Mom always appropriately answered, "No. God gave us all of you, and we love you all the same. Besides, who would you want to do without?" My response depended on which sibling I needed to get one up on at the time!

From my birth to one or two years old, we lived on a small rental "farmette" in GreenBank, where Daddy raised crops in the fertile farmland and tended a herd of steer. My older siblings simply walked across the street to GreenBank Elementary School. Mom recalled the time I toddled over to the door of the landlady, who lived on the other side of our two-family farmhouse, and knocked on her door, saying, "Nedna (Edna), let me in." She was a kind woman who provoked feelings of friendship and security. Besides Mom, this was the first relationship of an influential woman in my life.

During the Korean War, Anabaptist Mennonite young boys were exempted from armed services as conscientious objectors, believing in nonresistance to the enemy. Youth who were farmers received deferments because they were needed to sustain food and grain production stateside. The landlady's son qualified for such a deferment, and we had to move to allow him to do the farming on the homestead. To accommodate our growing family, we moved to Churchtown into a larger house on another farmette rental property about ten miles away but still in the middle of Amish country.

One day, Daddy brought Mom and the newest Martin addition home from Lancaster Osteopathic Hospital. I vaguely remember standing on the middle "hump" of the car on the back seat floorboard (this was before seat belt laws). I was puzzled and confused as I looked over my mom's shoulder. Why was she holding this small baby (my younger sister, Lorna) in her lap? I wondered why I was not the one sitting in Mom's lap, which was my usual arrangement. I stood quietly and stared.

Unless you were the baby sitting on Mom's lap, your seating arrangement in the family car when Daddy was behind the wheel, was either between Mom and Daddy in the middle of the front seat or in the back seat with other brothers and sisters. Over the years, many heated discussions derived from who deserved to be in the coveted middle front seat where you were less crowded and had a better view out the front windshield. The winner was always Mom or Daddy's decision. I'm sure that when they chose not to pick the winner of the "seating battle," the kid who won was the one who was either the strongest, most vocal, most behaved for the day, or the most convincing to Mom or Daddy at that time.

But back to the fact nobody remembered my birthday yesterday!

With my two dark-brown pigtails bouncing off my back, I ran into the kitchen, as the school bus pulled away from the front of our two-story duplex. Of course, Matt and Lenora reached the porch first. Mom faced the door and stood at the table, looking fresh in spite of it being midday. She looked up from her task of folding laundry. Piles of folded clothes of each family member were neatly stacked, some higher than others. A stack of folded towels about to tumble over and washcloths were in front of her. A worn oval straw-like woven laundry basket already emptied rested at her feet. I placed my school books on a cleared-off spot on the faded green oilcloth-covered kitchen table. As I fought back tears, I said in a sad voice, "Mom, my birthday was yesterday. We all forgot."

Mom continued to fold clothes and chuckled slightly. "Yes, I guess it was the seventh. Your seventh birthday, huh?" She changed the subject. "Do you remember the big snowstorm that we had on your fifth birthday when we got the new chest freezer delivered? That was some storm! After the roads were plowed, the snow piles were higher than Daddy's car. Today it is a beautiful fall day, so different from back then. Oh, well. Hopefully, we'll remember your birthday next year." She finished folding the last faded worn towel, added it to the top of the pile, and handed me my stack of clothing. "Here, put this away."

About five-foot two-inches tall, slightly overweight with nearly black hair and brown eyes, Mom was attractive with a shapely figure. Plus, she was a smart woman. Around five o'clock (before Daddy was expected home from work), Mom would look in the wall mirror and assess her appearance. She had worked hard all day gardening, cleaning, or doing laundry. Her dress would become somewhat soiled or her hair needed a little touch-up with the comb. Sometimes, Mom would simply freshen up and recomb the front of her hair and reapply her head covering. She would change her dress entirely if she thought it was too dirty for Daddy to see. Nicely dressed female secretaries worked in the business office where Daddy was employed. Even though he was a truck driver, he had opportunities to go into the office. She wasn't taking any chances on what would be the first thing Daddy would see when he came home each night. Kissing him as soon as he walked in the door, she was confident she could hold a candle up against any one of them!

Mom walked over to the kitchen wall mirror and checked her appearance. She used her fingers to fix the small waves that rested on both sides of her middle part. Mom removed the two small straight pins from the front of her white head covering and put them in her mouth and used her front teeth as a pincushion. She removed the covering and placed it carefully upside down on the edge of the sink. Then she used her hand to sweep any loose hair strands (sometimes with wet fingers) from the back of her head that might have fallen out of her bob and tucked them under it. She then carefully removed the straight pins from her mouth to pin her covering back on her head. Mom ran her hands over her dress bodice and her ample breasts, looked down at the dress's skirt, and determined if her dress was clean enough for Daddy.

Is it any wonder this cookie had her birthday forgotten by her family? I struggled to convince myself to stop any tears and forget about it. I opened up the door to the bedroom I shared with Lorna, who was sitting on the floor playing dress-up doll. Her stack of clothing, still on her side of the bed, hadn't yet found its home in her drawer. As I put away my undershirts, panties, slips, and colored knee-high socks in their proper place, I said sadly, "Nobody remembered my birthday yesterday."

Almost four-year-old Lorna was easily recognized as my sister and Mom's daughter with the same brown hair and eyes sucked in a quick breath. "Oh, happy birthday."

More disappointments and hurts peppered my life's journey; some felt by me, some caused by me. Life is not a trek for the faint of heart. As we fight our battles, what would it look like for us at our journeys' ends to feel completely whole, healed, and…at home? Our path may require that we make hunkered-down choices while wearing combat boots. I've surely stepped on too many hidden land mines marked "Me." The consequences were devastating and difficult for me to realize I would need to sit in the results. Most times, I fought fiercely. My journey included taking crossroads I never predicted I would select and life goals I never dreamt I would achieve. There was a time I could not trust myself. When weary, I could only walk, stop, and breathe. Eventually, I realized nothing would work until I learned to trust in God's grace. As comforting as my mother's quilts, grace will beckon me through my last and final front door of home.

But until then…hold on…

Thought of the Day

Grace is bestowed by saying "I'm sorry" when I could be half-right, to keep peace, or to move beyond a stalemate.

Chapter 2

My Memorable Horse and Buggy Ride

> So that, just as sin reigned in death, so also grace
> might reign through righteousness to bring
> eternal life through Jesus Christ our Lord.
> —Romans 5:21

Paternal grandparents' "Pike" Old Order Mennonite Church

HOW TO DESCRIBE DADDY? IN my young child's eyes, he was the head of our household, the main breadwinner, a hard worker, and provider for our family—facts he was so proud of. We knew mealtimes could not start until after "grace." Daddy directed us in a silent prayer.

After sitting down at the head of the table, Daddy simply bowed his head, a cue to the rest of his family; it was time for us to do the same. You knew the prayer was over when Daddy inhaled; his signal we could lift our heads and open our eyes. While eating, he rested his left hand on the edge of the table while forking his food items with his right hand. He, somewhat nosily, drank his water. Though at times, I think he embellished it just to be funny.

Mealtime was mostly a happy time of lively conversation of teasing and joking between us kids. If we got too rowdy, a look from Daddy was enough to straighten us out. We pushed the limits pretty far. I do not remember any one getting a spanking for misbehaving at the table. But I am sure Daddy threatened when someone crossed the line. In other words, Mom and Daddy put up with a lot of bickering, pinching, or giggling among their misbehaving kids, even during prayers at times.

I don't remember anyone talking at the supper table about what went on at school that day or about a problem to be solved. Receiving school report cards were mentioned to Daddy, especially if you wanted to brag about it. After all, getting Daddy's approval was always being sought. More times than not, conversations around the dinner table were most likely a continuation of the teasing that occurred prior to being called to the table. Siblings often used it as an opportunity to try to get someone in trouble. Daddy was definitely the one who spoke the least. Mom shared what she did that day, but the muffled conversation we heard behind their bedroom door each night made me believe their sharing about their day's activities occurred when we kids were not within earshot.

My earliest memory of spending time alone with Daddy occurred when I was about five years old. While living on the farmette, Daddy worked full-time driving a truck and also raised steers and grew tobacco and field corn. One hot summer night after supper, he stood up, grabbed a toothpick from the container in the cupboard, and headed for the kitchen screen door. As the screen door squeaked behind him, he noticed I was trailing him. "I'm going across the road to check on the progress of the corn crop." Saying nothing, I followed him down off the badly needed-painted wooden porch and walked across our small front yard. My dirty bare feet felt the somewhat cool grass, then the hot sticky macadam road, ending with the semisoft ground, as we reached the edge of the cornfield.

Daddy started walking down a long row, which consisted of cornstalks taller than him, who stood about five-feet seven-inches tall. Most cornstalks held about four cobs. Sometimes, Daddy tore back the husk partway and checked out the color and size of the corn kernels. After walking past about a dozen or so more stalks, while swatting at a bumblebee buzzing around his head, he became suddenly still. "Do you hear it? Listen, if you are quiet enough, you can hear the corn grow." Hearing corn tassels moving in the slight wind, I leaned in and agreed. Pleased with his assessment, he cut across the next row and headed back to the house. I had to hurry to keep up with his stride, as I tried to walk in his dusty shoeprints. He did not ask to hold my hand to walk beside him nor make any further conversation with me.

Once back in the house, he proceeded to follow his evening weeknight ritual. Daddy faithfully listened to the state's daily weather forecast broadcast from State College. Because of his various responsibilities of driving truck and raising crops over the years, Daddy faithfully tuned in. You could set your clock to Daddy's turning on the radio (since we did not have a TV) after supper to hear updates on the local weather conditions. Static caused the announcer's voice to be unclear many times.

I have no other childhood memory of any other one-on-one time alone with my daddy, albeit a short one at that. Naïve youngsters do not miss what they do not have. One could only assume my horse and buggy Plain "Wenger" Mennonite grandparents did not show their children open displays of affection or be generous with "I love yous" because Daddy didn't show us.

Daddy, the sixth child and third son, was born on September 19, 1923, to parents, Jacob and Elsie (Weaver) Martin, who resided on a farm in Hahnstown, near Martindale in Lancaster County, Pennsylvania. Jacob and Elsie had eight children who survived infancy: five boys and three girls. Daddy had blond hair, hazel eyes, and was light complexioned, the opposite of Mom. Daddy only started school at the age of seven when his family moved to a farm that Grandpa Martin had purchased. Fryville School was within walking distance. However, four older siblings had already finished eighth grade by the time Daddy was enrolled in first grade.

Living "plainly" without modern conveniences, "Wenger" Mennonite homes had no running water, electricity, bathrooms, or telephones. Lighting was provided by either kerosene lamps that sat on a tabletop or by lanterns with handles that, at times, were carried from room to room, as needed. Lanterns hung on a hook from the ceiling to be the most effective. As the family grew, and more rooms required lighting for additional family members, more kerosene lamps were added. They no longer were the lighting source for several rooms but remained stationary in each room.

When I was about six years old, our lively supper conversation one summer evening was about going to our mountain cabin, called Clay Mine Camp in northern Lycoming County, about a four-hour-drive away. Our table seating consisted of two seven-foot-long wooden benches for our brood. Two handcrafted chairs for Mom and Daddy sat at both ends of the table. Starting with Aaron Jr. to Daddy's right, Elvin, Marlin, and Mervin in birth order, filled the one bench. The seating was the opposite on Mom's right. The youngest, Lorna, once she graduated out of the red plastic high chair, sat next to her. I, Matt, and Lenora, in that order, completed the seating to Daddy's left. Slightly intimidated, I was glad I did not have to sit next to Daddy. To be within his arm's length and a possible smack was unsettling, for sure.

As the dishes of mounds of mashed potatoes, gravy, brown-buttered noodles, fresh cut-off-the-cob sweet corn, and hunks of roast beef served on a platter were passed around, Daddy rattled off the names of the other cabin family owners, who were planning to travel to Clay Mine the upcoming weekend. Realizing that not one of the families had a daughter near my age, I made a plan.

MY LAST LAST NAME IS GRACE

"Mom, can I stay with Grandpa and Grandma Martin instead of going along to the mountains?" I asked as I spooned up my packed-with-starches meal.

"Sure, I'll drive up tonight and ask Grandma. I don't see why not. We won't be home until late-Sunday afternoon. You'll have to go to church with them, you know," Mom answered. Before bedtime, Mom walked back in the front door and announced I should start packing my bag. Grandpa and Grandma were more than willing to have their granddaughter stay overnight, a first-time occurrence for me.

Friday evening, after Daddy got home from work and packed our '49 black Ford's trunk with two big suitcases, eight of us piled in the car. Two of the other cabin gang families stopped by and picked up Matt or Lenora so they could ride along with their friends. Besides, it was nearly impossible to fit nine people in the family car. Daddy's parents lived less than two miles from our home, so being squashed in the front seat temporarily was tolerable. After my parents dropped me off, Grandma and I stood in the front yard and waved good-bye to my parents and siblings. *I am ready for a new adventure.*

Grandma, round and plump, standing barely five feet tall, always wore a dark navy blue, green, brown, or black "cape" (double bodice) dress, which hung down to her ankles. "Plain" folk's church dress codes for women dictated the women be conservatively dressed in a hand-made small-print or non-printed fabric, have long sleeves, and aprons. Simple black shoes with dark black nylons were worn throughout all seasons. Women must style their uncut hair in a bun using bobby pins, no elaborate barrettes, and apply a large white starched see-through head covering.

Men who are church members must wear plain white, blue, or gray long-sleeved shirts and black plain suit coats without a lapel. Suspenders, not belts, held up nonpleated black trousers. However, other dark colors such as dark-brown, gray, or navy blue trousers may be worn during the week called "everyday" clothes. Mustaches are not allowed, and haircuts are bowl-shaped, allowing for slight movement as they shake their heads.

The rooms of my grandparents' home felt strange to me because their light source came from kerosene lamps. Scary shadows grew on walls, and stairsteps were somewhat dark and eerie. Grandma allowed me to select some Pepto-Bismal-looking pink candy from a quart jar. She read me a book, and I spent some time playing with a marble roller; it was time to retire.

"Grandma, walk in front of me and hold the light," I said to her as I climbed the stairs to the guest bedroom, looking around and behind me. The darkened room held a plain wooden twin bed, a two-drawer nightstand, and a dark walnut three-drawer dresser, which appeared as she hung the hissing kerosene lamp on a ceiling hook.

"I'll wait until you are settled in bed before I leave the room and take the lantern with me." Pointing to a small, two-gallon sized white chamber pot standing in the corner of the small room, Grandma smiled. "Leanne, sit on that if you have to go to the bathroom in the middle of the night." Cool! Using the potty is cooler than my parents having to use the cabin outhouse.

The most memorable moment that weekend was my first horse and buggy ride on Sunday morning going to my grandparents' "Plain" Pike Church (so named because it set back along the Pike, a name given to the road) several miles away near Martindale. There was only room enough for a small number of people to sit in Grandpa's black buggy, which smelled like sweet hay. It had a bench-style, soft-fabric black seat. Grandpa needed to sit on the left side to guide the chestnut-colored horse named Sam. Because Grandma took up most of the right side of the seat, I needed to sit between them on the floor of the buggy.

What an education! I was within reach-out-and-touch distance of the horse's tail. Being mesmerized by watching the horse's legs, feet, and hind quarters "dance" as it carried the weight of the load of us (around four hundred pounds) in the buggy, suddenly my eyes grew larger. The horse's tail lifted up, and within seconds, poop was being forced out in perfect circular plops. I guess, as with most creatures after a meal, upon some activity, nature takes its course. I witnessed the horse's contribution to "road pies" (manure). The smell did not bother me as much as the fascination of the "dance" continued without the horse "skipping a beat" as it carried out its business. Wouldn't you think sitting that close left some kind of residue on us? With my mouth wide open, I sat speechless. My reaction gave Grandma and Grandpa a great laugh.

One Christmas, my parents gave each sibling a book, *A Pleasant View of Martindale* (Saul Printing, 1994), about the history of the area Daddy and us kids were raised in. I read in it one historian wrote of Martindale, "Home to many of Lancaster's Old Order Mennonite population, the town has been described as the 'most conservative community in the world.' Conservative it may be, small, rural and mostly untouched by the outside world. Even so, Martindale certainly possesses a history and heritage well worth preserving…" The paradox is that separation from the world is the very thing that today attracts thousands of visitors to the county each year.

"Frysville was named for the Fry family, who immigrated to America in 1653. In 1780, Hans Martin Frey moved downstream a mile to the present Frysville with his son, John Martin Frey Sr., who had recently returned from four battles of the Revolutionary War. They bought the mill at a sheriff sale after Martin Bowman, the owner, went bankrupt due to poor engineering and insufficient water power to drive the waterwheel. Martin Bowman bought it from the estate of Peter Gundy in 1722, who in turn gotten it from Thomas and Richard Penn in 1752, the sons of William Penn. A large tract of land that includes the entire Commonwealth of Pennsylvania and all of Delaware was granted to William Penn by the King of England, Charles II. It was a payment of a royal debt owed to William Penn's father, who had served as an admiral in the British Navy."

Not aware of the familiar route from my grandparents' home to church was historically noteworthy, I simply enjoyed riding at this slower pace. Now I was someone riding in a buggy and observing car passengers and not the other way around, for a change. Gazing around the Martindale area I called home during our slow drive to church, we passed many big farms and laden-filled gardens. Some gardens were hemmed in with a row of bright pink chrysanthemums or tall yellow sunflowers. Nearly perfect straight rows of a bountiful crop of sugar peas, potatoes, and green beans (only a few noticeable weeds) stretched before me. Tall gray windmills, slowly moving in the breeze, were located near barns. A dark gray water trough and pump sat underneath the windmills in some cases. Partially opened barn doors revealed steeled-wheeled tractors (no rubber wheels allowed), hay mowers, and other farm equipment.

I was also fascinated by how many other horse and buggy families were traveling in the road on their way to church. One doesn't notice this as much when traveling in a car. It wasn't long before Grandpa's younger horse caught up with a slower buggy in front of us. One rule of the road: it is rude to pass another slower-moving buggy. Donning black hats, young boys, facing out the back, waved to me from the open buggy flap.

"Grandpa, you're getting too close," I nervously said as I waved back. Grandpa chuckled but did not give Sam any instructions, nor did he pull back on the horse's reins. Why was Grandpa allowing his horse to follow so closely? To me, it looked like our horse was almost up against the buggy and the boys. If they wanted to, they could have reached out and petted Sam as he trotted along.

We approached the last intersection where our buggy and five other horse and buggies were lined up to make a right turn onto the busy Route 522. Within a few hundred yards, the Pike Church was located on the right side of the road. Along with both Grandpa and Grandma, I too helped to watch for the safest time to tell Grandpa when it was okay to pull out onto the road in-between the cars that went buzzing on by. At one point, I gasped and grabbed hold with white knuckles to the front of the buggy, when I thought antsy Sam was about to start pulling out directly into the path of a car! At Grandpa's mouth signals and whoas, obedient Sam settled down his prancing feet, shook his head several times, and snorted instead. He seemed to be communicating: *ready whenever you are.*

Though my first buggy ride was exhilarating, I was glad when Grandpa pulled into the church's horse shed. We arrived safely at church; I survived my first horse and buggy ride! A dozen horses were already tied in the shed, which had a mixture of odors of sweat and stinky manure. After Grandpa tied Sam with a strong brown rope to a hitching post, he helped Grandma down from the buggy. I contemplated whether to get out of the buggy by going backward using the one and only small step provided. Or do I step down facing forward while holding on to the side of the buggy? I decided to go down backward. *My grandparents and cousins made this act look so graceful.*

Carrying no Bibles, we walked toward the simple medium-sized plain-white steepleless church building. Grandpa walked up to the water pump and trough, which sat on a concrete slab near the front door, pumped a few times on the pump handle, and filled a tin cup with water. The cup was tied to the pump with a black cord. Handing it to me, he said, "Here, Leanne. Want a drink before we go inside?" I took it from him and drank the refreshing cold slightly metal-tasting water. *I guess we all drink from the same cup?* I replaced the cup back to its home.

The three of us entered the somewhat-dark, reverently quiet sanctuary. Grandpa walked over to the right side of the church and shook hands with whispering men. Some men were busy hanging their hats of varying sizes on the wall hooks, which lined halfway around the barren room. Other men were finding seats and shaking hands with the men already seated on the hard wooden benches. Young boys were sitting next to their fathers, while teenaged boys sat in the rear of the church.

Since Grandma and Grandpa were not allowed to sit together, Grandma and I walked up to the third row near the minister's table and sat in the last two seats available, filling up the bench in the women and children's section. I noticed the white plain walls and hardwood floor. Though my Martindale church didn't have any steeple or stained-glass windows, either, this church was definitely more plain and boring-looking than my church. All the adults were dressed in black and white.

I had no choice but sit quietly next to Grandma and wait for the sermon, which was given in Pennsylvania Dutch, to end. Not standing behind a pulpit, but next to a small table, three different ministers in a singsong voice took turns leading the church service. Most times, they did not read out of the German Bible but had huge portions memorized. Worship songs were sang a cappella without any organ and piano. I spent some time gazing out of the opened windows and anticipated our buggy ride home. My thoughts were interrupted when I realized I needed to mimic Grandma. It was expected I rise, turn around, get down on my knees, and face the back of the pew for all prayers.

Finally, the church service ended. Grandpa unhitched Sam, and we started our slow uneventful buggy ride back home. The last mile or so from my grandparents' house, Sam started a full-gallop run. "He knows he is almost back in his barn, and I will be feeding him," Grandpa explained to me noticing my tighter grip.

Handing me a scoop, Grandpa put down fresh straw in his stall, as I filled Sam's bucket with grain following Grandpa's instructions. *Sam is so tall and powerful-looking. Is that white foam coming from Sam's mouth? His body looks damp too.* I stepped back nervously while looking for the barn door. "Grandpa, Sam's all wet."

"Yes, it is hard work to pull the three of us in the buggy. He'll be all right." Sensing my reluctance, Grandpa took the grain bucket. Sam's face was in it before Grandpa had a chance to set it down on the barn floor.

We walked back into the house where the inviting smells of home cooking greeted us. Grandma, who had remained in her Sunday dress, served us a good dinner (the noon meal) of potato soup, which was heated up on the coal stove, and sweet bologna sandwiches. For dessert, Grandma brought out from the icebox homemade apple pie and topped our slices with fresh-whipped cream. After dinner, I played outdoors with my cousin, Lena, who lived next door to my grandparents.

Right before supper, Mom picked me up to take me home. The next week, while driving in the car, I made sure to wave to any children riding in buggies. I now know what it feels like to have a buggy jerk from an antsy horse and witnessed firsthand the making of "road pies." When I see a fast-trotting horse pulling a buggy behind, I can only assume he is heading for his barn and a meal.

The sons of Grandpa Martin got their sense of humor and gumption from their dad. Grandpa Martin bragged that he was going to do a handstand or cartwheel on his eightieth birthday—and he did! Relatives remember seeing him, while walking along the road, suddenly step out in the middle of the road and perform two cartwheels.

Grandpa Martin died in 1970, the year I graduated from Cocalico High School. Yes, I was the first to graduate in my family. Still employed part-time in his eighties to do yard work for a local doctor, Grandpa was coming home from work one day driving his horse and buggy. While attempting to cross an intersection in Reamstown, a car hit his horse and buggy. Sustaining serious injuries, he was sent to the hospital. Someone who came upon the scene of the accident later told my cousin that he could not see how anyone could possibly survive such a mangled mess! During healing from his injuries, Grandpa developed pneumonia and expired on July 29. (Today, hospital patients are kept as active as possible, participating in physical therapy sessions to minimize developing pneumonia.)

Ten months later, Grandma fell at home and fractured her hip (or did she fracture her hip first, causing her to fall?). She died on the operating table on May 25, 1971. My grandparents were reunited once again.

Several months later, Daddy and his siblings planned a public auction for my grandparents' estate. To save expenses, I was asked, and gladly accepted, to assist the auctioneer and be his clerk. I was responsible to write down each item and the price it brought on the auctioneer's log. *No daydreaming allowed.* My brothers and cousins were responsible to be the "runners." They, taking only short breaks, ran around and handed the purchased items to the highest bidder.

One day earlier Grandpa had attended a similar auction while sitting on a wooden bench; a photographer snapped a picture of him. His calm countenance was one of peace. Little did he know, three generations later, many college students in the suburbs of

Philadelphia would gaze upon this conservative "plain" Old Order Mennonite elderly man. This photograph is among a wall display on "Pennsylvania Folk Art" in the library of a college where professors' teachings would be so foreign to him. Fraktur, the artistic and elaborate hand-illuminated folk art was inspired by a member of a German cloister, which originated in Lancaster County. Hopefully, they will read in Grandpa's expression—grace.

Three items were purchased by me that day: a colorful vase of Grandma's, which hospital flowers were delivered in; the half-full glass quart candy jar of pink candy that all of us grandchildren reached into, which Grandma kept on her hutch, and a brown buggy lap blanket, still smelling slightly of stale hay. Smiling in remembrance, I carefully wrapped both fragile items in the lap blanket and placed them in my brand-new pine cedar chest, my graduation present from my parents. I had no intention of eating any of the candy. *Just as my memories, I'll keep it all intact.*

Thought of the Day

Bestow grace on others by agreeing to disagree and realizing their perspective matters to *them*.

Chapter 3

The Luxury of Cars and Radios

But he said to me, my grace is sufficient for you,
for my power is made perfect in weakness.
—2 Corinthians 12:9

Maternal grandparents, parents and three older brothers

ONE APRIL MORNING IN 1962, when I was in fourth grade, while Mom was braiding my hair for school, the phone rang. Grandpa

Fisher called to tell Mom that Grandma Fisher had passed away earlier that morning.

"Leanne and Lorna, you can skip school today. Grandma Fisher died," Mom excitedly said as she hung up the black kitchen wall phone, as tears welled up. Finishing my last braid a little less gentle, Mom hurriedly applied the rubber band to my pigtail. Mom grabbed her pocketbook and scurried out the door; my sister and I trailed behind.

Since death is every bit as much a part of life, Mom allowed only me, not Lorna, to go with her into Grandma's bedroom, which was located off the kitchen. Because all the shades were pulled down, the room was dark. With dilated pupils, I noticed Grandma's too-white face, and her mouth was surprisingly open. The colorful, fading quilt was pulled all the way up to her chin. Mom pulled back Grandma's bedcovers using short jerky movements. Her cream-colored nightgown's six buttons were all unbuttoned. Mom carefully pushed back the gown into Grandma's left armpit. Instead of a flesh-colored breast, an orange-sized foul-smelling black "meaty" area remained. I gasped and stepped back, hitting the tall dresser.

"Oh, Mom," Mom said while shaking out her hands. "Why didn't you see Dr. Hess sooner?" Biting my lips, I hurried out of the room.

Eavesdropping, I later heard Mom describe the gangrenous wound to Aunt Lucy and others as a "black hole." Grandpa Fisher claimed, and Grandma's diary confirmed, he knew nothing about the extent of her illness. She kept her breast cancer a secret from Grandpa and the doctor until it was too late.

For months afterward, I dreamt about the sight I saw that morning. I will not call them nightmares, as I do not remember ever of crawling into my parents' bedroom to be comforted over a nightmare as a child. But, as with most frightening experiences, dreams embellish details. In my dream, I hesitantly walked into Grandma's room and over to her dead body lying on her bed. I noticed a strand of saliva perfectly attached from her lower and upper lip. Just as I was using my finger to wipe it away, Grandma opened her glazed eyes!

In a cold sweat, I awoke, sat up in bed, and started shaking. Seeing Lorna in bed beside me sleeping soundly and noticing my comfortable, familiar surroundings of our bedroom, I lay back down and attempted to stop holding my breath. I took a deep breath. *It's only a dream. Stop thinking about it and go back to sleep.* Unfortunately, it took several months before my sleep was undisturbed.

Mom, Elizabeth Anne, was the first daughter, second child, born to Isaac and Priscilla Anne (Weaver) Fisher in Churchtown, Pennsylvania, on January 12, 1924. Having been born in the same house in which her mother was born (which today is used as a bed-and-breakfast), she was named after her two grandmothers—Anne Fisher and Elizabeth Weaver. Mom's grandma became ill and was bedbound for seven weeks. Thus, her parents moved into my great-grandma's widowed Mom's home, where Mom lived until she was two. Grandma was thirty-two years of age when she had her first child. They had five children in all: three boys (Charles, Edwin, and Theodore) and two girls (Elizabeth and Lucy).

Uncle Edwin lived for only about one month and died the same year Great-grandma died. Grandma journaled: "This is the second time death visited our home." Grandma sold her parents' property for $1,500 and obtained a mortgage. My grandparents bought a four-acre farm. Mom recalls "a man came to Pop and offered a price and he sold it 'on the spot.'" So they bought six lots and moved to Main Street, Cambridge. Here, Grandpa started his love of woodworking and built several crude buildings on the property to store tools and farm equipment. Selling farm vegetables to various markets paid the bills, and Grandpa bought eight acres nearby. Having a car had to make his job easier and more profitable.

Uncle Theodore developed a "soft bone" condition around two and a half years of age. Also as a toddler, he fell down the outside cellar steps and broke his back, unbeknownst to his family. Thus, Theodore had a protruding shoulder blade that gave him a slight humpback appearance. His appearance was a little unnerving to me as a small child. He had an eye that did not focus properly and gums and teeth that appeared to be too large for his mouth.

Grandpa's brother, Elias, never married and lived with my grandparents until his death. Uncle Elias will always be remembered as a tall man with a big round belly, who wore suspenders to keep his pants up, and had poor vision. His nieces and nephews knew him as the uncle who reached into his big pant pockets and handed out pink candy to the children during visits to our grandparents. Uncle Elias's favorite pastime was setting up the Viewfinder toy for my cousins and me. This toy was stored in Grandma's parlor. Therefore, we usually only played with it on Sundays. Uncle Elias spent time with us looking at pictures until we were bored and headed outside to play.

My grandparents were members of Weaverland Mennonite Church of the Lancaster Conference. It was neither liberal nor too conservative, as they had electricity and modern conveniences. I doubt Henry Ford realized his invention would cause much contention over whether or not a church would allow members to drive cars. In 1927, this was the issue that split churches. Daddy's parents joined the remaining horse-and-buggy driving portion. Mom's parents accepted the modern mode of transportation, believed separation from the world would be evident in conservative dress, and not accepting of the fashions of the 1920s nor promoted short hairstyles for women.

Simple and of "plain" dress described Grandma Fisher's attire. Though not as conservative as Grandma Martin, she was allowed to dress in more color choices, not just black, grays, browns, or blues. Reaching well halfway between her knee and ankle, Grandma's dress fit the label of being a "cape" dress because it had an extra layer of matching material over her bosom. Causing no offense to the opposite sex nor showing off any form, a cape dress was necessary for everyday apparel, not simply to be worn on Sundays. Busy working around the house, Grandma always wore an apron over her cape dress as well.

At a time when most women wore only a head covering to church (some coverings stayed hanging on the church wall pegs from Sunday to Sunday), Anabaptist women were asked to forfeit fancy hats and remain "conservative." When stores stopped providing the simple bonnet, Mennonite women were forced to start sewing their own. Eventually, a wise woman started a covering and bonnet business and serviced several counties, fulfilling a huge need. Grandma honored another church requirement when she wore a fairly large white head covering. On Sundays, or when Grandma attended church functions or funerals, she wore a different white head covering that had white ribbon strings attached to it, as did other conservative Lancaster Conference Mennonite women. Plus, a black bonnet also was worn that fit perfectly over her white head covering. If you were married, your covering strings were tied in the front under your chin. If single, the covering strings hung loosely down the back untied.

As a teenager, Mom was baptized in the Weaverland Mennonite Church. Thus, she also was required to start wearing a head covering, although it was smaller in size than Grandma's covering. Becoming less conservative, Mom's covering did not have strings attached.

Mom recalled her childhood as not having many reasons to smile. I have no recollection of any childhood story that Mom told me. Grandma sewed most of her dresses, and Mom only owned a few pairs of shoes at a time. Mom remembered two of her teachers' names who taught in Chester County: Mrs. Pennypacker and Mr. Seabolt. When she was younger and during inclement weather, she was driven to school. However, when older, she and Uncle Charles walked together, carrying lunch pails. Mom spent her recess time jumping rope and riding the seesaw. Students were also expected to memorize Bible verses.

She was a good student, and learning came easy to her. Her favorite subject was math. (In her late eighties, Mom could perform math problems in her head.) She loved to read books too, as I do. But I do not remember her simply sitting down and taking the time to read them very often. Perhaps raising her nine kids kept her a little occupied. Mom remembers taking two "big trips" when she was a teenager: riding a train to visit relatives in Youngstown, Ohio, when she was fourteen in 1938. At sixteen, she visited Niagara Falls.

The home I remember visiting my grandparents was the one Grandpa Fisher built after he sold the farm in Churchtown. He became a carpenter by trade and continued his love for gardening, picking fruit from fruit trees grown on his property and raising chickens and small animals. I always thought he was old-looking with a face of wrinkles.

Grandma Fisher was a homemaker who sang along with the religious hymns on the radio while busy working in the kitchen. Just as I have a love of music, Grandma listened to Christian radio broadcasting throughout the day. As they did not have any TV, the radio was their one contact with the outside world.

The initial Mennonite reaction to the advent of the radio varied widely by conference and regional groups (another reason for contention). As early as 1924, it was deemed wrong to have a radio. Owning a radio was discouraged in the Lancaster Conference until the late 1950s. In some conferences, members left the church or were excommunicated when they began using the radio for gospel broadcasts. In fact, ministers often sold their radios upon ordination. Although perceived to be less of a threat than television, the radio was seen as a source of worldly influence that could corrupt the minds of members and weaken their separation from the world. Eventually, the sanctioning of the Mennonite Hour as the official radio voice of the Mennonite Church in 1951 effectively ended resistance to the radio among the Mennonites.

When Grandpa was older and retired, listening to his Christian radio broadcasts became a pastime. Because of his generous spirit, Grandpa received much junk mail, as his name and address were added to many of the radio evangelists' lists who were frequently asking for another donation.

Charles, Mom's oldest brother, joined the army in WWII, serving from December 1942 until January 1946. He left home for Germany the year Mom and Daddy married. However, being a member of the Mennonite Church, which believed in pacifism and nonresistance, Uncle Charles was "kicked out" of the church for his choice. After his four years of enlistment ended, Uncle Charles chose to dedicate another two years for his country. It was during this time that Uncle Charles met my Aunt Doris. Having been raised Catholic,

Aunt Doris and Uncle Charles were married in the Catholic Church. However, being a German war bride, Aunt Doris had to be married by the army chaplain in order to move to the States. Thus, Uncle Charles and Aunt Doris had to have two wedding ceremonies. With my two cousins, one a toddler and the other an infant, the family of four moved back to Pennsylvania.

Missing her family and friends and moving into a Mennonite family and conservative Lancaster County, Aunt Doris had a very difficult time adjusting to her new life and country. She remained a member of the Catholic Church. I will always remember her as the aunt who had a wardrobe of bright colorful clothing, wore hats and jewelry, and spoke with a funny accent. They were the only relatives who put up an envious, beautiful, sparkling Christmas tree.

But the devotion to her husband that lead her to move across the Big Blue spoke volumes to me as a little girl. Mom recalled her brother, Charles, returned into the States from the war and visited her on the very night she gave birth to my brother, Mervin.

Having only an eighth-grade graduation, Mom, at age sixteen, moved out from her parents' home. She went to live with and work for her Uncle Lester and Aunt Bertha Fisher, who lived in Ephrata. By the time she married Daddy, Mom was employed by a second couple, Harold and Florence Auker, while continuing full-time employment at Walter W. Moyer's factory in Ephrata.

The Aukers influenced Mom in two significant ways: First, Florence was raised Lutheran and fell in love with Harold, who was raised Old Order (horse-and-buggy) Mennonite. Florence's dad hired Harold's dad to paint their house. He brought his helper-son along to tackle the job. Florence and Harold's eyes locked; it was love at first sight. Within a year, they eloped to Elton, Maryland. They compromised and settled on attending Martindale Mennonite Church. Florence "grew out" her short bob haircut, combed her longer hair into a bob, and applied a head covering that honored a church ordinance. Love compels one to do things one would never imagine! Mom sat back and watched this swooning couple grow as soul mates.

Second, Mom also started attending Martindale Church, instead of Weaverland, her parents' church. This connection was beneficial when she learned Daddy started attending Martindale Church. With the influence of three horse-and-buggy-raised friends, he decided to acquire a car and participated in Martindale's youth group activities.

As a small child, I remember my families' visit to my grandparents' house often coincided with my Aunt Lucy and my seven or eight cousins' visit. I do not remember eating a lot of meals at Grandma Fisher's table. I am sure she fed the gang a meal of chicken, fruits from her garden, and canned goods. Grandma's house always had a unique smell. I do have great memories in the 1960s being in my grandparents' somewhat dark and dreary basement simply hanging out with my cousins. We listened to country western music and sang along loudly to Johnny Cash's "Ring of Fire," Conway Twitty's popular country western tunes, and many other country western hits of the 1960s until our parents called for us to come up, as it was time to leave.

In the 1960s, Daddy purchased a camera, slide projector, and projector screen when I was elementary-school aged. He enjoyed his new hobby of taking pictures, especially of nature, deer-hunting events, and his trucks. One picture Daddy took was of my grandparents, their friend who did the driving for longer trips, Uncle Theodore and my family in our Lycoming County hunting cabin of all of us sitting on a bench. It is still amazing to me how Grandma and Mom were able to cook on the small stove to feed the entire hungry gang and, besides, make room for all of us to sleep in our two-room cabin! This picture was the last one taken of Grandma and Grandpa Fisher and Uncle Theodore together.

During my high school years, after my grandparents passed away, Mom invited Theodore to move in with us, which he accepted. Having an abnormal back and unusual teeth and gums, he was somewhat scary-looking to my teenage friends until they became more comfortable around him. He always greeted them with a big smile. One time, he answered the door for my first-date boyfriend, who was slightly taken back. I was quick to explain he was not my dad but my uncle. (Okay, okay, forgive me; I was a shallow sixteen-year-old.) Altogether, Theodore lived with us for about eight years. He loved to read the newspaper, took naps while stretching out his legs, and had an easy smile. He collected Social Security Disability and never held a full-time job. Uncle Theodore got around town by riding his bicycle and made many acquaintances. His nickname was Fish or Fisher.

Uncle Theodore and Mom shared close January birthdays. On Mom's ninety-second birthday, Cousin Jane brought Uncle Theodore over to visit my mom, her aunt. He was thrilled to visit with other family members at the same time, who were present to celebrate Mom's birthday. Within a week, Uncle Theodore was hospitalized for pneumonia and passed away four days later.

Years earlier, $100 each was donated by nieces and nephews and enabled Uncle Theodore to have a funeral service and burial next to his parents' cemetery plot. Feeling good about always having some cash in his wallet to buy a cup of coffee, candy bars, or chips, Uncle Theodore did set aside monies though over the years to pay for a beautiful casket. As requested by Uncle Theodore, a dear friend and pastor led his memorial service on February 2016, a service that would have made him smile.

Thought of the Day

Bestow grace by not being a shamer. "You should be ashamed" should never leave my lips. I have problems at times. Well, because I am human.

Chapter 4

Folklore, Witchcraft, and Satan

> The Lord bestows favor and honor; no good thing does he withhold from those whose walk is blameless.
> —Psalm 84:11

Author on mother's lap with six older siblings

MOST OF MY FRIENDS HAVE warm memories sitting on their nurturing grandma's lap and having Mother Goose nursery rhymes read to them. I have no memories of anything close to that.

One balmy spring day Grandma Fisher was planting flowers along the fence that graced the length of their four-acre property.

40

Grandpa's four fruit trees flanked the other side of the stone driveway leading up to the small white barn, home to five sheep, several chickens, and a rooster.

At eight years old, my job was to have the five-gallon bucket half-full (the most weight I could carry) of water and ready to pour into each prepared hole for the flowers. Suddenly, Grandma jumped back while dropping her trowel, shouted, "Snake!"

I ran into the driveway, a safe enough distance away, and I yelled, "Yikes!" Confident there were no more slithering disturbances, she later motioned for me to come to her side, as my heart stopped racing.

"Leanne, never look a snake in the eye. Every snake is Satan in disguise. Ever since God cursed the serpent to crawl on its belly in the Garden of Eden, he wants to harm you," she said with furrowing brows. According to Grandma, dinosaurs too became crawling serpents because of the curse. Standing farther away, I waited until she needed me to pour before I gingerly walked over to finish our planting. *Whew! No more Satan.*

That was the only theory Grandma ever passed onto me directly. Other folklore and frightening stories were passed down from generation to generation through Mom. She would share these stories as we were doing household chores together.

Mom passed along stories that affected me greatly in hopes of instructing her daughters to always be cautious and aware of your surroundings. White slavery and superstitious stories had the most impact. In the 1920s, journalists created the term *white slavery* in reference to the vast amounts of prostitution that occurred in urban America. The 1920s ushered in the era of modernity, and sexual activity was no exception. Commercialism and mass media promoted sexual promiscuity that was not only more intense than customs of previous ages, but reached a much greater audience due to the ease with which movies and radio shows were distributed.

Grandma Fisher passed on the following white slavery story onto Mom, as follows:

> A group of teenage girls were attending a local Mennonite church. One of the teenage girls became ill. (Some remember the reason to be due to a white slavery stranger adding something to the victim's hanky or from a med discreetly injected by the stranger while sitting side by side in the church pew.) The stranger offered to go out with the girl, who was ill enough to want to get up and walk out of the church. But a wise teenager friend, aware of white slavery, offered, instead, to tend to her friend and accompanied the ill girl out of the church. One more innocent Mennonite girl remained a virgin or was protected from this potentially evil plan.

As an adolescent and not understanding prostitution, I asked Mom what had become of those "taken girls." She informed me most likely they were driven to another state or even Canada. The point being, their families never heard from them again. "You be careful and trust no stranger," Mom warned us.

The most puzzling and scary of all was the story of how gypsies visited neighborhoods in hopes of selling chickens for income. Someone witnessed a gypsy walking in a field come upon a tree. Instead of walking around a tree, she walked right through it! She was hexed. With the intent and purpose of making an impact, Grandma Fisher passed on this story to prove the evidence of the power of hexing and how casting evil spells was definitely an evil to be avoided.

Grandma recited tales about witches who changed form at will. I heard the following passed-on story about her two great uncles, who dabbled in witchcraft for a short period of time. Uncle Ralph was studying witchcraft and how to cast a spell. His brother Abe found the book lying in his brother's bedroom and secretly started studying it also. In this book was a picture of an old man sporting a long white beard that flowed to the floor. At one point, when Uncle Ralph glanced up to look at his brother, he saw, temporarily, this forty-year-old, not looking his current age, but exactly as the old man pictured in the witchcraft book!

"Mom, I'm confused," I said with narrowed eyes. "Uncle Abe instantly became an old man?"

"No, but Satan had control of his mind temporarily. Satan made his brother look exactly like the old man in the witchcraft book. Satan has evil powers! As soon as their mom found out about the witchcraft book, she burned it in the trash barrel immediately. Rightfully so," Mom explained.

Hearing this folklore, my young mind could not comprehend evil to this extent. However, more seeds were planted to not trust strangers or even unfamiliar, weird relatives. When my older brothers participated in a mission trip to Red Lake, Canada, as teenagers in the 1960s, they witnessed firsthand the results of casting evil spells on others (details are in a later chapter). Yikes! Gypsies, witchcraft, and crawling Satans make for a scary world for little Mennonite girls.

Filled with theories, explanations, and ideas, Grandma, with good intentions, prepared Mom for dating days in hopes of meeting a husband. Mom dated a few guys before meeting Daddy, but she did not talk about them much. One story she told empowered her daughters to always be wise and diligent about getting out of uncomfortable situations while on a date. You should know your dates and his intentions at all times. As a young child, upon hearing her story over and over, I knew how her story ended. Once again, her teachings put another layer of fear in my young mind.

For teenagers, the New Holland fair was a good reason to have a date or, at the very least, hang out with friends. Uncle Charles took Mom along with him to attend the fair. Later on that night, she was ready to go home. Mom found her brother and asked if he was ready to take her home, which he declined. A friend of her brother overheard the conversation and offered to do so.

After the guy opened the car door for Mom to get in, he walked around the back of the car, got in and then said, "Now that I got you, I will take you home when I am ready." Immediately sensing his ill intentions, Mom grabbed the door handle and tried to get out of his car. But she was unable to do so because the door must have been locked (or in her hurry, she was unable to open the door). Giving credit to her Protector, Mom tried again. On her second attempt, the door opened, and Mom ran out. Shortly thereafter, she saw some trustworthy neighbors who were willing to drive her home. As the saying goes, you need to kiss a few frogs before your handsome prince comes along.

At barely eighteen years of age, one cold January night, Mom and a girlfriend drove to the Five and Dime store in Ephrata, another town a few miles away. A handsome man, Aaron Martin, and his buddy, were shopping in the store. He was thin, about 5'7" tall with medium-brown hair, hazel-green eyes, and a great smile. After their initial meeting and some conversation, Aaron Martin asked if he could drive Elizabeth Fisher home. She agreed. But Aaron had a problem; he did not own a car! So Aaron asked to borrow his friend's car and drove Elizabeth home.

One day, Elizabeth was asked to be hired out as a maid to a couple, Harold and Florence Auker. She agreed and moved into their home and left her aunt's and uncle's employment. With the blessing of this couple, Mom and Daddy often held their dates in the Auker's parlor. Florence, who later became like another grandmother to me, taught Mom how to be a "particular" (neat) housekeeper, including ironing rags, underwear, and sheets.

It wasn't long before Elizabeth saw the caring personality of Aaron. Holding down two jobs led to Elizabeth falling asleep at her sewing machine at her Moyer's factory job. Mom was not getting sufficient sleep. She frequently hit her pillow late at night because she was cooking, cleaning, and ironing. Feeling sorry for her, since she also added dating to her already-maxed schedule, Aaron asked Mom to quit her factory job. She needed to spend time with him!

Good-looking, sporting a derby hat, which he only wore on Sundays or to church events, Daddy had sex appeal, gumption, and was a bit "wild." Why? Because he smoked cigarettes! Daddy smoked those cancer sticks until around the time of my older sister, Lenora, was born. Mom told him, "I do not want my baby to be a nicotine addict."

I was shocked the first time I noticed the family picture of Mom and Daddy, along with my three older brothers, standing on someone's porch. Daddy was posing to the far left of the picture. Sure enough, Daddy was holding a lighted cigarette. When I confronted Mom, she did not want to really talk about it except to simply say, "Yes, as a teenager and young adult, he used to smoke. But he knew it was wrong, so he quit." The topic was dropped. My oldest brother Aaron Jr. remembers Daddy smoking sometimes and having an occasional beer until Aaron Jr. turned fourteen years of age. My guess is some beer drinking and smoking occurred during all those deer hunting, men-only excursions. Perhaps Daddy realized he needed to be a better example to his teenaged sons and finally put the nasty habits to rest.

When Daddy found out where Mom worked, he too, applied for a job at the same factory in hopes of making a stronger connection. Without her knowledge, Mr. Gumption requested a job and was hired on the spot. For forty cents an hour, he became a stockroom clerk. What a surprise when sexy Aaron walked up to Elizabeth, who was busy working at her sewing machine. "Wanna have lunch together? I work here." His grin was as wide as the Niagara Falls. Mom understood gumption! How? Because when it was not customary for women to be driving cars (driving duties were left to men), Elizabeth asked Aaron to teach her how to drive. After being hired at Moyer's Factory, Daddy purchased his car from his buddy for $150. The 1936 Ford Tudor sedan did not have hydraulic brakes but cable brakes. Sometimes the cables would stretch and needed to be adjusted frequently, a real headache compared to modern cars of today. Those cable brakes would rust out. Water got inside the connecting tubes and rusted or froze in the winter. Therefore, the brakes needed to be tested before descending a hill. You needed to be prepared and think through: *what would I do if the brakes gave out?* Mom proved to be a successful driver, and Daddy proved to be a patient teacher. Their destiny was sealed.

By October 17 of that year, the smitten couple tied the knot and was married by Bishop Paul Graybill, the same man who baptized Mom and, years later, me and most of my older siblings. What a handsome couple! Daddy was sporting a necktie with a medium brown suit. Mom had sewn her own wedding dress: a white satin, midlength "cape" dress worn with off-black nylons and black shoes with a stacked heel. Mom was proud to show off her wedding photos, which were taken at a professional studio in Ephrata. She remembered how sick she had been on her wedding day. In spite of a less-than-perfect start, Mom and Daddy's bliss continued throughout their married life. They truly became helpmates, partners, supporters, and friends to each other.

The first home Mr. and Mrs. Right "set up house" (as it was called) was in a small house outside of New Holland near Ivan Martin's Quarry. Perhaps seeing trucks hauling limestone out of the quarry nearby piqued Daddy's interest for some day when he too could be holding down such a job.

Daddy had several loyal dogs in his lifetime, whether as a child or a teenager, and they shared a devotion that led to a great lesson on how devoted he would be to his future wife. Of course, he planned to take his faithful dog, Sparky, with him to his new home and acquaint him to his new wife. However, Sparky ran off and eventually found his way eighteen miles back to my grandparents' farm, albeit a little muddy. Another attempt was made to get Sparky to stay in Daddy's new home. This time, Daddy kept the dog in the trunk of the car, thinking he would lose his sense of direction and not be able to run back home again. The plan did not work; Sparky again wanted the comfort of the familiar, faded, worn-out rug of the front porch. Daddy had no choice but to center all his attention on his bride—a win-win for both.

My parents lost no time in having babies, which allowed Daddy to avoid having to serve in Alternate Service during WWII. Along with his recently married buddy, when faced with the draft, both married men chose opposite directions. Daddy chose to apply for a farming exemption and was accepted. His nonchurch-member friend, Henry, chose instead to serve in the military and enlisted in the United States Army on November 13, 1943. He was killed in the battle in which Rennes, France, was liberated by American forces. Henry's wife was pregnant at the time and received $500 compensation for his service. Henry was posthumously awarded both the Bronze Star and Purple Heart for his duties. Perhaps, Daddy talked to my older brothers about this tragedy, which had to greatly affect him. But I never heard Daddy or Mom discuss it.

In fact, it was exactly one year, one month, and one day from their wedding day when my oldest brother, Aaron Jr., was born. One year, one month, and one day later, my brother Elvin was born. By the time baby number three, Marlin, was born, Daddy's chances of being sent off to war was no longer an issue. Mom was a hard worker and jumped right into her role of being a mother and wife. For a short time, all three babies were in diapers. One Monday morning, Mom counted one hundred cloth diapers on the wash line!

Daddy needed more than forty cents an hour to support a wife. He quit the factory job and was hired by a chicken farmer in Elm. They also needed a larger home; Daddy and Mom moved onto a farmette near Churchtown where son number two, three, and four were born. They rented here for five years—the longest length of time until our new home was built.

Daddy helped to plant, strip, and harvest tobacco. During the war years, machinery was scarce, and Daddy rebuilt a tractor out of old parts and assembled a boiler on an old truck, which he used to steam tobacco beds. Tobacco was grown from seed in small beds, and then later, the seedling was planted in the larger field. Before the tobacco seed was planted, these beds were steamed to kill any weed seeds. Steaming tobacco became a second source of income for the family. He made forty to fifty cents per bed. Daddy was willing to drive some distance to supplement their income and to pay an assistant as well.

Eventually, Daddy held down several farm-related jobs during the day and started working night shift to run a mixer for making concrete pipes (very noisy and rough work in those days). Along with his friend Titus, they built a well driller. Later, Titus started his own well driller business, who was hired when my parents needed a well drilled many years later. Perhaps, my brothers were inspired by Daddy's ability to "putz" with machinery and create a necessary tool. When they decided to become mechanics, they felt like maybe Daddy's gift was passed onto them. At seventeen, Matt purchased two used Chevelles. Using parts from both, he "built" his 1967 Chevelle Supersport and drove it around for many years.

Eventually in the late 1940s, Daddy borrowed $900 and purchased a truck and trailer to haul block and pipe for New Holland Block or Pipe Plant. As he hauled concrete materials to construct a portion of the Pennsylvania turnpike near Harrisburg, a special relationship between rig and driver began. Just as his marriage was successful and fulfilling, Daddy found his third love: Lord, first Mother, and family next, and now the trucking industry.

While living in their home in Churchtown, Mom had an experience she said caused her to truly feel "scared skinny." It happened when Daddy was hunting with his buddies in the mountains, and she was home alone with her young family. In the middle of the night, she heard a terrible crash. She assumed it was coming from the kitchen area. She stayed in her bedroom terrorized, awaiting some evil plot. No doubt, her mind was conjuring up all the stories of fearing strangers, hexing, and other evil stories from her past. Mom was too paralyzed to do anything else but pray. When no other strange noises were heard anywhere else in the house, she finally fell back to sleep. The next morning as she entered the kitchen, she saw the kitchen blind had fallen down and was lying over the kitchen sink. Only then could she laugh at herself.

With three children born close in age, Mom did not plan on Daddy babysitting in the evenings. Mothers of that era stayed home and very seldom ventured out at night by themselves. Parents ran errands together. Mom did recall one evening she had to go to a doctor's appointment. Daddy was in charge of babysitting three young toddlers with instructions on how and when to put them all to bed. She came home to find Daddy had put comfy quilts and blankets on the floor. The three toddlers, wearing their same dirty playclothes, were sound asleep lying next to their sleeping Daddy.

Because Daddy was compassionate and recognized that Mom needed some recuperation time after delivery, Daddy did something that earned him many brownie points in Mom's eyes. Not only had he hired a maid to take care of the remaining siblings and run the household; he hired a second maid (albeit for only a short time) to only meet Mom's and the newborn infant's needs. Without saying words, Daddy taught his boys how to treat their wife, the "weaker sex." Mom felt cherished.

Thought of the Day

Be gracious by being a wife that a husband finds easy to live with and easy to love, so he is willing to die for you.

Chapter 5

Rumspringa and Shunning

Once you were alienated from God and were enemies in your minds because of your evil behavior. But now he has reconciled you by Christ's physical body through death to present you holy in his sight, without blemish and free from accusation.
—Colossians 1:21–22

Parents' wedding picture

As a teenager, Daddy had no plans to join his parent's Plain "Wenger" Church. His chance came when he reached the age to participate in the expected Old Order Mennonite's rite of passage called Rumspringa, meaning "running around." Starting around age sixteen, Rumspringa was a time to "sow your wild oats" before settling down, raising a family, and becoming a church member. The youth spent weekends at barn dances or "singing." Daddy's parents and church leaders overlooked a certain amount of misbehavior and temporarily disregarded church ordinances during his adolescent period. Some eighteen-year-old teenagers bought cars. Both cars and buggies were parked on the church parking lot.

Attending a "singing" for Daddy was meant to be a time to select a future wife. His plain, boring clothes were exchanged for clothes the "English" wore: jeans and short-sleeved or brightly colored, bold-plaid flannel shirts. A barber restyled his hair from the bowl-shaped cut to a crew cut.

The girls were attired in nonplain garb as well. Daddy couldn't help but notice their tight jeans. I recalled attending a hot-air balloon fest, I didn't know where to look; Daddy's eyes also didn't know where to look. He scanned the room for a willing partner for the night. Though their long hair was never cut, the girls let their hair down literally and figuratively. Smoking, drinking alcohol, and having sex went on behind the barn doors. The hay mound was a soft spot to lose one's virginity. However, Daddy had no intention of selecting a spouse from this available pool. Rumspringa was his ticket out of the horse-and-buggy lifestyle. Just as his older brothers and sisters came upon the same crossroad, Daddy had a choice to make.

Daddy wasn't the only sixteen-year-old to have his eye on owning a vehicle someday. In between drawing on cigarettes and drinking Jack Daniels, Daddy became good friends with Henry, Phares, and Levi. This group of rowdy friends developed a lifelong friendship. After all, what happens during Rumpsringa stays in the barn. All four decided they were going to purchase a car. The answer to which church should they attend was answered in befriending a Lancaster Conference neighbor, Titus, who hung out with the Martindale youth group.

By the time Daddy met Mom, he gave no one the impression or a hint of a more conservative lifestyle from his past. Daddy too worked hard and succeeded losing any Pennsylvania Dutch accent. My grandparents had no choice but to accept the fact that their prodigal son was never going to join their church, as most of his siblings had.

Having made the decision, Daddy was allowed to learn how to drive using his brother's car. In exchange for a tank of gas, Daddy put the pedal to the medal and perfected his driving skills. All my aunts decided to join the "Pike" or "Wenger" Old Order Church, following their parents' footsteps. The uncle who allowed Daddy to drive his car did sell his car and joined the horse-and-buggy church. However, when in his midtwenties, he decided to join the "Black Bumper" (translation: paint your chrome bumpers black) Horning Mennonite Church after he married my aunt. Once again, his buggy reins were exchanged for a steering wheel.

My daddy's childhood was eclipsed by a change in church affiliation when he was eleven years old. Not understanding all of the details why, I learned when Grandpa Martin was in his late twenties or early thirties, he was kicked out of the Plain "Wenger" Mennonite Church by the bishop. Wanting clarification, I asked my "plain" aunt and less conservative Mennonite cousin about the reason why my grandparents stopped attending one horse-and-buggy-church for another. In Pennsylvania Dutch, my aunt answered, "Ungle ich heit." My aunt then looked to her niece for the English interpretation: "Causing disunity."

Long story short, several church members were asked by the bishop to make a confession in front of the entire congregation, as was the tradition, for committing fornication (sex before marriage). The ritual of confession continues today. In Grandpa's eyes, at least, some members did publicly confess, and others did not. The clincher came when my aunt was not allowed to take communion. Being persistent, vocal, and opinionated, Grandpa met with the bishop and spoke his mind. After some time, the bishop had had enough and determined that Grandpa be kicked out of his church for "ungle ich heit." Bestowing grace on behalf of Grandpa Martin, I do not feel it is necessary to know all the specifics of the sexual sins that occurred. Just as I have no plans on exposing all my sins, I will let "sleeping dogs lie."

My grandparents remained church members of the Plain "Pike" Mennonite Church for quite a few years. Because of the communion issue, my Aunt Alta and Uncle Lester also left the Plain "Wenger" Church at the same time and joined the Plain "Pike" Mennonite Church with her parents. However, some years later, they rejoined the Plain "Wenger" Church, as their burial plot today is in the Plain "Wenger" Mennonite Church's cemetery. I assume these somewhat embarrassing facts assisted Daddy in making the decision not to join either of the two "plain" horse-and-buggy churches, as his parents had.

The division among church members occurred in 1927 when Groffdale Conference (Wenger) Mennonite Church was the result of a seventeen-year dispute within the Weaverland Old Order Mennonite Conference over the use of the automobiles. In order to retain horse-drawn transportation, half of the Weaverland conference of the more traditional members formed this new group.

Today, Wenger Mennonite Church is the largest Old Order Mennonite group to use horse-drawn carriages for transportation. Their black carriages distinguish them from the Amish, who use gray ones. They are mainly rural people, using steel-wheeled tractors to work small farms. Along with the automobile, they continue to reject most modern conveniences but do allow electricity in their homes.

The German language was used in worship services, and Pennsylvania German was spoken at home. They met in plain church buildings to worship but did not have Sunday schools. Practicing nonresistance like other traditional Mennonite groups during World War II, they advised young men who did not qualify for a farm deferment to accept jail terms instead of Civilian Public Service, the alternate used by other Anabaptist conscientious objectors.

As a teenager, I learned the results of Daddy's sister, Aunt Beulah's Rumspringa days. "It explains why your cousin Julia looks so different than the Martins," Mom pointed out. My aunt enjoyed the time spent "singing" and courting a very-dark-olive-complexioned handsome neighbor boy in the barn or down in some farmer's meadow. She, within two years, saw the writing on the wall and realized it was time to stop sowing her wild oats, settle down, and become a horse-and-buggy church member.

But the handsome boyfriend had no interest in joining the church or stopping the freeing lifestyle of driving a car and wearing regular clothes. Aunt Belulah faced a dilemma. She chose to join church, and her closet went through a makeover. Within a few months, she met and married my Uncle Paul. Did the boyfriend leave her alone and respect her decision? No. When he drove by my aunt, who was riding her bicycle on a return trip from the local grocery store, he stopped and harassed her about "getting in" his car. After several wooing kisses, her body couldn't resist him. Her bicycle with the small strapped grocery box on the back was hidden behind a tree as the car slightly rocked with hanky-panky. Having no respect for my aunt's plans to marry a "plain" Mennonite guy, Mr. Handsome was a relentless pursuer.

One day, my aunt's fiancé noticed her bicycle hidden in the back of her lover's barn. My aunt promised to stop two-timing. Unfortunately, Mr. Handsome only saw it as more of a challenge. I guess being able to wear a belt (does it have notches for each lover?) and a shiny belt buckle (unlike his "plain" rivalry) gave him some kind of boldness. They simply became smarter in the location of their rendezvous. My Uncle Paul looked the other way and tolerated the shenanigans of his love-struck wife. Guess what? Anatomy works! Six months after she married my uncle, my cousin, Julia, was born. Who is the father? What a l-o-n-g wait during her birth. Her mother looked into the beautiful face of a familiar very-dark-complexion, and the answer was obvious to both parents. Holding her child filled my aunt with mixed emotions—love and shame. Only then did my aunt have the strength to tell Mr. Handsome to move on. Her confession in church and to her heavenly Father wiped her slate clean.

Who suffered the most? Julia! Whispering behind her back and obvious snickering from both adults and children over the years were hard to swallow. Julia was the one who felt she should be called Hestor Prynne (remember *Scarlet Letter?*) and was wearing a "red A" on her forehead, not her mom. I have great memories of Julia filling the big black witchlike "brewing pot" on my cousin's back porch for the family's Saturday night weekly bath. She, along with her brothers, started a small fire under the kettle and filled it with pumped water from the well. It was too laborious to empty and refill each time someone bathed.

Again, when I was about eight years old, I chose to stay with my horse-and-buggy cousins instead of going to the mountains with my family. I couldn't wait to join my cousin in this pot when it finally came our turn. It was intriguing to have my "bathtub" be the biggest black kettle I have ever seen. Yep, the bathing order occurred from the oldest to the youngest. My cousin and I were about the fourth set to hop in together after Julia added some reheated water. I didn't think too long and hard as to what possibly could have been in the reused bath water!

At a quilting bee many years later, Julia learned about the death of her father. The quilters totally forgot the name someone mentioned was Julia's father. Only when she dropped her thimble and pricked her finger did the women look up and mouthed a silent "Ohh." *Yes, our passed-on sins from generation to generation cause such havoc.*

My brother Elvin, at seventeen years old, was asked to drive an eighteen-year-old "Pike" Mennonite guy going through Rumpspringa to the West Coast. Before he became a church member, settled down, and got married, he wanted to see more of the United States. All of Elvin's expenses, including a new set of tires, were paid by him. Elvin remembers that the fella' smoked a cigarette one after another until his car reeked of smoke. It took several months before the stinky smell wafted out of his car.

Mom was the one who mostly educated us kids about Daddy's upbringing and his somewhat rebellious ways. Another source of information was Daddy's grandmother's diary, which she journaled in for many years. One entry of hers described Daddy as somewhat "sickly" at some point in his infancy. When my sister Lorna completed a family genealogy tree, it was noted that one of Daddy's brothers died at nine days old. Later on, an aunt commented; perhaps, it was due to the fact that her mother's milk supply had dried up when her brother-in-law had committed suicide over financial difficulties during the Depression. During the 1930s, Pennsylvania Mennonite farmers living in small rural communities were close-knit and used to living frugally. Accustomed to living off the land, they were less dependent on the local grocery store to be their supply line. They were in a much better position to fend for themselves. However, times were hard.

When Daddy was seven years old, his family moved from one farm to another several times until Grandpa bought the Frysville farm in 1930. Upon this final move, his siblings stopped attending the public school and started attending the one-room schoolhouse within walking distance. Most, but not all, students were of the horse-and-buggy "Wenger" or "Pike" Mennonite faith. Teachers were usually the smarter, well-behaved students, who just completed eighth grade the previous year. No high school or college education was required to teach and, in fact, not possible because as a church member, higher education was frowned upon.

Having an education beyond eighth grade was not needed, as it was expected boys were to grow up to become farmers, carpenters, or other trade smiths passed down from father to son. Unmarried girls were either employed as schoolteachers, hired-out "maids" (especially those who never married and did not have their own children to raise) by other Mennonite families requiring an additional hand. Others became factory workers or hired help for businesses of similar faith, perhaps at a market stand, fabric, or grocery store. Of course, many girls were never employed and moved from helping their mother raise their brothers and sisters right into marriage and starting their own families. Some aunts and uncles used the assistance of nieces without pay to raise their families, especially widowers.

Serving as a teacher for the local parochial school meant you were most likely the teacher for your younger brothers and sisters, cousins, neighbors, and familial children of your congregation. One avenue of keeping control and limited exposure was to select only teachers of the same faith, which kept any potential "outside world" influences at bay.

When the youth of a neighborhood reached dating age, it was acceptable to date members of the opposite sex from other churches. Dress code, head coverings, or whether or not you had modern conveniences in a home had little to do with one's choice. For example, my aunt of the Plain "Wenger" Mennonite faith dated a boy from the local United Zion Church. The United Zion pastor married many horse-and-buggy couples, who chose not to become Old Order Mennonites.

An aunt described Daddy as "a teaser." She remembered him siccing his dog, a mean-spirited German shepherd, on her as she was walking to the bus stop and forced her to run away from the dog. Having a "soft heart," just in the nick of time, Daddy called after his dog, which immediately stopped pursuing his sister and returned to him. Knowing she would be scared to death, he thought it was hilarious to tease her in this manner. Other opportunities arose for this mischievous youngster to be disciplined. In fact, it was Daddy's oldest brother, Daniel, who disciplined him, not Grandpa or Grandma. Huh?

When Daddy was older, my aunt remembered, he added a motor to his bicycle to make it easier to pedal. While a little boy, he also developed his love and craft of winning at the game of checkers. I doubt his love for trucks started with his childhood toys, as modern transportation had been frowned upon.

Willard Fry (from the lineage of the county's early settlers), though seven to eight years younger than Daddy, was a childhood neighbor and friend. He recalled several stories of their youth. Daddy liked to trap skunks for spending money. Back then, Slabach paid $2–$4 per skunk hide. Daddy designed a skunk trap using a box and bait, which was parts of dead chickens confiscated from the chicken house. The skunks were baited in the box, but once inside, they could not escape. You have a trapped skunk. But how do you get it to be saleable hide? You shoot it! Willard said he held the skunk by the tail while Daddy shot the skunk in the head. Of course, while dying, the skunk sprayed them both causing quite an offensive stink. Daddy kept the dead skunks in the tobacco cellar until he had several of them to take to Slabach's to trade for cash.

Willard recalled a childhood prank that occurred when Daddy was assigned by Grandpa to get an old field crop roller, hook it up to a team of horses, and guide the horses around the fields so the roller could flatten ground lumps before planting crops. Willard hopped on the seat next to Daddy and decided to tease him and make his job more difficult by dragging his feet along the ground. Unfortunately, it wasn't long before Willard's foot got caught, and it pulled him off the seat. Thank God, his head landed on the soft ground and not on any rocks! Once Daddy realized Willard wasn't injured, he laughed and laughed at the prank that backfired.

Grandpa's dilapidated farm equipment, including an old field crop roller having shown many years of wear, had always been an embarrassment for Daddy. This was one reason for Daddy's philosophy of life to buy the best item that you could in a price range you could afford. Daddy and Mom saved up to pay cash for their cars (at least when they reached middle age and older). Wanting nice, affordable things and keeping cars maintained and somewhat clean was important to him.

One of Daddy's favorite tricks was to shock someone from an electrical wire. Willard remembers Daddy putting a wire around his car. When the car door was opened, you got a jolt. Each of his children, I am sure, at least once experienced Daddy's tricking us by causing an electric shock. He held onto the hook end of the electric fence, reached out, and asked us to hold his hand. Of course, with Daddy acting as the conductor, as soon as we touched him, we felt the jolt!

My experience occurred when we lived in Hinkletown when I was about eight or nine years old. Mom had one cow that she milked twice a day to supply the family with fresh raw (unpasteurized) milk. My favorite food item from Bessie's production was the salty homemade butter—*hmmm*. Bessie had an electric fence to keep her on a path behind Hinkletown Mill along the creek and away from the road.

"Leanne." Daddy mischievously grinned. "Hold my hand." He had unhooked the electric fence for Mom in order for her to milk Bessie. She turned the five-gallon bucket upside down, which became her seat. That's an unusual request from Daddy. Just as I grabbed ahold of Daddy's somewhat warm calloused hands, I felt a jolt run through my body from the top of my head to the bottom of my dirty feet. All my hairs seemed to stand on end.

"Ahhh!" I loudly screamed, dropped his hand, jumped back, turned around, and hightailed back across the road to our backyard. As I ran, I could hear Daddy heartily laughing. Of course, one only falls for this trick one time. To this day, I am uneasy around any potential electrical current shocks.

Being raised in the country near Muddy Creek, Daddy and his brothers and sisters had a great scenic backdrop: a covered bridge, which allowed horses to get out of the elements and gave them a chance to rest until they continued on their journey when other traffic came along. Many teenagers remember stopping in the middle of the covered bridge to take advantage of the opportunity to steal a kiss in this more private setting.

Some of the local churches used the Muddy Creek for baptisms. One spring day in 1939, my uncle remembered watching the local United Zion pastor baptize converts in the creek below the Frysville Bridge near Daddy's home. By the time the pastor had completed his three dunks: "In the Name of the Father (dunk), the Son (dunk), and Holy Ghost (dunk)…" the observers felt sorry for the ones being baptized and shivered from the cold water.

After Grandpa and Grandma Martin quit farming, they moved into a new small home that was built on the farm property. Aunt Hannah, after becoming a widow, lived with them for several years and helped take care of them. Their home was only a few miles from my home. Grandkids remember Grandma Martin's glass quart jar filled with the Pepo Dismal pink candy she handed out to us when we visited. I am sure we did visit them from time to time, but I do not have too many memories of playing with cousins who lived nearby while visiting my grandparents.

My "plain" Aunt Alta made the best homemade sweet bologna. My cousins and I often volunteered to help with weeding tobacco beds in exchange for all the bologna we could eat. To this day, I can recall quite vividly their farmette's musky smell of growing and drying tobacco and fresh rolls of sweet bologna hanging from hooks on the back porch. I watched in awe as she cooked meals on the coal stove.

Something else was mystifying about this aunt and uncle. Mom commented this aunt was totally shocked when the doctor told her she was pregnant. Apparently not understanding the birds and the bees, my aunt was convinced she too must have had a second virgin birth! In 1935, one month after my aunt and uncle married, their son was born. My cousins and I joked about the situation and said this was our aunt "who got pregnant through the long johns' buttonhole." But they were a gracious couple who showed hospitality to their nieces and nephews quite often throughout the summer months.

Another amazing observation for me was a practiced tradition held by all my aunts and uncles on Daddy's side of the family called "shunning or ex-communication." During the time my grandparents were kicked out of the Wenger Church and joined the Pike Mennonite Church, my aunt, like her parents, left to attend the Pike Mennonite Church as well. The consequences were, whether married or not, church members who left one church for the other were "shunned" and not allowed to eat (break bread) together. That meant my aunt and uncle could not sit down at the same table at mealtimes. My uncle and cousins were served the food by my aunt. But then, my aunt cleared their dishes off the table, filled her plate, and ate alone.

Many years later, when my parents decided to host a Martin family reunion for Daddy's relatives in our front lawn, two separate seating areas were required. Daddy set up picnic tables under one tree for the "shunned" relatives and placed several more tables around for the majority of my aunts, uncles, and cousins in a different part of our lawn. A specific church membership is that important?

Five years ago, I attended my Plain aunt's funeral, which was held in my cousin's home. Hopefully, I could reconnect with my cousins I had lost track of. My sister Lorna pointed out my one cousin Jacob, who was standing against the kitchen wall lined up with other relatives.

"Do you see anything different about him, Leanne?" she asked.

With squished-together eyebrows, I said, "Wait. I thought Jacob went 'English.' Why is he wearing a plain coat again? Did he join his parents' horse-and-buggy church?"

Lorna proceeded to fill in the details of my cousin's choices, which left me stupefied. Jacob left his roots behind during Rumspringa, when he met his wife, Janet. After moving out of his parents' home, he rented a small apartment in Ephrata, close to his place of employment. One night, Janet and some friends entered the same small bar Jacob frequented after work and on weekends. Within a year, they married and later on had two children. Janet was introduced to her in-laws' religion and lifestyle. But it never caused a problem. She respected them for who they were. Jacob and his family attended the Nazarene Church in town.

When Jacob's youngest daughter turned ten, he decided to move out. His upbringing had such strong ties on him. The pull of possibly going to hell because he had not joined the Wenger church after Rumspringa was greater than any reason to remain a family of four. Jacob did not comprehend the assurance of salvation and sustaining grace given from our heavenly Father, who counts believers as righteous.

In spite of all his actions and guilt-ridden choices, Jacob was warmly welcomed by the church leadership, as his sins occurred prior to becoming a church member. He was baptized and received into the fold. Faithful to his parental duties, Jacob held visitations with his daughters and paid their child support in full. He divorced Janet so she could remarry if she so chose. Janet is never referred to as the typical "worldly" term: ex-wife. He simply refers to her as "the girls' mom."

Though Rumspringa was never practiced by me and the more liberal Mennonites, I saw the effects of it in two astounding ways. During my clinical rotations in nursing school, my eyes were opened to the results of sowing wild oats. First, I learned nothing levels the playing field like an abortion clinic! During my clinical rotation of spending time in an ob-gyn clinic in Bucks County, I was shocked as to how many horse-and-buggy Mennonite girls had elected (or been forced?) to have an abortion. For these poor girls, whether it was an unwanted pregnancy from failed birth control from a Rumspringa "romp" in the hay or an incest situation, the tears were as universal as red lipstick. Though my mom taught us a lot about the evil in the world, I was sheltered about incest. I didn't have any friend whose dad was her sexual partner; it was as foreign to me as the spice anardana.

The doctor's notes I read in the clinic I was assigned to were full of sad stories. Just as a diverse group of singing our national anthem unites us, this diverse groups of "victims" was threaded with events that made me blush. One daughter, who was asked to come out to the barn to finish her barn chores, was met by a horny dad who violated her in the most obscene way, while the Mom was milking a cow in the next stall! Or for the sixteen-year-old virgin during her first night at a "singing" had no idea what it meant when she allowed the willing, breathing-heavy boy spread her legs. I learned the percentage of Plain moms (no dads ever showed up in the offices), who made appointments for their daughters with doctors located a county away, made up a small percentage of the clients.

When my sister was earning her doctorate, her dissertation was about the incest among Mennonites, including church leaders, starting in the late 1800s to the 1930s. Lorna found plenty of research material for her two-hundred-plus-page submission. Keeping things hush-hush about personal family matters gnawed at innocent girls for years. Driven by much fear, survivors would only consider penning their stories until after the perpetrator (perhaps a neighbor, preacher, brother, grandpa, uncle, or cousin) passed away. Healing does come—eventually.

Thank God, victors write the books!

No, I can't make this only about Mennonites. But each faith community needs to clean up their smelly litter boxes.

Secondly, my clinical rotation held in the local psychiatric ward was full of more surprises. As a nursing student, I was asked to complete several therapeutic conversations with a mental patient (twelve pages typed of homework when finished). I was astonished as to how many religious Plain folks spend time behind these walls. Another mental hospital nearby had a wing sectioned off for just the Plain and Amish folks! Religious confusion, unforgiveness toward oneself, and boulder-sized guilt and condemnation weighed heavily on their shoulders. One man couldn't believe that God would forgive him and his wife for fornication prior to their marriage. No, it wasn't a year or two after they got married, but a decade later and after he fathered three children. The guilt bogged him down until he no longer felt worthy enough to even *ask* his heavenly Father to forgive his trespasses.

He was also forlorn about the never-ending lustful sexual images that penetrated his mind 24-7. The concept of having the Holy Spirit give one assistance for his inner turmoil seemed as foreign as reading a Chinese menu and way too simple of a solution. If I look closely, I probably could see Satan running amuck laughing and giggling in the tortured patients' ears, "Tee hee hee." But I guess I can't include that thought in my nursing school homework.

Yes, I'm proud that cousin Jacob made a decision—for his sanity's sake.

Thought of the Day

Grace is understanding the gospel of grace is not just a moment in time but a new way of life that forever changes us.

Chapter 6

Aunt Lucy's Life-Changing Decision

But where sin increased, grace increased all the more.
—Romans 5:20

"You're about to have a nervous breakdown, Lucy," Dr. Kurtz softly said to my aunt. She twisted the hanky nervously on her lap. "Why don't you plan a little vacation away from your normal routine for a little while?" Even though my aunt did follow her doctor's advice, the "vacation" she chose changed her and her children's lives forever!

Lucy was my mom's only sister, younger by six years, who did not leave home, until she was married. She became very close to her brother, Theodore. She worked in a factory and married at a young age. In spite of red flag alerts about her fiancé, Lucy found out she was pregnant within a few short months of dating my uncle. As was expected by both their parents, they opted to tie the knot. Shortly into the marriage, Aunt Lucy realized her fate. But, as was expected when divorces were few and far in between in the 1960s, she never divorced my uncle. Even though the marriage was mostly loveless, "anatomy works" I say, and many children were conceived.

Mom told us the story many times how she and Aunt Lucy went to a fortune-teller when they were teenagers at the local fair. The fortune-teller took an egg and broke it open. Mom's egg yolk stayed intact, but Aunt Lucy's egg yolk broke apart. The prediction was Mom would eventually be happily married; Aunt Lucy would not have an intact marriage.

Sure enough, Aunt Lucy's cracked-egg prediction came true. She began running a household, attempted to make her husband happy, and raised babies. As the Lord would have it, Aunt Lucy and Uncle Samuel had eight children before she was forty. My uncle was not a good provider for his family. Unlike Daddy, he had short periods of employment; mostly, he was self-employed. One day, he proudly pulled his 1949 Jeep into our driveway and gave a sales pitch to Mom as to why she should buy the 18" trout he had on ice. Mom noticed three more like it in the ice chest. I guess he's now selling fish! Out of pity for her sister's family, Mom did purchase one.

Aunt Lucy had neither the time nor energy to work outside the home to contribute to their dire, bleak financial situation. My cousins were truly as poor as church mice. In fact, they were the recipients of their Dunkard Brethren Church's annual fruit baskets, clothing drives, and gift of monies at times. If it were not for the very low rent the landlord charged and financial assistance from two unmarried relatives, they possibly were saved from being homeless.

It soon became apparent to my mom and grandma that Aunt Lucy was not a tidy housekeeper. She chose to spend time outdoors frolicking with her kids, rather than being inside cleaning Lucy's two-story house, which soon looked like a pigsty. It made you feel like you had better keep up with your tetanus shot! Housework simply did not get done. Aunt Lucy found it more fun and interesting to spend time with her children out in the backyard building a snowman or teaching things about nature to her children. Sometimes, reading, as an escape, was more appealing to Aunt Lucy.

My aunt and uncle and cousins' living conditions were so unlike anything I experienced. Dirty kitchen floors—no, that's right, you could not see the floor! If one rummaged beneath the piles of dirt and filth, you might find soiled diapers, a few broken toys, and piles of dirty, stinky laundry. But it did not stop with the kitchen floor; it was repeated in the living room, down the hallway, and into some bedrooms.

At times, Aunt Lucy attempted to crack down on her kids and yelled, "Get this mess cleaned up now before your father gets home!" Some cleanup did occur, but unfortunately, it merely lasted only a day or two. With twelve people living in a moderate-sized house with no electricity, no running water, flushing toilets, and a hard-to-heat home, it was most difficult. Dirty dishes were always in the sink or in the perpetual drying rack, seldom finding their home in the cupboard.

A time Grandma Fisher, my mom and the kids, along with my cousins, did clean the house was when a *Lancaster Newspaper* reporter made plans to visit the house. The following day, my aunt was the subject of an article about giving birth to her youngest child during a severe winter storm by the light of a kerosene lamp. You cannot miss Aunt Lucy's big smile as she holds her infant in her arms.

Piles of laundry greeted us when my mom and my brother and sisters visited our cousins. Assisting my cousin with laundry (using the wringer washer that ran on a generator) had to occur first before we could start playing outside in their surrounding woods. Mom assumed she frequently needed to help her sister with the never-ending piled laundry while they caught up with each other's lives. This was the first family I knew who used a laundromat at times.

Though their home never had been voted to participate in the "House of the Year" flyer, abundant love did abide among Aunt Lucy and her children. She was always ready to give them a warm hug and a big smile. Unlike her older sister's home, the "I love yous" were said sincerely and left her lips often.

Having children close together was not the only reason for Aunt Lucy's state of exhaustion. The fact her husband had his own separate living quarters in a remodeled shed on one side of the dirt driveway had to take its toll. Being amply heated, clean and tidy, and always stocked with food, my uncle's home was for him only, and no kids were allowed inside. I can remember only peeping once inside my uncle's house, totally confused why a dad would do this to his wife and kids. Being that selfish was hard for me to fathom coming from my middle-class home. Loving to fish and hunt, my uncle will always be remembered as the one who cooked and served us squirrel as an entrée.

Aunt Lucy recognized early on that her older sons needed to find employment to help financially support her growing family. Aunt Lucy encouraged their being employed by Weaver's Poultry (the original company name of Tyson Foods). In fact, she was the one who drove them back and forth to work. The night shift paid the best hourly rate. Samuel Jr. (Sammy) and Gregory started on that shift catching chickens for processing. It was not long before they befriended some Hispanic coworkers from Vermont.

The Hispanic boys asked Aunt Lucy, "Would you please be so kind to drive us back up to Vermont so we can visit our families this weekend?" She had not forgotten her doctor's advice. Aunt Lucy compassionately answered, "Yes." With a tankful of gas, paid for by the teenagers, Aunt Lucy, her two oldest sons, and their two new friends, started their several-hundred-miles road trip from Pennsylvania to Vermont. This decision was life-changing for my cousins and aunt and uncle. Fourteen-year-old cousin Jane was put in charge of her siblings. However, her two maiden aunts (Uncle Samuel's sisters) stopped by and made meals for the family. After the third week of helping their nieces and nephews and no return of Aunt Lucy, the aunts became very concerned. Feeling they had no choice, they called the Pennsylvania Children and Youth Services.

Upon investigation, they found out my aunt's home of six children was unattended by a mom and had a mostly absentee dad (deadbeat was not a term used back then). A visit by the state agency found a fourteen-year-old daughter overseeing a filthy house and trying to be a caregiver for seven siblings, ranging in the ages of one and a half years to twelve. Because there was little food in the house and little monies to buy groceries, the social worker was forced to make a radical, immediate decision. A newspaper article was on file about this family and probably did not help any the situation for this family's demise. By the time Aunt Lucy found out about the situation, six of her children had already been disbursed to various local foster homes.

In the end, my cousins became wards of the state and were placed, as follows: the toddler and the four-year old were sent to live in the home of a childless horse-and-buggy Mennonite family in the neighboring county. They do not remember being raised in the Dunkard Brethren faith. The seven-year old was taken in by a local foster family in a nearby town. Two sisters were taken in by a Horning "Black Bumper" (church rules dictated all chrome bumpers be painted black) Mennonite family, who shortly, after their arrival, moved to Mississippi. Jill, my favorite cousin, moved in with a Mennonite family, who was a relative of my friend, Marilyn.

Meantime, in Vermont, the Hispanic boys found themselves facing a dire situation. What should have been a happy family reunion for the boys and their parents was unsettling. They walked into a dark house because the parents were unable to pay their electricity bill. Being gracious and kind, Aunt Lucy used her return-trip gas money and paid the family's electricity bill. She needed to call my mom, her sister, to have some money wired to her; it became a priority.

My part in this tragedy occurred when I was about eight years old.

The kitchen wall phone rang out three short rings. It was the signal it was a call meant for our family on the public telephone line we shared with two other neighbors. I stopped from playing Tag with my neighbor, Peggy, and ran into the house to answer the phone.

"Collect call from Lucy Stauffer to Elizabeth Martin. Will you accept the call, please?" the professional-sounding female operator asked me.

Since I had never answered a collect call of this type, I said hesitantly, "My mom's not home."

The operator then said, "Ma'am, would you like to leave a phone number where you can be reached?" I proceeded to write with the small pencil that was always tied to the notepad the return number.

Aunt Lucy was out of money and wanted to ask Mom for some gas money to be wired to her immediately, so she could start her journey back home. As with most youngsters, play was more important than passing on a message onto your parent. By the time my mom saw the posted phone number by the phone the following day, followed up with the call, my cousins' lives were already following a different journey.

Having not heard from my mom, Aunt Lucy was forced to get a job to earn some money to return home. By the time she did, some of her children were already being raised in uncrowded always-plenty-of-food-in-the-fridge, dishes-done, clean, heated homes. Eventually, wanting to reunite her family, she did her best to meet the social worker's demands upon her return back to Pennsylvania. But the social worker's first assessment, once again, revealed little or no income from Dad and unsanitary living conditions. Thus, she was not granted custody of her children. Feeling defeated, Aunt Lucy drove back up to Vermont.

My mom and Jane, the oldest daughter, acting as the fill-in mom, planned a family reunion the following summer in the park across the street where I lived. What I witnessed during this reunion will always be remembered. My cousins' foster families started planning their trip back to Lancaster County to reconnect. The horse-and-buggy family hired a driver, and other foster families were willing to drive whatever distance, so these children could be reunited with their siblings, and most of all, with their mommy.

It is forever engraved in my mind the memory of watching these, by then, three-and-five-year-old boys climb up on Mommy's lap. "Hi, how are you?" Aunt Lucy said with a big smile. "You know I love you, right?" So naturally, they were soaking up her love and warm hugs, so fulfilling, and so necessary. It didn't matter what had occurred to cause the separation or what her wrong choices were—this was Mommy!

After several hours of visiting between foster families, families, aunts and uncles and cousins, and plenty of picnic foods, the reunion was over. Foster parents, who by now dearly loved their cute foster children, with a sigh of relief, were ready to climb back into buggies and cars and return home. Whew! This was only a reunion and the birth Mom didn't try to snatch them away from their foster parents, after all.

The saddest tragedy of all about this dilemma was what occurred to my favorite cousin, Jill, who also was taken in by a local Mennonite family. One Saturday morning, just as I was finishing up my Saturday chore of cleaning the parlor (name given to our living room), the telephone rang. My fifteen-year-old mind could barely wrap around what I was about to hear. Cousin Jane, stammering and stuttering, was on the other end of the line.

"Leanne, this is Jane. I just got off the phone with my dad. Feel free to tell your parents and the rest of your family what I am about to tell you," she said between sniffles. "We just got word that Jill is pregnant."

I gasped. *Wait!? What? That's impossible! She's not allowed to date. She didn't tell me about any boyfriend.* A sudden coldness hit my core. With my mouth falling open, I managed to ask, "But how? Did she just recently have a boyfriend? Did you talk to Jill?"

"No, Daniel Hoover, her foster dad, got her knocked up," she said with a rising voice. "Yes, I talked to Jill," slightly softening, she went on to explain, "apparently, her foster parents had a TV in their bedroom. If the kids didn't want to watch what was on TV in the living room, they could watch it in their parents' bedroom if they asked for permission. Jill said the last several months Daniel and she watched *Star Trek* together. Nobody else in the family cared about the show."

I don't know much about that TV show. But I believe *Star Trek* isn't exactly full of sex scenes. What happened that Jill gets naked in front of Captain Kirk or Spock?

In a disbelieving voice, Jane continued, "At first, Daniel and Jill were sitting up in the bed to watch the show. Then one day, when Jill walked in his bedroom, he was lying on top of the covers with only his underwear on." In a voice I could barely hear, she mumbled, "That led to their having sex. Jill said it only happened three times."

Covering my other ear, I squealed, "Why did he have to have sex with her? Isn't that what his wife is for?"

Jane sniffled some more. Ignoring my outburst, she continued, "Jill always said the Hoovers were very lovey-dovey people. They hugged each other a lot. I know Jill grew accustomed to all that attention. Of course, Jill realizes now, after I explained it to her, she was simply seeking the love of a father. None of this is her fault."

I calmed down as I touched my throat and asked, "What happens now? Where is she living?"

Jane proceeded to tell me the plan for the remaining six months of Jill's pregnancy. She was removed from the Hoover family and moved into the church-supported Millersville Home for Unwed Mothers.

"Her baby is due when?" I asked.

"June 14," Jane answered. After a deep breath, she added, "So tell your mom I'll call her next week when I get more details about the Home's visiting hours."

Shaking my head, I hung up the phone and collapsed in the chair parked below the phone. *Oh, Jill. You must be so scared. I know I would be.*

Mom entered the kitchen, clumsily carrying three bags of groceries. "Leanne, go get the rest of the groceries…what? What happened?" she asked as she noticed my sad demeanor.

I stood up, feeling slightly dizzy. "Jane just called and reported sad news. Jill got knocked up by her foster dad, Daniel."

Mom suddenly dropped the three bags, which barely ended up safely on the table. Slapping one hand on her cheek, she said loudly, "Oh, for Pete's sake! What is wrong with that man?" She clutched her chest and walked to the phone to immediately call Jane. "What in God's name is this world coming to?" she commented as her fingers had difficulty using the rotary phone to dial the number.

As I went to the car to carry the remaining two bags of groceries into the house, my mind was whirling. *Daddy doesn't even let us girls see him when he's wearing his undershirt and trousers. I feel so bad for Jill.*

Eventually, Jill made the decision only her immediate family was invited to visit her. Other family members were asked to write letters or cards and keep in touch by phone calls. Jane dictated the contents of our letters and phone calls. We were not to mention the pregnancy; simply talk about what was going on in our lives. I can do that.

Letters of varying lengths, which I took the time to write in between my fifteen-year-old activities, arrived in Jill's mailbox. I regret that I didn't write more of them. Mom found out that my Uncle Samuel was adamant that Jill may *not*, in any way, shape, or form keep her baby. He threatened to disown her if she did. *Disown from what? His good name? His $20 in his wallet?*

On June 20, 1967, a beautiful baby girl, weighing six pounds and ten ounces, was whisked away from Jill's arms. One lucky, childless couple adopted Christy Lynn—and Jill's life was never the same. A permanent ache lived inside her, and a false smile formed on her lips for years.

Reunions continued on a regular basis. But, as time would have it, they became more infrequent or only partially attended by family members. Aunt Lucy eventually moved back to Pennsylvania, left my uncle, moved to a different county, got a job working in a factory, and took up woodworking as a hobby (just like her dad).

Eventually, Aunt Lucy started a long-term relationship with a man, but she never married him. Her family grew up, and soon, my cousins started their own families. Jane continues to be the thread that keeps the communication open, the best she can, between two counties and three different states and plans ongoing large family reunions.

As young adults, my two oldest cousins moved to Alaska to help build the oil pipeline. Eventually, they convinced their younger brother to join them in this lucrative job. He did and moved out from his foster family's home. As fate would have it, within five years of his move to Alaska to be reunited with his brothers, he fell overboard on a fishing boat. Though his body was never found, he was later declared dead by state authorities—another tragedy for this family.

The following is a memoir I wrote following Aunt Lucy's funeral in April 2010:

MY LAST LAST NAME IS GRACE

"Regrets and Forgiveness"

I recently attended my Aunt Lucy's viewing and funeral last Tuesday and Wednesday. My tears flowed during the service when cousin Gregory her second-oldest son, read parts of a letter his mother wrote prior to her death for her children. She spoke of asking for their forgiveness and having many regrets.

Six years ago, after the death of her long-term male companion, Aunt Lucy moved back to the Ephrata area, giving opportunity for her and Gregory to hold many conversations. She confided in him about the many regrets of how their lives were affected by her choices.

Gregory wisely informed her, "The past is the past, and it can't be changed. We can only forgive you and move forward." Aunt Lucy had renewed her relationship with the Lord as well. The more she stepped into God's river of grace, the more Aunt Lucy felt her sinful past was forgiven.

For one and one-half years, she fought, but lost, her battle of lung cancer, which metastasized into breast and brain cancer. But she was ready to meet her Lord and Savior. Aunt Lucy's biggest concern, portrayed in her funeral service, was that all her children and grandchildren would know her Lord, the One who truly and freely forgives.

I and my two sisters took some time to analyze Aunt Lucy's viewing and funeral service. We did not notice lots of tears or raw emotion at the funeral nor at the graveside. The only time my cousins had to mourn privately was during the family viewing around Aunt Lucy's casket prior to the final closing of it, which we did not observe. Cousin Susan, as tears welled up, told my sister that she felt some tinges of sadness around her mom's casket.

But what we did notice was the closeness between the siblings. It appeared that the religious differences and the conservative dress for some made little difference in their closeness and affection. Perhaps, this was due to their common-ground journey of being placed in foster homes. Plus, as taught by their mom, openly displaying affection was something shown to them often.

Forgiveness is definitely for the benefit of the one hurt. What a testimony for their grandchildren to see their mother and father, my cousins, forgiving Grandma for the error of her ways. I listed some areas, below, I imagine, are some of the reasons my cousins need to forgive, as God has forgiven them:

* Their deadbeat dad (who died four years ago of heart disease) on his part of their demise (I later learned from Jane her dad too asked his family for their forgiveness);
* Mom, who did not provide adequate babysitting; thus, changing the course of their lives forever.
* Me for not passing onto Mom, their aunt, the timely message.
* Aunt Elizabeth, who did not return their mom's call when she requested money for her return trip home.
* Foster dad of Jill, who got her pregnant at fourteen, when a teenager starving for the

love of a father, was taken advantage of, and to forgive their dad too, for saying he would disown Jill if she even thought about keeping her baby and insisted she be put up for adoption.
- God, for allowing Jill to die of lung cancer at the age of thirty-five, leaving behind a four-year-old son and a nine-year-old daughter (I miss you, Jill).
- The driver of the boat who perhaps caused the drowning of their brother—could he have done more to prevent his drowning?
- And many more reasons to forgive not mentioned here, I'm sure, my ten cousins have had to deal with I cannot begin to imagine, so they can experience peace and freedom, not bondage.

As my pastor preached the previous Sunday, forgiving is like expelling carbon dioxide from your body because you know holding it in will only hurt you. The Word tells us to forgive as we have been forgiven by Christ (Mark 11:24–25). In fact, I am to do this *before* I open my mouth in prayer. I need to sincerely ask my heavenly Father to search my heart and reveal to me the need to forgive someone before I start to pray. It's being intentional and is required to walk in holiness.

May God take all regrets and broken hearts and fill you with His abundant grace!

BEATY MILLER

Thought of the Day

Grace is realizing, as with King David's adopted son, many people gather around a table with crippled feet. We all limp through our lives. But one day we'll sit at the King's table and be treated as royalty too, as one who didn't ask for any of it but was simply given an invitation. Now that's being shown *super*abundant grace!

Chapter 7

"Where You See, I Have Done Good…"

Now to him who is able to do immeasurably more than all we ask or imagine according to his power that is at work within us.
—Ephesians 3:20

I KNEW I WAS LOVED by Daddy, but you did not expect to be asked "How are you?" or "What's up?" Daddy was not one to display affection to his children. But to Mother, that was a different matter. They openly hugged and kissed in front of us. Sunday afternoons were a time they rested together on the parlor sofa. If time allowed, some smooching took place.

Daddy wanted to teach his four growing boys responsibility, a good work ethic, how to keep busy, and to stay out of Mom's way. Both of my parents wanted their family to have the connection with nature and appreciate the value of hard work, as they had. My parents soon desired to live on a property that had plenty of room for the children to romp and play. Such a property was located, and we moved back, into Lancaster County on Good Drive in the Garden Spot School District. Daddy was working days for New Holland Brick and Pipe hauling items in his privately owned truck. He only worked on the farm part-time in the evenings or on Saturdays, as he expected the boys to do the farming during the day.

Switching jobs to be employed by Ivan W. Martin's Quarry, Daddy drove a truck, hauling limestone and worked his way up to become a foreman at the Limeville plant. Daddy got up early, kissed Mom good-bye, and left the house to go to work with a beverage thermos and a lunch box filled with a sandwich (Mom called a sammich), a snack food, and some fruit, which was lovingly packed by Mom. After work, he came home, kissed Mom hello, and expected to sit down to a quiet (seriously?) table set for ten people, for a simple evening meal of meat and potatoes, starches, and desserts, which Mom was always too happy to oblige.

As a teenager, I was grateful Daddy was willing to drive me to my friend's house. But I felt uncomfortable being alone with him because I felt pressured to think about the perfect conversation where we both felt at ease. More times than not, little conversation went on during those travels back and forth. When I was younger and spent time alone with Daddy's parents, I do not remember having any teachable moments with either Grandpa or Grandma Martin. So, monkey see, monkey do, I guess.

Often, Daddy was more than happy to drive me over to my friend, Nancy's house because he liked to spend a few hours foxhunting with her dad. Equipped with an actual fox caller and gun in hand, those two men hid somewhere in the local woods in anticipation. They already envisioned a fox's stuffed hide proudly displayed on one's basement wall. I do not remember Daddy ever being successful. The joy was in the hunt.

Convenient for me, when I was a teenager, Daddy had a full-time job and a part-time job of driving his own truck hauling block. So we did not interact very often. I would already be in my bedroom when he would arrive home around 10:00 p.m. each weekday night. Daddy was out the door well before the time I needed to get up for school.

Once married, I do not recall ever answering the phone and hearing Daddy's voice on the other end of the line. Mom was the one who always placed phone calls to their married kids' homes.

If Daddy wanted to make a point about something, Mom was expected to pass it on. When I was thirteen years old, Mom said to me, "Leanne, Daddy said I need to stop trimming your hair shorter so you have long-enough hair to put up in your bob (anticipating me joining church soon and wearing my hair under the head covering)." Or "Daddy said he does not want you girls going swimming when you have your periods (which we all did anyway)." How would he know when we had our monthly cycle? Oh, I guess with two teenaged girls in the house at one time and only one main bathroom, he could monitor the bathroom trash can? Ah, that's right; Daddy *does* have a sensitive side somewhat when it comes to women.

Being a man's man and raised out of his generation, Daddy and Mom definitely had definitive roles around the house on who handled which household chores. Daddy never cooked. Mom said, smiling proudly, "The poor guy can't even boil water if he'd ever needed a reason to." Nor did he run a vacuum cleaner, pick up a dustcloth, or help with laundry. I do remember seeing him sweep off the porch, burn trash, and clean out his garage. Since we did not own a barbecue grill, Daddy wasn't a grill chef either. However, he became the one who barbequed and gave oversight to some awesome chicken barbeques (over a huge wire rack that rested on cement blocks), for our huge family gatherings down in "the park." He helped Mom with making homemade root beer and dandelion wine. He did some lawn mowing, but, well into her seventies, Mom was seen more times than not on the riding lawn mower. While washing his truck, Daddy sometimes included washing the family cars as well.

Conversations around the Haas card table were lively for our competitive family. As a youngster, we focused on the game and strived to show Daddy we were paying attention to his lessons on how to bid, win the hand, and be competitive. Again, it was about the game and not about a time to talk about life. Being emotional, sharing warm fuzzy feelings were not in Daddy's nature; we simply accepted him for who he was.

As an adult, we geared around-the-card table conversations as a time to make announcements (i.e., "We're moving" or "I'm going to nursing school," or "I've changed jobs."). But it was not because you were asked "what's new?" It was because you initiated the conversation and took advantage of the opportunity to have your parents be aware of your life's happenings. Some discussions never came up, and I preferred it that way. At other times, you left after a visit back home and asked yourself, "Why bother? Does Daddy really care all that much?"

One fall day in September 1990, I walked into my English composition class, a prerequisite course required before I could start Nursing I through VI for my RN (registered nurse) degree.

Mrs. Bolten, leaning on her elbows, motioned for me to come to her desk. She was holding my last written assignment in her hands. "A" in red ink glared up at me from the top right corner. Whew! "Leanne, would you please be so kind and read your composition out loud for the entire class to hear. It is so touching."

Taken aback with furrowed brows, I mumbled, "Sure," still glowing from the good grade.

As soon as the approximately fifteen students were seated, Mrs. Bolten handed out the remaining compositions to my classmates. "I would like you to give your attention to two of the assignments. Leanne will go first." Mrs. Bolten, not bothering to look through her glasses, perched halfway down her nose, announced to the class.

Standing in front of the room while leaning against Mrs. Bolten's desk, I began reading using great voice inflection:

Piling Dinner Plates: September 27, 1990

Here I am at my age of thirty-eight, and I'm still worried about what my parents think, especially Daddy! My dad, Mother, Lenora (my older sister), and I were congregated in my parents' living room one Friday night last spring playing the card game Haas. As we placed our bets, the subject of our occupations came up. I thought, *Now's a good time to announce my choice of a new career and watch for Daddy's reaction.*

I had told Mother of my decision during her hospital stay for kidney stones four weeks earlier. After questioning one of Mother's nurses at some length in Mother's presence about her choice of career, I broke the news to my mother. "Mother, I'm seriously thinking about taking part-time courses at Reading Area Community College to earn a nursing degree. I decided I'm not interested in sitting in front of a computer for the next thirty years until I retire, keypunching in thousands of numbers every day."

She looked at me quizzically, and I could tell she wasn't taking me very seriously. "How will you manage your big house? What about the children at night? You'll never be home." Then the clincher: "You're going to work yourself sick!" After some discussion (no, more like convincing), I diminished some of her unfounded fears. Unlike my Daddy, Mother is easier to get to understand my views and is certainly more open minded.

(Anticipating the next paragraph, I slowed down my reading, gulped, and continued reading in a dropped voice.) I certainly was not expecting Daddy to slap me on the back or give me words of encouragement, but I was unprepared for his five-word comment to me that night sitting at the card table: "What's the matter with ya?"

(Breaking eye contact, I felt my eyes watering. I titled my chin down, swallowed hard, and began reading.) There have been many instances before when my dad hurt me deeply. The hurt slowly, incident by incident, has been piling up like a stack of dinner plates inside that mysterious cavity they call my soul. (*Whose strange voice is that?*) Amazingly, I've learned not to be too resentful or bitter at Dad. My sisters, who both love to dabble in psychology and have been counseled professionally because of my dad's effect on our lives, insist I'm choosing to deny my true feelings, which is a cop-out. Well, maybe, but the plates will keep piling until they fall over.

Pressing my hand to my abdomen, I slinked to my seat. I guess it is one thing to compile the assignment, but another thing to read it aloud when sharing such a private, painful moment.

Over time, the dishes continued to pile up, but eventually, they got washed by grace.

I do not remember doing any chores side by side with Daddy, such as washing the car. The only chore he taught me was when I was in sixth grade; he wanted to teach me how to use the lawn mower. Being a property of almost five acres of land, the lawn required much attention. Thus, I was needed at times to mow the front lawn. After some time of mowing, walking up and down the huge lawn, the mower ran out of gas. I proceeded to get the gas can out of the garage, walked up to the still-running mower, and started pouring in gasoline. Next thing I know, Daddy was running across the lawn, yelling, "Turn it off first! Turn it off!" A hand came around and turned off the mower. Looking back, it wasn't a scolding, but I definitely understood the lesson. I believe Daddy took some responsibility of assuming I knew about such things when I actually did not. I can tell you, I never made that mistake again.

Daddy's laugh was very unique. Sometimes, it was more of a chuckle than a laugh. At times, it was exaggerated and louder than what fit the occasion, especially if he was the originator of a prank or a silly comment. He was not a moody person, and we were not fearful of him, but in his presence, we knew to toe the line. A time of fooling around had occurred when Daddy tried to say the word *spaghetti*. He purposefully mispronounced the word, saying, "I can't sssaaayyy sssss-ggg-e-ttt-iii. So if I can't say it, it's not fit to eat."

I acquired the love for 5th Avenue candy bars from Daddy. I learned to appreciate his treats for an ice-cream cone for me and my brothers and sisters a couple of times a month. When we lived in Hinkletown, a small grocery store was easily accessible across the street. In the boring winter months, men gathered around the pot-bellied stove and "shot the breeze" with the store owner and other neighbor men. Under the guise of purchasing his kids an ice cream cone, Daddy frequented the store sometimes in the evenings. As time went on, I believe Mom put her foot down about how often and long Daddy was to spend time away from home and hang out over there.

I have only witnessed Daddy cry in public one time. It occurred during a funeral for a son of one of our hunting cabin gang families. The fourteen-year-old teenager drowned during a family beach vacation. It was a sad day for all of us, as we were a close-knit group that shared many a weekends in the mountains together at the jointly owned cabin. Perhaps, Daddy did cry at both his parents' funerals, but I do not remember seeing actual tears run down his cheeks, as on this occasion. It made me realize that day Daddy does have a soft spot.

I have only one recollection of Daddy making Mom cry. I was about five or six years old. My parents were discussing who would be invited to go along to the cabin with them the following weekend. Whomever Daddy had suggested did not sit well with Mom. The opinions went back and forth. Suddenly, Mom, in a strange crying voice I had never heard before, broke down crying and put her hand over her eyes. Daddy gave in and said, "Fine, we'll go with your suggestion." *Those hormones!* Though this occurred only once, I have learned by Mom's example that wives do not use tears to get their own way. But husbands are to be sensitive to women's moods.

If Mom and Daddy did not want the kids to eavesdrop on a conversation, they spoke Pennsylvania Dutch. My brothers learned the language by Daddy conversing with them in Dutch and by the cousins who spoke it as well. Because both parents were fluent in speaking Pennsylvania Dutch, they enjoyed participating in the annual Martindale Dutch bee (much like a spelling bee, except you were to translate an English word into the Dutch translation). They often won both first- or second-place prizes.

Daddy was a meat-and-potatoes man. Mom had a simple menu plan; she cooked to please him. I was not raised on casseroles or pizza, as Daddy did not even like tomatoes. Steaks and roasts, pork, and chicken were plentiful. Venison also filled the freezer when Daddy or one of my brothers, or both, were successful during doe or buck hunting seasons.

It was not until I was dating and eating out in a restaurant I learned to appreciate a good medium (or medium rare) steak. Whether it was a roast or a steak, Mom seemed to cook them in similar ways. Sometimes, a thick piece of meat (a roast?), I remember, simmered on the stove in a covered skillet for hours. Not having or wanting a grill, Mom, at other times, placed two pieces of thinner meat (steaks?) in a frying pan and simmered them on the stove for hours also. A definite thick too-large-for-skillet-sized piece of meat (roast?) was placed in the oven to bake for hours (often served for company).

Mixed green salads (Daddy said lettuce was only rabbit food) were not served often, either, unless it was cut lettuce fresh from Mom's garden, a cucumber salad, or coleslaw. Mostly, gelatin salads of all colors were served at meals. Because gelatin salads lasted for more than one meal, it was an easy, inexpensive food to serve her big family. Mom had earned a beautiful set of copper salad molds as a hostess gift from one of her home parties. But plastic salad molds were used frequently as well.

Buttered noodles, stewed crackers, and fried potatoes were often served along with mashed potatoes and gravy. Who cares about two or more starches being served at a meal? It was what Daddy liked, and Mom, not being up on the latest home economics lessons on meal preparation, willingly served the food items he enjoyed. Boy, did he ever enjoy his gravy bread too.

Later on, when Mom and Daddy frequented a restaurant, Daddy's favorite menu choice, being a picky eater, was to order a hot roast beef sandwich. Mom spoiled him so much. Once they were invited to someone's home for a meal, Mom feared the food served might not be to Daddy's liking; she brought along a hamburger patty to cook and serve Daddy instead. Yep, I witnessed it with my own eyes when my cousin Jill invited us over for dinner. Now Daddy felt cherished.

Daddy definitely had more rapport with my brothers. But they received the most spankings from Daddy as well. Frequently, my four oldest brothers shared one room that held two double beds. Since the apple doesn't fall far from the tree, energetic, rowdy boys made for some awful racket—Daddy's favorite word for any irritating noise. One can only imagine all the testosterone in that one room from four growing boys. Whether it was a floor wrestling match that got out of hand and the bumping sounds entering through the kitchen ceiling below made for too much racket, or their yelling match hit the highest decibel allowed, Daddy or Mom had their fill. Daddy did not even ask who was at fault. He simply entered the room, took off his belt, and spanked them all.

I am sure a brother often became "Pop" at times and doled out his own punishments to his brothers trying to prevent hearing Daddy's footsteps coming up the stairs. If one was not at fault, he was not about to bear a faultless spanking. So many times, they dished out their own threats and handled the pecking order quite well. After all, unless it was unpreventable that Daddy had to walk through the boys' room to go to the bathroom, handing out punishments was the only reason Daddy ever had to enter their rooms!

Having lots of time and reasons to spend time with the boys, who were his farmhands, Daddy definitely built a different relationship with them than his two younger daughters. (My older sister, the first girl of the family, shared a special bond with him as well.) Yes, the four older boys probably received more spankings than the four younger kids. But I do not believe any of the boys worried about what to discuss during a one-on-one conversation with Daddy, like my younger sister and I did. By the time baby Douglas came along, he had won Daddy's heart in the most special way. He cannot fathom what I or other siblings have experienced, or have *not* experienced, with Daddy.

The contrast is profound, as written below by Doug, as posted on his privately owned trucking transport business's website today:

Tribute to Dad

I owe the love of trucks to my father, who worked most of his life at Martin Limestone, Inc. or hauling for them. For many years, he had two jobs: driving truck and/or working in the quarry. He started in the late '40s with a single-axle tractor with a single-axle trailer hauling block and pipe for New Holland Block or Pipe Plant. He talked about hauling four cubes of block, loading and unloading them by hand; no need for a gym (membership) in those days! He also hauled pipe for the Pennsylvania Turnpike from the Morgantown exit on east. For a few years, he turned the truck driving over to some of my older brothers while he worked for the quarry and drove night shift part-time. I would go along, if he was driving, in the evening.

My first gear jamming was when I was around six years old. The truck my dad had at the time was a 1966 Chevy with a 454-gas engine and 4 × 4 transmission. Dad would shift the one stick, and I would move the second one. He was foreman of the Limeville plant until 1974, when he resigned. He then returned to trucking full-time.

At that time, he bought a new 1974 Brockway to haul for the quarry. He did a short haul for the quarry, supplying material to the New Holland Block plant. He became known as the "Red Yuke" with his bright red Brockway. I can remember going along with Dad. He would come home for dinner at 4:00 p.m., eat a bite, take a short snooze, and then be back at the quarry at 6:30 p.m. I would go along in the evening because Dad was the only person working, and he had to load his own truck. When we switched material, I would drive the truck to the other pile while Dad moved the loader.

He bought his favorite truck in 1979, a Peterbilt with a 400 Cummins engine. They started calling Dad the "Flying Dutchman," when he drove the Peterbilt. When I became old enough to drive at eighteen years old, I also drove this same truck. They started calling me "Little Dutchman" because of Dad's nickname, since I was driving the same one. The block plant was busy in those days, and they had a full-time night shift. I drove days, and Dad drove nights. We kept the wheels turning almost around the clock.

I worked for Dad until 1986. I then bought my first truck and became an owner-operator. Dad passed away from cancer in March 2001. Thanks for the memories, Dad!

Unfortunately, Daddy will never be able to read this tribute in his honor written by Doug. If so, he would be so proud of Doug today.

Typical of Mennonite families, the boys were assured a vehicle at sixteen years of age, while the girls were given "hope" (cedar) chests sometime before their wedding day. I received mine as a graduation present (which I still have—how many of my brothers still have their first car? None!). After all, boys need a method of transportation to start earning a paycheck. Girls did not need a vehicle, as it was assumed they would be dating, and the boyfriend owned a car as a means of transportation. Daddy bought my oldest brother his first used car. Of course, that car was passed on to the next boy in line when he turned sixteen about a year later.

So how did I get to work? Thankfully, my neighbor who owned a car drove us both to the factory for our after-school jobs. I paid her money for gas each week. When I was seventeen and started my first office job at Mennonite Central Committee (MCC) right after high school, I had to do some research for my own means of transportation. Luckily, a former high school classmate's sister lived a few miles from my home and also worked at MCC. Charging five dollars a week for gas, she drove out of her way a short distance, picked me up, and took me to MCC.

As with most teenagers, I could not wait for my sixteenth birthday to get my driver's permit and pass my driver's test. John, my boyfriend-turned-husband, drove me to my high school parking lot where I frequently practiced parking his 1968 Chevy II. Sometimes, I practiced my driving skills in Esther's or Cheryl's car. I nicknamed my parents' car Bessie. The jalopy was a 1958 light-green Chevy with chrome trim along both sides. A few times John had me practice in Bessie (I have no recollection of Daddy, only Mom, helping me to learn how to drive). Finally, with the assistance of a driver's education class at school, I felt confident and prepared to take my driver's test. Bessie, Esther, and I headed to the Lancaster testing site one Saturday.

On the outset, as per their protocol, the police officer first walked around my parents' Chevy to inspect its tires and checked for functioning brake lights and turn signals. When finished, the police officer asked Esther and me to step out of the car and return inside. So we did. The police officer informed me two of the Chevy's tires were too "bald" and need replaced before a driver's test could be completed.

Needless to say, when I got home, Daddy heard a mouthful from me! Already a ball of nerves, I vented, and he listened, sensing my frustration. It was not like him to neglect his car maintenance duties, and perhaps, he already had plans to replace the worn-out tires. Being a teenager and not fully appreciative of Daddy's handling two jobs, I did return the following Saturday to take my driver's test in Bessie, sporting two new tires. In my first attempt, I failed for parking too far from the curb, but the second time was a charm.

Daddy was more comfortable sitting up at the table for a Checkers or Haas game, being alone in the woods hunting, or sitting behind the wheel of his truck. I do remember being asked once if I wanted to accompany Daddy on his truck run during the summer, which I did. Sitting in a noisy cab was not conducive to a two-way conversation, but I could tell he thoroughly enjoyed mastering the gearshifts and being "king of the hill."

One oops moment occurred near our home. Daddy was attempting to cross a covered bridge with his dump truck. It had rained earlier in the day. So Daddy had put the dump truck bed in the up position to drain the water. Unbeknownst to him, the bed was still in the up position while he was attempting to cross the covered bridge. Needless to say, the dump truck came to an abrupt halt!

Those who work hard, play hard. Daddy was no exception. His hunting trips to the mountains of Pennsylvania, which started the weekend after Thanksgiving along with his buddies, were always a highlight. Many jokes and one-ups were played among the men. One story is told how Daddy bragged about his good Noodle Doosie water he brought along with him in a thermos from home. Dumping out the water, the men refilled it with the water from the cabin faucet. Daddy kept bragging about how great his water tasted. At the end of the hunting trip right before leaving for home, his buddies confessed to the trick. I do not believe Daddy bothered to take water from home again after that episode.

During my rebellious years and when far from God (an upcoming chapter explains this), I seldom visited my parents and held few phone conversations with Mom. Partly due to shame and disappointment, my visits with them were limited. So I missed out on hearing a lot about their life during that time, and they of mine. I was never invited to stay overnight at their hunting cabin as Mom and Daddy believed, as a divorcee, I was committing ongoing adultery when I remarried. They wanted no part of ever being under the same roof at bedtime with a man other than my first husband. Thus, I only visited their cabin on a day trip and drove back home the same day.

Think about that! I could never invite them to go on vacation with my family or travel out of town to visit relatives if my husband was traveling with me. They have missed out on so many family memories with my own immediate family. This saddens me.

Turns out Daddy was employed by Martin's Quarry for over thirty-five years before owning and operating his own stone-hauling business until he retired in 1988 at the age of sixty-four. Unfortunately, his occupation choice most likely caused his demise due to the rampant limestone dust (details in a later chapter).

I found out Daddy was a Sunday school teacher from his obituary. During his viewing, comments were made about him, and I learned about some aspects of Daddy I did not know. He was the man who frequently handed out candy on Sunday mornings to the children I was told. From his officiating minister at his funeral service, I heard stories for the first time about his volunteer job at Christian Aid Ministries.

In summary, Daddy was somewhat a different man viewed by his daughter than how the rest of the world saw him. At the end of his life, recognizing some shortcomings, he passed onto his family the saying: "Where you see I have done good, do good. Where I didn't do good, do better." *By the grace of God, I am trying, Daddy.*

Thought of the Day

Bestow grace by releasing others to God and realizing their decisions may cause scars. I am *not* one's Holy Spirit, either.

Chapter 8

Bugsy and Aunt Joyce

> What a wretched man I am! Who will rescue
> me from this body of death?
> —Romans 7:24

My sister Lorna was born in Lancaster Osteopathic Hospital, the first child in our family not to be born at home. Because we moved to Churchtown shortly after her birth, Lorna's makeshift bed on moving day was one of the dresser drawers. I do not have any recollection of living here. But for kicks and giggles, I enjoy looking at a black-and-white photo of all of us kids sitting on a porch lined up by our ages, from Junior, the oldest, to me, the baby at the time.

When I was about four years old, we moved again to a rental farmette near Fivepointville. Mom never cared for the layout of the home, as she felt the living room was much too small for her growing family. It was a house that sat real close to the road, unlike the previous rental property located at the end of a long lane. Thus, within a year, Daddy started looking for another house for his family. Needing a larger home, Daddy heard about another rental property, which had more bedrooms to accommodate his growing family. Having a barn, some acres to raise crops on, and plenty of grounds and meadow to rump and play, it seemed perfect for us. So we moved again into the Cocalico School District.

The rented double house (calling them *duplexes* came later) had a circular gravel driveway, so you could enter it from either the right or left side. This house also set fairly close to the road. The smallest end was the home of our landlord; the largest part was home to my family. It had two separate front doors. The main big yard was off to the side and the back of the house. It was understood we did not play in the small side yard on the landlord's side of the house. On the landlord's side, white wooden stairsteps led from the ground to a second-floor door. But the landlord usually used the front or back door just as we did. The back of the house had a wooden porch the entire length of the house, also with two more separate entry doors.

A small two-bedroom gray-shingled bungalow sat at the curve of our circular driveway at the back of our house. When we first moved, nobody lived in it. But within a few months, a family of four, including a sixth-grade girl and a fourth-grade boy, moved in it and became our landlord's second tenants.

My first memory in this house is "playing church" in the bathroom behind closed doors. My pretended pulpit was the clothes hamper. Not much higher than it, I tucked in my brother's shirtsleeve, which was hanging partially out from under the closed lid. Then I had to gather all the soiled underwear that missed the hamper opening (the boys loved to play hoops with their dirty clothing) before moving the hamper away from the wall. I stood behind my "pulpit" and began the first part of my pretended church service using a lower voice, "Please open your hymnal to page 312. Page 312, please. 'What A Friend We Have in Jesus.'"

A pitiful key of "C" sounded between my lips mimicking the church chorister's pitch pipe. Waving my hand as though leading singing, I belted out parts of the memorized song: "What a friend we have in Jesus. All my sins and griefs to bear…." If I heard any of my siblings outside the bathroom door, I would pause. After pretending to be the song leader led to mimicking the preacher. Mom's Bible was lying on top of the hamper and randomly opened. Not being able to read much beyond "God is good" at five years old, I pretended to be reading scripture while preaching.

"Church, communion Sunday is coming up. Are you ready? (pause for impact) Have you repented of all your sins? (looking down at the open Bible) Are you living for Jesus? (raising my voice) Or are you on the path to hell?" I pounded on the hamper lid for emphasis. "Hell is a hot place, and nobody should want to go there!" My only audience members of the tub and washbowl sat in respectful silence.

"Leanne." I heard a rattled locked bathroom door. "I got to go to the bathroom. Open up. Get out," said my brother Elvin. *Oh, well, I'm done preaching. I'm gonna go outside and play.*

The landlord, nicknamed Bugsy (that should give one a hint about his personality), was of the horse-and-buggy faith; he mostly got around by driving his bicycle. He also did not own a telephone, which was forbidden by the church. Soon Daddy became suspicious the landlord, using his own key, was entering our home while we were away, using our phone. The first trick done for proof was to place a small folded piece of paper underneath the mouthpiece of the wall phone. Too small to be seen, if you did not know it was there, anybody using the phone would cause the folded paper to slip onto the floor when you took the phone off the receiver. Lo and behold, one Sunday we came home from church and Daddy found the paper lying on the floor. I am uncertain if Daddy had ever confronted Bugsy, but I believe he did. Not having any success, Daddy tried another trick.

One Sunday morning shortly after this incident, several of us younger children were not feeling well. We were allowed to stay home from church with an older brother as the babysitter. Expecting the landlord to enter our home again, we moved the living room sofa away from the wall slightly and crawled behind it to hide. Sure enough, the landlord entered our home, went right to the phone, lifted the receiver, dialed a number, and started a phone conversation with someone. Shortly into it, we three kids on cue stood up at the same time and yelled, "Hey, you!" Startled, Bugsy hung up without saying good-bye and scurried out of our home. We have every reason to believe the use of our phone by him stopped. If he had asked for permission, I'm sure Daddy, of course, would have allowed him to use the phone sometimes.

Being thrilled, Mom had a grape arbor on this property plentiful enough to allow her to can grape juice. Two wooden swings hung from the arbor as well. Over time, the wooden seats rotted out. Thus, one day, while in a full high swing, my wooden seat broke away from the rope, which secured it to the top of the arbor. Down I went with the wooden seat scraping across my chest. Though the injury required a bandage and some first aid, I returned to my swinging using the unbroken swing. Thus, I now have a permanent scar.

One day, I was busy swinging on the swing that hung from the arbor. I suddenly heard a lady's voice shouting loudly. Sounding as though it came from the landlord's side of the house, I ran around to his side of the house confused, as I knew Bugsy was a bachelor and lived alone. I stopped in my tracks. There, standing on the landing on the top of the stairs was my Aunt Joyce (on my dad's side). Why isn't Aunt Joyce visiting with Mom? Does she know our landlord, Bugsy?

Aunt Joyce was standing at the screen door raising her fist at, assumedly, Bugsy, who was standing on the other side of it.

"Why did I see your bicycle parked along the side of the white house at 7415 E. Main Street in Ephrata yesterday? I know who lives there. A lady whose husband is a long-distance truck driver, and he is hardly ever home, that's who! What were you doing in her house?" Aunt Joyce screamed. "I demand to know!" Her blonde bob started to unravel in her fury.

Apparently, not liking Bugsy's response, she yelled again. "You had no business being there. Tell me *now*." Aunt Joyce kept yanking on the screen doorknob in an attempt to open the locked door. But it only slightly budged. Red-faced, she turned and stormed down the stairs. I quickly ran back to the swing, so she would not see me. Aunt Joyce backed up her green Dodge out of the driveway while spinning her tires, causing small gravel to go flying.

In hindsight, could the conversation I had overheard be about my aunt yelling at the landlord because she was already pregnant by him? When I was older, Mom told me my favorite cousin (on my dad's side of the family) was not my uncle's child but our previous landlord's child. Several years later, my aunt had another child by him who looked very much like Bugsy. Kudos to him, my uncle raised his large family as though every child was his. Grace is granted when asked.

Ah, yes, all families have their secrets. Hearing about my Aunt Joyce's indiscretions, it made perfect sense to me later on as to why Daddy did not say much about my mom's sister, Lucy's behaviors. How could he?

Living in the country, it was common in the summertime to have "road bums" (homeless men?) knock on our front door and ask for some food at times. Mom fixed them a plate and had them sit on the front porch. Remember, these were strangers, and she did *not* think of inviting them inside. If we saw one walking down the hill, we gave Mom the heads-up. I have learned you share your food but with caution.

Besides the road bums, another occurrence gave me and Lorna some fright. In the summertime when the bedroom windows were opened in hopes for a slight breeze, we could hear if any car was proceeding down the hill near the front of our house. Sometimes, a car would stop on top of the hill. Full of Mom's folklore stories, we could only assume it was a gypsy behind the wheel or definitely a thief up to no good. In hindsight, it probably was a dating couple stopping for a kiss, but the Martin girls stretched their imagination. We scurried into bed and buried our heads under the covers until we heard the car drive on by.

As is commonplace for those who lived on farms, we had a pet dog. Somehow, Daddy convinced Mom to allow him also to get a pet goat. Well, this billy goat was not too friendly and seemed to be proud of it. The more bucking he did toward you, the better; he definitely was not a pet. Whoever got too close to bucking billy at one time or another got their nudge. Some bucking was because Daddy encouraged it, and he laughed and laughed when it took us by surprise. Needless to say, at Mom's insistence, the billy goat was soon sold.

The pet dog did not fare as well. When Daddy or one of my older brothers was mowing the hayfield, the dog ran too near the equipment. They did not realize it until it was too late. The dog had two of his legs partially cut off by the mower. Saddened, Daddy sent it to doggy heaven by shooting it and taking it out of its misery and then buried it in the meadow.

One day while carrying a quart of milk, Mom dropped it, spilling the contents all over the floor. After seeing her physician, Mom was diagnosed with arthritis, which eventually affected her knees as well. Believing to be much too young for this diagnosis, she was determined to find a cure and took the matter into her own hands. Besides praying to her heavenly Father for healing, Mom heard about a homeopathic remedy: calamus root. For several times a day, she chewed on tiny pieces of this root.

This cream-colored root was kept in a small plastic bag in the freezer. Having a pungent lemony smell, the calamus root was routinely nibbled on by Mom, who anticipated its working cure. Though not being very pleasant for other household members, the strong root smell revealed when Mom was chewing it. Sure enough, in time, Mom was no longer affected by arthritis. Action mixed with faith wins every time.

To keep arthritis at bay, for many years, Mom kept a small amount in her freezer and nibbled on it on occasion. Her proof of not being afflicted again with arthritis was in the several dozens of quilts she ended up sewing for her family—a nearly impossible feat had she been dealing with arthritis the rest of her life. By God's grace, she was one of the fortunate ones who experienced arthritic pain for only a short period of time.

Can anybody recall an early dream? I can. No idea what the significance of it means, but I know it occurred when I was about five or six years old. I shared it with my cousin Jill. (Dream interpretation was not a hot topic at the time.) Here is the dream: I woke up in the middle of the night and went to the bathroom. Passing a mirror on the way to the commode, I happened to look in the mirror and saw my left cheek was full of holes.

After dreaming this, I woke up scared to death. First thing I did was put my tongue in my left cheek. Whew, no holes! But just to be sure, I went to the bathroom to double check in the mirror that both cheeks were just fine. So I fell back to sleep again. Who knows, perhaps, I had eaten Swiss cheese earlier in the day.

As you can predict, childhood diseases were passed around amongst us eight kids. Amazingly, not all eight of us had both the measles and the chicken pox at the same time. Only my brother Matt and I had the measles. Instructed by Dr. Hess to put us together in separate twin beds in the same darkened room, Mom made my temporary bedroom in Matt's bedroom and moved another brother out. Matt and I felt special having our meals brought to our room by Mom. Having lots of quiet time, I colored a lot and played with my doll. Later on, several other family members, including Lenora, came down with the chicken pox, but I never did get them.

My mom, being a busy housewife, took the time though to tuck her children into bed each night when we were younger. But, first, we had to kneel down by our bed, fold our hands, and say our bedtime prayers. Mom said one line at a time quickly, then we were to repeat after her. She said:

> Now, I lay me down to sleep
> I pray the Lord my soul to keep
> Ifishoulddie (yes, pronounced as one word)
> Before I wake,
> I pray the Lord my soul to take.

It wasn't until I saw the prayer printed in a *Little Golden Book*, when I was a little older and able to read, I realized I was saying "If I should die" not "ifishoulddie." I guess because Mom was talking too fast and hurrying to put the young ones to bed, the third line sounded like one word to me. Any busy mom can relate.

When it came time to have my own children repeat a bedtime prayer, it was changed to a less-scary version:

> Now I lay me down to sleep,
> I pray the Lord my soul to keep;
> Keep me safe all through the night, and
> Wake me with the morning light.

Another flaw of the landlord, Bugsy, came to light, though I did not understand the whole impact of his actions until I was a teenager. One fall day, just as Daddy was pulling into our driveway after work, he noticed Bugsy whistling, coming out of the small bungalow. The boy was outside throwing a ball up over the roof. His sister was nowhere to be seen. Realizing the children's parents were not home from work yet, Daddy became concerned as to Bugsy's purposes for being in the bungalow—being a landlord or not.

The muffled conversation behind my parents' bedroom door that evening was louder than ever. "Bugsy this" and "Bugsy that" was all that I could understand. At one point, I thought I heard Daddy say, "Lenora is not that much younger than that girl…"

After church the following Sunday morning, Bugsy was getting on his bicycle, which was propped against the side of the barn, just as Daddy was parking our car in front of our yard. Daddy barely got the car put in park before he got out and all but stormed over to him. I have never seen Daddy so angry. Whatever had him blasting Bugsy in such a manner almost had fire coming out of his ears. Daddy was holding onto the bicycle handlebar with one hand while slapping the air near Bugsy's head. Mom and my two older brothers ran to the scene. Junior and Mervin grabbed Daddy, forcing him to walk backward while trying to calm him down. Mom was walking beside Daddy and kept repeating, "Daddy, he's not worth it. Just drop it. Leave it be. You have no proof." Bugsy's bike made the most crooked line as he rode up the hill.

Within the month, the Martins were moving again. Protective Hubby and Daddy was not going to take one more chance of Bugsy defiling *his* family. Within the month, the Martins were planning another move.

The relationship continued on between Aunt Joyce and her lover Bugsy for many years. In fact, years later, our previous landlord paid my older brother, Junior, a nice sum of money to drive him down to Florida to "visit some friends." Guess who had moved to Florida earlier? Aunt Joyce! After pulling into the motel parking lot, my brother was handed money. "Go see a movie. I'll see you in the morning," our former landlord instructed Junior. A movie! What a special treat! It was only later, my brother realized, he drove the guy down to Florida to visit his own aunt to continue their affair.

As grace would have it, both Bugsy and Aunt Joyce, in time had asked God for forgiveness. The Man who walked upon the water wiped their slate clean and cast their sins into the bottom of the ocean floor of amazing grace with a "No Fishing" sign.

Thought of the Day

Grace is pretending I have tape over my mouth when noticing the faults of others because when I look in the mirror, imperfections stare back at me. Looking into my heart reveals my own clogged-up junk. Only God's grace clears my "hardening of the arteries." Sure, help someone remove the splinter from their eye, but not without first removing your own log (Matthew 7:5).

Chapter 9

Learning to Sing Alto in Second Grade

My heart is steadfast, O God; I will sing and make music with all my soul…for great is your love, higher than the heavens.
—Psalms 108:1, 4

First grade picture

SECOND GRADE SUNDAY SCHOOL AT Martindale Mennonite Church was unforgettable and helped to shape who I am today. The sewing circle room on the second floor at the front of the church doubled as my makeshift Sunday school classroom. Cold metal brown folding chairs circled the room. My Sunday school teacher, Irene Witmer (she helped author the book *The Pleasant View of Martindale*) wrote with perfect printed penmanship the words to two songs in big block letters on large sheets of white paper: "This is My Father's World" and "How Great Thou Art." Over time, Miss Witmer separated the altos from the sopranos. Sunday after Sunday, about nine of us girls sang in harmony those hymns over and over again.

"Class, please rise," Miss Witmer said, smiling. Having never married, she delighted in giving herself and sharing her talents with her young students. Dressed in a more conservative style than Mom, Miss Witmer's dress almost reached her ankles. She wore a larger head covering too. Miss Witmer stood proudly next to the easel. As the previous months of Sundays, we gathered in front of the easel, taller girls standing in the back, shorter girls, such as myself, made up the front row.

"This is my Father's world…" we belted out in a cappella style.

It was during this time I realized that I could sing alto. We were expected to memorize the words to these two songs. Acting as the directing chorister, Miss Witmer was devoted to her calling as a Sunday school teacher, not only to teach us girls God's Word, but she was preparing us to join in with the larger corporate worship of hymn singing. Thanks to my girlfriend, Lena, who was standing behind me and sang alto beautifully, I learned to sing alto also, as I would attempt to sing the same notes as she.

Besides learning to be an alto, memorization of scripture derived from my early Sunday school years. Each time you attended Sunday school, you were handed a blue ticket. Five blue tickets were exchanged for one red ticket. After collecting twelve red tickets (sixty weeks), you earned a small black King James Bible. Thus, you were expected to memorize and recite to your Sunday school teacher's memory verses weekly, sometimes individually or as a class. I received my first Bible in 1962 when I was nine years old, and it has its home in my cedar chest to this day.

Both sets of my grandparents lived through historical church divisions. As early as 1893, vocal bishops spoke against reasons why they could not endorse all of the Lancaster Conference activities, such as holding Sunday school. But how can a small split-away congregation afford to build their own building? They cannot. Thus, the sharing of buildings evolved. It was called the "off" Sunday. At one time, three different conferences used the same white plain wood building.

In 1948, the "brick" Martindale Church, where my parents attended, was built, and the congregants no longer needed to hold "shared" services. Martindale Mennonite Church remained my parents' home congregation their entire lives. As a child, when answering which church I attended, I quickly pointed out "the red brick one" lest the inquirer believed my parents drove a black-bumper car, as the Horning Mennonites was a sect that shared a building with horse-and-buggy Mennonites.

One Sunday in the late '90s on a weekend Daddy had gone hunting, I attended church with Mom. I was amazed! In summary, the women and men dressed more conservatively overall than when I attended it in the '60s. What is going on? Even though Mom had not changed in her style of dress all that much, she *did* indeed change somewhat: her hair was styled differently (a slight bit of hair was pulled down over the tip of her ear), and a skirt and blouse set was added to her wardrobe. Many women wore the not-required cape dress or a simple dress. Few skirts and blouses were noticed. More men were wearing "plain" suit coats than regular coats with a lapel.

On the way home, Mom explained to me that quite a few couples from the local "Black Bumper" Horning Mennonite Church dropped their church membership to join Martindale. Why? It was not because they did not have to paint their bumpers black. It was to be allowed to own a radio or a DVD player. The results: they did not bother to spend a lot of money on a closet makeover or bother to change the size of their head coverings. Thus, the church was actually more conservative than what I remembered it. Of course, those church members who recognized more plainness creeping into the church stopped attending Martindale. The more liberal Mennonite church memberships experienced a small growth during this time.

Martindale made the news February 1952, the year of my birth. One Sunday morning, an Air Force plane accidentally dropped an auxiliary fuel tank in the area between two churches. The pilot was forced to balance the plane; the second tank landed in the lawn of one of our hunting cabin families. Officers from Delaware Air Force Base probably never, prior or since, walked on Martindale soil. They roped off the areas where the tanks landed until they could be removed. Thank God, no one was hurt.

Attending church on a Sunday morning was a given. Mennonite churches not only had a minisermon before the main sermon, but everybody from preschool to the elderly was expected to arrive on time to first attend your Sunday school class. Mennonite churches did not have a choir, organ, or piano. The congregation sang hymns like "What a Friend We Have in Jesus" or "When the Roll is Called Up Yonder" a cappella-style with a male chorister (not choir director) leading the congregants, using only a pitch pipe.

As was common for plain churches, men and women were seated separately in the pews, with men on one side of the church and women on the other side. Teenagers and young adult sat in the rear of the auditorium. Leaving the first row empty usually, grandparents sat nearest to the front of the church. Next section was the middle-aged and young-married adult congregants, followed by the elementary-grade students who no longer required they be seated with their parents. Younger children of the opposite sex were allowed to sit with a parent.

I probably did sit with Daddy a time or two in the men's section of the congregation, but I remember mostly sitting next to Mother, where I was the most comfortable. You didn't want the stares of the congregation felt on your back if you were unruly and your parent felt the need to stand up and direct you out to the anteroom. If so, here at the very least, you received a scolding, a threat of a spanking once you were home, or a spanking right on the spot.

Being disciplined, quiet, and obedient during church services were expected behaviors. In my family, you better have a good reason to cause a disturbance needing to leave your seat, walk to the end of the pew, and then out the aisle exiting the auditorium during a sermon or hymn. Needing to go to the bathroom was not one of them, as you were expected to attend to such matters between Sunday school class and the sermon.

As a preschooler to keep me occupied for the sermon hour, Mom had a small entourage of items in her pocketbook. My fun, quiet activities consisted of one small book, black-and-white Trick magnetic dogs, a small pad and pencil for drawing, and a "hanky doll." You see, Mom would take her pretty flowered handkerchief and fold it in such a manner that it looked like a wrapped baby doll was in the center of the hanky. I would spend a long time rocking my "doll."

Playing with the magnetic Scottie dogs, which repelled each other when placed on top or the bottom of the hymnbook page, kept my interest for a while. But then, I would move on to drawing on a small tablet. Not being too creative, I would create a simple picture of a two-story house with a chimney bellowing smoke, flower-filled window boxes, and a flower-lined short walkway to a mailbox. A big tree stood next to the house. Only the flowers drawn by me changed week after week. If anyone was even able to determine what type of flower was drawn beside the walk, the easiest ones to attempt to draw were daisies, roses, or tulips. I drew this picture over and over. On occasion, I would discover in the bottom of Mom's pocketbook a packet of Life Savers or Chicklets, which she would usually allow me to have.

After the service was dismissed, children were allowed to play outside briefly until parents were ready to leave, but usually only a fairly quiet game of tag, Simon Says or Red Light, Green Light, or similar games. Watching for moving cars and not playing too rowdy was a given.

Every time there was a call for prayer, you stood up, turned around, and kneeled down facing the back of the pew. Being mischievous, this was a time in my later years when my girlfriends and I, out of view from our parents, would whisper to each other. After the prayer ended, of course, wearing a somber face, we stood up and resumed sitting in our seats.

Sunday school lessons of Bible stories were printed on small simple booklets. Graduating from coloring when we were preschoolers, we went to using flannel-board stories as the methods used to teach us the Bible. For teenagers, Sunday school lessons came in book form with several months-worth of printed lessons. Teachers expected you to have read the SS lesson prior to Sunday morning. Daddy often tuned in to the Christian radio station, WDAC, and listened to his lesson Saturday night prior to his Sunday school class. His sincerity of studying his lesson prior to class served him well. After retirement, Daddy was a Sunday school teacher for elementary-aged boys.

Later on, other avenues of showing off our musical abilities were when my sisters and I sang one or two hymns for Mom and Daddy on a Sunday afternoon, disturbing their afternoon nap, I'm sure. Other times, we sang at the Fisher family reunion.

Ever since the Reformation, the Anabaptist-Mennonite Church family has made church music important and had many hymnals published over four centuries. In 1969, one hymnal was simply named The Mennonite Hymnal. I, at the age of seventeen, using this newly published hymnal, joined a mixed male and female Mennonite youth chorus as an alto. During December and January, our choral group was scheduled throughout several Lancaster County churches and a nursing home on Sunday evenings to present free programs of hymn singing. Without any instrumental accompaniments, we harmonized our voices beautifully. Some hymns were memorized, and stanzas of some songs remain with me today. (In the inside back cover of my hymnal, I had written the dates and locations of our itinerary, along with the list of page numbers of the songs assigned for each service.)

I love music. Sunday school songs led to patriotic songs that we learned in school. As soon as opportunity presented itself, I signed up for chorus in high school and was selected to participate in an all-girl group called Sing Out. When a teenager, my clock radio, set to WFIL, a Philadelphia radio station, woke me up to the golden oldies.

Teaching grandchildren to sing the same songs I learned as a child was time well spent in Nana's car. Today, my home is usually filled with varying background music, mostly praise-and-worship songs. The local Christian radio stations supply uplifting Christian music in my car.

The gift of singing has been passed on down through generations. My nephew was the lead singer in a rock-and-roll band for many years. Many a karaoke bar has been filled with his and my son's duets during summer vacations together. In fact, my beautiful granddaughter, Taylor, posts videos of her singing and playing her guitar regularly on YouTube. Look out the *Voice*!

Music completes me.

Thought of the Day

Bestow grace when someone attempts to influence others in misguided ways, but they are "falling as flat" as the person behind you singing loudly off-key. It takes grace to not allow boisterous ones to silence me completely. Eventually, off-key and songbird will blend together beautifully singing heavenly music.

Chapter 10

My Mennonite Heritage

And if by grace, then it cannot be based on works;
if it were, grace would no longer be grace.
—Romans 11:6

Maternal great-grandparents

I NEVER HEARD MY PARENTS take the Lord's name in vain or heard a curse or anything close to a swear word slip out of their mouths. In fact, Daddy said in its place, "Bop deckle," which means *cardboard* in Pennsylvania Dutch or "*Ach du lieber*" loosely translated into "Oh, dear." I guess they sounded like good, clean replacements. Knowing that we were not allowed to say even "gosh" or "geez," my vocabulary broadened the day a new family moved into a house on my school bus route. The mom's name was Erma Gosh (rhyming with *douse*).

One day, a dish of red-fruited gelatin, not yet solidified, fell out of my hands and spilled over the kitchen floor. I "swore," Er…rrrr…maaaa gosh!"

Mom, who was sitting in the living room mending a hole in Daddy's trousers (never called jeans), asked, "What did you just say?"

I answered, giggling, "I just said Erma Gosh," as I proceeded to clean up the mess.

Not too pleased, she simply smiled and shook her head. Of course, that only lasted for a week before that smart-aleck trick was buried. As I recall, none of us ever had to bite soap or have our mouths washed out by it. Watching our mouths and being accountable for our words in front of our parents was a given.

Swearing, if at all, during an oath is a no-no. "I affirm" is the substitute phrase one would say, if need be, according to Mennonite church doctrine. No cursing is only one of the tidbits I was taught as part of my Mennonite roots. Listed below are some more. Some may sound familiar, and some will have you saying "huh?"

Hand over paychecks

By 1961, three of my four older brothers had completed eighth grade and quit school by fifteen years of age. They couldn't wait to hold down a full-time job. Their paychecks weren't placed in their own banking accounts at first because Mennonites held a tradition that was passed down from generations. Though the occupation might have changed for both the parents and the wage earners, the method on how to handle a paycheck remained the same.

Here were my parents' expectations that affected me: Any monies I earned babysitting (which wasn't very often), when I was either fourteen or fifteen years old, I was allowed to keep in its entirety.

Any paychecks earned between sixteen and seventeen years of age were signed by me and turned over to Mom. She gave me $5 a week allowance. This was spending money that I could choose to spend foolishly or wisely. Buying the latest top-hit record, makeup, or sexy nylons is how I spent my five bucks. However, my parents bought all of my necessities. From the ages of seventeen to nineteen years of age, you cashed your own paycheck and gave half the monies earned over to Mom. You were now responsible to support yourself. If you were unmarried and still lived with your parents at nineteen, you were required to start paying $10 a week for room and board.

What income did our family live off from 1959 to 1961? The three eldest sons' paychecks! Depending on their ages, either all or half of my brothers' paychecks supported the Martin family, not Daddy's paychecks. However, to be fair, Daddy *did* invest wisely in his kids' hard work and toil. By the fall of 1961, after saving his paychecks for two whole years, my parents bought land from Daddy's brother, Uncle Weaver.

At fifteen years of age and no longer attending school, my oldest brother, Junior, was hired out as a hired hand for a local Mennonite farmer, who paid Daddy an annual salary of $1,000. Hours of laboring kept Junior sweating and aching by the time he crawled into bed each night. The next year, Elvin was old enough to quit school and he too was hired out by the same farmer earning another $1,000 for my parents. Within days of hiring, he scolded Junior, "Why didn't you tell me he was such a jerk?" Hard work was a given, but having a tyrant for a boss was another. The verbal agreement couldn't end fast enough for Junior, who endured the entire year. Elvin quit after nine months and simply told Daddy he's not going back. Fool me once, fool me twice.

Work hard

To be a hard worker and not a slacker was one of several great ethics passed on from my heritage. Though my ancestors might have been mostly farmers, whatever occupation one chose, it was expected that you performed your job well, was dependable, and committed to the task at hand.

As written in an earlier chapter, Mom was hired out as a maid to her aunt and uncle long before she got married. Her aunt and a second employer, Florence, both gave her the opportunity to work hard and keep a tidy house while employed by them. Mom had plenty of opportunities later on to practice what she learned on her own large family.

One aspect of hard work was ironing while paying attention to details. How? Ironing white shirts that were first dampened with sprinkles of water and placed in the refrigerator for a few hours led to neatly pressed shirts. When one opened up the refrigerator door and pulled out the bottom vegetable drawer, do not expect to find fruits or vegetables in one of them. No, instead, you saw Mom's plastic bag filled with starched white long-sleeved Sunday shirts belonging to Daddy and my four older brothers. (As soon as I was old enough, ironing those many shirts became of one of my weekly chores.)

Even though she seemed to have an abundance of dresses in her closet, Mom had indeed sewn most of them herself. In fact, to save money, she handmade many of her daughters' clothing. It was just understood, if a Mennonite, you were expected to learn how to be a good seamstress. Appearance was not about being stylish nor bejeweled. But one could always look put together and polished. If you walked into our kitchen and noticed four pairs of men's shoes lined up sitting on newspaper, you knew that it must be a Saturday afternoon. Mom was busy polishing shoes for the boys' Saturday night dates or Daddy's Sunday dress shoes. (Eventually, she turned that chore over to her girls too.)

For the seven family members who have not received college degrees, all have either gotten their GEDs or gone on to learn a trade and own their own businesses. Since higher education was frowned upon, two of my older siblings, who were of the age to be attending college, decided to open up a garage back in the mid-1960s in New Holland, near the town where I was born. After studying various books and manuals used by mechanics, as well as personal experiences from servicing their own cars, they felt they were proficient and ready with the help of Mr. Banker to open their own business, Martin Brothers' Garage. A strong work ethic was needed, as many long hours were spent under the hoods and in the bodies of cars, pickup trucks, and vans for my mechanic brothers. Their days were filled providing service to local customers. They pumped gas, checked fluids, and washed windshields with a smile.

At sixteen, I volunteered for them a few Saturdays and evenings to help collect some overdue bills from nonpaying customers. They could not afford to pay me even a stipend. The stress of running their own business and the long hours eventually took its toll on my one brother and caused a near nervous breakdown. After a little more than two years, enough customers hadn't pay their bills, and the Martin's Brothers Garage was forced to close. My theory is word got around that "the Martin Brothers are Mennonites, and they won't sue you." As with most life lessons, understanding what worked and what didn't work, plus having had business ownership experience under his belt, enabled one brother to open his own electric motor shop. Today, it is profitable enough to support both his and his son's families.

The Martin children followed in their father's footsteps and either became a foreman, manager, supervisor, or business owner. My sister Lenora later on pursued a chaplaincy certification, which enabled her to work as a chaplain in a large Pennsylvania hospital. Lorna, the first and only sibling to earn a doctorate in our family, worked hard to achieve her goal. Today, she pastors a Mennonite church in the suburbs of Philadelphia. Yes, hard work and determination pay off. Observing and following this trait will allow our children and grandchildren, if they continue to follow the work ethic, to reap the benefit from the rewards of not being a sluggard. After all, scripture promotes passing on an inheritance onto your family, which Mom and Daddy were proud to do.

Inventions Originating from Lancaster County, Pennsylvania

Lancaster County has been considered one of the "bread baskets" of the New World. Rural areas named *Frog Hollow* and *Hog Swamp* were farmed by the early European settlers. Hardships and natural disasters plagued them. However, not everyone continued farming. Two German settlers were credited for creating two revolutionary items: the Conestoga-covered wagon and the Pennsylvania long rifle.

The Conestoga wagon, introduced by a Mennonite, was named after the local Native American Indian tribe. In colonial times, the wagon was eighteen feet long and able to carry up to six tons. Oxen, horses, or mules did the hard work of pulling the covered wagon over the Great Wagon Road and the Appalachian Mountains to carry cargo for those migrating southward. After the American Revolution, the use of the wagon opened up commerce as far as Ohio. Tar-patched seams allowed the wagon to cross rivers. It is believed the custom of driving on the right side began with the Conestoga-covered-wagon train.

Some historians believe the stogie (a shortened word from Conestoga) cigar originated from Conestoga, Pennsylvania. Conestoga wagon drivers were fond of one particular type of long thin cigar, which came to be known as a stogie. Today, it is a slang term applied to any cheap cigar of which both ends are cut.

The fact that Lancaster County was the home to nonresistant Mennonites, Amish, Moravians, and Quakers, the Pennsylvania long rifle (named a hog or Kentucky rifle) was the first American firearm. Created in 1730s in Lancaster, this rifle was designed by a skillful German/Swiss immigrant. It was lighter and more slender and the preferred gun for the first American colonists.

In 1895, a visionary, Abe Zimmerman, opened a one-man farm-machine repair shop. His plan was to sell his machines in every continent. New Holland Machine Shop was purchased by Sperry-

Rand Corporation in 1947. By 1975, it grew to be the fifth largest farm equipment company. By 1999, after Ford Motor Company earlier expanded its line, a merger with Case Corporation (whose parent company is Fiat) propelled it to become the world's largest equipment producer, today titled CNH.

Keep Things Fair

Another concern that is steeped heavily in Mennonite culture is the principle of keeping all things fair. As written about later in another chapter, I married at barely nineteen years of age. I realized that it would be difficult to pay my parents their share, plus save up for wedding expenses and purchase household items for our first new home. I asked my parents if they would make an exception for me, which they did. Instead of turning over half of my paycheck, I began banking the entire amount (minus tithing).

Because my older brothers and sister had already turned over their monies, in order to keep things fair, I had to pay back the money to my parents. The reality was: from my engagement at eighteen and a half years old on and up until I got married, on every payday, I logged what amount was due my parents. For a whole year after I was married, my husband and I had to take a portion from our monthly milk paycheck and pay back my parents! Thank goodness, my husband was from a more conservative Mennonite family, and he understood the paycheck-gets-turned-over philosophy. Otherwise, it would have been a bit embarrassing to explain to hubby this line-budget item.

Be a Good Money Manager, Including Tithing

Another lesson taught to their kids by our parents was the concept that a wife should be an expert at household budgeting and be trusted with Daddy's turned-over-to-Mom-paycheck. Mom passed with flying colors. She was the one who did all of the banking and handled the finances, including tithing, in our family. Mom drove to Blue Ball National Bank every Monday morning and deposited Daddy's paychecks (this was long before direct deposits). Mom kept the tithes monies in a Mason jar in the bottom dresser drawer. We all know that, if in a bind, we could take money out of the jar *but* not before writing a note and explaining the use of the emergency money (of course, she replaced any borrowed money by Sunday for the offering plate).

Mom earned some monies and household items when she began selling vitamins and catalog items out of Popular Club Plan to family and friends. Earning a percentage of her sales, she selected items, such as bedsheets, an iron, a popcorn maker, etc. (Of course, she did *not* consider selling to strangers.) When I was younger, drinking glasses were packed in oatmeal boxes. Over time, Mom had collected two dozens of them. Today, my hutch proudly displays a pretty set of water glasses, which Mom passed down on to her daughters.

Who doesn't remember S&H Green Stamps? It was a fun day when we saw Mom finishing up pasting the stamps into the book. That meant we were about to head to the redemption store and bring home new items: linens, cookware, small lamps, etc. It was second only to Christmas day.

I believe being thrifty is part of the reason Mom hosted home parties, which became popular in the 1960s. Earning hostess gifts (often items she would not have purchased) was one way to cut down household expenses. She earned a small ceramic Christmas tree, gold-plated silverware, silk poinsettias, and copper candelabras, for example. (Guess who later on loved hostessing home parties too?)

The grocery store my parents frequented during my childhood was in Martindale called Eby's General Store. A family-owned business that started in 1916, it doubled as a post office for a time. The store was closed on Wednesday nights, as the owners attended the weekly prayer meeting. To be closed on a Sunday continues to this day.

Sometimes, Mom or Daddy bought my favorite candy, 5th Avenue, from the candy display. But more times than not, purchased grocery items were centered on Daddy's packed lunches. I stayed home more often than the times I accompanied Mom to go boring grocery shopping. The one time of year I always went along was during the month of December. Why? The owner had a big box of rolled-up and tied wall calendars for the following year sitting near the cash register. No amount of purchase was required. Each customer could select one as an "in appreciation, thank you" gift for their patronage. Five samples of the free gift were hanging on the wall. Do I like the winter snow scene, the deer and mountain scene, the waterfall scene, the lovely flower garden, or the country cottage calendar best? More times than not, Mom allowed us kids to select the preferred calendar. Sometimes my vote counted, sometimes not. If more than one brother was in attendance, the deer and mountain scene won and was proudly displayed on the Martins's wall. Mr. Eby was no fool. It was a form of advertising, as it graced our kitchen wall from one year to the next.

Mennonites Attend and Support the Amish Mud Sales

Being generous and opening up closed fists to share with others was a passed-down trait. Many paragraphs could be added about the generosity of the Amish and Old Order Mennonites, who do not accept government Medicare assistance or believe in life insurance plans. Barn raising and Amish mud sales are combined community efforts. Mud sales evolved from a community that recognized that a combined pool of resources could make a priceless difference. A mud sale is so named because it is usually held every Saturday starting in February, when the winter thaw requires one to wear boots, as it is guaranteed your footwear *will* get muddy.

They are major fundraisers for the volunteer fire companies throughout Amish communities. They are huge events, sometimes drawing as many as twenty thousand people, where everything from hand-stitched quilts (donated by the Amish women's groups) and locally made crafts to livestock, furniture, produce, baked goods, antiques, and housewares. Someone joked, "Even the kitchen sink is up for bid." In a sight, that may seem like organized chaos to novice mud-sale visitors, six or seven auctions are conducted simultaneously as Amish and "English" mill together over the many items bound for the auction block. Any visitor during this time to Lancaster County will enjoy the delicious homemade baked goods and chow-chow. My suggestion: graze all day and nibble on something from each food stand. Walk off the calories as you labor a little harder walking through the mud. After all, it is all for a great cause.

Be a Seamstress

I asked a conservative relative one time, "What if you just did *not* have the talent to sew very well? Not every Mennonite girl can expect to be a great seamstress." She answered, "Well, you did the best you could. Sometimes people bartered and exchanged services, but usually the woman was expected to sew for her family, talented or not."

Fortunately, for my mom, she not only could sew, but she loved to quilt and held many quilting bees in our home. Providing quilts for our large family's beds was definitely one way of saving money. Being invited to a quilting bee by other Mennonite women meant that you passed a rite of passage: you could sew with small, even, envious stitches. Similar to the fact that not all Mennonite girls were the best seamstresses, not all women were precise quilters either.

Here is how to make a quilt and prepare for a quilting bee: First, select your quilt pattern. After determining color choices and size (single, double, queen or king), purchase the material from a local fabric shop (a profitable business in Lancaster County). Next, sew together the quilt pieces following the pattern into the desired quilt size. Once finished, you have a quilt top. Attaching some type of batting and material that will become the backside of the quilt (picture a large white sheet), these three pieces then become the unfinished, unquilted product (some call it a "quilt sandwich"). The next step is to stretch and fasten the three-layered quilt top to a homemade wooden quilt frame using straight and safety pins. Of course, the larger-sized quilts needed a large room to spread out the quilt. There were times we could barely walk around the edge of the parlor or living room because once mom's quilt was set up in the frame, it took up most of its space. As children, we didn't mind crawling under the quilt to get from point A to point B.

Finally, you are at the point where you invite fellow quilters (Mom usually invited friends at church or by placing a phone call) to assist in applying the stitches to your quilt top. Planning on serving some light refreshments and a beverage, Mom made her food purchases, and the day for the quilting bee arrived. It became a time of great fellowship for the women, as they talked while they quilted. The invitation was extended to several days. Before the close of the evening, refreshments were served, a small thank you for this time-consuming task. Once quilted, you would then bind all four sides to have a finished product ready to use and proudly display.

Depending on the size of the quilt, the size of the quilting bee, and or if Mom chose to quilt it mostly herself, this process could take weeks to months. Mostly a winter project, quilting bees were held throughout many of my friends' homes as well. Somewhat competitive women who were "pros" could master designing an intricate and more-detailed quilt, causing some envy. Putting in a quilt, then later knocking one out allowed women to beautify their homes with gorgeous quilts gracing their beds.

It was common when visiting family and friends to hear the woman of the house say, "Let me show you what I was working on recently." If I had a dollar for every time I saw Mom show off her quilt to company, or upon entering someone's home as company, having them show me their quilt or quilt top, it would cover the cost of my last purchased (not homemade) one!

By the time my mom passed away, she had quilted over three dozen quilts, becoming precious family heirlooms. More quilts were passed on and given to each one of her children and grandchildren than she actually kept for herself. For several years, Mom regularly donated a handmade quilt to be auctioned off at Mennonite Central Committee's (MCC) popular annual relief sale. It was always exciting to watch the auction results of all the beautiful handmade quilts that were lovingly stitched by Mennonite women and how high a willing buyer paid for them. It was not uncommon for one of Mom's quilts to be sold between $400 to $500. Though she no longer put in a quilt once she moved into the personal care wing of the nursing home, she did donate new quilts from her supply for the nursing home's fund-raising auction. Once, my cousin's family had flood damage in their home. What did Mom do? Hand them a quilt!

Though I never perfected the art of quilting like Mom, I completed a simple quilt pattern called Nine Patch when I was in my twenties. (Mom and her friends did the actual quilting of it for me.) My quilt rack in my bedroom today proudly displays six beautiful handmade quilts, though some are tattered and torn in places. Some patterns are the wedding ring, Dresden plate, and an appliqued nine patch. One of the most recent quilts Mom gave me prior to her death graces my bed and looks so lovely! Perhaps, later on when life is less hectic, I'll resume this passed-down art. I truly hope a granddaughter or great-granddaughter of mine will pick up this torch and make Mom proud. If not, it would be a shame.

Be a Great Cook and Gardener

Every Mennonite girl most likely has a cookbook titled *Mennonite Community Cookbook: Favorite Family Recipes* by Mary Emma Showalter (1957). I received mine as a shower gift from my parents. Filled with a collection of recipes from Mennonite women throughout the United States and Canada, it has been used so many times by me that pages have dried food residue on them. The edges now have a dark-brownish tint that once was tan. Missing a cover by now, this cookbook definitely was my go-to cookbook as a young bride. Just as owning a car doesn't make me Andretti, owning this cookbook doesn't make me Paula Dean, either. But watching my mom cook at times and being forced, as a teenager, to prepare for cooking for a husband someday, practice makes (almost) perfect. I'll be the first to admit I am not the best cook among my three sisters; Lenora wins that title, hands down.

Using lots of lard, sugar, and flour makes for a delicious fattening meal. Chow-chow, cornstarch pudding (but we'd drop the full name and call it simply cornstarch), lepp cakes (best soft cookie), pickled pigs' feet or souse, pig's stomach, schnitz and knepp, homemade noodles, seven-day or fourteen-day pickles are items from my childhood that my mom or grandma made one time or another from the *Mennonite Community Cookbook.*

When my children were young, the local Christian radio station, WDAC, was a godsend, as it broadened my menu selections. The announcer read off a recipe each weekday at 4:00 p.m. I diligently prepared to listen and copied it down as the announcer slowly read it. I still have the spiral notebook that is filled with handwritten recipes, four to a page. Presently, its pages are also splattered with foodstuffs on the most-frequently used ones. Little checkmarks next to the title meant it was a recipe that was a hit with my family and one to consider repeating.

Gardening, canning, and freezing are surely not only a Mennonite homemaker's job. But for these women, it was expected if you had the land to garden, you did so. The larger the family, the more foodstuffs were needed to fill the canning shelves and freezers. Roastin' corn was the name we had for corn on the cob, a summertime treat. Freezing corn was one of the messiest jobs; I was always glad when the task was completed. But what a sense of accomplishment when you lined up the forty- or fifty-pint-sized bags of corn ready to be put in your freezer! The competition between me and my sisters-in-law was great when reporting on our hard work. "Today, I froze fifty pints of corn and canned twenty-five quarts of peaches yesterday..." Hoping that my sister-in-law had not accomplished more, I'd hold my breath. Sometimes I'd win; sometimes, I'd lose. Oh, the pressure!

Fattening food items found aplenty in Lancaster County are whoopie pies, shoo-fly pies, chicken pot pie (made from homemade dough rolled out and cut into squares, not the double-crusted chicken and corn pies I see in stores and restaurants). Lancaster County is known for having one of the state's most famous smorgasbords. The main highway that weaves through the Amish country is loaded with restaurants, all good selections serving family-style meals and good ole' Pennsylvania Dutch cooking. They line both sides of the highway. Be brave! Try some pig stomach, schnitz and knepp, and scrapple with your eggs. Of course, if you leave hungry, it is your own fault.

I realize Southerners are big on their sweet tea. But Mennonites can hold a candle to ya'll with our brewed meadow tea. Sweetened to taste, meadow tea was an inexpensive beverage to serve others. Mom grew the tea around various areas of our yard or garden. Then she placed it on newspaper on the floor of the attic or storage room to dry. Once dried completely, the tea was packed in plastic containers and placed in the freezer. Having tea leaves available to boil in water, strain, and lastly, to add sugar, Mom's beverage was a breeze to serve on short notice.

Who can forget making homemade vanilla, strawberry, or peach ice cream using the hand-cranked wooden ice cream maker? On a hot summer day, my mom on occasion served homemade ice cream as the dessert for company. After Mom had mixed the ice cream base, it was the men's job to crank it until their efforts produced a perfect creamy consistency. Hmm, what a taste this side of heaven!

Most Mennonite families did not go out to eat in restaurants. It was expected meals be prepared from stocked pantry, canning shelves, or freezer items. Even when I had my own young family, the cheaper fast-food restaurants had been the restaurant of choice to keep the bill to a minimum. It was a family treat and only done occasionally.

Teenage Activities

Scouting a dating couple was a fun pastime. Here's how it works: Most Mennonite families had a living room designated for their daughter who was of dating age called a parlor. Blinds may or may not have been pulled down during a date. Only one small light is turned on for romantic ambience. Imagine a carload of teenagers driving up to someone's home, perhaps your own home to spy on your dating sister. Hoping to have a window with partially closed blinds to gaze through, you hoped to watch a couple kiss. Everyone kept quiet. The couple at first was usually oblivious that they were being watched. However, it is difficult to keep a gang of teenagers from giggling and not making too much noise as you take turns peeping, then step back, and allow someone else their turn to peep through the window.

Sooner or later, the couple opened the door and chased you away from the window. On a boring night, scouting was a last-resort activity. You made it worthwhile by scouting more than one couple. Most often, the couple was on their first date, and we didn't see any activity of interest. Knowing that you were one who also did the scouting at times when on a date, you were always anticipating this to happen at your home. If you did not want to be a couple scouted, your date was either held away from your home, or you were simply dropped off. Your date would leave, so there was no time spent hanging out in your parlor, you pulled down the blinds completely or did not kiss in view of the window and gave the peepers a boring show.

Only once did I see a couple partially naked and heavily petting during scouting (of course, they will remain nameless) through a blind that was only partially closed. Having never seen my dad walking around in his T-shirt, this was quite an education for my inexperienced eyes. After the three of us each got one turn to gaze for a few seconds, "the peeping Janes" left.

Playing walk a mile was first learned from my Plain horse-and-buggy cousins. Our countryside had miles of roads with little traffic late at night, which became a perfect backdrop for walk a mile, a game played by Mennonite teenagers. While playing this fun activity, we were totally oblivious how this could have been totally unexpected for drivers cresting a hill, for example, and seeing a huge crowd of teenagers walking along a country road.

Here is how it worked: All the girls started walking single file alongside the road. The goal is for a boy to select you to continue to walk beside. Giving the girls a few minutes to have walked a short distance, the boys started walking. If one was interested in walking beside a certain girl, he stopped moving onward and walked by the selected girl's side. If there was an odd number of guys (which happened frequently), someone walked up and down the paired couples, tapped a guy on his shoulder and directed him to another spot: "move front three" or "move back five." Having to follow the command, some boy was always directing another to start walking beside a different girl. The girls had no idea who or when her partner would be changing during the walking up to a mile or more.

Eventually, it became quieter as paired couples talked softly between themselves and stole a kiss at times. This game allowed for shy boys to have an opportunity to give a hint to a desired girlfriend. Simply by his stopping by her side spoke volumes. As with any group, some poor girl was the wallflower, the one whom most guys did *not* want to walk beside. Guess who was the girl the guys kept "sending each other" to? She! (But I must say, in my experience, even the shyest guy was grateful to have a walking partner.)

Of course, the last couple taking up the rear had the most envious private spot. The couple could lag way on behind, giving them more privacy. It was a huge complement to you, while walking together, when eventually your walking partner said, when tapped on his shoulder and about to be directed to move along, "Forget it, Buddy." Hmm…I think he likes me. I have many memories of meeting new boyfriends who did not always run around in my same circle of friends while playing walk a mile.

Sometimes, during a slumber party weekend, if no guys were around to hang out with us, and we were bored, we walked along the road by ourselves. One unforgettable memory sticks in my mind. My friend Lena's family was in charge of cleaning the church I attended; thus, they had a key. Lena knew that her brother and three other guys were planning on sleeping inside the church in their sleeping bags one Saturday night. So we decided to surprise them.

About 2:00 a.m., after walking about one-half mile, we arrived at the church. Peeping in the windows, we could tell the unsuspected snoozers were sleeping on the floor directly in front of the pulpit.

Using the second key, I, Lena, and two girlfriends quietly entered through the front door. Once inside, we turned on the auditorium lights. Suddenly, we saw her brother, totally shocked, standing up in his underwear beside his sleeping bag. Whew! It's only my crazy sister and her three friends. Hurrying to get back inside his sleeping bag and under cover, her brother was giggling so hard, he had awakened his buddies by then.

Having accomplished our purpose laughing hysterically, we started our trek back home for some shut-eye. I must say, later that Sunday morning, while we girls were sitting in the pew of the same church, it was hard not to picture the hilarious scene from just a few hours earlier. The chorister was standing at the exact same spot that snoozing, unsuspecting victims were scared out of their wits by some bored slumber-party teenagers.

The cost of having good, clean fun back then was priceless.

How Wedding Reception Expenses Were Shared

Mennonite wedding expenses are handled very differently than present day. Parents of the bride did not pay for all the wedding reception expenses. Since both the bride and groom were expected to have a large number of family members and friends attending the wedding and reception, the bill was split right down the middle between the parents of the bride and groom. Wedding receptions were not held in "worldly" ballrooms or banquet rooms of grand hotels but at the local fire hall. The cost was reasonable, and selecting a local one meant that, most likely, some Mennonite women were part of the kitchen staff that helped cook the meal. Besides, why not put monies back into the bank accounts of volunteer fire companies?

If a family consisted of mostly daughters or mostly sons, splitting the reception expenses also kept things more fair. A Mennonite father with a large family of daughters could go broke pretty quickly if things were done in today's standards.

Personally, I paid for my wedding dress and the material for my bridesmaid, gift receivers, and guest registrar (Mom did pay a stipend to my sister-in-law for handmaking them though.) The bill for the flowers was paid by me as well. Not sure how it was for my Mennonite girlfriends, but that was my experience. The honeymoon was also our own expense.

An extension of the wedding party, gift receivers and guest registrars had dual duties. One was to ensure the bride and groom's gifts were placed on the designated table in the fire hall. Later on, they were to help pack all the gifts in the groomsmen's cars to schlep them to the bride's house after the reception was over. Secondly, they performed waitress-like duties assisting the fire hall's kitchen staff with filling and refilling water glasses as needed and serving coffee. The reception was a family-style meal. So these girls were the ones to carry the filled plates to the wedding guests. Upon the wedding cake being cut, the gift receivers and guest registrar handed out the small plates that held slices of wedding cake and dipped ice cream. One of my favorite desserts was white wedding cake with vanilla ice cream.

How did one know she was "fit for marriage"? My future mother-in-law made a comment to me one day while I was washing dishes in her home a few months before my wedding day. "Well, Leanne, you are able to wash the dishes fast enough to keep *two* dish dryers busy without returning items back into the sink to be rewashed. You are now ready to get married." Whew!

Nonresistance/Pacifism

Conservative Mennonites believe that church and the state are completely separate. Joining the military definitely caused one to lose their church membership. Matthew 5:44 says "Love your enemies and pray for those who persecute you" and is interpreted to mean one should not carry arms and fight in a war.

Secular governments are expected to govern their earthy realm, while church members answer to a higher authority as only temporary earthly citizens. They believe the government has no right to interfere with the affairs of the church. This is the reason conservative Mennonites do not vote, hold public office, participate in unions, sit on jury duty, sue, or claim bankruptcy.

Some conservative groups do not participate in social security benefits and feel it is the church's responsibility to take care of their elderly. Since life insurance is banned, hospital funds are set up to take care of expenses for church members. Fire, storm damage, and other great losses are also covered from a combined fund that a deacon oversees.

Years later, there began a notable shift from nonresistance to peace activism. Mennonite church leaders, under the General Conference in the 1960s, revisited church regulations that were looked upon as bondage. Modern pacifism does not have the same definitive line between church and state. Teaching Christ's way of peace is carried into all walks of life and positions. In summary, the 2006 Mennonite World Conference General Council's list of "shared convictions" reads:

> The Spirit of Jesus empowers us to trust God in all areas of life so we become peacemakers who renounce violence, love our enemies, seek justice, and share our possessions with those in need… In these convictions we draw inspiration from Anabaptist forbearers of the 16th century, who modeled radical discipleship to Jesus Christ. We seek to walk in His name by the power of the Holy Spirit, as we confidently await Christ's return and the final fulfillment of God's kingdom.

Conscientious Objectors

As an alternative service, men of the Mennonite nonresistance faith were allowed to serve in civilian posts or in hospitals for two years as an alternative to serving in the armed forces. Some of my brothers served in Colorado or New Hampshire hospitals as orderlies or maintenance men. My brother-in-law eventually moved up from orderly to sous chef in a busy city hospital. This was the beginning of his experience, which led him to owning today one of the most popular smorgasbords in Pennsylvania.

During the late 1960s, an upheaval arose among five more conservative bishops of the Lancaster Conference that affected two of my older brothers. Believing it wrong to serve communion to church members who had televisions or did not abide by the strict dress code, these bishops chose to leave and took quite a few youth with them. The new conference was named Mennonite Messianic Mission (Three Ms, for short). Thus, under this bishop's influence, eventually, Marlin and Mervin believed if they remained part of the Lancaster Conference, they too could "go down the wrong path." They left to join the Three M Church.

Junior said Daddy was totally blindsided when his son stood up during a church meeting and made this announcement to the church leadership. Daddy wished he could have fallen through the floor! I say today that as much as my and my sister's divorce caused great pain to my parents, they were also hurt to be told by two sons that the church they chose to raise their family up in was going to hell. That did not sit very well, either.

Soon, these bishops devised their own voluntary service named Northern Light Gospel Mission for conscientious objectors. In 1964–65, my two older brothers (one went first, and the other brother about a year later) joined about twelve other youth on a mission trip that was led by the newly formed mission. They volunteered to minister to the Indian tribes of Red Lake, Canada, in northern Ontario. Marlin went to serve when he was nineteen years of age. Arriving at Popular Hill on Sandy Lake without a passport (none was required back then), my brother's eyes were opened to another whole world. His volunteer job was to drive a caterpillar and cut firewood for the long-term missionary family who resided there and taught at the school for the Indians.

Being a large group and unexpected guests, the boys were told to sleep out in the woodshed. The problem was that they had no sleeping bags. The temperatures dropped to −35 and −40 degrees Fahrenheit at night! My brother remembers shivering and freezing all night and not really ever getting warm in spite of the group of boys sleeping close together for warmth. About one year later, my other brother Mervin volunteered for the same missionary family. His job was to assist sled trains across the frozen lake carrying fifty-five-gallon drums of diesel fuel. This provided fuel for the family's generators to supply electricity.

Their eyes were opened to evils of this world that they had never heard their ministers preach about—witchcraft. For example, a witch doctor placed a curse on another tribe causing a newborn infant to have a deformed face or other side effects. One witch doctor was eventually converted to Christianity. He then disclosed how the witch doctors actually "spoke with the devil on any full-moon night, especially on October 31." Being empowered by Satan, for example, they believed they had power over women and money. Yes, my naïve brothers had been exposed to a whole new world. It went far beyond any witchcraft stories they had ever heard their grandmother talk about.

Upon my brothers' return back home, they were so dedicated to the missionaries' cause that they decided to schedule a travelogue of sorts. After booking a local fire hall one weekend, Marlin and Mervin shared dozens of slides from their Red Lake mission trip. All the proceeds from the goodwill offering were sent to the missionary family in Red Lake.

No, my brothers might not have gone around the other side of the world as a veteran, but they did bear "arms" for Christ, showing Christian love and a whole other way of a peaceful life to the native Canadians, who desperately needed saving from Satan's grasp.

Casting Lots to Fill Church Leadership Positions

Acts 1:15–26 holds the biblical precedent for using this method to fill leadership positions. Proverbs 16:33 reads, "The lot is cast into the lap, but its every decision is from the Lord." Since higher education is frowned upon, the Mennonite brethren who adhered to the church's rules, doctrines, and practices usually held some kind of position in the church (i.e., as a chorister, Sunday school superintendent or teacher). Casting the lot method was ascertained for four of my brothers throughout the years. One brother has retired in his leadership position, but three of my four brothers continue to hold their positions by this no-financial cost method.

Here is how it works: The deacon or bishop will announce to the congregation the need for a certain leadership position to be filled, for example, a preacher, bishop, or deacon. The congregation then is to seek the Lord's guidance on whom the Lord has "put on their heart" as a prospective candidate. The sermons were geared around scripture that spoke on the expected conduct of church leadership. After some time of prayerful consideration and after a Sunday-morning sermon, men (no women) were expected to submit their appropriate nominee in private to the church leadership team. The team sat in the anteroom, and the men entered, one person at a time, to offer their selection's name, whomever the Lord laid upon their heart.

To assure the Lord's leading in this serious matter, most congregations wanted a name to be selected at least two times by congregants. This was done in each of my brothers' cases. By the end of that Sunday's sermon, the bishop announced all the names of the male candidates. The following week, the leadership team met in the privacy of each nominee's home. This gave opportunity for both husband and wife to voice their opinion on whether or not they both were in agreement of the Lord's leading to be part of the lot. If one did not feel led to be part of the lot at that time in their lives, the bishop or deacon respected any declination. The following Sunday, the announcement was made of at least two candidate's names.

On the day of the scheduled casting of lots, another sermon appropriately reiterated the expected church leadership conduct. The nominees sat on the front row; wives sat behind them. In the presence of the congregation, an exact number of Bibles to match the number of candidates was used. One included a paper that was slipped in the inside front cover of one of the Bibles. It contained similar words, such as: "This certifies that _____has been called to the office of Minister of the Martindale congregation of the Lancaster Mennonite Conference on _____, 1990 (signed by bishop)." The Bibles are then shuffled so that no one knows which Bible holds the slip of paper and placed on the edge of the pulpit. At this point, man's job was done. Now the rest was up to the Lord.

One at a time, the men were asked to prayerfully consider which Bible to choose, come forward, carry it back to their seat, and wait for the bishop to look for the paper inside of it (my brother said when it was his time to select a Bible, he only saw one). The silence in the congregation is deafening as we all wait expectantly. The bishop moved off the pulpit, faced the nominee, and checked the inside cover for the paper. When no paper was found, you could visually see the wife's shoulders relaxing. Upon checking each one, the bishop then announced to the congregation, when found, which brethren is immediately ordained. Believed to be led by the Holy Spirit, this method proved to be tried and true.

Thought of the Day

Bestow grace by acknowledging that this side of heaven, believers are going to disagree. The good Lord could have taken us home to heaven immediately on the day we accepted Him as our Lord and Savior. But since He didn't, plan to get along with others. Be committed to the Lord and His Word, not to rules and regulations because they may change.

Chapter 11

My Reoccurring Frightful Dream

> I lift up my eyes to the hills—where does my help come from?
> My help comes from the Lord, the Maker of heaven and earth.
> —Psalm 121:1

MY DREAMS MIGHT NOT ALWAYS take me to a happy place, but they are composites of not-quite-correct details that make little sense: floating scenes that allow me to simply turn over, refluff my pillow, and soon fall back to sleep. Nightmares are not puzzling snippets of portions of your reality but scenes that cause one to become wide-eyed and wide awake. Most kids who experience heart-racing nightmares run into Mom and Daddy's room for comforting, soothing, assuring words and climb into a safe bed to resume, hopefully, a nightmare-free sleep. None of the nine kids ever climbed into our parents' bed because of an unsettling nightmare. We just dealt with them. Thus, the confusion for this chapter title: should I call it a nightmare or a frightful dream?

In 1961, Mom and Daddy, along with two other couples whom they considered some of their best friends, invested in a small one-bedroom cabin named Clay Mine Camp. Located in upper Lycoming County in the Pine Creek Valley near Slate Run, Clay Mine Camp became our frequent weekend home throughout the spring, summer, and fall. Set back off PA Route 44, the two-room gray cabin with its tin roof and one smokestack stood off a dirt lane flanked with plentiful ferns and the Pennsylvania state flower, pink mountain laurel. Forests of fewer white pine and scores of hemlock trees spread across several counties, providing shelter for black bear, white-tailed deer, and other forest creatures.

The true reason for purchasing the cabin was for the men to have a place to lodge on their late-fall hunting trips. This was the same year Daddy purchased his first camera. Over the years, he was able to take many pictures of these enjoyable male-bonding getaways, including the results of a successful hunting spree of the deer hanging off the designated for-our-trophies wooden log (called the deer rail or jokingly named by some as the meat pole). Certainly, the three investors, eventually dubbed the cabin gang, got their money's worth.

Our family chose the cabin over ocean or Chesapeake Bay vacations. We visited our cabin frequently, as it was only about four hours away to the northwest. I marvel how, indeed, did two or three families all fit inside this cozy two-room cabin? It had electricity, a wood stove for heating but no indoor plumbing. One entered into the kitchen and walked straight through to get to the bedroom. It had two sets of bunk beds stacked three high that were built into the wall, allowing room for six double-bed-sized mattresses.

The parents claimed the bottom two bunk beds, while the children slept in either the middle or top bunks. Being the coveted sleeping spot, the top bunks were usually selected by the older kids. When the brothers got too old to travel with their parents, the girls graduated to the top bunks.

So what creative sleeping arrangements accommodated ten to twelve kids? Three in a bed sleeping sideways, that's how. What priceless memories were made amongst the cabin gang. We reminisced during many great dinner conversations years later. (By the time, the grandchildren came along, watching Great-grandpa's slides on his slide projector providing some cheap educational entertainment about their parents' or aunts' and uncles' mountain vacations—especially laughable clothing styles and glasses.)

At bedtime, each of the sixteen found our sleeping areas, after using the outhouse, of course. Using a flashlight to stay on the short path, the adults oversaw the kids taking their turn toileting while trying not to joke loudly about seeing a hungry bear, a crawling snake, or a skunk at the opportune, or is that inopportune, time? Of course, Daddy was one of the worst culprits to tease with my oldest brothers, a close second. Sitting on a cold wooden toilet seat, you answered nature's call, and then scurried back inside the cabin, while telling yourself there will *not* be any middle-of-the-night toileting needs.

If you were on the top bunk, you had to bend your head down as the roof and ceiling line were on a slant and didn't allow you to sit up in bed. To put on our pajamas in the dark for privacy made for a fun challenge. If you were the first one up in the morning, you had to step around many outfits that were thrown from the bunks and landed on the floor until one of the moms picked them up.

Just when we were all settled down for our winter's nap, someone in the quiet room let one rip. Being jam-packed into this room with adults and youngsters alike, the guilty party was just as often one of the men as one of the boys. The giggling and laughing abounded, as the wife scolded the perpetrator. Just as it got all quiet again, you heard, "Oh, boy, it stinks!" as the affected wife was pulling back the bedcovers. Then the roar of laughter lasted louder and longer than the first round. Eventually, our tired bodies snuggled under the warm blankets and succumbed to our dreams about spooky outhouses, mountain wildlife, deer spotting, or potential deer trophies for the hunters hanging on the deer rail from the upcoming successful deer season.

Many times, the men planned a deer-spotting night at least once a weekend. With the use of a bright spotlight, we all piled in two or three cars to spot deer. It was really great when we were allowed in the summertime to pile in the back of one of the pickup trucks. The older boys were the ones who had the honor of holding the spotlight out the window as they sat in the front passenger-side seat. Sometimes, we were successful; other times, not so much. It was an adventure driving up and down the hardly passable dirt roads. With steep embankments on one side of the road and high mountains on the other side, driving the roads at times were hazardous, especially if it had snowed.

Daddy turned driving around spotting for deer into a game as a time to frighten us youngsters. Those of us who sat in the car with the steep embankments to our right would be wide-eyed seeing how close it seemed Daddy was driving on the edge of the mountainous road. The more one commented, "Don't get too close, Daddy," he would drive even closer to the edge of the road and laugh. Of course, he never put us in true danger. But it seemed so to us, little ones. Having many hairpin turns, the dirt road was not to be driven on by the faint of heart. After a while, Mom would scold Daddy and say, "Enough now. You're scaring them."

I was always so glad when we finally drove on the public road that was more flat and led to an apple orchard, an almost guaranteed spot to find feasting deer. When Daddy had his fill of deer spotting for the night, Daddy eventually headed back to the cabin on a less-treacherous road. By the time we arrived at the cabin and I had climbed into my bunk I shared with my sister, my little fast-beating heart had settled down.

The cabin gang men spent many years either hunting for turkey, doe, buck, or bear around Clay Mine Camp. As my older brothers became gun-carrying age, each passed his rite of passage of being allowed to experience the men-only club and be invited to be part of the hunting gang at the mountains. Daddy bought Junior, the oldest son, a gun first. But it was eventually passed on to the brother next in line, and more guns purchased. At times, I believe, Daddy purchased a new gun for himself and passed his old gun on to a son.

Daddy, a hard worker, looked so forward to his days of packing up and heading to the mountains for a few days several times a year starting in November to go hunting. Not wanting to know all the details of what went on at the cabin during hunting season, Mom fully trusted Daddy to behave and to look out for their boys' safety. Being able to tattletale on Daddy, the brothers came back home and reported on many a late night was spent playing competitive Haas games with lots of laughing and away-from-work-stress free days.

The passed-around deer hunting joke did not apply to Daddy and the cabin gang: "A wife inquired of her hubby, 'How was your hunting trip?' He answered, 'Great, but I didn't shoot any deer.' 'I can see why,' answered the wife, 'you forgot your gun.'" In fact, Daddy's opinion was if you didn't go hunting, you weren't a true man (a comment he later told my nonhunting husband when I remarried).

Each brother has a story to tell about his first hunting experience. But the scariest event happened to my brother Mervin, when he was around thirteen or fourteen years of age. At dusk, he was actually lost in the woods for a time. By God's grace, he trekked his way back to Daddy and the rest of the hunting gang. This is one not-so-pleasant-hunting story that Mom had to hear about later.

Over the years, deer hunting tales grew similar to fish tales. But one of Daddy's success stories led him to feel the need to pass it on to other deer hunters. Years later, after I was in high school and had taken typing class, Daddy had asked me to type up one of his hunting experiences when he bagged an eleven-point buck, which I gladly obliged. He wanted to submit an article to *Pennsylvania Game News* (unfortunately, it was never published).

Later, upon his death and disbursement of Daddy's possessions, most items were evidence of his greatest hobby: hunting. Guns, bullets, hunting gear, and Daddy's old hunting licenses were up for the taking. Several brothers and grandsons were proud to select Daddy's mounted deer heads for their own wall, so the bagged-the-big-one stories could continue to be passed down through the generations.

At the cabin, Mom and the other women would be busy cooking the meals and doing the dishes. But some time was spent sitting out in the yard on lawn chairs visiting with each other, while we kids would play outside in the mostly-weeds yard or would climb on the wooden logs, always on the look out for rattlesnakes.

Daddy was eager to take a picture of his family using nature as his backdrop. Daddy would walk first into the fauna to be assured he disturbed any snakes, which were expected to crawl away. Once satisfied, he would ask us to stand in a field of ferns and pink mountain laurel near the cabin driveway and pose.

One day, we were allowed to walk to the end of the road near the cabin, cross over to the other side, and play in a larger forest clearing. Heading back for lunch, one had to jump over an old fallen-down log to reach the road. In single-file fashion, we jumped over the old insect-infested decaying log. By the time the third or fourth kid did so, someone heard a rattle sound and yelled "Snake!"

I was one of the few who had *not* jumped over the log yet and was next in line. We quickly stepped back and waited wide-eyed. After silence and the assumption the snake crawled away, my brother directed me to jump. I reluctantly jumped over the log. The rest followed behind me. In a run-Forest-run-like scene, the little ones had a hard time catching up with the older ones. Without stopping, I ran all the way back to the safety of the cabin, exhausted. Grateful no one was bitten, our moms served us lunch while listening to the excitement of the "near rattlesnake bite."

Pennsylvania northern forests are home to rattlesnakes and copperheads. It was just a matter of time until one rattler moseyed up near our cabin porch. Having no men around to kill it, Mom took the matter into her own hands. Using a shovel (*where did she find that?*), Mom-Eve smashed its head over and over again until it was as dead as a doornail. Take that, serpent! Mom proudly posed for Daddy holding the dead about-three-foot-long snake by its tail. Oh, this was on the same day that the men decided to go rattlesnake hunting and came back to camp empty-handed.

Most likely not a hunter himself, one mountain man's hobby was feeding a tame deer a piece of bread that he held in his mouth. Forming a special bond over years, several deer would routinely come into his yard to feed on ears of corn, apples, and other delicacies. A passerby would soon notice this rarity and spread the word in the community. Thus, a cheap Saturday night mountain-family entertainment began. At dusk, this man would display his talent for the public.

Whenever we were in the mountains, weather permitting, we drove to his home and watched. Parking along both sides of the road or wherever one found a makeshift parking spot, a small crowd stood quietly in awe and watched this feat. If someone closed a car door too loudly, temporarily the deer might run back into the woods. Invariably the small herd soon came back out to finish their supper.

Another mountain tradition was to attend the woodsmen's convention hosted in a nearby town. The contest was held between competitors to see who could cut through a log with an axe the fastest. Wearing flannel shirts and blue jeans, the men displayed bulging muscles as they swung their axes, released it, and chopped some more. It wasn't long until the smell of sawdust filled the autumn skies.

One memorable summer weekend when I was eight years old, one Saturday morning, the women decided to go shopping. The closest town was Jersey Shore, located about ten miles away that had one red light. Having about a dollar to spend, I was eager to pick out a trinket. The first store was a general five-and-dime-type store. After a process of elimination, I was torn between buying a paper doll or a cute pink plastic mirror. Being undecided and choosing not to purchase something in the first store, I started looking around the store for my mom and the other women. But after looking up and down each aisle twice to no avail, I started getting scared. *Am I lost? Perhaps they left the store without me and were headed back to the cabin?*

With an ache in the back of my throat, I started to walk to the car parked along a street of the lady who drove us to confirm they had not left. Arriving at the car, I tried to open the back seat car door. *Of course, it is locked!* Nobody familiar was around. I figured I might as well go back into the store, find a cashier, and tell her that I could not find my mom. Arms crossing my stomach, while fighting back tears, I walked heavy-footed back toward the store.

The more I recognized strangers around me, I became more frightened. Suddenly, I noticed a tall dark man with sharp features whistling and walking toward me. As I was getting closer to him, he started walking away from the inside of the sidewalk but toward the curb side, while stretching both arms out, as he was heading toward me. Believing he was about to kidnap me, I quickly turned around and ran across the street as fast as my little shaky legs could carry me.

One miracle in this story is that I never even bothered to look before crossing the street and running out into the traffic between cars approaching the red light. I just wanted to get safely back into the store and get some help. Walking up to the first cashier I saw, I confessed that I believed my mom left the store without me. Sensing how frightened and shaken up I was, she pulled up a chair and asked me to sit down. Relieved, I made it safely back into the store, I wearily sat down with a weighted chest as my heart was pounding away.

What probably seemed a lot longer than it really was, one of the ladies from our cabin gang finally walked into the store and found me sitting down near the checkout. How do you spell relief? *Being found!* Sure enough, Mom didn't realize I had not walked out of the store with the group of them until they had gone into the next store. A search party by her was soon put into action. I told Mom about the man who was walking toward me with his hands outstretched and how I ran away. Yes, of course, a stranger was *not* to be trusted. I don't remember Mom hugging me, but I could tell she was glad to see me. "Stay closer," she advised.

Various routes could be driven to get to the cabin. As with most choices either way, you had to cross over a bridge on the Susquehanna River. After this event, I started "dreaming" how the man heading toward me *did* catch me, roughly shoved me into his car (just like Mom's story when she was a teenager), I couldn't get out of the locked passenger side door. After he drove partway over the same bridge, he would stop his car, grab me out of the back seat, and throw me over the bridge. No, I never landed into the river. But I did wake up with my heart pounding and was relieved to know it was only a dream. So I dealt with it.

Sometime that year, I learned about the word *rape*. One of my evening activities after supper dishes were done was to place our newspaper on the floor and read it while on all fours. Of course, I had to share one side with my brother Matt. This led to another whole world my parents didn't talk about much. Besides reading the funny comics, I eagerly read the short articles from the local police log. I remember looking up the word *rape* in the dictionary after seeing it listed as a charge against a criminal. I read it had to do with a sexual act and something that a girl wanted no part of, but I was still confused.

After that bit of newspaper education, my altered dreams included an additional step in the chain of events: grabbed, thrown in car, driven to bridge, raped (no recollection on how I envisioned this act) by him, and then an attempt to be thrown over into the river. Eventually, I awakened in the middle of the dream at the point where we were simply driving in his car before the rape ever occurred. By the time I started fourth grade, I finally stopped reliving my potential disaster and had more pleasant dreams.

To this day, I can't read the sign Jersey Shore or drive through the town in the Pine Creek area and not think about God's sparing grace.

Over time, the cabin gang built an addition onto the small cabin, making room for a large family room. At the back of the living room was a curtained-off area that held two double beds for parents only. The heating system was improved too, with a more efficient wood stove. With the additional sleeping space, the cabin could more easily accommodate the growing families to include sons and my brothers as a hunting lodge. Just as their dads, they too have a great love for this sport and the thrill of the hunt.

Eventually, Daddy bought out the other two families' share of the cabin. Deciding to sell it for a cabin that did have indoor plumbing, Daddy later on sold the Clay Mine Camp at a handsome profit. Then Mom and Daddy bought another larger cabin near Shunk, the cabin where grandchildren shared many family fun-filled memories.

In fact, the gun-carrying licensed hunters in the Martin family eventually included women: my sister, Lorna, and my daughter, Steph, to name a few. Though not allowed to stay in the men-only cabin, women hunters had to stay in a cabin nearby along with women and children. For the kids, spending time in the cabin during hunting season is one of the highlights of November.

Lorna's hunting excursion was short-lived. Not being allowed to select deer hunting (that was absolutely forbidden by Daddy), Lorna decided to take up small-game hunting. Her ulterior motive was to be able to spend some quality time with her daddy. Well, not so much. Holding a passed-down gun, Lorna was instructed by Daddy to stay at her designated post and watch for game to come by, then he moved quite a distance away from her. Well, that failed miserably, so Lorna quickly lost an interest in hunting with Daddy.

It reminds me of the story I heard about the man who took his naughty dog to obedience school. Only the dog passed the course.

Thought of the Day

Grace is understanding God is sovereign and almighty. Don't allow problems and circumstances to consume you to the point where you doubt if God even cares. Don't doubt for one second if He even has the ability to handle things in His own way and in His own timing. He holds his prodigal sons and daughters in the palm of His hands!

Chapter 12

From Country Living to In-Town Living

However, I consider my life worth nothing to me, if only I may finish the race and complete the task the Lord Jesus has given me—the task of testifying to the gospel of God's grace.
—Acts 20:24

Author, front row, second girl from left, posing with her family

AS THOUGH IMPREGNATING MY AUNT wasn't enough, Bugsy, our landlord, began to have other alarming rumors spread around about him across the countryside, such as he fathered several children around town. Being fed up, Daddy made plans to move off the farmette.

MY LAST LAST NAME IS GRACE

Standing at a fork of a road, he had a huge decision to make that would impact his family tremendously: Should we continue to move around from farm to farm raising crops and steers? Would he have any need for his farm equipment? He didn't want to walk down the wrong prong.

By this time, Daddy was driving truck part-time while working full-time at Martin's Limestone Quarry. His boys were getting older; they would soon hold down jobs of their own. To make the decision easier for him, a fourteen-room historic house became available to rent in Hinkletown. Sitting on the corner of Hahnstown Road and Route 522, the former Black Horse Hotel was plenty big enough for his quiver-full of kids and affordable. After a visit to the historic two-story large house, Mom and Daddy made the decision to move off the farmette. We became town dwellers, renting from the Gehr family.

So in the spring of 1960, Daddy held a farm implement and small tool sale, confident he was walking down the correct prong of his fork. The sale led way to successful downsizing and for us to start packing for yet another move. Even though we would miss country adventures, I was excited about living in a town and having close-by neighbors. However, I was not thrilled about moving out of the Cocalico School District and into the Ephrata School District in the middle of my third-grade year. One's got to do what one's got to do.

Being mostly an A or B student, I felt really stupid on my first day when I attended Bergstrasse Elementary School that first Monday morning. Why? Because Bergstrasse's students had already been taught how to perform math problems called division. Since I was not taught how to do that yet, I was totally lost when the teacher, Mrs. Warren, handed out a math sheet with about eight division problems to solve. Watching all the other students busy completing the teacher's assignment before recess, I began to cry. Finally, the teacher noticed I was staring down at my paper, my left hand under my chin, and not writing anything.

"Johnny, go help the baby." Mrs. Warren sighed, looking at the neighbor boy who sat across the aisle. After wiping away tears and getting some tutoring help, I proceeded to complete the assignment with Johnny's help. After recess, Mrs. Warren asked three students go to the chalkboard and participate in a division-solving race. On her cue, the teacher wanted to see who could finish first a division problem while the classmates were looking on.

After some time of watching this performance, I mimicked under my breath, "Teacher, someday I'm going to show you. You won't be calling me 'baby' after I win your math race." Yep, over time, I delighted in volunteering (only a few girls did so) to be one of the students to participate in the division competition. I often won first or second place. But Jay, my toughest competition, was a math whiz. Math did eventually become one of my favorite subjects in my elementary years.

I'm not sure Mom would miss gathering eggs from under mean pecking hens in the small chicken house or killing chickens sometimes for food, though. Yes, I can still visualize Mom chasing a chicken, grabbing it as it was squawking, laying its neck on a stump, taking an axe, and chopping its head off. Did you know that dead chickens still flop around in the barnyard for a little while after being beheaded? The first time I witnessed this, I was unprepared for one to start flopping toward me. I screamed and ran away to get up on the porch.

After the flopping stopped, Mom then prepared the chicken. First, she placed the chicken in boiling water in the biggest pot she owned to loosen the feathers. Next, she plucked the feathers off the chicken in the outside water trough out in the yard to keep the mess out of her kitchen. As skilled as most chefs, Mom then gutted the chicken using a knife and a scissors. "Watch out for the bile sac. That holds all the poisons," she taught her little awestruck helpers.

By the time the protein-packed fowl would be ready for frying, Mom would had expertly cut out the gizzard, liver, and heart, which, when cut up in small pieces, made the best giblet gravy. Drumsticks, breasts, and wings were thrown sometimes into the pressure cooker, but not before two of us would fight over the wishbone. Hmmm. Fried chicken served with creamy, buttery mashed potatoes topped with giblet gravy and fresh corn was one of my favorite meals Mom cooked.

Within a few hours' time, one sacrificed chicken gave its neck literally for the chopping block and was lying on supper plates for one hungry family. Because it required a lot of work, Mom slaughtered several chickens at a time. Uncooked portions were wrapped in white or brown freezer paper (we called butcher paper) and placed in the freezer. The chest freezer my parents bought on my fifth birthday was still operable, though not considered energy efficient, in 2014.

The boys surely won't miss the hard labor in raising tobacco either. The process from small tobacco seeds to fifty-pound bales ready to be sold to a tobacco company consists of many hours of toiling, spanning over several months.

The process of growing and harvesting our tobacco crop follows: After purchasing the small tobacco plants from a farmer who had tobacco beds that grew from seeds, Daddy drove the tractor, pulling a tobacco planter across the prepared field. Two brothers sat on the back of the tobacco planter in barely above-ground low metal seats. The tobacco planter made rows, a hole, and supplied some water for the hole. My brothers' job was to place a tobacco plant into the holes that were made by the planter. An attached water tank had a hose that somehow squirted some water into the hole to aid in having a successful tobacco crop from the outset.

Then someone had to literally walk down the straight rows of the newly planted tobacco plants behind the tobacco planter with a hoe and place dirt around the stalk to cover up the hole. Over time, the tobacco grew, as well as some weeds. My brothers spent many hours in the hot summer sun hoeing loose weeds in the tobacco field.

At a certain point in the growth season, tobacco plants needed to be topped and suckered. Topping removed unwanted flowers on top of the tobacco plant; suckering removed unwanted leaves that were unproductive. This time-consuming practice did provide for a healthier, heavier plant (making for a more profitable crop, as the bales were sold by the pound). Harvesting time began when the tobacco plants needed to be "speared" onto a lathe so they could be hung in the barn and air-cured. Using a sharp small spear, one would fill a wooden lathe with cut tobacco stalks and let them lie on the ground for pick up.

    Once a wagon was stacked as high as possible of the prepared tobacco without tumbling off, the driver of the tractor backed the wagon into the barn; the men would then start a relay process. One removed the tobacco lathe from the wagon and handed the lathe off to someone. That person then handed it off to the one hanging the lathes off the barn rafters. In time, the entire barn was full of musky, sweet-smelling tobacco leaves. Warm autumn days and cool nights aided in perfectly curing the leaves, as evidenced by the tobacco leaves eventually turning colors from green to yellow to brown.

    January evenings are usually spent in more leisurely activities for farm families. However, this is not the case for tobacco growers. Stripping tobacco (the next step) filled many after-work hours for Daddy and my brothers. Having rented another nearby barn to do the stripping in, Daddy headed over there most weekday evenings. I have a few memories of going along with them to watch the process. Once the rafters of our barn were cleared of the lathes of dried tobacco, they were transported by tractor and wagon over to the stripping area.

    The leaves were stripped, and bundles of tobacco were put in a tobacco press. It was a wooden box that had a lid on it. The lid was connected with chains. Near the bottom of the box was a ratchet. A pole was placed in the ratchet and cranked by the handle to compress the tobacco. The only help I could be was to place the dead leaves into the box. Once compressed, each bale, weighing about fifty pounds, was stacked high in the hayloft. Eventually, an entire tobacco crop was harvested. Soon a salesman arrived to assess the quality of the crop and gave Daddy a price-per-pound offer for his hard work.

    No, I don't believe my brothers will miss harvesting tobacco when they become a Hinkletown resident.

    When we lived in the country, my older brothers chose not to attend the public Reamstown Elementary School and had to walk to and from Napierville School, the same school that our cousins attended. It was a one-room parochial schoolhouse for local Mennonite and Plain Mennonite families that my horse-and-buggy cousins dubbed Corn Cob College. Quitting school after eighth grade, my brothers, by law, only had to attend school on Fridays for three hours until the age of fifteen. Having a December birthday, Junior, for example, only attended school as a three-hour-Friday-grade student for four months.

Junior would be singing while throwing a stone up in the air and catching it, as he walked down the hill coming home from school. I never saw him carry a textbook. I guess he got all his homework completed while at school. Moving to Hinkletown meant that my brothers would be forced to attend the public school, which must have been somewhat of a culture shock for them. Unfortunately, they quit school as soon as they were allowed.

Hinkletown was founded by George Hinkle in 1787. He built the first mill over the Muddy Creek; the second mill was built by Jonathan Hinkle in 1797. It was a sturdy stone construction that had four and one-half stories. Later on, in 1830, another mill was built. Still in use when we moved across the street, the Hinkletown mill, at its production peak, produced fifty barrels of flour a day. The mill operation was accomplished by three turbines to power sometimes flour, grist (ground grain), and as a saw mill.

The grist was placed in pretty, colorful feed bags for transportation. Guess whose mother went across the street, purchased some unused feed bags, and sewed Sunday school dresses for her three girls? Sewing either a fancy dress with complimentary white collars or a simple straight A-line-jumper-like dress, Mom was proud of her pastel-colored dresses she had sewn for her girls or to add to her own wardrobe and to save money. Not being allowed to wear sleeveless dresses or tops, the only purchase needed to complete my outfit was a white blouse to be worn under the jumper.

Once a rich farming area with pleasant homes, churches, and schools, Hinkletown was located between Ephrata and New Holland. Our home was an actual hotel at one time and doubled as a stop for a stagecoach between Philadelphia and Pittsburgh. It held an intriguing mystery for us.

Later on, to refresh my memory about Hinkletown's history, I browsed through the Gehr and Wenger family's scrapbook about the Black Horse Hotel. A log of deeds showed the second owner was Samuel Hinkle in 1794. (George and Susanna Hinkle's ownership was not recorded in courthouse records.) It eventually became the residence of Colonel Allen Yundt.

With a sign proudly displaying a black horse, the hotel served meals and a bottle of ale for less than seventeen cents. One of the hotel's postcards reads: "B. W. Sheaffer, proprietor, boating and fishing, choice wines, liquors and cigars." Several pictures show men wearing black hats and suits, while the ladies were dressed in simple attire, as they posed in front or the side of the hotel or while gathered around the horse and buggies tied to the hotel's porch posts. During renovations, the Gehr family found scraps of papers in one wall: pages from a Bible, a log of guests in neatly written penmanship: "Martha Mult came on the 16th of August 1844," a handwritten hotel menu with prices, and a homework paper of practiced cursive penmanship.

But most impressive, a piece of a page of a *Lancaster Intelligencer Journal* newspaper of Monday morning, September 30, 1918, was found in a wall. The headlines read: "Draft Lottery Will Be Held Today at Noon" and "French Advance Two Miles on A Wide Front." History was preserved, albeit in a wall.

Heating so many rooms became a problem. Mom hung a curtain at the beginning of the short hallway to make a barrier for three unused upstairs' bedrooms. These rooms, named the front rooms, were on the upper right side of the house nearest the driveway. I remember playing hide-and-seek in this area, but only if it was in daylight. After all, one didn't know what could be lurking in the dark shadows.

An unexpected surprise was discovered in the large cool musty-smelling basement of our home. Although imperfect, a piano was missing some ivory on a few keys. I assume the prior owner realized that once taken down the rackety old stairs, the piano found its permanent home. After her chores were completed for the day, Mom would go downstairs and start playing the piano. Using only one hymn book, Mom kept practicing and taught herself how to read music. Requiring a badly needed tune-up, the piano playing could be heard two stories away. Over time, Mom could play any song—ah, let me clarify, any song in the key of C.

Eventually, I took an interest in playing the piano as well and played songs in the easier key of C. Soon, Mom gave me permission to take piano lessons from the owner of the local popular Hinkletown music store. About a quarter mile up the road, I needed to bike or walk to get to my piano lessons that summer. For several weeks, I gladly did so to be able to learn how to play songs other than in one key.

One day, something weird happened. While sitting on the piano bench next to my older male music teacher, I began to feel uncomfortable. My personal space was invaded by his sitting so close to me that his one leg was up against mine. Just as I started playing the second tune, he put his one arm around me. Playing the keys with less fervency, I finished playing my simple tunes. Hurriedly, I ran out of the music store, got on my bike, and hightailed it home. Breathless, I told Mom what had happened. Next thing I know, she was placing a phone call to the music store owner. "Leanne Martin won't be taking piano lessons from you anymore…and you know why," she snapped.

Mom hung up the phone, looked at me, and announced simply, "You're done with that!"

My older brother Junior started taking guitar lessons. Within a short period of time, it seemed Elvin could play an accordion, harmonica, and a guitar; Marlin, a mandolin and guitar; and Mervin too could play a guitar. Daddy's collection of pictures included many of the Martin boys sitting in the living room and playing their musical instruments on the weekends. The Martin boys were the cheap entertainment at my mom's Fisher family reunions. It was the highlight of our summer.

My Aunt Alta Fisher had no children, but she enjoyed starting the tradition of playing a unique version of Go, Fish. She hung a tight clothesline between two tall trees and pinned a blanket, using clothespins on the clothesline. The fishing pole was a long stick with a string and a clothespin attached on the end of it. Aunt Alta hid behind the blanket with her "fish." Each child (from infant to fourteen) stood in line and "fished" for a small gift, candy bar, or a pack of gum. Guess what is a passed-on tradition at family reunions that the grandchildren and great-grandchildren look forward to? Go Fish.

The other favorite at the Fisher reunion was Uncle Eli's homemade lemonade. It was so refreshing on hot summer days. Lemonade was not a beverage my mom served very often. What a special treat!

During the two and one-half years we lived in Hinkletown, my three older brothers reached sixteen years of age and started driving their own cars. Marlin owned a small red motorcycle. Town living didn't give way for a big driveway. So Daddy gave permission for the boys to park their cars in the yard beside the driveway. Mom and Daddy would park their two cars beside the barn under a tree at the top of the driveway. We had a minicar lot.

One day, my mom's friend made a comment that they would have stopped by the previous Sunday afternoon to stop in and visit with our family. But she commented, "I saw that you already had company, as I saw all these cars parked at your house."

"Oh, no, nobody was visiting us," Mom answered. "Those cars belong to our boys. You should have stopped in."

One picture Daddy took showed the family car, a '56 black Buick, a '61 red Pontiac that Junior drove, Elvin's black '57 Ford and Daddy's 1949 black Plymouth, dubbed the pitch wagon, that he drove to work. Junior and Elvin would ask their sisters to wash their cars for them for $0.25 so they would be nice and clean for their Saturday night dates. We were thrilled to oblige.

Our home had a well-planned-out layout: a kitchen the width of the house, a bathroom behind it, and a family room off the kitchen that led into a room called the front living room, which was the entrance from the front porch. When standing in the front living room, to the left was my parents' bedroom. To the right was the parlor, a room used for special occasions, weekends, and visiting friends. In fact, our home hosted the Martindale Mennonite Church's youth group song fest. My parents removed the furniture from the kitchen and set up borrowed folding chairs from the church to accompany dozens of Martindale youth singing hymns. For several hours that night, it was filled with praises of combined singing voices lifted heavenward. For the treat (refreshments), my mom proudly served the crowd homemade doughnuts.

All of the children understood that our parents' bedroom was off-limits. We only went in when we were asked to do so. But the one time I was escorted into that room by my dad was memorable. I was about to get my first (and last) spanking by him with his belt. It was a Sunday and on Daddy's birthday, nonetheless. On the way home from church, while sitting in the back seat, Mom looked back at me and demanded, "Leanne, I saw you talking in church to Nancy throughout most of the sermon. Daddy, I gave her a warning look, and she ignored me. You need to spank her when we get home!"

So the inevitable wait began. Like the long walk to your boss's office to pick up your pink slip or what must have been the dreaded walk in front of your entire church congregation for one to confess sins to your pastor, I was full of anxiety the minute I got out of the car. *Is Daddy going to spank me before or after lunch?* As it turned out, most effectively, making me wait until *after* I ate (did I eat much?), he got up from the table and stressed, "Leanne, follow me." I walked behind him slowly through one room, then another, and another; finally, we turned right and entered his bedroom.

As soon as he closed the door, while taking off his belt, he prompted, "Mom wants me to do this. So lie down across the bed." The deserved smack of the belt across my legs began. This is one time wearing a dress that reaches to your knees helps. I yelled immediately and started crying out. I had learned from watching older brothers and sisters that you need to cry out from the outset. The punishment does not seem to be as severe. After three smacks, he stopped and stated, "Stop talking in church." I felt bad as I, with hunched shoulders, walked upstairs to my bedroom to sulk. Mom made him do this on his birthday!

Another lesson in life we learned by example was how Daddy handled an uncomfortable situation. We were sitting at the supper table and someone knocked on the back door. Mom answered it and found one of the neighbor men with his son standing outside. "Daddy, they are asking for you," she pointed out.

Within a few minutes, Daddy came back inside, sat down, and simply announced, "The Pop was making his kid return my watch he stole in the washhouse and to say he's sorry. Let that be a lesson. Your sin will find you out." The man of few words finished his supper.

Living along a main route from Blue Ball to Ephrata, I remember how challenging it was to fall asleep. My bedroom was in the front of our home facing the busy road. Passing tractor trailers were noisy with hissing brakes that caused the house to slightly shake at times. We witnessed quite a few accidents in front of our home. The record for us was three accidents in one day! One morning, I was sitting on the side porch shelling peas for Mom when a car pulled up to the stop sign; the driver looked to her left before pulling out. But unfortunately, she did not see the car traveling west. The minor accident occurred with little injuries.

Shortly after lunch, we heard the screeching of tires. Knowing what that could mean, we all held our breaths. Then we heard the crashing sound of metal on metal. Upon investigation, a tractor trailer truck had T-boned the side of a car that did not see the car crossing its path. Thank God again, only minor injuries ensued.

That evening, we went grocery shopping. While paying for the bill, Daddy was busy talking to the grocery store owner who knew where we lived. He informed us that someone told him that an accident had occurred that included a car being up over our front porch. Daddy asked for clarification, "Are you talking about the one that happened with the tractor trailer and car earlier today?"

"No," he answered. "Apparently, there is a car up on your porch now." We rushed home to investigate ourselves.

Lo and behold, a police officer was standing on our porch talking with a nervous teenager with, presumably, her dad standing nearby. Turns out the driver was learning how to drive. While attempting to make a right turn off Route 522 unto Hahnstown Road, she hit the gas pedal instead of the brake pedal. Thus, she crashed into one of the porch pillars and came to a stop on our porch within a finger breadth from hitting the corner of the house.

It was time for accidents to stop. Eventually, a red light replaced the stop sign; the old depilated mill was torn down to make room to widen Route 522 and replace the bridge.

As much as I enjoyed watching TV at my neighbor girl's house, my mom also enjoyed watching it. She would visit our elderly neighbor lady, Mrs. Gehr, who lived alone with her pet dog, Peewee. Mrs. Gehr enjoyed our company. It wasn't long before Mom realized a good night to visit Mrs. Gehr was on a Tuesday night when the TV show *Dr. Kildare*, about a handsome young doctor, was on. Not normally wanting to volunteer to go along with Mom to visit our elderly neighbor lady, I learned to appreciate the opportunity to visit her one or two times a month to view my TV heartthrob.

Another humorous memory from Mrs. Gehr was when she would stand on her front porch and call after her little pet dog to come back into the house. "Peewee! Peewee!" she yelled in a singsong manner. Obeying her, Peewee would run quickly back up on the porch. My siblings and I often imitated her by calling out for Peewee in our best Mrs. Gehr-sounding voice. Poor Peewee had to be so confused.

Mom's chore list for me at age eight or nine included to dust the hall baseboards and furniture. Sometimes, displeased Mom ran a finger along the upstairs' hall baseboard and demanded, "See this dust? Do it again, Leanne."

Behind the barn, rhubarb plants grew. It was my job to cut the rhubarb so Mom could make an awesome rhubarb pie. Of course, the huge garden produced plentiful crops of sugar and snap peas, wax and string beans, potatoes and cut lettuce, to name a few. "Many hands make light work" was proven over and over as we all pitched in to help with canning and freezing vegetables for the winter.

Living two doors down from a furniture store, Mom and Daddy purchased a new bedroom suite for themselves. That was a big deal. They used that same bedroom suite for over twenty years. Using a smart marketing tool, our neighbor gave away a new 1964 Ford Falcon that year. Simply by stopping in at the store and browsing, your name was put in the drawing to have a chance to win the car. The Martins were not the lucky winners, so the pitch wagon's services continued.

Living in town gave more opportunities for door-to-door salesmen to visit. One day, our front door bell rang. I was standing next to Mom being nosy. "Don't look this stranger in the eye, Leanne," she alluded as she opened the door. A salesman, selling knives, was eager to show Mom his wares. But it had to be somewhat awkward for him to be friendly and attempting to have eye contact from his prospective customer. The lady of the house was looking down at the screen door handle the whole time and kindly dismissed him.

My one memory of being too ill to attend school was when I lived there, and I had a bad chest cold. (During my elementary school years, I held either a perfect attendance or one-day-only-missed record.) I remember Mom making me an onion poultice, a hot pack of sorts. Believing in homeopathic household remedies, Mom simply fried sliced onions, placed them in a dishtowel, and, once it was cooled down slightly, put the poultice on my chest. My chest and throat was lathered with liberal amounts of Vicks Vapor Rub. How can anyone forget the menthol smell of dabs of Vicks on your nose? Being cheap and effective, Mom's remedy did the trick.

Besides TV viewing where I watched couples kissing, I also got some education from reading my brother's romantic comic books, named *Archie*. Having easy access to the comic book rack across the street in the small grocery store, my brother could get his hands on one pretty quickly. Sometimes, it was my job to clean my four older brothers' bedroom. I didn't mind on those days I found a comic book or two lying around. I would study those comic scenes (especially couples on a moonlit night) and duplicate them in my mind before falling asleep. How beautiful was Veronica with her long gorgeous flowing brunette hair, full lips, and perfectly made-up face. What does it feel like to be kissed and hugged?

Another source for learning about my upcoming dating life was from Mom as she was educating her older sons. One night, she told Elvin, who was combing his hair in front of the kitchen mirror before heading out on a date with Linda, "If you take Linda out for ice cream and she says 'no,' don't push the issue. She may have her monthly and not want one." Laughing his unique laugh (sounding similar to Daddy), Elvin left the house.

Either because Daddy had a camera and started taking pictures of Christmas celebrations or they had some extra monies to spend on gifts, my favorite childhood Christmases were spent while living in Hinkletown. Though not standing around a tree, we stood up against the front door proudly holding up a gift or two. We got about three or four presents each. When I was eight, I received a set of plastic cookware for the times my sisters and I played house. It was bright pink and included a frying pan and two kettles. What to put them on was answered when I noticed Mom pulling out from behind her bedroom door a small two-foot-high white wooden stove. Mom explained that my cousin made it. The burners were four gray tin can lids (two large and two smaller ones) with big black buttons, which turned as knobs. There was no oven door I could open, but my cousin did a good job of painting on a picture of an apple pie baking in the oven. Practicing cutting perfectly with a scissors was possible from my gift of a set of two paper dolls. On rainy days, cutting out the paper dolls and a dozen paper outfits kept me busy for hours.

But my favorite gift was a pencil color set of American birds when I was nine years old. I spent hours staying within the lines and producing a colorful picture I could be proud of. As much as I loved my gift of two new dolls, I was envious of the new pair of ice skates both Matt and Lenora received that year. However, Mom gave me my new pair of ice skates when I was thirteen, and boy, did I wear them out!

Mom started her hobby of growing violets, selling vitamins (only to family and friends; house-to-house selling to strangers was not an option), and collecting a beautiful set of white and green magnolia-designed china. She continued her collection of glassware from the oatmeal and laundry powder boxes when we lived in Hinkletown. The method for me and my siblings to get some free gifts was using coupons we cut out of the newspaper. How? We discovered through Matt's friend, Ned, in the neighborhood, you could redeem them at the grocery store across the street. We all stood there confused and asked him what he meant. "Redeem a coupon?" asked Matt, pulling on his ear. "How do you do that?" Ned explained that you took the cut-out coupon and exchanged it for a candy bar or a pack of gum. "If it says ten cents, you get ten cents worth of candy for free." His eyes sparkled as he enlighten his clambering-closer neighbor kids.

As soon as we finished our chores that evening, Matt and I could not wait to spread the newspaper on the floor between us to look for and cut out coupons. We needed to wait until it was our turn after Daddy, Junior, Elvin, Marlin, and Mervin in that order. Our scanning revealed two coupons on cleaning supplies worth twenty cents. We need four coupons. I guess we're sharing our candy bar or pack of gum with Lenora and Lorna. Matt, Lorna, and I ran across the street clutching the two coupons in our hands.

The candy and gum rack was so enticing. We licked our lips. "I would like two packs of Juicy Fruit, please," I said to Mr. Althouse, the grocery store owner. He turned around from restocking the shelves. Matt selected two Snickers bar. As he handed over the two coupons, Mr. Althouse observed. "Oh, I see you must have been talking to Ned. Okay, enjoy your candy." He opened the big black cash register and placed the paper coupon in the back of the drawer. We ran back home and shared our free candy and gum with Lenora. Wow! I want to do that six ways from Sunday.

1965 was the beginning of serious coupon clipping for housewives (though my mom did not do a lot of it). Unfortunately, the coupon exchange for free candy for the Martin children only occurred about four times that summer. The salesman for the cleaning product put an end to it. I believe it didn't take long to figure out the number of coupons didn't match the number of bottles sold off the shelf!

Our only Saturday road trip occurred in 1962 when Daddy drove half of his family (from Lenora on down) to the Poconos to visit Bushkill Falls. It was special because it was the few times my parents splurged on a souvenir. Daddy took a photograph of both Matt and I each standing in front of the black Buick's headlight. I'm holding a small Indian doll; Matt, a toy tomahawk. Both of us are grinning as wide as one of the falls.

For two to three years, the Martins were town dwellers. I had to endure one more move when my parents had a new home built next to my cousins' house. Yes, that meant another transfer over to Cocalico School District, the same school district that I had attended first through half of third grade. Starting in 1962, when I was mid-year in sixth grade, I attended Cocalico Junior and High School until my graduation (the first sibling to do so) in 1970.

Thought of the Day

Grace in its fullness means faith (my part) and grace (God's part) must coexist. Faith alone and grace alone miss the mark. Together, they will allow streams of living water to flow from me.

Chapter 13

"Mauh De Dara Ztu!" (Make the Door Shut!)

> But he gives us more grace. That is why Scripture says:
> God opposes the proud but shows favor to the humble.
> —James 4:6

JUST AS MY TWO DAUGHTERS are really close and best friends, in their younger years, my mom and Aunt Lucy were very close. Sisters who get along with each other have a special bond. My Aunt Lucy, along with her brood of kids, visited my family in the summer frequently during the week, as they only lived a few miles down the road. During my early elementary years, living out in the country on the farmette gave us all an ample place to play with my cousins in the yard, down in the meadow or in the barn.

The sisters spent hours together despite the hard work it took them to raise their large families: Mom eventually had nine children, and Aunt Lucy, ten. I cannot imagine doing what my mom did. She frequently prepared lunch for two families during these summer visits. It surely had to seem like cooking for company. Unlike her sister, my mom did keep after laundry, ironing, growing a large garden, canning and freezing, and other household duties. Perhaps, so she wouldn't have to face her many unclean rooms and stack of dirty dishes, piles of dirty laundry, is why Aunt Lucy visited her sister frequently? (Hmm or perhaps here is the clue why my cousins' house was so dirty because the family rarely stayed home?)

So that the sisters could converse about adult matters such as money, husbands, and life's woes that erupted in the early '60s, Mom chased all the kids outside to play out of earshot. Smart woman! I am quite sure the two sisters, while conversing, probably got more work done in the house, garden, or hanging out laundry without twenty-four feet underfoot.

I was thrilled to have my cousin Jill visit so often and hang out with me. Having my chores done before lunch enabled Jill and me immediately to go outside and play. Sitting on the front yard, I remember excitedly watching in anticipation for my Aunt Lucy's black Nash to round the corner at the top of the hill and enter our gravel driveway.

Weather permitting, we would play house sometimes down in the meadow. I would be the wife to my cousin Robert, Matt was the hubby for Jill, and Lenora and Gregory hooked up. One or two dolls completed our families. Our "home" consisted of crushing the hay with our feet until it would lie flat. Building three or four small rooms, we then played house mimicking our parents. "Hi, honey," I greeted Robert, "how was your day at work?" Robert entered into the kitchen and gave me a hug and a pretend kiss. Thank goodness, I don't remember playing house much beyond a kitchen scene so the bedroom never got used. We soon tired of playing house and moved on to the next item of play: tag, hide-and-go-seek, kick the tin can, throwing a ball, jacks, or swinging on the grape arbor swing set.

With adult supervision (Aunt Lucy often volunteered), on the hottest days, we were allowed to swim in the creek beyond our meadow. I will never forget the day a five-year-old girl (not much younger than me), who lived in the nearby city of Reading, drowned in the creek. A police car and an ambulance arrived on the scene. But looking back, it seemed pretty calm for such a life-changing incident for the affected family. Directed to get out of the water and stand on the bank, we stared in awe watching the scene unfold in front of us. Mostly hidden from view, the little girl's body was whisked away, and the cause of her drowning unknown. One can only assume the mom did not see the little girl go under the water. Had she slipped on a rock and got into too deep water in the middle of the creek and was unable to swim?

Never becoming a great swimmer, I learned how to doggy paddle and swim from observing my older brothers and sisters. (As a parent, I made sure my kids took swimming lessons.)

Daddy rented the farmette to raise steer as extra income and keep my older brothers busy and out of Mom's hair. Daddy always held a full-time day job and tended to the farm duties evenings and Saturdays. One of our favorite pastimes (especially on rainy days) was playing barn blumsock together. This was a more-the-merrier tag-type game. You simply tied a big knot in an empty brown burlap bag. That became your tag item. Since the barn consisted of two floors, stacked hay bales, wooden tobacco rafters, and many cubbyholes, hiding spots from the one who was "it" were plentiful. Being bigger and stronger, when my brothers threw the blumsock to tag you, you felt it! Not having much of an arm throwing distance or climbing ability up on the rafters, I hoped, when I was "it," I would be able to tag the person who was still running around on the barn floor selecting their hiding place. (Throwing and aiming the blumsock successfully was great practice later on for my baseball throws.)

Not surprisingly, the younger kids always seemed to be the ones who were doing the running around and tagging others. The older brothers and cousins could take long periods of rest sitting up on rafters, knowing the little ones surely couldn't throw the blumsock that far. When it became too boring, my brother would grab the blumsock, take over as "it", and chase the older cousins, making it a livelier game once again. Ducking from the blumsock, running zig-zag, making their aimed throw difficult, or diving behind a hay bale in the nick of time made for a fun-filled afternoon. To this day, I can still smell the more pleasant barn aromas: used old burlap, hay tossed around from scurrying feet stirring up dust, and drying pungent, sweet-smelling tobacco that hung from wooden barn rafters.

In the late fall, the second floor of the barn was filled with stacks of hay and straw bales. Here is the difference: hay is used for feeding; straw is used for bedding the steers housed in the lower level or in the barnyard. Rearranging them provided no-cost entertainment. With my older brothers and cousins' help to construct it, a long winding tunnel held hours of crawling fun.

The most exciting time to travel through the newly built tunnel was your first run. Constructed to make you think, the tunnel had surprise drops, where strategic hay bales were removed. If you came to a dead end, you had to figure out if you were to make a left or right turn. Perhaps you needed to climb up over two stacked hay bales to be able to continue crawling out of the tunnel to the end. If you had any fear of the dark, playing in the tunnel was not for the faint of heart. If you wanted to scare someone, temporarily blocking one end of the tunnel did the trick.

Even though our arms and legs got scratched from the hay, we repeated this over and over again, especially on rainy days. There is nothing like climbing out of a tunnel with your nose tickling with hay bale dust and your pigtails full of hay. What fun!

Our farmette housed several dozen steers, which could roam either in the barn or out in the barnyard, causing some unpleasant barn smells. Another one of our favorite summer pastimes, until Daddy caught on, was to get a resting steer to pass gas. I am sure an older brother of mine, responsible for feeding them, first discovered this unspeakable, hilarious act. After a meal, you poked a stick through the fence or gate. You got the resting steer to arise onto its feet. About fifty percent of the time, they would let one rip. The contest was which one of us had poked the steer with the longest-lasting one or most musical-sounding fart. Of course, it only worked one time and for only those steers where a stick could reach. We laughed so hard and almost wet our pants! For the longest time, Mom and Aunt Lucy couldn't figure out why we were all in such a hurry to leave the lunch table and run toward the barnyard.

A TV, not permitted anyway, was not needed to entertain us.

I was seldom allowed to stay overnight at Jill's unkempt house. That was fine with me, as their house was somewhat spooky. Not having electricity made Jill's bedroom, which she shared with her sisters, scary and mysterious by the light of the kerosene lamp or flashlight. I can remember looking out at a big full moon through the curtain-less windows, finding it difficult to fall asleep. What was that noise outside my door? Was it footsteps? Was that the bogeyman walking outside around the house with a gun? Was he under my bed?

The more pleasant memories at Jill's house occurred after a winter snowstorm. My aunt and uncle's house had a hilly backyard. Using potato chip can and pretzel can tin lids to sit in as snow toboggans, we would ride down their snow-packed hill. Once the path was reused, those homemade toboggans picked up speed. Aunt Lucy would play with us outside as well for hours until we all had red-rosy cheeks and running noses.

After my family's move to Hinkletown, when I was in the middle of third grade, our type of indoor and outdoor childhood games changed drastically. Our fourteen-room house set fairly close to the road along busy Route 522 and had a cement front porch the length of the house. I spent many hours on that porch watching the passing cars. By the time I had lived there a few months, a fun game that I played with my siblings was to shout out the year and make of cars as they passed by. With practice, it wasn't long until I was just as good at playing this game as Matt was. Only my older brothers, who already were of car-driving age, were better at it. Many a Sunday afternoon would be spent on the front porch shouting out, "'58 Chevy, '59 Ford, '61 Dodge!" Of course, we could have been wrong at times, but we got pretty good at knowing our makes and models of cars.

Living in town gave way to having close neighbors who lived right down the street. This was so different from our previous homes that were located in the country. The only neighbor girl, Charlene, who was in my same grade, lived only two houses down. Her family owned a furniture store. The neighborhood gang consisted of kids mostly older than me (my brother or sister's ages), but there were a few younger ones.

I was delighted to learn that Charlene had a TV. My education about the world and entertainment was broadened and changed forever! On occasion, I was allowed to stay overnight at her house on a Friday night. We would watch TV, powered by rabbit ear antennas, until the stations turned off and made an annoying, buzzing sound with only gray flickering lines and a no-picture screen. (These were the days when the stations did not run 24-7.) With instructions on how to turn on the TV, I would be the first to awake, turn it on, and started watching Saturday morning cartoons with eyes glued to the TV screen. It wasn't long before Charlene's parents had figured out the little Mennonite neighbor girl was intrigued and fascinated by TV viewing. Even so, they limited the hours we spent inside on nice summer days watching the boob tube.

Taking time out for breakfast was a total annoyance and disruptive to my TV viewing. Sometimes, Charlene's mom allowed us to eat cereal on TV trays (a new household item I learned about) and watch TV in the living room while eating our breakfast. My mom knew I was watching TV while visiting my friend's house and simply trusted that her parents were only allowing shows that did not include violence, guns, and murder, for example.

I am sure Charlene watched more hours of TV the times I visited than she would have if I had not been visiting. Still fascinating to me, I was thrilled when I learned that Charlene's dad purchased a color TV to replace their black-and-white one. He was the first to do so in Hinkletown. Now watching *Wonderful World of Disney* on Sunday nights, if invited over, was even more appealing.

Once the thrill of TV wore off for me (though I never turned down the opportunity to watch), Charlene and I joined her two brothers and other neighborhood kids who were playing outside. Kick the tin can, hide-and-seek, red light, green light, and four squares on the driveway, or catching fireflies at night filled many evenings of play and exercise. Using the furniture store parking lot, many games requiring space were played here when the store was closed. From morning to night, we spent hours outside playing.

In between my few chores of cleaning my room, dusting, and hanging up or taking down laundry, I spent my time hanging out with neighborhood kids or my cousins who continued to visit, though less frequently. Evening chores of sweeping the floor after supper or doing the dishes were hurried through so we could continue our play. Mom did not have to call after us; we just knew when to come in at bedtime.

Nor did she fear for our safety. It was understood we were either outside playing in our own yard or at some other neighbor's house. We had many "neighborhood moms" who could yell and scold us if we misbehaved; likewise for Mom, if the neighborhood kids needed correcting. So different from this generation of kids.

One of the best memories was playing around the dam and under the Hinkletown mill bridge. Using a makeshift fishing rod, we would tie a string around our big toe, drop the hooked fish line in the water and wait for a bite. Though someone may have caught a fish a time or two, it was tiny and thrown back into the water.

Soon bored with little fishing luck, we would walk behind the mill and start swimming in the creek. A dam spread clear across the creek. Hours were spent sliding down the slippery moss-covered dam until swimsuit bottoms were worn clear through. In fact, we would go through several swimsuits a summer. At Daddy's suggestion, Mom was asked to take us swimming suit shopping at the next local rummage (the original yard) sale, so we could replace our swimming suits that started having quarter-sized holes that Daddy was getting embarrassed about. So we got several new swimming suits each summer.

It never fazed us as to what exactly could have been swimming in the creek water with us as well. In fact, you could see our cow and the neighbors' cows upstream wading in the water too, at times relieving themselves! (Hmm…doesn't all that wash downstream?) Getting suntanned, bathed in the creek frequently, and getting plenty of outdoor exercise kept us healthy. I don't remember any one of us kids visiting a doctor or having any broken bones during this time.

Located across the street from our home was the Hinkletown Park. It was so named because it held a few picnic tables, an old sliding board, and a seesaw. It was the best place to enter to go swimming in the creek, as it had a small sandy area. A strong thick-knotted rope hung from a tall tree along the creek bank that was used to swing across from one side to another.

Part of Mennonite tradition was for church families and relatives to visit each other on either Saturday, Sunday afternoon or evenings. It was called company. Mom would say, "We need to clean the house first before we go shopping today. We could get company." Or after receiving a phone call inquiring of Mom, "Are you going to be home this evening?" Mom would say, "Leanne, go sweep the porch off. Company's coming soon."

Our company's kids and our cousins during visits would be a time for us to go swim in the creek in the park. Mom and the other women would sit on blankets and watch us while visiting with each other. I remember Mom putting on a swimsuit and getting in the water only a few times. I saw my dad wearing swim trunks only once; that was when we took a day trip down to the Chesapeake Bay clamming with my aunt and uncle and cousins. To leisurely go swimming didn't occur for Daddy even on Sundays. Whether it was because he was so light-complexioned and didn't want a suntan or whether he was too modest; I believe it was the latter. The time I saw Daddy wearing the least amount of clothes was when he came out of the bathroom, and we passed in the hall. He was wearing only his athletic shirt and trousers while heading to his bedroom that was located across the hall from my bedroom.

Childhood items required for play were cheap and inexpensive compared to today's entertainment gadgets. They consisted of a ball and bat, gloves, used bikes, jacks, bouncing balls, black inner tubes for swimming, and jars to catch fireflies. Flip-flops may have been worn at times, but we mostly went barefoot.

To be funny or when lazy, sometimes we would use the outhouse located beside the barn near the driveway instead of going into the house to use the bathroom if we were busy playing outside. But you wanted to sneak in unseen, as invariably someone would try to scare you while seated on the throne. Having spider webs, lots of dust, and being odoriferous, the outhouse did have a cutout-quarter moon on its wooden door. An old Sears and Roebuck catalog was used for toilet paper. I do not remember using it two times in one day for obvious sanitary reasons.

Wearing homemade or rummage-sale-purchased Halloween outfits (no monsters' or witch's masks were allowed), we, while living in town, warranted a reason to go trick-or-treating. That was the only time I remember doing so in my childhood. But I do not remember Mom handing out candy from our house to other neighborhood trick or treaters. My parents allowed us to go have the fun of roaming our safe neighborhood collecting candy, but they were not going to participate in this manner.

In 1962, when I was in sixth grade, Mom and Daddy bought several acres of land in East Cocalico township from my aunt and uncle, cleared it of trees and brush, and built a new one and a-half story five-bedroom white Holland stone house on it. Thus, I have quite a few memories of living next door to my horse-and-buggy cousins. I do not remember Lucille, the cousin who was the closest to my age, coming down to my house to play very often. The times she did visit my house to play was spent playing school with my sister Lenora as our school teacher. Lucille remembers to this day that she was way too strict of a teacher.

But I mostly played over at Lucille's house. Even though she and I had plenty of playtime (while babysitting her four younger brothers and sisters playing outside with us too), Lucille did do some chores during my visit, like hanging up laundry on the wash line, or removing it, or doing the dishes.

But hurrying through her chore list, Lucille and I spent many a summer afternoon playing together. Speaking Pennsylvania Dutch among themselves, my cousins would converse without my understanding what they were saying. With simple repetition over time, I did learn simple phrases, such as, *"Kum essa"* (Come eat), *"Vee bisht?"* (How are you?), and *"Vos is di noma?"* (What is your name?). Even though my brothers learned the language from my dad and cousins, my sisters and I never had enough interest to do so.

There was one phrase I heard my aunt repeat many times during my playtime with Lucille, but I paid little attention to it, since I did not understand it. One day when summer was almost over, I heard my aunt yell to us kids once more, *"Mauh de dara ztu!"* While hurrying outside, I turned to Lucille and finally asked, "What is your Mom yelling?" She answered, "Make the door shut. She hates flies." Oops, I guess I should have cared enough to pay attention to my aunt's command long before this.

My uncle's farmette, located about a football-field length away from our home, had the horse's meadow located next to our pond. It was quite a distance for me to walk or run before reaching Lucille's safe yard. In the evenings, when it would get dark earlier, before my playtime curfew was up, I remember being very scared to walk back and forth in between our homes.

Remembering all of Mom's scary stories about fearing strangers, I felt sure that the oncoming car was a driver with ill intentions. So if I saw car headlights in a distance, I would lie down in the ditch beside the road and wait until the car or truck would pass me by. (Of course, I never feared horse-and-buggy drivers.) A trip home could include throwing myself down into the ditch thwarting off danger twice before reaching my driveway. Most likely, the car probably held another Mennonite family. But I was not taking any chances!

Reinforcing Mom's warnings, an experience had occurred to Lucille and me. One day, Lucille and I were walking along the road. A lady known around the area as being somewhat eccentric and weird drove by us. The car slowed, was put in reverse, and the passenger window was being turned down. We noticed her son was driving, and she was sitting on the passenger side. She held out a cigar box to us and asked if we wanted some candy. We answered, "No, thanks," and kept on walking. With a witchlike laugh, she threw the box out of the window. Curious, after they drove on, we walked back, picked up the cigar box to check out what candy could be inside. But, instead, it was only a few banana peels. God forbid she would ever be driving by when I was walking home alone in the dark! So the ditch-diving continued for many a summer until I was older and my fears subsided.

My other neighbor and girlfriend, Cheryl, had a pond on her property. Many summer afternoons and early evenings were spent there sunbathing and diving off the diving board. One August, I noticed a small boil under my left armpit. Mom believed it was due to the germs in the pond. Explaining how to draw out the pus, Mom had me use one of her empty saffron plastic vial-like containers, heat it to a boiling point, and after cooling slightly, place it over the boil. As it cooled down, sure enough, disgusting yellowish pus was sucked up into the container. Repeating this method a few times, my boil eventually went away. No need to visit a doctor. But the boil did not stop more swims in Cheryl's pond.

As with all new homes set in a country setting consisting of several acres of land, landscaping is a must. Once the number of trees was removed to Daddy's satisfaction, grass was planted in our front yard. Mom planted lovely flowers, such as pansies and daffodils, around some of the tree trunks. When completed, our new home had a huge front yard about half the size of a football field.

That sufficient-sized yard provided hours of learning how to bat, pitch, catch, and play baseball from my older brother Elvin. Until I could no longer catch my breath, he played with his brothers and sisters chasing us around the makeshift bases, often tagging us before we ever made it on base. Changing it up by hitting high pop ups or at times hitting grounders to us, Elvin helped us to not be afraid of a baseball. He taught us how to hold a glove, squeeze it to hold the ball in, and throw straight toward his glove. "Hit me!" he'd say. Terms like "Save the stick" or "Big stick" (on two outs) or "Come on, slugger" was yelled. Being Mennonite, I was not allowed to join any high school sports of any kind. Besides, Mom did not have the time nor desire to drive me back and forth from school to participate in after-school sporting events. So this time spent with my brothers and sisters made up for it.

Listening to the Phillies' ball games on the radio was one of Elvin's favorite pastimes. He gets the credit for my love of baseball. In fact, when the opportunity arose when I was in my thirties, my friend Janie invited me to play softball on a women's league. She was the pitcher, and I was the catcher. Janie's restaurant The Elton was the sponsor of our team. Thus, we proudly displayed her restaurant name on our red team T-shirts. Not having participated in any school sports, I jumped at the opportunity and played on the team for several summers.

Whether high-school aged or not, squabbling that went on between some teammates was frustrating, especially if one was highly competitive. But it was a great exercise program for me after sitting in the office all day. After several years of being a mediocre player and base runner, I quit the team, allowing for the younger and faster-running twenty-something girls to take my place.

After the old Noodle Doosie (more on this later) church that was crumbling down from age was removed from the front corner of our property, Daddy had a medium-sized pond built to the right of our long driveway. Mom planted pretty pink flowers that quickly spread around the pond's bank, setting it ablaze. Though it was seldom used by us to swim in, it was an excellent area to go ice-skating on. Matt and his cousins, just as his Daddy did, tried his hand at trapping muskrats to sell the hides for cash too from the pond.

Over time, Daddy cleared the large area behind our house, and it was nicknamed the park. Located along the Muddy Creek, the park was used to hold covered-dish suppers, chicken barbeques, and our church's young people's events that drew a crowd. I have a few memories of us three sisters playing doll or a board game on a blanket in the park. Later, I spent some time with my date sitting on a blanket by the water and talking. It had no lights, so it was not a place to hang out after dark.

Being older and wiser about not swimming in the possibly snake-and turtle-filled-literally-muddy disgusting creek, we only rowed a boat on the creek at times. As a teenager, I would invite a gang of both guys and gals to take the rowboat out under the moonlight. Yes, the clearing acres of land for a park were a wise choice of land use, Daddy.

With the monies from my mom's inheritance, Mom and Daddy later purchased more land to the right of our home from the neighbor, making the property now all total about five acres. Mom turned some of the land into a larger garden, but the rest gave way for more yards to play in. Over time, my parents watched two generations of their large family of children and grandchildren make great use of the large property, which was planned with love and many hours of toil and hard work.

Thought of the Day

Grace is hooking up with my supply line, granting me efficiency in everything I do. As a babe in Christ, I understood I needed to accept grace. But as I matured, it became clear to me. I need grace to consume me because I surely have no confidence in myself.

Chapter 14

Cousin Rachel Stricken with Polio

The thief comes only to steal and kill and destroy; I have come that they may have life, and have it to the full.
—John 10:10

My cousin Rachel intrigued me because she was the only handicapped, wheelchair-bound relative I had growing up. She contracted polio, an infectious disease especially of young children caused by the polio virus. It is a serious disease that affects the neurons of the spine and causes a person to be permanently unable to move particular muscles. Polio can cause paralysis. One of fifteen children born to my aunt and uncle, Rachel's illness could have been a great burden to her family. But by God's grace, Aunt Alice (her mom's sister) and Uncle Martin, a childless couple, were gracious enough to have their niece reside with them.

When my siblings and I helped my parents downsize, I was thrilled to find some history among my parents' belongings. In their one-and-a-half story home, the one-half served as Mom's attic. We three sisters tackled the one side, while the sisters-in-law tackled the other side. Canning jars, unused linoleum, drying tea leaves spread out on newspapers, and Daddy's hunting gear greeted us as we entered the warm dusty area. In the highest area of the attic where one could stand up completely, unstacked boxes spilled across our narrow path. One old box, no longer squared, had one lid open, the other closed. Daddy's Stuff was written across the closed lid.

As typical of cleaning-out plans, more time was spent rooting through stuff (invaluables are just that: stuff) than actually cleaning out. Today was no exception. I reached down for the marked box and placed it on top of the waist-high stack of canning jars.

"Wonder what's in here? Have any of you ever seen this box before?" I inquired. Both Lenora and Lorna shook their heads as they started refolding Daddy's hunting gear and placing it neatly back in its assigned box.

Inside, I noticed my grandparents' 1971 public sale notice, an Ephrata Bank savings account book of my grandma's—who can't resist being nosy when it comes to people's monies? "December 3, 1970 Cash Deposit $20.00. Balance: $192.00," I read. The next item that barely fit inside the box was a stapled booklet. "No Time to Settle" was typed and centered on the plain white cover page. Leafing through it, I noticed twenty-plus typed pages filled with thoughts, poems, and humorous stories about my cousins.

"Hey, guys. Did you know that Uncle Weaver wrote about Daddy and his upbringing? He titled it *No Time to Settle*. It was written in 1995. I'm going to ask Daddy if I can have this. Or at least read and return it."

"Nope," Lenora answered. Lorna nonchalantly gave a be-my-guest wave.

Here is Cousin Rachel's story as written in Uncle Weaver's (her dad's) booklet titled *No Time to Settle* (July 1940 to December, 1995):

> I was born July 19, 1954…at four months old I had the whooping cough. One Sunday (when I was five years old) we visited an aunt, who was taking care of an elderly woman, who was sitting in a wheelchair…little did anyone realize how soon I was to be an occupant of one…
>
> Monday I started complaining about not feeling well. I had a fever, and I'm not sure what

all my symptoms were, but my parents had no reason to think it was anything serious. I did not get any better. By Wednesday I was unable to use my arms. The doctor was summoned without delay. He came out to check on me the next two days. By Friday he decided I needed to be hospitalized, telling my parents I may have spinal meningitis or polio…the doctor summoned an ambulance to transfer me to Lancaster General Hospital.

The spinal tap revealed it was polio, and I experienced a lot of pain as the virus attacked the nervous system and caused many of my muscles to start wasting away. I lost most of the function of my arms and legs and needed an iron lung to help me breathe…in the hospital nine weeks…

Having no children of their own, Aunt Alice and Uncle Martin's life was changed drastically when they opened their hearts and home to their five-year-old niece, who needed round-the-clock care…there were many more 'attacks' in store for me that I had to fight through. By the grace of God and encouragement from family and friends, I was able to endure.

Uncle Weaver wrote this poem shortly after Rachel was released from the hospital:

A Darling Girl
'Twas a darling little girl
At the age of five,
Was happy as any child
That was ever alive.

I could run and I could jump,
Would ride high in my swing,

BEATY MILLER

Did play with my sisters,
Also Daniel, James, and Tim.

Then the last week of August
I became so very ill.
It's a disease called 'polio'
That made me lie so still.

In an ambulance they put me,
With a lady by my side,
Oh, where will they take me?
But, I enjoyed the long ride.

I was in aches and pains
From my head to my toes.
In an iron lung they put me
With only my head exposed.

The doctors and nurses
Looked down at my pale face
"O Rachel, dear Rachel,
Hope you'll win the big race."

Friends came to see me,
My piggy bank they filled.
Hung cards on my wall
So my heart could be thrilled.

Hours were like days
And days were like months.
I want to go home,
When will the day come?

After three weeks in the iron lung,
In a crib I was laid.

MY LAST LAST NAME IS GRACE

They wrapped me in woolens
Till a scare crow I made.

In the Lancaster General Hospital
For sixty-two days and one.
They now take care of me
In the bed of my own.

I look out the window,
See the yard where I played.
Up to the apple tree
Is a path my feet made.

Although I can't walk,
Not yet for awhile
But if you stop in
I'll give you a big smile.

By Weaver Martin (*No Time to Settle*, December 1995)

Several times a year, Mom would take us kids over to visit Cousin Rachel in her aunt's home. With a small toy in hand to be presented as a gift for Rachel, I remember seeing a weak, frail, thin girl lying on a hospital bed by the light of a bright kerosene lamp. During the entire visit, Rachel's sister, Elsie or Mary lovingly would be exercising her arms and legs to keep them stimulated and as strong as possible, which they were willing to do for their sister. Smiling, Rachel was always so appreciative of every visit, card, and gift. She would have preferred to jump off that hospital bed and go outside and catch fireflies or play tag with her visiting cousins. By the grace of God, I go.

By the time Rachel died at fifty-eight years of age in 2013, she was survived by fourteen brothers and sisters, forty-four nieces and nephews, and ninety-nine great nieces and nephews. As written on her memorial pamphlet, she will be fondly remembered for her cheerful smile and giving spirit. She worked as a typist for some publications and volunteered at a local nursing home.

Here is the poem, so applicable, that was printed on her memorial pamphlet:

Sharing

There isn't much that I can do.
But I can share my bread with you.
And sometimes share a sorrow too,
As on our way we go.

There isn't much that I can do.
But I can sit an hour with you.
And I can share a joke with you
And sometimes share verses too
As on our way we go.

There isn't much that I can do.
But I can share my flowers with you.
And I can share my books
And sometimes share your burdens, too.
As on our way we go.

There isn't much that I can do.
But I can share songs with you.
And I can share my mirth with you
And sometimes come and laugh with you.
As on our way we go.

There isn't much that I can do.
But, I can share my hopes with you.
And I can share my fears with you

And sometimes shed some tears with you
As on our way we go.

There isn't much that I can do.
But I can share my friends with you.
And I can share my life with you
And oftentimes share a prayer with you
As on our way we go.

Maud V. Preston *(Ideals Magazine, 2000)*

Thought of the Day

Be gracious to yourself when day in and day out you are hoping, praying, seeking, and asking of God to end whatever you are so sick and tired of being sick and tired. And if He does not, then open up yourself to Him because someone who is doing mighty things for Him is a recipient of God's amazing grace.

Chapter 15

Moving to Noodle Doosie

From the fullness of his grace we have all
received one blessing after another.

—John 1:16

PART OF THE PROCESS OF building a new house on uncleared land is finding your best water source and digging a well. Remember those witch lore stories that were passed down? Certain relatives, including Mom, had the ability to smell water. How? Mom and Daddy walked through the brush until they found the best Y-shaped stick to act as a divining rod. Holding it out in front of her, she walked around our newly purchased property. The idea was that once the best underground water supply was walked over, the handler's stick would automatically start pulling downward.

Mom started walking around the property. The stick moved slightly in Mom's hands at some areas as she walked around the four acres. But in an area that later became our backyard, sure enough, the Y-stick, with no effort on my mom's part, moved downward quickly and easily at the best spot to dig a well. Daddy called a church member friend, who had a well drilling business. The well was dug at that exact spot. As God's grace would have it, Mom, once she was educated on these generational sins that were tied to witchcraft and satanic activity, asked God for forgiveness. His mercy and grace not only covered Mom's sins but allowed a break in this evil generational chain. In fact, she was totally embarrassed by the whole thing later and did not want to discuss it. Who can relate to that? I can!

Lancaster County settlers in Pennsylvania have been known to give their communities unusual names: Bird-in-Hand, Intercourse, and Blue Ball, to name a few. Whatever were they thinking? Since its founding in the mid-1700s, Noodle Doosie is another community name that piques one's curiosity. I wanted to understand its meaning when we were told we were moving to the same neighborhood next to my Plain horse-and-buggy cousins. I thought I'd ask someone who probably knew---my parents. How does Noodle Doosie translate in English? (Hmm, here is a warning, reader. It has a sexual connotation.)

So imagine asking your daddy then what your community name means in English. He directed us to Mom. She is the one who interpreted for us: *doosie* means "to her." The story has been passed down that two boys and one girl were nearing the covered bridge while driving in their horse and buggy. The two boys were fighting over her. One said to the other in Pennsylvania Dutch, "*Noodle doosie.*" (Now you can "noodle" her).

Many jokes, newspaper articles, and conversations have abounded over the years around this small community name. One reporter, Larry Alexander of *Lancaster Newspapers*, wrote the following on September 10, 2008:

Noodle Doosie contains a dozen or so homes and one business that is, by some strange oversight, not a pizza shop. Pennsylvania-German folklore regarding how the village earned its name involves two overeager men who got into trouble "noodling" with the same women. Since its founding in the mid-1700s, Noodle Doosie has spawned enough colorful characters to resemble a Pennsylvania Dutch version of Hooterville.

My favorite is a former Hessian soldier named Gen. Willembrock, who settled there about 1800. About 30 years earlier, while fighting for England in the American Revolution, Willembrock had been captured at either the battle of Saratoga or Trenton, or possibly both. After the war, he decided to stay in America. Every Saturday night, Willembrock rode his horse to a nearby tavern named Die Rotie Kuh, the Red Cow, which still stands at Red Run and Fivepointville roads. There, at 3 cents a drink, he proceeded to prove that Germans invented beer and beer-drinking.

One night, too inebriated to get on his horse unaided, he was loaded onto it by some of the young bucks of the village. Since the horse knew the way home, they slapped its rump and sent it off with Willembrock hanging on.

Meanwhile, the young men ran ahead to a stone bridge that spanned Muddy Creek, arriving before the general. They donned white sheets and hid beneath the structure until the general's horse arrived. They then sprang out in surprise. The horse reared up and galloped away, carrying the pickled general, who hurled unprintable German words loudly into the night.

Then there was Jacob Fry, who was carrying a load of apples home to his mother one night when he too stopped at Die Rotie Kuh for rejuvenation. After tipping a few, he departed, then stumbled on a rutted dirt road and fell. Hastily picking up the fruit, he accidentally retrieved some "apples" of the horse variety. So that's Noodle Doosie.

Realizing a poked-fun opportunity about his Pennsylvania Dutch heritage and being the son of an Old Order horse-and-buggy Mennonite, Mel Horst developed his alter ego, Jakey Budderschnip of Noodle Doosie. Expounding on his Dutch accent, his weekly WIOV-FM radio station spot was heard for many years. Daddy would tune into this show often and be cheaply entertained, as he could appreciate more than most people Mel's humor, since Daddy was born and raised in the Noodle Doosie area. So in 1961, our family returned to the Cocalico School District and out of Hinkletown (by the way, in Pennsylvania Dutch *Hinkletown* means "chicken town").

Daddy purchased some land from his brother, Weaver. It included a crumbling-down historic church named Noodle Doosie Church. My brother and cousins finished tearing it down, as it was an eyesore on the corner of our property. While destroying this historical building, they could only imagine what events had occurred in it—if only the walls could talk. One story that occurred involved a distant relative. On a hot summer day, when the church door was wide open to aid in circulating air, a mischievous youngster pulled a stunt. He tied a dead animal on the end of a string. At the perfect opportune time, during the sermon, the youngster, upon spying his dog outside, pulled on the string that would make this dead animal snake from one end of the church to the other and back out of the door again. His hungry dog came running in and out of the church, chasing and eying his lunch. Any sleeping members of the church were now awake, I'm sure!

Speaking of "sins," one of our funniest stories that we continue to laugh about happened while living in Noodle Doosie. Unlike when living in town, one could burn trash in a trash barrel in the 1960s at any time without any township or borough regulations. One of my siblings was given an Ouija board as a present. Not allowing it in the house, Mom immediately took it and threw it out back in the trash barrel planning on destroying it by fire. Unbeknownst to Mom, earlier Daddy had thrown out an old pair of work gloves and threw them in the trash barrel. As per her regular routine, once Mom started burning the trash with a match, she would observe the fire for a few seconds to make sure the fire stayed contained inside the barrel. Lo and behold! Within a few minutes, Mom saw this dark-shaped hand on top of the burning board game. Oh, Satan is furious, and he is letting me know! It wasn't long before she recognized Daddy's old work gloves and realized what had happened. Oh, the laughs!

On a lighter note, another Mom-story that has been passed around is this one: Shortly after moving into our new home, Mom was outside hanging up wash on her two newly installed wash lines. Nearby in the backyard was our sewer system. At the same time, my brother Junior had gotten up out of bed, went to the bathroom, and flushed the toilet. Startled by the swooshing unfamiliar sound, Mom, puzzled, looked heavenward. "Are you returning today, Lord?" Still earthbound and holding laundry, in the next blink of an eye, Mom looked over and noticed the sewer pipe. She put two and two together and remembered that this was about the time that Junior had needed to get up to go to work and must be in the bathroom. Sorry, Mom, you'll need to finish hanging up your family's big laundry load. The Lord was not returning today.

Next to our property was a summer cottage with a white fence laden with lilacs owned by a family, who had a car dealership in Reading. I have no memories of ever playing over there, as the family had no children my age. Daddy, showing neighborly love, would do light handyman projects for the owner, who only visited on holidays and some weekends. One day, in preparation of trimming trees for the neighbor, Daddy climbed up on the ladder and onto the roof. A trimmed branch, as it fell to the ground, knocked the ladder over. Mom's big garden was between the neighbor's cottage and our home. Daddy knew Mom would not hear his yelling. His plan was to wait until a car would pass by, and he would then call out. Not living along a heavily traveled road, this took some time. Since car windows were closed or with too-noisy road sounds, the drivers of cars passed by Daddy, who was up on the roof flailing his arms and yelling.

Finally, his nephew Amos, driving a horse and spring wagon, drove by him. Since a spring wagon is not enclosed but has one wooden bench seat, he could hear Daddy's shouts. Seeing the of-no-help ladder lying on the ground, Amos soon realized his uncle's dilemma. He tied the horse to the fence post and propped the ladder back up against the side of the house. Bantering and teasing probably ensued between them. It wasn't long before the story was passed around among family members about Uncle Aaron's helpless situation.

While living next door to my horse-and-buggy cousins until my first marriage, I learned a lot about my Plain aunt, uncle, and cousins' lifestyles. When older and having a driver's license, I would follow behind or pass horse-and-buggies in my travels. It was only when I observed my aunt and uncle, who eventually had fifteen children, pile into their various buggies to go to church that I got an education on the varying types and their purposes. A buggy used for going to church or family outings that enabled the highest amount of people to fit inside was the two-seater carriage. It had a flap in the back that could be opened or closed, weather permitting. Having no heat source, carriage riders used blankets for warmth.

When about nine or ten years old and believed to be strong enough to rein in a horse, my oldest cousin, Rueben, drove the second horse that pulled a trotting buggy. This single-seat open buggy held two or three people. It was common to have a woman sit on another woman's lap. By the time baby number fifteen came along, Rueben was already driving two siblings to church, meaning two buggies were required to haul this large family to church.

The spring wagon (was this named after the season? Winter carriage was no longer needed; let's get out the spring open wagon?) was used to haul large items: groceries, wheelbarrow, hardware, and tools, for example, equivalent to a bed of a pickup truck. Because it was time-consuming to prepare the horse and buggy, running errands needed to be completed in one outing. Occasionally, I would see Rueben or his brothers saddle up and ride a horse to go somewhere that did not require a buggy or wagon.

Legend has it that both Amish and Old Order Mennonites carried out a tradition for dating young adults. If it was winter and one would have to prepare the horse and buggy requiring lots of time and effort, the gentleman was allowed to stay at the girlfriend's home overnight. So his horse was tied in her parents' barn. Having no extra beds, the couple was allowed to sleep in the same one. However, Pop first placed a board in the bed between them. If no board was used, the guy was wrapped in cloths like a mummy, called bundling. Guess that helped one behave!

Living in the country that had many horse and buggy drivers, when driving a car, one had to always be on the alert when approaching a crest of a hill or rounding a sharp turn. You needed to assume that a slow horse and buggy could be ahead of you in your path. My family was involved only once in a car accident that involved a horse and buggy. One morning coming home from church, Daddy was attempting to pass someone in a buggy. Getting too close while passing, Daddy caused the spinning buggy wheel to scrape some paint off the side of our car. The buggy wheel wasn't damaged. However, Daddy got a scolding from Mom. Smiling, he continued to head home and later confirmed the minimal damage. Having been raised in a horse-and-buggy family, Daddy bestowed grace on his family by his wanting to drive a car. By the grace of God, go I.

The journal entries from my uncle's booklet titled *No Time to Settle* helped me to understand more about Daddy's family and heritage. Following are more excerpts:

> I went to a regular barber for $.35 for the bowl-shaped haircut.

In 1929 we moved to the farm in Stevens near Reamstown. A brooder house (for chickens) was ordered (purchased), built off property, and then later on had to be moved to our farm. It turns out the brooder house got stuck in the covered bridge; "braces" had to be removed to allow the shed to fit through it. In hind sight, we should have moved, and then ordered, and had the brooder house built.

Around 1929 a neighboring barn caught on fire. Women were asked to call the local fire company from the closest farm phone. (The church allowed a few strategically placed farm phones, but phones were not allowed in the home). Two different people were asked by the telephone operator for the name of the location of the fire and both were too excited and couldn't remember their own relative's name. The tragedy took the lives of a dog and a few hogs.

I worked for Miles Fry for $1 day making $525 a year with bonuses. A pea company delivered a pea sheller and supplied the Fry's farm with it. (I remember helping my mother in the '60s take bushels of peas to be shelled for a small fee at Fry's…what a great relief from a tedious chore!)

(Under the "that-was-stupid" category) Adam, (another one of Daddy's brothers), walked in front of his brother, who was aiming a 22 revolver at a tin can.

(Under the "I'm-safe" category) I remember Daddy needed to request to borrow a lantern from a neighbor to walk across a huge, dark field to get home…he could have been lost in the dark of night.

July 20, 1940 local paper headlines: 'Weaver Martin and Martin Weaver marry Martin Sisters' (when my aunt, Mabel, and uncle married on the same day as my aunt's sister, Alice). It's certainly true that the dust the buggy wheels kicked up as they pulled out of the minister's driveway never really settled. Or did it?

It was not uncommon to have what we would think of as a last name be a first name (i.e., Weaver Martin). Sometimes, men were given nicknames related to their occupation. I recall my parents mentioning names such as Paperhanger Eddie, Clover Seed Pete, Buffalo Bill, Preacher Frank, etc. My own uncle, because he had one eye that was nearly closed at all times, was nicknamed Blinky Martin.

No Time to Settle lists another story about my cousin Elsie, proving the humor of the Martin boys:

> In a catalog Elsie saw what she thought was the most beautiful doll she had ever seen. The doll could walk, talk, wet, and even close her eyes. Elsie knew that there was no point in asking for her because there would be no money for such an expensive doll. But the longer Elsie studied her, the more intense was her longing for it. Elsie decided it didn't hurt to at least make her wishes known.
>
> As Elsie showed Dad the catalog picture, she named all the things the doll could do. Dad was holding her little sister on his lap. "We have a doll right here," he said. "She can walk, she can cry, she can sleep, and she can wet." That was not what Elsie wanted to hear, nor did she see the humor in it. Elsie did not get the doll, although later she did get a beautiful doll they ordered from a cereal box.

Out of the mouths of babes: Daniel was pleased with his new baby brother. But there was something he just couldn't figure out. "Why do we boil the baby's water?" he asked. "To kill the germs," Dad replied. "You mean, you feed the baby DEAD germs?"

Many a boring summer afternoon was filled by taking a walk down to the Fry's covered bridge about one mile from my home with my cousins or neighbors. Just as it provided cheap entertainment for Daddy when he was a youngster, many lazy days were spent walking to the covered bridge, walking across it, and then back out again. After all, you did not want to be in the bridge, spanning ninety-five feet, when a car needed to travel through it; it was only a single-span structure.

The following are notes about Fry's bridge taken from *A Pleasant View of Martindale*:

> Built in 1849 by mainly the Fry family, costing them $934, a fifty-fifty deal was struck with the county. The structure 130 years later was much like it was then. The Fry family carved their initials on the brace of the bridge: great-grandfather carved his initials in 1869. To celebrate Morton Fry carved his under them in 1969 just to celebrate history.
>
> Unfortunately, on March 1, 1980, a $100,000 fire, suspected to be arson, destroyed the Fry's covered bridge. "This is a tragedy, a real tragedy! It's a senseless act by a mindless person, someone with no concept of history. It's like the death of an old man...an unnatural death," commented Morton S. Fry, obviously shaken by the incident, whose great-grandfather helped to build the bridge.

By the time the firemen got the blaze under control, all that remained was a tangle of charred timbers; lying like blackened pickup-sticks in the partially frozen Muddy Creek…the structure was eventually replaced by a concrete bridge… and the dwindling number of remaining country covered bridges remains at 31; down from 140 such structures at the turn of the century.

My uncle, who made the awesome homemade bologna, decided to take a burnt log out of the ruins and store it in his barn. Many years later at his public sale, the historical log was sold for $85. Someone appreciates history after all.

Miles Fry Sr. said he never wanted to drive over the new reconstructed bridge, as he was so hurt someone would actually set an historical landmark on fire. He made his sons promise upon his death, even the hearse carrying his body for his burial, would do the same; he did not want to be driven over the bridge. His great-grandfather is smiling down from heaven.

I had an aha moment one day when I read another story in *A Pleasant View of Martindale* about newlyweds killed in a car accident in 1934. It had to make an impact on Daddy and, perhaps, aided in my uncle making the decision to join the Plain Old Order Mennonite Church.

During the church's disputes over using cars for transportation, my dad's maternal grandparents and uncles decided to side with the "Black Bumper" Mennonite group, while their daughter sided with the group that retained the horse and buggy. Then an event happened that had everybody trembling and caused some teenagers to be convicted about driving a car. An aunt of my dad's friend, a bride of only three days, and her husband both died en route home from their Niagara Falls honeymoon. A truck driver reported the car had passed him, and a short distance ahead, he noticed the car swerve from side to side and roll off the road onto its roof. Both occupants were thrown out of the car—the groom, ten feet, and his bride, thirty feet. He died of a crushed chest, and she, a broken neck.

The local community showed up at the double funeral to show their support. Ministers from the Lancaster Conference, Horning Conference, and United Zion Church officiated. It was at that time the largest funeral ever held in the "Pike" church. The obituary itself issued a strong warning for young people to make it right with God "for you know not when the summons may come." Later, Daddy simply became a more cautious driver; his brothers and sisters were grateful to be in a less-accident-prone means of transportation and held on more tightly to their horses' reigns.

Throughout the years when I proudly announce that I once lived in Noodle Doosie (not listed on any map) always brings on puzzled looks and smiles, even from other Lancaster County folk. Though the area is now considered Napierville, my family homestead holds priceless memories. From 1962 until 1997, my parents lived in their love-filled home until Daddy was diagnosed with multiple myeloma. After a successful real estate auction, they sold the property for over $252,000 (I later learned that the new owners were relatives of my ex-husband).

The second homeowner made many great upgrades to the property. In December 2015, after eighteen years of enjoying their living quarters and the park, they decided to downsize and held their own public auction. The selling price reached $503,000! Mom was so excited when she told me about the sale results. "Wouldn't Daddy turn over in his grave if he knew the home we built together sold for over a half a million dollars?"

May the new homeowner, number three, enjoy the property as much as the Martins did and may grace and love abound.

Thought of the Day

Be gracious to yourself. Get off the detour you are on; stop looking in the rearview mirror. Open the window and expect the sunbeam of a new day, filled with promise and hope, to flood all passengers in life around you. Crossroads will be inevitable; forks need to be selected. Grace will mark the path that leads you home.

Chapter 16

Joining Church and Wearing a Head Covering

> Your beauty should not come from outward adornment, such as braided hair and the wearing of gold jewelry and fine clothes. Instead, it should be that of your inner self, the unfading beauty of a gentle and quiet spirit, which is of great worth in God's sight.
> —1 Peter 3:3–4

Tenth grade picture

MARTINDALE CHURCH WAS A PART of the Lancaster Conference and upheld seven ordinances. Joining church meant you were expected to follow these rules: (1) marriage, (2) baptism, (3) communion,

(4) foot washing, (5) women wear the head covering (prayer veil), (6) holy kiss among the brethren, and (7) anointing with oil, as requested, when sick.

As a child, I stood at times on the scary edge of the big stone quarry where Daddy worked. What a big limestone hole! Similarly, there was a gap in my life that needed bridged over that I, and only I, was responsible for. My bridge that needed built was to make a decision from my present state of being unsaved and without church membership, accept Jesus Christ as my Lord and Savior, and to start the process of securing a home in heaven. At fourteen years old, I was well past the age of accountability. To continue to resist joining church would probably soon have led ministers to come knocking at our door and speak to me about the reason I am not joining church. Plus, hell had a fury that I needed to fight against at any cost!

Summer and winter Bible schools or revival meetings were held to give opportunity for preteens or teens (or anyone) in the congregation to make a commitment for joining the church and following its doctrines. Once you made the decision to join church, one method used for your outward display of this act was to stand up in church during the congregation's singing of a repentance-type song (equivalent to walking to an altar during an invitation).

Just as with most of my older brothers and sisters, I had an idea of when that would occur. A fire-and-brimstone sermon would be preached, at times, scaring young converts out of their seats and onto their feet. The opportunities to join church were offered during the last song on the last day of Bible school or the last song of a revival meeting. The preacher or bishop remained standing at the pulpit during the hymn singing, scanned the room for people to stand to their feet. In between each stanza, he would pound on the pulpit and plea: "Jesus is calling" or "Today's the day of your salvation" or "Escape hell and secure a home in heaven" or "Jesus could return tonight. Are you ready?"

Older ladies sitting near the front of the church, including my former Sunday school teachers, turned around in their seats and sized up the prospects, who they believed were of the age of accountability and should be making this serious decision. For three years, I firmly gazed back and did not stand to my feet, even though Lena, Nancy, and other Sunday school classmates had done so either during the last Bible school or during an earlier revival meeting opportunity. For a girl, after joining church, my life was never to be the same! I was expected to wear the head covering, put my hair up, wear a cape dress to church, and participate in council meeting, communion, and foot washing.

My mom did her part in preparing me for this step. How? She had about one-half of my thick coarse hair thinned out so I would be able to manage styling my hair up in a bob. By the time Mom's friend, who did the thinning, was finished, her bathroom floor had a large pile of dark hair that looked like someone's wig was thrown on it! Daddy had already given Mom the instructions to stop cutting my hair so it would grow beyond shoulder length.

On a Friday evening in 1967, at fourteen years old at the end of the two-week summer Bible school I joined church. Again, my current and previous Sunday school teachers were turning around and gazing upon the several benches of teenagers noticing any covering-less girls, probably thinking, "Don't you think it is your time to 'stand up' for Jesus?"

The last song of the evening started. With heart palpitations and feeling very nervous at the beginning of the third (first is too soon) verse, I stood to my feet. Once I got the head nod from the bishop, that he noticed my commitment, I sat back down. I prayed, "Okay, Lord, this is the next step in my journey with you. I'm a Christian now, and with Your help I'm going to heaven, not hell. I know I need to start wearing the covering in submission of your designed headship. But please don't have the schoolkids make fun of me in September."

My outward appearance was expected now to separate me from the world. So the next day on Saturday, Mom took me to covering shopping. As was expected, I wore my covering for the first time in church on Sunday. Mrs. Harnish was known as the covering lady. A front room of her home was set aside for her sewing business of mainly selling coverings to the local Mennonite women. Her shop was full of many shelves of coverings in varying sizes. Mirrors for viewing were placed throughout the room. Passing the coverings that were either too small or too large, I walked over to the shelf that held the sizes that were equivalent to what my girlfriends of similar age were wearing. Following the church's head covering guidelines for baptism and church membership, the appropriate-sized covering was purchased.

I went home and started practicing how to wrap my long thick hair into a round bob slightly above the nape of my neck, hair pin it all into place, and attach the covering with two straight pins. As much as it took an art to wrap long hair into a bob, it was also an art to style the front of your hair as well that did not fit under the head covering. Do I want a middle part, side part, or none at all? I decided on only a partial part and usually teased the front of my hair. Styling it to be unteased was too conservative-looking and made me look too much like my mother! Practicing over and over, I finally was satisfied with my "masterpiece."

My sister Lenora joined church at twelve and started to wear her covering. Paving the way for a younger sister ends up being a positive thing in most areas. But being an older Mennonite sister, Lenora's stories on how she was made fun of at school gave me no comfort. I dreaded the day it would happen to me. Since we rode on the same school bus, I could overhear the kids' comments to Lenora: "Hey. The war's over. Take off your helmet" or "Soup strainer" or "Yonie" (the nickname given to Plain folk who drove horse and buggy). Unfortunately, the teasing began toward me as well, and it occurred on the school bus, in the hallways, or on the playground. The same cruel treatment occurred to me and my Mennonite girlfriends as we walked about the school halls. Of course, over time, the teasing eventually stopped as the kids somewhat matured upon reaching high school.

I always thought it was so unfair that my older brothers could join church and not face the firing-insults gang. After all, Mennonite boys can become a church member, and school classmates do not know any difference. Making them hardly discernible, boys had few new restrictions that were required for them to follow.

At thirteen and no longer being allowed to have my hair cut shoulder-length, I would comb and style my hair. The best hairdo I came up with was to pull some hair over the top of my ears and make a low ponytail. Parting my hair to one side, my only creativity used was in my selection of colorful bright barrettes or ponytail holders. Looking at my ninth (last grade before I wore my covering) grade school picture today, I say, "Yep, I can see why some people believe man came from monkeys. I looked like one."

To write about one of my most embarrassing moments for my Creative Writing class recently, it certainly made sense that it would have to do with the wearing of my covering. It follows:

> Having been raised in a Mennonite family in Lancaster County, PA, I wore a traditional head covering as per our tradition for about five years. Once married and no longer under my parents' roof, I transferred my membership to join a different Mennonite church which did not require my wearing a head covering. Needless to say, as a teenager and not at all thrilled about this requirement for women, I resented having to wear one. Having it blown off my head one day while running to the public school bus is one of the most embarrassing moments in my life!
>
> In ninth grade when I was 14 my family lived about eight miles from my public high school. In fact we lived in the farthest corner of the township at a triangle of three different school districts. One neighbor girl who lived across the creek attended one school and the kids that lived across two fields went to a different school entirely. There were only about five or six

kids on the bus when this embarrassing incident happened, but it was six too many.

Not being a morning person, I stayed in bed on school mornings until the very last minute. After all, my bed pillow was my friend. First, Mom would rattle my locked bedroom door and announce it was time to get up. Secondly, a few minutes later, since she saw neither "hide nor hair" of me, she would walk by my bedroom door again, but this time would loudly knock, insisting, "Leanne, get up or you are going to miss the bus." (Interpretation: don't expect me to drive you that far!)

Probably after her third attempt, I'd slowly get out of bed, shower, get dressed, and comb my hair. Making the perfect bob out of my long hair to fit under the head covering, plus pin it fast to my hair with two straight pins, (yes, straight pins, not bobby pins), my twenty minutes to get ready for school flew by. I had each step down to a science and knew exactly how long each step took, including a breakfast of toast and a cup of hot chocolate.

While watching out the kitchen window for the approaching bus on the country road, I finished the hot chocolate. My forty-something year old male bus driver had a competition with himself to see how many seconds could be shaved off his eight-mile long bus route. He had a heavy foot. Our front yard was about 70 yards long, so I had to run fast to meet the bus, often being the last one to board at my bus stop. This particular morning, I had to actually eat my last piece of toast, while running to the bus stop. I thought I heard Mom calling my name, but I had no time to stop.

Catching my breath while climbing the bus steps, I looked through the bus windows and saw my mother standing on the porch holding my covering. The bus driver, with a smirk on his face, said, "Go ahead. Go get it. I'll wait." I wanted to crawl in a hole. I guess in my hurrying to get dressed, I forgot to pin my covering on.

I mumbled "Thanks," turned around and once again ran back across the front yard to Mom. I angrily grabbed it out of her hands noticing she had two straight pins fastened to it. Not bothering to take the time to pin it on right then and there with "Speedy Gonzalez" waiting for me, I just held it while I ran back to the bus.

Boarding the bus the second time breathless, "covering-less" and eager to reach a seat, I passed the seat of the other Mennonite neighbor girl making eye contact. With big eyes and a frightened look on her face, I could tell she was thinking "Rather you than me!"

Turns out I wore a covering for over five years before I removed it. Over time, each new covering purchase was in selecting a smaller and smaller-sized one. My round bob was replaced with a more square-like bob that my less-conservative friend taught me how to style. My side part was changed to a middle part when I chose a hairstyle that allowed for my small covering to be placed more on the crown of my head, rather than an attempt to cover a bun in the back.

I became a member of the same Mennonite church where I was married. It was less conservative and did not require women to wear cape dresses or big coverings. Later on, by the time we had children, we chose to become members of a more liberal Mennonite church. Meanwhile, I started to observe the smaller-sized covering worn by my younger sister Lorna, who still lived at home under Daddy's roof. Lorna no longer wore her hair up in a bun to put a covering over. Her covering became quite small and was pinned on top of her beautiful flowing long hair. If she can do it, then I can do it! Out from under Daddy's rules, I had my hair cut into a shoulder-length shag (a popular hairstyle in the '70s).

Eventually, my covering was replaced by a black prayer veiling I nicknamed my doily, since it was only about four inches in circumference and purchased at the local Catholic shop. In time, the pastors required the covering of your choosing be worn only on Sundays, not during the week. Arriving at the church, I would take my doily out of the glove compartment, pin it fast, and enter church. Following the church service, I would remove it and stuff it back in the glove compartment until the following Sunday.

What followed the losing of my covering? Much to my parents' dismay, the wearing of slacks, shorts, and sleeveless blouses. However, out of respect toward our parents, we girls wore skirts or dresses when returning back home to visit our parents for over ten years before we felt comfortable enough to wear slacks during visits (never shorts though).

Purchasing the forbidden television followed. Early on, my husband and I would hide the TV in a hall closet and would only bring it out in the living room if it was well past the hour of any chance his conservative parents would be dropping by. Having shorter hair, wearing shorts, and watching a TV out on display in the living room occurred while a member of a Mennonite church. Obviously, one chooses to join the church that you feel you can honor their disciplines and doctrines.

Just as a mouse has a difficult time running through a maze, non-Mennonites must be thoroughly confused when around Mennonite and Amish women. Why the different sized coverings? Why do some have strings attached? Why are hairstyles worn so differently? The simplest explanation is that it all depends on which church's doctrine do you feel is the best fit for you. The church leadership has evolved in their applicable scripture interpretation too. Even my mother changed in her style of dress somewhat over the years. The same Bible was read by her at eighteen as well as eighty-eight.

Please understand. I respect those women who wear their hairstyle basically the same way since they were fourteen. That is not me. But bravo to you who can style your hair with your eyes closed.

Part of my frustration when I was growing up was looking around and seeing liberal Mennonite and non-Mennonite Christian women who were bareheaded. Perhaps, some church leadership disagreed, but I felt in my heart that they too were going to heaven, just as I was. But my church dictated I wear an outward symbol of my submission to Christ and to an (eventual) husband. If you were an unmarried woman, your submission was to the church.

As a teenager, it was hard for me to believe that the Mennonite Church was the only sect that had the correct interpretation of scripture, compared to the Methodist, United Church of Christ, Baptist, and Presbyterian—and the list goes on. I would rationalize ordained men of God, such as Billy Graham or Catherine Marshall, a Christian author, both read the scriptures too. They did not believe women needed to wear a head covering. Why were scriptures pulled out by Mennonites and an ordinance derived from Paul's words to literally mean a "woman's head was for a covering?" I did not know any Catholic nuns. But from the books I had read, I understood that they wore a habit because, in my mind, they prayed to God probably twenty out of twenty-four hours a day. They were Christ's bride and not allowed to marry. But why was this issue a deal-breaker between going to heaven or hell for covering-less women?

As I was older, I seldom went to the mountains for the weekend with my parents. Instead, I held a slumber party at my home. As most teens, I was living in the now and not-now. Saturday morning, upon waking up in an empty house, I would not bother to put my hair up and add my head covering. Instead, in the name of letting my hair dry (all day), I left my long hair hang freely and kept my covering off. A small ribbon kept my hair from falling over my eyes and out of my face. I felt free as a bird as I cleaned my parlor and bedroom or hung out laundry in the backyard. It took bravery to run to the mailbox with my hairstyle, as I was taking a chance of my neighbor-relatives noticing me and my misbehaving.

Monday morning, Mom answered the phone. I heard her footsteps come down the hall; she rattled my locked bedroom door. "Leanne. Polly told me you had your hair down all weekend, and you didn't have your covering on. What's the matter with you? You know better than that," she scolded. Polly, you little tattletale! From then on, the times I let my hair down, I hung out in my backyard for hours and did not bother to go to the mailbox until Sunday. My parents did not mind while I was sunbathing out in the backyard to allow my hair to hang freely. But that was the only exception, unless you truly *were* drying your hair.

The name I heard my mom use sometimes for non-Mennonite women was *worldly*, though never said in their presence. When I would see a worldly woman who was allowed to have her hair cut short and in any style of preference she chose, but her hair was unkempt, I'd shake my head. I thought, *Lady, you can wear your hair any way you want to, and you're choosing* that *style?"* I vowed to my thirteen-year self, *Self, when you are older, and if you are no longer a member of a Mennonite church and are allowed to wear your hair as you please, you are never going to go out in public looking like that.*

As much as we had a name for bareheaded women as worldly, the conservatives had a nickname for us former-conservative-now-has-her-hair-cut women: "curly top." Here is how I learned this fact: When I was six-months pregnant with my second child, I was attending a funeral of my husband's conservative Mennonite uncle on a hot summer day. Only about four of us relatives in attendance did not wear a covering. The long-winded preacher at the graveside seemed to go on and on and on. Feeling myself becoming slightly dizzy, I started to lean back against a gravestone that was directly behind me. Having no effect of decreasing my dizziness, I turned to my sister-in-law, looking quite pale, and emphasized, "I don't feel well." Since men and women did not stand together at the graveside, my husband and I were not standing side by side. Next thing I know, I am lying on my back on the ground between gravestones. Coming out of my fainting spell, I heard my husband's cousin, an EMT, informing the small crowd, "Stand back. Give her some air, please."

Having a terrible headache, I opened my eyes and glanced up. In-between beautiful clouds above me, I observed women walking by me and looking down at me. One of the Mennonite woman dressed in all-black: black dress, black nylons, and black bonnet while holding her hanky over her mouth, mumbled to her other Mennonite friend, "It's the curly top."

Yes, the preacher stopped his graveside sermon and the funeral attendees moved inside the church, finally, for the actual funeral service. But my husband took his curly top home.

My next story is about a time that I am totally ashamed of my conduct and have had to repent because of it. Remember how peeved I would get when others would make fun of me for wearing my covering? Well, even though several years had gone by since it happened to me, when it did occur once again, as a young adult, I had a knee-jerk reaction. Here it is: I was walking down Main Street of Myerstown at twenty years of age. Being a newlywed, I was wearing (albeit a smaller one) a covering. I was coming out of a store and was heading toward my car. Suddenly, a convertible full of four teenaged boys drove down the street. Just as I was noticed by, one of the guys who was sitting in the back seat and had moved out of his seat to sit up on the back of the convertible, loudly called out, "Hey, the war's over! Take off your helmet!" Without hesitating, I flashed him my middle finger! Turning my face away while hurrying toward my car, I heard, "Whoa!" and peals of laughter as they drove on by.

I am no better than the teacher who justifies having sex with one of their students, or the eighteen-year-old guy (presently in the news) who is now imprisoned for mimicking another "Bonnie and Clyde" excursion with a thirteen-year-old girl. Pulling others into our muck and mire is never beneficial. By the time I had reached my car, I had asked the Good Lord for forgiveness and vowed to get a better handle on teasing, misguided immature kids.

Was it payback time? It brought to mind the time I got a spanking from Mom when my brother Matt tattletaled on me (rightfully so). When I was in third grade, we rode on the school bus where we often selected the same seat. One day after boarding the bus, I noticed a girl sitting in my seat. Because I did not think she was very attractive, I called her "dog face," as I walked by her to go sit in a different seat toward the back of the bus.

I have surely heard enough of stories about my mom's childhood and how she felt somewhat that she did not quite measure up, since they were poor; she did not wear the nicest dresses or shoes. Thus, her classmates made fun of her sometimes. After Matt ran into the house to tell Mom about my misbehaving, she did not hesitate to get a belt and give me a lickin'. With each strike of the belt on my backside or legs, she would say a word, "No (smack) child (smack) of mine (smack) will (smack) ever (smack) make (smack) fun (smack) of anyone (smack)! You tell her you are sorry tomorrow!"

It was a little difficult to sit up at the supper table that night, as my legs were still stinging a bit. But I am sure not as severely as the sting of my cruel words were to this undeserving girl. I pray to this day that she can forgive me for being so unkind and that she is not permanently scarred because of my rude, inappropriate comment, especially if she had already been dealing with low self-esteem issues.

About five years ago I thought she possibly could have been sitting in front of me in church. After the service ended, I asked if she had lived near Reamstown and attended Reamstown School. This lady answered, "No." I proceeded to tell her that, if so, I had to ask her for forgiveness for something I said when I was a big third-grade brat.

Though a head covering is no longer worn by me to follow a Mennonite Church ordinance, I truly understand God's headship. He is my Bridegroom, and I'm His bride. Designed for my protection, He has designated, if married, a husband as head of the home. Women are to submit to their husbands as husbands submit to the Lord. I liken it to a president and vice president arrangement. Both give opinions on the subject. Then the husband-president needs to pray about a solution. I have no trouble submitting to any husband who loves Christ with all his soul, might, and strength, respecting His design.

I jokingly told my friends that I had no concerns about marrying Mike. It was a sealed deal when Mike asked me one day, while dating, after attending a church service at the Worship Center, "What actually does submission mean for you, women?" *Yep,* I said to myself, *Self, you are marrying him!*

I bridged the gap with Christ's death and resurrection, and my eternity is sure. By God's grace, He covers me completely from head to toe with His love as I journey on toward heaven's door.

Thought of the Day

Grace is shown to me by my Jesus, my Lord, when I don't deserve it. No striving, doing, or performing are expected to win God's favor (feels like Old Testament law, an impossibility anyway). His endless grace is a rich inheritance with an enormous supply, like a banking account that never runs dry.

Chapter 17

Baptism, Council Meeting, Communion, and Foot Washing

> I am the Bread of life. He who comes to me will never go hungry, and he who believes in me will never be thirsty.
> —John 6:35

ONCE I MADE THE DECISION to join church, I needed to attend a few weekly instructional classes, a requirement prior to my being baptized. By the time the classes had begun, I had become successful in combing and styling my hair into the right-sized bob. The front of my hair was teased to my satisfaction.

Most classes were led by the pastor, deacon, or bishop of my church. Being one of about seven or eight people in my class, there was only one other girl who was in attendance. She wore a bigger covering than I did. It appeared that she was from a more conservative Mennonite family but was choosing Martindale to be her home church. It was common for teenagers to join our church, even though their parents chose not to.

Following the instructional booklet about baptism and other ordinances of the Lancaster Conference, most classes were uneventful. Typical for most fourteen-year-olds, the instructional classes were mostly boring and did not seem to be reviewing any new material. However, that evening, the teaching was about headship, the head covering ordinance, and the women's roles in the church was unforgettable for me.

My ears perked up that particular night when I heard the pastor say, "And some coverings I can't even see from the front." Knowing that the other girl in my instructional class was more conservative than me and was wearing a fairly large head covering that was visible from the front, I knew the comment was directed toward me. While staring back at the pastor, I thought, *Hmm…Preach, I'd be happy to show you a covering that you can see from the front, buddy. It will be the size of a saucer. It will be so small I'll simply plop it on top of my head!* With warming cheeks, I dropped my eyes and pretended to be reading a scripture verse.

I went home and complained to Mom and Daddy how I felt picked on. Of course, my parents did not take me back to see Mrs. Harnish and purchase a larger-sized covering. Thank goodness. They agreed with me, my present covering size was sufficient and met the church requirements to be baptized. (Nothing was said about how high I teased my hair either.)

One October Saturday morning, along with the rest of the instructional class, I was baptized by the same bishop who baptized Mom. My mom had made me a navy blue cape dress that was longer than most of my other dresses that I wore to church on Sundays. Years earlier, Mom had explained to my sister, when she had to start wearing a cape dress when she turned twelve and joined church, the reason the extra layer was needed was to help ensure a dress is not too form-fitting. How much form of a twelve-year old needs hidden? Plus, Mom explained to her daughters, "The reason plain people are told they need to have their sleeves be long-sleeved ones is because some man in a church leadership position came to a conclusion: the point of a bent-elbow for a woman can look too much like a breast nipple. So cover it up!" Her smirk widened. Huh?

My baptismal dress came down below my knees. My other dresses were midknee in length. Off-black nylons were worn with black-heeled pumps. Directed to sit in the front of the church, we listened to scriptures about baptism being an outward expression of an inner transformation.

Then the entire class rose to its feet, walked to the front of the church, knelt down, and lined up in front of the pulpit. Both the bishop and the deacon had a role. One held the water pitcher and spoke the baptismal words over us, while the other cupped his hands, making an area for the other one to pour water over our heads. It was enough water that it did literally run off my head and onto my dress somewhat. Then the bishop would help us to our feet. The wife of the bishop would rise out of her seat, walk over, shake my and the other girl's hand, and give us a holy kiss on the lips while welcoming us into the family of God. *Did I use mouthwash?* Of course, the boys received their holy kiss from the bishop.

During the church service, it was difficult to concentrate. My thoughts escaped to my plans that were to be held that very night. I was allowed to go to my friend, Lillian's house, and then go on a hayride and hang out with my friends. After the baptism service ended, I looked at my friend, Lena, Lillian's cousin, and cajoled, "Let's get out of these clothes and go have some fun."

I might have worn that blue dress on one other occasion; probably for the first Communion service after my baptism. I wore a cape dress on Sundays for only about nine months. A modest dress was always the expected dress code. But over time, the cape dress was no longer a requirement. Of course, my mother wore a cape dress on Sundays only. But as restrictions were lifted, she eventually stopped wearing them too.

For the less conservative teenage girls, pushing the dress code limits, we did not wear cape dresses. Dresses were to continue to reach midknee or longer. Eventually, my dress length reached the top of my knee (in school, my sister can remember being told to get on her knees and her dress must reach the floor). If it became too short, Daddy scolded me. Mom had purchased some store-bought dresses modest enough for me to wear to church. Many dresses and skirts required that she needed to let out the hem and rehem it with the smallest hem possible in order to keep it the more-acceptable skirt length.

My high school graduation class was the last class not to be allowed to wear slacks to school. All the girls were attired in dresses or skirts and blouses. In the '60s miniskirts became popular. I would wear skirts and blouses to school more times than I would wear a dress. Wearing a skirt gave me the liberty to roll up the skirt and wear a big belt hiding the excess material. It was never a miniskirt length, but it was definitely two or three inches above my knee.

On the days I would forget to let the roll out of my skirt, by the time I got off the school bus and Daddy would happen to see me, he would yell at me for my miniskirt.

Hands on hips, I frowned and sneered, "Trust me. This is not a miniskirt. I'd be happy to show you one." But, of course, the skirt returned to its proper length, as I did not want to be denied my weekend privileges because Daddy was mad at me for my back talk.

I did learn to be more careful after that incident. Girlfriends would look out for me and remind me at the end of the school day, "Hey, Leanne. Roll your skirt back down." Once, while shopping, Mom wanted to buy me a pleated skirt. But I declined that style because I knew it wouldn't roll up very easily, nor would it be very becoming. Wearing a head covering and a too-short "immodest" skirt just does not fit well together, and often the Mennonite girls wore the longest length of skirt or dress at school.

Mennonites do not observe Advent or Lent. But twice-yearly communion services, including foot washing, are strictly enforced, and all church members were expected to participate in these ordinances. Having become a church member, I was now allowed to participate. First, I had to attend the preparatory service and council meeting, including a minimum of a one-meal fast. In lieu of eating, I was to use this time for introspection and prayer. In my family, we fasted breakfast on the Saturday morning of the preparatory service before the scheduled Communion Sunday.

The scriptures reviewed at preparatory service pointed out the need to have our relationship with Jesus Christ in right standing and without known practiced sins. The bishop or deacon would review the Lancaster Conference expectations on dress codes and lifestyle practices. We would hear about the church being against TVs, dancing, drinking, smoking, and fornication (sex outside of marriage). It seemed to me the list was more restrictive for women than men. Men were warned against the wearing of neckties (which meant they did not wear the expected plain suit coat) and not to own a too flashy colored car in either white or bright red.

The preparatory service included a time for one-on-one with the church leadership. After the applicable scriptures were reviewed, the minister, bishop, and deacon would move off the pulpit and go into the small anteroom behind the pulpit. As the result of my introspection, if I had any sin that I needed to confess and repent of prior to participating in Communion the following day, this was the time to reveal any known sins to be granted a pardon, forgiveness from your heavenly Father, and a clear conscience to participate in Communion.

After the three leaders would move into the anteroom, there was opportunity for a private session for those individuals who preferred not to be in a group of ten to twelve for the public confession of faith and obedience to the ordinances. For a few minutes, the silence in the congregation was palpable! For those of us who remained seated, we looked around and waited for someone to get out of his seat and head to the anteroom. If you were one who *did* get out of your seat and walk toward the "confessional" room, you knew that people were curious as to what sin you were about to confess.

Most times, in my recollection, young couples would confess to having committed fornication. It was obvious to all, if you saw a young man go into the room, and after his return, a young lady, who was his girlfriend, entered as well, you assumed it was for committing fornication. That was surely scary enough for me, when older, to behave during my dates! Another sin someone needed to confess was the sin of unforgiveness toward his fellowman, which was dealt with immediately.

After the private sessions ended, filing out one row at a time, a group (I was among other teenage girls) would crowd into the anteroom. After the introspection, we were asked by a nod of our heads if we, to the best of our knowledge, were at peace with God and man. One group left and returned to their seats, and another group proceeded to do the same until the entire congregation had participated.

When the three leaders returned back to the pulpit, the bishop would reveal the name and reason for each confession made. Yikes! In closing, having prayed over those who confessed their sins, and for the remainder of us who affirmed by a head nod, implying all is well with our soul, the bishop deemed the entire congregation now at peace with God and their fellow man. We were worthy to participate in the Communion service the following day.

After reading scriptures pertaining to following Christ's example of the Passover feast and the Last Supper, the pastoral team was in charge of the Communion service. Prior to the event, the ministers' wives prepared by pouring grape juice into stainless steel water pitchers, which were then poured into large-sized stainless steel tumblers. They broke a loaf of bread in small pieces and placed them in matching stainless-steel plates.

Two of the leaders holding a pitcher of grape juice would stand at each end of the pew on the women's side. The remaining two leaders holding tumblers of grape juice would stand on the end of the pew on the men's side. At the designated time, they passed the tumbler down the row. Church members took a small sip from it and passed it on, remembering the symbol of Christ's shed blood on the cross for our redemption of sins. *I hope I am not getting too many germs or backwash.* Thank goodness, the method of communion has changed, keeping in mind infection-control practices. Tumblers were refilled as needed.

Plates of small pieces of bread were passed in similar fashion. One held the bit of bread until the bishop prayed over it, emphasizing the symbol of Jesus Christ's broken body on the cross. On cue, we all ate of the bread together.

Lastly, the foot-washing ordinance was practiced. Since women and men were already seated separately in the congregation, this event went smoothly. The leadership team's wives had small basins of water half-full of lukewarm water and plenty of white (symbolic of purity) towels handy. After scriptures were reviewed on Jesus's humble service of washing His disciples' feet, on cue you removed your socks and shoes. Then you stood in line facing the back of the church where the basins of water were lined up on the floor in front of several folding chairs. The oldest church members had basins and towels prepared for them in the front of the church on both sides of the pews for the men and women. I attempted to stand next in line with a girlfriend because of the holy kiss at the end.

When it was the next team's turn to participate in the foot washing, one person sat down and placed one foot in the basin of water. The other person knelt down and placed the white towel on her lap. As an act of service, she washed the one foot and dried it off and repeated this with the other foot. Then they switched places, and the one who did the washing and drying of feet had her feet washed and dried. I can truly say the smell that morning was not the most pleasant one!

Most teenage girls wore panty hose. Nevertheless, some little (and not so little?) boys would sneak glances over in our direction in hopes of getting a glimpse of some bare leg, anticipating the girls to lift their dresses somewhat too high while removing thigh-high nylons (or when younger knee-high socks). Sorry, boys, in the name of modesty, we performed foot washing while wearing hosiery.

When finished, you shook hands and gave each other the holy kiss (dry kiss on the lips), a true sign of humility and lowliness. The congregation was now to follow the Holy Scriptures and live, to the best of its ability, the expectations of the church disciplines until the next communion service.

Between the biannual preparatory and communion services, our family had heard about cases where the church leadership team felt the need to make a house call to address a concern with a fellow church member. When my sister Lenora was about sixteen years old, the unexpected knock was heard on our door one hot summer evening. Uncertain if Mom and Daddy knew ahead of time about the visit, I stood shyly by as the minister and the deacon proceeded to tell my parents of their concern.

"You are aware that we have recently put down new macadam around the entire church. A troubling thing has occurred this summer. Dozens of high-heeled shoe holes are visible on the macadam throughout the back door area where the teenagers stand. We have every reason to believe that your daughter is one of the culprits, though we can't be sure." Kindly, Daddy listened to their concern, and they soon left. My sister was never asked to stop wearing her high heel shoes by her smart parents. How long does macadam stay soft? Isn't the damage already done? How is this my sister's fault?

As much as following our church's ordinances with respect was a privilege, I can remember one time my girlfriends and I were totally disrespectful during a church service. I was attending a wedding of my Plain horse-and-buggy cousin at her Sunday morning wedding at the Pike church. Yes, per tradition, weddings sometimes were held as part of the regular Sunday morning church service. I was about fifteen, bored and ready to get on with a fun-filled afternoon. The girlfriend, who was the driver, and my other friend I had invited to attend church that morning, made a plan. The next time we were asked to bow our knees for prayer, we were going to crawl out of the church on our hands and knees. So, shortly thereafter, the minister asked us to kneel. We stood up, turned around, and got on our knees facing the pew. On cue, we made the decision to start the crawl. Who should be watching us? They are supposed to have their eyes closed, correct?

The friend who was sitting on the end of the row started crawling out. Single file, our crawl started. I was in the middle, and my other friend took up the rear. We crawled to the top of the aisle and behind the back row of pews. Beyond the door, we stood up and laughed hysterically. Many of Daddy's relatives attended this particular church, and I was not confident that I would not be found out for our mischievous behavior. But nothing was ever mentioned. That kind of thing can only happen once—no one gets lucky the second time!

Another activity as a teenager that my friends and I participated in during a boring church service, as passed down by my older sister, follows: Open up a hymnal and add the words *under the covers* behind each title. For example, "Amazing Grace (Under the Covers)" or "What A Friend We Have in Jesus (Under the Covers)." One would randomly open the hymnal. The one who opened the hymnal to the silliest-sounding-remade title was the winner for that morning. The closed-mouth giggling probably caused the pew to shake somewhat, but at least, it was an activity that I did not get yelled out for talking too much during a church service.

Sometimes, my required grace needed to be only thimble-full sized; other times a high waterfall was needed to flow over me. Either one, poured-out grace refreshes the soul.

Thought of the Day

Bestow grace by remembering His church is His body, imperfect members who fall so short of displaying Christlike characteristics. As soon as I joined the body, I helped to fill the pews of sinners saved by grace.

Chapter 18

My 1967 Brag Book

*Our mouths were filled with laughter, our tongues
with songs of joy. Then it was said among the nations,
"The Lord has done great things for them."*
—Psalms 126:2

Oh, to be fourteen again and know what I know now.

I won a small brag book as a bingo prize at someone's party when I was fourteen years old. A brag book was an autograph-type book that you asked friends to sign and to write a comment about you; you did the same in their brag book. Of course, as a fourteen-year-old, not much else was on our minds, except school and boys. It is similar to what is done today in school yearbooks, except this was done in a much smaller book. I used this method, as my parents didn't buy me a school yearbook each time one was published. The only high school yearbook I received was the one published in my senior year, 1970.

The following are some excerpts from my brag book. I have eliminated my friend's names to protect the guilty:

In the inside cover, I wrote: "This is the property of Leanne Martin, Ephrata R D 3, 733-7707 age 14, 5/5/67 at bingo."

The first page was folded down: on the front, I wrote "For the girls only." And when you opened the flap, it reads "I knew you boys would look."

Page 2 (where the date would be on the top right-hand corner of the page, instead of a date), it reads "No date needed, you'll have plenty…"

Entries read:

Dear Leanne,
    Love is a peculiar thing
It's something like a lizard
It wraps its tail around your heart
And crawls into your gizzard.
…the cutest kid around, lots of fun…the girl that gets all the guys…has the neatest clothes.

To Leanne,
    To a really neat kid in my section. Remember all the fun we had in English class. I hope you get Stanley back soon. Good luck in the future.
2 old
+2 cry
4 milk

To Leanne,
    They walked down the lane together,
The sky was full of stars,
They reached the gate in silence,
He lifted up the bars;
She neither smiled nor thanked him,
For she knew not how,
For he was just a farmer boy,
And she……a Jersey cow.

Dear Leanne,
    Doors are locked
Keys in the cellar
Nobody is home

MY LAST LAST NAME IS GRACE

But Leanne and her "fellow."

Leanne,
    I wish you luck,
I wish you joy,
I wish you first
A baby boy.
And when his hair
Starts to curl
I wish you than
A baby girl
And when she starts
To pick up pins
I wish you than a set
Of twins
And if that isn't plenty
I wish God would
Send you twenty.

A friend,
2 good
2 be
4 gotten

Pink makes the boys "wink."

To Leanne,
    Never forget the fun we had together in American Studies and that story teller, Ruthie, (the little liar). Remember, never believe anything she says (it's not true). Forget me not, A.F.A. (A Friend Always)
2 young
2 go
4 boys

Leanne,
       Don't make love behind the garden gate,
Love is blind but the neighbors ain't. A.F.A.

Dear Leanne,
       May the lad you take in life,
Be as kindhearted as his wife,
And whether his eyes be brown or blue
May they always look lovingly on you.
A real cool and tuff kid I'm glad I know. A riot to be with.
A.F.A.

Dear Leanne,
       My grandma has a habit of chewing in her sleep,
She chewed on grandpa's whiskers and thought
It was shredded wheat. A.F.A.
To a real cute, tuff kid. Never forget all the riots we had. Keep your personality and sweet smile. I cherish your neat wardrobe and tuff hair.

Leanne Babe,
       To the cutest and neatest kid who is a good friend of mine. Never forget the rare times we had together. Keep your great personality and you'll succeed. Love Ya,

Sailors like ships
Babies like toys
But all that Leanne likes
Is Boys, Boys, Boys!!
A.F.A.

Leanne,

    To a real cute, sweet, and pretty girl who lives in the big town of Noodle…(can't spell it). Remember all the swinging Sunday afternoons and those neat Jeep rides. Best of luck with all those cute guys, Me Always,

Leanne,

    To a real nice, cute kid. Don't forget the times we spent together. Take care of Earl now. Good luck in your future years. A.F.A. (then written upside down in the corner: Only monkeys look in corners)

Dearest Leanne,

    To one of the greatest kids I ever knew. Remember all those good times we had together, Sunday afternoons and other times too. There was never a dull moment! The best of luck with Stanley and all the other guys. Stay as nice and sweet as you are now and you will always be a success. Do you remember the times we slept out last summer and walked the streets of Noodle Doosie with our nighties on? And ran and hid when a car came? Moonlight boat rides at your slumber party and that crowd? Remember the time you, Lena and I walked down to the bridge and saw them guys painting? Remember that Sunday afternoon you, Irene and I went to Dutch Bowl (ask Leanne what her score was) Remember all those Jeep rides? Remember the times we went roller skating? Remember Lena and Lillian's slumber party? And the time we went to Martindale Black Bumper Church (or whatever they call it?) we stuffed our Bibles in our pocketbooks and those white shoes we had on? Well some of us did. Remember the time we tried to scout Lenora and Polly and Frank and the time we were counting the blocks in Yoder's store and that dog came along or whatever it was? Boy, I am writing a book! Remember all those other rare times we had but I can't think of them now. Boy I better stop. No one could have a nicer, cuter, sweeter, loveable, greater and every- thing- else-neighbor than I have. I look forward to the time we can double date. Wow can you imagine that!

Just a neighbor,

A page of quotes only:

Hey Babe…Always remember: Make love, not war…Love is the ultimate trip …Love conquers all…Love makes the world go around…Flower power…Luv power…Disorder is fun…Send your parents to camp…Let it all hang out.

Leanne Babes,
I wish you the "Best of Luck" in your future years. The neatest kid around. Cute, tough. Never forget those long unforgettable times with _____ and _____, Kid, let it all hang out. "Forever" your friend,

Dear Leanne,
Best wishes to the grooviest and rarest kid. Never forget those rare slumber parties, like dancing under the bridge, playing walk-a-mile in the moonlight. Never forget our odd talks we

had together. Good luck and keep the ball rolling. Lots of love,

Dear Leanne,
    When you get married and live down South,
Remember me and my big mouth. Love,
Yours until Mississippi uses bobby pins to keep its waves in,

Leanne,
    When you get married and have 25,
Don't call it a family, call it a tribe. A nice sister,

Leanne,
    To a real swell kid I met way back when. One of the cutest, sweetest, and nuttiest kids I ever knew. Remember all those rare times we had together and never, ever forget your slumber party and "_____." Good luck in the future with all those cute boys. A.F.A.

    How many married sisters-in-law choose to hang out with fourteen- and fifteen-year-olds? Linda my sister-in-law, who married my brother Elvin, offered to drive me and my three friends down to Ocean City, Maryland, for the day. I saw the awesome wide ocean when I was fifteen years old for the first time. How awestruck I was to see the varying colors and shades of blues and blue-grays of the ocean, as it stretched for miles in front of me. The ocean seemed to kiss the hem of heaven. What fun to have waves twice your size throw you toward shore while drinking mouthfuls of saltwater and dousing your hair and bathing suit with sand! That summer, I learned the effect of baby oil lathered on one's body while sunbathing. By the time I arrived home, my mom said my skin had turned two shades darker. Unfortunately, this act was repeated way too many times when a teenager.

One Saturday night, my three girlfriends and I spent our evening in a very different fashion. Having no date this particular night, we scanned the newspaper for youth events in our nearby city. Lillian, Lena, Cheryl, and I decided we were not going to do the usual Mennonite activities but something out of character for us. I noticed the newspaper clip about Youth for Christ holding a swimming pool event. After about an hour of swimming, they were holding a short Bible study. Perfect! A little leisure time combined with scripture.

Daddy allowed me to have the '58 Chevy that night. I drove the four of us to the pool about ten miles away. As we were driving in, I fantasized about meeting a cool, non-Mennonite guy. Who knows? I may start dating someone from the city. I said, "Hey, girls, when asked, I am *not* going to say, 'My name is Leanne Martin.' Let's change our names. I am going to be Desiree Rutt." Within seconds, each one of my Mennonite-sounding-named girlfriends (Cheryl's name was fine) had a different name they planned on using.

Christian music was blaring through the loudspeakers as we headed toward the locker rooms to change into our one-piece swimsuits. Lillian was in a stall next to me. I jokingly said, "Hey, Lillian, I was stopped on the way in here. The Youth for Christ president asked if one of us, and I selected you, would be so kind to lead us in prayer. You will need to use the mic so it can be broadcasted over the loud speaker. I volunteered you and said you would be perfect," I specified, trying not to laugh.

"Oh, goodness, I guess I can. What phrases should I say in my prayer?" She proceeded to practice her prayer, changing her sentences, and rephrasing. This went on for several minutes until Lena, Cheryl, and I could no longer hold back and burst out laughing. By then, Lillian (or should I say Vivian) realized I was only kidding. Only once or so did I have the opportunity to tell some interested guy that my name was Desiree. Perhaps the city youth could detect we were totally out of our element?

As I learned from my sister and older friends, I had to determine my values early on. Having a healthy view of sex as displayed by my parents, I knew it was something designed to give marital pleasure and totally God's idea. Mom gave her daughters the idea that women had the upper hand when it came how to handle ornery boys. What power!

One Saturday, I was ironing my outfit I was planning on wearing that night. Mom strolled into her sewing room where I was attempting to press perfect pleats on my skirt. While rummaging through her sewing machine drawer for a needle and thread, she hinted, "Leanne, Daddy thinks you're doing too much running around for your age." She did not look at me but started threading the needle with her wet fingers.

While the iron hissed out steam, I stepped back. "You mean you won't drive me over to Lillian's for her slumber party tonight?"

"Yes," she continued. "Daddy knows you'll never have trouble with having boys around you. You be careful out there." I went back to ironing sounding a *pffff* out of my mouth. Yeah, right, always plenty of boys standing in a long line!

I saw the effects of girls getting a "bad reputation" if they did *not* put the brakes on during dating or alone times with the opposite sex when the boys got fresh. However, I also overheard guys complaining about my girlfriends who wouldn't even kiss and got labeled a prude. Because I determined I did not want to be labeled a prude and saw no danger in kissing a guy, I decided I would play it safe somewhere down the middle of easy and prude. Some of my girlfriends' brag books revealed some embarrassing moments by certain entries ornery boys wrote about; my friend, Sally, was one. Yikes!

Well, I guess my older brothers felt it was their duty to coach me on watching out who I hung with, like Sally, so I didn't get a bad reputation before I even reached dating age. If that wasn't enough, my sister Lenora sent me letters mentioning how her friends were concerned for me because of my hanging out with "wild" Sally. What's the solution? She's my friend. I don't know what goes on behind her closed doors or in a parked car.

During a hot bubble bath, I came to the conclusion to stop hanging out with her. Bummer! Sure enough. The next day, Sally called to invite me to her slumber party Saturday night. Within seconds, I heard myself answer, "Sure. Is Cheryl invited too?" Not only was it a slumber party, but Sally and her sister planned a scavenger hunt. Dave Hollinger asked me, along with Cheryl and Lillian, to ride in his '66 red Chevelle for the evening. Unfortunately, at the end of the evening, Cheryl's Jeep wouldn't start. So Dave offered to take Cheryl and me home. He made sure I was the last one to be dropped off. As soon as he pulled up to my house, he put his arm around me and gave me my first French kiss. Now I know why I was to attend Sally's party. My journal entry reads "I hate French kisses…signing off as 'Puzzled and Petrified!" *Really? Hmmm.*

On both weeknights and on many weekends, I had girlfriends stay over at my house for a sleepover. Esther was one of the girlfriends who spent many Saturdays overnight at my house. Thus, on Sunday morning, it was expected that we both had to go to church with my parents. After several combined months of this occurring, Esther realized that my Lancaster Conference church's teaching was more appealing and made more sense than the teaching of her parents' "Black Bumper" church. Plus, she did not have to dress as conservatively if she became a church member of Martindale Mennonite Church. Because of God's convicting Holy Spirit, Esther made the decision to join church. After informing the deacon of her decision, she participated in the instructional class and was baptized. A few years later, Esther was married by my minister and asked John and me to be in their wedding party, which we were more than happy to do so. Little did I realize back then how Esther, my middle-school friend, would truly be a supportive one when I so needed her.

Thought of the Day

Bestow grace by encouraging those discouraged to box up their failures and put them in the attic or to drop their sins in the ocean and not dredge them back up. Remember who you are in Christ.

Chapter 19

Needle and Thread and Cutout Letters

All the days ordained for me were written in your
book before one of them came to be.
—Psalm 139:16b

To my grandgirls:
"Pull up a chair,
I'll pour you some tea,
I want to share with you
More stories about me."

GRANDGIRLS: (THE REST OF YOU are allowed to eavesdrop) this chapter will disclose things about my life when I was fourteen through sixteen years old from my journaling. The diary was a Christmas gift from my mom and daddy in 1967. Pretend Nana is with you gathered around a fancy-dressed table, attired in our Sunday-best outfits, just like we did the last Friday before the upcoming school year when Nana invited you over for my tea party to celebrate the end of summer.

I have categorized varying themes from my diary. You'll learn how I filled my evenings and weekends with activities since I didn't have any TV, for example. You'll read diary entries that revealed secrets and my feelings toward my boyfriends when I experienced puppy love. You will learn about what it was like being a Mennonite teenager in the late 1960s. Slang words used in my entries may seem strange to you. You'll read about some silly methods of future predictions.

Pretend we are gathered around the table drinking tea with our pinkies extended outward, like we used to do. The tea has been poured. Here goes:

Birth of my Baby Brother, Douglas

One summer, the supper table conversation was about Mom trying to convince Daddy she wanted to get a part-time job. I'm uncertain how serious she really was or what actual job she had an interest in doing. Of course, the money would have been helpful. But I got the impression it was more about a different way of spending two or three days a week, as her family was empty nesting. By the time I was fourteen years old, I had two older brothers already married and starting their own families. A sister and more brothers followed by the time I was sixteen. Then Mom stopped bringing up the subject of working outside of the home. She seemed more tired and worn out.

By fall, Mom's tune completely changed. One day, the remaining women of the house were in the kitchen. Mom was cooking, I was emptying the dishwasher, and Lorna was setting the table. "Well, girls," Mom gloated. "You are going to have another baby brother or sister. Dr. Hess predicts around May 23rd." *Wait? What! Pregnant? At forty-two years old?* I all but dropped the glass in my hand. "Whatever do you mean?" I blurted out as I gave her a darting glance. "I will *not* tell any of my friends my mom is pregnant with her ninth child at forty-two years old! *Never*! How embarrassing!" I lamented. Lorna took a step back then started running around the table while yelling, "Yippee!" Guess she doesn't care about no longer being the baby of this family.

Mom stirred the water-flour mixture into boiling water to make gravy. "Oh, don't worry. You will be the one thrilled most of all among your brothers and sisters," Mom predicted.

That night during supper, Daddy, who obviously knew the news for some time, proclaimed, "Well, Mom, you can forget about your part-time job. By the time you raise this baby, you'll be too old to get a job." The matter was settled.

Of course, over time, my emotions went from embarrassment to acceptance. By the time Mom was six months pregnant and attending my brother's wedding (how many grooms have a pregnant Mom in attendance?), reality had set in.

Douglas, whom Dr. Hess called a "bouncing baby, who is all boy," was born May 21, and the Martin household was forever changed! Later on, as for most forty-four-year-olds, Mom's patience was worn thin when trying to raise an active toddler. Many times, I left my bedroom to intervene for Doug, who was getting a scolding from an exhausted mom. "Come here, buddy," I suggested. "Let's go back to my bedroom. I need help doing some homework." Many delightful hours were spent with Doug or babysitting nieces and nephews. Once spring arrived, Mom spent hours mowing our four acres. Thus, I was the one to keep an active toddler out of harm's way. Or when Mom and Daddy had evening plans, I was expected to babysit Doug. He was never a burden.

Spoiled Doug had a childhood no other sibling could fathom. Daddy bought him a puppy and a used truck tire, which became a sandbox. Doug and his nephew Keith, and niece Charlotte, all spent hours together playing with trucks and tractors in the sandbox. Yard-sale bought tricycles and riding toys were driven around and around our circular driveway. Baby fat turned into muscle for the three musketeers. Doug was frequently noted in the background of many of my photographs taken in my bedroom. Like a faithful puppy, he followed me around from room to room; I never felt he was bothersome. Today, I stake claims to being the one who raised him.

My parents had an open-door policy at all times: no need to call ahead of time; stop in and visit us at any time. Thus, my married brothers and their young families stopped in frequently on weeknights. It was rare if no one visited or I was not babysitting Doug. I only journaled a few times of alone activities: "Went back to my bedroom and listened to records" (I had a small tan record player, which played 78 vinyl records, not the 33 ½ size though) or simply "did homework" or "read a book."

Winter Activities

When fifteen, our Pennsylvania winter was such we could go ice-skating by December 30th. Frigid temperatures hardened the ponds to a point of safety for the many feet of us skaters. Car full of teenagers would be dropped off. Sometimes a concerned owner of the pond would chase handfuls off the pond because he felt there were too many of us warranting it too unsafe. Most times on weekdays, my brother, Matt, was my driver. Ice-skating games were tag, cross tag, and crack the whip.

Here are the directions for playing cross tag: The guys lined up on one edge of the pond, and the girls lined up on the other side. Whoever had the most team members skate to the other side without being tagged won. The strategy was knowing who and how many girls should stay behind to skate out and tag the guys who were attempting to cross to the other side, and which girls were the best ones to attempt to skate over to the other side without getting tagged.

Here are the directions for playing crack the whip: One of the better skaters started forming a line. The rest of the skaters held hands and continued the lineup. Altogether, the skaters started to skate forward. At any point, the lead skater started skating in a circle, causing a sharp turn, and the end skater goes fastest. The second-to-last skater let go of the end skater's hand. He or she was to stop skating and start coasting. The winner was the one who coasted the farthest. What fun!

I have many memories of hanging out at my friend, Nancy's house; she had a pond. Daddy drove me over to her house while he spent time with her dad foxhunting. Sometimes, Nancy's mom invited my mom to attend a quilting bee. Thus, I tagged along to ice-skate. As long as Nancy and I were in the house in time to serve the refreshments to the quilters, we could skate to our hearts' content.

Being a wintertime activity, getting a quilt out (finished) required Mom to assist Nancy's mom twice in the same week, much to my delight. Putting in a quilt took many, many hours from start to completion.

Many instances of puppy love warmed my heart on those cold winter nights. Lucky for me if a prospective boyfriend showed up on the same night! One struck gold when a boy offered to lace up your skates or lovingly removed them for you. I wrote in my diary that night, while my cold cheeks were still warming up, "Stanley not only removed my ice skates, but he put his arm around me… we graduated from holding hands. I was shaking and shaking, and I don't know why."

The times Matt was my driver and since I was with a brother, I guess Mom didn't give me a curfew before midnight on weekends. Frequently throughout the winter months, I went ice-skating and was out late also on school nights. I did not get home until 11:45 p.m. at times.

Sledding and roasting hot dogs were another great Pennsylvania winter pastime for those friends who had a huge hill on their property and a spot for a huge bonfire. What a thrill to be sledding down the hill double with your boyfriend! After four nights of hanging out with friends from Friday through Monday, I frequently took bubble baths on Tuesdays and went to bed early.

Teenagers became our own weather prediction "experts," who paid attention to the weather forecasts and pond conditions. When there were perfect conditions, local creeks (some called cricks) were full of ice-skaters, and sledding hills were full of sledders.

If weather conditions did not allow for outdoor activities, we teenagers would flock to the local roller-skating rink. It was one of my favorite indoor activities; I could roller-skate at a B-level. Stomachs held butterflies as one waited for a cute guy to ask you to skate with you for several trips around the rink during the couples-only skate. I turned down a few offers and was quite selective in whom I skated with from time to time. But you really hit the jackpot if a guy asked to drive you home.

Slumber (Named If More Than Two Girlfriends Stayed Overnight) Parties

Slumber parties were held year round. My friends and I hung out in my parlor listening to '60s music while watching out the big picture window for headlights of some guy's car coming in my driveway. It was always exciting to see how the grapevine among Mennonite youth included the whereabouts of a slumber party location. Somehow, cute guys knew where to hang out. These visitors came as late as 11:30 p.m. Sometimes, it was Marlin and his friends arriving in his '66 blue Grand Sport or Victor's gang in his '65 dark green Dodge Dart. All the girls piled in and rode around the countryside while laughing and carrying on until 12:30 a.m. or so.

We would finally settle down on our makeshift beds on the parlor floor around 2:30 a.m. Of course, we would be way too tired to get up and go to church Sunday morning. But we knew better than to try and get out of skipping church. It amazed me how Mom had no idea sometimes how many extra people there would be sitting at her breakfast table the next morning. Of course, the same was true for my friend's mom when I would decide late at night to stay at a friend's house (after a phone call to Mom).

When invited to my friend's older sister's slumber party, it was always an honor. That meant you were about to meet older boys and a new circle of guys who did not attend your same church. At Lucy's sister's slumber party was the first time I laid eyes on your grandpa, who started "dating" Lucy (she was not allowed to officially date, as she was only fifteen). That night, I played walk-a-mile with Marlin Hoover; he wanted to be the one to walk with me without switching with any other guy. I was not certain I wanted to do that, so I ended up walking with Galen Hurst. He even kissed me! Lucy and Sara's parents weren't home, so the guys sprawled out on the sofa or floor and slept (of course, fully dressed). It was my first time to lie down beside a guy until early morning. They left at 5:10 a.m. Some had to go home and milk the cows. The following

Monday, Lucy called to inform me that John was drunk Saturday night. *Really?* I had no clue.

Within a few weeks at Lillian's slumber party, a different gang of older guys showed up and invited us to drive around, which we did until 1:00 a.m. My notes on that sleepover read: "Once I climbed into the back seat, Marvin hopped in beside me. He put his arm around me and within minutes attempted to kiss me. But I refused, so he just held my hand...he's a neat and groovy guy but fast (interpretation: fresh)...Vic allowed me to drive his car for "about twenty feet" (on a back country road)...Lucy and John were hanging out... Barry asked me to go for a motorcycle ride. At one point, he went 102 mph! *Neat!*" (No, don't even think of doing that!)

Sleepovers

Once, my friend Lucy was asked to babysit for a neighbor. She received permission to bring along a friend—me. That night was my first all-night TV viewing, once we put the kids to bed. *Picnic* was the first movie we watched. Having no TV in my house, to watch ten shows in a row was big stuff. Finally, the TV was turned off at five o'clock in the morning.

Other weekend journal entries read: "Esther stayed overnight.... took guys for a boat ride on the creek behind our house...Earl held my hand." Or "boring night...we messed up Jay's car and wrapped pink toilet paper all around it...went with Esther to take her driver's test; first was her eye exam, which she passed...then on to the driver's skill section...wouldn't you know...Murphy's law...her car battery went dead. We had to wait an hour at the driver's exam for her pop to bring and install a new car battery. But in spite of her beginnings, she passed her driver's test."

Silly Future Predictions

One weekend during a slumber party at my house with Lucy and Lillian, Lucy exploded with excitement about two methods to predict future events she had recently learned about.

"Leanne, go get me a threaded needle, an old magazine, and a basin," she excitedly said. I brought the desired items into my parlor and joined my two friends, who were sitting Indian-style on the floor.

"Okay." Lucy grabbed my mom's foot-long brown thread with the sharp needle out of my hand. "Now watch closely. Lillian, I'm going to do this on you first. Stretch your left hand out in front of you."

Lillian obeyed. "This prediction using this needle and thread will tell us how many children you will have and what sex they will be," Lucy explained. She held the thread against Lillian's inner wrist at about the halfway point, leaving six inches of the threaded needle dangling. Slowly, Lucy started moving the thread in an up-and-down motion, not allowing the needle to actually hit Lillian's wrist. After about three times of this, Lucy held the needle about an inch above Lillian's wrist. Suddenly, the needle dangled in a circle.

"I am not making this circle," Lucy pointed out. "Circles mean you will have a girl. If the needle swings back and forth in a straight line that means you will have a boy."

"Wow," Lillian and I said in unison.

"Now, you do this motion until the needle does not swing in either a circle or back and forth. That means there are no more children," Lucy smiled with big eyes. "Guess what? My sister learned this from her friend, and she did this on me. I am going to have two children each: two girls and two boys! Cool, right?"

The next ten minutes, we learned I was going to have four children also: three girls and one son. Lillian's needle trick predicted three children: two sons and one girl. Then I came up with the brainy idea of having the needle trick repeated on me and Lillian to see if we would get the same results. Yep, and Lucy swore she was not manipulating the outcome.

Later on, I could not wait to do it on Mom. What better way to get proof than for someone who is finished with childbearing? With my younger sister Lorna present, I repeated the needle trick to her and Mom. It dangled correctly the proper order of my siblings: four boys, two girls.

"Wait. Your miscarriage, Mom," I quickly explained.

"You know the order and are making the needle go in a circle or straight," Mom said, convinced all of this was silliness.

"A boy, then two girls," I called out as the needle swung away. Just for the fun of it, I continued to rub the needle against her wrist again. The needle dangled over Mom one more time, indicating another boy was to be born into this family. Mom simply laughed and said, "Put it away. It's nonsense. No, you are *not* doing this on Lorna." Ten months later, Baby Douglas was born!

"Now what is the magazine and basin for?" I asked Lucy.

"Well," she answered, beaming. "This prediction will tell you the initials of our future husbands. I'm marrying JW. Oh, I forgot. We'll need three scissors." She cracked up laughing until her belly shook. I raided Mom's sewing supplies and returned with three scissors.

"There are four rules. The letters must be of the same weight, meaning out of the same magazine or newspaper, not mixed. They shouldn't be real small letters, but about one-half inch high," as she pointed to an appropriate "A" on the magazine cover. "You place them upside down in a basin of water. Slip the basin under your bed before you go to sleep. In the morning, the two letters that are turned over will be your husband's initials."

"Geezzzz," Lillian hissed.

"Whoa," I responded. "Let's get started cutting out letters, girls." I grabbed the magazine and started ripping it in thirds. "I'll cut out letters A to G. Lillian, you find H to N, and Lucy, the rest."

Eager to see my results, I convinced my girlfriends to retire earlier than most sleepovers. Lights were out around midnight. The blue basin under my bed held a promise for me more exciting than Santa Claus. Before my alarm clock sounded, I awoke. It took me a few seconds to realize I had one girlfriend sleeping beside me while another friend was curled up in her sleeping bag. That's right—the letters!

I shook Lillian awake, as she was in my way to reach under the bed for the basin. "I'm right here. I'll pull it out so we can all look together, okay?" she said as she rubbed sandman from her eyes. Filled with anticipation, I held my breath, as she carefully pulled the basin out from under my bed. By now, Lucy was also awake, yawning and sitting up in bed, smacked up against me so she too could see the results.

"R, Q, V, U" we called out in unison reading the overturned letters. With furrowed brow, I turned to Lucy and asked, "Am I marrying an Egyptian?" And we all burst out laughing. Lillian announced she could not wait to try her basin-letter trick that night, and she would call us both with her results.

That Sunday night, I cut out an entirely different set of letters and placed them in the bottom-covered basin of water. On Monday morning, the basin looked exactly the same as when I pushed it under the bed: no letters were turned over. "Hmm, I guess I'm not getting married." I giggled over the phone when I called both Lillian and Lucy to report the results of my second attempt. Lillian reported her letters were C, W, Z.

Years later, when I was engaged to John Weaver, Lucy explained, "The basin gave you a U and a V. Perhaps it was trying to give you a W." Lucy's predicted letters of J and W; the J part for John was correct. Lillian's letters were correct with the only last name of her husband: Z for Zimmerman.

Perhaps, in reality, it is good that six letters of three future husbands did not turn over. If it had, I would have thought the prediction was downright silly. To believe there was a possibility that the six letters would be the initials of three husbands would not have crossed my mind, any more than the four letters could have meant there would be two marriages for me.

Red Run, Dutch Bowl, and Twin Kiss

Summer activities were packed with swimming at Red Run, an awesome local pond where teenagers and families hung out at on hot humid days. Many couples met here and started dating. Many Sunday afternoons, I had fun times swimming and sunbathing at Red Run. (Who can forget the smell of coconut oil?) I lathered it on to produce a healthy tan. Since I am dark-complexioned, I tan quite easily (much to my blonde daughter's dismay). As we sunbathed, a transistor radio blasted top hits from WFIL, a radio station located in Philadelphia. On Sunday, Clyde Martin took me for a motorcycle ride, and we ran out of gas. Just as the sun heated up my body temperature, my heart melted the day my boyfriend, Earl, showed up to swim also. I labeled that afternoon coolness, groovy. While carousing around with Lillian and Lucy in Earl's car, I took my first puffs on a cigarette, four puffs total.

Though the parking lot wasn't conducive for frequent drive-throughs for guys showing off their cars, the Twin Kiss was a stop en route to the Dutch Bowl from my home. Mennonite youth, after purchasing an ice cream cone for sixty cents hung out together until it became too boring.

Another fun backdrop was the local bowling alley named Dutch Bowl. Guys, proud of their wheels, circled through the long parking lot several times an hour. Admiring girls would be asked to hop in and go for a spin. Earl was noticed by his parents hanging out at the Dutch Bowl; they drove by the exact moment Earl and I were standing at the edge of the entrance.

"Oh, boy," he pointed out. "I am going to get heck (scolded)." The following week, Earl indeed broke up with me. My fifteen-year-old heart mourned—until the next slumber party.

Martindale Dutch and Spelling Bees

Held in the local Martindale fire hall, Dutch and spelling bees were fantastic opportunities to hang out with friends on a school night. When in my elementary years, my sisters and I were brave enough to go up front, walked on the stage, and participated in our appropriate grade bees. I held my own for quite some time spelling words correctly for several rounds but never won. However, both Mom and Daddy over the years won either first or second place in the Dutch bees. The leader would say a word in English, and you had to say the word in Pennsylvania Dutch.

Church and Youth Group Activities

Twice a year, in the spring and the fall, church families house-cleaned the church. While catching up on our weekend activities, Lena, Nancy, and I wiped down the pews, the job assigned to teen-aged girls.

My parents seldom attended the midweek Wednesday prayer meetings; nor was I expected to attend. However, my parents offered to host the prayer meeting at our house. One entry reads, "55 attended prayer meeting tonight here…" Thank goodness, we had a large basement.

Of course, whether I hosted a slumber party or not, it was expected the group of us girls attend my church service Sunday morning. Many Saturday nights were spent attending Young People's Meeting at varying churches in my district. For both summer and winter Bible school and revival meetings, I had to promise to attend, if at all possible. One night, at sixteen, I begged Daddy for the use of Bessie, the family car. I was allowed, but only if I promised to attend the Young People's Meeting first.

"Sure," I exclaimed. Lena, Lillian, Cheryl, and I piled into the jalopy. I drove to Weaverland Church where we dutifully attended the service—well, only through the singing. Daddy didn't make me promise I would attend the *whole* service, right? Memorizing which scripture text was used, in case I would be asked by Daddy, I, along with my friends, quietly left the back row. Dutch Bowl, here we come! There was only one time where I actually journaled the topic title of the Young People's Meeting I had attended when I was sixteen: Christian's view of sex. My conclusion: Mennonite youth—no "third base" during dating, no lying down on the sofa, and stay pure.

Group Dating Allowed Before I Was Sixteen

District church youth group activities were perfect avenues to meet other young people other than the youth who attended your church. We gathered for weekend retreats for two different scheduled events, which the ministerial team of the Mennonite church had scheduled. Both broadened my world beyond Martindale Mennonite Church. One was to witness Sunday afternoons by handing out pamphlets, called tracts, in neighborhoods in a bordering county. The pamphlet was named *Star of Hope*. If someone was sitting on the porch, we simply handed them a tract and said, "God bless you." No actual conversation was ever held by me with a stranger to witness.

The second planned activity, held in the spring and fall, was a bus trip to Bowery Mission in New York City, using loaned Mennonite school buses. We were in charge of the mission's Sunday night church service. Some of the boys, never girls, were assigned to be the chorister and lead the hymn singing; two presented a short sermon ending with an altar call invitation.

What was exciting for the girls was to be asked by a boy to share his bus seat with you. Guys who were interested in you got up the nerve to ask you if they could sit with you for the long bus ride either one way or both ways. Picture a bunch of anxious girls waiting around a school bus. Suddenly, a guy walked up and asked if you would like to sit together. Most girls accepted the invitation. My first date was with my friend, Marion's brother, Dave. Being a little older than me, he was able to convince someone that he deserved the back seat. Needless to say, first kisses were shared for many of us Mennonite girls on the way home on a dark school bus leaving New York City, including me.

My parents did not call it a date if a guy dropped you off from an event. My brother Matt and his girlfriend, Renee, would often drive me to fun activities. Then a love-interest, such as Dave, would ask if they could drive me home. Most cars in the 1960s had a bench seat. It was easy for a girl to sit right beside the driver. In fact, "first base," while driving in a car, was when a guy put his arm around you. When bucket seats became popular, the girl simply sat in between both front seats the best she could. The most fun was when the car had a stick shift. How does a driver shift gears and put his right arm around his girl? The girl does the shifting.

The second guy to kiss me was Stanley, but it was a little embarrassing. Mom had just entered the kitchen prior to Stanley's car pulling into the driveway. Good-bye smooching was going on between us. Mom was warming up a bottle for my little brother, Doug. She happened to be looking out the window at the exact same time. As I entered the kitchen, I noticed her grin. "Long goodnight kiss?"

"Hmmm," I replied with a big smile and headed down the hall to my bedroom. My diary entry on that night reads: "Real groovy" (a slang word we used for *awesome*). I replayed the conversation for Stanley the following weekend while we were both busy lacing up our ice skates. "Your mom didn't scold you?" he asked with raised eyebrows. "No," I looked puzzled. "Why should she? It was only a kiss." He shook his head as he stood up and balanced himself on his skates. "You got one cool Mom!" Reaching out for my hand, he and I skated until our toes became too cold and numb.

A Sad Event

Dave and Marion Hollinger's dad's business, Hollinger's Farm Market, burned down! By 2014, Dave or his family had experienced three more fire tragedies. In 1991, a candle in the lower level was to burn itself out, but it malfunctioned and caused smoke damage throughout their beautiful large home. In 2008, their rental property where their daughter lived caught on fire and caused much damage. In 2014, their one-million-dollar-house under construction burned down. During a newspaper interview, Mrs. Hollinger remarked, "I think we have had our share of fires. Enough is enough."

Misbehaving

Mom used to make dandelion wine and stored it in the coal cellar. One weekend, my house was full of visiting boys. Stanley's brother, Jimmy, who was two years older than most of us, was experienced. Jimmy noticed the dandelion wine quart jars neatly lined up on Mom's canning shelves. He asked if he could taste it. I proceeded to serve the four guys a small amount of dandelion wine in a paper cup. Unbeknownst to me, while Lucy and I were talking, Jimmy went back down to the cellar for some more dandelion wine. By the time the evening ended, Jimmy said he was "sorta dizzy" (this was before I knew what *tipsy* or *buzz* meant). Without my knowledge, Mom told the guys that it was time for them to leave. I and my girlfriends were ordered to bed, as it was 11:45 p.m. About a month later, Jimmy and some (eager?) guys returned for some more of "your Mom's great dandelion wine." Daddy found out and exclaimed, "Absolutely not!" and made it known to them to never ask again. Of course, I got a scolding. After that incident, Mom stopped her "dandelion brewery."

The following unfortunate event occurred within two weeks of Matt's and Renee's dating. One winter Sunday afternoon, my boyfriend, Stanley, and some guys, showed up at my house to hang out. Several girlfriends of mine were visiting. We decided to go for a drive. For some reason, the girls and guys were in separate cars. Stanley decided to drive Renee's parents' car. Somehow, he got stuck and during the process of attempting to get the car unstuck, he hit a tree. The car ended up with a small dent in the fender. He was upset, and I felt so bad for him.

Turns out Renee was just as frightened to try to explain to her dad why a male friend had driven his car without permission. If it had been Matt driving the car, that would have made a little more sense. But Stanley? Of course, Renee's dad was mad. Stanley had to pay every dime of the cost of the repairs, which amounted to $100—quite a bit of money back then. I offered to pay the bill, but Stanley would not hear of it. It took him over a month, but by taking some money out of each paycheck, he paid his debt in full.

Though frowned upon by our parents, an Ouija board filled up a boring Sunday afternoon pretty quickly when at Lillian's house. One entry reads: "Ouija says I am breaking up with Stanley, and then Lena and Stanley will start dating. I will start dating a former boyfriend, Luke." The predictions had me stressed for weeks. Of course, later on I have had to confess the sin of playing with an Ouija board, reading horoscopes, and fortune telling.

Years later when in my midforties, my friend convinced me to visit a psychic who lived in my same development. Sensing my hesitation, Suzie asked, "Aren't you a bit curious about your future after nursing school or life happenings for you a decade from now?" After an appointment was made within the week, Suzie and I walked into his incense-spice-scented home. She took her turn first, while I waited in the waiting room and flipped through a *Lancaster County* magazine. A half-hour later, it was my turn. Mr. Young placed gray tarot cards in front of me on the card table between us. I remember only one quote of his: "Hmm, you will always have money on your mind, how to spend, save, or invest." Suzie and I both received a cassette tape of our psychic readings. Because I discarded it after my repentance, I have no more recollections of its contents.

I guess Mr. Young missed that Suzie's future would be filled with a sad tragedy of finding her fifty-four-year-old husband dead in bed! Plus, I heard nothing about my upcoming second divorce, or finally, happiness nestled inside a third marriage, and a return back to God. Praise God, our path is marked in trust and not in palm readings or tarot cards.

Thought of the Day

Grace is recognizing what God says about me. I'm valuable and capable of stretching my faith. That's what He expects of me. God will continue to help me to perform, as He has created me, to fulfill a purpose. Grace knows the engineer has hidden features inside of me to accomplish His intent.

Chapter 20

Have T-shirts Gone Out of Style Yet?

> But you will receive power when the Holy Spirit comes on you; and you will be my witnesses in Jerusalem, and in all Judea and Samaria, and to the ends of the earth.
> —Acts. 1:8

ONCE I WAS GRANTED PERMISSION to graduate from high school, I made plans, which was expected by my parents, to work part-time after school, as soon as possible, after my sixteenth birthday on November 7. My neighbor Cheryl was already employed at a garment factory named Cinderella Garment Factory. It was an easy decision for me as I needed a means of transportation. Her 1961 Jeep fit the bill. After a doctor's physical and the appropriate paperwork were submitted, I started work on November 19. My assignment was working in the sleeves division, putting sleeves on men's white T-shirts. My pay was figured by using a base rate called piece rate, which was 45.5 cents per bundle. Within one week time, I was able to complete five bundles within the pay period.

I was dropped off by the school bus around 3:20 p.m. Barely having time to freshen up and to grab my bagged supper, I was scheduled to work from 4:00 p.m. to 9:00 p.m., Monday through Friday. Holding down that job kept me busy the remainder of my junior year. During Christmas break and the summer months between eleventh and twelfth grades, my hours increased to full-time at forty hours per week. As time went on, I joked how factory work could easily motivate any school student to graduate and find a worthwhile career. At the beginning of my shift, I frequently asked my coworker, Terri, who was sitting at the machine next to me, with an expression that appeared pained, "Haven't men's T-shirts gone out of style yet?"

Laughing, she'd jeer, "Nope, Leanne. Get to work. I'm about to end my shift, and you're just getting started." Terri would leave her post promptly at 5:00 p.m. No one wanted to stay a minute longer.

Here is the process the best I can remember it: The body of the T-shirts without sleeves would be bundled up in huge bundles. Stacks of turned inside-out sleeves were bundled up in the matching count as the sleeveless T-shirts. Using a specific sewing machine for this chore, one would untie the bundled sleeves and one by one open it and put it through your right (if right-handed) arm. Thus, when finished, I would have about forty-eight sleeves scrunched together from the top of my arm to my wrist. To the left of my sewing machine was the stack of forty-eight sleeveless T-shirts. Pulling the top T-shirt off and aligning it up next to the needle, a sleeve was pulled off my right arm and lined up with the T-shirt. Adding a sleeve was to be done in two steps or whirls of the sewing machine without cutting off more than $\frac{1}{8}$" of the T-shirt seam. After assured of the proper alignment, I would start the first sewing machine run from the bottom of the T-shirt seam to the top to the sleeve, realign or make adjustments for proper T-shirt "waste," and finish off with sewing from the top of the sleeve ending at the bottom while aligning up at the seam. Repeat the same process for the second sleeve.

Our factory floor lady Edith's job was to examine the trough in front of each machine filled with the cut-off waste. Several times during this job, my friend and I would be scolded for not working fast enough or having too much waste cut off the T-shirt, warranting the T-shirt to be a "second." Once sleeves were added, another department's staff, named examiners, where Cheryl was assigned, would inspect the completed T-shirt to be sure the underarm seams met perfectly and no holes occurred. If not perfect, it was considered a "second."

A white film of dust from white fabric and thread bathed all over everything—your clothes, hair, and the floor. Mennonite girls, who were one of the fastest workers and produced the highest number of bundles hourly, stood up to leave and started walking out with poor posture. It seemed like they were still in their leaning-over position at their machines! Tell me that wasn't motivating to get a high school diploma. As Terri proceeded to walk toward the time clock behind some slouched-over Mennonite girl, she exaggerated her straightened-up posture while pushing her chest out. I laughed so hard I had trouble containing it. Thank goodness for the WIOV radio station blaring throughout the factory too loud for Edith to hear me.

Unfortunately, T-shirts never have gone out of style.

My first paycheck was $24.30 for nineteen hours worked. Yahoo!

Jenny, another after-school employee, was assigned to Terri's machine. Being a junior at the same high school, we held many conversations about our mutual high school teachers while we slaved over our machines.

Donning short-sleeved dresses year-round in the warm room, Edith proceeded to walk down Jenny's and my aisle. Uh-oh. Here comes the boss. As my machine whirled, I watched her from the corner of my eye, picked up material scraps or waste, and assessed for the proper trimmed size in the low trough, which ran in front all the sewing machines.

Edith stopped and stood in between Jenny's and my machine as she dropped the assessed waste. "Leanne, you only completed 3.5 bundles. Your numbers are dropping. You two are talking too much. Concentrate on your work, please." After Jenny and I both nodded in agreement, she strolled off as she made a note on a log she was holding.

When Edith turned her back to us and started to walk away, Jenny and I looked at each other and broke out in a noiseless, open-mouth, belly laugh. I have more than Edith to worry about. Mom surely will be observant and notice too if my paychecks don't increase as I gain experience.

By the end of December, my performance improved. Jenny, Terri, and I simply got smarter with our ongoing carrying-on while the completed bundles increased. During that time, my diary entries read: "Did 5.5 bundles in 5 hours…can do 6 shirts (12 sleeves) in 10 minutes, instead of 15 minutes…my second paycheck: $27.68 for 21.75 hours…got out six…seven…nine bundles…Started $5 savings account."

Every payday, I turned over my paycheck to Mom; she handed me a $5 bill. I could either save it or waste it. I did little of both depending on my mood. Oftentimes, with permission, after work, Cheryl and I would go to our Friday night hangout called Green Dragon, a flea market, farmer's market, and auction combination. It was a great avenue for teenagers from varying Mennonite or Brethren churches to gather, flirt, and, if lucky, be asked out on a date. By the time we left Green Dragon, my wallet was nearly empty. More times than not, my five-dollar bill was spent on the latest hit record, such as, *Moni, Moni* or *Sugar, Sugar*. Other times, I just had to have a sexy pair of black nylons with fake diamonds running along the back seam or a new brand of mascara. Occasionally, the savings account was fattened.

One night while mulling around the farmer's market, Cheryl and I decided we were tired; time to head home. Just then, four guys walked up to me and one asked me, pointing, "Why do you wear that cap on your head?" Another guy nudged him and giggled. Without even answering him, flapping my hand in dismissal, I turned around and headed toward the parking lot. Will it ever stop?

Thought of the Day

Grace is realizing I am a "be." Grace will enable me to live the lifestyle I am to live to be on mission for God. I win when God is glorified, not when others glorify me. Find all the good in Him.

Chapter 21

First to Graduate in My Family

The fear of the Lord is the beginning of knowledge,
but fools despise wisdom and discipline.
—Proverbs 1:7

Senior Class picture

AH, TO REMINISCE ABOUT ELEMENTARY, middle-school, junior, and senior high school years—events seemed so monumental. Little did I know, when I was a student, that God would give me the opportunity to teach at a two-room parochial school when I would be barely nineteen years of age. (I hope those students of mine can read and write today.)

Miss Kurtz (later becoming Mrs. Shelby), my shorthand and typing teacher, was one of the most influential people in my life. She looked out over her tenth-grade class one day and made a profound statement: "Girls, don't expect a man to take care of you. Choose a career and earn your own paycheck so you can pay your own way. Don't expect a husband to support you. You become your own breadwinner."

Miss Kurtz gave many examples that year during homeroom, shorthand, or typing classes on the advantages of her being hired as a secretary and working her way up to become a manager for Flexsteel of Lancaster, prior to her becoming a teacher. Not getting married until a middle-aged adult, Miss Kurtz was a perfect example of needing to earn her own monies to support herself as a single woman.

Wow! This was the total opposite of what my Mennonite upbringing taught me. Being totally dependent on your man and following the footsteps of your mother, a housewife, and dutiful wife was the only aspirations a little Mennonite girl of Lancaster County needed. One could confidently assume that we would marry and rely on our husbands as the financial supporter, just as my daddy had.

The message Miss Kurtz gave resonated with me. It made perfect sense to not assume you will be married and expect a man, married or not, to support you. After all, plenty of married women have become widows (Lena's sister was one) in their twenties or thirties and have lost husbands in various forms of tragedies. Then, what?

So by the end of tenth grade, I signed up optimistically for my eleventh-grade classes, having no idea if I would be allowed to graduate or not. It was a long maybe. I knew Daddy had to make the decision by my sixteenth birthday in November of eleventh grade. If he came to the conclusion that I was not allowed to graduate, then it meant that I would be getting a full-time job and turning over one-half of my paycheck to my parents, just as my older nongraduating siblings had done. Yikes!

My sister Lenora, who would have graduated in the class of 1967, had begged to be allowed to graduate. But Daddy's lame excuse he gave her was that because she was put on detention once in ninth grade, "You're not taking school seriously." So, much to her heartbreak and dismay, she was forced to quit. Lenora became employed by Moyer's Factory and worked full-time. At barely eighteen years of age, she got married and moved to Williamsport, where her husband was assigned to work in a hospital for his two-year IW stint as a conscientious objector. Upon her moving out, I moved into Lenora's bedroom, no longer needing to share a room with Lorna.

My brother Matt, who was next in line, did not have the desire to finish high school. He could not wait to quit school and become employed. Eventually, at eighteen, he started driving truck for Daddy.

Other Mennonite and Brethren classmates and friends, Esther, Lois, and Sara, who frequently stayed at my house overnight on the weekends, were given permission to graduate. Esther recalls her mom being her advocate: "Daddy, if she does her farm chores morning and night, can she graduate then?" Carrying a load that was difficult for most adult city slickers, let alone a teenager, brainy Esther pulled it off and came in Number 8 in her senior class! I think that helped to make up my parents' mind also. My older brother, Junior, being in his midtwenties and perhaps regretting his own decision to quit school, argued on my behalf and helped to reason with Daddy too that I should be allowed to finish high school. After all, the times were a changing by 1970.

I always enjoyed attending school and doing homework. I did not go to kindergarten; I was only five when I entered first grade at Reamstown School. Being short and petite, I was usually one of the smaller-sized kids in my class. My first-grade picture displays a smiling little girl with two pigtails trailing down the front of my buttoned-up sweater. I had dark-brown eyes and dark-brown hair parted in the middle with small braids that began on the top of my head. Suddenly, right before the photographer snapped the picture, he reached down and placed my pigtails to rest on the front of me instead of hanging off my back. He wanted them to be visible.

Second grade was taught by Mrs. Weinhold. She allowed her favorite students—okay, okay, I'll say, teacher's pets—to grade spelling and math papers for her instead of going out for recess, if we chose to. One of my favorite grade-school pictures was the one taken in second grade. One weekend while my parents went to the mountains, I selected to stay overnight with Harold and Florence, who were like another set of grandparents to me. Getting one-to-one attention from them and not having to share a room nor a View Finder toy with my sister, I was pampered on these excursions.

But the icing on the cake was when Florence took me shopping and bought me a brand-new Sunday dress. Proudly wearing the gray-and-white big-blocked, thin chiffon-like dress with a black silk flower pinned on the left side, I beamed for the camera. Wearing a pin was the only acceptable jewelry. Earrings, necklaces, and bracelets were forbidden. I think another reason that I always liked my second-grade school picture was because I had shoulder-length hair, and it was not necessarily styled like a little Mennonite girl—one with pigtails.

We moved to Hinkletown when I was in third grade. I needed to attend part of the school year in both Reamstown and Bergstrasse schools. I made friends pretty easily, and I adapted quickly to my new surroundings. I had Sunday school classmates attending both schools, which helped with the ease of adjustments. In fourth grade, I learned about world events from the Friday's class called Weekly Reader. We did not have a TV. Thus, I was educated about other races, religions, and world events through this once-a-week class. I loved it when our teacher read storybooks to us right after lunch each day. Loving to read, I relished the day when we were allowed to go to the library and select new reading material.

My favorite part about attending a public school (my private school friends had to pack their lunches) was eating cafeteria food. Eating Mom's cooking of simple meals and mostly those food items that Daddy would eat, I learned to eat sauerkraut, pizza, casseroles, such as, shepherd's pie, goulash, and tuna noodle casserole. I only had one embarrassing experience during third grade of running out of the cafeteria while vomiting, as I could not make it to the bathroom in time. What was I eating at the time? Sauerkraut. So to this day, I do not eat the stuff. The entire cafeteria would get noisy every time our school janitor would come into an affected area with his mop and bucket. Dutifully, with a smile on his face, he cleaned up our vomitus, art supply spills, and overflowing lavatory toilets throughout the years.

However, it was in fourth grade that I learned a hard lesson about one who slacks off gets Bs and Cs and not As and Bs. Our teacher had the class divided into four groups named after birds: red, blue, yellow, and black. Being one of the smart students put you in the red bird class; black bird class was for the students who had the lowest reading scores, with blue bird and yellow bird in between. The classroom was actually set up in a square-like pattern: red birds to the top right; across the aisle was number 2 blue bird section. Below these desks were the number 3 yellow bird students next to the teacher's desk. To her right was the lowest section, the black birds. (Thank goodness, this discrimination in classrooms has stopped.)

After report cards were handed out for the marking period, the teacher reassigned your seating arrangement. I had slipped into the "yellow bird" section. Yikes! I was much too proud to be labeled a yellow bird reader. So I was motivated to study hard and move up into the red bird section once again. I moved up to the blue bird section, as my efforts paid off. Unfortunately, school ended before I could be awarded a seat in the red bird section again.

Fourth grade recess gave me opportunity to run races and be named the fastest girl runner in my grade. Being short and petite, my little legs made me a fast one. However, math whiz Jay was the fastest runner overall. Along with only a few other girls playing baseball at times helped to perfect my throwing, batting, and catching skills. Sometimes, we held a feed-bag race. You and your partner put only one leg each in the bag, held it up, and ran to the finish line. Recess was never long enough.

Mrs. Wenger, my fifth-grade teacher, was wise enough to know her job was about more than grading papers and being an educator. Recognizing her role as one who influences, she made a comment to me one day that had a positive impact. Recognizing that I was short and small for my age, she said to me, as I was handing in a test paper before recess, "Great things come in small packages."

Beaming and empowered, I ran out to play for recess with my non-Mennonite friend, Wanda. She was the only friend who did not attend my church and whose house I was allowed to stay overnight. Why was I allowed? Because our dads worked together at the same stone quarry, so that did not make her parents total strangers.

Pretty, perky, and with an adorable, envious short haircut, I admired Wanda's shoes. Unlike my shoes that were bought at Weaver's Clothing Store that catered to plain folks or purchased at a rummage sale, Wanda would wear cute little boot-like shoes at the beginning of the school year. When Christmas vacation was over, she would return to school wearing another pair of desired shoes that she received as a Christmas present. Allowed to wear short skirts and cute outfits, Wanda was definitely one to watch and was probably destined to be a future cheerleader. She had it all—looks, brains, and the neatest wardrobe.

One late morning in November when I was in sixth grade, Mr. Mink, our school principal, made an announcement over the school intercom: President Kennedy has been shot and killed! Gasping and with mouths open wide, we all looked to our teacher. She put her head in both hands and started weeping. Just as this event affected our country greatly, my move back into the Cocalico School District also had a lasting effect on me.

When I was in the middle of sixth grade, my parents moved out of Hinkletown and to Rural Route 3 (later named Landis Road), Ephrata, in the small community outside of Reamstown, called Noodle Doosie. But at Cocalico, sixth graders were considered junior high. I was thrilled to brag to my church friends that I had graduated to junior high a bit earlier.

Within the first week, I met other Mennonite girls, and we became fast friends. Just as birds of a feather flock together, Esther, Sara and I were great pals all through middle and high school (Esther remains a dear friend to this day). Lois too later became a friend, who turned out to be a distant relative of mine. I found out later, another underclassmen friend was actually a relative of the foster dad who got my cousin Jill pregnant. Having strength in numbers, we Mennonite and Brethren girls, who eventually all wore head coverings, stuck together to battle the demons of childish teasing classmates because of our coverings.

One of my earliest memories in sixth grade at my new school was during home economics class (boys were attending industrial arts at this same scheduled time). Just as we sat down at the table to eat our casserole we baked together that morning, my classmate who was sitting at the end of the row simply fainted and fell off her chair! We hadn't tasted anything yet, so, no, it couldn't be the food.

Mrs. Graham, in a slight panic, patted the girl on the cheek until she "came to." Helping her to her feet, Mrs. Graham walked her down to the nurse's office. Soon, Mrs. Graham walked back into the now-turned-silent room; we waited for an explanation. If it wasn't the food, then what was it?

Mrs. Graham announced, "She got her period today, ladies. You remember that when you get your monthlies, no skipping meals and don't forget to drink." Gee. I thought I wanted to become a young lady and eagerly anticipate my monthly. But now I'm not so sure.

Because sixth grade was considered a part of junior high, I participated in a real gym class. The expected uniform was a one-piece polyester blue-and-white striped sleeveless top with shorts. Loved it! My parents agreed that I would be allowed to wear it. The same gym was shared by both girls and boys, and the in-between gym partition wasn't always closed. After all, girls were running and jumping around, possibly showing off more than bare legs in view of curious gawking adolescent boys. A few of my more conservative friends, like Lois, were not allowed to wear the "immodest" gym uniform. So they wore the same selected skirt and blouse during gym class instead.

The next rite of passage was sharing a locker room with your female classmates knowing that Mrs. Woods, my gym and health teacher, could walk in on you any time, as well as when you were showering, dressing, or undressing. This was also another adjustment for me. But coming from a family of three girls and one main bathroom, modesty flew the coop a long time ago.

Senior high kids loved to tease and initiate ninth graders, who were the peons on the bottom of the totem pole. They pulled your books out from under your arm while walking in the halls and had them crash to the floor, which was a favorite. Second was holding a door shut at the top of the stairs between classes for a few minutes, hoping to make you late for your next class. Someone simply tugged on your pigtail or ponytail as they walked by you was lovingly done.

Handsome young teachers, like Mr. Hall, made homeroom worthwhile. Turns out Mr. Hall, Mrs. Woods, as well as some classmates of mine who became teachers and were hired by Cocalico School District became my kids' schoolteachers as well. We girls were all thrilled when we heard that Mr. Hall would be the chaperone for our eighth grade spring fling. Not being allowed to dance, I twisted the truth when I asked Mom if she would please drive me to school Friday night to attend game night. She did. Wallflower is what Leanne Martin expected to be that night. *Oh no, wait! Is David asking me to slow dance?* Clumsily and most likely uncoordinated, I attempted not to step on the poor guy's feet while lightly resting one hand on his shoulder and holding his hand with the other just as I saw occur on TV. I was relieved when the next dance was a square dance a chance to practice what we learned in gym class recently. Except for "dancing" to the oldies in the privacy of my living room, I had no clue how to go about a fast dance. With my best-body twisting motion, Esther and I, along with the rest of our classmates, enjoyed twisting to Chubby Checkers. Therefore, as not to have told Mom a total lie, I did take the time to play the games that were lined up on one side of the dance floor. Ah, I mean, gym.

Recess included mostly playing four square or simply hanging out with my friends. Chorus practice took up some free time as well. Along with my Mennonite friends, we participated in choral activities throughout all six grades, singing both secular and religious songs. Sing Out was a group of only seven girls, which Esther and I were members. We participated in separate song selections as directed by our music teacher. In tenth grade, we sang in baccalaureate for the seniors' graduation.

Many high-school diary pages I wrote on the top: "Another riot (fun) day in school." Strong friendships began to be cemented, as I recognized early on, your choice of friends had an impact. High school experiences also are building blocks that mold who you become; our belief systems become foundational, hormones are causing havoc, and the chances to choose right and wrong smack you in the face daily. But our incorrect choices had greater consequences, unfortunately.

Ninth grade started to challenge my brain, as I had selected more difficult academic courses versus business courses. These courses taxed my brain: chemistry, world geography, earth science I and II to name a few. When I received a D in earth science for the first time on my report card, I made the decision to immediately switch to easier business courses. You could do so if you did it before the second marking period. I rationalized: *I don't know if I'm even going to be allowed to graduate. Why should I be stressing out over these tougher subjects?*

So I switched to business courses, which included typing, shorthand, and bookkeeping. Mrs. Boggs, my English teacher, got kudos for being strict. After handing out writing composition assignments, she would write on the chalkboard: "Linking verbs are (circled) no-nos!" To satisfy Mrs. Boggs's expectations, one did not hurry through these assignments and expect to get a good grade. The extra effort I made not to use linking verbs paid off for me when I took English composition while attending college to become a registered nurse.

It was a proud moment during tenth grade gym class to document I scored the winning point, making the final soccer score 1–0.

Monday morning classes by tenth grade became difficult for me to be the most bright-eyed and bushy-tailed, as I was up late Sunday night involved with various weekend activities with my friends. Mr. Becker's class was one of the classes that I would pass around notes to my girlfriends, sharing tidbits about my previous weekend. If one is doing that, surely you cannot be answering questions in class. Mr.

Becker would look out over his inattentive class and say, "You people have diarrhea of the mouth and constipation of the brain."

During one of Mr. Becker's classes, I wrote the following poem about my boyfriend. I pasted it inside my locker for the remainder of that year:

Romancing in the Moonlight
Leanne and John, who are very much in love,
Walk in the moonlight while the stars shine above.
His hand in hers, they slowly stroll along,
Filling the air with sounds of their favorite song.

They stop awhile for a rest beside the lake,
Watching the cool, serene, glittering waters make,
A romantic picture for all lovers to see,
Of moonlight, loveliness and harmony.

Now as he whispers sweet words of love in her ear,
She lovingly smiles at him, for what she hears
Means more than words could ever express
And fills her heart with everlasting happiness.

Being more laid back, Mr. Becker would do things in one speed: slow. He'd talk and walk slow. Because his class was held first thing on a Monday morning, I often fought to stay awake. One day, some classmates decided to play a trick on Mr. Becker to spice things up a bit in his classroom. The student who sat in front of me had a history of epileptic seizures. Having attended various classes together, I personally witnessed these events about three or four times before graduation.

His best friend came up with a plan and informed the rest of the class of their intentions. After all, as with most misbehaved teenagers, two heads together can have behaviors spiraling downhill quickly. Within about five minutes of Mr. Becker's entering the classroom and starting his class lecture, this guy was to pretend he was having a seizure. Sure enough, as Mr. Becker had his back turned and was writing on the chalkboard, on cue, he started twitching, eye rolling, and sprawled himself clumsily over his desk in front of me.

The rest of us who were in on the trick, were to stay sober, not smile and act alarmed, which was difficult to do. Mr. Becker turned around and witnessed an assumed epileptic seizure. Looking at the student, who sat closest to the door, he said in his fastest speech I've ever heard, "Go get Merla" Who? The school nurse? Yep, he forgot to call her by her last name in his excitement. The guy pretending to have the seizure started shaking in laughter and couldn't resume his twitching. He lifted up his head and pointed out, "Gotcha!" Mr. Becker just shook his head and had to smile. He was just relieved that it *wasn't* indeed a true medical emergency and did not require the attention of the nurse—ah, Merla. Those who cry wolf.

Having switched to business courses in ninth grade allowed me to earn honor roll status once again each marking period. Loving to learn how to type, shorthand (which paid off for writing those thoughts I didn't want anybody to read in my diary), and German, my language choice, took less time of my time for studying. That allowed for more weekend fun to hang out with my friends and not consume me with doing only homework. Sometimes during the week, I was able to enjoy roller and ice-skating too.

Misbehaving, I passed notes to Sara, Marilyn, and Esther at times. I had just finished mouthing words to Esther when Mr. Schaeffer noticed me. "Since you're a good student, I'll allow you to deliver the message." How embarrassing! In biology, Esther and I learned how to determine one's blood type. For our class project that year, we tested eight classmates for their blood-type test.

That same year, Esther and I both signed up to volunteer as Ephrata Hospital's Candy Striper Program (a volunteer position traditionally held by young females performing nonmedical tasks in a hospital). To assist in lightening the workload of nurses, Candy

Striper's title refers to the candy cane look of the red-and-white-striped pinafore that was worn. We were assigned every Wednesday from 3:00 p.m. to 6:00 p.m. This commitment lasted through my freshman and sophomore years. Of course, this gave us ample time to discuss her cousin, Harold, who drove me home from the Martindale spelling bee.

One November Sunday afternoon, soon after my fourteenth birthday, Lorna and I were playing a game of Monopoly. I felt twinges in my abdomen, so I went to the bathroom. Hmm, I became a woman today! Every girl knows your life is never the same. I had both extremes in my family. Mom started menstruating at ten years of age (being uneducated, she thought she was dying), and my aunt was fifteen.

Even though Mom was not the one who actually did the education, I did proudly announce to her after arriving home from school on the day I received the booklet about growing into a woman. She was glad the school was proactive about informing sixth-grade girls about this natural phenomenon. Later, during health class, Mrs. Woods showed a film, titled, *A Girl to a Woman*. Learned from an older girlfriend, I too nicknamed my monthly *granny*. Many diary entries started out with "Got granny today…" I would get a certain look in my eye when I would start menstruating. I simply looked in the mirror and knew I got granny overnight. Yep, going to the bathroom confirmed it; I can't explain it physiologically.

Tenth grade is when I began the love of clothes. I expanded my wardrobe to include jackets, sweaters, suits, vests, various colors of sleeveless shells (today named camisoles), and both long and short skirts. It wasn't long before my closet was packed full of good-buys, on-sale items, and hand-me-downs, which I accepted eagerly. To this day, I am a bargain shopper and peruse thrift stores and boutiques.

Since I had to hand over my paycheck to Mom, I was not responsible to support myself until I received half my paychecks at seventeen. However, I must say, if I was in a shopping mood at sixteen, Mom obliged and took me shopping (I could simply drive myself, but then Mom wouldn't be along to fork out the money to pay the bill). Albeit it was never for a full outfit, nor did it happen too often, as my crazy schedule didn't allow for too much time for such a leisure activity. My favorite store was a dress shop in Ephrata called Verties. One such Saturday morning, I asked to go shopping for a new dating dress.

"Sure, we can go to Verties," Mom agreed. "But first, we need to get all the cleaning done around here. When we get home from running around, we're not going to feel much like cleaning then. So get your parlor and bedroom cleaned and the kitchen floor washed up. Then we'll head out."

Mom was exactly right. Cleaning, then shopping (put in the correct order) made for a great feeling when we walked back into a clean house after being fatigued from shopping. I passed down the same advice to my girls, and I practice this routine today.

Health teacher, Mrs. Woods, weighed each one of us in her class. I documented "got weighed at school: 105.5 pounds." About a month later, I wrote: "I now weigh 109 pounds." I believe I know why. The school cafeteria had a sign posted on the food line that read: "Maximum pieces of bread: 4." My two farm girlfriends, along with many football players, took four pieces of bread to eat with their chili. I started to do that also many times. One night, I started buttering my second piece of bread to eat along with my supper meal. Mom warned me, "You'll get fat if you keep eating the way you do."

At the end of tenth grade, the driver's ed instructor wanted to compile a list for the following fall's eleventh-grade students who anticipated needing to take his course. With determination and a lot of faith, I signed up, believing I would be returning in the fall. How thrilled I was that October night later when Daddy told me that I would be allowed to graduate from high school! In my defense, I guess, he saw how I had made the honor roll frequently and still pulled good grades in spite of my busy social life. Being too embarrassed about my chance of not being allowed to graduate, I never told the teachers that I was so close to having to quit school. Knowing that my more conservative friends were allowed to graduate, and the possibility that I might not be able to, was something I did not even want to disclose.

With new determination of proving Daddy made a wise choice of allowing me to finish school spurred me on to get the best grades possible. Well, as high as possible for the time I allotted on weekends to do homework and extra studying. My next dilemma was how to answer the question when teachers asked of us, "What college do you plan to attend? Have you thought about your major?" I knew that answer was a definite one: no college in my future. (Doesn't God have a sense of humor?) You don't realize, Teach, I barely got permission to graduate.

Blending growing up, dating, dealing with teenage problems, girlfriend conflicts, working a part-time after-school job, and not getting enough sleep paved the way for a balancing act during both eleventh and twelfth grades. Continuing on with a near-perfect attendance record, I looked forward to going to school. Playing hooky was not an option. After all, that would not have been the message I wanted to send to Daddy. Until that actual walk up on stage to receive your high school diploma, Daddy could have yanked my privilege at any time. I would then have been forced to get a full-time job and hand over a paycheck. I surely did not want to succumb to that.

Optional school clubs that I had selected to become a member of, besides chorus, was Future Business Leaders of America, the club that made the most sense for business-course selectees. Attending a local business meeting in the Ephrata area broadened my knowledge on the various opportunities for secretaries. If efficient and proficient, secretaries were looked upon as a most valuable employee to company presidents. It spurred me on to continue to get good grades and achieve my next milestone of graduating.

My shorthand was perfected to the point that most diary entries about my dates were written in shorthand. After all, I could not take the chance that my nosy sisters would not cut my diary flap and try to read about my activity on dates. Sure enough! One night, I came to journal in my diary and noticed the flap was cut. (Unfortunately, today I can no longer read shorthand.)

As soon as I turned sixteen in November of my eleventh-grade year, I started working at the Cinderella Garment Factory after school. I worked Monday through Friday from 4:00 p.m. to 9:00 p.m. After returning home, I would finish my homework that I was not able to complete in study hall and crawl into bed, only to repeat the cycle five days a week. If I wanted to go roller-skating or ice-skating with my friends at times, I had to get permission from Mom to take off from work. She did not like it, but at times, she allowed me to only work four nights that week. After all, that led to a smaller handed-over paycheck.

The summer before twelfth grade was motivating enough to continue to pursue good grades and select a career option as a secretary or bookkeeper from my business course selections. Who wants to end up an old maid and work in a factory all your life? *Not me!*

My friend Pat also worked at Cinderella. What memories! Sitting a few rows in front of me meant that she would turn around frequently and mouth something to me. Sometimes it was about the song on the radio blaring overhead or about the floor lady, in our eyes, who was much too critical. One can't always sew a preferred ⅛" seam on the T-shirt, can one?

One day, Pat and I walked outside to have lunch while sitting on the factory lawn. The front door was facing another industrial building. We noticed a construction crew of young men working on the roof. "Whoa! Who is that gorgeous, shirtless creature working on the roof of that building?" I asked Pat. "Hey, I know him. He goes to my church," she answered.

Pat called out loudly, "Hi, Roy. This is my friend, Leanne Martin." Roy, along with the rest of the crew, looked over, waved, and checked us out. While eating our lunches, Pat gave me the scoop on him. She knew that he attended a less conservative Mennonite church and drove a cool '68 green Mustang. That was all I needed to know.

Who do you think was the first person I saw when Cheryl and I walked into Green Dragon to hang out that night? Roy! (Isn't God great?) Seeing him walking in from the parking lot about the same time we were entering was God-ordained. Whoa! How sexy did this guy look in his cool shades? I was smitten. My heart started pounding, and I began to wonder if the stars and the moon could possibly line up in a miracle and allow Roy to ask me for a date for Saturday night.

Not only did the stars and the moon line up; a beautiful rainbow was added to the mix. Boldly, Roy *did* ask me for a date within the hour. We dated for about two or three months. Every time Roy pulled into my driveway, wearing his cool sunglasses and driving his '68 Mustang, I experienced sweaty palms. In great anticipation, I cleaned my parlor, prepared refreshments, ironed my outfits, and planned many double dates with friends. Roy and I dated through most of the summer attending many church youth group events.

One weekend, we were allowed to attend the countywide Mennonite youth group event held in Camp Hebron, a county away. Just as too much chocolate cake served daily was no longer desired, Roy and I felt our attraction to each other slipping away. On the way back home that weekend, having an over-one-hour drive to discuss our relationship, we mutually decided to break up and go our separate ways, even though we could not explain exactly why. My guess is that I was a little too conservative for him. So I saw the taillights of Roy's Mustang drive out of my driveway one last time.

Senior year at last! By the time graduation came in the spring of 1970, I was going steady with John. Darcy, a wiser, experienced woman in her thirties, spent some time trying to convince me, as our machines worked on T-shirts, not to go steady. "You're too young, Leanne," she scolded. "Plenty of fish in the sea. These are the years you should be dating them all. Kiss 'em and leave 'em," Darcy implored me. Unfortunately, I did not follow her advice.

We were definitely planning a future together as husband and wife. It was never an option to attend college. Remember, all that Mennonite women are good for is to get married and have babies, just like their mothers. But my high school diploma was not going to be wasted. I planned a secretarial career after high school. I could hold that position at any age, I reasoned. Thanks, Miss Kurtz.

One day, my life changed. Mom asked me if I wanted to work as a receptionist and duster for the furniture store across the corner from our home. Of course! Hmm, let me see. White factory T-shirt dust everywhere or furniture dust? A drive back into Denver or just walk a few hundred yards from my home? The decision was easy. After all, which one would look best on my resume? So, instead of being employed by Cinderella Garment Factory, I became employed by Yoder's Furniture Store. The store was large enough to have a moderate-sized showroom and enough business to require three delivery trucks. Mr. Yoder, a more conservative (translation: safe) Mennonite, hired me as his payroll clerk, secretary, receptionist, and furniture duster. While music was playing on the not-for-sale record payer, I gave Mr. Yoder my best efforts from 4:00 p.m. to 9:00 p.m., closing time five nights a week. Most of the time, Mr. Yoder was also in the showroom talking to customers. Sometimes, family or church events would dictate him not be able to be in the store. I gradually learned to become a great saleswoman. Payroll was done by simply following the government-driven Pennsylvania (state), Lancaster (county), and federal tax cheat sheets. A small machine printed out the employees' weekly paychecks (about six total), and then I finished the payroll process.

I innocently flirted with the handsome delivery truck drivers at times, which helped to pass the time between 4:00 p.m. and 5:00 p.m., when their day ended. Every night, Mom or Lorna would drop supper off for me around 5:30 p.m. It would be leftovers of the same meal Mom had prepared for the rest of the family covered with an elastic plastic bowl cover (using plastic or aluminum foil would have been too wasteful). Of course, it was expected that I return the cleaned-off plate each night and put it in the dishwasher.

About a month later, I entered the furniture store door and noticed that Mr. Yoder had moved my desk. Prior, his desk and my desk together (though not up against each other) used to form an L. Now my desk was facing his desk, which was about ten feet away and right inside the door against the wall. Moving a sofa and chair, my desk was sitting in its place. I had better make sure I keep my legs closed when preoccupied and working while sitting behind my desk now.

As per their usual routine, Mom, not Lorna, brought me my supper that night. She walked in, made small talk with Mr. Yoder, and noticed my desk's new position. With an ugly twist to her mouth, Mom turned around and walked out. The next day, I walked into the furniture store and saw that the sofa and chair and my desk were moved back to their original position. Mrs. Martin, I believe, made another phone call on her daughter's behalf!

One afternoon, I walked in just as the weekly published *Shopping Gazette's* salesman was leaving.

"Hey, Leanne," Mr. Yoder excitedly said. "I'm putting in an ad next week in the *Gazette*. I hope you can work more hours next Friday night." Is the store going to stay open until 10:00 p.m. for a sale or something? Mr. Yoder proceeded to inform me of his ingenious idea of the first-ever midnight madness sale (he swears he is the inventor of this phenomenon).

"Next Friday, the store will close at four o'clock and reopen at ten o'clock until midnight. I'm calling it midnight madness sale. Grab a tablet, please, and let's walk through the store. I'll call out the new prices."

I was amazed how many customers showed up at ten o'clock. Of course, there were some browsers-only, but Mr. Yoder's bottom line was well in the black that month. Some customers chose to go grocery shopping later than usual and stopped on the way home. Some newlyweds stopped in after finishing their workday. The midnight madness sale was so successful, Mr. Yoder repeated it quarterly until the store closed.

Yes, Mr. Yoder was a visionary, but his vision was cut short if he believed he could get a peep up my dress!

The remainder of my senior year, I continued to perfect my bookkeeping, secretarial, and answering-telephone skills. Upon graduation, I was hired as a full-time secretary with Mennonite Central Committee and quit the job with Yoder's Furniture.

Unlike my siblings, completing homework in twelfth grade at times during a weekend date was common for me, as John got some shut-eye. By year-end, my hard work paid off. When the principal posted the ranking of each senior, I was listed somewhere in the low 20's of 162 classmates.

My parents allowed me to buy my blue-and-white senior class jacket and a senior class yearbook appropriately named *1970 KO-KA-LE-KO Another Bridge to Cross*. Cocalico was named after the Indian tribe that had earlier settled in the southcentral Pennsylvania area. As dancing was forbidden, I was not allowed to attend either the junior or senior proms.

During the early 1970s, street unrest in Washington, DC, was reported in the media. This was the usual class trip selection for former Cocalico seniors. Rumor had it that other senior classes of Lancaster County, who had chosen our capitol for their class trip, had returned with broken bus windows! For our safety, our senior class alternate trip was a weekend to the Pocono Mountains in northeastern Pennsylvania. With suitcases, swimsuits, and smiles, we piled in the school buses and headed to a popular resort. What a ball!

Later, I learned that when I chose to get a few hours of much-needed sleep before 2:00 a.m., I had missed out on one of the shyest senior girls dancing on the table. It was cheap entertainment for the whooping and hollering crowd of rowdy away-from-home seniors. Unlikely to ever pair up, couples hooked up just for the weekend. As the saying goes, "What goes on in the Poconos, stays in the Poconos."

By early May, we were measured for our size of graduation gowns. Those who hung in the balance of graduating or not buckled down and worked hard to be guaranteed a spot in the commencement walk up on stage in early June.

One of the few times Daddy stepped inside the Cocalico High School auditorium was when he attended my graduation. Mom had attended my choral events, and the junior and senior class plays over the years. When my turn came, I walked across the stage beaming and grateful. I shook the hand of the superintendent as I accepted the piece of paper that meant more than he could possibly imagine. All six conservative girls made it! Teachers and teary-eyed classmates passed on "Congratulations!" From my parents, though, I cannot remember hearing any "at-a-boys."

1970 was the dawn of a new decade but ended full of tumultuous times. In some ways, the decade was a continuation of the 1960s. Various people groups continued their fight for equality, and many Americans joined the protest against the ongoing war in Vietnam. Americans were affected by higher gas prices and unemployment. Peace-loving youth sported bright colors and answered groovy whenever possible. Near the end of the decade, the nuclear accident occurred at Three Mile Island. What is this world coming to?

Sperry Rand of New Holland was one of the businesses whose ad was published in the back of our yearbook that addressed our class. Titled "The Decade Ahead," it reads:

> Will be one of realizing the potential which lies in our roots...a period of dramatic change for the entire globe. Your school years have equipped you with facts, thoughts, questions...and some of the answers. Your search for more answers begins now. It is a search that will never end, for the world, with its expanding horizons, is growing further from the simple answer. The excitement and knowledge gained from the search are valuable and will lead to greater, deeper thoughts and understandings. Know too that this search will inevitably lead to the answers of tomorrow...answers different from those of today. For tomorrow's world will be a changed world. You, the graduating class, can claim possession of the roots of knowledge. It is these roots that will direct the rate and course of tomorrow's growth toward a better world.

Only God could know what changes would unfold in my lifetime: two divorces, three marriages, the birth of three children, becoming a registered nurse in my forties, walking a path far from God for a time, and later on, moving out of Pennsylvania, leaving my roots behind. As encouraged above, as I explored questions, expanded my knowledge, broadened my search, and, finally, yes, achieved deeper thoughts and understanding, I grew up. But it cost me my marriage. People who crossed my path (starting with Darcy), and later, when I was in my midthirties had observed strengths in me that I had no idea existed. The old adage states people should change who they are six times before adulthood and selecting a marriage partner is so true and needs to be heeded.

Just as the rose, thriving on manure, opens beautifully to brilliant colors among thorns, my journey was one that eventually blossomed to full bloom under the Son.

Thought of the Day

Grace is recognizing my Source determines my potential. Living by the fruits of the Spirit is possible because I have inherent Christlike qualities. I can be loving, kind, and merciful, and also be a giver of grace.

Chapter 22

"Boys Have Needs"

> The grace of our Lord was poured out on me abundantly,
> along with the faith and love that are in Christ Jesus.
> —1 Timothy 1:14

EVER PLAY THE WHAT IF? game? I have. What if I had married one of the handsome MCC volunteers and not John? What if I had told John *nope* when he asked me for a date instead of getting back together again that fall when I had broken up at sixteen? What if, after my two-timing date with Stanley's older brother, Drew, I would have broken up with John and continued to date Drew and eventually marry him?

I learned later, Drew was fulfilling some kind of bet among his peers. "Bet you can't get Leanne out on a date while she's dating John?" he was challenged. "Bet I can!" He responded smugly. One Friday night at Green Dragon, Drew motioned for me to come over to him for a private conversation. John had not been seen anywhere around the Dragon that night. "Hey." Flashing his biggest smile, "I'd love to take you to a drive-in movie Monday night in Columbia. Can I stop by and pick you up around seven o'clock?" Okay, okay. This was too much of a thrill for this sixteen-year-old girl to handle. Several factors intrigued me: I had never been to a drive-in movie, a Monday night was a nondate night (I had to lie about my whereabouts to Mom), Columbia was about a forty-five-minute drive and safe distance from nosy friends and neighbors, and something about Drew's dark eyes, sexy smile, and curly hair expanded this girl's heart. But apparently, not her conscience.

"Sure," thinking quickly, I said, "Pick me up at Cheryl's house." My heart was practically beating out of my chest as I rejoined my circle of friends. Leanne, whatever are you thinking?

The weekend date with John was uneventful. We played cards Saturday night with Elvin and Linda and double-dated Sunday night with Nancy and Roy to watch the Garden Spot senior class play "Carousel." The storyline brought tears to my eyes. In spite of all my busyness, my mind frequently wandered to the upcoming Monday night planned with Drew.

Finally, Monday night came. I told Mom I was walking down to Cheryl's because she invited me to go shopping along with her and her mother. Previously, I had called Cheryl up on the phone and whispered my plans to spend the evening with Drew. I arrived at her house and convinced her as to why I said yes to such a scheme. Having had no boyfriend for several months, Cheryl simply shook her head and said, as I was leaving, "I sure hope you know what you're doing."

Drew pulled up in his cool black 1960 Pontiac, looking sharp in his mirrored shades. Breathless, I hopped in to the passenger side of the door he had reached over and opened for me. Staying in the car was important as Cheryl's parents could surely tell the driver behind the wheel was not John.

The long drive down to the Comet drive-in theater was filled with exchanged stories about our friends and funny events occurring during slumber parties and while scouting. I felt both naughty and relaxed with Drew. I decided not to sit right beside him but remained in the passenger seat.

At one point, I looked over at Drew and simply said, "I'm hoping this date clarifies some things for me." Arriving at the long lane of the drive-in, I read the marquee, Naughty Boy, Rated R. I pretended not to have noticed the title and continued on my conversation about my last slumber party.

Pulling into a designated row with a speaker box, Drew turned off the car engine. Turning toward me, he said, "Thanks for coming to the movies with me. I hope you find some answers. Don't worry. I'm not going to turn up the volume for the movie. How about I get us a soda and popcorn?" While he was at the refreshment stand, I nervously looked in the mirror and checked and double-checked my appearance. I squirted some breath mint in my mouth to refreshen my breath.

Before long, Cool Shades put the near-empty popcorn bag on the floorboard. He reached out and started softly kissing me. *Nice!* With the Supremes singing in the background on the radio, we kissed for several minutes. Somehow, I ended up with my upper body behind the steering wheel and my head covering smashed up against the window. Drew was partially on top of me and partially straddling the stick shift. The longer the kisses lasted, the heavier his breathing became. Just like John.

It wasn't exactly easy to forget about John with Drew's tongue in my mouth, but it all felt familiar. *I wonder if any other moviegoer is noticing the Mennonite head covering being smashed up against the window?*

At one point, Drew's hand started getting too close for comfort on my blouse where it did not belong. "Take me home, please." I sat up quickly. "Sorry," Drew mumbled and got out of the car on the passenger side. I moved out of the driver's seat and into the passenger seat as I straightened out my skirt. I reached back and felt my head covering was askew and practically falling off my head. *I lost one of my pins!*

"Please sit next to me driving home," Drew kindly asked me. "No one is going to see you. It's dark out." So I did. Unlike the drive into Columbia, the drive back into Ephrata was more subdued. We talked about the lyrics of songs on the radio and about the Beatles and the Beach Boys. More quiet filled the car than conversation.

Pulling up at the end of my driveway, Drew asked me, as I was getting out, "Did you get any answers?" Shrugging my shoulders, I ran up my nearly pitch black drive while holding my head covering in place with one hand. In my bedroom, I removed my head covering and examined it. How am I going to explain all these wrinkles to Mom? I snuck down the hall to the sewing room and picked up the iron. Using warm heat, I ironed my head covering on top of the bedcovers. This is the best I can do for now.

What if Daddy had allowed Cheryl and I to volunteer in Washington, DC, that summer when I was seventeen? The conversation about this between my dad and I impacted me greatly, and it was the final straw. The story goes: When I was seventeen and employed by Mennonite Central Committee (MCC), I was intrigued by the number of young adults who were entering into the mission field through MCC. Canadians selected the United States or overseas and Americans selected Canada and beyond as their mission fields. But all volunteers came for a two-week training session through the MCC headquarters in Akron. My eyes were opened to the world of missions.

Church publications frequently included a list of serving needs. My neighbor and friend, Cheryl, did not have a steady boyfriend. So she decided to consider applying for a short-term volunteer position she had read about, as a teacher's aide in Washington, DC. Not wanting to venture out alone, she asked if I would consider it so we could volunteer together. After spending that afternoon discussing the pros and cons, we became so excited about this opportunity. Why wouldn't it be God's will? Cheryl said she already had received *go* from her parents, and they were highly supportive. The next step was for me to get my parents' permission and blessing. Yes, it would be more difficult to put John and my relationship on hold. But I would deal with him later.

With a bounce in my step, I eagerly ran into the family room where Mom was glancing through the *Popular Plan* catalog, and Dad, his *Pennsylvania Game News*. Excited and talking way too fast, I threw at them, "Hey, Cheryl read about a volunteer position through MCC to assist teachers in Washington, DC. I would love to do this with her."

Before I could rattle on any further, Daddy, slapping closed the *Game News* on his lap, looked up at me and reprimanded, "No daughter of mine is going to go down to Washington, DC, to get raped, mugged, or robbed! You get that idea out of your head, or I will pound it out of your head!" Stunned with my mouth gaping open, I ran back into my bedroom. As I slammed the door, I yelled back, "Fine! Then I'm going to get married!"

The next morning, Mom woke me a littler earlier than usual and asked me to come out to the kitchen as Daddy wanted to say something. *Oh boy. This is not going to go away.* I sleepily put on my robe and dragged my feet as I walked down the long narrow hall into the brightly lit kitchen. Squinting, I sat down at the first available chair. Mom was scrambling eggs in the big black cast-iron skillet. She turned and looked at me. "Leanne, I could not sleep last night worrying about you two girls alone in DC. No way are you allowed to go." Just then, Daddy entered the kitchen through the front door. I saw his truck warming up in the driveway.

He drew in a big breath, gave me one quick glance but then kept looking down at his chair. "Leanne, there is no way I'm giving you permission to go to Washington. Have you gotten the idea out of your head yet?" I realized then, there were only a few times I heard my name in his mouth.

"Yes. I get it. We're not going. I gotta get ready for work." I got up and pushed my chair in and turned and walked toward the bathroom. I bet if I look back, I'd see them both vigorously rubbing their hands together in a that-settles-that fashion.

After dating from almost sixteen years old until our November 1971 wedding date, John and I dated for a little more than three years. Who takes the time to evaluate how your dating years will play out? Will you go steady with one particular guy? Will you play the field for a while? I know I certainly did not. I let the chips fall where they may. But I surely did not expect to be swept off my feet and land squarely on puppy love as quickly as we did. I truly figured *I would* be dating a new fella every couple of months. Sort of like dating Roy—easy come, easy go.

I learned all about this wavy hair, blue-eyed medium-brown handsome six-footer from Lucy. John and some other Lebanon

County friends showed up earlier that summer at her sister's slumber party. Lucy and John broke up by the end of summer when I was fifteen. John, a year older than me, received his brand-new green 1968 Chevy II for his sixteenth birthday—a thank you for being his parents' devoted farmhand for many years. He had wheels to drive down to Lancaster County and meet a prospective wife. Cheryl and I held a slumber party to celebrate the end of summer that September. On this date, "JOHN!!!" is written on the top of my diary page; the very next page reads "AGONY, PURE AGONY!" Looking back, it should have been an omen. Our relationship did not start out very well and certainly did not end well, as we divorced after twelve years of marriage.

In summary, John found out Lucy was hanging out with several other guys while supposedly going steady with him. Arriving at my and Cheryl's slumber party showing off his Chevy II, John invited us four girls for a ride in his car. Later on during the slumber party, he asked if I wanted to walk down to the local covered bridge while we discussed Lucy. It was slightly uncomfortable talking about my friend through the eyes of her previous boyfriend. I had no idea we would soon start dating. Around 1:00 p.m., John hugged me goodbye as he and his buddies left our slumber party.

The following Sunday evening, who showed up at the Twin Kiss? John! He asked to take me home, which he did. Using my kitchen phone, he called Lucy and held a thirty-minute phone conversation with her. While I was sitting in my parlor listening to records, John was breaking up with Lucy. He made Lucy promise she would not be mad at me. Later, I learned she begged him for a second chance.

Within five minutes after their conversation ended, my phone rang. Yep, it was Lucy bawling and yelling at me. I threw down the phone and asked John to speak to her; but he would not at that time. He asked me to tell Lucy he would talk to her later. By now, I am hurt and upset because Lucy was yelling at me and blaming me for their breaking up. Tears started to flow. In an attempt to comfort me, John gave me a hug and a short sweet kiss. *I guess this means he's my boyfriend.*

The following Tuesday, Lucy and three of her neighbor girlfriends stopped by at my house. She pretended the reason she was stopping in was to collect a picture I had of my previous boyfriend, Earl. Suddenly John, Johnny, Lester, and Marlin pulled into my driveway. *Horrors! I'm not dressed up enough to meet John.* I ran back into my bedroom and quickly changed my clothes. Again, John and Lucy talked together in my parlor while all the rest of us hung out in my front yard. After about fifteen minutes, Lucy came out and announced as she glanced my way, "I'll get over it, and we can go back to being friends, Leanne." She wiped her eyes with a tissue. That night I journaled, "I believe John and I are going together now, and with God's help, I'm never going to two-time him because I love him very much! Praying…"

Our first official date was September 14 on a bus trip to Bowery Mission in New York. We exchanged several kisses on our return trip. Since the cars were parked in the church parking lot, they were available for pranksters like Cheryl and Lucy. Bored (revenge for Lucy, perhaps?), they wrapped John's Chevy II with two rolls of green toilet paper. Before he left that evening and planted his last soft kiss on my lips, we planned a second date with his church youth group for another NYC bus trip to the Mission. After all, since I was not officially of dating age, bus trips to the Bowery Mission were the only events I was allowed to participate in according to Mom and Daddy.

The next weekend, I was invited to spend the night at Micky, Dave's sister's house. Her parents attended the same church where John attended. So I got to see him on Sunday morning. After church, a gang of us met at her house and planned a date to attend the Sunday evening church service. John drove me home. He walked me to the door. We kissed, and he hugged me tightly and said, "Leanne, I love you!" I died in his arms. I was shocked and did not know what to say to him. I simply responded, "You're the greatest." He said, "Goodnight, honey." Oh, dear. I'm shaking!

By Monday night, I felt a cold coming on; a sore throat and a headache plagued me. While trying to finish my homework, I shivered like a dog. Finishing up, I took some cold medicine and went to bed. As I tried to fall asleep, I kept hearing John's whisper of "I love you, Leanne," over and over again. Do I love him? How does he know he loves me so soon? I stayed home from school on Tuesday but knew I had to be well enough to go to school on Wednesday. Why? The Ephrata fair and parade was that night. My parents' rule was if you did not go to school, you do not run around that night either (a rule I also stuck to for my own children). As planned, Cheryl drove me to the Ephrata fair. We met up with John and some other friends. After a night of walking hand in hand, sharing some French fries, and going on some rides together, we parted. But not before John asked if we could meet again Saturday night in front of the Ferris wheel.

Saturday night is always a must-have-a-date for Ephrata fair. This was one of those occasions when guys would get the nerve to ask someone for a date to attend this fair, as it was one of the biggest fairs in Pennsylvania. Again, on Saturday night, Cheryl drove a carful of girls to the fair. Starting with a ride on the Ferris wheel, John and I hung out; I was proud to be holding his hand and to be noticed as John's girl. At the end of the night, he offered to drive me home (in my parents' mind, it was okay to be driven home one way, but a guy was not allowed to both pick me up and drive me home. That constituted a true date). Besides, I had not hit the official dating age of sixteen yet.

Right before John was walking to the door to say goodnight, he played the record "Beautiful People." He hugged and commented, "Leanne, you are so beautiful." I had to bend my head to look up into his eyes and answered, "We are so young, and we might not know what love really is." He simply pressed his lips on mine. As the song ended, he opened the door and left.

As my older siblings left home and married, Mom became less busy. She showed an interest in a new hobby: decorating cakes. Celebrating birthdays (finally!) and serving a cake at birthday parties was one avenue for Mom to show off her handiwork. Dad was more than happy to take pictures of the four-tiered white cake with red rosebuds skimming the edge of each layer. My sister-in-law, Linda, was the first to hold a surprise party in our family when Elvin turned eighteen. That event started a tradition for my parents to hold a surprise sixteenth birthday party, starting with my sister, Lenora. Keeping the secret about the date, sending out invitations (after spending time on the phone getting addresses from her girlfriends), and giving the house and yard an extra spit-and-shine routine, the long anticipated day came. Lenora was totally surprised when she walked into our parlor thinking she was retrieving her friend's forgotten pocketbook. The *surprise* yelled at her from a gang of about twenty friends would give one a heart attack! I sat through watching another sibling, Matt, be surprised over his sixteenth birthday party. Mom smartly held it a few weeks before his actual birthdate.

However, I was determined no one was going to be successful and pull the wool over my eyes when it was my turn a year and a half later. I would feign any surprise for Mom's sake. I figured I would pay close attention to any unexpected reasons to leave my home or enter my parlor during any time close to my sixteenth birthday. Guess what? They did it! Because Mom held it on a Tuesday night, I was totally unprepared for a birthday party. A friend I had not seen in months was the one who stopped by and asked me to go shopping. Around eight o'clock, we returned back home. Innocently, I walked right through the parlor front door, expecting to play for my friend the latest record I recently purchased. Having this song on my mind, I turned ghostly white the minute I saw light bulb flashes and heard yells of *surprise* from a group of sixty-four family and friends. Standing smack up front in the middle, John stood beaming.

How exciting to open up so many gifts! John gave me the softest brown leather gloves. All my girlfriends joked about having the chance to see their cute boyfriends during the week—an extra date. Everyone raved how Mom's cake looked professionally decorated. My parents informed me they purchased a new floor-model stereo "for the whole family. But since you're dating and using the parlor now, you'll get the most use from it." Boy, did I ever! While cleaning, sewing, doing homework, canning, freezing, and other indoor chores, I spun my favorite 33 1/3 rpm record albums over and over again. Some became so scratched and caused the needle to jump and skip lyrics. Behind closed parlor doors, my friends and I would do the twist and the jerk to our heart's content. The FM radio cranked out oldies so loudly, Daddy called it "racket." Of course, when Daddy was home, the volume was turned way down. Because I did not hear my parents come home and failed to turn down the radio, many times I was scolded for listening to such racket.

Eventually, my new stereo was the perfect spot to display my big senior class picture. John had his picture taken professionally when he turned eighteen because he did not graduate and had no senior picture. It flanked the other side. My parents enjoyed the stereo for over ten years until it spun its last record and played its last tune. But, until then, after arriving home with a date, I stacked four albums on the stereo to softly play as ambience and background music while smooching on the sofa. By the time Leslie Gore belted out the last song, it was time for my boyfriend to leave. Most times, not.

John and I dated every Saturday and Sunday night. Friday nights were spent mostly working at Cinderella or with girlfriends. The first weekend after my birthday, John pulled back from kissing me.

"Leanne, it is very important to me that I marry a virgin," he proposed. "I think it would please God too." I lovingly smiled at him and said determinedly, "Well, I want to be a virgin too. We can both make it happen." Having only kissing and touching be our only methods of expression, our kisses were so forceful at times my lips hurt by the time I visited My Friend, My Pillow.

By Christmas, John and I were regularly calling each other honey. We exchanged the exact same Christmas card (A Christmas Wish for You, Sweetheart) that year. Of course, we started out with both of us sitting up on the sofa facing each other. One night, I walked in from retrieving some snacks from the refrigerator and found John lying face up sleeping on the floor. Of course, my kissing him woke him up. The sitting-up-only days ended. Because John had to rise early to milk cows, he often fell asleep on the sofa while I studied and finished homework. But there were also plenty of times to misbehave. By the year's end at sixteen, John was talking regularly about me being his future wife someday.

Being around other Mennonite friends who were "behaving," attending church services about the Christian view of sex, reading a book titled *Why Wait 'til Marriage,* and simply trying to honor John's wish spurred us on to not indulge our desires. Sometimes we purposefully stayed late at our friends' house so John was forced to leave within fifteen minutes of dropping me off. Such planning and scheming to behave!

By our sixth month of dating, passionate kissing led to other misbehaving. My diary is full of prayers to God for guidance, for His will, and many outpourings of devotion for John. That spring, I was invited to go on a bus trip with MCC's mission field volunteers down to Washington, DC. Guys outnumbered the girls two to one. Their world of being raised Mennonite in Canada or Indiana was so different than my Lancaster County one. On the return trip, a cute guy, Lowell, asked if I wanted to sit with him to continue his stories about his upbringing. So I did. *I'm not misbehaving, John. It's only a bus trip!* By the time I crawled into bed, I decided on three things: (1) I am too young to be talking about being anyone's wife, (2) we'll never be able to keep our paws off each other for three years until I'm nineteen (an age I determined was old enough, since Lenora got married at barely eighteen), and (3) the only solution was to break up with John next Saturday night. I shed a few tears before I fell asleep thinking how shocked and hurt John would be; a sense of peace finally lulled me to sleep. *Darcy will be so proud when she learns I ended it.*

On Saturday afternoon, I was laundering my hand washables in the bathroom sink. Mom entered carrying a pile of bath towels. "Mom," I sighed, "what do I know about love at sixteen? Aren't I too young to be going steady? I'm breaking up with John tonight."

After placing the towels on the shelf, she turned toward me. "But I thought you said you love John."

"Mom, what's love? I can't keep him from touching me all over. We'll never going to make it and keep behaving for three more years," I said, exasperated.

Mom put her hand on one hip. "Well, John's a whole year older than you. Boys have needs." Just then, the kitchen phone rang, and she turned around to answer it. From the hall, she concluded, "When I met your Daddy, I just knew I loved him, and that was the end of that." *Hmmm, Mom recognizes the problem but has no solution. She thinks I'm wrong in breaking up?*

That night, John and I attended his cousin's bridal shower. The night seemed to drag. Even though on the way home I continued to sit in the middle of the car seat next to John, I am sure he sensed I was somewhat distant. As soon as we entered the parlor, without bothering to play my stereo, I asked him to sit down on the sofa. For the next fifteen minutes, I went on to explain I think I (can't speak for him) am too young to be going steady. It does not sit well with me to only date one person and go right into marriage.

John immediately teared up and started apologizing about any misbehaving. He grabbed both my hands and promised it would only be kissing and hugging from then on if that would make me happy.

"No, John. It's not that. I don't want to only date you. I shouldn't have to feel guilty wanting not to date only one boy. If it is meant to be, we'll get back together," I explained. Once my mind is made up, there is no changing it. I apologized, walked to the door, and held it open. "Go date around too" I suggested. He reached down and tilted my head back for a short peck before the parlor door closed behind him.

Before I walked back into my bedroom, I telephoned Cheryl, who was not dating anyone at the time. "Hey, girlfriend," I said. "I'm free next Saturday night, next Sunday night, and the next weekend after that. Whatcha' doin'?" I asked. She yelled. "What? Did you break up with John?" After she heard my short explanation, Cheryl chuckled, "Of course, you're too young. Good for you."

My summer included dating a few Brethren guys for several dates each (I believe it was important they marry someone of their own faith). Meeting a new circle of their friends was fun. But I could not get use to not knowing how my weekends would end. The unknown was more daunting than the familiarity of dating John, misbehaving or not. The most fun was dating Roy that summer. But it was not in the cards for us to go steady. Many guys who were almost eighteen were already going steady with their future wives. Helping Mom can seventy-four quarts of peaches kept me busy. By this time, Daddy had bought Doug a new puppy he named Dusty. My sister Lenora had a miscarriage. Mom drove me up to Williamsport so I could be her "maid" for two weeks. Lenora spent many hours confirming I need to date more than one fish in the sea.

Time spent with girlfriends was surely stress-free without worrying about going too far. But I missed hearing sweet nothings, sharing soft kisses, and simply holding John's warm calloused hands. Cheryl and Lillian did their best to keep me preoccupied bowling, taking long walks, going to church or school plays, and scouting other dating couples. Plenty of guys came around to take us for a ride, but they were already going steady.

That summer, I took my first puffs—four total—on a cigarette while carousing in Earl's car. Why? I wanted to see what all the thrill was about. For a short time, Esther secretly smoked in her car. I noticed John holding a lit cigarette one night when I unexpectedly walked up to him and his circle of friends at Green Dragon. What? A smoker? Bad boy! John proceeded to discreetly drop it and crushed it under his feet. *Too late, I already noticed.* I am uncertain how long John actually smoked Camel cigarettes. But by the time we were going steady, he could tell being a smoker was a deal breaker for me; this Mennonite girl was not going to be that rebellious.

Between birthday parties and slumber parties, my calendar was full enough. My favorite slumber party was staying over at Micky's house. It was common among teenaged girls that we would exchange outfits and wear them for a few weeks before returning them. For church, Micky styled my hair completely different and placed her smaller-sized covering on my head. She allowed me to keep it. As soon as I got home, I showed Mom my new hairstyle and begged her to take me covering shopping Monday night to purchase smaller coverings. Once granted permission, there was no going back. Not only did she purchase me a smaller head covering, but she took me to her friend who thinned out my hair again. Now it was much easier to handle my long hair in this new hairstyle called wearing your hair out.

MY LAST LAST NAME IS GRACE

One October Saturday night, Lillian and I walked into my friend, Ida's (nicknamed Pokey—wouldn't you want a nickname if you were an Ida?) house for a slumber party. John's six-foot frame was leaning against the far wall facing the door. Within seconds, I heard several whispers, "John's here alone…Leanne, John's here…hey…did you know John's here?"

By the time we were playing games, our entire group of friends saw to it we either sat beside each other or were pushed into the same corner, sitting beside one another while eating cake and ice cream. Walk-a-mile ended the evening, giving us opportunity to hold hands and spend time alone as we lagged behind on the walk. By the end of the evening, John asked me for a date the following Saturday night. My yes was as easy as low-hanging fruit. I felt a longing inside I immediately could not name. But as months turned into years, I named it love.

The following Saturday night, I took a deep breath, and ran full tilt into his arms literally and figuratively. As spring is a sign that winter's dormancy is over, our connection was strong and sure. John cherished me, smothered me with kisses, and continued whispers in my ear that moved me. He was as dependable and reliable as a seatbelt. I decided to latch on to his love and accept the future, come what may. One month from my seventeenth birthday, we were back to going steady.

Shortly after we were back together, my brother, Junior, thought he was being hilarious. At the breakfast table one Sunday in between his bites of bacon and eggs, he glanced at Daddy, then me, and asked, "Hey, Leanne." He smirked. "Didn't I see you carrying your panty hose down the hall toward your bedroom last night?"

My fork dropped on my plate of half-eaten eggs and toast. "What? No," I said with a puzzled look. "You know you didn't. I can easily see the front door when leaving the parlor. Wouldn't you think I would see you coming in the front door?" He just laughed and laughed. Daddy just shook his head and smiled. Mom scolded, "Now, Junior." Boys have needs, right?

The times when I was weak during petting sessions, John would be the strong one to honor our commitment. When he was the weak one desiring to go all the way, then I was the strong one. Vacillating, we struggled through our dates, not unlike other couples with the same goal of remaining virgins. Being a dairy farmer and having to get up at 5:00 a.m. daily, John was often so tired sometimes that when he would lie down on the couch, he'd fall asleep. On those nights, the struggle would lessen.

By February, after my eighteenth birthday, we planned to announce our engagement at Easter. As typical for Mennonite couples, you selected a favorite spot for someone to take your photograph, which was used in your engagement announcement. John and I selected the beautiful Poconos' Bushkills Falls as our backdrop. Nancy and Roy joined us for our milestone photography shot. We stood standing on a wooden bridge facing each other, smiling, while holding each other's two hands, as Roy took several pictures. As the power of the waterfalls sprayed slightly over us, our love for one another was spilling over.

Thought of the Day

Grace is understanding that as we live by correct priorities and cultivate our relationship with Christ on a daily basis, we will begin to experience a great joy resulting from a sense of security that we belong to God, the One in control of our lives.

Chapter 23

Planning a Wedding at Eighteen

> For your Maker is your husband—the Lord Almighty is his name—the Holy One of Israel is your Redeemer; he is called the God of all the earth. The Lord will call you back as you were a wife deserted and distressed in spirit—a wife who married young, only to be rejected says your God. For a brief moment I abandoned you, but with deep compassion I will bring you back.
> —Isaiah 54:5–7

ONCE ENGAGED, I WAS ALLOWED to have a date on Wednesday nights as well as on Saturday and Sunday nights. I have always said the reason we did not go all the way while dating was for two reasons: (1) I promised John I would be a virgin on our honeymoon night. Somehow in my mind it would be my fault if we did not meet our goal, and (2) having six older brothers or sisters having been through the dating regimen, and neither of them had to get married, I was not going to be the first Martin sibling to be the one to have to make a public church confession either. So I had great motivation. Besides, if we made it through two-and-one-half years, we can make it through six more months. Darcy, my factory-neighbor, wasn't too pleased I chose to go back to dating only John (of course, she did attend our wedding and gave us both encouragement to "make it work, guys").

Since John lived a county away, phone calls in between dates were few and far in-between and needed to have a purpose, not to just say *Hi*. Besides, they cost money. Even though I thoroughly enjoyed my job as Nevin Hostestter's secretary, I lived for Wednesday nights and weekends. In fact, I prayed God would hold off on His return for a few more months until John and I consummated our marriage.

Mid-March, John finally received his farm deferment from the government. During the Vietnam War, qualified young men could seek deferments if they could prove extreme hardship for dependents, if drafted. In John's case, he was needed to run his family farm, as his father was unable to do so. Only then could we plan a wedding date. We selected Saturday, November 20, eight months and four days away! My diary pages that year were marked up with a bold countdown from the twentieth of each month and from each Saturday date, such as "only twenty-four more Saturday nights, and we'll be on our honeymoon!"

In between my wedding plans, attending friends' bridal showers, and being a bridesmaid in weddings and freezing and canning produce for my own freezer kept me busy. However, I documented several incidents that year, which are noteworthy:

* I scolded John for calling someone a "b&%@+!".
* I wrote letters to cousin Jill, when she lived in the home for unwed mothers.
* During the week of Daddy's forty-eighth birthday, he required back surgery. I had to babysit Doug so Mom could visit him in the hospital. During his recuperation at home, Mom planned a song service (Martindale youth group sang hymns) at our house.
* John and I had our first disagreement over furniture selection. He wanted to purchase a dining set without my looking at it first.
* Two Corning glass cookware sets I was planning on giving as shower gifts for friends were stolen out of my car.
* My niece Karla Jean was born August 11.
* I embroidered a set of pillowcases (one and only sewing project of its kind).

* Saw Johnny Cash and June Carter at Allentown fair (what couple full of lust can't relate to the "Ring of Fire" song?).
* I clerked at Grandma Martin's public sale.
* My heavy monthly "granny" with bad cramps started by September to the point I almost fainted twice (more on this in a later chapter). One day when I was baking a chocolate cake to serve John as refreshments at the end of our weekend date, Mom reminded me, "Don't forget, your Grandma Fisher used to say that you are never to bake when you have your monthly. Your cakes will flop." Then she chuckled. "Of course, I never believed that."

Our weekend dates included enough church services and other avenues to keep us convicted to behave. Attending summer Bible school, "Youth Congress" events, which lectured about "The Holy Spirit Movement," or a Sunday evening church service topic of "The Second Coming of Christ," viewing of the film *The Cross and the Switchblade*, and MCC's guest speakers from time to time kept petting at bay. One night, my neighbor Polly invited John and I over to watch a TV program called *Billy Graham Crusade*. That night, John commented, "I'm so glad you are a virgin. You don't know what that means to me." Only forty-eight days to go!

At the local Provident bookstore, I purchased the book *Everything You Wanted to Know About Sex, but Were Afraid to Ask*. Honey, I can't wait until we can do what I'm reading about! My neighbor Polly educated me about the best birth control options. I selected the pill. I ended up getting my first packet less than a month away from my wedding night from my family doctor. I waited until my physical and blood tests to get my first packet of pills. Oops! I had to add another birth control method for extra protection. We were sorely tested when five unmarried couples went down to Ship Bottom for a beach weekend. The married chaperoned couple directed girls to sleep in the loft area, while the guys crashed in the two bunk rooms. Nothing like having your honey wake you up with a kiss and serve you breakfast!

I was wise enough to host a last beach week with some girlfriends in the summer of '71. But I missed John so much I could barely stand it. Our first date back together was rough. I journaled: "How can I say 'no' to roaming hands, kisses so sweet, and a passionate, demanding body that longs for me? I look into his beautiful deep blue eyes that plead for me, and his sweet murmurs are hard to resist. We both fell asleep on the couch and didn't wake up until 3:10 a.m. Yikes. Engaged or not, Mom will be mad."

Even though we were dating for years, my home was still a target for "scouters," mostly because John's two buddies were bored and simply stopped in to talk.

My dental checkup revealed two items requiring attention: I needed to have two cavities filled. Plus, my left front tooth was darkening, making my two front teeth unmatched. He inquired if I had had any recent injury. Does hearty French kissing cause damage? I had no idea what possibly could have been the cause. Mom agreed she will pay for my tooth to be crowned. After all, a bride should not be smiling for wedding photographs with a gray front tooth.

I paid for the two cavities to be filled costing me $15. At this time, I came up with a plan. The following evening at the supper table, I presented it to Mom and Daddy.

"Hey, giving you guys half of my paycheck, plus supporting myself is leaving me little money to put in my checking account. I can't possibly pay for my wedding and help John pay for some furniture with my leftover paycheck. Can I keep all of it?" I inquired.

Daddy slurped noisily on his water and looked across the table for Mom to answer me. "Well, we need to keep things fair. You write down what amount you would be handing over and pay us back later after you're married," Mom said as she got up and started clearing the table. God forbid things aren't kept fair!

I had no idea what wedding expenses Lenora ended up paying for, nor could I remember her purchasing any furniture. I was fourteen when I served as a gift receiver in her wedding. Because she moved 120 miles away, their apartment furniture was purchased after their wedding date. My sister-in-law also sewed Lenora's white satin cape dress and a matching shirt for the groom.

My older brothers had full-time jobs since they were sixteen. Because I graduated from high school, I was the only sibling to have less working hours under my belt.

It's interesting to read the cost of items during the early '70s:

> Fifty engagement announcements, $12.00
> Easter-engagement dress, 23
> Used dining set, 218
> Used bedroom set, 280
> Living room sofa and chair, 295
> Two end tables, 29
> Carpet, 200
> Stove, 229
> Refrigerator, 259
> Wedding gown and veil, 50
> Wedding shoes, 7
> Fall bridal party flowers, 96
> Cost of quartet, 25

Wednesday date nights were spent searching for the perfect wedding invitation, wedding book, napkins, and reception table centerpieces. After all, it would have been difficult to do all that planning on Saturdays, as most stores back then were not open on Sundays.

I helped Mom freeze strawberries and corn for my own freezer. John's mom put up peas for us. I also canned twenty-three quarts of peaches without Mom's assistance too. I had to prove to John that I was a good cook (like a good Mennonite girl should be able to do). How does one do that? Several times that fall, I invited John over for supper on a Saturday night or a Sunday lunch and served him a meal that I cooked all by myself with no help from Mom.

I was totally surprised the night of my August bridal shower because it was not held on a weekend, but on an unexpected Monday night. My friend Nancy, who was marrying in December, asked me to be a bridesmaid. On this particular night, she asked me to stop by to pick out material for her bridesmaids. The roar of *shower* was totally unexpected. John said I was the lightest-complexioned he had ever seen on me. I confiscated a corner in Mom's attic for all our lovely useful household products shower gifts until I moved them into our home. I can't wait to use my cookbook and cook meals for my sweetie.

John's parents bought their farm in the 1940s for $8,000. The ten-room farmhouse was built in 1864, the date proudly displayed on the side of the house, which faced the driveway. It was partly gray stone and white siding. A cement front porch graced the entire length of the house. A small side, entrance porch led into a kitchen, which was remodeled in the 1950s. When they had to move out of their homestead for John and I to move in, they purchased a two-story red-brick home in Schaefferstown. What a switch to no longer hear mooing cows but cars traveling on Route 502 directly in front of their home. As exciting as it was for me to visualize our furniture in our "new" home, his parents had fun downsizing.

I knew immediately I wanted to drop my Martindale church membership and become a member of John's less conservative Indiantown Mennonite church. Being allowed to marry in this church meant I could do things a little differently than what the Martindale bishop would allow for my wedding. Of course, his church leadership accepted my church membership transfer.

About the same time we were addressing our 254 wedding invitations, John and I met with our bishop, Lester, to review wedding details and expectations. I'll start with the yeses: the bride may wear white shoes and a floor-length gown, the bridal party may carry bouquet of flowers, and the church benches may be decorated with bows.

Nos: the bridal party may not stand during the entire sermon; eight folding chairs will be placed in front of the altar; no decorating the cars on church property, and no sacrilegious music may be played at the fire hall during our wedding reception. It was understood there would be no exchange of wedding rings, nor was my father walking me down the aisle. My submitted list of wedding songs the quartet would be singing was reviewed and approved.

My only disappointment was not being allowed to stand during the wedding ceremony. However, being allowed a gown that reached to my shoe tips was a plus. John had no opinion and left the planning up to me. His only job was to assure his Chevy II was ready for our Florida road trip for our honeymoon.

Our weekend dates in November were spent folding wedding bulletins and napkins, addressing thank-you notes and frequently reviewing my detailed to-do list. Mennonites did not practice the tradition of the groom's parents paying for a dinner for the bridal party and family after the wedding rehearsal. The bride's and groom's parents did split the cost of the wedding reception, which we selected the New Holland fire hall. Since I was a secretary, I typed and mimeographed our church bulletins.

My beautiful wedding dress was purchased at JC Penney using the layaway plan. It was an A-line gown with lace bodice and sleeves with pointed cuffs. It featured a lace scalloped stand-up collar and had an (added) satin bow on the back. It included a beautiful scalloped-edge veil. Having no use for it (my head covering was my veil), the veil was cut up and turned into a lacy covering for a satin bow and attached to the back of my dress at my waist. What a difference in Lenora's and my wedding gown! My sister-in-law Linda was also my great inexpensive seamstress. She turned dark-chocolate velvet material into beautiful gowns for my bridesmaids. The bodice was tan lace, which complemented it very nicely. My receptionist's and gift receivers' velvet dresses were made of the same soft material, but in gold, cranberry, and green. Mom and John's mom both wore handmade navy blue dresses.

The second most fun in my wedding preparations was selecting my wedding flowers. Fall colors filled our cascade-style bouquets. I carried a cascade of white mums and pompons with orange sweetheart roses, ivy, and croton foliage. Cheryl, Nancy, and Lorna carried cascades of yellow mums and yellow and bronze pompons. The men's corsages were gold and rust pompons; John's was, naturally, white. How stunning the gowns and flowers will look together!

Once my gown hung in my closet, I could not keep my fingers off it. I would try it on and retry it on. I can't wait to wear this on my big day! "Leanne," Mom scolded, as she noticed me again standing in front of the full-length mirror right outside my bedroom. "Take it off. You'll have it ruined before your big day." That night, I dreamt I could not find my glasses on my wedding day. As I was getting dressed, I tore my wedding dress with my heel.

Since I was doing most of the work planning for my wedding, Mom had time to put in a quilt the end of October. The only time Mom went with me was when I went to Achenbach's and ordered the wedding cake because she paid that bill.

My November diary entries read: "applied for marriage license… purchased a camera for my birthday for our honeymoon…I turned 19!....started packing for my honeymoon....I won a carry-all at a bingo game....Lucy called from Texas to wish us a happy marriage… we went to a different church the Sunday morning our wedding date was to be announced over the pulpit…last day at work as a single woman, Leanne Martin…beginning of a twelve-day vacation…John brought a pickup truck to load up our shower gifts to take to our home…our kitchen linoleum was laid today…I pressed my wedding gown one last time and Linda pressed the bridesmaid's dresses…finished packing for my honeymoon…"

Tick, tock, tick, tock—I can't believe it, our wedding day is almost here!

Then on November 18, two days before our wedding, Lorna asked me to return a call to the Ephrata Flower Boutique to finalize my flower order. Say what? I walked in his shop four months ago and discussed possibly using them as my florist.

With a racing heartbeat, I dialed the number. For the next five minutes, I was cussed and yelled at. I was shocked! (This was my first encounter of someone swearing at me.) My stomach lurched as I sat down on a chair. I tried to explain he should have had a clue that I had not selected his floral shop since he had not heard from me for several months. What bride waits until two days before her wedding day to finalize flower choices? The owner continued to tell me he was looking at an order from a discussion we had earlier. Slam—he hung up on me. For the first time during all of my wedding plans, I burst into tears. I shook while I dialed Nancy's phone number to tell her about my upsetting phone call and how the man was so angry, he swore at me.

My friend, Sara's brother, was in a quartet and was frequently booked for evening church services and events. It was an easy choice to have his group scheduled to sing at our wedding. Rehearsal night finally arrived; all went off without a hitch. The quartet's male voices blended beautifully and had a chance to practice five times before I was satisfied with the results of the bridal party's timing in walking down the aisle. The fire hall was decorated by my florist by Friday night. My last night to sleep by myself as a single girl.

November 20 finally arrived. Yipee! I awoke at 6:30 a.m. and soon left for the church with all my stuff for our 10:00 a.m. wedding. It was a cloudy day; though it never rained. My honey said I was the most beautiful bride ever! The girls looked great, and the flowers were gorgeous. I cried while being congratulated. Burt, the MCC photographer, captured lots of photographs (some posed, some not). After the ceremony, we drove to Miller's Studio to have pictures taken professionally. We were a little late in arriving to the fire hall for the noon meal. My friend Sharon played background music on the piano during the reception. Around two hundred guests enjoyed ham, mashed potatoes, ham gravy, peas, potato, and macaroni salad. Of course, white wedding cake with vanilla ice cream was dessert. Yum! The clinging of the glasses, a signal John and I were to kiss, made it difficult to consume our meal without interruptions.

By 3:30 p.m., we had changed into our going-away clothes in my bedroom (yes that felt strange), and we headed to Hunt Valley Inn in Cockeysville, Maryland. The hotel room cost $30—a little pricey because the inn was less than a year old. I suggested we get a bite to eat at Burger Chef, a fast-food restaurant across the street, before retiring for the night. "If you insist," John joked as he looked at me with starry eyes, "you're really thinking about food?"

In spite of stalling until it was darker outside, I realized 6:15 p.m. was bedtime and entered our honeymoon suite. John loved my negligee showing a big red heart with *I love you* written inside it. Well, what a night for Mr. and Mrs. John Weaver!! Between 6:15 p.m. and 10:00 a.m., we made love x times (Hmmm, none of your business). But later on, when discussing my honeymoon with some close girl-friends, one jeered, "Doesn't that border on sex abuse?" I laughed, rolled over onto my bed, and held my stomach in remembrance. "Let's just say this Mrs. Weaver slowly walked out of the motel the next morning. John said if you divide the honeymoon suite cost by the number of times we made love, it is a single digit number—and it was all worth it."

Sunday morning, after a good hearty breakfast at Schrafts, we started our trek to Disney World in Orlando, Florida. The clothing rod hung across our back seat and made it easy to select our desired wardrobes before entering the three different hotels we slept in before we arrived at Cape Kennedy. The average hotel cost was $14, and some mattresses, we soon learned, were lumpier than others. However, tired lovers fall to sleep pretty quickly, lumpy mattresses or not.

By Wednesday, I called home to check in. It was fun to report to Lorna and my parents on Marineland, Cape Kennedy, Vero Beach, and Lion Safari at West Palm Beach. John learned I love bubble baths, as I spent some time soaking in different-sized hotel tubs. We joked about how this would have been a date night for us. "No more stopping me from going too far, Mrs. Weaver," he chided. I learned I am often interrupted by John in the mornings when I am busy getting dressed. After donning a blouse, he wants to take it off!

Thursday was Thanksgiving and spent at Parrot Jungle, Monkey Jungle and a drive down to the Everglades. A mom-and-pop diner was open to serve us the traditional turkey dinner. Friday was spent touring Cypress Gardens (where we planned to meet up with friends of ours who got married the same day) and the Citrus

Tower. Not surprisingly, I journaled, "Too tired to make love. We watched TV instead."

On Saturday, married one whole week, mister and missus spent all day at Disney World taking in the Haunted Mansion, 360 Screen, Bear Jamboree, and went on several rides. That night, we drove to Ocala to be closer to Silver Springs by Sunday. We took in Six Gun Territory, including a glass-bottom boat ride.

Not only was it enjoyable to be on my first ten-day vacation with a husband, but I removed my head covering and allowed my long hair to flow freely. A few pictures were taken with my head covering, which would be displayed in my honeymoon photo album for both sets of parents and family to view. But a few pictures with my hair down were kept in a bottom nightstand drawer.

Guess what? On day ten, John and I had our first misunderstanding (no clue exactly what about) and our need to make up. Fun! John allowed me to drive his Chevy II (after all, I was planning on driving it to work every weekday), and I drove 230 miles through the rest of Florida, Georgia, South Carolina, and most of North Carolina. That night, I journaled "sick of TV already so we just went to bed early to…"

I was anxious to get home, pick up our wedding gifts at my parents' house, which were still piled in my…oops, I guess I now need to say, Lorna's parlor. I was anxious to open up our gifts one by one and put them away in our kitchen cupboards or bathroom closet.

"November 30: home! We slept in John's old bed. Seemed silly—at least, it's legal. His parents are moving out tomorrow, as they had to do the farmwork in our absence. We had the best honeymoon two people could have had. I'm looking forward to doing life together. Lord, thanks! Most of all, I got the "tuffest," sweetest, dearest, sexiest, and best husband in the whole world" was journaled.

Only three days in the beginning of December had entries in my diary: "Our first grocery bill was $40 to stock the kitchen…I cooked my husband his first supper…did all the laundry from our honeymoon…hung new curtains.…I overslept, but made it in time for breakfast.…Lord guide us." The remaining pages were empty.

The honeymoon came to an end, and busy routine days turned into routine weeks, then months. I attempted to keep juggling all my balls as a newlywed, trying to impress my husband on my ability to put supper on the table after arriving home from my full-time secretarial job, grocery shopping, laundry, and ironing. My organizational skills were put to the test. I strived and accomplished.

I had my housework schedule down to a science, but when summer arrived, I needed to add gardening, canning, and freezing food. So, for obvious reasons, my diary entries stopped for about a year. Keeping a husband happy and satisfied led to lights out and no time for end-of-day diary entries, I suppose.

As a couple, we now attended church together on a regular basis and became members of the "young marrieds" Sunday school class and formed new friendships. Cinderella continued to love her prince charming and performed her wifely duties as she witnessed her mom do for her prince charming. But one day, Cinderella's prince charming broke her heart—something she never witnessed her daddy do toward her mother.

About six weeks into our wedded bliss, Lebanon County experienced a severe snowstorm. The potential consequence of a snowstorm can be worse for dairy farmers. Milk is stored after each milking in a huge stainless steel milk tank. A tractor trailer truck is scheduled routinely every two days to pick up the dairy farmers' milk supply. The milk tank must be emptied to make room for more milk that would be added each morning and evening. A blinding snowstorm, making driving treacherous, and the impossibility of following a pickup schedule or even the driver being late, could be serious.

I was in the kitchen doing my chores when the phone rang, sounding the neighbor's party line ring. (Back then, phone lines were called party lines because up to three people were on the same line. The difference was the amount of rings. One would have two short rings or one long and one short ring, for example.) I saw John walk over to the phone, pick it up, and eavesdrop on our neighbor's phone call. He was not saying anything, just listening in.

MY LAST LAST NAME IS GRACE

No one in my family ever listened in on our neighbor's conversation; I looked at him totally puzzled. When he turned his back to me and continued to listen in, I said, "Hey, hang up the phone." His ignoring me was troublesome. Appalled, I decided to talk louder, "Get off the phone."

John turned around, slammed the phone down, and with the reddest face I ever saw him have, yelled at me, "You b&¢$#*! I was trying to find out if and when the milk truck driver was going to arrive in this area."

I stopped what I was doing, ran through the living room, and up the front stairs to our bedroom. (The usual way I took to go upstairs would have had me passing John.) Throwing myself across the bed, I burst into tears. Of course, John was experiencing his own anxiety related to our livelihood (milk production). He apologized for swearing at me and proceeded to explain the purpose of his eavesdropping. Accepting his apology, I reminded him, "I have *never ever* heard my daddy raise his voice to my mom, let alone swear at her! I'm just shocked." Later on, the snowstorm gave opportunity not just for snuggle time; in our case, it was needed for make-up sex.

Just as icing has only one main purpose, open, honest communication between two people can be sweet and the icing on the cake. Since God did not design us to have the ability to read each other's minds, communication is a powerful tool, a way of staying connected, and needs to be made a priority of any successful marriage.

Our tower of love started leaning just slightly off-center.

Thought of the Day

Bestow grace by recognizing a husband is 98 percent lover and spouse and 2 percent irritant. God designed marriage as an institution to live under grace and love.

Chapter 24

Teaching in a Two-Room Parochial School

And this is my prayer: that your love may abound more and more in knowledge and depth of insight, so that you may be able to discern what is best and may be pure and blameless until the day of Christ.
—Philippians 1:9–10

Author at 19 years old

MY JOB IMMEDIATELY FOLLOWING MY high school graduation in 1970 was a supervisor for the central stenographic services department (information services) at Mennonite Central Committee (MCC) in Akron, Pennsylvania. MCC's office layout was designed so that executives' desks sat along the windows, while their secretary's desk was located in the middle of the room facing their boss. Several MCC executives did not have their own personal secretary. Thus, their letters of dictation or typing needs were completed by the central information services' secretaries.

My business English courses in high school and becoming a member of the "Future Business Leaders of America" acted as a springboard to my career. I became an organized, efficient secretary. I could type at a decent words-per-minute speed and was particular about turning in to the executive dictated letters with little or no white-out marks (correction fluid for typists using typewriters before word processors), minimal spelling, grammar, or punctuation errors. My organizational skills helped me keep my workload manageable and to have a tidy desk at all times.

I was thrilled when I walked in to the office first thing in the morning and noticed my desk was piled high with up to nine dictation folders, which an executive laid on my desk sometime prior to my arrival. My coworker Carol would see her desk piled high with dictation work and would groan. Setting priorities became important and quite easy for me. Being enthusiastic, having a great work ethic, being dependable, and a desire for a career path (however limited it was), I was soon promoted from the information services department to become the private secretary for Mennonite Disaster Services' executive, Nevin Hostetter. What an amazing Christian man and boss! I would have been content remaining in this position for several years until I became a stay-at-home mom.

However, one early August evening, my mother-in-law phoned me. I could tell she was so excited to pass on to me the conversation she and her Mennonite friends had that afternoon while quilting. "Leanne, Mrs. Allen Zimmerman said that they are still looking for a teacher at Cedar Cove School. School starts on August 30 for teachers, and they need a teacher, quick. I've told her that you graduated from high school, and I suggested that you could do it. Give Allen a call at 555-2810."

"But," I explained to her, "I've said that I'm intrigued by two-room parochial schools. It doesn't mean I think I should teach at one just because I graduated!"

Well, the conversation over the supper table that night was about my possibility of switching careers. My husband basically said that, yes, he thought I could handle it. He would rather have less mileage wracked up on his '68 Chevy II with a five-day-a-week, twelve-mile-round-trip to Cedar Cove School opposed to the thirty-mile round-trip to Akron (in a different county).

So thanks to the sparing of the '68 Chevy II's heavier engine use, tires, and desiring lesser odometer readings, and some confidence shown in me, I called Mr. Zimmerman. Before I knew it, a date and time was set for him and me to meet at Cedar Cove School. I pulled into a wide gravel driveway in front of a fairly new white rectangular building with a green roof. A cement porch with porch posts, almost the length of the dwelling, led into two different doors. To the left was the entrance into grades one to four. To the right was the entrance for grades five to eight. Lots of sunlight greeted us when we stepped into the wooden-floor room. Four neat rows of brown wooden desks were arranged in the classroom facing a gray metal teacher's desk. Behind the teacher's desk ran a blackboard mostly filling up the entire back wall space. A cursive A-B-C poster rested on top of the blackboard. I got a whiff of chalk. I love the smell of a freshly cleared chalkboard. *On that basis alone, I'll take the job, Mr. Zimmerman.*

Mr. Zimmerman gave me a building tour and explained the dwelling was only two years old. It was governed by a school board of fellow "Black Bumper" or Horning Mennonite men, who lived nearby in the same school district. Having separate indoor bathrooms for both boys and girls proved to be a luxury for most parochial schools at that time. The school had a partially finished basement with small windows, which could be used for recess when the weather did not allow for it to be held outside.

Reviewing all of the items housed in a closet or in the desk drawers, Mr. Zimmerman pointed out textbooks that lined four shelves and the stock for the blackboard and mimeograph supplies. He explained that a retired public school teacher had taught for several years and is now truly ready to retire from school teaching altogether. Opening desk drawers, he explained that the former teacher did indeed leave behind many master mimeographed forms, question and answer sheets for various tests for first to fourth grades, and other homework assignment answer sheets as well. One file folder was marked "Art" and held coloring pages, simple craft projects, and bulletin board ideas.

Envisioning myself in this classroom setting, I asked Mr. Zimmerman if the church officials would allow a nonchurch member of the Horning Mennonite Church to teach in their parochial schools. He assured me that the school board made the decision, and he as the present chairperson had no issue personally with teachers who are not of the Horning Mennonite faith. In fact, the prior teacher who was retiring was not a Mennonite. As long as teachers were willing to accept the salary and passed the school board's scrutiny, non-Mennonites were allowed to teach in their church schools. Realizing Mr. Zimmerman already knew of my church affiliation with one of the Lancaster Conference Mennonite churches (or he would not have set up the interview), I decided to truly consider being a school teacher for the lower four grades at Cedar Cove School.

I weighed approximately 108 pounds and stood only five feet two and one-half inch tall. I expressed a fear that potentially a fourth-grade student of mine, being raised on a farm and having a body of a muscular tween, could manhandle me and make it difficult for puny me to dole out punishments, if need be. Mr. Zimmerman assured me that the young lady who taught the fifth to eight grade classes was quite a husky farm girl herself and would assist with discipline issues. He emphasized she could handle any unruly girl or boy student who would try to pull any shenanigans. Later on, when I met Miss Vera Burkholder (also of the Horning faith), I had to agree.

My dilemma now was how to decide if I should switch careers. Being only nineteen years of age, I wanted input from someone at MCC, whose opinion I respected. Thus, I started the discussion and set up an impromptu meeting with the human resource director, Lavon Walton. I'll never forget his advice: "Leanne, we'd hate to see you leave us, as you are doing a great job here as the MDS secretary establishing the MDS office. But sometimes in life, God opens doors, and we need to walk through them. Teaching at a two-room school that needs a first- to fourth-grade teacher slot filled within weeks sounds like a huge problem that God was planning on using you to fill this need. This opportunity for you is a once-in-a-lifetime one."

Having the school located within a short distance to my home and my husband's blessing indicated this door was labeled "walk through." (Of course, later in life, I had learned all open doors are not ones that need walking through, nor have God's blessings.) But Lavon's advice set a great standard for me in my spiritual journey. Within two weeks of my mother-in-law's phone call, I signed payroll paperwork and accepted a salary equivalent to my secretarial wage.

One of my newly found friends made through MCC contacts, Brian and Priscilla, were both public school teachers. Prior to the first day of school, they took time out of their busy schedules to visit my classroom and briefly reviewed the textbooks. They gave priceless advice on lesson planning for four grades, since students of four grades were seated in the same room. I felt prepared and challenged to replace questions like, "Where should we eat lunch today in downtown Akron?" Or "When do you need this dictation completed?" to "Did you complete your homework?" or "Class, are you listening?"

Unlike today, during these times, teachers, especially parochial school ones, were allowed to spank, punish, and "not spare the rod and spoil the child" (Proverbs 13:24). Just as with my parents, the philosophy for students was: if you get spanked at school, you'll get another spanking when you get home. Thus, the teachers felt the support of the school board and were aware parents saw teachers as disciplinarians too. It was expected that Sunday school teachers and teachers were an extension for parents to help raise one's child, called fetchin' up. (When a parent myself later on, while scolding my child, I would jokingly say, "Ain't you had no fetchin' up?")

Asked to teach school for twenty-three students in less than a month was daunting. I did not find any instruction book in my desk on how to be a school teacher. Thus, it was a lot of trial and error—mostly error. My decision laid the groundwork for me to jump in with both eyes wide open and hoping, at times, they were also on the back of my head.

Mr. Zimmerman informed me there will be parent-teacher conferences held quarterly within the same week report cards were issued. Volunteer families of students were assigned to clean the school building weekly. An entire building housecleaning was scheduled every August (prior to a new school year) and in January. With the assistance of the older students, I was to wash the blackboards every Friday and clap clean the blackboard erasers.

The first day of school arrived. My packed lunch and briefcase left the house with me in plenty of time to walk up and down the aisle visualizing myself in my new role. A bouquet of fresh flowers was placed on the desk. My high-heel shoe bookends rested on the opposite corner. A Bible, devotional book, my library book choice for storytime, and extra tablets were displayed between the bookends.

Using my roll call log I was given earlier by Mr. Zimmerman, I placed folded colored construction paper name tags on each student's desk according to their grades. A sticker of either a flag (for boys) or a flower (for girls) graced the corner of each name tag. The end row to my right started the six first graders' seats. Behind them would be the three second graders (all girls). Weaving behind them and into the second row sat the seven third graders. Finishing off the fourth row were the remaining seven fourth graders.

I heard the crunch of tires driving on gravel stones. The first car pulled up, and several students stepped out. I hurried to stand at the door and greeted each student as they arrived.

"Good Morning. I'm Mrs. Weaver, and you are?" I asked. Within five minutes, I was introduced to all twenty-three students.

Once seated at their assigned desk, the students eagerly started rummaging through their desk items of several newly sharpened pencils, erasers, and a yellow-lined tablet.

Since the first day was a half-day class, I scheduled a time for each student to stand up front and tell the class about something they did over the summer. Some had new baby brothers or sisters join the family; some boys talked about their fishing successes. Only two students traveled out of the area to visit relatives.

The first moment for a good laugh occurred when Barry, a fourth grader, selected the hymn we were to sing during devotions. Excluding Barry and me, no one was familiar with the song. At the end of the first school day, one fourth-grade girl walked up to my desk and said shyly, "I like you, Mrs. Weaver. You didn't make us do any studying today or give us any homework." She picked up her lunch box and headed toward the door.

When I reread my journal entry for Tuesday, September 5, 1972, I read:

> Back again after a long time (almost a year) from journaling. Well, I am starting again because of my new and exciting job. I am a school teacher for Cedar Cove School. I am teaching grades 1–4 and have 23 pupils. Today was our first day of school, which ended at 1:00 p.m. Already each student has a spot in my heart. Help me, Lord, always! I was not scared or anything. Today we talked about what we did over the summer and handed out our books. I discussed all the rules and read for over an hour for story time. I am so looking forward to the coming year.

Wednesday, September 6: "I had everything organized for today, and things worked out fairly well. I can see already my biggest problem will be the first and second graders, especially Mary. We started playing baseball together. Well, Lord, it has been a busy day, and I see busier ones in the future, especially now when I have to start planning a schedule of sixteen lesson plans a day, four for each grade. Give me that extra boost of strength, Lord."

Common sense told me that minor infractions should entail less severe punishment: pinching a student on a cheek, swatting their hand with a ruler, or having them stay inside during recess. Not having homework completed repeatedly, lying, or class interruptions were grounds for a walk down to the basement for a spanking. They were learning to see how far they could push my buttons and whether or not I meant what I said.

Thinking quickly on my feet, I learned shortly into the first week, was a necessary character trait for a teacher. For example, do I address the very first time I see a note being passed? Do I allow one small whisper between neighbors? Do I address a boy pulling the pigtail of the little girl in front of him if she is laughing about it? Elias fell out of his desk, bumped his head, and started crying. Now what? Since the desks were connected, I could not easily separate them. It was way too tempting to not pinch someone beside you, color uninvited on someone else's paper, or try to cheat looking over a shoulder. By the second week, Alta, my third grader, felt comfortable to press me for my first name, which I did not disclose. On rainy days, several girls would hang out around my desk and ask silly questions, like, "Do you kiss Mr. Weaver before you leave to come to school?"

By the end of the first week, I had settled on my final draft of the lesson plan as follows:

AM
8:15...............Singing and Bible reading...............
8:25 Grade 1 Arithmetic
8:40 Grade 2 Arithmetic
8:55 Grade 3 Arithmetic
9:10 Grade 4 Arithmetic
9:30 Grade 1 Spelling
9:50 Grade 2 Spelling

..................Recess...
10:05 Grade 3 English and Spelling
10:30 Grade 4 English and Spelling
10:50 Grade 1 Reading
11:10 Grade 2 Reading
11:20 Grade 3 Reading
11:40 Grade 4 Reading
12:00......................Lunch and Recess..................
12:45 PM................Story Time* M–TH...............
1:00 Grade 1 Penmanship
1:20 Grade 2 Penmanship
1:40 Grade 3 Geography/History/Science
2:00 Grade 4 Geography/History/Science
2:20 Grade 3 Health/History
2:40 Grade 4 Health/History
3:00
............................Dismissal.......................

1st Friday: Art project, 3rd Friday: Language Arts
2nd Friday: *Weekly Reader* Review, 4th Friday: Nature Study

There were plenty of documentations I journaled about which had me in stitches, such as: "I forgot the ten o'clock recess. Since the class was too afraid to interrupt fourth grade spelling (a strict rule), I continued teaching right through it…I asked a first grader what her favorite food was. She answered me, but I could not understand her. I asked her to repeat it. She said it over and over, and I had no idea what she was saying. Then it occurred to me she was answering me in Pennsylvania Dutch. Thus, I asked her older third-grade sister to translate. "Oh, an Italian sandwich." Too much…During health class, while discussing a picture from the chapter "Staying Well," I asked, "What does a boy lying in bed have to do with health?" Ruthie answered, "Because he has his mouth shut, and when he sleeps, he doesn't get germs in his mouth." Or after the devotional reading and during our discussion about sins, Elias raised his hand and demonstrated: "If you put this (middle) finger upward, our fresh air girl said that's a sin." Can't make it up!

On a more sobering thought, by the end of September, Brian and Priscilla performed placement tests on all the students of the top two grades. Fourth graders came in at a third-grade level, and third graders second-grade level. Yikes! They believed that due to the students not having English as their first language, but instead, Pennsylvania Dutch, they decided to wait to test the first and second graders in April. Boy, my work is cut out for me!

Much documentation was made about the students being "naughty." For example, I wrote how I had to "talk, talk, talk" all day long. I cut back story time to only five minutes today. I stomped my foot on the floor and told everyone to stop what they are doing, to look around, and pick up all the paper off the floor *now*! "I'm tired of seeing this place looking like a pig pen!" What brats today: Elias did not have his coloring finished, again. Carl had to clean up crayon marks he put on the floor. Mark had to stay in at recess because he was gawking out of the window instead of finishing his spelling test.

Then peppered in between the craziness were moments that I wished I had an "everything you wanted to know about teaching first to fourth graders, but were afraid to ask" manual to refer to. I was correcting math papers. Suddenly, I looked up and noticed a wet puddle under Barry's, a first grader, desk.

"Barry, is anything wrong?" I inquired, glancing at the wet spot. "Oh, it's nothing, Mrs. Weaver. I spilled my thermos at lunchtime," he answered while he avoided eye contact and continued to color. "Really? No, I think you wet your pants! Now what?" I then quickly made a decision for his older brother, Jake, to feel Barry's pants to see whether or not they were wet. I sent Barry to the restroom to get some wet and dry paper towels. "Yep, he peed himself," Jake reported, as I sent him to wash his hands.

"Oh, I didn't know I did it," Barry explained. Knowing that Barry and Jake lived in the farm right behind the school, I sent him home for a change of clothes. I phoned his mother to expect his arrival shortly and updated her on the situation. "Yes. Barry is still a little nervous about coming to school, knowing that you don't understand Pennsylvania Dutch. He's afraid he'll say the wrong thing." *Whatever! Your son failed to go to the bathroom at lunchtime.*

Realizing that I myself had visited parochial schools during my public school breaks and how Janie, a friend and fellow schoolteacher, and I would visit each other's schools, I was prepared at any time for a car to pull up and out would jump my first visitors. Who were they? Mom and my sister, Lenora. I was so grateful for their support.

The first day for student family visitors came on October 2. I heard the car pull up on the gravel drive. Four ladies were observed getting out of the car. They were all dressed in dark blue or green dresses, black stockings and shoes and wearing black bonnets over their head coverings.

After acknowledging them and having the entire class in unison say "welcome, visitors," they stood on one side of the classroom in front of the long line of windows. As an unspoken rule of etiquette, visitors do not stay any longer than the length of observing two different class subjects or up until the next recess. As I walked out with them at recess, I heard one mother say, "Well, I observed just what Gerald told me. Ralph, who sits behind him, is a pest. He was tickling his neck and poking him on his back with his pencil eraser. I realize he waits until your back is turned. But something needs to be done." Of course, Ralph's mother was not one of the visitors Gerald's mom invited to visit Cedar Cove with her that day. How embarrassing!

As soon as recess was over, I took Ralph downstairs to the basement and gave him my first paddling using the yardstick. After three whacks, I directed him to head back upstairs. I followed behind. As soon as we walked in the classroom, of course, all eyes were on us. First and second graders had eyes as big as marbles. Then I noticed Ralph snickering as he glanced at Barry. Needless to say, we marched right back downstairs again. Four harder smacks blessed his backside that time!

MY LAST LAST NAME IS GRACE

Then my first PTA meeting was scheduled, and report cards were ready to be handed out. It took until one o'clock in the morning to finish them. There was only one family that was not of the "Black Bumper" Horning Mennonite faith. Mrs. Esh, my oldest brother's age, became someone I felt comfortable talking to. She was the first one to enter my class room that night of the PTA meeting. After several encouraging comments about the buzz among my students' families at the grocery store, she put me at ease.

All but one set of parents arrived to meet the new Mrs. Weaver. Parents, indeed, were empathetic about the difficult task of teaching four grades and twenty-three students. It was plain to see the classroom had a nice variety of art projects on display, star charts for homework completion, and a new bookshelf labeled *Library*. I felt comfortable discussing my challenging student's behavior and future lesson plans. I crawled into bed that night exhausted, yet with a smile on my face. I survived my first PTA!

On October 18, we had our first snowfall. That energized the students! Marion, my fourth grader, missed school for a whole week. I offered to drive her weeks' worth of homework to her home, since her mother had just given birth to her baby brother.

By the end of November, it was time to visit the local bookstore where I could purchase any school supplies, bulletin board material, and mimeograph carbon. I simply turned in the bill to Mr. Zimmerman. Except for one minor cold, I was not sick enough to have to call off that winter.

In November, more discipline needed to be done. Ralph waited a week but then kicked Gerald for being a tattletale. One day, I saw a ball of paper go flying to the back of the room. Elias scribbled on his desktop, and for the third time that week, he had not completed his homework. Two out of the three second graders had not finished their reading homework, making it difficult to follow my lesson plan for the day.

Then the clincher: Elias again did not have his homework completed. Probably because it was a Friday afternoon and my last nerve was spent, I decided on a different punishment. But I was out of options and had no reference book, except the Bible. Enlightened, I walked over to the other classroom and asked Vera for her advice. Answer in hand, I directed Elias to come front center stage, stand in front of the blackboard, and hold out both arms straight out. I then proceeded to place heavy dictionaries on his arms. Even though he was a strong farmhand, one cannot hold up a stack of seven heavy books for very long. Of course, they fell down on the ground. Smack went the ruler across his hands. Elias picked them up and handed them to me. I again piled the books on his arms. Determined to not have them fall, he began to sweat. His arms started shaking, and down the books fell. Again, smack. Of course, the entire time, I am reiterating the importance of doing homework and following rules. Naturally, the length of time he could hold the heavy load was getting shorter and shorter, even though I lessened the number to five books. Elias began to weep.

"Well, Elias. Just as you are tired of holding these heavy dictionaries, I'm tired of hearing your homework isn't finished. Make sense?" I turned to face the entire class. All faces were solemn and staring at Elias. "Yes, Mrs. Weaver," he mumbled, head hanging. "That was worse than a spanking," he interjected as he walked back to his seat.

Within a week, I needed to punish Mary for not having her homework done. Her punishment: she leaned on her two pointer fingers on the blackboard as I smacked her hands with the ruler (another idea of Vera's). Just when I needed to laugh, it happened. Carl asked me for a scissors to finish his art project. But he failed to add "please."

"You didn't ask for it nicely, Carl," I hinted.

"May I have a scissors," he said softer and kinder. I kept repeating what he had said, hoping he would correct it and add *please*, but to no avail.

"You want a scissors." (pause).

"Yes, may I have a scissors?"

After five more times of going back and forth, I asked, "How do you ask?" By now he is staring at me, clueless.

"May I *please* have a scissors?" I finally said loudly, exasperated.

"I know. That's what I said," he answered. *Geezzz, just like the Martin siblings, I guess.*

Then back to more serious times. One boy asked to sharpen his pencil; I allowed it. Two minutes later, the boy who sat in front of him asked to do the same. I asked him if he would please hold up his pencil in order for me to see the pencil tip. A spanking new tip was on it. I asked him if indeed he believed he needed to sharpen his pencil, and whether or not it was wise to interrupt my class for such a request.

"No. I just wanted to go for a walk," he commented as he looked down at his history book. Another child asked if she could go to the bathroom five minutes before recess. "No. I think you can wait until recess."

The second PTA was scheduled for Monday of Thanksgiving week. Similar to the first session, I felt comfortable discussing my world of teaching and all that it entailed. I was learning to put names with faces of the mothers (few fathers attended, except school board members). The Friday after Thanksgiving (we did not have off), Mr. Zimmerman came into my classroom as a visitor during the last class.

As I was erasing the blackboard, he started to ask me if I had heard anything about the results of his Horning Church's fall council meeting. "No," I said with furrowed brows.

"Good," he said as he twirled around his black hat over and over again in his hand. He sat down on the top of one desk and propped his one leg on the seat. "Two fathers of your students made a comment to our church's bishop during our council meeting."

"Oh? About what?" I asked point-blank.

"Well, they brought up the question with our leadership team why we don't hire teachers of our own kind. They weren't sure they wanted their students taught by teachers who wear blue shoes." Only when I noticed his smile did a chuckle escape. "What?" I said. "They don't like that I wear navy blue shoes?" I held the back of my hand over my mouth.

"Don't worry about a thing. The bishop has no issues with anything. They felt they needed to inform me as the school board president. We have no dress code for our teachers. I am the one who hired you, and I wanted you to be our Cedar Cove teacher. I just wanted to stop by first in case you heard the rumor. I didn't want you to fret over the council meeting. You're doing a good job. Keep it up." Only in my car on the drive home did I burst out laughing again about Mr. Zimmerman's comments. Of course, I braced myself for the spring council meeting, but no more visits were held by Mr. Zimmerman ever again.

Then, on February 6, the worst day of that school year occurred. I read in my diary:

> What a day! If I would have a day like this every day, I'd go simply nuts. Here's the story:
>
> I was in the lav during the last recess. I heard my two second graders discussing homework. Mary asked Beulah if she could copy from her reading workbook. Beluah answered, "Sure." I could not believe it! I did not know what would be the best way of handling the matter; I went over to ask Vera, the other teacher.
>
> She advised, "Just ask the class and make the two girls admit it. That's all. No other punishment. Just tell them why it is wrong." The bell rang at 1:50 p.m. I stood in front of my desk and announced, "I know cheating is going on, and I would like those involved to stand up." I waited, avoiding eye contact with Mary and Beluah. Nobody did. Now what? I decided to go around the classroom, starting with first graders. Each person was to stand by their desk and tell me whether or not they were planning on cheating. My! Look at all the pale faces! We went all around the classroom, and nobody fessed up. Stalling, I sat down and started working at my desk.

"Until the two culprits admit to their planned sinning, all classes will be stopped," I said. At 2:00 p.m., I tried again to have each person repeat after me, "Mrs. Weaver, I have made no plans to cheat" to no avail. I was so sick and hurt…I could have cried. I don't know what to do! I glanced over at the second-grade row. Mary looks guilty and seems like she could start crying any minute. Beluah sure doesn't, though. I interrupted Vera's class and asked her what should I do next. She suggested I call them out. "But, Leanne. Now you must punish them for lying."

I walked back into the classroom and said, "Okay, I was in the girl's bathroom at recess…" It was amazing how all of a sudden, many of the boys relaxed a bit and slid down in their seats, as if thinking, *Whew, not me this time.*

I had each girl repeat back to me, "Mrs. Weaver, I did not plan to cheat while in the bathroom today." Again, both Mary and Beluah stared right back at me and lied to my face. At my wit's end, I finally called out the two culprits' names. "You didn't know that I was in one of the bathroom stalls at the time. I overheard you two discussing it. You two are my only female second graders, Mary and Beluah."

Finally, Mary admitted she asked to copy, but Beluah wouldn't admit she said she could copy. She said she didn't say anything. I had them both go to the blackboard and turn around facing it. I paddled them both hard, especially Mary. Then before I paddled Beluah, I asked her again, and she finally admitted to it. Then I smacked their hands twice with a ruler. I really blew my top. I let them know that I was punishing them because I loved them.

School ended; the hall phone rang. It was Beluah's mother on the other end of the line. "Mrs. Weaver, Beluah tells me that she had to admit to cheating or you were going to hit her anyway. I'm calling to hear your side of the story."

I explained how I was in the bathroom stall unbeknownst to the two second graders. She agreed that I surely know the voices of each of my students. "Well, then Beluah gets a spanking by me too." Whew! I'm glad she believed me.

Today was a day I surely am not getting paid enough!

My schedule of preparing sixteen lesson plans daily, weekly art projects, selecting which books to read aloud for story time, choosing a devotional, grading test, and homework papers, plus removing and adding seasonal room decorations made for a quickly passing ten-hour day. Having eyes in back of my head, being alert to possible cheating and passing of notes, and having a smile on my face wore me out. Realizing I too need to be an encourager, one who influences and not just one who teaches subjects while showing no partiality, was difficult. But I did the best job I could with the materials, skill level, and support systems available to me.

I hope and pray these former students of mine can read and write today!

Thought of the Day

Grace is when no visible footprints were in the sand, and I realize I was being carried by my Heavenly Father.

Chapter 25

A Replica of Me Running Around in Heaven?

I lie in the dust; revive me by your word. I told you my plans, and you answered…I weep with sorrow; encourage me by your word.
—Psalm 119: 25a, 26a, 28 (NLT)

THOUGH BUSY CARRYING MY TEACHING load and household responsibilities, I noticed I had missed my monthly period once, then twice. I had not planned on becoming pregnant. Besides, we were using birth control. But you know the saying, "Anatomy works!" I told my husband, "I think I'm pregnant!" Excited and willing to keep it a secret, John encouraged me to make a doctor's appointment. It was scheduled for the following Friday after work. The rabbit died, and I phoned Mom. Well, I guess I'll only be teaching school for one year. I'm going to be a mommy. Wanting to share with my parents our great news, I asked if we could stop by Sunday afternoon for a visit. The only other people we told our life-changing news to were the couple, who was our best man in our wedding. We arranged to have lunch with them after church before we headed over to visit my parents.

We arrived at my parents' home and started to play Haas. Not wanting to keep back the secret any longer, I spilled the beans about being pregnant during the first round of card playing. Mom and

Daddy, of course, were happy for us. In between the second and third hand of cards, I went to the bathroom. I noticed a tiny eraser-tip-sized blood in my underwear. Both hands flew up to my cheeks, and I screamed, "Mom!" Having had two miscarriages, Mom, I knew, would be able to ascertain the situation. Unlocking the bathroom door for her, I showed her the bloodstain. "Call your doctor," she advised grimly.

So, pushing aside the Haas game, after explaining what I saw to John, I called directory assistance to get my doctor's phone number, a doctor I had just had my first appointment with this past Friday. Within minutes, Dr. Courtney called me back. He told me, "This could go fifty-fifty. Go home and get off your feet for forty-eight hours, except for going to the bathroom. If you are starting to miscarriage, you'll know in two or three days."

What was supposed to be a day for making memories by telling your parents they will be grandparents again turned out to be an anxious, fretful one. The drive home gave opportunity for John to assure me everything will be fine with our baby. My to-do list grew in my mind as I rested my head on the car seat and sat with my eyes closed. First thing I needed to do was to place an urgent phone call to Mr. Zimmerman, the school board president, so he could find a substitute teacher for me in short notice.

But wait! Mr. Zimmerman doesn't even know I'm pregnant. He assumed I planned to teach for at least two years, as I had informed him earlier; we had no immediate plans to start a family. Besides, this conservative Mennonite sect calls it "being in the family way" and did not use the word *pregnant*. It surely is not discussed between the opposite sexes! But having no choice, I reluctantly picked up the phone to inform Mr. Zimmerman of my situation and of the doctor's orders that I needed to follow. Being sympathetic and understanding, he said he'll find a teacher substitute for me and to keep him informed. After placing one more phone call to the other higher-grades teacher, Vera, to update her, I then crawled into bed to wait.

Putting out fleeces (as read about in the Bible), begging, loudly crying out, making promises to God are desperate acts from desperate people. Being bedbound and not able to concentrate on reading, I did nothing but think and pray. Thinking positive thoughts, believing for the best, and visualizing a healthy baby being held in my arms calmed me.

Then the cramping started. The bleeding turned from an eraser-sized area to need for pad protection. Oh no! God, please let our baby live and grow. Do not let me miscarry. Another phone call to Dr. Courtney was not too comforting. "Time will only tell. Stay off your feet. Keep me posted."

Throughout Sunday night and all day Monday, the cramping and bleeding continued, and the bargaining with God started. If you let this baby live, I promise to read the Bible every day. I'll read it twice a day, morning and night, if that will help! Having had caught up with my sleep, I did resort to starting to read the newspaper and a book. Why did I suddenly notice every comic seemed to have a picture of a baby in it? Tears flowed as I flipped through a magazine; diaper ads jumped out at me like never before.

After returning from the bathroom and noticing no change, I crawled into bed with tears streaming down my face while pleading and praying to God with a heavy heart. Husbands, feeling helpless in these situations, can do nothing but wait and pray as well.

By Tuesday morning, when John was out milking the cows and I was lying in bed, I began to feel lousy. My body ached, my cramps worsened, and I became very pale-looking. Directed by Dr. Courtney, we headed off to his office, which was located about five miles away. I sat on bath towels in the car in preparation; I didn't feel much like talking. John drove right up to the door and dropped me off. I walked into the already-crowded doctor's office. The receptionist gave me one look and asked, "Do you have the flu too?" After being updated on my potential miscarriage, a nurse had me bypass the usual wait in the waiting room and quickly led me down the hall to the last exam room on the right. She helped me up on the exam table, took my vital signs, assured me the doctor would be in soon and disappeared.

What does an anxious person do while lying on an exam table and was miscarrying at that exact moment? In my pain, I reached down for the exam table drawer knob, which was below me, and started opening and closing it. *Bang, bang, bang.* Visualizing liquid vials falling over, perfectly lined-up exam equipment being thrown in disarray or pill bottles falling over, I continued the gotta-do-something ritual. I didn't know, and I didn't care. When that brought little relief, I started pulling on my hair (I later told my friends that experiencing my miscarriage at three months pregnant was just about as painful as delivering a baby).

Finally, my hubby and Dr. Courtney walked in. Upon examination, he confirmed indeed, "I believe that just now you lost the fetus." Dr. Courtney saw the sadness on my face and assured me. He patted my knee, smiled, and said, "Miscarriages are God's way of taking care of a deformed baby. You two are young. In three months, try again, okay?"

I passed the receptionist desk again, left, and thought *I wish it was the flu!* We headed home. I felt as though I left a piece of me behind in the doctor's office trash can. My bed, once again, became a haven to send prayers heavenward. Just as my mother and sister, Lenora, I too joined the I-had-a- miscarriage club.

I trusted God as being supreme, sovereign, and I knew He had my best interests at heart. I gradually accepted my fate. Plus, to aid in my healing, I pictured our perfectly formed little darlin' running around heaven with other family members. I was not able to visualize our little button as a human being created from our combined gene pools. I decided on an exact replica of me: dark hair and eyes, dark-complexioned, and petite. Today, the only time I am reminded of my miscarriage is when completing a new visit doctor's office forms and answering the question: "Number of pregnancies?"

After two weeks off from teaching, I returned back to school the following Monday. Eager to see my students, I told them I was so happy to be back in the classroom after being "so sick." Expecting our birth control method to resume doing its job, I planned on finishing the present school year and teaching the following year as well.

As God designed it, I did indeed teach the second year at Cedar Cove School. I became pregnant again the following winter. My blue-eyed, fair-complexioned blonde baby was born September 18, 1974. The nurse walked in to hand over the baby to its dark-haired, dark-eyed, dark-complexioned mommy. Amazed and puzzled, she looked at the blonde baby, glanced over at the mommy, double-checked the baby's name band again, and started to walk back out of the room. *This can't be right?*

"Yes, she's mine. Bring her here, please," I said as I sat up in bed, attempting to get into a better nursing position. My God has a great sense of humor. He's a giver of great gifts in His perfect timing!

Holding this precious bundle in my arms, I felt love cascading down from a waterfall like I have never experienced before. The late summer skies looked bluer, the moon later on shone brighter, and my purpose was rediscovered. My life was never to be the same again.

Thought of the Day

Grace grants me the wisdom to understand what true Christianity is: faith, period and not faith plus. Paul teaches us we do not add works to our faith, nor do we keep doing. It is a *done* not a *do* religion. Christ's complete work was done on the Cross.

Chapter 26

One of My Most Sacred Moments

As you do not know the way the path of the wind, or how the body is formed in a mother's womb, so you cannot understand the work of God, the Maker of all things.
—Ecclesiastes 11:5

Christian, left, Steph, center, Kiersten, right

NOTHING INSPIRED A MORE ENORMOUS devotion than the birth of my first child, Stephanie (meaning "crowned one") Ann. Creating something out of combined DNA with the Lord's help, while adding another human being to this planet's population, which we could get credit for, was astounding. Don't forget: anatomy works!

After a pregnancy of morning sickness in the first trimester and gaining over twenty pounds by the ninth month, I kept detailed notes in my *Care for You and Your Baby-to-Be* booklet from December 1973 to September 5, 1974, my due date. By August, my friends teased me as I was beginning to look top-heavy. "Don't start rolling down hill, Leanne. You're not going to stop once you get started."

September 5 due date came and went. A week later, September 12 passed by as well. Ticktock, ticktock. Finally, on the morning of Monday, September 16, I began to experience signs of early labor. Little did I know my little bundle would not show the expectant world her beautiful face until two full days later! Only those mothers who have experienced labor beyond forty-eight hours can relate to my story. Usually being upbeat and positive, I confess I was convinced I was the first mother to be carrying her child as long as an elephant does—almost two years.

Experiencing some discomfort and arriving at Lebanon Valley General Hospital by midmorning, as directed by Dr. Courtney, I was about to experience the unknown and this much-anticipated rite of passage. Like the lucky big slot-machine winner, one can only imagine the thrill of that ching-ching event, unless you are the one who pulled the one-arm bandit. On the cusp of being one who is no longer looking in from the outside, but as one who can stop imagining, I was about to become a member of the mommy club. My ching-ching would be priceless!

In those days, laboring women shared labor rooms. My first (yes, I had more than one) roommate was a fifteen-year-old single girl who was further along in her labor. So I figured I might as well watch closely and take lessons from her as she progressed to full transition, her final labor stage. Eventually, I enviously watched too young mom-to-be being wheeled out of the labor room and head toward the delivery room.

But by late afternoon, an internal exam revealed I was barely five centimeters dilated. With a barnful of dairy cows waiting to be milked, John went home. The nurse reassured him she would not hesitate to place the phone call when it was time for him to return. All during his evening milking, he had one ear tuned in to the wall barn phone. At bedtime, he went to bed expecting a middle-of-the-night phone call asking him to return back to the hospital. But no.

Meanwhile, back in the hospital, the evening shift nurses went off duty and the night shift staff came on. Those nurses too continued to check my slow progression. It got to the point where the nurses, after an examination, sighed, "No change." They made me feel after each one it was a waste of their time, let alone the waste of a good pair of gloves!

Sometime on Tuesday, another patient was admitted into my labor room. *Woman, go ahead. I know you'll come and go from this room too.* Sure enough, she too, after several hours, was wheeled out into the delivery room and joined the envious club. My baby elephant was growing.

Meanwhile, back on the farm, John was surprised he was able to sleep through the night without answering the anticipated phone call. Unbeknownst to me, he checked in with the nurses' station after his milking and was told he might as well finish his chores: "No urgency here." Late Tuesday morning, he drove back to the hospital to hold his wife's hand. After all, his training for comforting a late-stage about-to-deliver-wife was not necessary to put into practice yet.

By Tuesday evening milking time, again, the nurse sent my husband home, leaving me alone: "After all, you might as well go home and get some work done. We'll call you with any progression." In fact, John had lined up a hired hand to take his place and to assist his dad with milking the cows. Knowing this journey started Monday morning, and it was now his third time of facing the same decision about leaving his laboring wife to go home to milk the cows, he thought, "Will I miss my baby's birth?" (Actually, he was hoping he would get out of milking the cows.) Again, he drove back home. Ticktock, ticktock.

Evening shift nurses came and went. Night shift nurses clocked in. During shift report from nurse to nurse, I am sure they heard,

"Yep, Mrs. Weaver is still in labor room 2!" Uncomfortable back labor pains pressed on. Around 2:00 a.m., after another internal exam with undesired results, the nurse suggested I walk the halls to help to move my labor along. Sure, why not? My baby elephant remained incubated.

Stopping at times to hold the wall during back pain, I was getting more depressed. I begged God to please move this delivery along by allowing contractions not be wasted, but to open the cervix as He has designed it for this miraculous event. I remember well sitting in a chair at the end of a hallway resting in-between walks in the middle of the night, feeling frustrated and alone, atypical for me. Though I was privy to observe a glorious morning sunrise (a rare event for me) over the Lebanon horizon still laboring on day 3 of labor, I was quite disheartened.

Remember how smart teachers realize their job is more than teaching students? It is about being an influence. Well, compassionate nurses realize too, their job isn't only performing assessments, administering medications, and following nursing procedures. Their words can be powerful and impactful too.

Night shift nurses punched out, and day shift nurses punched in. "Yep, Mrs. Weaver is still in labor room 2." But then, I experienced the effects of a cheerful attitude of my fresh shift-change nurse. With a big smile, she gave the prediction I surely will *indeed* be holding my baby by noon. Maybe my baby will finally see the light of day today? John arrived back at the hospital truly believing too, today *had* to be the day.

Meantime, I resigned to the fact the medical staff may follow through on any doctor's orders during this "two-year" pregnancy. Want an X-ray to check on the baby's head position? Go right ahead. Want to complete another internal to manually check the baby's head position and take the chance of wasting another pair of gloves, after all this time, before wheeling me down to the X-ray department? Be my guest.

Then Miss Cheery nurse said the X-ray would not be necessary, as I progressed to about seven centimeters. Since I learned I will soon feel like swearing at the next stage from my teenager-teacher, I prepared mentally for the worse stage. Plus, I have never been so glad for back pain and discomfort to be gone and sweet sleep to envelope me!

Next thing I know, Miss Cheery was telling me to push. What? No worsening pain! No feeling as though I needed to swear! God was with me this whole entire time and did answer my prayers in more ways than I could imagine. How do you spell relief? "P-U-S-H!" Sounding like a howling cat in heat, I was motivated to follow Miss Cheery's advice, which was quite a chore. But "expelling the swallowed watermelon," as one comedian labeled it, this sweet-pain effort only lasted about ten minutes. At 12:18 p.m., beautiful, healthy Stephanie Ann, God's gift and blessing to our family, was born close to Miss Cheery's predicted time frame. When my baby was placed in my arms, the tears flowed. John and I, in awe, just stared at the most awesome creature this side of heaven—a most scared moment!

It was appreciated when Mom and Daddy drove to the hospital, located twenty miles away, to visit me and their newest granddaughter. As I was carefully getting out of bed to shuffle down the hall two days postdelivery to gaze through the nursery window, Daddy looked over at my belly and teased, "Did you have your baby yet?" Mom nudged Daddy in his side and scolded, "Now, Daddy." I couldn't laugh too hard because I knew it would hurt too much. Instead, I blew out a *pffff* and said, "Geez." I believe starting out at a weight of 110 was fifteen pounds less than Mom's pre-pregnancy weight ever was.

Adjusting to mommyhood was pretty much a breeze, once I learned the knack of breastfeeding, or should I say once Steph got the hang of it? Back in the 1970s, mothers and newborn infants stayed home for about a week before taking their little one out into the elements and in a public setting, such as attending church. On the day of our first outing, unlike today, I wrapped Steph tightly in a receiving blanket. Only exposing mostly her face, beaming Mom showed off her precious little bundle to her church friends.

The first and last time (to date) I ever got a speeding ticket was when Steph was about six weeks old. I had gone to the grocery store. As we headed back home, Steph decided she was hungry and wanted to be nursed *now*. Her crying jags led to her becoming red-faced and angry. I, being a dutiful mommy, put the pedal to the metal and hightailed it toward home, going 55 mph in a 45 mph zone on Route 422. But, lo and behold, a police officer's flashing lights behind me got my attention in short order. You would think a screaming baby making conversation difficult would cause an officer to be a little sensitive and believe my excuse for speeding was reasonable. But no. I drove away with a ticket in hand.

Steph has several early memories, unsure which is the actual earliest one. She remembers being out in the barn with her daddy and enjoying it. However, she was afraid of the cows, even though they were secured in individual stalls. Steph was afraid they would escape and step on her. She was fascinated by the milking and pipeline system and how the milk traveled through clear pipes and ended up in the milk tank, which had a large paddle used to stir the milk. Steph wanted to jump right in too.

Steph remembers waking up early to watch Saturday morning cartoons while playing with her toys. She remembers too my listening to country music while working around the house as well as Paul Harvey's *The Rest of the Story*. During playtime, she would hear me baking in the kitchen. Once she heard the whirring of the mixer, Steph ran into the kitchen, grabbed a table chair, and moved it close to the mixer. She knew Mommy was making a yummy dessert and waited ever so patiently to be able to lick the beater and the bowl when I was finished.

Having witnessed a car accident, Steph lists that event as one of her earliest memories too, and it is no wonder. One night, a drunk driver plowed into our fence. As his car clipped off several of our meadow fence posts, he leaned over in his drunken state toward the passenger seat. Lucky for him, a fence post went perfectly through the windshield and over top of the driver's seat. He was lucky to be alive! Steph's bedroom faced toward the road. She heard the crash and went outside without our knowledge. Thank God, the neighbor girl was on the scene as well. As much as Steph was nosy and wanted to watch the rescue scene unfold in front of her, she was fearful the cows in the meadow would chase her. The neighbor assured her the cows were far down in the meadow, and she was safe. Steph witnessed the ambulance driver pull the drunk driver out of the car. Today, she can still describe his appearance and the bloody scene. She remembers me being shocked as she stood there and watched the ambulance drivers work and eventually pull away. I thanked the neighbor girl for watching over her and returned Steph back to her bed.

Steph's nursery Sunday school friends remained as elementary school friends too. A group of four adorable toddlers shared combined first birthdays, cakes, and parties, which led to repeats for their second and third birthdays as well. We first-time parents spent hours together visiting in each other's homes playing cards and hanging out, as our children played together and cemented life-long relationships.

Since we had no close neighbors, and it was only occasionally playmates came over, when I was babysitting for friends or vice versa, I was concerned Steph was not having enough social interaction other than her grandparents and Sunday school friends. I did some homework on reviewing the closest nursery schools. Satisfied with what I learned, I enrolled Steph in classes for Tuesday and Thursday mornings from 9:00 a.m. to 11:00 a.m. Shyly, Steph made new friends and beheld a whole new world of different toys and coloring books. Sharing was a new word she had to learn. She slowly adjusted to Mommy dropping her off and returning a few hours later. I used that time to go grocery shopping or ran errands. In the end, the cost of the nursery school was so worth it.

Having been a teacher prior to becoming a mommy, I was looking forward to Steph's attending school. Along with her other Sunday school friends, she was enrolled in Grace Christian School's kindergarten at four years old, but she was turning five in a few weeks. By the end of the first marking period, I had regretted not holding Steph back and waited to enroll her the following school year, when she would have entered kindergarten at age five, almost six years old. Why? Well, for one, she had a difficult time with weekly scripture verse memorization. Being a former teacher who wanted her child to be one of the brightest brains in the class, after all, I had put great expectations on Steph. Many nights we spent reviewing memory verses and her homework. There were many weeks, Steph told me, she practiced her memorization at school and was prepared to recite them to the teacher the following morning. I had no reason to assist her, or so I thought.

Well, what a shock when I went to Steph's first teacher's PTA meeting! Posted on the bulletin board for all eyes to see was the students' scripture memorization chart. There were many "holes" missing smiley stickers on Steph's chart. Not just one or two, but half of Steph's blocks were empty. When I questioned Steph, she just shrugged her shoulders like "What's the big deal, Mom?" I was shocked when I realized my precious child had the nerve to lie to her mother! My world was rocked to its core. Yes, I knew a sinful nature is in every child; no one has to teach one how to be naughty, selfish about sharing toys, and how they frequently use the word *No*! But I did not expect my precious angel to lie to her mother. Sigh, sigh, what a rude awakening.

As the blonde-haired, blue-eyed thin, petite Stephanie grew into a cute little first grader, so did a bad habit—sucking two fingers. Desperate Mommy read many articles on it and discussed the matter with the family doctor. Applying a disgusting-tasting liquid on her fingers or having her wear gloves at bedtime did not solve the problem. I had no choice but to wait until she made up her own mind to stop. Of course, as predicted by the dentist, Steph needed extensive dental work and wore braces eventually to straighten out her slightly protruding front teeth. Today, Steph's teeth are as perfect as one could hope for. Too bad one can't see into a crystal ball; if able, perhaps, Mom would have chilled out a bit about it all.

By the time Steph was about two and one-half years old, she became a big sister to her brother, Darrin. As much as they grew to fight, scold, and yell at each other, I always said they would kill for each other. Living on the farm gave them plenty of opportunity to run and play in the front and backyards. They might not have had close neighbors, but they grew to enjoy spending day and night with each other as playmates and best friends.

It wasn't long before Daddy thought they needed a pet dog. Eric, a gentle Saint Bernard, joined the household (of course, he was a barn dog and not an inside dog). Big enough to knock either child over, he was also a protector of sorts. Barking to let us know if any vehicle pulled into the driveway, Eric was a refreshing sight whenever we too arrived home, knowing he stood guard over our property.

Many years later, I babysat for my brother Doug and my nephew Keith, who were about nine years old and only nine months apart (remember, Mom was pregnant at my brother's wedding). Deciding they wanted to get up early and help John in the barn with milking the cows, they ran into the barn. Who was totally surprised? Eric, as he wasn't prepared for any young children to enter his territory. He pounced on Keith, knocked him down, and dug his claws into the side of his face. I can only imagine how frightened Keith must have been with a big Saint Bernard on top of him barking just inches from his face. Poor Doug stood by and could only watch and yell for his Uncle Keith. John came running and rescued crying, hysterical Keith.

Upon assessing the wound beneath Keith's ear, I realized it required stitches; I drove him to the doctor. Doug rode along for emotional support. I accompanied Keith into the doctor's exam room, leaving Doug out in the waiting room with other patients. Still traumatized, Keith was inconsolable (he probably wanted his mom by his side, not Aunt Leanne). His crying continued while waiting for the doctor and, of course, during the wound repair. At one point, I heard Doug say to the patients in the waiting room, "Oh, that's just my Uncle Keith crying." Sure enough, when we were passing through the waiting room, we most certainly received some quizzical looks. Oh, Uncle Keith is a child!

I personally don't like strange, unfamiliar mean dogs. After Keith's episode, I certainly was not going to have an unpredictable pet causing fright in others. After some research, we found Eric another loving home. Eventually, the second pet dog, Mikey, a mild-tempered mutt, joined our household.

MY LAST LAST NAME IS GRACE

Another memory occurred when Stephanie and Darrin were younger. We opened up our home to a Hispanic young man who had passed the first stage of his drug rehab. Our pastor called us one day and asked if we would please consider having someone live with us for a few months to get away from the drug use temptation, which was so prevalent in the city. Our church had an outreach program named Jubilee Prison Ministries, which assisted men to reform, become drug-free, and hold down respectable jobs.

Our pastor knew we lived in a large farmhouse and had an extra bedroom. John and I agreed to do a trial and invited Miquel from New York to live with us. What a far cry from living in a big city to living on a dairy farm! Though Miquel did not get up at the crack of dawn, while watching or assisting John with milking the cows, he certainly had some lessons on how bottled milk ends up on the grocery shelf.

What I remember most about Miquel's stay with us was how he was a neat and sharp dresser. One day, he asked me where I kept the ironing board and iron. Next thing I know, fifteen minutes later, Miquel was still pressing the same pair of jeans. Over and over and over, press in the crease, one leg, then the other leg, one side, and then the other side. Who irons jeans?

We have taken quite a few photographs of Miquel playing with Darrin sitting in his high chair laughing hysterically at some funny face of Miquel's. He teased Darrin by coming from behind his high chair and squeezing one of his noisy toys. Darrin's laughter rose louder and louder until he could not laugh anymore.

Miquel traveled with me sometimes when I had a scheduled Rubbermaid party (details in a later chapter) at a far distance from my home. He was a gentleman schlepping in my four product boxes for me and assisted me in setting up my display of wares. I am sure I had some hostesses shaking their heads as to why I had this young man accompanying me. I sure enjoyed his company when driving home alone late at night during those times.

Unfortunately, Miquel's trial ended, and he returned to his family in New York as a clean, sober young man with some cow manure on his boots and straw in his hair. I pray today he has remained responsible, drug-free, and stayed the course of a changed man and looks fondly on the memories of spending that summer on the Weaver farm.

Another similar opportunity came from the local psychiatric hospital. Administrators were looking for families to take in young girls who were approved to be released from the hospital but were not (or it was not appropriate) to resume living in their prior living arrangements. Once again, we opened up our home and arms to a thirteen-year-old girl I'll name Trudy.

She moved into Steph's bedroom; we temporarily moved Steph into Darrin's nursery. Trudy spent hours watching Steph and Darrin play together while she crocheted. My only job was to drive her to the psych hospital for her biweekly outpatient appointments, which I did. Trudy never seemed to fit in with our family as much as I would have liked. She always seemed to be holding us at arm's length. Not being privy to her private life, we could only assume what traumatic episodes this poor teenager had endured. We simply loved her and prayed with her.

One day, we noticed some items were missing around the house. John could not find his watch, and I could not find our camera. Lo and behold, sometime later that week, I found the missing items in Trudy's bedroom trash can. I reported the scenario to her case manager. We were informed Trudy has to do something so we won't love her. "With all the unfortunate things that occurred in her past, she has a hard time accepting your love and kindness," the case manager explained to John and me.

It wasn't long until we received a phone call about a very personal matter (which will not be disclosed here), which she revealed during one of her outpatient sessions. The case manager felt Trudy needed more hospitalization. I hope and pray that today Trudy is a vessel of forgiveness and lives a blessed life, knowing God is our vindicator when injustices are done to us. Our children watched and learned that Christians need to live a life of service. It is not about me all the time.

Making the same mistake of most parents, I wanted Steph to live out my own dream. Which one? Learn how to play a guitar. At barely seven years old, holding an oversized guitar, Steph plucked away on the strings, pretending to be enthused. Since Mom wasn't totally clueless and wise enough to know when you have to continually nag someone to practice their lessons, I resigned to the fact it was my dream and not hers. Steph laid the guitar down and later picked up horse's reins.

Within a few years, she exchanged hours spent learning how to play a guitar with riding a horse. Because she learned how to ride at summer camp and spent some time with another friend, who had a horse named Lady, Steph begged her father to purchase her a horse. One birthday, she looked up to see her dad holding the reins of a horse. He had literally walked into the house to surprise her! Steph screamed and startled the horse, which she named Ringo. Needless to say, their initial bonding had to take place in the driveway and out of the house. As horse lovers understand, the union meets needs for both.

Unfortunately, an incident occurred that affected Steph for many years to come. Steph and her friend both entered their horses, Ringo and Lady, in a local fair event. Suddenly, Lady reared up. Steph, while attempting to grab the horse's reins to calm her, had Lady lunge and stepped on both of Steph's feet. Her ankles now remain injury-prone and twist entirely too easily. Thus, she was forced to give up playing soccer. Several times a year, she twisted her ankle forcing her to wear a foot brace for long periods of time.

Despite the injury, Steph's love for 4-H, bareback competitions at local shows and running Ringo full speed up and down the meadow was exhilarating. When Ringo died, her love for horses would be replaced by working full-time and experiencing puppy love with her first boyfriend.

Another important lesson I taught my children when they were younger was to thank God for a healthy body. The lesson was taught every time we noticed a disabled child either sitting in a wheelchair or walking with crutches. Out of earshot of the child, I would say,

"Thank you, Jesus, for my healthy body." After repeatedly saying this, when the opportunity arose, the children eventually said it first. Mommy did not have to remind them. After all, they knew about Mommy's cousin Rachel, who was stricken with polio and lived in a wheelchair.

By the grace of God, go I.

Thought of the Day

Grace is taking my too-heavy backpack, full of hurts, mistakes, and problems, pulling it off my shoulder, and laying it at my Master's feet. He not only empties it, but He promises to share any heavy burdens, especially those that cause me to bend over and stoop.

Chapter 27

My Only Son, the Army Officer

I have no greater joy than to hear my children are walking in truth.
—3 John 4

Heather and Darrin, second row, Madison,
1st row left, Taylor, 1st row, right

ANOTHER RABBIT DIED, AND MY pregnancy test read positive after I had no longer gotten granny (remember my name for my monthly?)

after April 1976. Similar to my last pregnancy, I experienced both morning and evening sickness at times. My three-month doctor visit weigh-in showed I had gained one pound more than my baseline weight. In spite of having nausea, feeling dizzy and tired, my weight slowly climbed and my mysterious human being grew. My due date was January 18. By the fifth month of my pregnancy, my doctor was scolding me for gaining too much weight between doctor visits. My goal was to be no more than three pounds.

Eventually, I began to feel better by my fourth month of my pregnancy. One Sunday morning, John and I had a visitor at our church. Who? Rollin, a former coworker of mine from MCC. It was great catching up on each other's lives. Monday morning, my phone rang. It was Rollin asking me an important question: "Leanne, I would love for you to be my fill-in secretary while my personal secretary is out on maternity leave until January. Would you, please, seriously consider it?" he asked me.

I sucked in my breath, "Say what? You want a fat five-month pregnant woman as your secretary?" I started to chuckle. "I know your work, and I would love to have you as my secretary. Isn't it perfect timing? By the time my secretary returns, you'll need to quit," he said, sounding convincing.

Once again, John and I had a serious conversation around the supper table. "Any reason why I can't drive down to New Holland to Power Plus until I go into labor to earn some extra money? Rollin is practically begging me to be his fill-in secretary," I entreated. "I'll find a babysitter for Steph."

John agreed I could do it as long as they paid me an hourly wage $2 more than what I was paid when I taught school. The extra $2 an hour was to aid in covering childcare costs. Excited, I phoned Rollin, who did not bat an eye about my hourly wage request. John and I decided all paychecks be put in a savings account to buy a new bedroom suite for us. I am about to punch a time clock once again.

Having confirmed a babysitter with the wife of my former boyfriend, Dave, who lived along the route to New Holland, Steph and I and my big girth started our Monday through Friday trek. Dave and

Debbie had a little girl who was close to Steph's age. Thank God, she enjoyed being dropped off and barely noticed Mommy walking back out the door. Being organized assisted in my crazy morning schedule, as all working women understand. I followed a routine of both having Steph bathed in the evenings and her playclothes laid out.

Serving simple supper meals and getting to bed earlier provided a way to survive this stressful time. Power Plus was located close to John's brother's grocery store, and it gave me more opportunities to do my weekly grocery shopping, which was a rare event. I had plenty of energy and looked forward to going to work. Rollin was an easy-going boss, and I made new friends.

As my belly's size grew, it forced me to push my chair farther back from my work desk as the months went on. By the eighth month, I could have sworn I was having twins with all the activity going on below my rib cage and navel. One doctor appointment was moved back when I felt as though I had the flu and couldn't keep anything down, other than ginger ale. Thus, I had to call off one day from work. However, the scale showed climbing numbers.

By mid-November, I felt so fat and uncomfortable sitting at a desk and typing or doing payroll all day long. Hoping Rollin would understand, I told him my last day would be the Wednesday before Thanksgiving. "There is no way I want to continue with my schedule and sit at my desk for another two months," I explained, rubbing my big belly. He understood and mailed my last paycheck. The following week, John and I purchased a lovely dark pine suite for our bedroom, which we used for many years. By mid-December, I was assured I was not having twins. I inquired whether or not the doctor believed I would have back labor, as I did with Steph. He had no reason to believe why my labor would not be normal and across my abdomen. The doctor estimated my baby to be about 7.5 pounds at birth. Wrong in both counts!

Again, not surprisingly, my due date came and went. Six days later, true labor pains dictated a trip to the hospital. Steph was dropped off at her grandparents' house with a promise to soon have Grandma bring her in to the hospital to see Mommy and her new baby brother or sister. I braced myself for more back labor, which was all I knew. Yep, no front labor pains again. All my pain was pressure in my lower back. As in my previous labor with Steph, I asked John to "take the Mack truck off my back." Able to again endure labor naturally, I couldn't wait to hear the good news: "Push with all you got."

I faithfully logged monthly notes after each doctor visit in my *Care for You and Your Baby-to-Be* booklet. My chart indicated my total weight gain was twenty-six pounds. Finally, on the morning of January 24, my beautiful bouncing baby boy was born! Weighing eight pounds and six ounces, our baby was named Darrin Joel. Darrin (meaning "a gift" or "great") was selected from a baby book, and Joel, from the Bible. As I nursed and bonded with my adorable healthy baby, John and I again marveled how blessed we were to have one of each, a girl and now a boy.

Grandma and Grandpa brought in big sister Stephanie to see her baby brother. She was totally displeased why she couldn't climb on my lap whenever she felt like it. Before long, the family of four started their new normal. Within a few months of his birth, Darrin was dedicated at church. I remember it vividly as it was the first time I truly felt the effect of Darrin's large birth size. I have permanent damage from giving birth to such a brute. What do I mean? Well, whenever I am in a nervous situation I feel as though pins and needles are pricking all over my lower back. On Darrin's dedication Sunday, John and I, along with several other parents, stood up in front of the church and had our babies dedicated; a prayer for the parents and grandparents followed. As soon as I sat back down on the church pew, my lower back began to hurt. It took my breath away. I couldn't imagine what was going on. I have not ever felt anything quite like it. But I have learned to anticipate the pain, lasting about ten seconds, whenever I sit down after a nervous situation. I simply have learned to live with this permanent nerve damage (my diagnosis).

Being Daddy's namesake, Darrin wasted no time in putting on muscle and baby fat, causing pudgy legs and pudgy cheeks, so pudgy one could not keep their hands from pinching his cheeks, especially his mommy. Because he had an unlimited amount of raw milk, he was able to drink and ate finger food cereal whenever he was placed in his high chair to keep him occupied, while I finished making supper. Darrin grew and grew. Along with his stature, his forming mind was inquisitive. Darrin was full of questions. Day in and day out, he asked questions of anybody who listened. "Mommy, how high is that telephone pole?" Having no idea, I threw out an answer: "Thirty-six feet high." The next day, he asked the same question while I was driving down the road. I answered, "I dunno, honey. Thirty feet high?" "No, Mommy," he commented, "you said thirty-six yesterday." "If you know, why did you ask me again?" I asked, exasperated by the daily twenty questions. He remembers my answer, but I don't. Kids can wear you out with their whys and how comes.

Typical for my toddler children, Darrin needed a spanking at times to tow the line. One day, after scolding Darrin about something, he asked me, "Mommy, good boy sometimes?" This phrase, thirty years later, is still today a favorite family line, which is used and abused. On many occasions, we asked each other, "Good boy sometimes?" It always brings in a smile.

When Darrin was about five or six years old, his punishment was to brush Mommy's hair one hundred times. Since I love when my hair is played with, I frequently had made this my kids' spanking. Darrin was asked to bring Mommy her hairbrush and start brushing more times than the girls. "One, two, three,…" he'd brush away begrudgingly. Of course, the longer it went on, the shorter and ineffective each brush stroke became. By the time he said fifty-six, the brush was barely connecting with my hair (I don't think I ever got the full one hundred strokes out of them, but I received some delight). Perhaps later, when Darrin's platoon was asked in boot camp to "hit the deck and give me one hundred push-ups," he thought about his mom.

Darrin's first memory occurred when he was about three years old. He remembers standing at the end of our driveway with me waiting with his older sister Stephanie on the first day of school. She was entering first grade. Typical for me, my camera snapped pictures of this milestone. However, Darrin was upset his sister was waiting for a big yellow school bus to take her to school (whatever that means), while he was left behind on the farm. He was not very happy! Stephanie, the older and wiser one, assured him, "Believe you me, I am not going to have much fun. I will be home soon."

Standing together at the end of the driveway holds another memory for both Steph and Darrin they wish they could forget. At least one other school bus first passed their bus stop and was not assigned to pick them up. One morning, their pet dog, Mickey, ran into the path of the school bus which was passing them by and not stopping for them. Too late, both Steph and Darrin yelled for Mickey to stop. Unfortunately, the thud was heard as Mickey was hit by the bus's wheels and thrown to the side of the road. With tears streaming down both their faces, within seconds after they witnessed this tragedy, Steph and Darrin boarded their school bus. John and I were both oblivious to what had occurred. It was only when the school bus driver who hit Mickey stopped by within an hour to sincerely apologize that we learned of the event. Of course, John got busy burying Mickey down in the meadow before the children got home from school. The supper table conversation that evening was both lively and subdued: Steph and Darrin both wanted to tell the story about their morning at the same time with their parents. They grieved for several months for Mickey, rightfully so.

Living around three other farms, we saw many acres of crops as opportunities to see God's colorful creation during all seasons. The farmer neighbor, whose farm bordered ours, grew vegetables for Campbell's Soup. Requiring many hours of hard labor to raise many acres of crops forced the farmer to hire minority groups to assist in harvesting. One day, Steph and Darrin were outside playing in the yard. One of the hired hands, having reached the end of the row behind our barn, walked across our drive when he noticed our outside water faucet. He asked the children if he would be allowed to get a drink. After being told yes, he offered the drink to a few other hired hands, including a woman. By the time I arrived on the scene, about five people were drinking water from the hose. I noticed the woman's white blouse had two obvious dirty dusty hand marks exactly at her breasts! *Hmmm, some hanky-panky is going on.* I quickly chased the children to the other yard. But, of course, observant Darrin commented, once they were out of earshot, "Mom, she got really dirty."

Having children raised on a farm gave this mom plenty of reason to be nervous at times around Daddy's driving his farm equipment, tall silos, which had ladders reaching to the top and a corn shed filled with tons of loose shelled corn. A child could be playing in this tempting pile and be buried in short order. One Saturday, my niece was babysitting our three children so John and I could attend a farmer's event in town. The exact time we were pulling into the drive, I noticed five-year-old Darrin climbing about halfway up the silo ladder! Do I start screaming? No, this is the time to talk quietly and soothly—easier said than done.

With my heart pounding out of my chest, I stood at the bottom of the rung and looked up, up, up. "Darrin, honey, we're home. Come on back down very carefully, okay?" I stood on tiptoe reaching toward him. *Please, dear God! Self, just shush and don't distract him.* Does this child have no fear? I wouldn't think of being enticed by forty steps on the side of a tall silo.

Darrin casually climbed back down as though this was an everyday occurrence. He gave me a glance, as though saying, "What's the big deal, Mom?" Sometimes he would back down without looking; other times, he would turn around and look for the rung below. Until he was within reach, I had a sore taste in my mouth. After hitting the ground with his last step, he got a scolding that he won't forget. But the bigger scolding was laid on my niece who was busy watching TV. Thank God, no child ever again had the nerve to explore the world at the top of a silo ladder and the shiny tin round dome.

Uncertain if this continues today, a handwritten two-sided letter was sent home attached to Darrin's kindergarten report card. Having been a teacher, I took much interest in any teacher's letter. It read:

> I'm afraid Darrin isn't doing his best in regards to neatness. I know he is capable of nicer work—he has done a few really nice papers. But on the

> whole, his coloring and printing is in need of improvement. Darrin is doing well in reading. He knows his letters, their sounds and can blend them into words. Daily practice in reading at home will ensure success as we continue to get harder work. He is doing very well in math and also understands the concepts covered. Darrin has done well with his Bible verses, but they could be better memorized. He seems to understand what we're doing in class, but he does not volunteer as often as he should. Basically, I feel Darrin could do much better than he is doing. He seems tired a lot of the time (especially after nap), and he is becoming very "pokey" when doing his work, and I need to remind him to keep busy..."

I remember his first-grade teacher also requested my help in improving Darrin's forgetfulness and following instructions more closely. She recommended, "For example, tell Darrin to put the green ball in the brown chair, a specific toy on the sofa, and a certain channel on the TV." Prayer requests logged around this time included asking the Lord to give me understanding and to change my attitude on Darrin's restlessness.

Darrin struggled throughout his elementary years with similar issues, which started as a child. Later, his English and reading teacher wrote back to me:

> I want to thank you for "cracking the whip" with Darrin! You wouldn't believe the improvement you've initiated. He's still a bit forgetful, but he is much more conscientious about doing his work and doing it well. You can see the evidence by looking at his last composition. When I read your original note about Darrin's "disgusting" report card, I cracked up. "This," I thought,

"is great! She is not afraid to lay it on the line and make Darrin responsible for himself." You wouldn't believe how refreshing it is to see a parent take control of a situation rather than call a teacher and complain. So whatever you're doing, keep it up! Darrin's done a complete turn-around for me. Thanks so much.

Eventually, Darrin figured out his responsibility and his part on getting an education and how no one could do it for him. Much to Steph's and Rochelle's dismay, retaining class discussions and what the teacher taught became one of Darrin's strength. He did not spend much time studying for tests outside of the classroom or study halls. He seldom brought homework home. Darrin's grades remained above average and acceptable without putting forth, what seemed to be to others, much effort. He preferred, instead, to hang out with friends, be involved with sports, or work out in the school gym. Later on, receiving a paycheck and the freedom that came with it fueled having part-time after-school jobs and during the summer. He preferred being employed over studying, and it worked for him.

Today, Heather and his girls realize "Dad is forgetful. You'll need to send him a text and remind him later." As with most of his generation, Darrin seldom writes using cursive penmanship. Everything is either printed, looking very similar to his school homework, or typed. Well, I guess he turned out okay. After all, he did earn a bachelor's of science degree in business management.

Because I paid close attention to what TV shows my children watched, they were somewhat protected from the world's evils. Darrin remembers, as a child, watching *Little House on the Prairie*, *Dukes of Hazzard*, and *Hee Haw* (unlike today, these shows were viewed during prime time hours). When questioned if he remembers what TV shows he was not allowed to watch, which his buddies were allowed to, Darrin answered *Night Rider* and *Airwolf*.

So much for protecting my children from inappropriate material shown on TV; their babysitter I hired when I was a single mom (details in a later chapter) allowed them to watch trash! At first, Steph and Darrin did not tell me, but I soon learned this babysitter had no qualms about allowing her slightly older daughter and younger son and my children to watch R-rated movies. I spoke my mind and told the babysitter I would appreciate it if they saved watching those types of movies in the evening when my children were not present. By the end of that summer, Steph convinced me she could be responsible for her siblings and not hire a babysitter. Besides, they confessed later they both often left her lunch table still hungry. It was a win-win for both.

While living at East Petersburg during his visits, Darrin was fortunate enough to have Marcus, who was the same age, live right down the street. Marcus was a hemophilic. Being an entirely new situation for him, Darrin learned playtime with a friend who had this type of serious bleeding disorder meant he had to make some changes. No rough-housing, wrestling, nor taking a chance of any kind of bumping could occur. Marcus and Darrin played for hours in the park behind our home and on the running trails, which ran through it, without incident.

The following winter Darrin and Marcus were playing in the freshly falling snow. What boy can resist making snowballs? At one point, Darrin made one. He did not throw it toward Marcus but straight up in the air. Unfortunately, Marcus was hit in the face by the snowball. He screamed and ran home. Within minutes, Marcus's mom called me up on the phone and reported the incident. Funny how I never heard about the episode from Darrin until that moment. Of course, I educated Darrin once again on how careful he needed to be and to always think before he acted with every little thing. Thank God, Marcus was fine.

As most siblings do, Steph and Darrin had some fierce battles. But the conflicts made them closer and, in the end, enabled them to look out for each other. What a contrast from my childhood! I had not viewed fighting with my siblings as an opportunity for conflict resolution. Steph and Darrin's battles most times were arguments about clothing. Steph liked a new sweatshirt I bought Darrin and wanted to pull it out of his closet and wear it. Darrin was firm about getting the first chance to wear his new sweatshirt. In between the yelling matches, I couldn't believe my scolding was needed to tell my daughter she needed to pick out something feminine from her own closet. Why would she want to wear her brother's clothes? I couldn't fathom it.

Because I preferred it that way, our home became the neighborhood hangout. Most times, it worked out fine. Other times, not so much. On the days there was no school, I could expect a tornado to have gone through my home. In spite of the rule, Steph and Darrin were expected to clean up the house prior to our coming home from work. My rule fell on deaf ears way too many times. Probably PMSing, I overdid it one night coming home to a messy house. I quickly cleaned up the house before expected guests arrived. But later on that evening, after Darrin got home, I messed up the house again, similar to how I found it, told Darrin to clean up behind me, and then, as punishment, "go to bed *now*!"

Not liking clutter in my home, I also raised my children to follow household rules. "No touching Mom's Soft Batch cookies." My breakfast for years was two cookies with a cup of hot chocolate when I had to be at work by 6:00 a.m. Yikes! When they did not finish their chores, especially over the summer months when they were home alone (including some neighborhood kids as well) gave me ample opportunity to scold and yell. I regret today not handling stress over unfinished household chores very well. Looking back, I should have come home, and if I came upon any messed-up room, I should have grabbed a glass of wine, ignored it, walked through the house, and simply gone out on the deck giving them five minutes to clean it up before I walked back in. Okay, forget the wine part. But as my kids told me, "Mom, you had to know, we waited until the last ten minutes before you got home to clean up the house. You arrived home a little earlier today, and we just weren't ready for you." Sigh, sigh.

Not one to ask to go shopping very often, but when Darrin did, he expected me to buy name-brand clothes to keep up with his best friend, Davis. One night, Darrin went with me to buy Steph a used computer for her birthday. The seller had a bar built in one corner of his basement. Darrin was in awe playing the jukebox and admiring his miniature car collection and other expensive paraphernalia. On the way home, Darrin excitedly started talking about all of the "toys" the guy had. I used it as a lesson to teach him why he needed to get good grades in school, go to college, and become whatever he wanted to be so he was able to buy all that name-brand clothing and more.

Darrin's choice of high school sports was soccer and wrestling. His first position in soccer was goalie. Later, the coach placed him in defense positions. Not being used to all the running the position entailed, he learned to appreciate why his coaches made the team run laps. The second year, he never got to play one soccer game. Why? He broke his right femur during a summer pickup game scheduled to get them prepared for the season ahead. I was notified via a phone call about the situation and asked to go to the emergency room of Ephrata Hospital. Though it was not a serious reason to be hospitalized, it seemed strange to have my child be in the hospital and not his mother. Having his leg put in traction for a week, Darrin was limited to not doing much of anything but answering the phone, watching TV, and hanging out with his visitors.

Darrin's full-time job that summer was to babysit for my coworker's son, Pete. She paid Darrin $60 a week, a lot of money for a teenager back then. Coming home on crutches, Darrin was quite dependent on others to help him get around or have his needs met. If Rochelle thought she catered to her brother before, she surely was catering to him now. However, mischievous Pete took advantage of the situation. Laughing hysterically, Pete hid Darrin's crutches and made a game out of his being unable to chase after him. I don't even want to know the yelling and words that flew around in the air over that time!

Getting extra attention, Darrin had both solicited and unsolicited friends sign his leg cast. The worse part of the entire healing process was when they removed the pin later on in the doctor's office. It was extremely painful for him and difficult for me to watch. After the cast was removed and his fractured leg healed, Darrin was amazed how weak his right leg was when he first started walking on it again. Once again, Darrin joined his teammates on the soccer field. One of Darrin's senior year pictures was taken while performing the difficult bicycle kick (hitting the soccer ball with your foot while upside down). After many hours of practice, he was ready for the photographer (a relative) to take the picture midkick. It is a picture proving hard work pays off.

Watching Darrin during his wrestling matches made me so nervous. And you know what happens then? My lower back starts killing me. In the middle of certain wrestling holds, when it appeared as though Darrin was losing the match, my voice echoed in the crowded gym as I yelled, "Darrin, get out of that now!" Needless to say, later on, Darrin instructed his mother to "cool it." Cocalico's wrestling team did make it into the district tournament his senior year. Who was his wrestling opponent? One of his best friends from another high school. Unfortunately, Darrin lost.

As with most teenagers, they cannot wait to get behind a wheel and drive a car; Darrin was no exception. However, Darrin had to wait six months longer. Why? This was part of his punishment from a situation that occurred when he was fourteen between eighth and ninth grade. My thinking was he would have plenty of opportunity to explain to his buddies and classmates why he was still not driving. Each time, hopefully, his explanation reinforced in his mind how he made a huge mistake when he broke the law.

One day, I answered a phone call to hear a police officer on the other end. Long story short, Darrin and one of the neighbor boys were caught on the local bank's videotape. The two culprits were standing at the bank drive-up window holding socks stuffed full of quarters hoping to get them exchanged for one and five dollar bills. Were the quarters removed from their piggy banks? No! They were stolen from a pinball machine, which required quarters to work, in a park near our home. Earlier, the neighbor boy had stolen some monies from the machine. Believing a partner in crime made it more fun, he began to show Darrin how to play the game without actually using a quarter and how to empty the coin box. What do you do with dozens of quarters? Remove your socks and fill them with quarters. As with most youngsters who don't think of the consequences, they did not realize all bank activity at the drive-up window was videoed. The police officer reported back to the owner of the park and the pinball machines on which two neighborhood boys were the culprits. The owner decided to press charges.

The magistrate sentenced Darrin to pay back full retribution, plus serve thirty hours of community service. Feeling this was unfair, as he was for a full month simply the lookout guy before he actually committed a crime, Darrin thought the punishment should be less for him. But both criminals were sentenced alike. Thus, while most of Darrin's friends were enjoying their summer at the swimming pool, he was painting a fence as punishment. My punishment, in addition, was to write the victim a letter of apology, to write a letter to the local newspaper's letter to the editor to inform other teenagers breaking the law had serious consequences, and he needed to wait six months (at sixteen and a half years of age) before applying for his driver's license.

Other less serious pranks occurred in the neighborhood, which Darrin was also part of. I learned of his inappropriate behavior from an uninvolved neighbor boy, who thought it would be funny to get Darrin into trouble. He called our home, disguised his voice, and made me believe he was the neighbor man who lived closest to the affected area. I was informed Darrin was a part of a group of rowdy boys who participated in making homemade bombs, then setting them off in a nearby construction site. Just as I was getting ready to march Darrin over to the neighbor man to apologize, I learned the full correct story.

No parent wants to receive a phone call about your child caught shoplifting. What was the item for Darrin? A pack of baseball cards. This bad choice occurred between ninth and tenth grade. The security guard of the local mall called me and told me that his partner in crime was picked up by his father, but he did not offer to give Darrin a ride home. Thus, I needed to come down to the mall to pick up my son. Since the cards were unopened and still intact, they were returned back to the shelf without incident. How embarrassing! My scolding to Darrin on our ride back home was as necessary as the car fuel. I vented, and he listened the whole way home.

Being bored apparently, he and two buddies who lived in a different area did some mischievous things, which led to my receiving a phone call from yet another town's police officer when Darrin was in eleventh grade. One Saturday night, the driver decided to break into the local car wash coin box. Darrin and one other buddy were adamant they were not going to participate and stayed in the car. The break-in failed but did set off an alarm. A neighbor alerted the police and gave a full description of the car. Since it was a unique car that was difficult to hide, the police soon spotted the car with three boys inside. After a search of the car, the police officer found tools, which one could only assume, were used to attempt the break-in. All three were taken to the police station and interrogated separately. Both Darrin and the other innocent party told the truth of not participating in the actual crime and staying behind in the car.

I walked into the police station that Sunday morning so disappointed with Darrin. He noticed my stern angry face and high chin. "Mom, I swear I had nothing to do with this. I stayed in the car," Darrin enumerated with a pained stare.

"If you're guilty, you can go to jail and take the time to sit and think about some new improved choices you had better start making!" I threatened. The police officer asked for a few days to do more investigation, and he would be in touch with me. Darrin had told the police officer that he was planning on joining the marines immediately following his high school graduation. For two whole weeks, Darrin was sweating bullets while awaiting his verdict. I saw his having to wait was punishment too. Thankfully, the police officer believed him and did not charge him. Unfortunately, the other innocent buddy was not so lucky.

Eventually, participating in sports and holding down part-time jobs filled his days with no time or desire to break laws. Thankfully, none of these incidents prevented him from joining the marines. Yes, perhaps, if Mom had a crystal ball to see into the future, one would relax a bit when raising teenagers, especially a boy.

Early January 1995, when Darrin turned eighteen, he received his Selective Service form to be completed. It was an easy form to complete as Darrin had his immediate future already figured out at sixteen. How? Darrin's buddy, Dwight, had a cousin who joined the Marine Corps. He influenced Dwight to join. Thus, Dwight decided to discuss with Darrin about joining together. Something resonated with Darrin. Perhaps because deciding what college or major to select was a daunting choice, Darrin agreed and signed up for the Delayed Entry Program, as he still had to complete twelfth grade. Darrin was planning on going to boot camp immediately following his high school graduation. Before the first day of his senior year, he had passed his testing and physical for the corps.

One Friday night, I was watching the TV show *20/20*. What was the show about? Inappropriate hazing causing the death of a young man in boot camp in the Marine Corps. Feeling sorry for any parent who had believed their child would survive boot camp and return a man, I was appalled such craziness went on. Within minutes of viewing the hazing incident, Darrin walked through the door.

With eyes beaming and a wide grin, he announced he decided to join the marines. "Someone will be contacting you about signing your name to the paperwork, Mom." He could not stop moving.

"Wait! What? The marines? Are you aware, Darrin, about the hazing I just heard about on *20/20*? No way!" I stressed. "Oh, Mom," Darrin sneered. "That stuff really doesn't go on. How would they get more recruits to join if that really happens? Dwight's cousin survived it, and he didn't say anything about that. Dwight and I are signing up." Over time, he convinced me his future was sure—at least for four years.

For the remainder of twelfth grade, Darrin and we parents, also, regularly attended Marine Corps meetings (more like pep rallies). Darrin took on the challenge of remaining physically fit. Many long hours were spent in the high school gym workout room lifting weights, doing pull-ups, sit-ups, push-ups, and rope climbing; outdoors, he ran around the track for miles. Improving his results gave him staying power and fueled his enthusiasm. I learned about the terms *jarhead, cammies, chow hall* (to name a few), and the saying *oohrah*.

Of course, we parents were delighted not to have the expense of paying for partial college tuition, but sending my eighteen-year-old off to Parris Island gave me much trepidation. The backyard graduation and kick-off party was held for family and friends. Heather (his future wife) was one of the guests. In the middle of his boot camp planning, I stayed in denial somewhat. It was hard to fathom Darrin would be picked up by an officer, driven to Harrisburg, and soon be on his way to Parris Island for Marine Corps boot camp! Families were instructed they were not allowed to place any phone calls nor expect to speak with their loved ones for the next three months. Care packages were not allowed to be sent either. If any serious tragedy occurred, we were told the Red Cross would be the organization contacting the responsible party.

With many hugs and prayers sent heavenward, I, along with his family and friends, said our good-byes to Darrin. Endlessly teased about returning as a real man, Darrin and his duffel bag, filled with must-have items, boarded a bus and stepped into an entirely unknown world. Praying for his safety and return back home, a real man or not, I couldn't wait to learn about his life as a recruit for the Marine Corps and to have him back home before he was shipped off to additional training called MOS school in Mississippi.

One day, I walked into a room of a resident who had the local TV station tuned in to a news channel. As I was administering the resident's medications, I heard the news anchor mention about some casualties on Parris Island due to an unexpected lightning and summer storm. Apparently, during a training session for several platoons in an open flat area, suddenly a storm arose. Lightning struck and killed one person and severely affected each person on either side of him, who were hospitalized. What? Is Darrin okay? Please, dear God.

For the rest of the day, I could only pray and worry. Every time the phone at my nurse's station rang, I held my breath, hoping and praying it would not be someone calling from the Red Cross informing me of any news about Darrin. Anybody I had contact with over the next several hours, I had asked to pray for Darrin's safety. Only after forty-eight hours did I finally relax and realized the Red Cross would have contacted me by then. Of course, some unfortunate parents did get the dreaded phone call from the Red Cross.

The three months of not having any contact with Darrin seemed strange. We devoured any letter we received from him. I could tell he was homesick and was being challenged beyond what he expected. As I heard from the earlier pep rallies, recruit training was all about physically and mentally challenging the recruits to produce basically trained disciplined, ethical marines. I could only hope he was being treated fairly and with dignity as they turned my boy into a man.

Graduation day in Parris Island finally arrived, and families were invited to the ceremony— quite a sight to see. Proud young marines marched before us in impressive platoons. This graduation day couldn't even compare to Darrin's high school graduation. However, it was similar to how my nursing school graduation (details in a later chapter) meant so much more to me too because of the hard work, sacrificing loss of sleep, and mounds of effort to survive it all.

During Darrin's Mediterranean six-month float, he started to pursue his bachelors of science degree in business management, which served him well later when he decided to start his own business (more on his marine career is discussed in a later chapter). He finished his four years of service to his country. Much later, he decided to pursue joining the marine's reserves division. Unfortunately, he missed the age-limit cut-off. Thus, he had to join the Army National Guard, which he did in September 2010. Influenced by one of his friends, he set and achieved a lofty goal: attend officer training and become a second lieutenant in the US Army. After speaking with the recruiter, his enrollment occurred within two months. Darrin signed up for the OCS class by April 2011. In less than five years he has been promoted to captain. By the time he has served his country twenty years, he plans to be Major Darrin Weaver. I have no doubt he'll achieve his goal.

Being raised Mennonite and being taught not to believe in fighting in wars, I never dreamt I would have a son who would follow in my uncle's footsteps. I am so proud of him!

Thought of the Day

Grace is needed to fuel our days, as this life is only a pit stop, not a destination.

Chapter 28

My Best Ever Christmas Present

Then make my joy complete by being like-minded, having the same love, being one in spirit and purpose.
—Philippians 2:2

Rochelle, Duane, Alex, rear, Hope and Talon, front row

MY LAST LAST NAME IS GRACE

MY BEST EVER CHRISTMAS PRESENT was the gift of the birth of my youngest daughter, Rochelle Lynn, in 1980. For the first time, I was slightly having trouble getting pregnant. So the morning temperature taking and charting of ovulation times occurred, as advised by my doctor. I faithfully recorded my temperatures, and we took advantage of the best time for anatomy to work. Yahoo! I'm pregnant! After experiencing an uneventful pregnancy, I eagerly anticipated a winter season of enjoying my newborn baby and all that entailed. As with the other two pregnancies, my due date, December 5, came and went. What was the effect of this? Gaining my last three pounds and maxing out to thirty-five pounds. I tried to tell my doctor a Tastykake truck had a spill in front of my house, but he would not believe me.

Around ten days late, I was desperate enough to drink some castor oil, a remedy to start labor. Yuck! The only effect had me running to the bathroom the next hour. On December 20, fifteen days late, during a full-moon weekend, irregular contractions finally began on Saturday afternoon. Paying attention to the intensity, I climbed into bed around 11:00 p.m. Around 1:00 a.m., I woke up with the pain! I knew this was it. John and I dropped off our two other children over at Grandma's house and headed to the hospital. After an examination, the doctor reported I was four centimeters dilated. Ouch! It hurt! Once again, I was experiencing mostly back labor. How could I not remember the pain? Why did I ever forget how labor pains feel? Why did I even imagine those earlier false labor pains even hurt?

With regular contractions three minutes apart, I progressed from four, five, six centimeters dilated and finally reached transition stage of eight centimeters. I started shaking uncontrollably, and dry heaving began. Having had my other two children naturally, I wasn't about to ask for pain medication for this delivery either. Back rubs from hubby were quite helpful.

As soon as the nurse saw the baby crowning, I was wheeled into the delivery room. Rochelle (nicknamed Shelly) blessed this world with her presence on Sunday, December 21, around 8:15 a.m. Unlike her older cute blue-eyed, blonde sister, this beautiful eight-pound bundle had dark hair and brown eyes. Finally, all those aches and pains, nausea, kicks and squirms from inside of me for several months became a reality; it was all worth it! Realizing that my family and friends were all in church and unable to receive the phone call about my family's newest addition, I had to wait several hours before repeating the great news. That was tough.

After spending four days bonding in the hospital, Rochelle and I were discharged on Christmas morning. Stephanie and Darrin's best present that Christmas wasn't under the tree but was found in Mommy's arms. After some time hugging and kissing Mommy and Rochelle, big sister and big brother headed off with Daddy back to Grandma's house for a family Christmas meal. Darrin was more than happy to inform Rochelle later on, he was not all that thrilled with her being a Christmas present, making him no longer the baby.

Once again, Mommy and baby Rochelle were home alone for a few hours celebrating Christmas. Thrilled to be home amongst my children's newly opened Christmas gifts of toys and books, I awaited my promised plateful of Grandma's delicious Christmas meal. I was in my glory. A nursing baby filled my lap, and an awesome home-cooked meal brought a huge smile to my face. Merry Christmas, Jesus!

After innumerable times of dipping soiled cloth diapers in the commode, washing dishes and many other reasons for making my hands wet throughout the day, my hands started with a bad case of eczema. Yikes! My hands look wrinkly, like Grandma's. And I am only thirty years old! Eczema started to plague me when I was a teenager. Loving hot baths didn't help the situation any. At times, the itching on my inner thighs drove me batty. I would grab my hairbrush (my finger nails were too soft) and scratched away until I drew blood. Mom made a doctor's appointment for me when she noticed the red blotches all over my upper legs. Dr. Hess determined I was having a reaction and planned a process of elimination of items. He wanted me to stop wearing my panty hose for two weeks to determine if my nylons were a cause.

"Seriously, Dr. Hess"—I looked at him as though he had two heads—"I'm a secretary at a professional office. I can't go without wearing panty hose." As Mom and I walked out to the car, she wrapped it up. "Fine. You figure it out."

After trying various home remedies to no avail, I finally consulted my doctor for proper treatment. Dr. Courtney explained, my hands did not have a chance to allow the natural oils to replenish my skin before they are being attacked again with water, which stripped the oils away; the cycle continued. Thank God, as Rochelle grew out of the use for diapers, my hands were wetted less often, and my eczema slowly disappeared. My love for using hand cream started at this time. Every night, I lathered them with hope and a promise before retiring.

Different from my own childhood, all three children had the chicken pox illness at the same time. I prayed to God I would have enough immunity to be spared this contagious disease while caring for them, as I realized, as an adult, getting the chicken pox would not be a fun experience. He answered me. There is a picture of all three smiling kids standing against the bathroom door only wearing their underwear with red pox marks all over their body—and Mommy's not in the picture.

As much as Rochelle and Steph were far apart enough in age to forge a friendship more than sibling rivalry, Rochelle and Darrin's relationship was strained from the very beginning. Why? Rochelle's first memory around three years old was the time Darrin and she were fighting over who should be the one lying on the couch. Rochelle had laid down and tried to hide her arms because Darrin was pulling on her arms trying to get her off the sofa. Suddenly, he pulled her right arm out of joint. Screaming, she ran to me while Darrin became petrified. After calling for an emergency doctor appointment, I took her to Dr. Courtney to put her arm back in joint. Rochelle cried and cried while Dr. Courtney was soothingly talking to her. He fixed her arm, and Rochelle immediately stopped crying and accepted her googly eyed sticker from him.

With all of my three children, I would wake them up each morning by walking in their room and singing a song to them. If it was a Sunday morning, I simply added the word *Sunday*. Here it goes:

> Wake up, wake up, you sleepyhead,
> It's time for school today,
> Wake up, wake you, sleepy head,
> It's time to learn the Golden Rule;
> When the school (or church) bell rings Ding Dong
> And the bus is on its way
> Wake up, wake up, you sleepyhead
> It's time for school today.

It made for a much more pleasant way of facing the morning. I seldom had to reenter their room and nag them, but if I did, I simply said, "Rise and shine, sleepy head." I have no clue how Mom got me awake for school when I was elementary age.

Around four years of age, I noticed Rochelle was having trouble with pronunciation of certain letters, like R. After a few speech therapy sessions and simply growing out of it, she improved to normal speech. Around ten years of age, Rochelle had to have orthodontist work on her gums—her first experience with laughing gas. Her oral surgeon said she passed "because she laughed at my not-so-funny jokes." It was so worth it as today she too has beautiful teeth and smile.

Adding the third child to the household caused me to have plenty of opportunity to yell, scold, and discipline. I always felt under control but only barely—my breaking point was just right out of my reach, but it would not take much to reach it. Many prayer requests I logged during the children's younger years included "Help me guard my tongue. Help me not get too angry at the kids when they do wrong. Give me patience. Help me give more hugs and praises."

Much later, I journaled: "I feel so guilty. I lost my cool and was really yelling at the kids. Then I had to drop them off at their Dad's for the weekend. But at the same time, issues still remain. I am working full-time, attending four classes a week, plus doing homework, keeping the house and family together...it is not easy! I'm only asking for some cooperation and help (which they shouldn't have to be told) until we all get through this rough time. I'll have to talk and hug and patch things up Sunday night. Showing empathy for my heavy schedule, Shelly brings me breakfast in bed sometimes...what a nice way to wake up."

Regrettably, Rochelle did not have a cousin close to her age who could become a best friend, like both Steph and Darrin had been. However, at six years old, she was the perfect choice to be the cute flower girl for her cousin Karen's summer wedding. With her shoulder-length hairstyled, Rochelle, except for the bride, stole the show, especially when she fainted! Feeling hot and woozy, she tumbled over onto her left side and promptly fell to the ground while standing among the bridal party. I helplessly watched it all in slow motion. Someone nearby offered her a glass a water; the officiating minister did not skip a beat.

Instead of preschool, Rochelle was dropped off at a babysitter when she was four years old. As written about later, Rochelle and Mommy were living together without either of her sister and brother. We formed a bond necessary to survive the troublesome road ahead of us.

Since death is as much a part of life, I, like my own childhood, did not shelter my children from attending funerals and viewings. When Rochelle was around five years old, I took all three children to a neighbor boy's viewing. While serving in the navy, he had fallen to his death while jumping onto a ship. The family lived a few doors down from our home. His mother was a good friend of my sister. Thus, I wanted to show her support and attended the viewing. As we were leaving the funeral parlor, I heard Rochelle ask, "Mommy, why didn't the boy have X in his eyes?" Puzzled, I said, "What? I don't understand." Then I heard big brother Darrin scold her. "Shelly, you are so stupid. That is so dumb." Still not understanding, I asked Darrin what she meant by her question. "You know, Mom, in cartoons they show X in the eyes of characters when they want to show they died." No, I did not know that either. This busy Mom doesn't watch cartoons. But I laughed and laughed until I cried as we walked back home. Oh, the memories you just can't make up!

Rochelle's fifth-grade teacher was teaching her class about incubation. After a dozen chicks were hatched and survived, the teacher allowed her students to take one home. Being a parent who said yes on matters of indifference, I allowed Rochelle to bring a chick in the house. How much can the little thing possibly eat? Friday night, Twinkie, so named, chirped away all evening. Unless Rochelle would pick it up and pet it, it never shut up. Guess what the overnight hours entailed? Because Twinkie chirped all night long, the entire household was not too pleased. Saturday night, Rochelle got the brainy idea to take Twinkie in bed with her to keep it happy and quiet.

Sunday morning, Rochelle awoke lying on her stomach. She slowly opened her eyes and remembered she had a bed partner. But Twinkie was not on its side of the bed when she felt around under the covers, nor was Twinkie on the pillow. Rochelle slowly raised herself into a sitting position. There laid Twinkie—flat as a pancake! She shed a few tears and buried it in the backyard. As the last bit of dirt was covering Twinkie's body, Rochelle concluded, "Good riddance."

Rochelle's name means "little rock." She is a beautiful person inside and out. As her name depicts, she does things her way when she wants, where she wants, and how she wants. Rochelle is a great listener and tells it like it is. She is loyal and trustworthy and fun to be around. As her hubby says, smiling, "She is her own person." Yes, Rochelle has made some mistakes too. But I am so proud how quickly she has applied learned lessons and put them to work, rose to the top from inappropriate labels placed on her, and overcame too many years of having to listen to way too much stinkin' thinkin'. She is a survivor!

My family of three children have made it easy for me to answer when asked, "Whom do you love the most?" I sincerely answer, "I love Steph the "most-est" (as the children said) because she was my firstborn. I love Darrin "the most-est" because he is my only son. I love Rochelle the "most-est" because she is my baby. I love you all sooo much!"

Thought of the Day

Grace is needed to acknowledge my own sins I ignore and then gives me more grace to repent deeply.

Chapter 29

Ironing with a Twist

It is good that the heart be established by grace.
—Hebrews 13:9

MY NON-MENNONITE FRIEND JOAN INVITED me to attend a two-night seminar entitled The Total Woman that was to be held at the local high school. She explained that the author had written a book, and it became a best seller. The author decided to tour cities and promote her marriage philosophy to groups of women. *Of course, count me in.* Looking forward to two nights out and away from my childcare duties, I picked up Joan and drove to the event location.

After a brief introduction, the guest speaker, Marabel Morgan, entered from stage left during a round of applause. A beautiful, sharply dressed woman walked to the podium to begin her speech.

Someday, that will be you. I looked over at Joan to see if she was the one doing the talking. No, she is busy clapping. Besides, I would not have been able to hear her comment that easily among this noise. *Hmm…*

For two hours or so, Joan and I, along with an auditorium full of women, listened intently to Mrs. Morgan's ideas on how to cater to our men. Her lessons reiterated that a wife needs to appreciate, adore, and adapt to her husband. Hmm, this sounds like Mom: "Take care of your man." With humor and scripture, Mrs. Morgan gave applicable examples of how a wife could go about doing this. By the time our first lecture had ended, we were assigned homework: "Before tomorrow night, wrap yourself in Saran Wrap and greet your husband at the door."

Leaving the building feeling giddy and challenged, Joan and I discussed on the way home how impractical this would be for her to accomplish, as her son was much older than my child. Not having a husband with a nine to five job, but a stay-at-home farmer, I had the challenge of figuring out how to carry out my homework also.

The following afternoon, I made a plan to complete my ironing chore, with a twist. The idea was to wait until John came in for lunch and the baby was down for her nap. As per John's usual routine, after lunch, he either sits or lies down on the sofa with the newspaper for about half an hour. So, after lunch, John and the newspaper bonded. I set up the ironing board at the end of the kitchen counter six feet or so from the sofa and placed the clothing items to be ironed nearby. Engrossed in his newspaper, John kept his nose in it, while I was preparing the scene.

I stepped into the bathroom and removed my bra and blouse. Returning to the kitchen and facing the sofa and ironing board, I picked up my first piece of clothing and began to iron. Several minutes passed. *Hmm, I better ask him a question to get him to notice me.*

"Did you schedule the neighbor to do the milking the weekend we are going to the cabin? What hourly wage did you agree on?" I inquired as the iron smoothed out my dress sleeve.

"Yep," John answered me behind the newspaper without putting the paper aside. "No, we'll talk wages later on." He kept on reading the comics. *Well, Mrs. Morgan, now what?* After I finished ironing the entire first piece to no avail, I walked over and picked up the second piece of clothing. Prince charming was more interested in what Beetle Bailey had to say than to look at his wife.

Finally, while ironing my third piece, I lamented, "Well, this homework got an F." Puzzled, John peeped around the newspaper, noticed me, smiled, and asked, "What are you doing? Homework from last night, huh?" His attention returned to his reading. Shaking my head, topless Leanne got redressed. *Maybe the Saran Wrap would have worked.*

So I listened to the second night's lecture on Marabel Morgan's suggestions on how to be full of surprises and keep hubby guessing while wearing costumes as a cowgirl or showgirl or simply a naked lady wearing only high heels to spice up one's sex life. Practically guaranteeing a surrendering, serving wife earns one an appreciative, happy, and fulfilled hubby, Mrs. Morgan claimed to be proof. I pulled bits and pieces from her lecture, as I did not want to throw the baby out with the bathwater entirely. Understanding her clear message, I did purchase her book though.

Eventually, as our marriage deteriorated, our sex life became rather lackluster. There were too many c-days and not enough of knocked-my-socks-off ones. I became way too nonchalant. Farm chores, housework, and raising our family became more important than recognizing the need to keep date nights, spend weekends away together without kids to polish and hone our relational skills. Besides, my parents did not teach me any of that; Mom and Daddy made marriage look so easy. By the time a pastor recognized our dilemma, the *Titanic* was already sinking.

Much later, after sharing this tidbit with hubby about my failed experiment, he challenged me to reenact the same scene once again. Beetle Bailey would not keep his attention!

Thought of the Day

Grace is recognizing God is not the God of "I was." He is the God of "I am" and "I will." He is building His church. The Glory of God will reign at the end of time. Hallelujah!

Chapter 30

If She Can Wear Mary Kay

> A worthy wife is a crown for her husband, but a
> disgraceful woman is like cancer in his bones.
> —Proverbs 12:4

ONE DAY, I ANSWERED THE phone and accepted a Mary Kay facial. My friend Janie was stopping by to share the wonderful skin care products she could not stop raving about. Thus, she signed up to become a Mary Kay cosmetics consultant when offered the opportunity.

I first met Janie when I was a little girl. Our dads were hunting buddies together. Though Janie has more memories of my family visiting her family in Lebanon County, I do not have as many memories of our parents visiting at each other's homes. But I was reacquainted with Janie when I was a schoolteacher at Cedar Cove School. You see, Janie was the teacher for another parochial school. Calling it a field trip, we took our students for a visit at each other's school. Thus, she was another teacher whom I could unload to and one who understood my gripes and complaints about unruly students.

After Janie got married, she and her husband chose to become church members of a different Mennonite congregation than her childhood congregation. Being somewhat conservative, her church had strict dress code and guidelines that had to be followed.

So when I answered the door on the day of my scheduled facial, I was shocked! Before me stood a gorgeous lady (okay, she was always gorgeous, but now her face looked radiant) with teased hair in front of her head covering, perfectly penciled eyebrows, mascara-laden eyelashes, wearing eye shadow, rouge, and lip gloss. Her cape dress had all the ruffles, lace, and frills her church allowed. Since her dress was handmade, the added one-and-a-half-inch lacey ruffle made her dress midcalf length acceptable.

After a quick hi, I said, laughing, "If you can wear it, I can wear it. Come on in and show me your stuff." Perhaps becoming one of her fastest customers, I was thrilled with the Mary Kay facial results and purchased the full skin care set (without consulting hubby). Again, I rationalized John too would understand: "If Janie can wear it, I surely can." He did indeed agree.

Then as any competent consultant should, Janie gave me the speech about becoming a Mary Kay cosmetics consultant like her. "We need more consultants in Lebanon County, and you would be perfect for this, Leanne. It's a great part-time job," she concluded. *Hmm, I have heard these similar words before this.*

About two years earlier, I had been invited to attend a Rubbermaid party at my friend Joan's house. The demonstrator, Faye, feisty and convincing, proudly demonstrated her wares to the prospective customers, her hostess and her guests. By the time Faye was handing me my copy of the sales receipt, she looked me in the eye and said, "Leanne, we need more demonstrators in Lebanon County. I would love to start a sales territory up here extending beyond Lancaster County. Is there any reason why I can't stop by sometime next week and talk to you more about this great income opportunity with Rubbermaid?"

Within one week, I was signing the contract to become a Rubbermaid party plan dealer. But not before sweetly convincing John why I should even consider doing this. The following evening, he was sitting at the desk reviewing farming paperwork. I went to him and sat on his lap. What followed was a speech about why it is good for our children to have their daddy give them their baths and put them to bed one or two nights a week, while I am out earning some money. "They are with me day in and day out. I am the one who tucks them into bed every night. Having you spending time with them would be most beneficial," I reiterated. He was hesitant about my driving back and forth alone late at night from who-knows-where and putting extra mileage on our car. But John eventually agreed for me to give it a try. After all, who cannot use more income?

So, once again, Leanne was back in the workforce. On Monday mornings, I dropped off my children at the babysitter, usually Grandma or my friend, Karen's house, and drove down to Faye's home for a weekly sales meeting. Learning how to be equipped to sell our products, keep generating income by ongoing bookings of parties, and reviewing new product lines, I took on the challenge of being one of Faye's top saleswomen.

It wasn't long before John realized we needed a different car, which could haul my four large cardboard boxes stuffed full of my Rubbermaid products. Thus, we bought a Volero station wagon, trusting it would be dependable and cheap-running. For almost two years, I completed my household chores, made dinner, kissed hubby and kids good-bye, and took off to fill varying county homes with the best household products available through a party plan. Making new friends, learning how to become organized from tried-and-true tips from Faye, realizing the great income from just three or four hours of work per night, I thrived on trying to increase my weekly sales amounts and seeing my income steadily rise. Our household monthly budget bottom line held more positive outcomes than negative ones, finally.

On the day the monthly corporate office's list of sales amounts arrived in my mailbox was always a cause for excitement. With anticipation, I eagerly scanned the list and looked for my name on the list of Pennsylvania's "Top Fifty Sales". What joy when I saw my name listed! At times, I was in the top forty; other times, top twenty. My sales totals led to my being one of Faye's top consistent saleswomen.

One day, Faye told me I earned a spot to fly to Chillicothe, Ohio, to visit the Rubbermaid headquarters. Being excited about my first airplane ride, I was eagerly anticipating a two-day trip with other saleswomen. Flying out of Lancaster Airport, I boarded a small airplane that held our luggage in the rear. I was awestruck appearing down on God's beautiful country from a bird's-eye view. Countryside of rolling hills, snaking rivers, many miles of turnpike concrete, and beautiful patchwork farms greeted me as I gazed downward out of my small window. Thank you, Wright Brothers, for this memorable experience. Except for a few air pockets, our flight was smooth and uneventful. Before long, our plane landed, thankfully safely, and we were taxied to our hotel.

I was excited to be a part of this all-expense-paid trip; I felt proud to be named among the hardworking sales team from Lancaster, Pennsylvania. We toured the manufacturing plant and determined picky quality control people make for good quality products to ensure satisfied end users. The demonstrators witnessed firsthand our company's methods and were proud of our company's quality control.

Upon our return trip home, we were spurred on and more psyched than ever to continue to sell household products, which we could proudly display. To bring on new products each quarter kept the sales totals climbing for me and put more money in my wallet.

Lo and behold, Faye asked me to please consider being one of the guest speakers at our next district meeting in Hazelton held a county away in a Holiday Inn. Like any other good sales meeting agenda, top sellers were encouraged to share tricks of the trade and what led to their great successes. So I consented.

I was excited about an overnight stay and a break from mommy duties. I packed a suitcase, my speech notes, and carpooled to our sales meeting. My presentation was scheduled for Saturday morning. Feeling nervous, I stood in front of my peers and simply spoke about what worked for me. I owed a huge amount of credit to my district leader, Faye, and I shared tidbits on what I had learned from her and what had proven to be a success.

At the end, while returning to my seat in the midst of the applause, I said to myself, "Okay, Lord, I remembered the setting when I heard you say 'one day that will be you.' I just shared in front of about forty to fifty ladies. There you go." *No, Leanne, this is not it,* I sensed in my spirit.

For one or two, and if I was lucky, three nights a week, I peddled fantastic, durable products from plastic hanging planters, cutting boards, and storage containers giving Tupperware (a swear word) competition. I've learned cutting boards are great spanking tools. I still use mine today over forty years later (not to spank, though, but for its original use).

Yes, there were plenty of times when my scheduled parties were canceled by the hostess at the last minute. Having a datebook with two or three parties scheduled did not mean that was the actual number of parties held. So my income varied from week to week. I admit, sometimes I was glad to have a party cancelled if I had to drive forty miles, for example. Or after a day of working hard canning and freezing, I did not mind not having to work that evening.

One day, Faye announced (and a corporate office letter in my mailbox confirmed) the division of home party plan for Rubbermaid was folding. We soon all would be without our jobs, as they were planning on expanding their retail product lines.

So the timing for Janie to stop by and give me a Mary Kay facial was perfect. As a satisfied customer and needing to replace my part-time job, it wasn't long before I signed my second contract and became a Mary Kay cosmetics consultant. Though the size of the party attendees may have been somewhat smaller and was held around a kitchen or dining room table, I promoted their awesome skin-care line.

With previous party plan experience under my belt, I jumped in with two feet to achieve the same sale's goal for my new senior consultant, Romaine. Soon I was awarded for being one of the top weekly salespersons. Both of us being competitive, Janie and I soared as our sales amounts rose consistently, offering facials to different circles of family and friends. Mary Kay was a product that required reordering (unlike Rubbermaid); thus, Mary Kay customers needed to call six months later to order refills on their cleanser, mask, or moisturizers. What a grand idea: sell an item that would require repeat business. Yep, Mary Kay Ash was a wise woman.

Once again, though in a different part of Lancaster County, I drove down and started to attend Romaine's weekly sales meetings. Making more new friends, which promoted a sisterhood, though my competitors, I filled my datebook, was as busy as I wanted to be, scheduling facials and selling Mary Kay. My UPS driver was soon known on a first-name basis as he delivered many packages of products, including quarterly prizes, such as jewelry, household items, and organizational items to help boost my career.

One day at our weekly meeting, Romaine announced the dates for the upcoming annual Mary Kay cosmetics seminar to be held in Dallas, Texas. Romaine informed Janie and me that we earned the privilege, due to our sales volume, to be part of a select group who were invited to tour Mary Kay Ash's pink office. Along with other high-ranking senior consultants, Romaine had also planned a sales recognition meeting during a breakout session. Again, I was asked to share in front of the group how I reach my sales goals. After scheduling babysitting, selecting the right outfits, and packing a large suitcase, I bought a plane ticket with my earnings. The day finally arrived when the excited consultants boarded our flight to Dallas.

Able to hold a candle against any Miss America pageant, Mary Kay cosmetics' bevy of beautiful competent women dressed in their finest and wearing envious jewelry filled the auditorium. As the names of queens of sales and queens of recruiting were announced from the various areas throughout the country, glowing radiant women accepted their awards on stage. Women, who had quit other careers to climb the Mary Kay ladder, were now excelling in leadership, some overseeing a few consultants, others over hundreds of them. Some were handed keys to a hard-earned free pink Cadillac, while others became millionaires from recruiting commissions.

Besides myself, Janie had recruited other ladies to become consultants; thus, she earned the award for having the highest number of recruits for Romaine that year. The time came for Janie and me, along with other successful saleswomen, to share our success stories in front of our peers in a sales meeting, which was attended by seventy to eighty women. Once again, while sitting back down, I said to the Lord, "Okay, I spoke in front of a larger group tonight. I get why You said 'one day that will be you.'" *No, Leanne,* I sensed in my spirit, *that was not it.*

Eating fabulous four-course meals in a most stunning hotel dining room, listening to motivational speakers, such as Zig Ziegler and Roger Staubach, and personally touring Mary Kay's pink office, Janie and I were flying high as we headed home on our own wings (okay, I admit, we did need the wings of US Air after all). But we definitely soared as we left Dallas with dreams of our own pink Cadillacs parked in our driveways. The closest I came to that goal was to win Romaine's contest of drive my pink Cadillac for a day. *Oh, well.*

One day, an invitation arrived in my mailbox to attend my seventh year Cocalico class reunion. Because I had not attended my fifth-class reunion when I was eight months pregnant, I decided I wanted to attend this one. Sporting a popular shag haircut and wearing Mary Kay to cover any flaws, I looked forward to dressing up for the "night out." As typical of high school class reunions, former classmates were busy catching up with each other's lives. I was looking forward to the shock when surprised classmates would notice I no longer wore my head covering and wore more makeup. Esther and I walked over to a group of guys. She began to talk comfortably with some of the guys, whom she had seen around town from time to time over the last eight years. Most did not seem surprised she no longer wore her head covering.

At one point, a former classmate looked at me and inquired, "So whose wife are you?"

"You don't recognize me. Did I change that much?" I smiled with a playful grin. "I'm one of your classmates." In disbelief, several exchanged confused glances. Finally, Dave, my eighth-grade dance partner, spoke up and said, "Oh, yes. Wow! I know who you are."

However, the remaining guys, holding their beer bottle close, remained confused. The worst culprit, and the one who teased me the most about wearing the head covering during my high school years, opened his mouth wide and gasped. "Wait. I would remember if you were one of my classmates." I smiled and teased, "You guys couldn't picture my head covering eventually being taken off at night, having my long hair flowing down, and you couldn't date me for my personality. Well, it was your loss." I emphasized, snickering.

They walked over to the on-display class yearbook and thumbed through it. One guy stepped back away from the table, gave me a quick once-over glance, and back again to my senior class picture. "Leanne…it's you!"

"As I said, you couldn't see beyond the covering," I chided, laughing, as I thumbed through the yearbook.

Eventually, John was no longer supportive of my being a Mary Kay cosmetics' consultant, so I quit. When I became a single mom, I realized I could easily activate my consultant status. But I knew leaving my children at home so I could sell Mary Kay in the evening, after working full-time, would not be wise. That would be showing them the wrong priority. Thus, to Romaine's dismay, I ceased holding parties.

Today, I still wear Mary Kay proudly. I cannot help but smile when I hear someone say to me in the presence of my granddaughters, "Your daughters…"

> Aerodynamically, the bumble bee shouldn't be able to fly, but the bumble bee doesn't know it so it goes on flying anyway…God didn't have time to create a nobody, just a somebody…I believe that each of us has God-given talents within us waiting to be brought to fruition…There are four kinds of people in this world:
>
> * those who make things happen,
> * those who watch things happen,
> * those who wonder what happened, and
> * those who don't know that anything happened! (Mary Kay Ash)

MY LAST LAST NAME IS GRACE

Thought of the Day

Grace is understanding you are beautiful inside and out as your perfect Creator designed you. You are beautiful because you reflect His holiness.

Chapter 31

Leanne's Bargain Boutique

> He has saved us and called us to a holy life—not because of anything we have done but because of his own purpose and grace. This grace was given us in Christ Jesus before the beginning of time.
> —2 Timothy 1:9

JOHN'S FAMILY WAS GATHERED AROUND our living room one Sunday afternoon. Somehow, the topic of conversation changed to discussing my Mary Kay part-time job. His brother came up with what he thought was a brilliant idea. "John, why don't you build an addition onto the front of the barn in order to add about five or six more cows on each side of the barn walkway? Then, Leanne, you can stop running around the county selling your stuff and stay home and help John milk the cows. The income from those additional ten to twelve cows' milk would generate more, I'm sure, than what you are making now. No?" he asked as he twirled a toothpick around in his mouth.

Swallowing hard and biting my tongue, my mind started to process an appropriate answer. *Should I slap him on the left or right side of his head? Are you kidding me? Are you my husband?* I swallowed hard and gave a feeble explanation of why I like getting out of the house a few hours each week. I believed it was necessary for John to have one-on-one time with the kids in the evening. Unsmiling, I glanced over at John for eye contact and support. I got neither. What I heard come out of his mouth instead sounded like an echo in the room.

As I looked to various sisters-in-law or to my mother-in-law for someone to side with me, I met more silence. So I began once again to rationalize, "Besides, you guys know I wasn't raised on a farm. I have no interest in milking cows." I purposely changed the subject.

After everyone left to go home and the children were tucked into bed, in our bedroom I brought the subject up again with John. "You know, I didn't appreciate that you didn't stand up to your brother on my behalf. He's not my husband. You are." I reiterated as I lathered on hand cream.

Not looking at me, John started undressing and laying his clothes on the radiator. I continued, "You gave me your blessing a long time ago to sell Mary Kay as a part-time job. Yes, I realize that the income is inconsistent and not money we can always count on. But when I do have a party, I make a great hourly wage." I pulled the covers back and crawled into bed. As I tucked the quilt under my chin, I mumbled, "I won't ever be milking our cows or anybody's cows."

I turned over in bed away from John and tried to get some sleep. But just as a ruminating cow, I chewed and regurgitated again and again John's brother's comments in my mind. *Who does he think he is? How dare he, in my own house, stick his nose in our business about our income?* I finally fell asleep. But I felt like a drifting untied canoe. Though there were two of us in this bed, I started to feel so alone.

Shortly after this incident, I was shopping in a consignment shop in Lebanon. The owner started telling me how she was forced to close her store due to a rent increase and other personal problems. She informed me that all her racks, shelving, and signage were also for sale. My mind started churning, and I began to ask her lots of questions about how to open my own thrift shop. With a promise to hold on to any start-up items for me, she encouraged me to call her the next day; thus, we exchanged phone numbers. The following day, she continued to answer more questions about where to purchase the price tags, how to register a business name, and how to report quarterly taxes on certain items, like pocketbooks and baby strollers, etc.

Feeling equipped to answer many questions that John could possibly have, I presented my dream to him one evening over the dinner table. Realizing that we had to make the decision in three weeks before the owner's lease ended, and she would be emptying the building of its contents, John and I seriously discussed how feasible it would be to bring my idea to fruition.

As with all business ideas, pros and cons need to be visited. The pros were: (1) I would have the shop open from 10:00 a.m. to 4:00 p.m., and Saturdays 10:00 a.m. to 3:00 p.m. Obviously, I would no longer schedule any Mary Kay facials or parties during the day, but only in the evenings. It would mean that I would be home during the shop's business hours. (2) Having small children would not be a hindrance, as I could take them with me into the shop as needed. (3) There is no expense outlay for stock, as I would be given clothing and other items as donations to sell on consignment. (4) I could spend my time selecting or pricing clothing while watching TV in the same room with John in the evening. (5) It would help our clothing budget, as I would purchase items for our own children at a reduced price.

The cons were: (1) The initial investment to fix up the washhouse. It would require new flooring, a new door, a heating system, overhead lighting, a countertop, and a cash register for starters. (2) The expense of building an arbor so the washhouse and house would be connected to satisfy borough regulations. (3) The outlay for the racks and shelves, pricing supplies, and signage from the previous owner. (4) The cost of registering a new business and advertising.

Not sure exactly what all reasons John had for agreeing with me to start up my own consignment shop, within a short period of time, Leanne's Bargain Boutique, selling items from size infants through fourteen, was registered in Pennsylvania.

Just as with my other previous jobs, I jumped in with two feet. We found a reasonably priced carpenter to do the required construction. As the word went out among family and friends, as well as with the help of a weekly ad in the local newspaper, the bags of donations started to be dropped off. Many hours were spent selecting clothing, pricing items, and arranging the clothing on the racks and shelves in the store.

Opening day finally arrived! The shop was stocked, organized, and racks were mostly full. The sign on the door was turned to Open. And then, I waited. The first shoppers were friends, neighbors, and family who arrived to show me support. Though the cash register was opened and closed several times a day, it was going to mean selling lots of baby onesies, cute toddler dresses, and boy's pants to start showing numbers in the black.

That first month, every time I heard a car drive up our driveway, my heart skipped a beat. A customer! Stopping what I was doing, I simply walked outside my door a few steps and entered the shop a little later, giving the potential customer time to browse. Sometimes, donations were simply dropped off, and no purchases were made by the customers. But buying customers were too few and far in between, unfortunately. Being small, the washhouse was not big enough to sell big-ticket items like strollers and playpens.

Bookkeeping needed to be meticulous to keep track of who gets what amount of money. Checks were written and mailed to my consignees. Quarterly taxes were filed and paid on nonclothing items to keep Uncle Sam happy. Other stresses started to crop up over time, like when I felt inconvenienced about when I could go grocery shopping, for example. Oh, that's right. My shop sign says Open. I can't leave right now.

Eventually, I wanted to live my life and not have it dictated by a sign on my shop. Sometimes, I would take chances and turn the sign around to Close and leave to go shopping or whatever. Since John was home and took a break over lunch, I would leave during that hour, knowing he could tend to the boutique if need be.

Even though we lived along a well-traveled road, location, location, location makes sense. I learned that ladies who worked did not feel like stopping in at my shop while heading home from work; they had dinner to prepare. In time, yard sales became my competition.

I wrote in my prayer journal that year: "Help the shop's business to grow or definitely close the door." Gradually, customers lessened. There were days when I had only one customer, then only a few for the entire week, and then no customers for days. Leanne's

Bargain Boutique became a statistic, a business that could not survive the three-year mark. *Well, well. That failed. But I'm not going to start milking cows.*

Extra time in my schedule was soon replaced with sitting on the board for developing a brand-new Christian school in the Lebanon area. After being asked to consider and pray about it, I decided this was a challenge I wanted to be a part of. Having selling experience under my belt, I was the perfect candidate for becoming a board member for New Covenant Christian School. Many phone calls and visits were made by us to local businesses asking for donations to assist in this huge endeavor. With God's blessings and timing, in spite of our inexperience, our first benefit auction proceeds totaled $16,000!

Today, more than thirty years later, New Covenant Christian School's website states: "A K4 to 12th grade school dedicated to transforming our community through deeper relationships: students and families, church communities, local community, and world community…New Covenant has been developing people of intelligence and integrity through high academic standards combined with the application of the Word of God in daily living. New Covenant Christian School is building leaders for our world." Now that accomplishment I am proud of!

Thought of the Day

Grace is getting up over and over and over and over and over again, while keeping your eyes on the Lord. Sometimes, we are asked to walk on water. Sometimes, we need to simply reach out in faith and grab ahold of His hand.

Chapter 32

From Dairy Farm to Poultry Farm

*In his heart a man plans his course, but
the Lord determines his steps.*

—Proverbs 16:9

ONE DAY, JOHN CAME HOME after visiting a local farm supply store. He said he ran into a representative for Buttercup, a local wholesale egg producer, who was trying to have farmers and landowners in Lebanon County build huge chicken houses that contain sixty thousand chickens. I could not fathom a building that would be so huge to hold that amount of chickens, plus have a room large enough to be able to pack eggs for shipping.

As with any good business idea (sounds familiar?), we discussed the pros and cons. Pros: chickens replace cows. Cons: chickens replace cows. Okay, seriously, we knew we had to visit a successful poultry farmer in our area first to even begin to make sense out of why we should stop dairy farming. We might have driven by large poultry farms, but until you have a reason to be interested, you simply do that—just pass them on by.

With the Buttercup's salesman's assistance, we had an appointment to observe a local poultry farmer during the time he would be packaging eggs to observe this process firsthand. We drove up the farmer's lane. One could not help noticing the building that seemed to be as long as a football field. Inside, the tour began on the second floor at the beginning of a row of several tiers of metal cages packed with white chickens. Once you got beyond the cackling noise and the smell, initially, one noticed how a trough was designed to catch all the eggs that were rolling down from the slightly slanted floor of the cage. When turned on, a conveyor belt of sort would move all the eggs to the end of the row, travel across the front, and finally, through a window in the wall and into the automated egg packing room.

If your eye followed the trough full of eggs or the length of cages, it appeared to reach beyond your vision. You could not see the other end. The building had six rows total of three-tiered-high cages. We then proceeded to the egg packaging room. Oh, wait, what's that lying on the aisle? A dead chicken? "Yes," the poultry farmer explained. "It is not uncommon for a chicken house this size to have up to nine dead chickens a day." Yikes!

Like any well-oiled machine, the automation of how the eggs were packed by machines in perfect timing was amazing to watch. Filling the egg cartons one whole row at a time, the machine selected and dropped eggs quickly, repeating the process in an assembly-line fashion. Once the egg carton was filled, it was moved to another section of the assembly line ready to be stacked six high. Once that was done, the eggs were packaged into specific egg boxes, placed on pallets, and lined up in a cool temperature-regulated room. Several times a week, a refrigerated Buttercup truck driver would pick up a minimum of eight egg pallets. The Weavers would be one of the poultry farmers for the egg wholesale business to supply eggs to restaurants, schools, and grocery stores.

John asked questions of the representative and the poultry farmer and seemed pleased with their answers. "Discuss it with your wife and let us know your answer soon," the rep said. Once again, the Weaver household was abuzz discussing new possibilities. The following day, John answered the phone and heard the rep on the other end. "One question: You own the dairy farm, correct?" John answered, "No. We rent from my parents."

"Oh, boy, that's a problem," he answered. "You need to own it. Is there any chance of your buying the farm from them?"

Not only did we have to make the decision of whether or not we even wanted to pursue poultry farming versus dairy farming; we had to start the conversation with John's parents about this new venture. They had no idea at all what their son and his wife were even contemplating. Plus, would we even qualify for a loan to purchase the farm? Shortly thereafter, we invited John's parents over to the house to discuss Buttercup's proposal.

The obvious pros were that John did not have to be up as early to process eggs, as he needed to be to milk cows. The work was not as difficult, and his dad could assist, just as he enjoyed helping out at times with milking the cows. (Eventually, his dad could do the egg processing work all by himself—something he could not do when milking cows.) During those few times a year when we went to the mountains, and John wasn't home to do the work, egg processing should be a lot easier to hire someone in his absence. But most of all, John was simply ready for a change. He had been milking cows since he was a young boy.

Liking the idea of selling the farm to their son, his parents gave us the green light to start the inquiry of obtaining a mortgage for both purchasing the farm and a loan to build the chicken house. Should not one assume his parents would sell the farm at a slightly below market price to their son (especially to the one son, out of three sons, who chose to stay working on it and took over the farm management since he was fourteen)? Ah, no.

Lo and behold, John's brother found out about what was about to happen and, of course, had to add his own two cents. Not only did we have to pay full market value for the farm, but we found out later the money was loaned to the other son to reinvest in his business, who in turn paid his parents a higher interest rate. It was a win-win for father and *one* son.

Within a short period of time, John and I had an appointment with a loan officer. After listening to him rattle off monthly mortgage amounts, the actual total of money that would be paid by the end of the loan, and being reminded of the consequences of loan defaulting, John and I signed our "John Henry's" on a fifteen-year loan. Whew! Are we crazy?

Buttercup's contracted construction company, Emerald Construction's crew started bringing building materials, construction vehicles, and laborers to an area behind the house onto a field that once was used to raise crops. Upon the completion of the huge chicken house, inside and out, the last final step ensued: washing and cleaning the entire interior. Next, we watched the tractor trailers, filled with stacked-high crates of sixty thousand chickens, arrive and place them in their new clean home. Pallets of empty egg cartons and egg boxes filled the processing area.

The Weavers became poultry famers! An amazing automated process from eggs rolling into a trough to being packaged for the end user became a new normal for John and his dad twice a day. Buttercup's delivery trucks arrived and carried away pallets of eggs, guaranteeing a monthly check. Devising a simple plan of always transferring into our savings account regularly what amount needed to be pulled out of our paycheck to meet the mortgage payment, I always had money to pay the huge mortgage.

By fourth grade, Darrin was a great help to his dad. He felt so grown up to be running the hand-drawn skid loader backing the pallets into their proper place in the refrigerated storage area. Watching Dad break the necks of diseased chicken was a daily occurrence. The not-so-pleasant part was carrying dead chickens to the dumpster. It was paramount to keep the huge poultry operation running full tilt.

Year in and year out, things went well—until the avian flu hit. This devastating poultry disease was running rampant, spreading throughout Lancaster and Lebanon counties. In the 1980s, H5N2 struck Pennsylvania and destroyed seventeen million, our worst bird flu outbreak in the United States to date. Holding our breaths, we prayed that our poultry farm would be one of the lucky ones, but no.

We emptied the entire chicken house and assisted Buttercup's staff to disinfect every nook and cranny that any operating room doctor would have been pleased when finished. Then we waited for the Buttercup rep and the Department of Agriculture to give us the green light to refill the house once again with a fresh shipment of birds and be back in business. No, our first white-glove inspection failed. Stricter disinfecting ensued, and again, we waited. Yes! We passed! We survived the flu outbreak. Then salmonella pummeled the Northeast. Enough is enough.

Eventually, more than the avian flu and a spread of salmonella were the downfall of the poultry farm. Equipment started breaking down, requiring John to call a repairman. No downtime was affordable. Thus, John summoned one, and he arrived within hours. Unfortunately, along with his presence was a $150 (expensive back then) hourly fee the minute his boots hit the ground. Okay, anybody can slip that expense into your budget a time or two. But soon, it became way too frequent and expensive for a building that was to be paid off in fifteen years (usually half of the amount of time a house is mortgaged). Yet, the equipment was not lasting half of that time before John needed replacing and repairing it. Later on, Emerald Construction admitted to using recycled material in their new poultry house constructions. It was simply a poorly engineered product.

Failure and disappointments were occurring in the poultry farming aspect at the same time the poultry farmer's marriage was being way too taxed as well. After I had moved out (details later), John was forced to claim bankruptcy and hold an auction to get as much money as he could out of the remaining stock and barrel. No, Mennonites don't sue, but won't somebody hold Emerald responsible for not playing fair?

Facing the dilemma of what job should he seek after his farming days ended, John was hired by his brother as one of the managers in his huge grocery store, a job he holds to this day.

Thought of the Day

Grace is the ability of God to always do in me what I need to do. Grace is needed for all my assignments when in His will.

Chapter 33

The Agony of Being Destoned

Look upon my suffering and rescue me, for I have not forgotten your instructions. Argue my case; take my side! Protect my life as you promised.
—Psalm 119:153–54

WHAT A THIRTIETH BIRTHDAY PRESENT! I spent it recuperating in a hospital after a right partial nephrectomy (surgical removal of one or both kidneys). The surgery was necessary to remove a large kidney stone, called a staghorn calculus, in my right kidney. Instead of the stone passing through, it attached itself to my kidney wall and grew over time.

During my nine-month pregnancy with my third child, Rochelle, my urine was routinely tested by my family doctor from March to December of 1980. Several urine tests were positive for blood. Thus, my family doctor prescribed antibiotics, but to no avail. After Rochelle's birth, I had no reason to check more urine tests, and I totally forgot about my prior positive test results.

By the following fall, John and I decided we were not having any more children—three were enough. We planned a special weekend getaway in November to celebrate our tenth wedding anniversary. Not desiring to continue with birth control, we discussed a permanent solution. What a better time to not have to worry about becoming pregnant? Either John needed to undergo a vasectomy, or

I needed to have a tubal ligation. Believing giving birth three times had me winning hands down, I clearly voiced my opinion: John needed to have a vasectomy. Did he agree with me? No! "I don't want to go through any pain," he commented. Women are not the weaker sex, are they?

My tubal ligation was scheduled for October 1981, one month prior to our anniversary trip. But first, my doctor scheduled a chest X-ray to rule out any cause for concern prior to my surgical procedure. Being deemed fit for surgery, I made childcare arrangements for Rochelle. John and I arrived at the hospital. Since October is small-game hunting season, John arranged to go hunting as soon as I was under the knife. Before I became drowsy and was wheeled into the operating room, the nurse informed me that my chest X-ray showed gravel in my right kidney. Having the upcoming tubal ligation in my mind, I totally forgot about the important observation the nurse made until it was too late.

I awoke in the recovery room and felt a slight ache in my lower abdomen, which had a small dressing. The nurse instructed me to sit up, eat some crackers, and drink some water. Once assured I had no nausea and vomiting and no dizziness from walking down the hall, she planned to have the doctor discharge me. Unfortunately, I did have ill effects. Sitting up in bed made me dizzy, and simply drinking water had the nurse scurrying for an emesis basin. Finally, two hours later, I felt fine and wanted to be released.

"Your husband checked in earlier at the nurse's station in between his hunting. Since you weren't feeling well enough to be released, he decided to go home and first do his barn chores. He'll return around 6:30 p.m.," the nurse said. While I was enduring pain, John was having fun hunting?

Our tenth wedding anniversary celebration, Christmas, New Year, and January came and went. By February 1982, I realized for several months I had been experiencing signs and symptoms of some kind of infection: low-grade fever, body aches, and chills. I told my LPN friend, Darlene, "I wish I would simply get the flu and get it over with." She advised me to make an appointment with my doctor.

Honoring her advice, I went to my family doctor for my aches and fever. My urine specimen again tested positive for blood. Oh, dear! Last fall, my chest X-ray indicated gravel in my kidney too. I totally forgot. Dr. Courtney sent me home with another course of antibiotics and a consultation slip for a kidney specialist. All summer, I stayed busy gardening, canning and, freezing and caring for three children, including a toddler.

Finally, in August, I went to see the specialist, Dr. Sandoe, who ordered a specific test using dye that revealed the renal stone. Dr. Sandoe recommended surgery before my kidney ceased to function. Oh, how I wish I had followed through on my positive urine tests right after Rochelle's birth!

I went for a second opinion with Dr. Drago from Hershey Medical Center. In more detail, he basically told me the same thing as Dr. Sandoe. Dr. Drago asked me if I wore a bikini. "No, a two-piece suit," I answered. "Well, those days are over," he commented. "You will have a long, abdominal scar running around your right side of your waist to midback." Yikes! During my final consultation with Dr. Sandoe, he explained about all the surgical risks, including death. "You may not live through the surgery," he commented. Someone knocked on the door, opened it, and asked Dr. Sandoe a question. After the staff member closed the door, Dr. Sandoe gave me his full attention and asked, "So where was I?" I answered, smiling, "You could die." "Oh, yes, you could die. I have to tell all my patients that this is a possibility during this type of surgical procedure and the use of anesthesia," he answered. Conversations such as this one are a little unsettling for an almost thirty-year-old mommy of three.

While taking four antibiotics a day to keep me at my optimal best, I made plans for my household and family to run smoothly without me. I had scheduled two trustworthy "Black Bumper" neighbor girls to assist in getting Steph and Darrin off to school and making some meals. Lenora was scheduled to drive down and pick up Rochelle to babysit her until further notice. After I finished some fall housecleaning, I was prepared for my upcoming surgery scheduled for November 3.

My diary entry for November 1 reads: "I'm presently taking antibiotics four times a day. Some days I really ache, and they don't seem to help. I can tell when they wear off. God, guide me all the way."

John drove me to the hospital after I finished my Early Bird bowling league on Tuesday morning, November 2. After checking in at the admissions desk, the staff member stated, "Have a good stay." But the look on her face told me she was thinking otherwise. Next, we were instructed to go to the X-ray department where I had two chest X-rays taken. Asked to put on the infamous hospital gown, I gave the nurse two urine specimens. Throughout the remaining day and night, my vital signs were checked regularly.

At one point, both of my doctors came into my room to answer any questions I may have. My anesthesiologist said, "Boy! Am I glad I'm not you?" I had an EKG and four tubes of blood drawn by the nurse. After John left, the nurses started an IV. By evening, my pastor, John, an awesome Christian man, came to visit and pray with me prior to my surgery. Only during our conversation about keeping the faith and listening to his prayers for a full smooth recovery did my tears fall. I wanted to stay brave.

Wednesday, November 3 arrived. I was awoken every two hours throughout the night because of my jabbing IV. At 5:45 a.m., I started to read *Guideposts* and rested and waited. At 9:00 a.m., I had an abdominal X-ray. The nurse's aide gave me a bath, scrubbed me down, and put on elastic stockings. Soon, the nurse brought me the infamous green cap to wear, gave me an injection, and assisted me onto a gurney. Around 10:15 a.m., I was greeted by a nurse and two doctors on the third floor. I noticed several other patients were waiting in the hallway. I was wheeled into the operating room. I do not remember at what point they put the sleep medicine into my IV. After the surgery, I do not remember waking up in the recovery room either. But, apparently, I became fully conscious and was in the recovery room for one hour. Around 2:00 p.m., I was wheeled into room 207.

My first memory was awakening in my room and seeing John sitting in a chair in the corner of the room. I immediately asked for ice chips several times, but I was refused them. John remembers my first comment was "It hurts." I remember feeling a big ache on my right side. A huge dressing covered my twelve-inch surgical wound and wrapped around from midabdomen to midback.

Around 8:45 p.m., I was assisted by the nurse to go to the bathroom for the first time (earlier, I had refused to have a catheter inserted). I fainted on the commode! About every two or three hours, I was asking for help to go to the bathroom. I did fine the first four times, but not the fifth time. I was walking ahead of the nurse because she was busy with my IV pole friend. Suddenly, I fell at the bottom of the right corner of my hospital bed. The nurse yelled "Help!" I am not sure if I really fainted or not. I do not remember falling down, but I do remember being on the floor and saying "Ouch!" From then on, there was a joke passed on between the nurses: have a smelling salt taped in your cap and handy before going into room 207. Out of this experience, I have learned smelling salts have one unique smell. Boy, what an ingenious use for a nurses' cap too.

On both Thursday and Friday, I did not feel as though I was improving. By Thursday night, they gave me a pint of blood. My temperature climbed from normal to as high as 101 degrees on both days. Sometime either on Thursday or Friday, I noticed my family doctor walking down the hall outside my hospital room. After calling out his name, he turned around and entered my room. I questioned him if he was planning on visiting me? He answered, "I visited with you in the recovery room. We had a great talk. Don't you remember?" No, I had not. Now, that is a weird feeling!

By Saturday morning, I had conquered the lightheadedness. Finally, after five days, I lost my IV pole friend. On Saturday, I also had my second blood transfusion because my blood count remained too low. But by Saturday afternoon, I felt worse: gas pains started, my shoulder blades had sharp pains, and I had a headache. Up until Saturday, I had morphine injections every four hours for pain management. They were effective. I was able to sleep well at night until Saturday night. I could not understand why. My stomach felt like a marble roller. By 3:30 a.m., I still had not fallen asleep. I buzzed the nurse for a sleeping or pain pill. I explained to her I was experiencing a different kind of pain. She informed me all that rumbling was gas. I told her, jokingly, I thought the doctor had left a surgical sponge behind inside of me. I finally fell asleep.

Sunday was my thirtieth birthday! I had many visitors and received nine beautiful bouquets, a ceramic chicken, two books, a candy jar, and a cross. John bought me a beautiful tan dress from Ormonds. He said I needed something to cheer me up. I finally started looking like myself by Saturday night.

After my Sunday afternoon visitors left, I tried to nap, but to no avail. More family and friend visitors came to visit me on Sunday night. I figured since I did not nap during the day, I would have no problem falling asleep that evening. Wrong. After going to the bathroom and coughing (ouch!), I had pain in my back in my incision for the first time. At 1:30 a.m., I buzzed for the nurse and requested a sleeping pill.

When recuperating from abdominal surgery, coughing hurts. Patients were instructed by the nurse to hold a pillow over your stomach and press down gently during any coughing or sneezing episodes. An elderly male patient in his early eighties had a similar surgery as mine. He was located in a room across the hall from me. Not certain if he had been a smoker or had a chronic cough, I heard him cough frequently because his door was ajar. Immediately following his cough, I'd hear his low moan. In empathy, I held my pillow over my stomach during both his and my coughs!

Major surgery recovery is so different from maternity recovery. You don't always stay ahead of the game, but one can regress or start experiencing a totally different set of problems. Having thick dark hair meant my leg hair growth was endless (therefore, I got in the habit early on when a teenager to shave my legs nearly every day). While in the hospital, I was unable to do that chore for myself on a regular basis. By day five of my recuperation, my leg hair growth was out of control and drove me batty. I told the nurse that as much as rest and nourishment aided in my body's healing, mentally, shaving my legs was a must if she expected ongoing recovery. She understood.

The nurse had requested a dear kind nurse's aide to assist me in my first postsurgical shower. While trying to keep herself and my bandages as dry as possible, she did a great job helping me shave my legs in the shower. No easy task as I was not able to bend over very far. Bless her!

Monday was my first full day of eating foods on a regular diet. Dr. Sandoe came in and told me I could probably go home on Wednesday. He credited my shortened hospital stay of only nine days for this type of nephrectomy was due to my being slim and weighing 110 pounds, young, and generally healthy. Dr. Sandoe explained that the more stomach tissue that needed cutting for a partial kidney removal for an obese person, for example, the longer a healing time and hospitalization is required. He removed the Hemovac drain (ouch!), my second "friend." Informing me that they would test its contents, Dr. Sandoe eventually gave me the actual kidney stone for my safekeeping. Thanks! For years, I kept the kidney stone in a small vial in my cedar chest. Testing revealed my kidney stone contents were basically from my limestone drinking water, plentiful in my area where I lived. In fact, Dr. Sandoe named Southcentral Pennsylvania "part of a kidney stone belt."

By Monday night, my new dilemma was feeling bloated. But I had the best night's sleep without having to take any sleeping or pain pills. Tuesday morning, I felt fine. Dr. Sandoe removed my large abdominal dressing and applied only a small bandage. He told me to take care of my remaining one and one-half kidney. Also, he stated, many times patients end up with recurring kidney stones. God, I hope not. I may shower and go home Wednesday. Yahoo!

I can never be the same person after all that I experienced with this major surgery. God carried me all the way through this ordeal by His grace. Verses and song stanzas mean more to me than ever before. I thought I was sentimental before, but now I'm a basket case. Thank you, Lord, so much, for easing the pain and making me as comfortable as possible. I can now look back and say it was worth it all to be drawn so much closer to You. Help me to always show the love I was shown by my church, family, and friends.

All total, I had fifty visitors between family and friends (some repeats) and eleven phone calls during my hospitalization. One day, Janie brought in her scrabble game so we could feed our scrabble fix. Lenora ended up babysitting Rochelle until November 20. Being only about two years old and away from her mommy so long, Rochelle was confused as to who her mother was the day Lenora brought her back home. As Lenora handed Rochelle over to me, she hesitated and would not come into my arms at first. Lenora and I do sound alike, so I guess poor Rochelle was confused after not seeing her mommy for over three weeks—enough time for her to have forgotten about me. I started crying, "Honey, it's your mommy. Come here." It broke my heart, but Lenora thought it was so funny. Of course, Rochelle came into my arms and accepted the biggest warm hug.

Six weeks post-op, I had a reason to freak out. I awoke in the middle of the night and felt damp bed sheets beneath me. It was obvious that yellowish drainage was coming from some part of my incision. It was draining from the insertion point midback where the Hemovac had been inserted and later removed. For peace of mind, I went to the emergency room to be examined and assured there were no surgical healing complications. Having no temperature or pain, I was assured it was probably body fluids escaping through an available opening, which was to be expected.

Two consequences came from this kidney-removal surgery. One, I wear a one-piece swimming suit. Two, I have learned what internal scar tissue is, and how it can pull slightly during a sneeze. I'm limited in performing certain exercises that require bending with my right arm over my head and reaching down my left side. No kando!

Little did I know that a decade later, when I turned forty years old, I would be spending that birthday while attending nursing school. I have no doubt that my hospitalization experience played a huge role in that decision. It became my turn to once more appreciate nurse's aides and to give back to residents who were later entrusted to my care, which I did with pleasure.

By the grace of God, I have had no further issues with kidney stones.

BEATY MILLER

Thought of the Day

Grace is realizing results are God's responsibility, but responses are mine. Every spiritual blessing is a yes and amen.

Chapter 34

"Must It Be a Cruise?"

> Listen, my son, to your father's instruction and do not
> forsake your mother's teaching. They will be a garland
> to grace your head and a chain to adorn your neck.
> —Proverbs 1:8–9

OUR MARRIAGE COUNSELOR, LYNN, LOOKED at my husband and explained, "John, you need to take Leanne on a two-week cruise. During the first week, I want you two to get all your arguments out on the table. Fight your way through your opinions. Yell and scream if you must. Then during the second week, I want you to treat her like a queen. Pamper her like you have never done before. Make her feel like she is the most special wife in the whole world."

John looked at her and asked, "Must it be a cruise?" Lynn looked at me as though fully understanding for the first time. In her eyes, I read *Run, Leanne, run!* But first—

It was one thing to expect my prince charming to treat his Cinderella like I saw my daddy treat my mom. I also had placed expectations on John, which I learned from a friend in my new weekly neighborhood Bible study. While toddlers played with toys at our feet or while babies nursed at our breasts, we shared about our home life, churches, and families while sitting around our kitchen tables. Applying the Word, we realized, must start with the relationships in our homes. Not only did we as mothers and wives have the power to set the mood for the day, as queens in our castles, we understood we had a serious role to play in raising up godly children. But prayer and the Holy Spirit were the oil required for our smooth-running, spiritually slanted households.

My new friend, Elizabeth, made a comment one day in our women's Bible study, which intrigued me. "Every night before Jake and I fall asleep, we take turns reading the Bible to each other while lying in bed. But Jake will always be the one to pray, as the head of our home, while I lay my head on his chest. What an awesome way to end our day."

Wow! That sounds neat. I'm not sure John will feel comfortable enough praying out loud every time. So I'll guess I'll suggest we take turns. Following the pattern set by our parents, no Bible reading occurred around our family supper table during this time. You were responsible to have your own devotions at another time. Most times, grace was a silent prayer. That night at the dinner table, I shared with John Elizabeth's comment.

"Taking turns reading the Bible to each other and praying together in bed...wouldn't that just be the neatest way to end our day together as I snuggle up against you?" I inquired as I sat down at the supper table. Slightly shifting in his seat, John, not giving me eye contact, half agreed.

That night after I brushed my teeth and got ready for bed, I grabbed my Bible off the nightstand and crawled into bed. John was already in bed under the covers. "So I guess I'm doing the praying tonight," he observed. After selecting a passage of scripture, I started to read out loud. Finishing up, I closed my Bible, put it on the nightstand, laid my head on his chest, and closed my eyes in anticipation. John started his simple prayer, feeling as nervous and uncomfortable as a first grader in a new school. He struggled through praying about four sentences. I opened my eyes after the second sentence. *Hmmm, this is not working!* We kissed goodnight, turned over, and fell asleep.

Not one to give up easily, I was hopeful my plan would go much more smoothly the next night when it was my turn to pray and John's turn to read the scripture. Once again, snuggled under the covers, I handed him the open Bible at the next selection of verses for him to read and laid my head on his chest and hugged his waist.

What I heard next was embarrassing for both of us. John struggled with pronouncing words correctly and had so many pauses, I could not keep up with the verse's content, as I had to keep lifting my head to clarify how to pronounce a word for him. Shortening the number of verses he planned on reading out loud, he closed the Bible. In closing, with ease, I said a simple prayer. When finished, John remarked, "I'll never to be able to read the Bible and pray out loud like you do." So the dream died, was put away on a shelf, and never spoken about again.

Looking back, my expectation was totally unfair to John. Being raised in the "Horning" Mennonite Conference, Bibles were not brought to church with you. Yes, it was expected church members read their Bibles. But the concept of daily devotions as a couple, and your being responsible for your spiritual growth, was not emphasized. Having been raised in a church that did not include Sunday school, John had no opportunity to learn how to pray in front of others. Slowly, chances to do so occurred in our young adult Sunday school class. But the more I had opportunity to read scripture out loud, participated in answering questions (which John seldom did), and to lead out in group prayer at times in class, the more John was convinced he would never measure up.

I know what you are thinking: You never prayed and read the Bible together before marriage? No!

I knew Pennsylvania Dutch was John's first language. Struggling through first grade because of the language barrier, John barely passed first grade. Believing at first it would be beneficial to repeat first grade again, the teacher changed her mind and chose to pass him to second grade because John was so tall for his age. As typical for Mennonites, John only completed eighth grade; it was expected he work full-time on the farm. After his brother left home to fulfill his I-W (conscientious objector) two-year alternate service, John, as a teenager, was expected to manage all the farming workload, which he did.

My expectation to have a husband who was truly a head of my home was far from reality. It reminded me of the times I stepped into my hot bubble bath to soak and read. Putting on my reading glasses, I needed to wipe the fog off so I can see more clearly. The first wipe had no effect. So I wiped again, little clearer, but it took the third wipe for my glasses to adapt to the temperature and rising heat from my hot bath. Remove, adjust, remove, adjust.

Five years of marriage led to ten years of marriage. Raising three children on a bustling farm and assisting them to get good grades at their local Christian school, plus household management, intermittent part-time jobs, and wifehood kept me hopping. As I turned over the calendar years passing through my twenties, I not only wanted to discover who I was; I had to create who I was.

Bouncing ideas off John, I had read about earlier in the day in a book or newspaper had him unsettled. "You're crazy to think that. You weren't raised that way. You're nuts!" *Hmm, John sounds a lot like my scolding daddy. What is happening to the man who said at one time he worshipped the ground I walked on?*

At one point, our marriage counselor, Lynn, told me she and her husband supported two different political parties: one is a Republican and the other one a Democrat. "Yes, it makes for a very interesting breakfast table conversation," Lynn pointed out. How is that even possible in the same household? I could not fathom such a diverse union.

Some days in our heated discussions, John became unnerved as he felt his temper rising. Feeling hopeless, he frequently walked away from me, realizing it was the best way to keep his temper in check, retreated into the living room, and turned on the TV. Guess our discussion is over. You can't fight with a brick wall.

In the meantime, the divergent path was widening between us.

One day after church, our pastor, who also doubled as our Sunday school teacher, came up to me, held small talk with my kids, then asked how I was doing. Apparently, I shared a funny tidbit about my week with John. My pastor looked at me and said, "Leanne, please don't outgrow him. I see that happening." *Huh?*

Once again, people saw things in me I did not recognize in myself as I was creating me. Now older and wiser, I look back on this conversation and want to scream: "Pastor, why didn't someone sit John down and tell him if he did not shape up he was going to lose his wife?"

The children grew up and observed their mommy and daddy growing apart. The last two years of our marriage were more unhappy than happy. C-days became d ones. Sad to say, our kids witnessed way too many fights about stuff—who remembers anymore what all those subjects were? If our kids did not witness the fight, the overheard heated conversations from our bedroom were just as damaging.

Some arguments were about how the remaining $100 (the amount left over once all the monthly bills were paid) should be spent. Or they were about his lack of disciplining our children (confirming once again in my mind yet another area of his not being the head of our home). I recognized I surely did not want my kids to fear their daddy, like I feared mine somewhat, when we all sat around the dinner table. But I figured, since I was the main parent dishing out the punishments and the scoldings, most times, at least during mealtimes or in the evenings when Daddy was present, I would get a much-needed break. I was tired of doing all the policing.

One repeated discussion was about why could I not have the three kids and myself ready for church on time on Sunday morning by the time John milked thirty-six cows and got himself ready? To me, the answer was obvious! Apparently, it took longer to get three kids out of bed, give them all breakfast, including a toddler, clear the table of breakfast dishes, supervise their dressing, and also get myself dressed and ready, make the beds while thinking about what's for lunch.

Granted, in those days I did not want to believe my alarm clock had any five o'clock. Besides, just because farmer Daddy got up early did not mean his children and wife wanted to be up with the birds and get ready for church. But my planning on getting the kids up fifteen minutes earlier made for a happier car ride to church the following Sunday. But as Murphy's Law would have it, the inevitable happened—spilled milk at the kitchen table, soiled diaper change (sometimes a whole outfit) was required right before heading out the door—take your pick. I made hollow threats to change places, "I'll milk the cows, and you can get four people ready for church." But, obviously, that threat never went anywhere.

As I gradually lost respect for John, my love for him went right out the window. I remember crying myself to sleep many times, feeling so trapped. Tears flowed down my face as I rationalized, regretted, and begged God to help me find an acceptable solution. I wrote in my prayer log: "Help me to love John with Your love. Help me not to try and change him." My parents taught me, "You made your bed, now you lie in it."

Sunday afternoons were a great escape for me. It was a time when I wanted to be alone, to crawl into bed with my friend, Pillow, and take a nap. The kids knew, unless there was a fire, they had better not disturb mom. Keep the noise down to a minimum and stay off the second floor were some of their instructions. Looking back, I now realize this was my way of handling of my being somewhat depressed.

The wearing of a happy face started. In front of my church friends, I wore one mask. In front of my true friends, I confessed to my unfulfilled married life. Who would I complain and gripe to most? My single friends or sister, who were already separated or divorced, had the most attentive ears. Misery loves company.

One evening, my newly separated friend invited me to go to the Eden Hotel and Resort in Lancaster to listen to a country music band. Out of character and atypical for me, we danced, and I tasted my first Long Island Iced Tea. Neither feeling nor acting like a Mennonite, I began to enjoy these girlfriend-sharing, loud-music-blasting times.

By the time we had made this a routine event and invited more girlfriends to join us, our circle of desperate married, fed-up women grew. Smiling, having fun, feeling free, we slightly tipsy ladies got the attention of handsome guys in the room. What? Wait! You're asking me to slow dance?

Over several months, my eyes were opened to a whole other way of life. Not being able to comprehend at first my not being a

Mennonite, I was enlightened when my friend told me she stopped attending her Mennonite church right after her separation. Her truck driver hubby decided he liked having several women along his route to ease the pain of long-distance truck driving. I slowly comprehended the possibility of a different way of living for me and my children. In my mind, I started putting together a different reality. But it just was not coming together. I knew one of the Mary Kay consultants, Lynn, had a side business as a counselor. So I set up an appointment with her.

After hearing my story and sensing my frustration, Lynn advised me, "Leanne, why don't you get a job and think about something else? You dug yourself into a big hole, and now you need to take the necessary steps to get out." At the time, Rochelle, my youngest child, was about four years old. But, but, Mennonite mothers don't work outside the home, especially those who live on a farm.

Realizing our marriage was in big trouble, John agreed with me we should see a counselor. (I did not tell him I had already had one private session with Lynn.) Hesitant at first because he was not sure she was a Christian counselor, John joined me for our joint session.

Lynn took the opportunity to hear some of John's frustrations about our marriage. It was at this time she had disclosed at times couples "have to agree to disagree" and revealed how she and her husband are of opposing political parties. Her idea of a two-week cruise was advised at this point in our counseling session. This was when John looked at her and asked, "Must it be a cruise?"

Sigh, sigh.

When Lynn encouraged me to get a job, a possible picture of a new reality for me and my kids was coming more into focus. Since John was present and heard Lynn's advice, he had no leg to stand on to tell me I could not get a full-time job. So I started pursuing finding one. Knowing my old boyfriend had his own business, I phoned David, who in turn hired me practically over the phone as his sales secretary. As Paul Harvey said, "And now you know the rest of the story."

Once again, someone saw character traits I did not recognize in myself. Lynn was wise enough to realize I would get a full-time job, be able to support myself, and move out, if I so chose. Sure enough, one year later on the first Saturday in June after school ended, I and my three kids moved out of Lebanon County and back into Lancaster County. At thirty-two, I became a single mom after twelve years of marriage.

Our tower of love crumbled completely to the ground and smashed into dozens of pieces.

Meeting other men who gave me compliments, cared what I had to say, and instilled confidence in me telling me I could make it as a single mom were soaked up by me like a dry sponge. The big hole I dug myself into by time can be summed up, as the saying goes, "Sin will take you farther than you want to go, costs more than you want to pay, and lasts longer than you want to stay." In time, my big hole filled up of unbecoming behaviors and reeked of a cesspool!

Thought of the Day

Grace overflows like the Niagara Falls, where great and many sins abound. Praise God!

Chapter 35

My Dirty Laundry Flapping in the Wind

Remember, O Lord, your great mercy and love, for they are from of old. Remember not the sins of my youth and my rebellious ways; according to your love remember me, for you are good, O Lord.
—Psalm 25:6–7

Just as it only takes two sturdy bra straps to lift its load, I only needed two friends in my corner to spur me on to make the decision to move out from John. Once fear lost its crippling grip on me, I could move forward knowing I had the support of my sister, Lenora, and my friends, Janie, Esther, and Pat. Many friends walked away and dropped their friendship with me as casually as putting a trinket back on the shelf in a cheap souvenir shop.

Where to move? When? With whose help? Determined to move back into Lancaster County, I started considering which township would be far enough away from my parents' house, but not too far from my new church and place of employment. East Petersburg seemed to be the perfect spot. Yes, it was still Lancaster County, but not in a rural part where I would find many horse and buggies or nosy Mennonite relatives living in my backyard.

I found an affordable duplex with three bedrooms and paid the security deposit and the first month's rent to the landlord. The next step was to sit my kids down and discuss my plans that would greatly affect them. Of course, they were tired of Mom and Dad fighting.

But who wants to move out of one's home? Just as other single moms have lived through this heart-wrenching conversation, one side of my heart was breaking into pieces. The other side was gearing up to the beat of a totally different drummer.

I spoke separately to the two older children, Steph and Darrin and informed them of my plans and my wish to drive them down to see their new home. We toured the duplex, discussed who got which bedroom, assessed the backyard and community play area, and then drove around East Pete to familiarize ourselves where the pizza shop was.

One solution down. But when is moving day? The perfect opportunity came for me when I heard John had volunteered to help with the chicken barbecue at our children's Christian school's fundraiser the first Saturday in June. I had told my kids their dad knew I was moving out, but he just did not know the exact date. I emphasized with them Mommy truly feared his anger if he indeed found out. I made my kids promise they would not tell their dad about my plans. Thank goodness, it was only for one night.

Thanks to the help of Janie's restaurant crew, her male dishwashers became my much-needed muscle. Paid a hefty fee by me, they were hired to load up the moving van. I found it difficult to fall asleep that Friday night. My mind was racing with various lists: What do I pack from each room? What do I want out of the attic and storage rooms? Which toys and games do I leave behind? Which clothing pieces go or stay? I had to get a good night sleep to prepare for the hard work ahead the following day; I finally fell into a restless sleep.

By the time the moving van backed up to my front porch, I was one determined, let's-get-this-done-and-not-too-soon woman. Enduring struggles became my middle name. But this single mom saw a brighter future at a different address that was just beyond her grasp. I was going to pull myself up with my bootstraps, and the four of us would survive it all.

Thanks to being organized and one who lives by lists, the movers were in and out of each room loading up the selected items pretty quickly. The kids kept busy packing clothing in suitcases and boxes and selecting their toys of choice. I knew we had to be long gone before John arrived back home, and we had only one chance to move everything out for the four of us. I did not expect John to be gracious to allow me to come back into the house for any reason once we had moved out.

About two hours into the move, my phone rang. My friend informed me she heard someone drove by the house and noticed the moving van and put two and two together. The man was on his way to the same Christian private school where John was. Not certain of the details of what ensued next, my friend witnessed firsthand the events and was so appalled for me. Thus, she wanted me to know. Apparently during the auction, the auctioneer, once informed about John's wife's despicable actions at home, took a break from auctioning off items to say a prayer over the loudspeaker for the Weaver family. What? Wait. Did I hear you correctly?

Well, let me just summarize for you. From that point on, I became angrier and more frustrated about people not understanding how to deal with hurting people. I felt of little value by the body of Christ. Besides the fact of knowing my dirty laundry was now flapping in the wind over my kids' entire school, I became angry at God and my parents. Where was my parents' responsibility of allowing their too-young daughter to plan a wedding in all of this? What would have happened if I had gone to Washington, DC, to volunteer as I had wanted to (the best chance of not marrying someone more conservative than me)? How different would my life be now? Would I have married John?

No, I was not allowed to go to Washington, DC. Instead, I planned a wedding at eighteen years old.

With tears brimming my eyes, I reached down inside of me and got a tighter hold on my bootstraps. My anger simply fueled and empowered me to walk through a new door. The present door was slowly closing inch by inch literally and figuratively.

As I began to feel untethered, my journey of walking away from God carved deeper ruts.

BEATY MILLER

Thought of the Day

Grace is realizing our wilderness days can't simply be abandoned. They need to be consecrated. Let the Father's cloud of the day and the fire in the cloud by night guide you during all your travels.

Chapter 36

Against Marriage to Your Father

*But if anyone does not have them (fruit of the Spirit),
he is near-sighted and blind, and has forgotten that
he has been cleansed from his past sins.*

—2 Peter 1:9

REGARDLESS OF NOT ASKING FOR any of the changes, my children's lives were never again the same; a new normal was smacking them in the face. The moving van pulled out of the driveway and headed toward our new home. We needed to lead the way to our new address. They said good-bye using a flat monotone voice to their pet dog, Fluffy, and the children, feeling uprooted, piled into the car. They sat between the delicate items not suitable for a moving van.

The dreaded phone call from John was inevitable. "Yep, I moved out, and I am not even going to discuss again with you why. You know all the reasons." Trying to get John to see I was not being entirely cruel, I explained how I had moved out very few furniture pieces and even left the kids' bedroom furniture behind for their weekend visits with him.

When John found out I took about two thousand dollars from our checking account, that seemed to make him the angriest. I needed money to start my new checking account, plus have monies to buy used furniture and appliances. I had earned a great salary for the past year before my moving out; I felt I deserved to take this money. After all, I did leave him the money in the account, which was used to pay the monthly mortgage. Later, my lawyer questioned me as to why I had not emptied the account entirely? I devised a new budget. As a single mom, I lived by penny-pinching more than ever.

Our duplex, sitting on a cul de sac, was soon full of furniture, appliances, and new beginnings. Although he did not have large blocks of time to spend with him, Darrin, at least, slowly made a friend. Steph and Rochelle did not fare as well. At Pat's suggestion, we started attending her church, the Worship Center, which became one of the best decisions I ever made.

I knew that I did not want to make any mistakes that would interfere with my fight for full child custody. I searched for a local babysitter. I was lucky enough to find one nearby. Even though Steph was eleven years old and old enough to stay home alone for short periods of time, she was not old enough to be responsible for her siblings, eight and four. A huge line-budget item for me was paying for babysitting. (Turns out my naïve kids had a rude awakening about what other mothers allow their children to watch on TV.)

The following Friday night, John and I agreed on a halfway meeting for his weekend. After dropping off the kids, I started my new lifestyle. This pattern I followed for years.

Pat became my partner in crime. I will never forget the day when I told her over the phone about my decision to leave John. Pat said, "Wow, Leanne. I know we griped and complained. But I didn't think we could do anything about it!"

Over the years, Pat and I had tried to keep in touch on a regular basis. Sometimes we placed long-distance phone calls to catch up, made plans to meet at a restaurant over coffee, or visited in each other's home as a family. A tragedy befell Pat when her epileptic seizure-prone youngest daughter died at five years of age. Our times of meeting and sharing became more valuable and precious. Our coffee dates now also included how to grieve, questioning God, in addition to complaints about our unhappy marriages.

Well, who called me within weeks of my separation? Pat! Still shocked, she proceeded to tell me she and her husband were separating. As statistics prove, the percentage of divorcing parents after the death of a child is high. Grieving differently, she and her husband, six months after burying their child, separated. Shaky ground cannot endure a crumbling tower.

Having the same weekends free from our kids, Pat and I started going to the Jukebox Friday or Saturday nights (or both). Staying until wee hours of the morning dancing the night away, drinking Long Island Iced Teas and catching the eye of some cute guys, we drove back to our homes and crawled into bed exhausted but smiling.

Within months of my moving out, I filed for divorce. I started dating before it was final, even though I was in no hurry to tie the knot. In the beginning, I was careful not to have my older two kids meet any of my boyfriends. I explained to all three kids, "I'm not against marriage. I'm just against being married to your father. In order to do that, I need to date. When it is your weekend with me, I won't be dating." I realized whoever I dated that first summer, the kids were never going to accept. I told my friends, "It could have been God Himself, and they would have resented him for taking me away from their father."

As the DJ spinned the popular rock and roll hits, Pat and I had the chance to perfect our dancing. At times, we still felt a bit nervous when asked to slow dance. Are we going to step on toes and embarrass ourselves in this crowd?

As much as I enjoyed journeying on my new path of finding a non-Mennonite future husband (I guess I figured I was marrying way above my station), there were times I was still numb to my new reality. Pat danced with her date, returned to her seat, and asked me, "Hey, Leanne. Tim wants to know if you are mad at the world. You don't look too happy tonight."

Between coworkers, restaurant managers whom I met through my work, or guys whom I felt comfortable enough to be around or had good vibes about them before inviting them to my home, my testing the waters began. I was not necessarily comparing any prospect up against John, but I knew what I definitely did not want in a future husband.

At the outset, I apologize to any wife if I was told by your husband he was single, and we could date. I was not interested in simply dating; I wanted a husband. Dating a married man was not in the cards. The possibility of a man lying to me about being single could have been the one I dated who was in the area building cell towers. One to give complements about how proud he was of me to be making it as a single mom of three and understanding being raised Christian, he was definitely a future prospect—except he moved around the country making $80,000 a year.

One unforgettable weekend was when Pat and I drove over to Quakertown one Sunday night to meet up with each of our cell tower building buddies. We did so, and then we had to drive back at 5:30 a.m. to report to work by 8:00 a.m. One's gotta do what one's gotta do. Let's just say, by Monday night, I crashed and could not wait to have a date with my pillow. Eventually, he moved on and became just a memory.

As my one friend said while she was dating to find husband number 2, her life back then would have made great lyrics for a country and western song: a pickup truck in my driveway, his cowboy boots under my bed, the empty wine glass and beer bottle on my nightstand, along with antidepressants and antianxiety meds to melt away heartache, pain—reality! Ditto for me, minus the hard stuff and meds.

Dating allowed me to experience new things: how to pronounce words on an Italian menu, acquire a taste for wine coolers and sweet mixed drinks (never did acquire a taste for beer, and wine is only tolerated), and an opportunity to take on new interests, like boating on the Susquehanna. The downside was I had to start shaving my legs more regularly because I never knew when Pat would call me for a night out on the town at the last minute.

One guy I had met when Esther and I were at the Eden Resort sparked enough interest in me, I began to date him exclusively. I'll call him Mark. Having never been married, I was flattered he wanted to take on the whole package of me and my three kids. We spent that summer learning to know each other. I fell in love too with his kind parents, who graciously opened up their hearts and lives to my kids. Eventually, I felt comfortable enough to introduce Mark to my friends and coworkers. (No, not to Mamma. We weren't speaking much in those days. But that is for another chapter.)

Slowly our relationship deteriorated as I noticed some immaturity, and the love for beer was way beyond my tolerance scale. The clincher was when I noticed Mark was not feeling too comfortable around my kids. At times, he entered my kitchen and had not even acknowledged them. Ouch! So I broke up with him.

In my diary, I wrote, "I grew to love you, but we would never have worked. My expectations are far too high. I cannot settle for less. You are too immature for me, and I do not appreciate your foul language…not much depth…more concerned about showing off your dry humor. I have seen other dates talk to Rochelle more in one-half hour than you have had all summer. Besides, the kids would always resent you, believing my first relationship was the reason for my marriage breaking up. But I will always be grateful for your support when I needed it in taking the steps to move out."

Shortly thereafter, I had made plans to meet one of my restaurant managers, Bruce, after he realized I had broken things off with Mark. We set a date and time to meet at the country club he managed about an hour's drive away. I dressed up for yet another date, expecting only good things. As Bruce and I sat at the bar, we conversed about more personal matters. After all, since we had a phone relationship for several years under our belt, we needed to spend this time talking about more in-depths topics to find out how compatible we were.

Bruce was so tender and sweet and just could not keep his hands off my face. He gently ran his fingers down my face, talking sweet nothings. After sharing two short soft kisses, I happened to lean back in my bar stool to reposition in my seat while glancing to my right. Who is sitting two barstools down? Mark!

I shrieked and turned toward Bruce and quickly said, "And there he is! Mark!" Shocked with my heart pounding, I jumped down off the barstool and ran outside. Mark followed me to the end of the walkway, mumbling about missing me and wanting to start dating again. Ignoring his comment, facing him, I demanded, "How did you know I was even here? Were you following me?"

He answered me by saying one of my friends betrayed me and told him of my plans that night. Hysterical, I then noticed Bruce walking toward me. Staying cool while ignoring Mark, Bruce walked me to my car. Assured I was safe, we separated, but not before promising to call him the following day. Pat was the only one who knew of my plans to meet up with Bruce. Needing confirmation she never would have betrayed me, I drove to her home. It was quite late when I arrived at her home; she was still awake on a date with Tim. Of course, she had not told Mark my plans. Later on, she told me the look on my face when she opened her door was of pure terror—even an hour later.

Bruce and I had a second date at the restaurant, Log Cabin. After pulling into my drive after dinner, he confessed he has been seeing somebody else for quite some time. Feeling guilty, he needed to be up-front and tell me why he cannot continue the relationship with me. I wrote in my diary later: "I could have fallen in love with you…loved your muscles…you're a great kisser…we communicated well…I liked your ambition."

Since my sister Lenora was also going through a divorce, I planned weekends for my kids and me to visit with her and my nieces and nephews. I willingly drove the two and one-half hours to the outskirts of Williamsport. She was familiar with the city and learned hotel bars were a great place to hang out and have a good time. Some had live bands regularly scheduled to provide entertainment for the crowd. Let's just say it was never a dull moment when I spent time with Lenora as single moms. Though she was not interested in meeting someone to date (as she already was seriously dating her husband-to-be), she did enjoy going out with her unmarried best friend. Adding me to the mix was simply doubling the fun. As soon as all of our kids were settled for the night, we headed to the Sheraton.

One late fall evening, I was updating Lenora on my recent dates while hanging out at the Sheraton, which included how I ended the relationship earlier with Mark. As per our usual, we were laughing, as we sipped our alcoholic drinks (two at the most). At one point, the three of us decided to head to the bathroom to powder our noses.

Walking down the hotel corridor, we rounded a corner. Who was walking toward us? Mark! Since Lenora had never met him, she was totally clueless. Grabbing Lenora's arm, I stopped in my tracks and asked him loudly, "Whoa! Wait! What are you doing here?" Surmising this must be Mark, Lenora put two and two together. Mark explained he was on the way to his hunting camp and decided to stop in at the Sheraton. Shaking my head in disbelief, I hurried past him and ran into the bathroom with Lenora and her friend following me. Did Mark really want me to believe he selected this weekend to drive over three hours to his hunting camp? Of all the routes he could have taken, he just so happened to take Route 15? Yep, long before stalker was a household word, my ex-boyfriend now had another name.

My journaling for the course of the next twelve months included entries about various dates. Seeing facts on paper helped to clarify a few things. Entries about them read:

> A sharp dresser, but too much of a chain smoker…we communicate well…you're romantic…how handsome…what a neat car you drive…love how you talk freely with Rochelle…we have similar religious backgrounds…but being younger than me, I'm sure my "package deal of four" is frightening…nice alligator boots…you're a P.K (Baptist preacher's kid)…has four-year-old daughter…short, muscular built…ex-football player…nice BMW…smiles a lot….great kisser…feels comfortable around Rochelle….Hmm…smooth talker #1: 'I want an instant family…can't wait to meet your kids…hope your kids like me'…too much into your looks…you spend more time in front of the mirror than I do…gorgeous tan…

stares in my eyes a lot, but I have no idea what you are thinking…drives black Corvette…gentle kisser….

In the 1980s, when I was dating, HIV was one of the news topics. I learned it was a disease that was prone to occur between homosexuals only. Having no fear of getting pregnant, I tested the waters all right. By God's grace, I survived dating in the '80s—barely.

Then one night, Pat and I walked into the new local hangout called Corvairs just a few miles from my home. One young man sitting at the bar eventually won my heart, scars and all, ending my dating-around days. Little did I know this nonvoter would end up marrying a Democrat (more details to follow in another chapter).

Thought of the Day

Grace is divinely eternal. No amount of money can buy it, nor can death take it away. We are no longer orphans but beloved, adopted children of our Father, sealed, and set apart for Him.

Chapter 37

"Grandpa Said I Should Hate You"

> When they walk through the Valley of Weeping,
> it will become a place of refreshing springs. The
> autumn rains will clothe it with blessings.
> —Psalm 84:6 (NLT)

By the second week after moving out, I called my mom to give her my new phone number and address to assure her I lived in a safe area, the kids had a huge community park as a backyard, and to tell her I was now attending Pat's church.

"But, Leanne, if something happened to you, where in the world would we bury you?" she asked me. Keeping the conversation brief, I reminded her I have no plans to reunite with John, regardless what anybody says or how they try to talk me into it.

I do not recall having any family members visit me at that address or the next address the following year, except my nonjudgmental sisters. They were smart enough to realize I was not going to listen to any preaching.

I became determined, obstinate, and built a wall so thick that no one's words, opinions, or quoting scripture reading was going to penetrate my broken heart. As word got around I had left John, the phone calls, cards, and letters poured in. Through tinted lenses, I read only words that reached my brain. Words meant to penetrate bounced off into thin air because words cannot hit rock bottom if there are bleeding streams flowing out of one's soul. My bootstraps and I, working together, will be just fine.

I realized my decision to leave John was a new predicament for my Mennonite Church leadership. By the end of the month, I received the following letter (copy sent to John) from them:

> Helen and I think of you and your family often. We are a bit perplexed as to how to best communicate our love and concern, but want you to know that we remember you in prayer throughout the day as you come to our minds and in a more concentrated way at other times.
>
> I felt it was necessary to read the enclosed statement (see below) to the congregation on Sunday morning, June 23, 1985. It is my sincere hope that actions in the near future would enable us to notify the congregation of your restoration.
>
> Keep in mind that the necessity to keep your marriage vows faithfully is not merely a congregational idea but a scriptural commandment…also, I am sure you have considered the consequences of your move on your children, and hope you will rethink what effect this will have on them if your separation continues.
>
> I understand you are in communication with Pastor John. Since I carry the greatest discipline responsibility in the district, you may choose to continue meeting with him or any other leaders on the team.
>
> We wish you God's love and grace to overshadow you and pray for reconciliation, forgiveness, and faithfulness.
>
> Cordially in Christ

The enclosed statement read:

> With great regret and sadness, I inform you that Leanne Weaver, one of our members, is out of fellowship. This does not mean that she is no longer one of us nor that she is no longer a member of the congregation. It does mean that she has taken action which hurts reputation and witness of this congregation, which in the spirit of our congregational covenant should not have been taken prior to consultation and sanction by her spiritual leaders. We encourage you to continue contact with John and Leanne, and we will do this also, as we endeavor to understand her distress and to promote marital healing. We ask each of you to engage in much prayer on behalf of John, Leanne, and the family. It is our intention as leaders at this time to make no judgments, take no sides, and come to no conclusions in this matter other than the obvious, and we ask you to unify with us in this regard.

One of the least conservative pastors, the dad of one of my friends, wrote me a letter showing me he was truly concerned about my feelings about receiving the "out of fellowship" letter. In softer tones, he was hoping to meet me for breakfast "to talk with you and assure you that I have no scolding or put down for you…want you to feel free to share, and is there is any hurt from us? You might be able to help the leadership team to improve or change their method of dealing with others in the future…I hope you will not turn us off…and, Leanne, we still deeply love you…our prayer is that God's strength and wisdom will come to you to help you to make the right decisions for His glory and your joy, With great love.

I did end up meeting with this pastor twice over the course of the next year or so. Over breakfast, he soon realized no one's words or opinions were going to change my mind. I have moved back into Lancaster County and was embarking on a new, different path. Thankful for his love, concern, and feeling less condemned, I actually met with him later on one last time during my final divorce proceedings. One of his last comments was, "Boy, I wish someone took away my farm debt and handed me $7,000!" By July of the following year, I wrote my own letter and asked to have my name removed from my Mennonite church's membership list.

Since my address was posted in the church bulletin, I understood why most letters were sent. Some were more tolerable when I read:

> I refuse to take sides and blame either one. We believe problems are family problems and that placing blame never solves them. We feel for all of you in the pain we know each of you must feel. We do believe marriages are lifetime commitments and as such pray that yours will be mended. If at any time there is anything we can do, we are here and willing…our prayer is that you will find peace….

Or

> I feel like I know you through my husband (who was a coworker). I understand in part what you must be feeling. When my family found out I was seeing him, the things we went through with them were unreal (they were "black bumper" if that tells you anything), and the condemnation I felt from people (not only family) was so strong, I could hardly stand it. It gets better…hang in there! I had a brother who, although he didn't condone what I was doing, stood by me like a rock and showed me only what I called real love. He once told me, "They do love you. They just

are not able to separate between that and how firmly they believe what they believe." I think about that many times and somehow it helps and maybe you can relate to that too...If you ever feel like you need someone to talk to (without any preaching) please call me. I do understand some of the pressures! Hang in there and keep your chin up. Love.

Other letters infuriated me, like the one written by one of John's relatives. In it, she admitted to having had bad feelings toward me for years and now wanted to apologize and ask me for my forgiveness. Not only was it about how marriage is hard work, but it was full of her opinion on what went wrong between John and I. She wrote:

> I guess I would have to say my feelings against you were mainly the way you dressed and your heavy makeup, and I felt it showed up in your personality...I always felt and I still do if the heart is right, there is a limit to all things. So please forgive me where I might have failed you in word or deed. I'm sure you could sense this feeling I had toward you. So I want to say I'm sorry for the way I acted...it seems it has started from when you started working out in society... we cannot go to the world and live like the world and find peace...take your friend, Janie...you could have been a real spiritual help to her, but instead, you envied her when she left her husband...I am not saying the Mennonite way is the only right way and that you have to dress plain... not at all....there will be many people in heaven that do not dress plain. But only those that live according to the Bible...you cannot live like the world by going to night clubs and drinking and

> listening to rock music, and with that goes very low moral standards…maybe you think we are old-fashioned, but we know what is out there in the world…you and your sister are just running away from your problems…John was easy-going and was not demanding of you…I am sure a lot of your friends thought you had a great marriage…so what went wrong?…we are to be submissive to our husband in all things the Bible says. We know our husbands need to be good to us too…we would appreciate a reply or call from you, for we know there are always two sides in any situation like this…please reply so we can have an understanding…we do not want you to feel like we are preaching to you…we just want to be a help in any way we can because we love you and care about you and your family.
>
> Love and Prayers

Right! When pigs can fly!

Somewhere along the way, my parents must have spoken to John at length. I am sure he told them about my going out to bars with Esther, my hanging out with three other friends who were in the process of a divorce and who knows what else. Once people realized I was planning on filing for divorce and there was no hope for reconciliation with John, letters took a more scolding and preaching slant.

My dear mother sent me a letter that fall (the first of many), which broke my heart simply because I gave her plenty of reason to have to write such a letter! Excerpts from it:

> I have a burden on my heart for you and the life you are living. What if the Lord would take away your health for the life you are living…wake up before it is too late…one of Elvin's truckers saw you at a bar, and he knew you were Elvin's sis-

ter…if you want to settle for something like that, you will be living in misery the rest of your life… you can't tell me your marriage was that bad with John…you are just looking at the bad points and are not counting his good one…the devil is laughing, and your Savior is weeping…John told me that if I would know of all the things you have done since you got yourself in this mess, my hair would turn gray. I told him I don't want to know. The Lord knows. He is the one that wants to wash your sins away and make them white as snow. John wants you to be sorry for what you have done and a true confession through the church and with him…you can't upset the rest of the family by bringing someone else around… we had such good times together and could laugh and feel closeness, and now Satan has spoiled it…I would be afraid, Leanne, that the Good Lord would take away my health. What would you do if you would get sick and couldn't hold your job? You wouldn't have John to comfort you like he did when you were in the hospital… think on these things. Christ is the answer…out of concern,

Love and Prayers,
Your Mother

Sure enough! Sometime within the next year, I needed a babysitter for Rochelle. Lice had spread through her day care not once, or twice, but three times. The kids were sent home with instructions how to get rid of the lice. We followed them; Rochelle would be cleared of them, but then somebody else's child was not free of them. The cycle went around and around until all clothing items, bed sheets, and toys of all day care kids were properly cleaned. I had taken off from work when the day care called and asked for all children again to be picked up. By the third Monday morning, I was at my wit's end. Calling my mother as a last resort, I asked if I could please drop off Rochelle lice-free so I could return to work. Mom's first response was no, as she had planned to go to a quilting bee that afternoon.

"Fine, take her with you." But only when I broke down over the phone, begged and cried did Mom finally give in and allow me to bring Rochelle by for her to babysit. As I was getting back in my car that morning, I heard Mom say something about the Lord is punishing me. Of course, I dreaded to have to go back to Mom's to pick up Rochelle. I had to mentally prepare myself for more of her comments. It grieved me whenever my children had to hear these remarks.

But nothing could have me prepared for this scenario. One Monday morning after John's weekend, I was combing Rochelle's hair.

"Mommy, Grandpa says I should hate you. But I told him no, I love my mommy."

All the pent-up frustrations, anger, hurt, pain, and grief welled up inside me. Taking her into my arms to give her my biggest hug, buckets of tears poured out of from my eyes; heartache oozed from every pore in my body down to my toes and all the way back up. Thanking her for being a very smart little girl, I reassured her, as I often commented to my kids, No, I love you the "most-est!"

After I dropped her off at day care and I was alone once again, I cried and cried on the way to work (thank goodness for waterproof mascara). However, by the time evening came, Momma Bear was ready to fight. I could not dial John's number fast enough. Without saying hello, I reamed into him.

"If I ever again hear your dad is telling my kids to hate me, I will take you back to court so fast, your head is going to spin!"

John admitted he did not know anything about it. He was aware Rochelle had been sitting on Grandpa's lap yesterday at a family gathering. "I'll talk to him," John said. But I never heard an apology.

Our summer came and went that year. Knowing that Steph and Darrin were no longer going to be attending their former private school, I started to prepare them for attending the public school. I set up appointments to tour their new school in hopes of making them feel more comfortable.

Little did I know, by Labor Day, my worst battle was about to be waged. Mamma Bear needed more than a fighting spirit. It would take deep pockets, support of my friends, and many hours spent in a lawyer's office.

Thought of the Day

Grace is understanding the great exchange and the sufficiency in God's grace. It's the way we partake of His riches, an abundance of spiritual blessings. It has nothing to do with this world's treasures.

Chapter 38

Sea of Black

> Though I constantly take my life in my hands,
> I will not forget your law.
> —Psalm 119:109

"Oh my! I don't believe I have ever seen such a sea of black before in Lebanon County courthouse," exclaimed my lawyer, Pam, as she peeped through the courtroom doors.

I took a peep and busted out laughing, a much-needed relief. In one side of the courthouse, taking up several rows were seated a lot of John's relatives dressed in their typical conservative garb: black or dark blue plain suits for the men and dark green, navy blue, or black dresses for the women, wearing their head coverings. By their attendance that day, they were showing John their support. Their presence meant they believed he deserved to win full custody of the children and, presumably, that I was not a fit mother.

How did I get to this point?

As that summer ended, I had planned to do some fun things with the kids on Labor Day weekend. Earlier that week, John phoned me and practically begged me to switch weekends, so he could take the kids to his brother's cabin Labor Day weekend. I gave in, but only if he promised to meet me an hour earlier at our meeting spot that Monday night, as the following day was the first day of school. He agreed.

I dropped the kids off at the meeting spot and assumed John and the kids were heading straight for the mountains. With a change of plans, Mark and I decided to go boating all weekend, instead, since I was childless now. Upon our return back to my home later that Labor Day afternoon, I saw I had a message on my answering machine that was apparently left on Friday.

"I told you. You are not getting these kids. Darrin and Steph are going to attend their same school and are not going to go to East Pete!" John said in the angriest voice I had heard in a long time. Slam!

When the kids spent the weekend with their dad and I was alone, at times my empty house's silence was deafening to me. Right then, it roared with my scream, "*Nnnnoooo!*" With shaking fingers, I dialed John's number. Of course, he did not answer. Then I called his mom and asked if she had my kids.

"Yes, Leanne, I have the children, but I'm not supposed to allow you to talk to them. I'm sorry."

With crocodile-sized tears welling up, I looked at Mark and yelled, "We gotta' go" and ran out the door. Mark, knowing I was too upset to drive, got in the driver's side of my VW. The spinning of the fast car tires couldn't keep up with my pounding heartbeat. My hands were shaking as I tried to calm myself by holding onto the door handle. Having about a twenty-five-minute drive, we had plenty of time to try to put together a time line of what actually did happen the past Labor Day weekend. John lied to me!

Realizing that it was the time of day that John would be working in the chicken house, I guessed that he would have scheduled his mom to babysit, knowing that I most likely would be driving up to his house to retrieve the kids once I heard his message. But I was uncertain if Grandma would have taken the children back home, letting John face this battle.

What happened next can only be described as a scene out of a cops-and-robbers movie. As Mark pulled into the drive, I saw that the house was completely dark, and only the chicken house was lit up. That confirmed that the children were still at Grandma's. I told Mark to start driving the few miles to his parents' house. Dust scurried as he quickly backed out of the gravel driveway. He wanted to avoid being seen, if he could. But no. Within one mile of heading to his mom's house, I saw John's pickup truck pulling up the rear as he attempted to reach his parents' driveway ahead of us.

At the last second, as Mark was entering the drive, John, driving like a maniac, simply drove his pickup truck across his parents' yard and pulled in front of my car, stopping only about a foot away from us. John got out of the car and started shaking his fist and yelling for us to get off his parents' property. If I could have looked closer, I probably would have seen fire spewing from his ears.

Mark looked at me and asked, "Now what? I am not letting you get out of this car without me." Realizing that one or both of us would probably have gotten punched by John, if we would have attempted to go into his parents' house, we backed out of the drive and left.

Words cannot describe how defeated, helpless and hopeless I felt on our drive back home in a childless car. With a heavy heart, I began to put myself in Rochelle's shoes, my four-year-old baby who was expecting to wake up the following day and resume her schedule of going to nursery school, which she loved. Yes, Darrin and Steph were pawns too in the hands of their I'm-right parents, but they were older and could better understand decisions made on their behalf.

By the time I got back home, I phoned once again to both John's and his parents' house in hopes to talk to my children, but no one would answer the phone. Mark, not being a parent, tried to console me the best he could. I sent him home and crawled into bed. Soon, my pillow was drenched by floodgates of tears.

I started thinking about all the times John would ask me to move back in. Putting two and two together, I really believed he thought that I would choose to come back home if he knew I can't have the children. But it only angered me more. He wasn't going to know what hit him!

By early morning, when I finally was about to fall asleep, I had a plan in place to contact my attorney and get the ball rolling for full-time custody, with John having only visitation rights. Just because a wife leaves her husband and starts dating on her free weekends doesn't make her an unfit mother!

The second part of this story would make for another great scene in some movie about a naïve single mom going through a divorce. When I called Pam, my lawyer, the following day on my lunch break, our conversation was probably another first for her (long before her first sea of black in the courtroom).

"So, Leanne, let me get this straight. You said that you understood when I emphasized with you last week why it was very important that John, no ifs, ands, or buts about it, was not to have the children over Labor Day weekend. Remember? I was helping to assure that you would have them, and they would be waking up in your home to attend the first day of school Tuesday. Remember that conversation? What happened?"

"Well, John lied to me. I *never* thought he would lie to me." I answered. Can't you hear her ughs?

With a date set to meet to discuss the procedure for my child custody hearing, Pam asked me to think about two friends who would be great character witnesses for me that I could bring with me to start the process of my hearing. I was confident about a sure win and hung up the phone.

Work was a great distraction for me. Again, several times a day, I would attempt to phone John's house after school to talk with the children but to no avail. I began my list of supportive friends who, I thought, would testify in court on my behalf. Janie and Esther won hands down. I knew Pat would have been there for me, but she was going through her own custody battle.

Knowing that it was my weekend to have the kids, I began to count down the hours when I could talk with them and try to gauge their emotions of the previous weekend and since then. So many questions were spinning around my head. My arms were especially aching to cuddle Rochelle, my baby.

I was totally unprepared for John to answer my Thursday night phone call and the conversation that ensued. Long story short, he suggested, "I'll give you Rochelle back if you give me Steph and

Darrin's clothing for school." What? We're bartering our kids like cattle now?

Feeling like I had to give in for now, knowing that Pam was working on getting me a court date to settle this matter once and for all, I consented to pack up most of Steph and Darrin's clothes by Sunday night. At the very least, I needed to have Rochelle back home where she belongs with her mother. (I found out later that John had no idea what to do with Rochelle for all the times he needed a babysitter without burdening his mother.)

When Pam heard that I was asked to pack up Steph and Darrin's clothes for having Rochelle full time, she didn't hesitate to advise me. "Leanne, you have the kids this weekend. Don't meet him Sunday night. Lock the door and have them attend East Pete School Monday morning. They only missed four days thus far. Your court date is scheduled for early October. We'll get all of this behind us soon."

Friday night could not come fast enough. At the meeting place, John started on me again about why I couldn't have selected a town nearby to move to and stay in Lebanon County so the kids could have attended the same school. He just didn't understand my need to get as far from him and Lebanon County as possible.

I attempted to keep our conversation light during our drive back home. After many hugs, I asked Steph and Darrin the typical questions about their first day of school: what was their teacher's names and who of their friends were in their same classes. When I asked about what school clothes they wore for the first day (as I always made that a big deal), they informed me that Daddy had to quickly take them shopping "for everything…shoes, socks, and underwear." Rochelle had spent the week split between Grandma and my friend, Jackie's house.

That entire weekend, I spent time with the kids and struggled with a *huge* decision. What do I do? What do I do? How can I put Steph and Darrin in East Pete School after they have already started school where they are familiar? I found myself falling back on an old natural habit. I started to pray, "God, please help me!" As a single mom, I prayed every night that angels would surround my home and protect me and my precious babies. There were times I felt close to God, and there were other times I wanted to run in the opposite direction.

I wish I could share with you a more positive outcome to my next part of my story, but I can't. I wish I knew then what I know now. If I had, perhaps, I would have made an entirely different choice.

By the time Sunday night came and it was time to meet John, I felt at peace about my decision. No, I was *not* going to put the kids in the middle of this battle. This was about John and my issues. I would return Steph and Darrin, along with more packed outfits, as promised, confident that in six weeks, our custody court hearing would be over, and we would resume our household of four.

Once again, I sat them down and explained that for now, I agree that they need to continue to attend the private school. Rochelle and I would miss them terribly until they would once again live here with us. Reassuring them that great moms, like me, don't lose custody battles, I explained that no judge is going to say that children of their ages should live with their dad. Besides, if dad just did not want to pay his child support, and this was one way of lessening the amount due, the judge would be able to read into that too.

I was happy to have Rochelle back under my roof, but seeing Steph and Darrin's empty beds tugged on my heart that no words can describe. During those moments, I had to maul over in my mind why I made the decision I did and not second guess myself. Small waves of peace started to wash over me.

Several appointments were scheduled with Pam when Janie, Esther, and I were prepped and ready to answer John's lawyer's questions. We were full of confidence that John didn't have a leg to stand on. It was a sure win in Pam's eyes. Just as Pam's fee rose, so did my confidence. Feeling assured, I waited for the court date.

When our scheduled hearing date was confirmed, I asked off from work. Janie and Esther cleared their calendars as well. My day in court finally arrived. The judge had a full docket that particular morning. Our hearing was scheduled right after lunch.

We were seated in the hallway waiting for our turn. It was at this point when Pam peeped through the door and commented on "the sea of black." The laugh from all of us was so needed and cleansing. Weeks of anticipation and nerves stretched to the hilt, I accepted any break from the heavy strain all four of us were feeling.

I peeped the second time through the crack in the courthouse door. I was curious to see who in the world of my friends could John possibly have testify against me? Besides family members, I recognized two of John's friends and my friend, Jackie. Are you kidding me? Jackie? The woman who I would babysit her three kids, thinking it was only for a few hours because she had a dentist appointment. But she returned thirty hours later because she lost track of time getting high?

Ticktock, ticktock. The morning stretched before us so slowly. At one point, Janie went outside. She told me later that she ran into John's dad in the back stairs. Upon seeing her, he started screaming at her while getting red in the face, "This is all your fault. This is all your fault!" Fearing he would actually hit her, she scurried back up the stairs to our bench. The apple doesn't fall far from the tree.

Finally, after lunch break, Pam went to check on things. I will never forget the look on her face as she reentered the room. "Leanne, I am so sorry. But the judge will not be able to hear your case today. He's running out of time with all the other cases ahead of yours." Wait! What?

I turned and ran into Janie and Esther's arms. My heart was broken into a million pieces. Only half-listening to Pam's condolences and how she would plan on getting our court hearing rescheduled as quickly as possible, I picked up my purse and headed out toward my car, stunned.

Although I had a huge lawyer bill from today's logged hours, I had nothing to show for it. My mind and my tires went fifty miles an hour as I drove to pick up Rochelle at day care. I regretted my decision that I had not locked the door and forced Steph and Darrin to go to East Pete School. I wanted to go back in time and make a different decision.

I was not asking God to set the world on fire, part the waters, or burn a bush before me. I simply wanted God to hear the desperate pleas of a mom begging to have her family reunited.

When the time came to tell me about my rescheduled court date, Pam was hesitant to even call me. Between holidays, the judge's surgeries and vacation and who knows what else, our next hearing date was set for April. Say what? April?

I had to face the fact that I had no choice but to continue to allow Steph and Darrin to attend the same school and return them to their dads after my visitation weekend until something was determined by the courts. Yes, I could have pushed the issue, but again, that would have put them in the middle. I did not want to do that.

How does one live out disappointments, even if one understands circumstances are partially due to one's own choices? How can I possibly survive the pain of being separated during the school year from Steph and Darrin? Shouldn't my selfless decision of putting them first count for something, God? I continued to look to Him for a miracle to turn my very substance of life, my kids, into new wine: my redefined family nucleus.

Today, when sharing my testimony, I cannot talk about this painful period of my life. I simply say, choking up, that my saving grace for those dark years when my two older children did not live with me full time is only bearable because of "selective amnesia" (amnesia is defined as a loss of a large block of interrelated memory). The gaping wound on Steph's and Darrin's hearts will always have a permanent Band Aid.

During those years when the two older children lived with John full-time, he had time to influence them both in good and bad ways. My choices and actions were frequently discussed, and I am sure that I became the mealtime menu item. If I could have a dime every time during these years, my name was mentioned at either a Martin or Weaver family get-together, I am sure it would have been enough to pay my lawyer bill!

Thought of the Day

Grace is recognizing trials and tests are designed to turn you *toward* God, not away from Him. Genuine grace can only be proved via tests. A promised crown of life is our reward for genuine faith.

Chapter 39

Heart-to-Heart Letters

Search me, O God, and know my heart; test me and
know my anxious thoughts. See if there is any offensive
way in me, and lead me in the way everlasting.
—Psalm 139:23–24 (NIV)

REGARDLESS OF MY CHOICES AND feeling far from God, it was extremely important to me that my kids had no interruption in attending Sunday school somewhere. They soon settled into attending my new choice of church, the Worship Center, and enjoyed their time spent there. I might not have been attending to work on my spiritual growth, but it was a must for all of us to attend church on Sunday mornings. Pat and I sat near the back of the auditorium and spent more time whispering way too frequently about our dates the night before than about paying attention to the pastor. At least, we were warming the pews. John stopped attending our former Mennonite church. The children had to adjust to yet another Sunday school class when attending church with him.

Fun memories were peppered in between painful ones. As we had done prior to our divorces and trying to keep things as normal as possible, we continued to vacation with Lenora and her children. Spending the weekend together with their cousins and best friends at the beach in cheap cabins was a great get-away for all of us. This allowed me some time to have fun and not think about the tumultuous world of divorces and child custody issues.

I maxed out my time spent with all three children on my shoestring budget until school started. By fall, Rochelle and I started our new normal. She was enrolled in Brownies after school, which kept her busy at times. She enjoyed hanging out with Joy, Pat's daughter, when we shared a babysitter.

My budget was stretched beyond its limit when my VW required a new transmission. Even though my brother Elvin replaced it for me and offered a payment plan, I was too proud. Thus, my charge card was maxed out with a $2,000 car repair bill.

All during my preparation for my custody battle and beyond, the aforementioned hurtful letters and cards still frequented my mailbox. By this time, I skimmed them and threw them in a shoebox. A bleeding heart can only bleed so long.

One day after my November birthday, I received a note from Stephanie when she was eleven years old:

> Dear Mom,
>
> Hi, this is me, Steph. I decided to write a letter to you. Mostly questions. Well, did you have a good birthday? Did you like the earrings? Did you like the flowers? Did you like the cards (by the way signed "to my wonderful mother")? This is a heart-to-heart and woman-to-woman talk. Remember the time I asked you what did Dad do to make you so sad? You didn't really answer me the question. I don't want this letter to hert (sic) your feelings, ok? But, I thought by the way, it sounds, and the way I think I thought you moved because of Mark. You promise you won't tell Mark? Well, I don't like him. He kissed you when we were there, and I would really like you to tell him "get out of my life. I'm going home." I wrote because you won't listen to Dad, and I can't

talk face-to-face. Don't ask me why. I have no idea. I hope this letter touches your heart. Steph. PS: If you don't like this letter, you can chuck it. But I hope you like it.

With a wish and a prayer of understanding, while tears streamed down my face, I wrote Steph the following:

Dear Steph,

Thank you for your letter...of course, I won't throw it away! Yes, the flowers were so pretty. They still look okay. Thank you too for the earrings. I will try again to answer your question, but it's hard when I'm an adult and you're a child of eleven. But I will try.

Life is too short and precious not to be completely happy living it. Your dad never hurt me or harmed me to make me unhappy, but several years back, I began to feel "trapped" and knew I was not the kind of wife Daddy wanted. He always hoped he would have a farmwife, like Darlene, who would help him milk cows or help in the chicken house. I never lived on a farm and was afraid of the cows. I was a secretary when we met...not a farm girl. When you were a baby, I did Rubbermaid parties and later on Mary Kay shows and loved it. But Dad didn't...so I quit. How much can you do for somebody else...and still be happy inside?

I need to tell you too, I love Jesus and am a Christian now and always will be. My not living with Dad does not mean I'm going to hell. I have been "more" of a Christian than your Dad for so long. It's only recently that Dad took such an interest in church things...and I'm glad.

About Mark…I need to date to find another husband to start my life over again…because I want to be married sometime again…but not right away. Dating is the way to do that. I plan to date several men to find the one I will fall in love with again. But I want to tell you that my next husband will love my three kids as much as he loves me!

As I said before, Dad and I will always love you. You will be with each of us often, plus a new "family" (possibly in case my next husband would have children). I have been talking to Dad about you and Darrin living with me. I want that very much—because I miss you so much. Please talk to me or write to me any time you want to talk. There's nothing wrong in communicating through letters. Looking forward to this weekend. Love, Mother."

A postcard that Darrin gave me when he was about nine years old was addressed as: "To a favorite Mom." In the front was a picture of two little cute kittens stuffed inside a basket. It read: "It's lonely here without you." Several weeks later, I received a poem from Darrin:

Dear, Mom,
We pray for you each and every day.
I love you so much, I love you so.
So I just want to say
That kindness for you
Starts with a letter K.

Mom, please come back to Dad,
For he's so, so very sad,
You may be sad too,
But come back to Dad, please do.

MY LAST LAST NAME IS GRACE

> These poems I give to you now,
> So I just want to say that
> Every day for you is a happy day.
> Love,
> Darrin

The spigots start gushing from the depths of my soul. Please, dear God, help them someday understand.

Several months later, I received another letter from Steph after she heard from John I had filed for divorce. It reads:

> I love you very, very, etc., much. But I hate hate, etc., what you are doing. I pray every day that you will dump Mark and come home. Everybody at church is praying for you and Dad. Maybe you think that if you go to church, people would say, "Here comes the divorcer" or something like that. But I go there. I know what they would say. They would say "PRAISE THE LORD SHE CAME TO KNOW YOU, LORD, AND SHE IS GOING TO BE PART OF THE FAMILY." And if you don't, I know they will be disappointed. Oh, and another thing. I heard you want a divorce paper. Well, I REALLY hope, hope etc. you don't. I would like it if you showed this to Aunt Lenora or read it to her over the phone. The people that agree with you are the rough people...not saying I don't like them. But they should want you to go back with Dad.
> Well, I said everything I wanted to say. So saying good-bye, From Steph.
> PSSSSSSSSSSSSSSSSSSS GO BACK WITH DAD

On the same day that I read such heart-wrenching thoughts, I received another letter about straightening out my life. My emotions were flying all over the place like a wild racquetball. If it were not for the support of my friends, I do not think I would have made it through this dark time. As I say, amnesia is a great defense mechanism.

Beams of sunlight shone on my troubled path at times though few and far in between. One such day, I received a note from my sister, Lorna (she attended seminary during my separation and lived near Chicago). The meat of her message was about a recent book that she read spelled out great truths of God's compassion.

The author put His words in the following about it:

> I know you. I created you. I have loved you from your mother's womb. You have fled, as you now know, from my love, but I love you nevertheless and not-the-less however far you flee. It is I who sustains your very power of fleeing, and I will never finally let you go. I accept you as you are. You are forgiven. I know all your sufferings. I have always known them. Far beyond your understanding, when you suffer, I suffer. I also know all the little tricks by which you try to hide the ugliness you have made of your life from yourself and others. But you are beautiful. You are beautiful more deeply within than you can see. You are beautiful because you yourself, in the unique person that only you are, reflect already something of the beauty of my holiness in a way which shall never end. You are beautiful also because I and I alone see the beauty you shall become. Through the transforming power of my love which is made perfect in weakness you shall become perfectly beautiful in a uniquely irreplaceable way, which neither you nor I will work out alone, for we shall work it out together. (*People of the Lie: The Hope for Healing Human Evil* by M. Scott Peck, 1982, 1st edition, pp. 267–68, source: "Known" by Rev. Dr. Charles

MY LAST LAST NAME IS GRACE

K. Robinson, November 4, 1973 (*Duke Divinity School Review*, Winter 1979, Volume 44, p. 44)
I believe these words are truth. I know they are. Yet we humans struggle to even believe it.
Grace and peace to you,
Love, Lorna.

How beautiful are the feet of those who bring good news (Romans 10:15)! During painful days, these types of notes were the closest to reading a Bible or having devotions for me (besides hearing scripture readings in church). I knew deep down inside that God was watching over me from above. My God is able, and I was confident that I was not going to drown, even though my backpack was way too heavy for me to carry.

Yes, there were many days back then I would have like to have no memory of it all. But then, there were others that we laugh and laugh about today. My youngest sister, Lorna, and her hubby, Ray, were living in Chicago, and busy earning their degrees. Lenora and I, both single moms, got the brainy idea to borrow our brother Elvin's van and take our seven kids on a road trip to visit Aunt Lorna and Uncle Ray. What memories! After a whirlwind weekend of crashing on their small apartment floor and touring Chicago with them, our weekend wrapped up. Sunday evening, Lenora looked at me and asked, "Are you up to starting out tonight while the kids are sleeping?" "Sure," I answered. Having the kids dressed in their pajamas and after rounds of hugs and good-bye, we started out. Having traveled through the rest of Illinois, then Indiana, we finally entered the Ohio turnpike.

Around 4:00 a.m., we heard a *pop* and felt the bump of a flattened tire. Now what? We don't know how to change a flat tire! After some discussion on what to do, we decided we needed to wave down a trucker for some assistance. So while Lenora remained in the driver's seat, I walked to the back of the van and started to wave crazily when I noticed a tractor trailer truck approaching. After all, my family consists of many truck drivers. Any one of my brothers would stop and help a damsel in distress, right? Where are the police when you need one?

From any truck driver's perspective, he notices some lady waving for his attention. But who is in the back of the van? Someone who is ready to rob or murder him once he stops and offers assistance at 4:00 a.m.? After fifteen minutes of waving to no avail, we determined to drive on the flat tire to the next exit, get off, and seek help at the turnpike toll booth. From this experience, I can tell you that driving five miles an hour—*thump, thump, thump*—to reach our destination seemed like a long time. Of course, some of the kids were awoken and asked about the disturbing noise.

Arriving at the toll booth, we were informed that the police were tied up with a traffic accident nearby. After a phone call and paying a tow truck driver $80 for his tire-changing services, we resumed our journey home. While handing over the borrowed van keys to our kindhearted brother Elvin, he just shook his head and laughed about his crazy sisters not knowing how to change a tire (the wheel rim ended up being okay).

To help pay her share of the expenses that occurred on that road trip, Lenora came up with a brainy idea: "Leanne, why don't I take Steph and Darrin with us to visit Disney World?" I agreed. Suffice it to say, they made wonderful memories on another road trip once again with their Aunt Lenora and their favorite cousins. Five people crammed into her Escort; one person sat on a pillow that was placed over the emergency brake in the middle of the front seat, and two sat in the back seat. What was the worst part of all? Lenora's car air-conditioner was not working. It's a bit too much to expect a carful of kids to endure a long-distance trip in a small car traveling from Pennsylvania to Florida with no working air-conditioner. Lenora was glad when all could stretch their legs and had all of Disney World to explore. The road trip helped to bond the cousins closer than ever.

The following spring, I made plans to move to another town to be closer to work as soon as my rental lease expired in June. As the time drew closer to John's and my rescheduled hearing date, I decided I did not want to spend more money on lawyer fees. I was confident (probably, John too) I would win my custody battle, and Steph and Darrin would move back in with me full-time. Thus, they would have to finish school the last six weeks in a strange one. That just was not fair to them. What is six more weeks to have them live with their dad and finish out their school year? I had blocks of time when I spent with my kids during the summer as the weekend-only visits disappeared. When John wanted them, he asked. But basically over summer, I had them full-time, as he began dating as well.

My plan was that Steph and Darrin would conclude on their own to live with me full-time without using the courts by the following school year. After I moved, the school district they would be attending was one that they were more familiar.

But my well-laid plans failed. Both Steph and Darrin together decided to return to live with Dad for the following school year. By now, they were of the age that they did not need much supervision, while John was in the chicken house tending to his chores. Well, let's just say, I have heard some horror stories. Upon hearing about some of them, after the fact, I shook my head in disbelief and asked, "Where was your mother?"

By the following school year, I was engaged and planning on marrying Jeff. Using my divorce settlement money, we purchased a new duplex together in the Cocalico School District, the same one that I had graduated from. Starting her freshman year, Stephanie was so eager to get contact lenses. Call it a bribe if you want. But knowing that she was becoming a young lady and believing she should be with her mother during her early teen years, I promised to buy her contacts if she came to live with Jeff and me. Deciding that her life was changing in other ways as well, as her Dad was actively dating and seeking a wife, she said, "Okay." Since Steph agreed to move in with us, I assumed Darrin would agree as well. But no.

Being the sensitive guy that he is, Darrin did not like the idea that his dad had nobody to live with him until his remarriage. Darrin would say to me, "But, Mom, you got Steph, Rochelle, and Jeff, and Dad would not have anybody living here." So he decided to live with

John one more year. Darrin joined the local boy's baseball team for three years when he was in fourth to sixth grade. Unfortunately, I did not get to observe many of his games.

By sixth grade, John said Darrin had to attend the local school and was not paying for private school. But that only lasted one quarter. Darrin begged his dad to return to Grace Christian School. So he did. However, a form of bullying ensued for Darrin. Acting as though he betrayed them by going to the public school, his buddies did not treat him very well. In his eleven-year-old mind, he made a plan. With $30 in his pocket, he ran away from home. He walked several miles to a neighboring town along Route 422. Sunset occurred, and it became dark. But Darrin kept walking with no destination in mind.

Suddenly, a car pulled over. Uncertain of the driver's intentions, whether good or bad, he became scared and ran into a field. Realizing he needed to go back home, Darrin walked to his dad's girlfriend's house, who lived in the same town. Meanwhile, back home, worrying John, having no clue where his son was, called for prayer warriors to pray for Darrin and his safe return back home. Several buddies arrived to show John support. What relief when the phone call came in from his girlfriend! Relieved, John drove over and picked up Darrin. On the drive back home, John heard about the hurtful bullying that was occurring. Walking back into the house, noticing his dad's friends, Darrin felt stupid and embarrassed. After hearing about the situation, Darrin's principal permitted him to stay home from school for two weeks. Things were much improved from then on until the remainder of his school year.

However, when I heard about Darrin running away from home, the decision was made. "You must come and live with me, Darrin. It is time you start fresh with a new life and friends in Cocalico." The following year after Jeff and I purchased and moved into a new larger four-bedroom home, Darrin agreed to move in with us. The decision was confirmed later on for him once he realized his other choice would be to live with a stepbrother, stepsister, and his dad's new baby when John remarried.

Oh, want to know how that came about? Anatomy works! Less than three months of dating, John got his girlfriend pregnant. Janie overheard the news at her restaurant counter when John and Jackie's husband were having breakfast together. She could not wait to phone me. Boy, does he owe Steph an explanation and me an apology.

All I wanted from John was to explain to his teenage daughter why he could not keep his privates in his pants, while he is busy calling me a slut and a whore. An apology to me would be nice as well. I placed a call and told him of my expectations. "I knew you were going to love it when you heard the news from Janie," he embarrassingly said. He only followed through on one part of my request. I wish I could have been a fly on the wall for that conversation with his daughter. I never did get my apology. Oh well, his family now has some other news they can discuss, and it will not always be about Leanne.

Thought of the Day

Grace is being carried out of sinking sand, out of a pit, then lifted out by the strong arms of Jesus, and set on solid ground.

Chapter 40

I Said "I Do" But Then I Don't

A man's own folly ruins his life, yet his heart rages against the Lord.
—Proverbs 19:3

Here is the full story on how I met Jeff: Pat and I heard about a new hangout appropriately named Corvairs, which catered to those who loved listening and dancing to Solid Gold Oldies. Giving the Jukebox hangout competition, it was located closer to both of our homes. One Saturday night, we decided to check it out. We reasoned driving with two drinks in us over the course of the evening was better if we did not have as far to drive back home. What I discovered I liked most about Corvairs was the parking situation. I said a prayer for my safety many nights when I left the Jukebox while I walked to my car parked quite a distance away along Route 24. Most times, the parking lot was usually full by the time I arrived for our dancing-the-night-away evening and forced me to park away from the building. I did not particularly like that when I left alone many nights.

Pat and I entered Corvairs to the sound of the Supremes greeting us. Bright neon lights winked as we entered. We noticed car memorabilia displayed everywhere on the walls. The DJ stood in an actual half of a car. A shiny black Corvair was parked on the edge of the dance floor. Drinks were served out of oil can replicas and poured into small pint jars.

As per our usual routine, Pat and I did our first walkthrough to check out the "landscape." It was packed with other nosey newcomers; there were no tables available for us to sit down. Instead, we hung out at the bar and joined the others who remained standing. A second tier formed behind the people seated on the barstools. Seating at the bar slowly became available, as people moved onto the dance floor or away from the bar to join others at a table.

Pat and I noticed a group of four wholesome, good-looking, and clean-cut (safe?) guys hanging out between the bar and the Corvair. All four were drinking beer. We figured it was a group of friends who choose to investigate the new place in town also. They engaged in lots of laughter and felt comfortable with each other. The first thing I noticed about the guys was they did not seem to be the average age of the crowd who loved oldies. Perhaps, they were younger. Two of the four were at least six feet tall and thin; one was average height, had a great smile, slightly thinning hair, and sported a mustache. The other guy appeared to be average height also but was more serious-looking and already drunk. The group noticed that Pat and I and sneaked glances, shyly, from time to time.

It wasn't long before a slow song began playing. Mr. Great Smile shyly walked up to me and asked if I wanted to dance. I accepted his offer, and we approached the crowded dance floor. Near the edge of the dance floor and as far away as possible from the loud DJ, we began to slow dance somewhat uncomfortably, at least for me. We started playing the questions game. I learned over the course of the evening he was only twenty-nine years old, and his name was Jeff. The four close friends drove up from Berks County because they all loved the oldies. The proof was how well all of them could sing or mouth most of the words to the songs. No kidding. I thought I knew most of the lyrics, but they showed me up. They sang along with the varying record artists. As the evening went on and they emptied more beer bottles, the more their joyful noise reached higher levels as well.

From the conversation, Pat and I learned that one of the six-footers was a professional boxer and loved cars. Jeff, a service manager for one of Berks County's famous Cadillac dealers, did as well. The envious Corvair on display was a topic of conversation.

By the time the evening ended, plans were made to meet back at Corvairs the following weekend. I was impressed when I noticed someone was selected to be the designated driver from the outset. The following weekend, another friend was added to the mix: a good-looking muscular Italian who talked loudly the more brown liquid he consumed. I learned Jeff was the youngest of three boys, was never married, and still lived at home with his parents, whom he loved and respected dearly. His bed was shared with his pet dog. Jeff learned I was older than him by six years, was recently divorced, and a single mom of three who worked as the office manager for Four Seasons Produce.

After the second weekend of meeting at Corvairs, Jeff and I started dating regularly. On one date, we attended his friend's professional boxing match. What a first-time experience for me! I was on edge watching the rounds. I could not imagine being the one in the ring and having to watch your opponent's weapons of strength come toward your head. Jeff noticed I was not a beer drinker but a sweet mixed-drink kind of gal. Our dates were held at either one of his friend's home hanging out, playing cards, or circulating between the bars or fairs where various bands played Solid Gold Oldies between Berks and Lancaster counties. On occasion, we danced to the oldies. But it was more about hanging out and talking. More times than not, dates included going out to dinner with his friends and their wives or girlfriends to an exclusive Italian-owned, member-only club a few miles from Jeff's home.

Within a few weeks, I dated Jeff exclusively, and my hanging out at bars, seeking dates stopped. Apparently, I passed his expectation as potential marriage material, even after he learned about my conservative Mennonite background and my feelings on the importance of going to church. Because he arrived home late on Saturday nights, Jeff was seldom bright-eyed and bushy-tailed enough to attend his parents' Lutheran church on Sunday mornings. He mostly attended St. Mattress, he joked.

MY LAST LAST NAME IS GRACE

Our relationship grew to the point of nightly phone calls. Jeff was willing to drive the distance some weekday evenings to hang out in my home in East Petersburg. For Jeff, meeting my kids, observing my lifestyle, and learning what was important to me cemented our relationship. Learning about my mostly estranged family because of my divorce and being a black sheep did not scare Jeff away, either. Happy with what he learned about me and believing we were compatible, Jeff surprised me and said, "I love you" by the sixth week of dating and information gathering. Not prepared for his comment, I mumbled, "You are a great guy."

After meeting his parents, I was tickled to see how accepting they were of my three kids. They grew to love them as much as their other two grandchildren. Skeptical about marrying again, I stored those little tidbits in the back of my mind; eventually they proved to be priceless. We spent a lot of time together over dinner or picnics with Jeff's family. His two brothers and sisters-in-law were also reaching out with open arms to me and my children. I learned Jeff was highly respected as a manager by his coworkers, and he had common sense about handling money. Jeff introduced me to his boss, Bruce, and his lovely wife, Marlene. Everyone I met seemed to be down-to-earth, and I felt very comfortable to be around them. Over time, Jeff was introduced to some of my family members, sisters, and friends. We double-dated often with my coworkers. Eventually, the I love yous sincerely left my lips also.

When primary election time came around, I learned Jeff's family members were Democrats. In fact, his aunt and uncle served on the local committee. Treading new territory, as I had little knowledge or interest in politics, I was easily convinced by their rationale and political discussions why Bill Clinton should be president. So, I, the nonvoter, signed up for my first voter's registration as a Democrat (giving one more reason for Daddy, later on, to scold me).

I realized the best thing I could do with my divorce settlement money that I had banked was to put it in real estate. After my second rental lease expired, Jeff and I decided to buy a duplex together located in a small town. We sincerely considered moving into Berks

County, but the most affordable new housing was in the same school district where I attended as a child. Besides, it was not in an area where my relatives lived. Because I was in no hurry to get married, and I had placed God on a shelf (and pulled Him off when I wanted), I had no qualms about moving in together. Apparently, I believed that if God wasn't on my radar, I'm not accountable. Of course, I knew my parents disapproved. But I was not regularly visiting with my parents during this time. I placed short phone calls to Mom and pretty much geared the conversation. And yes, Mom's letters kept filling my mailbox.

One morning, upon my arrival at work, I tended to a few customers' phone calls. Then I placed a call to Jeff's mom around 8:30 a.m. and inquired about what food I could bring to the picnic that evening. She gave me her menu selection idea, but just as she was about to hang up the phone, she commented, "Leanne, it is an unspoken rule. So now I'm telling you. Unless it is an emergency, no one calls this house before 9:00 a.m." *Hmm, that is a new rule.* My mom called her friends anytime of the morning: 7:30 a.m. or 8:00 a.m. or whenever her little heart desired.

But, I can tell you, I never made that mistake again, and I live by that rule today.

Moving in together allowed Jeff to practice being a stepdad, and my kids had an opportunity to realize Mom most likely had selected her next husband. The kids enjoyed living in town. The pool and elementary school were both within walking distance, and some classmates lived nearby. Neighbors became good friends and were people who could be trusted to babysit my kids or had a home that I felt comfortable for my kids to hang out in. Since Jeff's parents were Lutheran, we started attending the convenient Lutheran church in town in our backyard.

Eventually, enough time had passed, and I felt we all blended fairly well as a family. Jeff got along with my kids and vice versa. No, it wasn't always a bed of roses, but my unwritten checklist of must-dos and must-haves concerning Jeff were being checked off. As with any young men who wanted to get married, he started to talk about our setting a date and finalizing plans. Having never been married, he wanted a traditional wedding.

For me, my second wedding was not going to include any Mennonite restrictions that my first wedding had. For instance, during my first wedding ceremony, we had eight chairs set in a semi-circle for the bridal party, as standing in front of the pulpit was not allowed. Why? The minister's sermon lasted longer, and you did not want to be standing the entire time. Plus, for this wedding, I would be wearing a veil over cut hair. Our Lutheran pastor agreed to marry us and set up four compatible premarriage counseling sessions, which we passed.

We chose a wedding date in April and started choosing our bridal party, photographer, soloist, caterer, and reception hall. Cute Rochelle was the flower girl, and the son of my coworker and friend, Wanda's son, Brandon, was the adorable ring bearer.

Obviously, Janie, who owned a restaurant and did a terrific job as a caterer, was an easy decision. Thankfully, she accepted when we asked her. Our reception was to be held at a local Berks County fire hall where we spent many date nights listening to various oldies bands. My niece Cyndy was the soloist, who sang beautifully. Pat was my maid of honor, and Esther and Janie, my bridesmaids. Jeff selected his best friend, Steven, as his best man, his boxer friend, Pete, and another friend, Gary, as his groomsmen. His boss, Bruce, was in charge of the fleet of cars (all Cadillac models, of course) and was assigned to be the driver for the wedding party.

My Friday diary entries one day prior to our wedding are below:

> I worked until noon on Friday. After meeting Jeff's mother at the fire hall and unloading some items, we drove up to Janie's restaurant, the Elton. We planned to assist her with any odd jobs in catering the reception. We made the punch, peeled onions, buttered buns, and then loaded up the station wagon with a lot of supplies. We drove back to the fire hall and assisted with dec-

orating the head table with a beautiful garland. My friend Bonni, was in charge of decorating the fire hall. Jeff and his dad also came to assist us in placing the table favors. It took us until 6:30 p.m. to finish decorating. Oh, how lovely it looked!

Jeff and I rushed home to change our clothes for our rehearsal scheduled at the church by 7:00 p.m. We were late, needless to say, and I felt too exhausted to enjoy the events of the evening. Everybody did fine. Some things were not in the order or the way I wanted them, but the minister had the final say. After rehearsal, we all went down to the Adamstown VFW for a great meal of your choice on Jeff's parents. We were all anxious to leave and get home for a good night's sleep. Nobody seemed to drink too much or stay out too late. Jeff stayed overnight at his parent's house.

My diary entry on my wedding day:

After a good night's sleep, I was up and about by 7:45 a.m., Saturday morning. The first part of the day seemed to drag. I had all the kids showered, nails done, hair shampooed, etc., and it was only 11:00 a.m. My friend Cory, the receptionist from Four Seasons, brought pizza for our lunch. From then on, time seemed to fly, and a lot of action started to take place. My friend Beverly came and helped me do my nails and get dressed into my gown. Of course, Pat and Esther came before 2:00 p.m., as they both needed assistance with their hair and makeup. Wanda brought Brandon, the ring bearer, but she had not allowed him to get dressed too early.

At one point, I counted twenty people were in our house. My sister Lenora (my only sibling to attend my wedding) and her four kids arrived. The photographer arrived around 2:00 p.m. and took many pictures of me, the bride around the house and in my messy bedroom. Janie, after checking in on things at the fire hall, arrived late. I did not panic because I knew she would arrive with her makeup already on and her hair done. Wrong! She arrived at 2:20 p.m. and announced she needed to hop in the shower. At 2:25 p.m., she asked, "Do you have a hair dryer?" I do not know why or how I remained calm. My friend, Cathy, arrived to help style Rochelle and Steph's hair.

As far as the weather, it was a rainy, dreary day. But it never rained when it mattered. Thank God! When Bruce, the driver, came to pick me up, it was not raining when I needed to get into the car to head to the church. We arrived at the church around 2:30 p.m. Every time I saw Jeff's uncle, I'd asked him, "How is Jeff holding up?" It seemed so long since I had seen him. Janie finally arrived at the church around twenty minutes before three, not wearing earrings. One of the drivers drove back down to the house and delivered them to her.

Next thing I remember, the music began playing. This is it! I will never forget the feeling of walking down the aisle while holding onto Jeff's uncle's arm (not my dad). I began crying before I started walking down the aisle. I was lucky to have met my new husband in three short years. Jeff looked so handsome in his tuxedo and was smiling from ear to ear. But he looked so nervous. He said later his knees were shaking. The soloist sang beautifully, and the ceremony went smoothly and quickly. Brandon and Rochelle did a great job of standing up front with us for as long as was needed. Before long, we were married.

Because of the rain the cars did not get decorated as much as Bruce would have liked. He did have some great champagne waiting for us. We decided to pass on driving to the Reading Museum for outdoor pictures. Instead, we drove around the Ephrata area, including past my parents' house, and blared the horns. My parents were aware of my wedding. But not believing in divorce and remarriage, they chose not to attend.

After arriving at the fire hall around 5:20 p.m., we were asked to stall entering because the macaroni and cheese was not quite ready. Panic! Because they could not find the tray initially, it needed more time to be heated up. There was a slight delay in serving the coffee too, and the ice cream was not served on the designated plates. But other than that, everybody commented on Janie's delicious meal of meatballs and baked beans.

The reception lasted until 10:00 p.m., and everybody seemed to be have a good old time. At one point, Pete picked me up and carried me around, ripping the elastic of my bustle. From then on, I had to carry it around with one hand. Accidentally, Gary knocked off my veil, and it came loose from the headpiece. But by 9:00 p.m., who cares? We made over $55 during our dollar dance. What better way to end a wedding reception than with a singing contest? It was held between my Four Seasons' coworkers who sang a Beach Boys song, "Help Me, Rhonda" and Jeff's friends, who sang "Brown Eyed Girl." We had a wonderful time!

Jeff and I honeymooned in Puerto Vallarta, Mexico. We continued to work on being a new family nucleus of Mom's new husband and Jeff becoming a stepdad to my three kids. The process went a little smoother as Steph and Darrin visited only on the weekends. Thus, a gradual blending occurred. I am uncertain if it is typical or not with most stepfamilies, but my son had the most difficult time adjusting to Jeff. If I got caught in the middle of choosing sides, most times, Mama Bear chose her cubs.

During the decade I was with Jeff, I learned about politics and had my eyes opened to political tactics, the effects of Congress stalling, and hardcore divisions among the left-right followers. As I sifted thoughts and ideas, I eventually landed on the Republican ticket.

A memorable trip Jeff and I took was to romantic Paris. Because his Cadillac dealership won one of the top awards in the county, he won an all-expense paid, five-day trip to France. Yahoo! Six other couples left the Philadelphia Airport, flew together over the Big Blue, and spent almost a week in lavish surroundings. It felt good to be holding onto the arm of a hard worker, one who takes his nine-to-five job seriously and a goal-setter. My claps were heard the loudest on the night of Pennsylvania's Award Night. Jeff grinned from ear to ear as he proudly held the plaque for the photographers.

In between a little business, we did get the chance to tour Paris and attended a popular show at Moulin Rouge. The six women were told to all dress in pink. Standing outside our gorgeous hotel in bright pink outfits (mine was a then-fashionable pink jumpsuit with gold-plated buttons), we all saluted the Cadillac CEO for such a grand time. We all took turns taking pictures of the twelve of us. It was the last time I saw Jeff wearing a pink necktie. No reaching into your wallet, unless you are buying a souvenir. It was the closest I ever came to feeling like royalty.

By the time nursing school ended (details in the following chapter) and I started my new career as a registered nurse, my marriage was unraveling. I threw myself into my career and climbed the nursing career ladder over the next five years. Just as a tapeworm is secretly causing havoc, subtle nuisances crept in. The differences between Jeff's and my upbringing were becoming too vast and more noticeable. By the eighth year of marriage, I was so unfulfilled and extremely unhappy. Of course, I was still far from God, so the restlessness connection did not compute.

Another cesspool began reeking once again; my sinful lifestyle continued to deepen the ruts of my path. My typical pattern of seeing something I desired just beyond my grasp was right around the corner in an unexpected source. He was someone on cyberspace with a nick of PA_Great Guy.

Yes, I said "I do" to Jeff, but then, I did not love him anymore. Eventually, I threw away another marriage like a pair of old shoes!

Thought of the Day

Grace is understanding God has made His love message so simple so we can all understand it. My pastor, Jay's Easter message was so clear when he shared about this: John: when I was confused, you gave me *faith*. Marlene Magdalena: when I was hurting, you gave me *hope*. Peter: when I was guilty, you showed me *grace*. Thomas: when I doubted, you gave me *truth*.

Chapter 41

Turning Forty During Nursing School

> You were taught, with regard to your former way of life, to put off your old self, which is being corrupted by its deceitful desires; to be made new in the attitude of your minds; and to put on the new self, created to be like God in true righteousness and holiness.
> —Ephesians 4:22–23

1993 RN Nursing Graduation Picture

"I CAN'T DECIDE WHETHER TO have a reversal on my tubal ligation and try to get pregnant for Jeff. Or should I become an RN?" I questioned my friend Janie over the phone one day. I took the phone with me out on my deck to finish my morning cup of coffee.

Janie chuckled. "Seriously, Leanne? You're considering having a baby? Wow. Your question shocked me. Is Jeff pressuring you to do this?"

"No, not at all. He said it is entirely up to me. Jeff was not counting on having a child with me, since he knew I had settled on three children years ago. Besides, from what I've been reading, the success rate of getting pregnant from tubal reversals is very small." I took a sip of the coffee.

Believing too the reversal would have a poor outcome, she suggested college. "Between those two choices, there is no reason to believe you'll have a hundred percent success rate of one day signing your name as a registered nurse. Go for it!" We caught up on each other's lives about our kids' activities, and after a few minutes hung up the phone. By the time, I completed nursing school, and Janie reminded me of my earlier questions, I could only shake my head. Thank God, I chose the latter.

Jeff's boss, Bruce, and his wife, Marlene, a registered nurse, became one of our close friends. One night, we met for dinner. Since Bruce and Marlene were childless at the time, Marlene enjoyed hearing me share stories about my teenage daughter, Steph. A frequent over-dinner conversation was about my family or about Four Seasons, where I worked as an office manager. One night during dinner, Marlene commented to me, "Leanne, you do such a good job handling your kids. You are a great analytical thinker. You should be a nurse." *Hmm, you hardly know me.* Haven't I heard this before? Someone sees something in me I do not even see in myself?

Little did Marlene know how her comment changed my life! For over seven years, I spent hours doing data entry and key punching produce codes and order quantities to print out on loading slips. Servicing the mid-Atlantic region, a fleet of trucks required much accurate paperwork from the data entry department to run efficiently. Thus, day in and day out, I keypunched produce codes and quantity amounts and oversaw loading slips for the various delivery routes for each truck driver. Although the job held plenty of challenge to be perfect (an incorrect punched number, such as 22 cases, instead of 2, could be disastrous), I began to feel I had more to offer the world other than being a keypuncher. I was ready for a change in careers (although I did not realize it at the time).

Marlene's other advice, which I acted on, was to attend the cheaper community college and forfeit attending any expensive, prestigious college, as she did. "After all, we all take the same state boards and write the same initials RN behind our names. Go through nursing school at the cheapest expense."

After taking some time studying the difference between an Associate of Applied Science degree and a diploma for a registered nurse, I attended an open house at Lancaster General Hospital's School of Nursing, a diploma school. The following week, I did the same at Reading Area Community College (RACC) and learned more about their associate degree program. I understood working in a hospital under the diploma program gave nursing students lots of hands-on experience on various clinical floors as free labor for the hospital. The associate degree program gave opportunity for less hands-on clinical experience, but participants learned the why behind rationale, strategies and obtained more knowledge. Attending RACC made the most sense, as it was located close to both my home and place of employment. Plus, I figured I could obtain clinical experience once I was hired as a registered nurse. Why not get paid while learning?

At the outset, Jeff was not too thrilled with my plans. With my usual gumption, I commented it was not the first time I was planning on doing something without much support from a husband. But whether he was on board or not, I was going to pursue a nursing career.

In less than two months after Marlene's comment, I pursued a new career (with Jeff's reluctance but permission). Within a short period of time, I scheduled an appointment with a RACC career counselor and planned my courses for over for the next three years. If I thought I was busy earlier in my life, I had no idea!

Want to know the other advantage of having an old boyfriend for your boss? Dave understood and was agreeable when I asked him if I could take a two-hour lunch to start taking prerequisite courses at RACC to become a registered nurse. Even though Dave realized it meant I would eventually be leaving his employment, he was supportive.

Whatever was I thinking? Starting nursing school at thirty-eight years old, when I had only half of my brain cells, made for many hours of knuckle-down studying. Anyone who has worked full-time while attending college with the younger nineteen-year-old college freshmen knows what I am talking about. I can simply sum up those three years—I had no life. It was rough. Probably to teach college freshmen about "life," professors, I learned, changed things up, not to rattle us, but to prepare us for the real world. One time, our biology professor decided against testing us on the expected material of definitions and illustrations. Instead, he called it an essay of think-it-through. After handing in their papers, classmate girls cried and ran out of the room while some guys threatened to commit suicide. While many flunked the biology test, I received a grade of 71 percent, barely passing it.

Being an office manager meant I worked extra shifts and was expected to stay until computer issues, if any, were resolved. One such expectation occurred on my thirty-eighth birthday. Jeff planned on surprising me by having a handful of relatives stop by for cake and ice cream. But I never made it home until after the guests had left. I journaled: "I can't believe it; only two more years until I'm 40. Forty sounds like such an old, old age!"

During nursing school, I met and made new friends, like Susie, I will always cherish. Being an older student like me, Susie became someone I could carpool with to help save expenses when I learned she lived within five miles of my home. She was a brain and the push that kept me studying harder.

Steph was the fill-in mom to Rochelle, who turned ten. Everybody had their chores; they were responsible to aid in the smooth running of our household. My kids knew their mom ate dinner and then hid out in her bedroom to study for hours. I missed wedding receptions, cut short family reunions, and declined many friends' offers to "let's just hang out."

My first EKG was done, and my first appointment to the doctor for shoulder pain was held early on during nursing school. My EKG, scheduled to rule out the cause of an irregular heartbeat at times, concluded I was simply drinking too much caffeine. The cause of my shoulder pain was due to the many heavy nursing schoolbooks I was schlepping around. I had better make some changes.

In spite of my heavy workload, my family took a trip to Williamsport one November weekend. My sister was marrying her boss, a man who was actually older than our dad. No, that did *not* go well when Lenora informed my parents she was marrying Jack. Being asked to be her matron of honor, I felt this was an important reason to take a break from my studies. Lenora told me she did not want any wedding present. "Your presence is present enough." We had a great time celebrating Lenora and Jack's new union that weekend—a much-needed break for me.

Eventually, all my prerequisite courses were met, and nursing 1 was upon me. Turning forty years of age during nursing school was a landmark year. Continuing to work as the office manager while finishing up microbiology I and II, biology, physiology, and anatomy kept me hopping. After the completion of six nursing phases, our class was prepared to start our clinical rotation at the various hospitals or nursing homes. By the time we came to this point, our class lost about 25 percent of the nursing students, who either dropped out or failed.

Mastery was by far the most difficult course throughout college. It was expected one had a reasonable understanding of the course material and be able to answer three of the professor's questions. If you passed mastery, you were allowed to wear your uniform and report to the assigned hospital by 6:30 a.m. for a clinical rotation. If you flunked, you were to report to the library and continue to study and review the homework to broaden your knowledge base. What pressure! The reading material, if stacked high, often made at least a one-inch pile of papers and charts. Covering all the various body systems, including medical terms, the material required many hours of preparation, as you had no idea which questions would be asked of you. Besides, who wanted to be known as the one who was not asked to report to clinical but, instead, sent to the library?

By the grace of God, there was only one time when I did not do well in mastery. It was during a week when a clinical rotation was not scheduled; I did not have to be ashamed after all! John and I had a court date to discuss my desire to have child support increased. Obviously, I was distracted. It simply forced me to study harder than ever before and not allow other life experiences to interfere or distract me. I was good at compartmentalizing, so that is what I did to get through my most challenging career preparation.

Another stressful moment during nursing school was when Jeff and I received a phone call from his mother. Our friend Leeza (the wife of the muscular handsome Italian, who was Jeff's groomsman) was found murdered in her home. After fact-gathering, we learned her two elementary-aged children came home from school and found their bludgeoned mother. She was stabbed over twenty times! Nothing ever happens in the quiet town of Progress, Pennsylvania. Leeza's murder has never been solved. To this day, my heart breaks for the emotional healing Leeza's poor children have had to endure. Who wants to unpack that?

During my attending college years, we moved out of our duplex and into a larger four-bedroom house located in a great, older development within a mile from our home (this was during the time Darrin finally consented to move in with us). Unlike Steph and Rochelle, Darrin soon became close friends (which continues today) with some neighborhood boys. From living on a farm, which had no close neighbors, to having several classmates live in the same development was a huge plus for Darrin. Yes, he no longer attended his familiar private Christian school, but he adjusted nicely to the public school. Eventually coaxed by his new friends, Darrin became active in sports signing up for both soccer and the wrestling team for

Cocalico High School. Attempting to go to most of Darrin's soccer games or wrestling matches made for a harrowing schedule.

Knuckle-down studying gave way to eventual entering the last clinical rotation of nursing school. We nursing students finally saw a light at the end of the tunnel. I realized I could no longer work full-time at Four Seasons Produce. Thus, my hours were cut back to part-time status. David hired my replacement. After nine years of employment, the door as an office manager closed behind me.

Being a visionary, David was wise in paying for several of his key management employees in the late 1980s to take the Dale Carnegie course when it was offered in our area. I will always be grateful for his footing the bill (which was not cheap) and this opportunity prior to my leaving Four Seasons. Homework included writing speeches, standing in front of people, and presenting it realizing both the instructor and your peers later critiqued it. Yikes!

Remembering my inner voice told me ten years ago I would be standing in front of a crowd of people someday in an unknown setting, I took the course very seriously to learn whatever I possibly could. At one point during our class, when the instructor was talking about improving upon our listening skills, he surprised me when he said, "See what Leanne is doing?" he asked. "She is showing me she is intently listening by having her head slightly tilted and is sitting with proper posture. This leads me to believe she cares about what I have to say." Oh boy, no more chance of ever daydreaming in this class.

Another grateful experience David offered me and my coworker Allen was the chance to stay at the gorgeous Opryland Hotel in Nashville, Tennessee, to attend a wholesale produce sales seminar in 1988. Who was the Dole representative that year who showed up for pictures and autographs? Kenny Rogers! While standing in line, after one of the lectures, to shake hands with Kenny, I kept thinking of a question most people had not asked of him. I got it. While reaching out to shake his hand, I asked Kenny, "How is your lovely wife, Marianne, doing?" He answered, "She is doing just great." Marianne was a cast member in *Hee Haw*, the hilarious cornfield comedy that was a TV syndicate at the time. Flanking both sides of Kenny, Allen and I smiled for the camera for our thirty-second-celebrity event to be in a photo with Kenny Rogers.

Thanksgiving and Christmas time at Four Seasons Produce was a profitable time for my kids. I put them to work helping me and a group of employees make fruit baskets. It was a true test of patience for Darrin. Oh, that's right. He has very little! After signing up our willingness, we watched a gifted fruit basket maker expertly design her fruit basket, spin it as it was being covered with cellophane paper using a hair dryer, and lastly, apply a big bow on top. What can be so hard about strategically arranging fruit in a too-small basket and plopping about one pound of grapes on top? It's difficult! By the time we were finished, incorrect-sized colorful cellophane paper was lying all over the floor. Grapes were rolling off the table and onto the floor. Several were squished, making it look like we were making wine instead of fruit baskets. The kids watched me make the first one to learn some tips. Done, one down. Several hundred to go!

In spite of my busy schedule, I offered sometimes to play a game with Rochelle before her bedtime. She either selected the game of Life, Monopoly or Hangman. More times than not, she often beat me. Somewhere in my child-rearing knowledge, I decided eight was the appropriate age to no longer be spanked; instead, groundings or removing privileges had occurred. I failed Rochelle. Perhaps from being stressed? When she was ten, I journaled, I "spanked Rochelle tonight for disobedience. Now, I need to go talk with her and give her a hug."

Finally, both graduation day and the pinning ceremony were scheduled for the remaining fifty-four (a small percentage from the outset) nursing students. The light at the end of the tunnel was beaming brighter. My husband and children, along with a few faithful, supportive friends: Roz, Pat, and Darcy attended my graduation and celebration. They were thrilled for me. Their presence somewhat lessened the painful reality my parents should have been in attendance but were not.

MY LAST LAST NAME IS GRACE

One of my proudest moments within recent years was when Rochelle submitted an article to *Country* magazine for the Editor's Page. Along with a beautiful picture of her and Steph, the published article read:

> Sister by her side:
> I'm very thankful for my sister, Stephanie. When we were girls, while our mother put herself through college, Steph would braid my hair for school and cook our supper. Years later, we were blessed to be pregnant together. Whenever I worried about my baby, Steph would calm my nerves. She was my rock when I struggled. She introduced me to my husband, an amazing man and partner for life.

It grabs me right in the middle of my chest every time I think about this article.

Instead of grabbing for a baby bottle or diaper, I grabbed for a blood pressure cuff or medicine pack and signed my name proudly with two letters behind it: RN!

Here is a tongue-in-cheek poem I wrote around 1995, within two years of being hired as a three-to-eleven RN charge nurse. I planned on submitting it when it was accepted through a poetry forum (until I realized they required $25 for publishing). One night, the LPNs and I overworked and, putting in overtime beyond our shift, were joking around. Wearily, we began discussing a solution. It takes a village to care for the elderly was our solution. I mean no disrespect and apologize if I offend anyone. It follows:

> HEALTH CARE REFORM
> Everybody knows today's buzzword is health care,
> Hillary has scratched her head and turned elsewhere.
> But, I have some answers to save time and money
> On hospital downsizing and the economy.

American nurses, like me, have had their fill;
Being overworked and underpaid is about to be killed;
To work smart for more money is the coming new way,
For we can find our OWN better solutions, I'd say.

Each morning each patient gets hosed off by a robot,
Are fed by local prisoners, who can also make cots.
All oral meds are given in an assembly-line style
Color-coded and prepackaged in error-free vials.

Daily suppositories are given from a barrel of a gun
As patients bend over and line up one by one.
"Now is the time to turn and reposition, please,"
An intercom reminder is announced quietly.

Visitors have a dual purpose when they come,
"No leaving until you've brushed Grandma's gums."
We can still push the pencil and chart expertly,
Because we have the time to give that needed TLC.

Thought of the Day

Grace is abounding most in deepest waters. You are worthy to be saved from drowning and worthy to be adopted into the family of God simply because He loves us.

Chapter 42

"Summr" Meets "Pa_Great Guy"

*For you know the grace of our Lord Jesus Christ, that
though he was rich, yet for your sakes he became poor,
so that you through his poverty might become rich.*
—2 Corinthians 8:9

IN THE FALL OF 1996, my friend Susie had purchased a new computer. "IRC? What is that?" I asked Susie. I had no idea what she was talking about when she was describing her newly found cyberworld. To me, a computer was mainly used as a word processor and a tool that got me through nursing school. Other times, I inserted a disc to search for recipes, or my hubby played a computer NASCAR game on it. Who knows why Rochelle used it.

Susie got more excited as she shared this new unknown world with me. I looked at her as though she had two heads. She said, "I know, I know. I get it, you have to be one of them to understand." She went into detail describing the usage of a nick (a nickname), chat rooms, and how she conversed with people from around the world by typing conversations.

Sometime later that week I went to Susie's house so she could show me on her own computer how IRC (internet relay chat) functioned. With Susie's assistance, I logged on to a chat room and began typing to chat with someone in Arizona. It reminded me of the times I had been in a similar situation when I made my produce sales calls to the same list of restaurant and store customers. During the placing of their produce order with me, we often chatted about our personal lives. We inquired about each other's weekend family activities, for example. However, I never met most of my customers. Chat rooms were a new method of discussing life with someone; instead of over the phone, it was now over cyberspace, although I had little opportunity to meet any of them.

Intrigued as Susie by the new cyberworld, I called my local phone company and hooked up to IRC. To get online, I was told, I needed a nick or puter name. I loved the name given recently to one of the nurse's aide's newborn girl, Kathlyn Summer. I selected Summr (without the *e*; catchy nicks were important). Summr seemed neutral enough, as I did not want to select a nick that implied anything sexual, like Hot Lips or Luscious Laci.

Within the first month I logged on to IRC, my free and TV viewing time was mainly replaced with IRC time. When I worked seven-to-three shift, I winded down chatting between 4:00 p.m. and 5:30 p.m. If I was scheduled for a three-to-eleven shift, I had my morning coffee while chatting in cyberspace. IRC became my pastime in between chores and errands.

I learned early on if you are a jerk or nice person in real life, you are the same type of person on IRC. Important things I learned about chat rooms over time were: have a sense of humor, hold your own in a chat room discussion, type fast, and be friendly and courteous. I had a lot of fun and a good experience in cyberspace my first weekend, and I also felt competent as a fairly fast typist. As with anything, there were both decent and indecent chat rooms to choose from.

As time went on, I recognized familiar nicks had frequented the same chat rooms. Getting a dcc (private conversation for your eyes only) was one method of scheduling meetings in the same chat room. You could set up an alert when certain nicks logged on.

Besides using a factitious nick, one did not disclose personal information about oneself. (Things have evolved in today's cyberworld where one can be more honest and truthful.) My standard cyber answer when asked the question "Please tell me a little about you" was only partially correct. I did not use my proper name, nor did I have any reason to be forthcoming with the virtual strangers I would never meet face-to-face.

One eventful day, I got dcc (a private chat signal) by PA_Guy. After his introductory question about some personal info, I gave him my standard answer: "I'm an RN who works at Holy Spirit Hospital… live in the Harrisburg area…have three kids…in my mid-thirties…"

He typed back and questioned me as to why was I using a local server Prolog? I ignored his question and reiterated again I was from Harrisburg. But he pressed me for honesty and commented I could not possibly be from the Harrisburg area. But, in fact, I had to be from Lancaster County. I began questioning him and getting a little frightened. "Who are you?" I typed. It was a rarity to be talking with someone in a chat room from your same state, let alone, your same county.

Holding back a little mystery, chat room users could be intriguing. One's personality, enthusiasm on favorite topics became evident, and discussions of day-to-day concerns were revealed. But it was understood your actual name and address, boss's names, true weight, dress size, or other personal matters were off-limit topics.

PA_Guy must be on the same local server as me. Yes, I finally admitted to him I actually did live in Lancaster County. But how did he find that out about me? He explained he was employed by the local phone company that handled the IRC accounts. With his computer knowledge, he knew how to do an online search for those female-sounding nicks using Prolog. We chatted for a little while; I did not learn much more about PA_Guy that night. Knowing he was from Lancaster County and worked for one of the largest businesses in the area, I let down my guard somewhat.

Chat rooms became a means of escape from my reality because of my unhappy marriage. By late fall, near my birthday, I learned PA_Guy made me laugh, had a sense of humor, and was just generally a nice guy. By this time, we had exchanged e-mail addresses. Another nick who befriended me informed me he lived near Pittsburg and held an eight-to-five computer job. He had chosen the same nick and was also called PA_ Guy. Since I had chatted with both of them early on, I could not remember what things I had discussed with whom. It soon became obvious to me one was logged on during the day, but never at night, and vice versa. Originally, we had connected several nights a week. Once local PA_Guy found out he had competition with the same nick, he changed his user name (appropriately) to PA_Great Guy to stop any confusion on my part.

On my forty-fourth birthday, I decided to subtract ten years when asked my age by my few cyberfriends. I answered thirty-four. PA_Great Guy was one of those acquaintances who inquired. I received a friendly cyberflower bouquet from him on my birthday. E-mail conversations eventually led to including a picture of me. Thank goodness, I had a recent one to attach, which was professionally done, as was the craze at the time.

By now, we had actually disclosed our real names, and I came to learn his name was Mike Miller, from a town near East Petersburg, where I used to live. Since he did not send me any picture of himself in a return e-mail, I inquired, "On a scale of one to ten, what number would you assign to your good looks?"

"Six," he answered.

By mid-January, we planned a face-to-face lunch at Pieros, a restaurant close to his work and the car dealer where I had made an appointment for my Camaro. Having a description of his pickup truck, I watched and waited for him to enter the parking lot. Suddenly, this tall dark-haired handsome guy wearing glasses and a big warm smile walked toward my car. *He is no six. He is more like an eight or a nine.*

I was only slightly nervous, and Mike appeared calm. After all, I knew so much about him already. I do not remember our first-words exchange. I do remember thinking what a sharp dresser he was in his green business suit and tie. He sported a corporate haircut.

We sat down in the restaurant and both ordered Italian Wedding Soup. Mike took several spoonfuls and pushed his soup bowl away, too nervous to eat. I had mostly finished mine. Conversation flowed easily between us. I noticed Mike used a lot of eye contact, smiled often, and had great table manners. At one point, he dropped his napkin. While I bent down to reach for it under the table, I observed strong thighs through his dress slacks.

"Okay," I commented. "Confession time, I just turned forty-four, not thirty-four."

"Wow!" he exclaimed. "You do not look forty-four. I would have believed you were thirty-four if you had not told me otherwise."

Having cleared up that lie, I questioned Mike as to exactly what were his intentions of me.

He answered, "I know you are a wonderful person, am blessed to have met you, and just want you to be my friend." No problem. I have had male friends before in my life. While working at Four Seasons, Allen, a great friend, sat in the desk next to mine. We shared many a conversation about our families and weekend excursions, which had us laughing until we cried. He knew a lot about my family. Sure, we can do lunch every couple of weeks. It is nice having a face with your nick.

After my car dealer appointment, I came home to a heart-warming complimentary e-mail, which made me smile. Of course, the e-mails and connections became more frequent, soon daily, and then several times a day. By the weekend, Mike disclosed he had wished he had kissed me good-bye, but he was too shy. *Hmmm, only friendship, huh?*

The Camaro needed a second appointment, so we made plans to meet for lunch again. Once scheduled, he started discussing what would I be wearing. "A surprise," I answered. I decided I was going to surprise him with a kiss and get it over with and out of the way (remember my unmet needs?).

The following Thursday, we met at the Greystone Restaurant for lunch. Walking toward the restaurant, Mike noticed my short skirt and commented, "Nice surprise!" After he complimented me, I grabbed him by his lapel and kissed him a warm, special, comfortable, French kiss lasting about five seconds. I pulled back and smiled. He said, "Wow! I thought your outfit was the surprise. You surprised me."

As we were walking hand in hand into the restaurant, I noticed Mike was wiping his lips with the back of his hand (taking off my lipstick?). He later commented, "No, I was still in shock of how awesome your kiss was." We ordered our lunch, and during our conversation, I noticed him grinning and laughing about that kiss. It was almost to the point where I started getting embarrassed and feeling uncomfortable about my initiating it.

During lunch, we shared pictures of our kids and more about our personal lives. Lunch ended. After more passionate kissing, I turned to get into my car. The heel of my shoe got caught somehow in the car door. I could not move. Poor Mike did not know how to help me without reaching out and touching my leg. But it suddenly broke free. We laughed. It was the first of many shared wonderful, hearty laughs—a need fulfilled for both of us. As I drove home, I thought, *I am not going to pursue this any further unless it can remain a friendship. But, at the same time, how I can live without those wonderful soft French kisses?*

Shortly thereafter, Susie had a suggestion for me. "Why don't you and Mike start e-mailing four questions to learn more about each other?" Over time, I learned Mike was a hard worker, was taking college courses two nights a week to earn his bachelor's degree, handled money wisely, took reasonable, affordable vacations, was a dedicated employee, had concerns for his son, and had one older sister living in the area. Mike described himself as an orphan since both parents died within a short period of time of each other when he was in his early thirties. Mike learned I was from Mennonite background, why my first marriage failed, and why I chose to change careers. But we did not discuss the compelling reason to pursue our friendship nor the cause of our unhappy marriages. Those were not questions we asked of each other.

About a month later, after one of our lunch dates at the same restaurant, Mike paid the bill and turned to lay the tip on the table. I watched him and said to myself, "Leanne, it is not him. Do not think about putting him through your scrutiny of the perfect man you are looking for." Then I heard an inner voice very clearly answer back,

'You do not know that.' I looked out the window and sighed. What a mess I made for myself once again! How and why did I allow this to happen? Besides, I cannot possibly hurt Jeff. He does not deserve it.

Many complimentary e-mails, e-cards, and e-bouquets poured in frequently from Mike. He started to call me by endearing words such as "my queen" and, later on, "sweet princess." The more I learned about Mike, I liked what I saw. In one e-mail, Mike wrote: "I have gazed into your eyes, peered into your soul, and know you love God."

Around Valentine's Day, Mike asked me if he could meet me for lunch as he had something very important he needed to share with me about an experience he recently had. He insisted we meet in person. I said that would be fine, as I had something I needed to clarify with him as well. We never made it inside the restaurant. We remained in the car in the parking lot and talked. Mike spoke for about three-fourths of an hour nonstop, while I listened.

He said, "One of the questions you asked me was 'When did I last have a full-blown cry?' Well, I had it on Saturday morning in the shower, and God spoke to me. I found Him again, and I cried and cried. I knelt down in front of the commode and gave my life back to God. I know I promised you I would never use the L word. But I know I love you, and in order to love you completely, I need to love God first."

Mike said he was prepared for me to end the relationship or to tell him we needed to keep our relationship to cyberspace time only. He had no motivation to tell me anything differently. He came to the conclusion he could no longer live out the lie of not loving his wife. In fact, he doubted if, indeed, he ever did love her. Mike said if nothing else came out of our short four-month friendship, he would be eternally grateful for my bringing him back to God.

I started to cry then gave him a gentle slap on the arm and said sarcastically, "That is funny because I have never felt so far away from God. Have fun with that!"

I repeatedly reminded him not to make any decisions believing I was part of his future if he chose to leave his wife. He needed to know he could end up all by himself. After sharing a wonderful kiss, we parted and drove back to our homes and jobs. Through me, through our sinning, Mike finds his Lord?

Thought of the Day

    Grace is fulfilled when we live by faith. Seeing through the eyes of faith, the end results before seeing it with our actual eyes is faith. Stepping out in faith is having a sure foundation of what we believe will become evident. Living by faith pleases God.

Chapter 43

Divorce Number Two

*For you know the grace of our Lord Jesus Christ, that
though he was rich, yet for your sakes he became poor,
so that you through his poverty might become rich.*
—2 Corinthians 8:9

WHEN I WAS YOUNG AND played dress-up with my dolls, different outfits gave my doll a totally different appearance. But the same doll remained. Wishing and hoping for my husband to become the man I needed him to be did not occur. The same husband remained. What if it was that easy to change a husband?

On a cold February morning, Darrin and Heather joined hearts and got married by her Lutheran pastor. Little did anyone know, except for Susie and Mike, of the inner turmoil I was going through that special day. While his mother's heart was turning cold toward her husband, Darrin's heart was melting. He beamed with his beautiful bride on his arm. It was a time of celebration and full of hope for the happy, young, handsome groom and his gorgeous bride. Emphasizing the contrast, Susie commented later, "I forgot how hopeful wedding days are."

What was Mike doing that same weekend? Leaving his wife, he temporarily moved into a motel and out of his present home. Eventually finding a rental property close by to both our places of employment, he later moved into a small two-bedroom apartment (which proved helpful during that next winter's snowstorm), which was owned by one of my RN coworkers.

I needed to return some wedding rental items to a business located near Mike's hotel the following week. During that visit, he proceeded to tell me about his unpleasant experience of telling his wife why he needed to move out. Of course, sitting his nine-year-old son down and explaining not loving his mother and needing to move on beyond his loveless marriage was the most difficult. The stress of it all caused him to lose over twenty pounds and reach a weight below 170 pounds that winter. I had no plans to change my address at the end of that discussion.

Shortly after that evening spent with Mike, I had a hair appointment. While waiting in my hairstylist's shop, I read a magazine article about mechanical sex. Gosh, that is what I had and have with both husbands! On the way home, I started crying hysterically, making driving safely difficult. I phoned Susie and updated her on Mike's leaving his wife and moving into a motel. She believed I respected Jeff too much to pursue an affair; thus, she understood my hysterics. Susie advised, "Stay married but get your needs met elsewhere."

Not believing that to be the best advice, I drove up to Janie's house. Nothing like a close friend's shoulder to cry on. A great listener, Janie understood my dilemma of unmet needs and the huge gap of what-I-have and what-I-need. Hearing more reasons why I was so unhappy with Jeff, she told me she supported me in whatever decision I made. Being in my corner when the chips were down was one thing Janie does best.

How do you explain to your spouse mechanical sex, missing passionate French kisses, and your feeling more like a roommate than a wife without hurting his feelings? Some mornings, while getting ready for work together, there were no words exchanged between us. I was drowning in a dead relationship. Trying to explain to Jeff, I believed he attended church because I had asked him to, and his not becoming the spiritual head of the home I was hoping for surely broke his heart. His drinking on weekends as a way of life was not what I was used to, either. Plus, his emotional detachment during my dad's illness was not appreciated. Surely, all these excuses for leaving him had to sound lame. But they were the ones I had and was using. Dare I even think about grabbing ahold of the lifeline Mike was throwing toward me for a more fulfilling future? It was a sliver of hope, but I was grabbing ahold.

One weekend, Jeff and I drove down to assist Darrin and Heather move into their new home in Jacksonville, North Carolina. At one point, I took a long walk around their neighborhood. My head and heart were in turmoil. Becoming determined and stubborn, once again I made up my mind. I came to the conclusion it was time I changed my address as well. Rochelle and I needed to start making plans about moving out. Divorce proceedings number two followed soon thereafter. Eventually, I headed back to Darrin's home. Receiving many puzzled looks from my family, I realized I had actually been gone for more than an hour; they were becoming quite concerned. Inner conflict causes one to lose track of time.

On the long trip back home to Pennsylvania, little conversation was held between Jeff and me. Oldies playing from the radio were appreciative background noise. It gave me time and space to continue with rationalizing my future move. Wanting to consider my family's feelings was in direct conflict with my heart. I felt like I was on the edge of the cliff ready to free fall, hoping to land directly in Mike's arms. Yes, it would be scary to announce to Jeff once again I had not chosen the correct hubby. My children certainly did not need the embarrassment of their mother seeking a second divorce. My heart won the inner battle. Not to take a chance on Mike and our future together was more frightening, believing he could just as easily slip away from me and seek his happiness elsewhere. I wanted to be his sweet princess and was not willing to hand him off to another lonely heart. I surely could not take that chance. Therefore, I jumped in. I had a knowing in my knower.

Later that week, I approached Jeff about my leaving him and the need to find an apartment for Rochelle and me. He was not completely shocked. His first comment to me was he knew something was wrong, as I had failed to give him a Valentine's Day card.

Whoops! After admitting to me he had searched through my pocketbook and could not find any strange addresses, phone numbers, or notes that appeared to be any information about my having an affair, Jeff came right out and asked me if I was having one. Not wanting to pursue an affair while living with Jeff, I explained I needed to move out. I admitted this had very little to do about him, but mostly about my needs. I took full responsibility for the failure of our marriage after eight years. Later, I said to my friends, "Poor guy did not know what hit him!"

When Jeff's friend heard about my wanting a separation, he encouraged Jeff to try some salvaging. "If you love Leanne, go fight for her." Jeff took off from work the following day and came to my workplace. He asked me if we could meet with our pastor. I did oblige to the counseling session, but simply went through the motions, making it clear to both of them I no longer love him. Our pastor gave Jeff a book to read about marriage. Both realized my mind was made up and wise enough to know you cannot force someone to love you in return. By the end of the counseling session, Jeff acknowledged his part in our failed marriage.

That evening, we continued the heart-wrenching conversation (the details are our personal business). Jeff said, "I now understand why you need to go. But please keep an open mind about us." Later on, Jeff admitted to learning quite a bit from the book on marriage. By the first weekend in March, Jeff was helping me pack my china and had lined up helpers to assist with moving into School Court apartments. Susie and Rochelle helped me pack up the rest of our belongings.

Then each dreaded conversation about my separation was held with the other two children. I phoned Darrin and Heather in Jacksonville and told them my marriage was over, and Rochelle and I were moving into an apartment. He commented, "I do not agree with your decision, Mom, but I want you to be happy."

Steph's responses were not as pleasant to hear. Realizing Jeff was assisting to help me move out had to speak volumes to her though. What husband does that unless one who feels guilty? Steph, busy dating herself and rarely home, was ignorant of how much time I had spent in chat rooms. Refusing to meet Mike initially when asked, she was making her point. She had a great understanding boss to whom she could vent. Steph's saving grace came when, within a month, she met her future husband, Eric, another sounding board for her.

With the help of Jeff's friends, Rochelle and I moved into our two-bedroom apartment. By the second weekend, our apartment looked cozy with familiar Home Interiors pictures displayed on the walls. I purchased a dining room set, bed, a vacuum cleaner, microwave oven, and bathroom accessories. Our apartment became home, at least to me.

One reason we picked School Court apartments, even though it was more expensive than most, was so Rochelle could always feel safe and would be within walking distance to her school. My nursing shifts at that time contained both seven-to-three and three-to-eleven shifts. Rochelle was home alone after school, which she preferred at times. Though I pulled myself up by my bootstraps once again, I kept busy working extra shifts.

Words cannot describe the pain I had put my children through with two divorces. Rochelle's anger and hatred toward my decisions and having to once again move out of her home and watch her mom date another man was cruel beyond words. She reached out to her brother, Darrin, who offered to have her move in with them if need be. I was wise enough to set up a phone counseling session for Rochelle with the pastor.

Initially, only a handful of friends and family members found out about my separation. Again, I was looked upon as being messed up, crazy, and foolish. Several friends understood my decision and supported me in it. Having someone in my corner was all I needed. Lenora found it hard to believe I was not considering dating anyone else other than Mike. She yelled, "Why in the world are you not in therapy?" One friend envisioned Mike going back to his wife. When he found out, he commented, "No way!" Another friend gave her opinion, "You will soon be bored with Mike." I lost the respect of one coworker when she found out I was divorcing

Jeff; she cut ties with me. However, she did remain friends with Jeff. As only the Holy Spirit can do, this coworker sent me a card many years later asking me to forgive her for her behavior, which brought tears to my eyes.

But the stress of it all took its toll. By mid-spring that year, my weight had dropped down to 112 pounds. Earlier, I had broken out in a rash, which my doctor diagnosed was due to nerves.

I continued to be far from God and had no conviction against sex before marriage. It was not long before Mike stayed overnight in my apartment. Mid-April, we took our first long weekend together and drove to Atlantic City to see Howie Mandell. It was one of the few times I was in a large let's-be-happy-and-party-all-night crowd. I had just sat down in the second row when a lady sat down beside me. Within seconds, she vomited all over my blue shoes! Yuck! This is why I don't drink much. Saying no apologies, she simply got up and left. Mike and I were one of the first couples to leave the show; we did not need alcohol to have a good time.

By the end of April that year, my siblings and spouses were all working together helping Mom and Daddy get ready for their public sale. It was during this time my family members got to meet Mike. My diary entry for that day reads: "Of course, Mike was accepted as one of us…the best he could have been under the circumstances." Lenora had forgotten her purse at my parents' house. She kindly asked if Mike and I would meet them at the halfway point near Harrisburg. So we did. Mike and Jack clicked from the very beginning. After all, their common ground was they were non-Mennonites riding in the same boat who married a Martin sibling "black sheep." Thank goodness, they were both Republicans.

The evenings and weekends of Mike's son's visitations were the only time he actually slept in his own bed in his apartment. Within a few months, he realized it was a huge waste of money for him to be paying rent too, when he rarely spent time there (by this time, we were past winter snowstorms). We made the decision to simply shack up together. Thus, Mike rescinded his apartment lease, moved into our apartment, and put some things in my storage unit as well.

My excuse to Rochelle about Mike's moving in had to sound pretty feeble, I am sure.

Mike's spiritual journey was just beginning during this time. Realizing his need to grow in the Lord, at my suggestion, he started attending the Worship Center. At times, we attended church together as a couple, and other times, Mike would go alone if it was my weekend to work. The first time he attended the Worship Center, he was alone. He came home and said how blown away he was with the contemporary praise-and-worship music led by a band. His tears flowed during worship. He was hooked and started reading his Bible. At times, we had devotions together. Over time, I began to notice he was truly a likely spiritual head of the home material. We were wise enough to know couples who live together cannot expect to join the recommended connecting small groups of our church. However, we were fed spiritual food by attending church on a regular basis.

As a sponge, I soaked up Mike's attention, love, words of adoration, and verbalized commitment. As a new couple, I introduced him eventually to friends and coworkers; weekend activities included time spent with them playing cards. Plus, we started new family vacation memories. I was falling more and more in love with Mike; he was filling my nearly empty glass. Within three months, I had filed for divorce from Jeff. Being matter of fact about it all and feeling numb, I barely listened as the preliminary divorce papers were reviewed by my lawyer. I gleaned through them and signed my Jane Henry. After I left her office heavyhearted, I sat in the car, shook, cried, and vowed I would never marry again!

During nursing school, I did some things differently to help to save expenses. For instance, I started wearing my contact lens (I only wear one in my right eye) for the second week instead of discarding it. After cleaning it and soaking it overnight, I reinserted it again to extend its wear.

However, I faithfully followed through on gynecological appointments. My health was not an avenue to try to save money. After a routine Pap smear, my family doctor informed me one day my test results showed some growth of abnormal cells. He explained they could lead to precancerous cells if not removed. Thus, I agreed to have a procedure done in his office to freeze them off.

At this time, Mike had just entered my life. From the time I had first heard about my abnormal test results until I had a negative follow-up Pap smear, I prayed fervently to God (see how I pull Him off the shelf when I need Him?). Several times of lying in the embarrassing position in the doctor's office with his unwanted cold instruments, I prayed while enduring yet another procedure.

If one is going to swim in the cesspool full of disgusting garbage, then the stench is not your worse concern. I was certain He was getting my attention on this very potential serious health issue. Repeatedly, I begged Him to give me a clean bill of health. I praised God for all the diseases I could have gotten, but did not, during my dating days in the mid-eighties. I promised to be forever faithful to Mike, my last and final lover, if He simply answered my prayer.

It took more than a year before my full recovery. With gratitude and thanksgiving, I was able to present to Mike a cleaned-up vessel with a promise never again, so help me God, will I be swimming in cesspools. Mike would forever be my one remaining partner.

Thought of the Day

Grace is having God open our minds to marvelous truths so we can become a blessing to others. As God nourishes us with mighty torrents of blessings, rivers broaden before us, and we had nothing to do with any overflow.

Chapter 44

I Do Love You, But I Will Not Remarry

> For the Lord your God is gracious and compassionate. He
> will not turn his face from you if you return to Him.
> —2 Chronicles 30:9b

Isn't it much easier to see the whole picture when you are not the one in the frame?

Determined to make three times a charm, I eventually pursued a lasting relationship outside of marriage with Mike with urgency and vigor. Who would not respond to romance, being made to feel like a queen, and shown so much attention? I was content in pursuing our relationship and had a good-enough idea of what substance my next permanent boyfriend (note: not husband) needed to consist of. Aware I was hungry for a spiritually compatible soul mate, Mike stepped up to the challenge after his shower conversion. In the throes of love, we plowed ahead.

My first marriage fell apart because we grew in two different directions and away from one another. I morphed into my second marriage with the belief that little went wrong on my part. I grew up, decided my own religious beliefs apart from any husband or parents, and received fulfillment elsewhere from more than being a wife and mother (I reasoned).

My choice for husband number two was someone who was so very different from my Mennonite background or circle of friends, and it coincided with my creating me. Not walking close to God at the time, I did not dig too deeply into Jeff's Christian walk or beliefs. He was a hope and a promise to fix whatever went wrong with round number one. He saw no big red flags on the reason why I had sought a divorce from my kid's dad.

After the failure of my second marriage, I hung on for dear life when Mike threw me a refreshing lifeline. I was not interested in repeating history and going out to bars to find a potential husband. But my thought process was wrinkled and flawed. Satisfied with the love and devotion shown to me by Mike, I never bothered nor was interested in dating anyone else after divorce number two. This certainly had to be flattering and comforting to Mike.

However, poor Mike had to surpass my expectations of two previous husbands and pass any scrutiny. I became nitpicky about his poor posture at times, his limited likes of the menu items I cooked, and how he was raising his son.

An aha moment came when I realized I did not trust myself with committing to Mike entirely. I did not have the best emotional competence score, either; Mike was paying the price. I always had in the back of my mind the slightly cracked open back door was possibly a way out (while I was still unmarried). I just did not feel like I deserved all the good that was happening in my life. I dwelled on my failures way too often and seldom felt trustworthy. It was time I figured out the rationale behind my choices and opinions. As Dr. Phil says, "You cannot change what you do not acknowledge."

I read in a *Smarten Up* magazine column, one psychologist says:

> You don't trust yourself because you constantly beat yourself up for not doing 'enough.' You hunt for solutions to motivation problems, because you don't trust yourself to do the things you know you should. You fret about creating structure in your life to protect yourself from yourself…is it a clever, verbal trap? Or is it tapping into something deeper?…either way you are your

own worst enemy...there's resistance, motivation doesn't flow easily and everything feels hard. You don't trust yourself. You're new to this place but the child inside of you has years of experience reveling against all the adults and their coercive insistence on doing things just because you have to. So when your fully developed adult mind voices its desires for those grown-up things too, your inner child has already put its fingers in its ears...Lalalalala! You've spent such a vast portion of your life being coerced into doing things you don't understand that, when you finally get the point, it's already too late. Your inner child is in rebellion. The self-sabotage has already begun... once established, the cycle is simple: Your inner child doesn't want to do the things you know you should, so you try to force it to grow up with structure and coercion. In response, your inner child rebels harder, inspiring even more irresponsible behavior. Your response to that is to...not trust yourself."

It was time I became my own best friend and stop self-perpetuating cycles. It was time I put down the (punishing) belt in my hand. I deserved to be happy, and the first step was stepping on the walk of promise while holding tightly onto Mike's hand. When I started trusting myself to know I could handle what came my way, I started trusting Mike and others. My future was fulfilling my fortune cookie message: "A new venture will be a success."

As any marriage counselor should tell you, it is not always about knowing what you want. It is about understanding what unmet needs you have and the causes behind marriage failures. Both husband and wife need to have an awareness of what does it entail for the success of a marriage and be willing to work at it. It is not a matter of *if* a marriage will have any problems, but *which* ones. It takes two to tango and two to work together to achieve golden anniversaries. Envisioning desired results becoming a reality (celebrating our fortieth anniversary, for example), I reverted to familiar patterns of "figure it out, self, and make a decision."

Understanding that communication is one tool to achieve anniversary milestones, we surveyed methods of improving it. Early in our relationship, we spent a lot of time alone for hours and hours doing just that. Somewhere, I purchased a couples' communication game called "His and Hers." It was packed full of cards of ten questions (five on each side). During road trips or sharing a bubble bath together, we asked each other communication-building questions. The little $9.99 pack was priceless! Sometimes, our answers were downright silly. We found we bonded over a sense of humor. However, our firm foundation was building.

Being thrilled to be romantic with me (unlike with his first wife), Mike made up for lost time. All I can say is, unless you live with one, you have no idea what you are missing. It is important to Mike, after getting in our car, we kiss before driving away. "You just never know when you might be in a serious accident." Kissing also occurs every time one leaves and returns back home.

In fact, early in our relationship that first summer, Mike wanted to kiss me during each TV commercial. At the outset, it was flattering, but in time, even good things must end. One time after kissing during a commercial, I got up off the couch and said, "Geez, you are smothering me!" Being sensitive not to hurt him, I quickly commented that I was thrilled and relished in all his romantic gestures. I was still getting used to all his attention. Did not Mike hear my complaint about my previous husband not being romantic enough? Was he not simply doing what he thought I expected? Instead, Mike took it all in stride and continued to adore me and lavished me with love.

In the back of my mind, I frequently thought no man deserves to be put on Leanne's potential relationship list nor have to live up to the perfect man I was looking for. In March 1998, I had journaled my feelings about our relationship and my struggles of wanting to assess it completely, tear apart pros and cons, and dissect potential areas of failure. Here are some excerpts:

> I am finally with a romantic...he tells me and writes me constantly that I am the most beautiful woman in the world (we all know that that is not true!)...he will always see me that way, he says, even when I am old and gray because he won't allow it to be any other way...he loves to touch...rubs my legs...rubs my back...is a "toucher" without implying sex or that it has to mean anything else...to truly appreciate me and mean it...to not take me for granted...he buys me small gifts on the 13th of each month...takes bubble baths with me, reads to me...goes to church without me on Sunday when I am at work and tells me how he has prayed for us... anybody living with a romantic has their own list. But the point is while all this is going on...I do not feel I deserve this because I caused pain to loved ones. It is too much pressure knowing that relationship 3 has to be the most perfect thing on earth, right?
>
> I know no one is perfect...and everyone knows that little flaws, of course, can be blown up to lead into larger problems...the handling of them is the key...God brought Mike into my life, and I again have so many things to be thankful for...and I cannot take for granted this forty-five-year old imperfect, nearly healthy body...three wonderful kids that I am so proud of...an extended family of an outstanding daughter-in-law...a soon-to-be son-in-law...friends...family...and a God who cares enough and loves me enough to continue to enlighten me with bits and pieces...just when I need them...Thank You, Jesus!

I continued to evaluate, observe, and listen to Mike and his thought processes. Three scheduled trips and vacations gave plenty of opportunity to continue to watch how Mike spent his money, tipped waitresses, handled stress during traveling, and his interactions with family and friends. Plus, Mike knew how to make a bed hospital-style with tight corners and cleaned our house better than I did!

That summer, Mike's employer sent him to San Diego for a business convention, and I accompanied him. We decided to extend the trip to include beautiful Arizona, a state that was on Mike's bucket list of places he hoped to visit someday. Relaxing by the pool of the Hyatt Hotel or shopping in Seaport Village, I enjoyed my time immensely while Mike attended his conferences. One night, we were shuttled to the local Indian reservation casino. I turned $20 into $62 when the one-arm bandit turned up three green sevens! Leaving foggy San Diego behind, we drove a rental car to Tucson, Arizona. For being a large city, Tucson seemed pretty quiet to us. After staying the night in a gorgeous bed and breakfast, we headed toward Phoenix. Along the way, we saw our first astounding cactus forest. Everybody needs to add to his or her bucket list: visit beautiful, stunning Sedona. What a view when one rounds the curve of the highway that leads into it! The huge red rock formations were so impressive and unexpected when you first laid eyes on them. God's natural museum was on display. How can one observe this magnificent creation and not believe in our Creator God? We soon headed back to Phoenix to catch our plane. Little did we know we would be returning the following April to get married in Sedona in beautiful Oak Creek Canyon.

That same summer our family vacation included time spent with both my sisters and their families at Atlantic Beach. Since Atlantic Beach was close to Darrin's marine base, Mike and I, his son, and Rochelle followed Darrin and Heather back home to Jacksonville, North Carolina, to visit in their home. Being a waitress while attending college, Heather suggested we eat in the restaurant where she worked. We were introduced to Southern sweet tea and hush puppies. Yum!

By the fall of 1998, my friend Pat moved out to Iowa with her third husband, Curt. To celebrate our forty-sixth birthday together (we were born eleven days apart), Mike and I planned a long weekend with them in Muscatine, Iowa. After seeing beautiful fall foliage on that trip, I journaled, "Pat and I both are with our new men and new 'leaves' in our lives." Unfortunately, Pat's marriage to Curt did not last—another devastating tragedy for her.

We continued to grow in our relationship, and I was thrilled with my romantic find. I was willing to plan a future with Mike beyond the time my apartment lease ended. We were committed to each other. Thankfully, Mike filled up my half-empty glass over time, and annoyances could be overlooked, as they should be.

Both divorce settlement monies were combined together. We knew it would be wise to invest it into real estate. Mike and I spent some time reviewing housing options, both older homes and building lots, in the same school district, so Rochelle would not to have to change schools. By April 1998, we had moved into our newly built colonial-style three-bedroom home in one of the newest developments outside of Denver. My friend Cathy stopped in to visit with me and to check out our new home. "Leanne, you sure know how to land on your two feet." Nothing is by accident, girlfriend.

As our relationship became cemented, I not only could start trusting myself, I started keeping promises to myself and not self-sabotage my success. Being a sanctuary for me, Mike enabled me to forgive and trust myself. He understands losing respect for my husband is a big serious deal for me. Frequent evaluations on this matter have proven successful. I couldn't afford a come-what-may outcome. I needed to accept ownership and responsibility.

I identified what values I had let slip and was kinder to myself by not letting my inner dialogue cause harmful actions or judgmental questions that caused me to spiral downward. As any wife knows, small irritants can open the door to full resentment. Resentments can color. Don't allow Satan to push through cracks and play mind games. Bringing compassion to myself and getting to the root of what derailed me, with God's help, I was better able to reduce slipups.

My growth in my insights incubated a start-up toward attainment. I stopped living enslaved and defeated; enduring struggles was part of who I've become. I was no longer a desperate girl doing desperate things fulfilling the empty not-worthy hole. I was sure my future would include golden anniversaries as sure as I was of any Hallmark movie plot ending on hope and a promise.

My lofty goal was authentic 100 percent *me*. I wanted my inner dialogue to be so pure, it could be made into a PowerPoint on Sunday morning for the entire world to see. As part of the minister's sermon, it would be full of only good, pure, lovely, and righteous thoughts.

But five percent of my inner dialogue is still not fit for print. It is full of some thoughts I'm ashamed of. I long for the day I speak my mind and freely give all my opinions seasoned with grace and love too. The buzzword today is cholesterol numbers, causes of hardening of the arteries, and fitting into a size four dress. I'm still growing on clearing out my mental arteries and securing every thought.

I pictured not becoming Mrs. Miller but continuing as his paramour. I felt grounded and was content on doing life together with Mike. However, the good Lord had other plans for me. He got my attention, and boy, did He ever make me take back some spoken words!

Thought of the Day

Grace calls you out from caterpillar crawling-on-the ground living while inhaling dust and into flying as a butterfly, where the sky is your realm.

Chapter 45

Our Sedona Wedding

> Yet, not what I will, but what you will.
> —Mark 14: 36b

Our Sedona Wedding Day

After two plus years of dating,
Our Special day finally arrived,
Sedona was the setting for
Our love to be sealed and tied.

With a matron of honor and best man
Along for the experience and plan,
We arrived a day early on Friday,
Into a gorgeous hotel oh, so grand!

Noticing the beautiful desert landscape
Among the Sedona Red Rocks,
We got our marriage license up to date,
And tried not to go into shock.

Knowing how serious was this decision,
And needing some reassurance this time,
In amazement I got up early and

BEATY MILLER

Watched a gorgeous Arizona sunrise sublime.

In stillness and quiet
With the sun rising high,
I prayed to my Lord
Expressing gratitude with sighs.

Words cannot describe the beauty of
Sedona expansive and wide
Sprouting red sandstone formations
Forming glorious mountains…oh my!

With assurance and excitement
Trepidation of the unknown,
A hardy breakfast of bacon
And eggs filled us 'til we groaned.

After several hours of primping and priming
While sipping on exotic wine,
The hairstylist aware of our timing
Worked her magic with results in kind.

Planning for a wedding at five
In Oak Creek Canyon, so fine,
We walked a quarter mile deep
Carrying high heels on tired feet.

Sporting a ponytail and full of message,
The preacher was kind,
Reminding us of love and promises,
I know we have found.

With birds sweetly singing
And a magnificent sunset aglow,
We promised to love each other,

With our Savior's guidance, we know.

Eighteen years and counting
And having no regrets,
Our astonishing Sedona wedding
Has been our best one yet!

On January 19, 1999, the Holy Spirit was heavily convicting me. Mike and I walked to our car after another powerful Spirit-filled sermon given by Pastor Sam at the Worship Center. After I slid into the driver's seat, I looked over at Mike and said, "Either we stop going to this particular church or attend another one. We need to stop sinning. I am under so much conviction about our living together. It's time we 'straighten up'!"

Mike agreed with me. He said he had been experiencing similar convicting pricks from the Holy Spirit too. We realized and agreed we needed to stop having any sexual relations until we were married. Because Mike had always hoped one day he would be a groom again and marry his beloved bride, this was music to his ears. Before the car engine turned over, we bowed our heads and prayed to our Lord asking for forgiveness and repented from all our selfishness.

Knowing we were about to become grandparents by spring, I told Mike to plan our elopement. Yes, yes, self, I know I had said I'd never marry again. But the Holy Spirit would not leave me alone. I knew we had to become better examples to our four children, and one way of doing that was to get married. Mike had frequently commented, "I do not want it to be said 'Here comes Nana and her boyfriend.' We are getting married before our grandchild is born."

That evening, we prayed together some more and rededicated our lives to the Lord. We both asked God to forgive us for our past sins and promised, with His help, to behave. We also dedicated our home, which had a large basement, to God's purposes (later it was used to host small group and children played in the basement family room). Within the week, I planned a special family meal to announce to my family our future plans—and no more sex before marriage.

Humbly, I asked my children to please forgive me for my being a bad example and the cause of so much pain. As only the Holy Spirit can do, I also felt led to write four separate letters (trust me, a difficult task) to Mike's ex-wife, his son, my ex-husband, John, and my parents (I held a private conversation with Jeff).

Updated e-mails were sent to some family members, including my two sisters and close friends revealing how the Holy Spirit convicted us, and we are making changes. Within a few hours, I received a phone call. I heard, "So you think that's how I'm praying for you? For you to get married?" Sigh, sigh. You can't please them all.

The next step was for Mike to decide if he wanted to include me in the decision of my engagement ring selection. He decided he would, and I did not mind. So the following Sunday, we stopped off at the local jeweler and selected a gorgeous, reasonably priced diamond ring (jewelry has never been that important to me) and our wedding band set. Mike hoped he could at least surprise me somewhat and not be aware of when and how he would actually propose. For me, every time we had a dinner date, I was filled with anticipation. On the actual night, I was distracted with other events that were going on at the time. So when Mike did get down on his knee and proposed over dinner at the Greenfield Inn, I can truly say I forgot to be prepared, and he pulled it off.

In the shadow of romantic candlelight, I said, "Yes! Yes!" and laughed. However, Mike had the biggest grin because he knew what obstacles he had to jump through. After some Internet research on elopement packages, Mike selected Arizona—no one was surprised. When we had visited Phoenix and Tucson on an extended business trip to San Diego a year earlier, Mike fell in love with the desert.

He proudly announced, for $400 he paid for a minister, groom's corsage, my small bouquet, a photographer, who later handed us the film (developing of wedding pictures was our expense), and our marriage certificate. The catch was one had to walk some distance to have the backdrop of Oak Creek Canyon in Sedona in our photographs. Knowing how stunning the landscape was in that area, we agreed it would be worth the effort. Our friends Karen and Harry, fellow bikers and hikers, agreed and were happy to stand in as our best man and matron of honor.

We set the date for April 17, 1999, through "Weddings in Sedona". Within two months, the four of us purchased plane tickets to Phoenix, arriving on Thursday, giving us plenty of time to prepare for the big event. Learning how simple an elopement can be, we signed a short form stating we were not related and paid $50 for our marriage license; no identification, blood test, or divorce decree was required. The clerk handed us a newlywed gift basket consisting of a roll paper towel, toilet paper, dishwashing liquid, and other household products. We then headed out of Phoenix toward Sedona.

Friday was spent sightseeing around the fantastic red rocks, strolling through an outdoor art show, hiking around the visitor center, and taking a "Pink Jeep" tour of ancient ruins. What a perfect way to end the day watching a gorgeous Sedona sunset! We four checked into the Village Lodge where a suite easily accompanied the ladies on one side and the men on the other.

Saturday, our wedding day, was a typical warm day. Atypical for me, I awoke at 5:30 a.m. and decided I was going to drive to the top of Cathedral Rock and watch the sunrise to spend some time alone with my Lord Almighty. After all, this day stretching in front of me was one of grave importance.

Being a morning person, Mike heard someone stirring from our side of the suite. He saw me, still wearing my pajamas, just as I was heading out. When I told him of my intent, he asked if he could join me. Of course, it was not how I pictured my morning playing out, but I felt I had to say sure. After about five minutes of driving around Cathedral Rock searching for the perfect sunrise spot, we finally settled on a point that had a view of a cell tower in it. But the sun beat us. Mike commented, "Too much technology in the way." We sat in silence, in awe of being able to sit in such a beautiful area of His creation. Then we took turns praying for our future set before us as mister and missus and submitted to His will for our remaining days on this earth.

After a hearty breakfast at Bell Rock Inn, we separated. Karen and I had an appointment for a massage and hairstyling. While Karen and I, feeling pampered, were sipping our wine, the men were at an outlet purchasing a shirt and tie for Harry.

Later, back in the suite, Mike was busy ironing my wedding dress (yep, that earned him brownie points) and his shirt. Protecting my hairdo, I later took a leisure bubble bath. That became my private moment to speak to Jesus. I was ready to say "Yes, 'til death do us part" to Mike Miller. At five o'clock, the four of us drove to Red Rock Crossing and met our minister, sporting a ponytail and a photographer. I should have known our weddings in Sedona minister could be a new age one. Yikes!

After introductions, I, carrying my high-heeled shoes, while wearing sneakers, started the trek to the perfect photographic shot. "This is it," the photographer said. Harry asked, "Are you sure? I see ants around here, and the sun is in my eyes." Assured we cannot move off this selected spot, the minister started reading from a booklet, while a boom box played soft ceremonial music in the background. Surprise! Our $400 *does* include music too.

Here are excerpts from our marriage ceremony booklet:

> We have come here today to witness your marriage and to celebrate the coming together of two separate lives. To share with you, Leanne and you, Mike, on this occasion of making a total commitment to each other. May this joyous occasion always be one of the most memorable and happy days of your lives. As we begin this ceremony of the uniting of your souls, let us share a moment of silence as we still our minds and enter into our hearts with the knowing that this is divine order that you have found each other and chosen to share your lives together. As Rumi says "Two lovers do not meet somewhere in time, but they are in each other all along."

MY LAST LAST NAME IS GRACE

As you know, no minister, no priest, no rabbi, no public official, can marry you. Only you can marry yourselves. You come here today with a mutual commitment to love each other; to work toward creating an atmosphere of care, consideration and respect, and a willingness to together face the problems and challenges that are brought to your wedded lives...You are adding to your life not only the affection and the response that your heart desires, not only the happy companionship of hours together, but a deep trust as well. You are finding in each other that which complements your life. You come together as two independent whole people, each bringing your gifts and love to this marriage... But love is not meant to be the possession of two people alone. Rather it should serve as a source of common energy, as a form in which you find the strength to live your lives with courage... your love should give you the strength to stand apart, to seek out your unique destinies, to make your special contributions to the world which is always part of us, yet more than us...Today, as you join yourselves in marriage, there is a vast unknown future stretching out before you. The possibilities and potentials of your married life are great; and now it falls upon your shoulders the task of choosing the values, morals and making real the dreams that you seek. In this way, you will create the meaning of your life. If your love is vital, it will make the choosing and acting easier for you.

I should like at this time to speak some of the things which many wish for you...First, we wish for you a love that makes both of you better people, that continues to give you joy and zest for living that provides you with energy to grow together and to face the responsibilities of life together...We wish for you a home—not a place of stone and wood, but an island of sanity and serenity in this frenzied world...we wish for you loving and close relationships with friends, family and children and the enrichment of yourself and others through your togetherness...we wish that at the end of your lives you will be able to say these two things to each other: "Because you have loved me, you have given me faith in myself, and because I have seen the good in you, I have received from you a faith in humanity"... So within the safety of your love, you may face challenges of things that need healing. Be kind to each other, knowing that because you love each other these things can be healed.

In this exceptionally beautiful location that is sacred to the Native American people, the Apache Wedding Prayer expresses your importance to each other, and I would like to speak it for you now:

> Now you will feel no rain, for each of you will be shelter to the other.
> Now you will feel no cold, for each of you will be warmth to the other.
> Now there is no more loneliness for you, for there is no more loneliness.
> Now you are two bodies, but there is only one life before you.
> Go now to your dwelling place, to enter into your days of Togetherness.
> And may your days be good and long upon the Earth.

Our wedding vows were:

> I, Mike/Leanne, join you, Leanne/Mike, in marriage, to know you as my wife/husband, to share all of life with you, its freedoms and responsibilities, its tensions and excitement, and its times of enlightening growth. To cherish, love and care for you and to be your best friend. This is my promise to you (tears ran as I repeated them).

While we exchanged wedding rings, the minister read:

> The wedding ring by its shape is a symbol of eternity without beginning or end and is a true emblem of the undying love that shall exist between you. These rings shine and reflect the beauty of their surroundings. So too may your love shine and reflect the beauty of God's creation. These rings are a symbol of your willingness to take all that you are and encircle all that the other is, leaving nothing out…With this ring, I wed you and with it, I give to you all the treasures of my mind, heart and hands.

Then the blessing:

> Leanne and Mike, please join hands for a blessing:
> May all blessings attend you
> May joy pervade your lives together,
> May you carry into your marriage the beauty and the tranquility of this place, and keep alive always the sense of exploration and the peace and intimacy you have shared here.
> May you find here a good beginning of your married life and the true fulfillment of many years together.

And now, in accordance with the institution of marriage by the state of Arizona and the power of your own love, I pronounce you husband and wife. You may kiss your bride.

We then posed for wedding photos I never dreamt would be held in such a lovely spot for my third wedding ceremony. We noticed a jogger along the trail had stopped to gawk for a little while too. After we all signed the marriage certificate and the minister left, Mike and I read cards to each other bringing in more of God to this celebratory moment. Mike had tears in his eyes. With a beautiful backdrop of God's awesome creation, I was willing to handcuff myself to Mike for the remainder of my life.

After a delicious dinner with Karen and Harry, we headed to a cute B and B named Adobe Hacienda for our honeymoon night. But, first, I felt very unsettled about our wedding ceremony. I asked Mike, "I only heard *God* mentioned once in our vows, never *Holy Spirit* or *Jesus*, did you?" He agreed with me and also said he was not surprised by the ponytailed minister. We stood at the bottom of the bed in front of a stone fireplace and repeated to each other a new set of ad-lib wedding vows and included our unseen invited guest, Jesus. Just as Sedona dazzled with sparkling lights, our eyes sparkled as we gazed into each other's eyes and professed a love everlasting as we once again made beautiful love after months of waiting.

The remainder of our Arizona vacation was spent together visiting Lake Powell, the Painted Desert, a Navaho Indian Reservation, and astounding mouth-dropping Grand Canyon (another must-see on your bucket list). At one point, I realized I left my wedding dress behind in the B and B's closet. So we had to backtrack to pick it up. Karen and Harry left for home a few days earlier than us, leaving the lovebirds to themselves. Little did I know how our lives would soon change in our new role as grandparents and a different career path for both of us to make our special contributions to the world and our true fulfilment, as listed in our wedding ceremony booklet.

We arrived back in Pennsylvania on April 22. I worked the weekend and took a second vacation on Sunday, April 25, to accompany Mike on a business seminar to Charlotte, North Carolina. We had no idea our first trip as husband and wife was to a state Mike would be holding a job in some day. We started out Sunday evening after work and drove to Virginia and stayed overnight at my sister, Lorna and Ray's home. It felt good to plan trips as a married couple if we were asking family to stay overnight in their home. From there, we drove to the Omni Hotel in Charlotte. Due to overbooking, the hotel put us up in the penthouse suite. As Mike attended his Information Technology (IT) seminars, I shopped, while exploring downtown Charlotte, and read a book. One journal entry reads: "We drove through several Charlotte suburbs and saw neat Southern-style homes." If someone had told me some day I'd be moving into one of those "neat Southern-style homes," I would have fallen over!

By August, we had a second opportunity to explore the South. My friend Roz and her boyfriend, Steve, invited us to join them for a few days at their Pawley's Island condo. We explored Hilton Head, Charleston, and Savannah, Georgia, cramming lots of sightseeing in a few days. Visiting the South had just begun for us.

On our first anniversary, Steph, through her travel agent job, booked us a long weekend in Las Vegas (no need to add "visit Las Vegas" on your bucket list). Yes, I am glad I saw the stunning hotels along the strip, which obviously were built to compete with one other. However, there is no need to return. My journal entry on our anniversary reads: "One year! What a fast year! God is both showing and teaching us so much."

The only way marriage number two (for Mike) and three (for me) will ever work is to live under the guidance of the Holy Spirit. Over the years, there have surely been trying times. The backdoor option to have it slightly cracked open and one foot partially in it to be ready to run when times get tough can never be opened by me. I have had to hunker down and start living with a different purpose as a twice-divorcee and nana.

I was aware of how losing respect for a husband had been my downfall. I needed to reach into my arsenal of weapons of scripture and say just-a-breath-away prayers. Any hint of disrespect toward my husband must be dealt with immediately. If I am not careful, negative thoughts can turn into negative words, and sarcasm flies out of my mouth much too quickly. I fail to zip it much too often. God knows negative thoughts can be annoying as a pesty barn fly.

Wouldn't marriages, whether in the church or out of the church, be much stronger if we all lived as Dr. Phil reiterates on his talk show: "You need to wake up every day and ask yourself, 'What can I do today to make my spouse's life easier?'"

Awaken the sleeping lion and the elephant in the room; communicate and don't harbor resentments. Bring items to the surface so they can be brought out of the light. Honest, kind communication and discussions bring clarity and insight when the Light is asked to shine on our miscommunications.

Over the years, our mutual love and respect, fulfilled in our foundation of Christ's love and three-strand cord, enables us to fly circles around the moon and make memories that will carry us into old age.

Mike has a picture of me on his desk at work. He added the following scripture verse and taped it to the bottom: "Guard the good deposit that was entrusted to you; guarded with the help of the Holy Spirit who lives in us" (2 Timothy 1:14). Now he is the spiritual head of my home my soul so hungered after!

Thought of the Day

Grace is understanding He who promises is able, and no one is too "dead" for a resurrection.

Chapter 46

One Church Hurt Me, Another Healed Me

> Because God has said, "Never will I leave
> you; never will I forsake you".
> —Hebrews 13:5b

MARTINDALE MENNONITE CHURCH'S CONSERVATISM AND legalism did not often pave the way for unbelievers to spill in through its doors to learn about Jesus Christ and Christianity. The less conservative Mennonite church, which John and I joined when we were first married, was a safe haven for unsaved searching souls. One could at least feel comfortable attending a service.

My friend Jackie, a leftover hippie from California, proved this point. Jackie and Ken met during the wild and free days of the early '70s. Answering the call to assist with a men's prison ministry in Lebanon County, Ken moved Jackie into a world that was foreign to her. A "Black Bumper" Mennonite family lived down the lane behind their house. Jackie was intrigued by the mother's simple, plain cape dress and her large head covering. After Jackie learned from the neighbor lady that a woman is to have her head covered, she decided she was going to start wearing one. She learned it is a symbol of submission to her husband (doesn't a move to Pennsylvania show enough of submission?). About the time she was contemplating on where she would be able to purchase such an item, her "Black Bumper" Mennonite neighbor lady handed her two of her large head coverings. After a short lesson on how to wrap her shoulder-length hair into a bun, Jackie managed to style her hair in a way that pleased her.

The following Sunday morning, Jackie, carrying her infant, proudly walked into church and selected the pew in front of me for her family to sit. Is that a cape dress that Jackie is wearing? I immediately cupped my hand over my mouth to stop any outburst of laughter. Her husband, Ken, turned around, smiled at me, and rolled his eyes. That only made my situation worse. By then, my silent, contained belly laugh was making my mouth hurt because I was pinching my lips together. No matter how hard I tried that Sunday morning, I could not stop the pew from shaking. Jackie had informed me earlier during a phone call about the gift of the head coverings from her neighbor and the lesson on submission. However, I was unaware the same lady also blessed her with four partially worn-out cape dresses.

Although I was already in a situation that was unable to be corrected, as an out-of-control tailspin, I raised my eyes. Keeping my eyes downcast was an attempt to avoid looking at Jackie's cape dress. I noticed the funniest thing yet. Jackie was wearing her head covering upside down (the middle seam is to be at the top)! I could not help the snicker that escaped out of my mouth. In John's scorn I read, "Get it together. We're in church." For the next few minutes, I turned my head and looked out the window until my belly shaking stopped. My friend Darlene behind me was also snickering, which did not help me any.

After church, Jackie proceeded to inform me and Darlene how her cape dresses were great for nursing mothers. Using her hands to mimic a demonstration, she began, "You just push this first material aside, pull out your girl, and voila, you're nursing your baby with modesty." You're speaking to the choir, Jackie. Ken rested his one hand on Jackie's shoulder and taunted, "I told her I give her two weeks before her cape dresses are donated to the Reuzit Shop."

"And the wearing of the head covering will last how long?" I inquired, giggling. "One week," Ken chuckled. Well, the following week, I drove by Ken and Jackie's home. The site I saw when I rounded the curve had me in hysterics. Jackie was busy hoeing weeds in her garden. She was wearing her head covering correctly—with a halter top and shorts! I better educate Mrs. Hippie that halter tops and shorts do not mesh with wearing a covering.

"It is much too hot to wear a cape dress out here," she claimed as she wiped her brow with the back of her hand and rested one elbow on the hoe. "I understand," I exclaimed as I walked up the green bean row. "But, then, please remove your covering. You'll confuse your neighbors." We both burst out laughing. By nightfall, Jackie packaged up the cape dresses and head coverings and returned the gifts to her neighbor. Lifting a T-shirt to nurse a baby worked just fine.

Many years later, as I sat under the teachings of the Holy Bible, I listened to Pastor Sam at the Worship Center use simple language and methods. Being raised in the Amish faith and out in the country, Pastor Sam made scriptures come to life when he talked about how he needed to control his horse with a bit when taught about how to control our powerful tongue. Watching the cows ruminate on their cud is how a Christian needs to digest scripture. Many examples of faith also came from his childhood stories of harvesting seeds into full crops.

At the start of each Sunday service, Pastor Sam held up his Bible and asked us to do the same. We proclaimed together: "This is my Bible. I am what it says I am. I can do what it says I can do. I have what is says I can have. I boldly confess, my mind is alert, my heart is receptive, and I'll never be the same. Amen." Taking notes on sermons and applying scriptural principles became a way of life. He taught me grace is needed for my complete wholeness. Grace upon grace was fully realized. One church hurt me, but another one was healing me.

I'll never forget one of the first Sunday morning services Mike and I attended at the Worship Center. One of the first praise-and-worship songs the worship team sang was about returning to the God of our Father. Getting my attention, it melted my heart. Tears coursed down my cheeks. My spirit was sensing a coming home, finally. My search for the source of peace and trust could be found in my Lord and Savior, Jesus Christ. My days of doing and "I did" and "I strived" and "I do" were over. The Holy Spirit set my feet on a path of wholeness and healing (though it was several months before I rededicated my life). God's love is not extended any more or less according to how well I carry out church doctrine. Freedom came from realizing that because I repented of all my sins, my huge stockpile, my heavy-laden backpack, and my overstuffed suitcases of past behaviors were laid at His feet. The Prince of Peace has forgiven me forever!

Just as a macadam road on a hot summer day has dancing, shimmering lines of heat waves rising above it, I visualize my Bible having shimmering, alive lines of soul nutrition rising above it also. Pick it up and read it until you are full.

Cesspool living and my actions of pulling-up-by-my-bootstraps days were over. Relying on myself, hoping my talents can push me through to the finish line and making poor, selfish decisions that ended marriage commitments were placed at His feet. The enemy at times tried to get me to think about an event in my past, when I heard a special love song on the radio, which had my mind go to an experience during cesspool living. I immediately prayed, "Thank you, Lord, for forgiving me for my stinkin', disgusting living of my past." At times, Satan wanted me to stay burdened, feeling like rat dung, and a pathetic, useless human being. But no, I'm a daughter of the King, and I belong to royalty. Christ is steadfast, trustworthy, and reliable to keep His promises. I surely am not!

Mike and I looked forward to the praise-and-worship portion on Sunday mornings. Hours spent praising my Father while singing helped to build fortresses and protective walls. I sent many prayers heavenward. Later, answered prayers affected others in my life. Learning to pray expectantly and with faith, knowing our heavenly Father is a giver of good gifts, opened my eyes to intentional living.

One weekend in February, shortly after Mike's and my rededication, our small group leader had invited us to go sledding on their snow-packed hill. My friend Pat was planning to spend the evening with me and she joined the sledding party. After several others had taken their turn to sled down the hill, someone handed me the sled. It was decided that I would lie on the bottom, and Pat would climb on top. Picking up speed, the sled flew down the slippery slope. Unexpectedly, I felt my face being smacked into the snow-packed ground. Ouch! Feeling stinging and burning around my eyes, I got up and assessed the situation as to what caused our abrupt stopping of the sled. Pat, lying a few feet away, admitted she was frightened about how fast we were going down the hill, she put her foot down to stop us.

Mike and our friends ran toward us to find out why we spilled off the sled. Mike looked at my face and asked if I was okay. I told him, except for some stinging on my face, I was fine, but I believed I had lost my contact lens. What turned out to be the first miracle Mike, as a young believer, witnessed started with our small group leader's wife, Ida, who immediately sprang into action. Asking them to gather around me and to lay hands on me while she touched my eyes, she began fervently praying. The group of us hardly noticed the cold air as we prayed for the Physician's healing. My face should have had one big bruise on it. But when I looked in the mirror Monday morning, before work, I noticed only a small bruise on the right side of my face. Prepared to explain many times throughout the day to curious onlookers, I was able to testify that my face should appear so much worse, but because of answered prayers, it was much milder than it could have been. God gets the glory.

Mike, whose past included coughing up a dollar bill for the offering plate Sunday mornings, listened to teaching on tithing and God's provision. Within weeks, our budget included tithing amounts—not the net but the gross amount of our paychecks. I was more than happy to resume tithing once again and reap the blessings. Daddy taught it is not always evident in the balance in your checkbook but in being granted good health, as simple as appliances lasting longer than normal, satisfying friendships, and an overall sense of connection to the storehouses of heaven. Once, our associate pastor, Don, asked us before the passing of the offering plate: "What if I asked you to get out your checkbook and show everybody here how you spend your money? Would it not tell us where your focus is?"

In general, my attitude has been: It's all yours, God. If you want me to spend $1,000 on repairing my Acura, fine. If my raise is only three percent to match inflation, okay. It made perfect sense to me you give your tithes cheerfully to your home church that feeds you, and offerings are given to other nonprofits or avenues of need. Honoring teaching on giving tithes and offerings pleases me and keeps my hands open and not close-fisted. Of course, our giving is also displayed in volunteering our time and talents.

As his heart was softened toward the true Source of this world's peace and His Creator, Mike gained freedom from the truth. Because he believed in science's methodology and all things that can be proven, the former Mike believed he deserved heaven because he was a "good" person. He did not smoke or drink, rarely swore, and was an upstanding, law-abiding citizen. The Holy Spirit taught Mike that only Jesus is the Way, Truth and the Life. Being good enough for heaven has nothing to do with one's right to be listed in the Book of Life. He learned through praise-and-worship songs and scripture that God paved his road to everlasting life by accepting His Son, Jesus's death and resurrection for him, and him alone. Being good enough and basing truths on man-made (*Star Trek?*) philosophies was way off base.

Our entire family attended the Worship Center the morning Mike got baptized. We did not hesitate to let him hear our support as he was brought up out of the baptismal water. The old, dead Mike was left at the bottom and a new, alive-in-Christ Mike was raised up out of the water. His testimony on how God has miraculously healed him from pornography and how the Holy Spirit enables him to live with a mostly pure thought life is astounding! He lives by what Associate Pastor Don also said one Sunday morning, "Gentlemen, you cannot help for the birds that fly around your head. But you can help having them build nests there."

Since it is difficult and a challenge to have a close friend in his life, Mike was devastated when his friend Nelson died at forty-two years old of pancreatic cancer. Nelson and Shelby became our fast friends once we got married and joined their small group. Nelson and Mike simply shared a sense of humor and a mutual respect for each other. Shelby, though younger than me, is gorgeous and a great woman of God. We bonded quickly too and felt privileged to have each other in our lives.

To walk the journey of cancer with Nelson and Shelby was a situation that first we did not want to even allow in our mind, let alone process it. The reality of this was a nightmare coming alive. I would be lying if I said fear did not creep in and all emotions were turned over to our Lord. But once reality did set in, we accepted the doctor's grim prognosis while fervently praying for Nelson's miraculous healing. It's one thing to have an elderly grandparent pass away, but a vibrant father of four daughters dying in middle age did not seem right. Our small group continued to plan fun events. Our three families went to the Outer Banks for a long weekend and shared a special time being hopeful we would have decades of summers to continue to repeat this memory over and over again. Enjoying the expanse of the ocean and its beauty brought on a power and peace, forcing us all to realize we have no choice but to rely on our Creator and turn over Nelson's disease to Him.

Another powerful truth-teaching Pastor Sam emphasized was God is 100 percent sovereign. But it is Satan who comes as a thief only to steal, kill, and destroy (John 10:10). As a Mennonite, I was taught that everything is God's will, and things happen in God's perfect timing. Comments made at a young child's funeral, for example, would be, "It's God's will" or "God needed another flower in His heavenly bouquet" or "Her young life was over here on earth, and God wanted her to walk the streets of heaven." God's word teaches we live in a fallen, evil world, and, yes, God is the Sovereign and Supreme Ruler. But He does not bring on rapists, terrorism, hurricanes, and perhaps my own death because I ate myself into gluttony or someone mismanaged their diabetes. God does not cause all horrible things. Of course, I have questions for Him about why certain things occurred on this earth. But God, as my loving heavenly Father, is a giver of good gifts.

Pastor Sam and his wife lost their eighteen-month-old son to a tragic tractor trailer accident. He toddled out onto a busy highway, unbeknownst to the mother, and was hit by a truck, which could not stop in time. This was a sad tragedy, but they never once blamed God but put the blame on the real enemy, Satan. Plenty of books have been written about why bad things happen to good people.

Nelson, after a few short years, found himself once again admitted in the Hershey Medical Center. During a visit to his bedside, Mike had an unforgettable experience. While praying healing scriptures over Nelson and laying his arm on him, Mike begged God to move, be merciful, and drip some grace out of heaven somehow. Yes, total healing could occur for Nelson by walking through the pearly gates, but Mike believed the mercy of God could come through one of His touches. Suddenly, Mike felt an electric jolt leave his arm. Seeing through the eyes of faith, Mike claimed Nelson's healing and his expectancy of a full recovery. Their shared good-bye hug in that hospital room is a special memory for Mike.

Surprising his doctors, Nelson was discharged from the hospital. We rejoiced through every meal that stayed down and on the days Nelson was able to go to work. We celebrated his clear mind, knowing pancreatic cancer messes with one's electrolytes causing confusion. The day came when Nelson was giving up the fight and sick and tired of being sick and tired. Shelby brought on hospice services to assist her with this journey as unfamiliar as, let's say, beekeeping would be for her. Our small group leaders, John and Ida, and Mike and I took turns sleeping on the living room floor next to Nelson's hospital bed. We continued to sing hymns and pray scripture over him, believing His confessed Word would bring about Nelson's healing. The begging prayers that left the lips of Shelby and their four daughters could not have been more fervent.

The thief took Nelson from us. Mike was asked to be one of the pallbearers, which he was more than happy to do for his best friend. Not having Nelson in his life left a huge gaping hole. But Mike continued to trust that God is sovereign and believes his prayer gave Nelson three more weeks to spend on this earth with his beautiful family.

Another life stolen from me was Cousin Jill. She left behind two wonderful children and a devoted husband. I recall the night of Jill's memorial service. This was during the time I was working full-time as a single mom. I was stopped for speeding driving near Green Dragon on my way home from work. As the police officer was walking toward my car, I wiped away falling tears. Jill's obituary was lying in the console beside my car seat. I simply showed it to the officer and explained how I must have been distracted and did not realize how fast I was going. I was concentrating on the upcoming memorial service to be held that evening. Jill's obituary picture revealed someone that could easily have been a relative, as she had long dark straight hair. Truth wins out! I did not get a citation.

As Job, we endure struggles and trials in this life. However, some people, like Jill, seem to have so many more and beyond their share. A highlight of Jill's life was God's gift of a compassionate, understanding husband in Gary, who married her in spite of her teenage pregnancy from her foster dad. Cousin Jill is living free and clear from any more of Satan's darts.

By 2009, a church member, whose business is publishing devotionals, was inviting others to submit an entry for *God Stories from South Central Pennsylvania, Volume Six* (Partnerships Publications, 2010). I decided to write about my experience of coming home. Based on Hebrews 4:16, I titled it "Transformed at the Cross."

> The church I attended in the mid-1980s had little idea how to deal with a thirty-five-year-old woman choosing to divorce her husband. As much as it took courage, strength and determination, the cost of it led to losing the respect of most of my siblings and losing many friends. Letters of opinions poured in from family members.
>
> My dad was furious and embarrassed of me. I saw my heavenly Father much like my earthly father. I felt judged on the basis of how well I followed all of the church practices and doctrines. I

became very angry at God and was tired of seesaw judgments. Thus my rebellion toward God began.

It was in the church that I was hurt deeply, but it was also a church that helped to heal me. Sitting under teaching for the truth for lost, hurting and broken people, I've learned how to forgive others and myself and to accept God's healing of all my wounds.

My transformation began when I realized that God is a righteous judge who deserved my utmost respect. I've never been the same since the Sunday I envisioned in my spirit my Lord hanging on the cross and calling me by all my last names. I felt His unconditional love, which in turn allowed me to completely trust Him and totally surrender my selfishness.

What is it that you need to recognize and admit at the foot of the Cross?

Thank you, Lord, that You are my High Priest and I can boldly come before You as my loving Father, full of grace and mercy."

That same year, events happened that sent me to my knees in a special way. Our neighbors, Kate and Frank, were members of our Bible study. Their daughter, Teresa, met her Columbian boyfriend, Pedro, in college. They dated, married, and moved to the Republic of Columbia. Her husband had big dreams of starting his own computer business. Their family and business grew; however, their marriage started failing. At times, Teresa felt like a beggar in her own home when she needed to ask for enough grocery money to feed her family of five. Being locked in her bedroom closet became a frequent occurrence. The abuse she was asked to tolerate and the infidelity she was to ignore was a far cry from the man I heard say to her once, "You are the most beautiful woman in this world that I have ever seen!" Words out of Pedro's mouth were false honey. If he opened his mouth, he most likely was lying. Promises of faithfulness or times of asking for forgiveness were as fake as the fur around my hooded coat. After years of living in an unfamiliar, strange foreign country, she felt so trapped. Teresa was riding a shaken-to-the-core, nearly empty boat named "Barely Any Faith."

By the time her mom found out about the dire situation and her son-in-law's treatment toward her daughter, it was obvious the parents acted none too soon. Teresa and her three children needed to return back to the Unites States, ASAP. The problem? Pedro hid her and her children's passports. It goes without saying Teresa did not have access to any extra money. Renewed passports were required to fly home. Teresa and her children were stuck temporarily in Columbia. Her saving grace came after her husband hit her once again. Teresa and her children moved in with a sympathetic friend and visited the local police station. Pedro understood his conduct behind closed doors was (finally) logged on a police form. His my-wife-the-punching-bag days ended, and Teresa's boat was now named "Hopeful."

As a mission field has a supply line and a front line, Teresa's resources came from her mom and Christian friends. God moved the chess pieces exactly how it was supposed to happen from: people working in the embassy office with a listening ear, a lawyer willing to take risks, a friend who drove the family to the airport, and an airline employee with a caring heart. As the tornado survivor said recently about the disaster response crew: "Nobody asked me how I voted. It's the people that matter."

Many prayer requests were spread far and wide on the actual day my neighbor's daughter and her children secretly left Columbia and returned to their mom and nana. That night, our Bible study members prayed fervently. We could not wait until I received the phone call from Kate that all four safely landed in the Philadelphia Airport. Thank You, Jesus, for hearing our prayers. What a testimony to these youngsters.

Today, Teresa is happily remarried to a wonderful Christian man who lives the evidence of anointed oil. Her husband jumped in and prayed earnestly on how to lead his newly formed broken stepfamily. With God at the helm, this blended family began navigating successfully in a boat named "Gotta' Have Faith."

Part of missionary living is serving. It makes one accountable. As I grew in my faith, I came to realize God valued me, and His church body came to value me too. While living in Pennsylvania and having a full-time job, I was limited on available hours for volunteering. However, upon our move South years later and not employed, I knew I needed to stay busy participating in more Bible studies and volunteering.

God has it designed that in each decade of our lives, we have a purpose and destiny. It was time I started giving back. If you have a willing heart, God will open doors for you to serve Him and others. Sometimes, they last for only a season, or you find out some doors you walked through turned out not to be the best match for you to cheerfully serve. Close the door and walk through another one.

It was an easy decision for me to volunteer in the local long-term care nursing home, Pleasant View, just right down the street. On my first day of volunteering, the activity director asked as why I chose to spend my morning with the assisted-living residents. Without hesitating, I answered, "I pray someone is doing for my mother in Pennsylvania, as I am doing here in the Carolinas." I have grown to love spending time with the residents, having devotions with them, teaching them about my Mennonite, Anabaptist heritage, and talking about current events. That night, Mike smiled and said, "That was the best choice and an easy fit for you."

Having a desire to serve together on Saturday mornings, Mike and I completed the paperwork and background checks to volunteer at the local Manor Street Homeless Shelter. It was held in a building that was once a car dealership and was open until 4:00 p.m. The shelter was run by a retired, dedicated Christian director. It provided shelter, snacks and drinks, computers, sofas for napping, TV viewing, and clothing. Mike was one of the room monitors who supervised snack time and appropriate material selected to be downloaded on the computers. When requested, he would gather clothing items from the closet. The director assisted with handing out free heating fuel vouchers, completed state-assistance paperwork, and directed them to avenues of recovery for drug or alcohol addictions.

My job was to be the receptionist and prepare client files for the over-one-hundred homeless men and women who sought, at times, a handout or a life-saving rope. One day, I used my nursing training and performed the Heimlich maneuver on a client, who was choking on his snack. Their stories were full of hopelessness, demons, and great despair. Sitting under the teaching of the Good Shepherd, who wants to put them on a path of still waters (rest), the clients slowly had good self-esteem. Once again, some hungry clients used Manor Street temporarily as a shelter during a storm or a period of in-between jobs.

Another door opened for us when Mike and I felt called to support the outreach program from our church. The Dream Center was looking for volunteers to help establish a clothing closet named Hand Up. It is a faith-based ministry serving the needs of people in our community who are struggling with life. The website enforces their purpose: "Our goal is to know the people as well as their needs. The store is a place where we engage the community and develop relationships for sharing the gospel. This is not just another store. It is an outreach ministry where we have the opportunity to meet people from our city and share the gospel through servitude and prayer."

By the grace of God, go I.

Thought of the Day

The body of Christ in our local church is one of God's greatest gift of grace to us believers. God's work never goes unfinished until we reach heaven's shores.

Chapter 47

Miracle of the Portable Potty

We will not hide them from their children; we will tell the next generation the praiseworthy deeds of the Lord, his power, and the wonders he has done.

—Psalm 78:4

Posing with Steph, left

MY LAST LAST NAME IS GRACE

At 6:45 p.m., our tour bus driver, Mr. Paul, cruised on down the motorway heading out of Rothenburg, Germany. Next stop: Munich. The bus's windshield wipers swished and removed beads of water out of Mr. Paul's field of vision. Priscila, our perky short tour guide announced, "I know we promised you toilet stops every two hours or so on this tour. However, Mr. Paul tells me that he has not been coming upon any bathroom facilities for the past thirty kilometers. So sorry, folks." She leaned front and spoke softly to the driver without the use of her microphone.

"Okay, I am going to pull over here," he said. Our Greyhound bus crawled to a stop. *Hissssss* went the brakes. Steph and I both gazed out of our side's wet bus window. It was obvious we must be in the country, as only a field and a few small trees along the side of the road came into view.

"Let's call this 'go natural,'" Priscila chuckled. "Mr. Paul is kind enough to give us an opportunity in case anybody needs to toilet." I looked up from my book I was reading and asked Steph, "I can wait. Can you?" She didn't bother to look up from her magazine and nodded.

Nobody bothered to get off the warm bus to brave the elements and "go natural" behind a tree. If the thirty-six people on the bus had the foresight to understand, it would not be until 8:45 p.m. until screaming bladders were emptied; perhaps, we would run to the tree, did our business, one at a time, and given the tree a special hug!

Mr. Paul continued down the road and headed toward our hotel destination several hours away. The bus was a flurry with sounds of rattling snack papers, turning of newspaper pages, people humming, and some muffled tones as seatmates and husband and wives held conversations between themselves. Occasionally, a laugh was heard, but the noise level was mostly subdued. No overhead CD was playing music at the time, either.

Just as I turned the page of my book, a pant leg slightly brushed against my right arm, which slightly protruded into the aisle. The Australian husband carefully walked down the bus aisle, grabbing ahold of the back of the seats to steady himself. He hunkered down next to Mr. Paul. After a brief conversation, the gentleman returned to his seat located off to the left side in the seat behind Steph and I. He leaned over and made a comment to his wife. I'm sure I know what that was about. He probably asked Mr. Paul to please stop at a bathroom facility for his wife. Poor thing.

The Greyhound bus's odometer continued to turn over ten miles, twenty, thirty. It became impossible to see anything out of the bus window except the reflections from inside our bus. Again, the same gentleman rose out of his seat but walked faster this time until he reached Mr. Paul's side. This time, the conversation wasn't quite as short. By this time, Steph and I were glad this man was speaking up on behalf of his wife, but by now, it was on behalf of most of us.

Again, the guy sat down next to his wife. The urgency in her voice was heard by the commuters around her. "Steve, I can't hold it anymore. This is ridiculous. I'm going to wet my pants if he does not stop in the next five minutes," his wife lamented. "Ohhh…" she whimpered.

Wow! I feel so bad for her. This bumpy road is not helping this poor woman either. Lord, please hear us now. We need a bathroom soon. In Your name, I pray.

The wheels of the bus turned for another few miles. Then I felt the bus attempt to come to an abrupt stop. Mr. Paul guided the bus to the right into a turnaround. "Folks, I missed my turnoff. Just give me a minute, and we'll be resuming our (pause) journey (pause) shortly." His words fell silent. Steph and I both groaned. No, no delays! Not now! I heard the neighbor's wife blow her nose.

Just as the bus slightly shook as it drove over a small bump in the middle of its wide turn, the headlights fell on… What? On a potty? Sure enough, as stunning as the Leaning Tower of Pisa would be to us later, this portable potty was parked on the edge of a cornfield. No one could talk as we were all stunned; our jaws dropped in disbelief. "Is that what I think it is?" or "Do you see that?" or "Thank you, Lord" were heard all around the bus. Steve quickly stepped out into the aisle, so his wife could gingerly hurry down it as soon as Mr. Paul stopped the bus. The sight of that toilet planted where we so desperately needed was astounding. In fact, the toilet had my vote over the tower!

Without anyone being told, we all waited for the woman to get off the bus first. As she walked by our seat, holding her stomach, I heard her say, "It's a miracle, isn't it?"

Priscila announced, pointing, "For those who may not be aware, there just so happens to be a potty in the edge of this field in front of us. Let's have ladies first, please."

We all took our turns spelling R-E-L-I-E-F. I could only imagine the pain this unfortunate woman was experiencing, as my bladder receptors were screaming to the point of my being afraid to move. By the time the men had their turn, we learned later the last dozen or so were using their wives' tissues, as the available roll of toilet paper emptied much too soon. When Steve's wife, wearing the biggest smile, walked back onto the bus, a loud cheer burst forth.

Later around the dinner table, Steph and I and the Australian family struck up a conversation. We ended up hanging out together for the remainder of the trip. We became fast friends; the connection of believing in a miracle-making God cemented us. In fact, it turns out, we e-mailed and sent Christmas cards to each other for over ten years.

Steph and I learned because the Olympics were being held in Sydney, Australia, the family of five chose to take a long vacation. They wanted to get out of Dodge. In fact, I never knew of a family who took a six-week holiday (as they called it). They started by visiting Disney Land in California, took the European Jewel Tour, planned a Viking Cruise next, and then ended the holiday by flying to a small island for the remaining weeks. We learned the wife's name was Carole; the children were Charlie, Amanda, and Jennifer. They were not of the upper class, but they decided to make family memories before Charlie headed off to college.

"Actually, this is our first vacation since Jennifer was a baby. We are so busy running our own trucking company," Carole explained. By the time our tour ended, we spent many a conversation on the bus and around mealtimes discussing and comparing our cultures.

The Australian family was fascinated by my Mennonite heritage and the Amish community. We had a blast; we regretted we had not connected from day one.

After graduating from Consolidated School of Business, Steph was employed by Destinations, a small travel agency owned by two women in New Holland, Pennsylvania. Her pay wasn't great, but she enjoyed nonpaycheck benefits occasionally. Sometime in early 2000, Steph knew that her workaholic hubby was not planning to take the time off to vacation with her. She asked me if I wanted to go to visit Europe with her at a discounted price. Hmm, let me think. Yes! At first, Mike was hesitant about my going on an overseas trip without him. However, we both realized this was a once-in-a-lifetime trip for me and a great way to spend some time with my married daughter.

As I was planning my European trip, Mike decided to travel during the same time period. He chose something I surely would not have any interest in—an archeological dig. He planned a trip to Colorado in hopes of getting a peek into our ancient history for this once-in-a-lifetime experience.

As planned, I switched weekends with another nurse and excitedly planned for our European Jewel Britain trip that started on Saturday, September 16, 2000, and ended on September 30, 2000. What made the trip special was that it occurred on Steph's twenty-sixth birthday.

My honey drove us down to the Philadelphia Airport without incident; we made good time for our British Airways direct flight to London. Mike cried as he kissed me good-bye; it was our first time of being apart for two weeks. Then Steph told me about my surprise. We were flying club class. That meant we were entitled to enjoy the buffet, open bar, and lounge. We felt special! After we boarded, we were served another meal on chilled china and with chilled silverware. Club class included socks (that's a first) and a free movie. I dozed off during the movie. We landed at 6:30 a.m. at Heathrow Airport, and I noticed my watch read two-thirty. Jet lag, here we go!

After going through customs, we checked our luggage and met our Cosmos guide, who was wearing a bright-red jacket (later on, we learned to look for the intentionally worn red jacket). We had to wait for more of the travelers in our group before being bussed to our hotel, the Jury's Inn. Upon arrival, we found out our hotel rooms were not ready for us. So we tried to sleep in the comfy lobby chairs or sat on the floor for over five hours. Our first scheduled tour to Windsor Castle wasn't until 12:20 p.m. We were exhausted by the time we hugged Mr. Pillow.

On Sunday morning, we awoke to a slightly chilly and mostly cloudy day; we wore sweaters. Our bus trip on the way to the castle was about a forty-five-minute drive. We passed Charles Dicken's home, Notting Hill (Julia Robert's movie setting), and Michael Caines's former home. The Windsor Castle, an over-nine-hundred-year-old working palace and the official residence of the queen, sat on the top of a hill at the end of a long lane. We followed a tour guide for one hour; the remaining time was a self-tour. The castle was beautiful, expansive, and so ornamental.

We were then bussed back to the Jury's Inn, where we again tried snoozing on and off. My last time for a good night's sleep seemed days ago. Steph and I just wanted to get a bite to eat, go to bed, and get some shut-eye. We walked a few blocks and selected Upper Bistro, where I ordered broccoli soup. Steph and I shared creamed strawberries. I started getting a headache, so I ordered some coffee, enough to nip the headache but a small enough amount to allow me to sleep. After writing in my journal and taking some Tylenol, I was ready to watch some TV to lull me to sleep.

Monday, September 18, was Steph's twenty-sixth birthday! We learned the weather was a typical day in London: cloudy, windy, and chilly. After a bagged continental breakfast was eaten in our room, we headed to the Cosmos desk to get advice on how to take the Tube around London for the day. Plus, I needed to get a cup of coffee to start my day. We exchanged $40 worth of traveler's checks for about £23.

We walked the few blocks to the subway (the Tube) and paid £3.90 for each ticket, which was good for the entire day. Our first stop was Buckingham Palace. What a lavish building! However, we were disappointed because there was no changing of the guards.

They only do it every other day. We walked through St. James Park to stunning Westminster Abbey, a living church, not a museum. The opulent quire room was jaw-dropping! My stretched neck hurt as I stared upward for quite some time. We spent about an hour in the abbey, but no picture taking was allowed. Shucks.

It started to drizzle; our umbrellas were back in our hotel room. We walked to famous Big Ben (notably a more drab gray building but proudly stretched skyward) and ate lunch at a sidewalk café, while the rain poured down. Steph and I shared a sandwich, dessert, and a hot chocolate. Then we took the Tube to historical Tower of London, where Henry VIII's wives lost their heads. We crossed over London Bridge and stood in line to view all the Crown Jewel attractions, and we learned more about London's nine-hundred-year history. My shopping spree limit in the Jewel House shop was a pittance; I spent it on a small replica of the queen's magnificent crown.

Unfortunately, it rained on and off all day long. Then, at the last minute, we remembered Princess Di's memorial was in London; we knew we could not leave without seeing it. We took the Tube to Kensington Palace. By now, we were soaked. You could only see Princess Di's memorial from the gate. But how impressive! It was worth getting soaked.

Later, Steph and I went to Harrods, an awesome department store. I purchased a Christmas ornament to remember our trip. Much to Steph's chagrin, we had difficulty trying to figure out London's transport system. Finally, we reached Piccadilly Circus (it reminded me of Times Square), a big downtown square with bright neon signs flashing on the side of buildings. For a celebratory birthday dinner, we chose Adam's Ribs. It was a good choice because it played golden oldies music. We were seated on the second floor at a table that overlooked the street. We selected from the menu ribs and wings for two, and a delicious blackberry crumble with ice cream and custard, for dessert. We clicked our water glasses, and I said, "Happy birthday, Steph. Thanks, Destinations!"

Stuffed, we headed once again to the Tube. When I inserted my ticket, the machine read "see attendant." Our ticket had expired.

Because we tipped the waiter using our last bills, we had no currency. After the third try, Steph got through the stall, and an attendant kindly put a ticket in for me. Whew! Thanks.

Finally, we were in our seats. I was thankful for being warm and to be heading home to our hotel, or so we thought. We found out we had to get off a stop earlier, as our stop closest to the hotel had closed. We had to walk to another bus stop, and that bus would take us back to our hotel. Finally, at 9:50 p.m., we saw a refreshing sight—our Jury's Inn hotel sign. After a quick hot shower, I was ready to relax, watch some TV, and get another good night's sleep. Thank you, God, we were not mugged, pickpocketed, or stranded.

The next day, Tuesday, we experienced what I called the most frustrating part about our European Jewels bus tour. In order for the bus driver to have time to load up all of our suitcases and to keep our travel schedule, suitcases had to be placed outside your hotel room door well in advance of our actually leaving the hotel. For our 8:30 a.m. departure, our suitcases had to be placed outside our hotel door by 6:45 a.m. That meant we had our wake-up call around 5:45 a.m. We had plenty of time to sip on several cups of coffee, if we chose. No, I would rather be spending extra time with Mr. Pillow.

Our bus drove through London, a city of seven million people. It was a typical bustling big city, some dirt and grime. Many women wore business attire and high-heel shoes, and men, carrying expensive briefcases, attired in business suits. But, of course, unlike the USA, it had beautiful, ancient architecture.

We were bussed toward Dover to catch a ferry to cross the English Channel. We were dropped off at a waiting area before we walked through airport-like tunnels to a huge ferry. Steph and I sat at a comfy table for four on the same level as the entry to the ferry. It held arcades, bars, coffee shops, more restaurants, and gift shops. After smooth sailing, we were greeted by four different bus tour guides. Priscila, a Dutch girl with multicolored hair, and an elderly man, Mr. Paul, our bus driver, were our specific guides.

Our first stop en route to Belgium was "toilets." Finally, we started our trek through Belgium, a narrow and flat country. We traveled on an eight-lane highway full of small Toyotas, through countrysides of cow pastures and cornfields. We arrived in Amsterdam, and after entering the Netherlands or Holland, we came to a truck stop. We were allotted an hour to eat our buffet-style meal. I selected a hamburger and fries, but the hamburger was served without a bun.

As we traveled, the tour guide explained about the sandy soil Holland tulips (not in season), which the natives loved so much, the reason for the Thirty Years' War, and pointed out windmills to us. Around 9:30 p.m., we arrived at the Golden Tulip hotel. It was very nice, large, and clean. The only pay TV channels were World and CNN. However, we watched part of the Olympics and applauded at the USA's successes.

The following morning, Wednesday, we learned, per European standards, even though the hotel was gorgeous, it had no hot water. Ugh! But the continental breakfast buffet was great. Then, we were off to visit a Van Beers diamond center in Amsterdam. We watched them grind and polish sparkling diamonds. Later, in the gift shop, I bought a Swarovski choker (equivalent to $52).

Then Steph and I went on a one-and-a-half-hour canal and town tour and took many pictures. How relaxing! Our next tour stop was at the nineteenth-century Van Gogh Museum. Perhaps an hour would not have been long enough to tour the more than two hundred paintings and five hundred drawings for some tourists, but it was long enough for me. We had lunch at a German restaurant where I ordered potato soup (it did not taste anything like Mom's), and Steph ordered an egg sandwich. By 2:30 p.m., we boarded the bus and headed toward Germany. We drove through the rest of Holland on an eight-lane highway. Within two hours, we stopped at a rest stop. It started to rain and poured for the remaining four hours. For the first time during the bus ride, I became acclimated and alternated between reading a book and napping.

We arrived in quaint Rhineland in time for dinner. I was starved! Our dinner was simple but good: vegetable soup (mostly broth), pressed meatloaf, potato puffs, mixed vegetables, and pancake kuchen for dessert. We sat with a couple that we met from

Connecticut, Lynn and Rob. After dinner, we strolled around the hotel to check things out, but it was still raining outside. Our hotel, which Steph loved, was the most rustic so far. It had twin beds, small-sized rooms and bathrooms, no phones and no porters. Thus, we had to schlep our own heavy suitcases up two flights of stairs. We went to bed by 10-ish and watched more of the Olympics on TV.

On Thursday morning, the twenty-first, because there were no phones, a loud knock on the door was our wake-up call. This hotel served us a complimentary breakfast of buns, slices of ham and cheese, orange juice, and coffee or tea. After taking a few pictures, we were off. Today, we had a choice of tours: ferry down the Rhine or a downtown bus tour. Steph and I selected the tour down the Rhine, which was about fifteen to twenty miles long. We snapped our camera taking quite a few pictures of many small Dutch towns and some neat castles nestled on the hills. Next, we had lunch at the best yet roadside restaurant and truck stop. It was drizzling and cloudy on and off all day until late afternoon, when it started to pour.

On the way to our next stop on the tour, Rothenberg, was when our miracle of Carole's potty occurred. Before bedtime, we went shopping in the Christmas Shop. Our buffet dinner ended up unexpectedly to be included in our tour expense because we were scheduled to stay in a hotel in Munich. Because of Oktoberfest, we were bussed to a hotel sixty kilometers out of the way. Thus, the Munich pub tour was cancelled. Steph and I got settled in our room. Once again, Steph blew a fuse while trying out her hair dryer at eleven o'clock. This TV had no English channels, either. Instead, I decided to finish reading my book.

On Friday, September 22, I journaled: "Our trip is already half over!" After a meager continental breakfast of cornflakes, fruit cocktail and coffee, we headed out for Innsbruck, Austria. We stopped at a quaint, beautiful shopping area. Since Austria is the home for Savorski's crystals, of course, I had to go shopping. I bought a crystal bracelet, and Steph purchased some earrings. We then headed toward the Dolomites. They are gorgeous high mountainous peaks (I'm guessing as high as the Sedona Red Rocks and our Rockies?).

Dolomites, made of limestone, were stunning! I later commented they were one of my top five favorite sights of the entire trip.

When we crossed into Italy, we turned $40 into L82. Due to heavy traffic, we did not arrive at our restaurant for lunch until 3:00 p.m., where we were served real spaghetti in Cordona. After taking more pictures, we headed toward Venice. On this trip, I finished one book and started a new one. Also, I got a nap (travelers got used to the lull of the bus ride over time). Again, because of heavy traffic and hairpin curves on our route, we arrived in Venice later than planned. But the delay was worth it. Mr. Paul allowed us plenty of time to capture the stunning views. There were beautiful gorges on our right and tall mountains on our left—truly the most beautiful part of our journey thus far.

We arrived at our Columbo Hotel in downtown Venice with its exquisite canals. The hotel was nice, small, but nothing fancy. For supper, we had fish, spaghetti, potatoes, salad, and ice cream, for dessert. After dinner, the majority of our tour group went into town. Steph, for the first time, planned an event without her mother; she went water-taxi bar hopping with Lynn and Rob. I decided to purchase postcards, filled them out, and placed a phone call to Rochelle. I relaxed and watched more of the Olympics. So far, USA had won twenty-five medals. Go America!

Saturday, September 23, would have been my weekend to work. Instead, I was on holiday, as my Australian friends called it. Because Steph and I woke up too late for the bus driver to take our luggage out to the bus, we had to schlep our own suitcases down the stairs. However, we made it on time for a relaxed breakfast of (only) a roll, jam, and coffee. We headed out to the Bridge of Freedom that connects old Venice with the new Venice. A water taxi took us to old Venice. Another tour guide took us to central market, St. Marcos church and to a glass-blowing factory. No wonder Venice is the world's favorite city! The market is a U-shaped mosque-type building full of various kiosks of jewelry, silk ties, pizza, etc. St. Marcos's tour was short—simply in and out—perhaps two minutes long. Why? We were not allowed to enter wearing shorts or sleeveless tops, so we were quickly corralled in and back out. After the glass-blowing tour, I purchased a pair of earrings for Rochelle.

After meeting at the Bell Tower, our tour guide directed us over to a canal for our gondola serenade ride. Performed only in breathtaking Venice, our men-driven gondola ride followed a narrow canal and went under several bridges. The relaxing excursion lasted about forty-five minutes. Little conversation was held; our cameras were busy snapping away. One couple celebrating their anniversary got their personal serenade from the gondola driver. Steve, Carole, and their family went with Steph and me to a pizza shop for lunch. We selected a thin-crust ham pizza and a gelato for dessert. Very good!

Our tour was to meet once again back at the Bell Tower at 2:15 p.m., to cross back over in the water taxi to our bus. All showed up but one person, David. The tour guide, Priscila, went to look for him, but to no avail. As per her instructions, the tour must go on, and anybody who missed the bus must find their own way back to the hotel. Poor David. Hope everything is okay. We headed out from Venice to Florence through hilly countryside and many tunnels. We stopped for a stretch, drink, or toilet break in Bologna, Italy. Then we started out for Hotel Florence. Turns out it was a much nicer hotel but still only had twin beds, small bathroom, and no tub. But it did have a hair dryer.

Dinner was included in the tour price, so we headed down to the buffet room for dinner. We were served pasta, chicken, mashed potatoes, carrots, rolls, and ice cream for dessert—one of our best meals yet. After dinner, we sat around and talked more with our new Australian friends to learn more about them. We promised after the trip was over to keep in touch.

Want to know what happened to David? We found out he wanted to surprise the group and arrive back to the hotel ahead of everybody. So he took a train back hoping to beat us but didn't. Weird.

I wanted to phone Mike, but I realized he would not be home yet. Rob and Lynn wanted to go out again tonight, but Steph was too tired and was ready to crash.

Sunday, September 24, started out with an adventure: the shower would not drain. Steph and I had to put towels down on the floor. I called the front desk too about having no hot water. When I was finally able to connect with Rochelle, I learned Mike was stranded in Denver airport due to a snowstorm. He was able to get a flight into Washington, DC, where he was put up in Hyatt. Eventually, Mike and I were able to catch up. But with Steph in the other room, we had to keep the smooching to a minimum.

After a breakfast of strong coffee, rolls and jam, and biscotti toast, we headed out for Florence. En route, we stopped off at a look out over the city and took more photographs. Another tour guide then took over. We stopped off at the huge St. Crux Church—gorgeous with twelve statues gracing the top. Next, we toured the Peruzzi leather shop, Gold Corner, and several town squares. Each one was magnificent in its own way, especially the Statue of David by Michelangelo. While eating another gelato for lunch, we watched a huge flock of pigeons that gathered in the town square looking for their own lunch. Surrounded with at least one hundred pigeons, one little girl was crying, while the parents looked on, laughed, and took pictures. They thought it was so funny. Some kids' parents.

At this time, an option was to select to be bussed out to Tuscany to the town of Pisa for the Leaning Tower of Pisa. Steph and I decided to go. The rest of the group went back to the hotel and had free time. I'm so glad we went. Because no one had been allowed inside the tower of Pisa for over ten years, we simply walked around the outside of it. Again, souvenirs were sold outside. I purchased a small orange jug that had the tower painted on it. We were hungry and ordered some frit (french fries). As we visited the three stunning cathedrals next to the leaning tower of Pisa, we nibbled on our frit.

Once again, we traveled though vineyards (which Tuscany is famous for) and beautiful hilly countrysides. By the time we arrived back at the Delta Florence Hotel for our dinner, it was six o'clock. Steph and I were starved. Then we found out another bus tour was using the restaurant. Apparently, there was a schedule glitch. We had to wait until 7:00 p.m. for our meal. Reluctantly, Priscila informed us we would not be able to use the restaurant at all.

At the front desk, I was informed by the clerk there was a La Stroda pizzeria within ten-minute walk. So we headed out. How safe was it for two female Americans to be walking the streets at night? Just then, the serenaded couple, who were also checking into restaurant options, came out of the hotel. Lucky for us, they decided to walk along with us to the restaurant. Thank God! Because after walking longer than ten minutes, there was no pizzeria in sight. Finally, another Italian restaurant came into view. Four starving people walked in. Of course, we had difficulty attempting to order from an Italian menu. The restaurant was serving six courses, and we didn't have a clue what to select from any of them. Steph and I both picked a linguini dish (believing it to be a pasta dish) as our first course and a Coke. The linguini had seafood mixed in and was not really a pasta dish at all but cuttlefish. It tasted rubbery, so I gave it a 5 on a 1 to 10 scale.

Because the charge card machine was not working, we then fretted over how to pay the bill. We sensed our waitress was ignoring us because of the language barrier, even though the other couple was planning on paying with cash. We truly were in a bind! The couple patiently waited for us to walk back together to the hotel. Finally, an observant customer in the restaurant, who understood English, assisted us in telling the waitress we had to pay by credit card. Steph, are you ready to wash dishes? Luckily, in one last attempt, the credit card machine started working. Thank you, Jesus!

So, once again, it was back outside to walk along the heavily traveled road in the dark. Finally, we safely arrived back at our hotel. Steph and I were ready to relax and watch TV. We watched a circus—universal entertainment with no interpreter needed. Lights were out early, as we had to be up at 6:00 a.m. again.

Monday, September 25, started the second week of our vacation: so much had already been experienced. As enticing as the queen's jewels, our upcoming schedule was packed full of culture and more sightseeing. We left memorable Florence and headed for

Lucerne, Switzerland. Around 9:30 a.m., we stopped off at another Auto Grill (truck stop) for toilets and headed for Lugano Lake for lunch. After traveling through hilly Italian countryside, flat lands were boring until we drove nearer to the lake, where the countryside scenery improved. Many tunnels were built into the mountains making it difficult to read on the bus. Lake Lugano was beautiful! We turned our Italian currency into Swiss francs, but it was not enough to buy lunch. We selected a café, so Steph and I could charge it. We shared a good lunch of a club sandwich and a salad.

After a two-hour break, we boarded the bus and headed to a souvenir shop. Steph and I both bought cuckoo clocks (which hung on my wall for about ten years and lasted through quite a few grandchildren's must-touch hands). Then we walked around the lake to the Lion Memorial and another half an hour of shopping. We both bought some yummy Swiss chocolates to take to our coworkers back home.

Next stop was our quaint hotel in Imensee, about thirty minutes away. Steph and I were assigned to our own rooms with twin beds; some men had to share a room with three other people. It's quite nice. Shortly after arriving at our hotel, we were served dinner: soup, salad, chicken breast, rice pilaf and custard ice cream for dessert. Excellent! Then an embarrassing thing happened. Because I had granny, I soiled the dining room chair. My new friend, Carole, donated some unmentionables in her purse and rescued me (an upcoming chapter tells about my much-needed hysterectomy). Because we were limited to one piece of luggage, I learned to pack lightly and rewear the same clothes. I was planning on wearing cream-colored slacks the next day. No kando! Before bed, I had to rearrange my suitcase so all my souvenirs would fit inside. A big problem. By this time, I was journaling nightly: "I miss my honey."

On Tuesday, we headed to Paris. After being served the best breakfast thus far (especially the orange juice), we left Lucerne and headed down to the lake for an hour-long cruise. Unfortunately, due to dense fog, it was difficult to see the shoreline landscape and buildings. Next stop, Paris! Since it was over a four-hundred-kilometer trip, we stopped midmorning for coffee and a toilet break. I purchased some chips, which satisfied my salt craving. Lunch was at a motorway restaurant. Steph and I each bought a salad but shared a chocolate mousse and an apple tart. For the umpteenth time, we boarded the bus again.

I finished the second book and starting reading my magazine. At one point, Steph and I began discussing a childhood memory about a time when her dad spanked her. But I got blamed for it. John told me, "Steph knows how to push your buttons." She was something else! I haven't spent two weeks of 24-7 with her alone in ages. At one point too, we both laughed hysterically at the tour guide's pronunciation of the word *scents*, when she was talking about Paris's "par fumes." She added a few extra syllables that sounded like "essencence."

We arrived into busy, traffic-jammed Paris around 6:00 p.m. and arrived to our Hotel Ibis around 7:00 p.m. This hotel's accommodations included a tub, and the bed was a double. After exchanging $20 for 120 francs, we joined the Australian family and another couple for dinner. We walked the bustling streets for a little while. We passed several restaurants but saw nothing appealing. Finally, we selected one of the restaurants. For 120 francs, Steph and I shared a salad, spaghetti, a caramel tart, and a Coke during a lively dinner conversation with our new friends. When we arrived back at the hotel, I used the last eight minutes on Steph's calling card and called my honey. I miss him so!

A rare treat occurred on Wednesday morning: we could sleep in! Due to the fact we were staying two nights in this hotel, we did not have to put out suitcases. After an average breakfast, we headed out to tour Paris. Our new tour guide was fifteen minutes late because of traffic. Our first stop was at the incredible Notre Dame, then onto the priceless Eiffel tower and the impressive Arc de Triomphe, where we did not stop but enjoyed from our bus window. Then Mr. Paul drove down the marvelous Avenue des Champs-Élysées.

Since we opted out of any optional tours for this day, we had free time until 3:30 p.m., when we had to meet back at the opera steps. Because our tour was coming to an end, we planned several locations to take pictures of the Australian family. They joined us to go souvenir shopping and have lunch. Looking for a restaurant that served French onion soup, we finally found a popular café that did. It was not as cheesy as we Americans make it, but it was good.

We probably walked ten blocks, which was a nice change from riding on a bus. The weather was perfect finally. Again, because of heavy traffic, it took a little longer to return to Hotel Ibis. We learned that one of our tour mates was hospitalized. She had complained about not feeling well and was dizzy. She went to the ER and was diagnosed with an ear infection and remained in the hospital until we left for home. This is a vacation she'll never forget!

After relaxing in our room until 6:30 p.m., the seven of us returned to the same restaurant for dinner. Because the restaurant opened, closed, and reopened, we had to wait for the restaurant to reopen. So we killed some time shopping in the nearby mall. I bought Rochelle a sweater and Mike a wallet.

After dinner, we hurried back to our hotel to dress for the cabaret show at Le Moulin Rouge. The bus made three other stops and picked up more groups of tourists to join us. After waiting in a long line, we were finally seated and served champagne. The show consisted of acrobats, jugglers, and audience participation and more nudity than what I remembered occurred in the previous show.

The show ended around twelve midnight; we had to wait quite some time for our bus. We were all tired but suddenly more awake. A fight broke out between two guys in the street in front of us. Facts weren't clear, but these two guys got into a brawl, and a third guy tried to break it up. Within an amazingly short period of time, six to eight cops showed up on the scene. Two men were just lying on the street, so we believe the cops used their stun guns on them. I believe America needs to take some lessons. By this time, Priscila, our tour guide, invited us to go inside the restaurant and bought us all a round of drinks. Nice! Shortly thereafter, our bus arrived to return us back to our hotel. Until the three other groups of people were dropped off at their respective hotels and we got ready for bed, we didn't crash until 1:30 a.m.

MY LAST LAST NAME IS GRACE

On Thursday, September 28, our saying good-bye started, as a portion of our tour group was heading for the airport. Because the Metro workers were on strike, there were more cars on the road causing more traffic jams. The bus driver decided to leave the hotel fifteen minutes earlier to meet the ferry to go to Dover. Traffic wasn't too bad in spite of two accidents, a one-half hour coffee and a much-needed toilet break. By 12:15 p.m., we arrived in Challis and boarded the ferry. Because of high winds, the water was choppy. I started feeling queasy. Eating a burger did wonders.

It was time to say our good-byes to Priscila, our tour guide, and our skillful bus driver. He certainly could be listed among the best of them based on his driving among Parisian drivers and navigating through those hairpin turns! The group tip collection ended up being $40 per person. We then headed toward London and the Thistle Euston Hotel. After the three-hour drive, we dropped off more tour mates and said our good-byes. After checking into our hotel, we reviewed our departure itinerary and relaxed until 6:30 p.m.

For one last time, our Australian friends had dinner with Steph and me at the Ibis Restaurant. Steph and I filled up on asparagus soup and a shared salad. Again, our lively dinner conversation included the difference in some terminology between the Americans and Australians. We didn't leave the restaurant until 8:30 p.m. and continued to gab in the hotel lobby as well. We did not want the night to end.

However, the time came when we realized we absolutely needed to say our good-byes to each other, so we did. We passed around big hugs. Steve whispered to me, "Take care of your wonderful family." I turned toward Carole, gave her a big, long hug and promised to write. A pen pal friendship had begun. After spending so much time together, it was a sad departure. It was hard to believe that we only knew each other for several days. Back in our room, I took a bath, read some devotions while soaking, and did our final packing for our early departure.

On our last day, Friday, September 29, we were up by 6:00 a.m., had our luggage out by 6:30 a.m., and ate a boxed breakfast before meeting in the lobby by 6:45 a.m. Our flight did not leave for Philadelphia from London Heathrow Airport until 11:25 a.m. But, as we experienced throughout the journey, Cosmos tour wanted to leave plenty of time for hiccups. I wrote: "Today, I'll finally see and feel my honey, and I won't be dreaming."

What an awesome site when I saw Mike grinning and holding a bouquet of flowers, as he waited at the baggage claim area for us. On our trip home, we exchanged vacation stories. Mike shared a dozen pictures with me about the Colorado digs and his great experience. Unfortunately, his sifting revealed only pottery shards and chicken (no dinosaur) bones. Sleeping in a hogan (a Navajo hut of logs and earth) with a loud snorer made for memorable long nights with little shut-eye. In spite of that, it was an unforgettable adventure.

What a wonderful trip of a lifetime packed full of wonderful memories that Steph and I experienced! I graded the Cosmos touring company an A-. All total, our journey took us through five countries and was over 3,600 kilometers in length. I completed a scrapbook about our European Jewels ten-day tour within a month and eventually shared it with my grandchildren. I will always cherish these memories spent with my daughter. I realized it would never be repeated once she became a mommy.

One day, I showed Steph my scrapbook, and we walked down memory lane. She commented, "My friend said she can't imagine spending 24-7 for ten days with her mom. She was shocked and asked how did I possibly do that?" Steph looked at me and smiled. "I told her it was no problem. We had a grand time."

Again, thank you, Lord.

Thought of the Day

Grace is evidenced by a surrendered servant growing more like Christ and living a life on mission for God's kingdom.

Chapter 48

How September 11 Affected Me

> Now I know in part; then I shall know
> fully, even as I am fully known.
> —1 Corinthians 13:12

MY NURSING CAREER HAS PROVED to be very rewarding and fulfilling; earning a nice paycheck was icing on the cake. I am so glad I decided to switch careers. Most nurses don't know exactly how their career paths will end up. I know I certainly did not. Susie and I decided we were going to take a break for one year, then continue on to earn our bachelor's degree. One day, Susie asked me if I was ready to start taking college courses once again. The heavy college caseload, while working, was still fresh in my mind. I said, "No, thanks. Perhaps, later on."

I graduated from nursing school in 1993 during Hilary Clinton's health care reform. Local hospitals had hiring freezes. Thus, several of my nursing school classmates did what we said we were never going to do, get a job working in a nursing home. My incentive to find employment was because the first student loan bill was coming due. I applied and got offered a job at a local long-term care nursing home. Another RN and I had basically applied about the same time. Since she had her bachelor's degree, she was offered the three-to-eleven RN house supervisor position. I accepted the RN three-to-eleven charge nurse position.

The Director of Nursing (DON) who hired me had previously worked as a nurse for the armed forces. I felt so blessed to have an intelligent, fair Christian boss. Being a brand-new RN, I've made my share of nonserious mistakes. She dealt gently but firmly with you when discussing areas of growth as a charge nurse. All of her staff meetings were opportunities to learn and grow in the nursing field. One could always feel she had your back. In that environment, I thrived.

What any charge nurse needs to do is to build teamwork among the staff. I made an effort to build rapport with my LPNs and nursing assistants. If I had time, I pitched in to lighten my staff's workload jokingly calling myself a "working RN" (versus a paper pusher and telephone receptionist for the nursing unit). If time allowed, I enjoyed helping the nurses' aides by feeding a resident during the noon meal on weekends.

Some friendships I have made with the nurses I met during my first job continue today (little did I know one of the LPNs would end up being the grandmother to my future step-grandson). Because I wanted to have a strong nursing unit between the RN, the LPN charge nurses, the nursing assistants, and myself, I started a tradition. Every Christmas, I hosted a meal in my home where the nurses provided a potluck dinner for the nursing assistants as a thank you for their hard work all year. Every nurse knows the attitude of the nurses' aides makes or breaks cohesiveness on a busy nursing floor. A houseful of staff members shared many laughs, sang Christmas carols together, and just had a grand ole time.

During a snowstorm in the 1990s, one of the resident's daughter, who resided on Sanibel Island, Florida, was visiting her mother. She was snowed in and needed to stay in one of our nursing home's nice motel-like rooms for two or three days. This particular daughter, Lizette, and I had spent many hours visiting and getting to know one another. By the time it came for her to leave, she had learned a lot about my family, and I learned a lot about her family. We became fast friends. The following summer, she invited me to come down to visit her on Sanibel Island to show her appreciation for all I and my staff had done for her mother while residing in the nursing home. Not believing I should take her offer very seriously, I repeatedly answered, "Hmmm, I don't know" during every one of Lizette's phone call invitations, when she called into the nursing unit. "Yes, indeed. I am very serious about my invitation, for either you and your hubby or a friend coming down to visit me and stay at my home."

Thus, one of my summer vacations that year was spent when Esther and I flew down to Sanibel Island to stay at my new friend, Lizette's, lovely home. Great memories! I have learned the difference between the habits of an owner of a million-dollar home and a humble abode like mine was: never apply red nail polish on a coffee table in a living room covered with white carpet. When Lizette saw me doing that, she kindly asked me to please do so in the bathroom using the counter. "I know you don't intend to spill it, Leanne. But if you did, the results could be disastrous." Of course, I obliged her. At times, even though I seldom wear red nail polish, I remember her wise words of advice: around white or light carpet, expensive or not, do not apply red nail polish.

One day in March 1998, after being employed by the nursing home for about five years, my administrator pointed out to me a posted position at the time clock for a director of nursing for one of the smaller nursing homes of the same faith-based affiliation. After my shock of his believing I could even handle such an important administrative position, I decided to consider the possibility. On the drive home that day, I decided my first step should be to drive to the nursing home, which was located in a different county, and determine if the distance from my home was too great before applying. Mike and I drove up late Sunday afternoon and logged fifty-four miles round-trip. Never having been in this facility, I decided to walk inside. I explained to a nurse, who introduced herself as the three-to-eleven shift supervisor, I was simply checking out the facility, told her where I worked, and the purpose of my visit. During our fifteen-minute conversation, I encouraged her to apply for the position.

Monday morning (news travels fast), I was summoned into the administrator's office. He commented, "You blew it. You can forget about the DON position." I'm confused. Is this not the same man who encouraged me to apply for the job but was now backing down? I attempted to explain to him it made no sense to even put in an application if I was not willing to drive the distance. I do not know who was saying ouch and why, but I apologized only for having to answer for my intentions. I reminded him it was at his recommendation that I even considered applying for the position. If someone did not agree with my decision process, so be it! Why didn't he have the guts to remind the complainer the job is posted at every time clock and any RN with two years long-term care experience qualifies to apply? I left his office feeling like I lost a whole lot of respect for this Christian-pastor-turned-administrator (thank God that was the one and only time I was called into his office).

My next step was to talk to my DON, whom I respected a lot. After informing her of what occurred, she made no comment about the administrator's responses, which I understood. But we did spend quite a bit of time talking about the responsibilities of a DON position, whether a small facility or not. She stated, twenty years ago, the best clinical RN would be the one to be promoted to DONs. But today, it was all about learning state regulations, needing to write policy and procedures, plus having management experience. She encouraged me not to apply for the position, as it is too stressful, and the life expectancy of DONs is eighteen months. She herself made the decision to change her nursing career path. She was going to eventually leave her director of nursing position to become a geriatrics consultant and earn a PhD. I had calmed down somewhat after talking with my boss. I was not interested in driving over two hundred miles a week for the job anyway. In reflection, I guess visiting the facility without an invite and speaking to the staff nurse was my mistake. But from that day on, I could never feel the same about my administrator.

From the position of working three-to-eleven shifts (seven to ten days a pay period, including every other weekend), I advanced to the position of being the seven-to-three RN charge nurse four days a week with the remaining up to six days on three-to-eleven shift.

Eventually, when the full-time seven-to-three day shift RN retired, I was promoted to her position. Even though I loved the varying schedule of being on both some seven-to-three and three-to-eleven shifts (allowing for me to sleep in some days), I was thrilled to finally be offered a permanent ten-day-a-pay-period schedule on day shift. What nurse does not feel they have paid their dues by getting off an eleven-to-seven or three-to-eleven shift? You can start a regular bedtime schedule, resume watching favorite evening TV shows, and be off work in the evenings.

As she desired, the DON left her post and was promoted to the home office as a consultant for all of the nursing homes under the same church affiliation. The newly hired DON, April, was much younger, pretty, and had a bounce in her step. Not unexpected by the nurses, her style of leadership was totally different. Shortly after April was hired, the day shift charge nurse position became available for me.

When April offered me the position, she shared a concern that some of the long-term residents and their family members might have. She explained they had built trust and a relationship with the previous RN charge nurse, who had worked there for many years. Besides, April pointed out, I was more than twenty years younger than my predecessor. My DON suggested I pray about that challenge. So I did. As typical of my personality, I took the bull by the horns and worked hard to win over the residents and family members' trust over the next year. During my next annual job performance, I asked April if, within the last year, in fact any resident or family member ever shared a concern of my competence as the RN charge nurse. She assured me no one ever did. My efforts paid off!

It wasn't long before the buzz began about how moody the new DON could be. She could be too critical at times and often overacted. The following Christmas, April handed out to her staff the most beautiful Christmas letter (I held onto it for many years) that was full of God's love, her appreciation of us all, and her desires and hopes for a successful upcoming year. Guess she was in a great mood when she penned her Christmas letter. All of the RN charge nurses continued to work hard to keep our units afloat and provide great care for our residents.

There were times when I heard April's high heels walking toward the nursing unit around 8:00 a.m. and wondered if I would get a "good morning" or be totally ignored. I soon learned to only answer back "good morning" if you were greeted first. One day, she made a very unfair, rude, inappropriate comment to the LPN at the public nursing station. In my fury, I knew that I had to leave the scene. I found myself walking down the hall toward the café counting to ten out loud because I didn't want to make any comment I would later regret. This is just one experience how staff began to lose respect for April and her leadership style.

Annual job performance reviews given by this DON were dreaded by staff. You hoped your review was to be held on a day when April was in a good mood. Some staff got lucky; I was one of the unlucky ones. In summary, my overall performance was mostly positive, showed in all areas evaluated I had met expectations, and I qualified for a raise. Once again, I found myself trying to defend my actions about situations that frequently arose on the nursing unit and how I determined priorities. I could tell April was mostly clueless on how nurses handled phone calls from the lab or our pharmacy. After the short performance review, I left her office totally frustrated. I had heard about many of other nurses' review results. Some were so ticked off about April's focus during their annual job performance, they called and complained to staff at the corporate office. Not a good idea! In conclusion, I realized little was going to change with administration.

Just as piling dinner plates eventually fall over, my tolerance met its limit. I went home and typed up my resignation letter, giving my thirty-day notice. Having heard many complaints over the recent years about some of the situations on my job, Mike fully supported my giving notice.

"However, can't you wait until you get another job first?" he asked me on our drive home from our couples' Bible study. "No, this must be done now. RNs have no trouble finding jobs," I answered, sounding hopeful.

Arriving on the floor before 7:00 a.m., I had time to place my resignation letter on my DON's desk. Sure enough, shortly after 8:00 a.m., I was called into April's office. Long story short, she asked me who knew about my resignation, and I answered, "Only Mike."

"Good, because I am ripping this up," she said as she ripped the letter in shreds. "There has been one big misunderstanding!" April complimented me on how well I had run the nursing unit and had built a great team. Oh, is this my real annual performance review?

That evening, after Mike and I hugged and kissed upon his arrival home, I pulled back and looked at him, smiling, "I'm staying. April would not accept my resignation and ripped it up."

About a year later on that beautiful fall morning on September 11, 2001, my busy calendar included overseeing scheduled residents' Care Conferences: weekly meetings that were held to satisfy state regulations. Residents who resided in long-term care homes were expected to have a conference held quarterly. The resident and his/her POA were updated by the interdisciplinary team, which consisted of the RN charge nurse, social worker, dietician, activity director, chaplain, physical therapist, and the nurse who was responsible for government-driven Medicare paperwork. As per the usual, the resident list for September 11 was quite lengthy. The Care Conference meetings started early in the shift.

But first, I was called into my Assistant Director of Nursing's (ADON) office shortly after 8:00 a.m. She was asking me to clarify why I didn't have time to help feed a resident the previous Sunday. Why am I being asked such a question? Who on my team had passed on such a complaint to the ADON? The team of nurses' aides who worked on my weekend understood RNs were not expected to assist with feeding residents, but they were appreciative when nurses did. After a short time of defending my actions of how that particular Sunday's workload did not warrant it, I left her office totally ticked off. I had time to process the conversation for only a few minutes as the Care Conferences were due to start and came to the conclusion the piling dinner plates were about to tumble down once again.

Sometime during our first scheduled Care Conference, a staff member ran into the room of eight and asked us to follow her to the nearest TV. She was attempting to explain to us something about a plane crash into one of the Twin Towers. With mouths gaping open wide, we watched in horror as the TV announcer commented on this tragedy and not understanding its cause. As we remember, it was only a few minutes later when both Twin Towers crumbled to the ground, taking more lives and spewing debris and enormous clouds of dust around bustling New York streets. This was so much worse than tumbling dinner plates! America as we knew it had forever changed.

We all remember what we were doing, where we were, and how we felt on that 9/11 morning. I took it as a sign that God was shouting from the sky "Get out of this job!" I remembered how frustrated I felt. Over and over again, I had so many reasons to lose respect for the nursing home's administration. After all, I threw away a husband I no longer respected. A place of employment can certainly be thrown out too. Dazed and confused about what a terrorist attack even meant for our country, I was not confused about this decision. After nine years of employment, I went home and typed up a second resignation letter. And no one was going to talk me out of it. April accepted my thirty-day notice the following morning, when she realized there was no changing my mind.

That same week, Mike's business trip planned for Reston, Virginia, was cancelled. The 9/11 crisis caused planes to be grounded. Once the ban was lifted, we flew to Arizona, since we both had scheduled time off from work. Since I was looking for another job anyway, Mike asked me to seriously consider relocating to Arizona, a desert state he had fallen in love with over recent years. That evening, I searched the Internet for an ADON position near the Phoenix area. Even though I look great in orange, I am only interested in an ADON position. DONs are the ones that get handcuffed and sent to jail. ADON is as far up the nursing career ladder I'm interested in climbing. I found three possibilities of job openings and tucked them in my purse.

Remaining open-minded, I entered a beautiful Scottsdale nursing home that we passed on the way from the airport to our hotel. It was one of the possibilities; I wanted to simply ask for a job application. Not dressed appropriately (I was wearing shorts) to face any facility administration, I expected to quickly be in and out. As soon as the DON overheard someone ask the receptionist for an application, she stepped around the corner and greeted me. Somewhat embarrassed, I explained I had seen the ADON job opening on the Internet and was considering applying for the position. The DON invited me back into her office and immediately put me at ease. Being laid back, she commented, after learning I was an RN from Pennsylvania, "I know you East Coast girls know how to work. Fill out the application and please return on Thursday so you can meet the CEO." Basically, she was hiring me on the spot after only a brief discussion of my career path.

Mike, so excited for my good fortune, had a second job interview and accepted a position working for a map company. On Wednesday morning, we were sitting in a lovely Denny's having breakfast while soaking up the breathtaking scenery around us. As Mike was rambling on about the logistics of our future move to Arizona, telling family and friends, and planning our relocation, I started getting an unsettled feeling in my stomach.

"Hon, I've learned not every open door is one which I am meant to walk through. Being offered this administration job, which sounds so laid-back and too good to be true, and one I am sure I would love, it simply means RNs find jobs," I explained in between sips of coffee. "I'm sorry. I just can't make the move. Our family needs us." We understood it needed to be God's will for both of us. It was a much too serious of a matter not to pray more about it in-depth and get confirmation by other Christians. After giving both hiring companies our regrets, Mike and I flew back home. We decided to keep it a secret from my family that we had included possible new jobs and a relocation during our last-minute planned Arizona vacation.

The next day, Steph, holding her abdomen, announced over dinner she was pregnant. As I rushed over to give her a big hug, I looked over my shoulder at Mike. He grinned and slowly shook his head. Yes, this is why God slammed the door shut. Grandbaby number two was on their way.

When retelling this story, Mike holds up his hand forming one-inch and announces, "I was *this close* to getting her to move to Arizona. *This close!*"

God was opening up another door for an awesome opportunity for me in my nursing career. No, it wasn't located in Arizona but in a beautiful, quaint Lancaster County town. The job offered to me was a day shift RN Case Manager position for another nonprofit long-term care retirement home, which I started the day after Christmas. First, I was hired by an insurance company to visit their doctor's offices to ensure they were following their criteria to be one of their clients. However, I knew it was only for a short term. I felt like a surveyor, and the tables were turned. I thoroughly enjoyed driving around various counties that beautiful fall, checking off the number of offices that required my attention.

Unlike ever before, with this new job, I realized I needed to depend on the Lord and Him only. I was grateful and recognized the awesome responsibility my job title held. Every morning, I prayed for God to walk beside me. I literally said aloud, as I entered my car, "Lord, *you* and I together will get through this day." On the way home, I said, "Thank you, Lord, for being with me and helping me today." Any successes were coming from my Good Shepherd.

My new coworkers and friends learned I was a "newlywed" of two years and befriended me during a time of growing strong in the Lord. My staff learned I had an open-door policy, and I was more than willing to pray with them if need be. I was an administrator who treated others as I wanted to be treated. The Christmas potlucks continued in my home, however, with a new set of LPNs and nurses' aides coworkers. My office over the years was a place of heaven-sent prayers before a family meeting, annual state surveys, or staff counseling sessions. For once, my private life was straightening out, and I could focus on my career. Again, I thrived under respectable Christian management. My boss, Joyce, and the management team, staff, coworkers, and residents will always hold a special place in my heart.

Working with the older generation remained my specialty. Did my residents feed a need in me that my grandparents never did? Early in my nursing career, after finding out I thoroughly enjoyed working in geriatrics, I told others, "You couldn't pay me enough to work in a hospital."

After thirteen years of climbing the nursing career ladder from the RN Case Manager position, I moved into the Assistant Director of Nursing position. Years later, when the opening became available, I became the Personal Care Home Administrator for the personal care wing, a position I held until I moved to South Carolina.

Choosing nursing as my second career, which spanned over twenty years, was one of my smartest decisions I had ever made.

Thought of the Day

Grace wins every time. What if the pearly gates are made up of the pain of saints? A making of a pearl from an oyster is a painful process. An irritating grain of sand, along with the oyster's secretions, turns the irritation eventually into great value. Joy does come in the morning.

Chapter 49

Having My Wild Eyelashes Pulled

> So that having been justified by His grace, we might become heirs having the hope of eternal life. This is a trustworthy saying. And I want you to stress these things, so that those who have trusted in God may be careful to devote themselves to doing what is good. These things are excellent and profitable for everyone.
> —Titus 3:7–8

ONE THING I LEARNED FROM my mom, which has always been intriguing to others was you need to have your "wild" eyelashes pulled out regularly. Yes, "wild" eyelashes are those lashes that grow inward toward your eye, instead of outward, and cause irritation. How to solve this problem? Make an appointment with the "Plain" Mennonite lady who will pull them out. The first time I learned about this was when Mom, during one of my visits, noticed I was battling seasonal allergies of itchy eyes and a runny nose. Mom was introduced the previous month to the eyelash puller from a fellow quilter.

"Leanne, you need to go see the lady who pulls out your wild eyelashes. That will fix you up," she commented to me, while we were working together in her kitchen preparing lunch. "I went last month because my eyes were itchy. I have had no problems since then," Mom assured me, as she filled the water glasses. Mom explained this horse-and-buggy Mennonite lady was taught by her mother on how to pull out the troublemakers. I figured I had nothing to lose but a few eyelashes (wild or not). I agreed to have Mom make an appointment the following week with Mrs. Nolt.

We pulled up in her gravel driveway, and I noticed the house was lighted by a bright kerosene lamp. Will this woman pull too many of my needed nonwild eyelashes and make me look like a freak because of poor lighting? As we walked up Mrs. Nolt's walk, Mom explained she was not allowed to display any business sign in her lawn nor charge a certain amount because she was not licensed to be in business. "Only by donation," Mom suggested as she knocked on the door. "I usually pay her $5 for both eyes."

After introductions, Mrs. Nolt asked me to sit down in a kitchen chair and to rest my head on several comfortable rolled-up towels. She wore a miner's-type-lamp and assured me it does not hurt when she plucks the wild eyelashes. "It only hurts a little when I pull out a good one," she said, smiling. Mrs. Nolt held tweezers in one hand and a magnifying glass in the other. She instructed me to lightly close both eyes. After turning on her bright miner's lamp, she started plucking away on my right eye. I felt a small tug as she worked. Every now and then, it hurt slightly. "Oops, that was a good one," she laughed and paused.

As she continued to work, while conversing with Mom, the lady lined up the wild eyelashes on the tip of her one finger to show me later on the amount pulled out from each eye. Asking me if I wanted a break before proceeding to my left eye, Mrs. Nolt allowed me to reposition and gave my neck a rest. Then she pointed out about eight eyelashes lying on her one finger. Yikes!

Feeling fine, I gave her the go-ahead to proceed and finish the remaining eye. When finished, she informed me my left eye did not have as many and showed me about one half-dozen of eyelashes displayed on her finger. After handing her a five-dollar bill, I promised to return in about a year (the recommended time frame to keep after the little buggers), if I believed it to be effective.

Well, I certainly was not taught about wild eyelashes during nursing school. However, I am going to side with the wild eyelash theory that they certainly could cause irritation if they were incorrectly growing inward and rubbing up against an eye. When allergy season was at its worse the following spring, I did return to have more wild eyelashes pulled out. All total, I made three appointments in the last decade with Mrs. Nolt for her services and found some relief. I hope this woman does pass her skills onto her daughter, the third generation.

Some things inherited from our parents one can be proud of; other things, not so much. I have often been told I look a lot like my mother. When looking serious or concentrating, I have frown lines that turn downward, making me look stern or somewhat angry, just as Mom used to. Once I realized this fact, I tried to remember to put a slight smile on my face to not appear stern.

Something else I inherited from my mother is while eating a bowl of soup, my nose runs. Our meal could be interrupted to blow our noses. Though mother never complained of allergy symptoms like me, she did carry one or several tissues with her at all times too. They would be stuffed in pocketbooks and pockets of dresses and jackets. In fact, when she was older, I noticed Mom stuffing a tissue up her sleeve. I do not think of leaving the house without having a tissue in at least one of my pockets. I would have a nice bank account if every time I had found the evidence of a shredded, forgotten tissue in my clothes dryer, I had put a dollar in the bank.

Mom never recognized that her daughters got their gumption from her. She could not understand how we girls could drive all over the creation alone at night or take road trips without our husbands. Perhaps our gumption was displayed in a different manner from hers, but Mom definitely passed on some spunk. She was opinionated and stubborn at times. Once her mind was made up, there was no changing it.

Mom had several girlfriends (especially women of the neighborhood), and she enjoyed speaking to her non-neighbor friends over the phone somewhat to catch up on life. But, unlike her daughters, mostly Mom's phone calls had a purpose and were not just a chatting session.

Being devoted to only one man in her life, Mom could not quite fathom my sister and me having more than one husband.

Several years after Daddy died, I teased Mom about accepting companionship and going on a date if any man asked her out, knowing she would be a good catch. Believing I was talking total nonsense, she commented, "Nope. Not interested. Too much hassle in mixing two families' money." I guess that subject is closed.

Thought of the Day

It takes grace not to look upon giants who can defeat us. Do not be afraid or be weak. Nevertheless, be strong and of good courage in the Lord.

Chapter 50

The Cost of Unhappy Marriages

> Grace and peace be yours in abundance through
> the knowledge of God and of Jesus our Lord.
> —2 Peter 1:2

OSWALD CHAMBERS WROTE, "GOD'S CALL has nothing to do with personal sanctification, but with being made broken bread and poured out wine. God can never make us wine if we object to the fingers He uses to crush us with…If ever we are going to be made into wine, we will have to be crushed; you cannot drink grapes. Grapes become wine only when they have been squeezed." Yikes! But, Lord, I want to pick and choose in what areas are squeezed and ask for gentler fingers.

One of the most influential books I have ever read (and remains part of my collection of books) was *The Wisdom of Menopause: Creating Physical and Emotional Health and Healing During the Change* by Christiane Northrup, MD (Bantam Books, 2001). Dr. Northrup opened my eyes to the connection between unfulfilling relationships and the growth of uterine fibroids—the cause of yet another major surgery.

> At midlife, we get the chance to make changes, to create lives that fit who we are—or, more accurately, who we have become. If, however, a woman cannot face the changes she needs to make in her

> life, her body may find a way to point them out to her, lit up in neon and impossible to ignore. It is at this stage that many women reach a crisis in the form of some kind of physical problem, a life-altering or even sometimes life-threatening illness. One very common physical problem in the years leading up to menopause, for example, is fibroid tumors in the uterus…we doctors are content to explain that the reason fibroids occur so frequently in women in their forties is because of changing hormone levels, with too much estrogen being produced…it is not the whole truth…bodily symptoms are not just physical in nature; often they contain a message for us about our lives—if only we can learn to decipher it… the message only becomes clear in stages…we attract precisely the illness or problem that best facilitates our access to our inner wisdom…a phenomenon that is both awe-inspiring and sometimes terrifying…it hits us harder and more directly during perimenopause and menopause, as though nature is trying to awaken us one last time before we leave our reproductive years, the era when our inner wisdom, mediated in part by our hormones, is loudest and most intense.

I too had to unlock the message behind the symptoms. Healing cannot be fully realized until you do. Dr. Northrup believes there are seven emotional energy centers, which connect emotions to specific areas of our bodies. The uterus and ovaries and other female anatomy are tied to the mental, emotional issues of: "personal power: sex, money, and relationships…boundaries in relationships: dependency vs. independence, giving vs. taking, assertiveness vs. passivity."

About five pounds of uterine fibroids (which I named as a "decades' worth of must I's" and "what have I done?") were surgically removed. Just as Dr. Northrup admits in her story, when going through her divorce, "it was the emotion of anger that gave me the energy to proceed with the onerous task of dismantling twenty four years of marriage…and building another kind of life. I used the volcanic energy of my anger to guide me toward identifying my needs and then getting them met."

Dr. Northrup wrote about how to navigate a road map of unknown territory, which includes steps "on your journey home to yourself." She herself ventured onto a new path that

> loses its intimidating aspects and becomes instead of a voyage of exploration and discovery…know that the fear of loss is often worse than the actual loss…discovering what my own needs and desires actually were…I experienced the crumbling of everything I had always thought I could count on. Paradoxically, that year also proved to be one of the most strengthening and exhilarating of my entire life…being willing to roll up my sleeves and rebuild my life, I've become infused with the energy of hope, relief, and new beginnings. Every day I'm reminded that the energy that supports new life abounds. We just have to believe in it, surrender to it, and ask for help.

I proved too, as Dr. Northrup believes, we're stronger and more resilient than we may think.

In January 2003, prior to my February surgery, I scheduled my first gynecological appointment, thanks to an abnormal abdominal ultrasound, which showed an increase in uterine fibroids. While still sitting on his rolling, backless chair, Dr. Kegalle looked at me, between my legs, and announced, "I recommend a hysterectomy." A biopsy of my uterine lining was pending. Reinforcing my need to agree with Dr. Kegalle's decision, I was required to change my soiled bedsheets twice within the week. In addition, the embarrassing times

MY LAST LAST NAME IS GRACE

I had soiled my white nursing uniform and the nurse's station's desk chair was one too many. Is this a coincidence? Don't think so.

By mid-February, Dr. Kegalle informed me he was unable to schedule my hysterectomy until April, unless I selected Dr. Martini to do the surgery. Mike and I discussed it and decided why wait? Thus, we met with Dr. Martini. He explained to me there are at least three fibroids and demonstrated the sizes with his hands: one is about the size of a grapefruit, one an orange, and the other one a lemon. No wonder, I have all this back pain! I dreamt for two nights in a row about the surgery. How do you prepare for three to four weeks off work?

Then I got a grand idea. Why don't I surprise Mike with a week of my recuperating in Arizona, his favorite state? The wheels churned until I had a plan in place. I called Mike's boss and told him about my plan to book a week's vacation for Mike without any of his knowledge. His boss agreed and secretly cleared Mike's calendar. I booked two plane tickets, a rental car, and packed both suitcases.

Dr. Martini didn't agree with playing my so-busy-at-work card and requesting only two weeks off. We compromised on three weeks' recuperation with his final say of "let's wait and see." He also didn't say no when I asked if I could recuperate in Arizona. The only question he had was "what is your planned method of travel?" When I told him we were flying, not driving, he said he'd consider it. I reassured him bottom line, Mike wouldn't let me do anything I shouldn't be doing.

On February 11, after a fairly decent good night's sleep and my last tub bath for a while, we headed off to the Women's Medical Center by 6:00 a.m. We were directed to the surgical admission desk, where I was handed a paper that outlined my schedule for the day and what I was to expect postsurgery. Next, a nurse reviewed med pain management with me and encouraged me to consider accepting the recommendation of the drug, Demerol, which had the most effectiveness if administered via an injection.

After signing more consent forms, I met the anesthesiologist and the nurse anesthetist and answered more questions. Finally, after giving them two vials of blood and changing into a hospital gown, I kissed Mike good-bye and walked beyond the double doors. I walked up to the OR table, while my nurse was holding the IV solution. What a weird feeling! I climbed on the OR table while one nurse explained she'll be adding "relaxing" meds into my IV; another nurse inserted a Foley catheter, while another nurse covered me with warm heated blankets. Then the anesthesiologist walked over to me. "So please tell me where is your cap?" *Hmm, this must be a question to see how alert I am.*

I patted my infamous green shower-like cap on my head and smiled and slowly answered, "Right here on my head." He burst out laughing. "Now I'm awake. I've never heard that answer before. No, I meant which of your front teeth is the capped one. I don't won't to place the tube on that side of your mouth." Geezzzz, who remembers you have a capped tooth?

My last memory was putting my arms in the arm boards and having the thought, *Hey, keep asking me questions. I'm still awake here...!*

My next memory was arousing in the recovery room. I again felt a Mack truck abusing my body. Only this time, it was parked on my belly. I heard a nurse say, "Mrs. Miller, you're in the recovery room. It's twenty after ten. I'm giving you some pain medicine in your IV." In my hazy field of vision, I noticed shadows of a nurse to my left who was fixing my blankets. She kept talking to me saying how good I was doing and how she was giving me pain medicine again. I frequently felt the automatic BP cuff expand in my right arm and heard the whirl of the pneumatic compression hose. The respiratory therapist had me breathe into the incentive spirometer and cough and deep breath. That hurts!

Soon, I was transported to my room, where Mike was waiting for me. The nurse asked Mike to step out of the room while they transferred me from the gurney to my bed. The nurse explained to Mike the recommended Demerol via injection every four hours and the use of a pain scale by number to determine my pain level. Mike joked, "Add a number. She handles pain well."

MY LAST LAST NAME IS GRACE

My first visitors were my mom, Steph, Eric, and Kiersten. I could hear all of the conversations, but I just couldn't keep my eyes open. Flower arrangements were being delivered, and Mike answered several phone calls. Sometime that day, an RN instructor asked me if I would grant permission to be assigned an LPN student. She introduced herself as Lori Anderson. I consented, as I surely understood what nursing students go through. I was frequently fussed over by my LPN student. I soon figured out why. She told me I was the only patient she was assigned to. Thus, she could give me lots of attention. Under the scrutiny of her RN instructor, Lori administered my injections. Later on, she noticed she gave me a golf-ball sized bruise on my right buttock from her injection administration inexperience. No problem; been there; done that.

While I was attempting to eat my lunch of clear liquids and gelatin, I sipped on some Sierra Mist. My family started playing cards in the corner of my room. Heather and Taylor came to visit later on in the afternoon and then later took my mom home.

My pain scale remained at an average of five or six. Sometimes, I answered eight, and another time two. My "friends" were an IV in my left arm, pneumatic hose, a Foley catheter, and oxygen tubing. Due to my hemoglobin dropping to 8.6 (normal is 12–13 for women), they kept me on supplemental oxygen. They didn't want to transfuse me with packed cells, unless they needed to. My boss, Joyce, and my friend Shelby stopped by in the evening to visit me. More flower arrangements arrived from my church, work, and Mike.

Lori frequently checked on me. Once, she announced she was going to check on my incision. Even though my family was present in the room, I gave her permission for them to not have to step out of the room. Mom, Steph, Heather, and Mike were anxious to get a peep. I simply wanted to see my flatter stomach! After loosening the incision dressing, Lori assessed the incision for drainage, a foul smell, or any notable complication. She commented on the great job the surgeon did, how clean it was, and how all the Steri-Strips were intact.

Lori left the room to document her assessment findings but quickly returned to my bedside. Even in my drowsy state, I could tell she was quite frazzled. "I wasn't supposed to open the dressing and assess the incision. My instructor said I was only to assess the dressing," she commented. "Let's make sure the tape is on so tight, no one can tell it had been open." She looked down at me nervously, as she resecured the tape. "Why did you let me do that?"

I softly answered I could only assume she had a doctor's order to check on the incision. "You'll never make that mistake again. You'll always remember this lesson. Trust me."

Guess who was the one, about ten years later, who was involved in our move to South Carolina? Lori and her husband purchased our home!

Some time at the end of three-to-eleven shift, two nurses assisted me to walk to the door while keeping tabs on my "friends." It didn't hurt too badly, except when having to sit up and get out of bed. I did sleep half decently that night in spite of the interruptions of getting my pain med injections. Eventually, the injections were switched to Percocet in pill form. Dr. Martini stopped by Wednesday morning, assessed my incision (I left him believe this was the first assessment) and reviewed my chart. Being pleased with the results, he announced I could go home on Thursday after his rounds. After saying goodbye and thanking the great nursing staff, an elderly volunteer, using a wheelchair, wheeled me to my car.

One monkey wrench was thrown in my plans to surprise Mike about part of my recuperation to be held in Arizona. He had two bosses: One boss, whom I had talked to, kept it a secret. The other boss didn't know it was meant to be one. Mike learned about his scheming wife when his boss walked into his office and wished him a safe flight. Oh well.

My journal entry was titled: "My Grand Idea: to Recuperate in Arizona - Friday, February 28, to Friday, March 7, 2003."

After two weeks of my recuperating, having visitors, going out for lunch, having Steph and Kiersten visiting for hours with me and some babysitting Taylor, Mike and I left for our vacation to Loewes Canyon Resort in Tucson. Because of another predicted snowstorm, we cancelled Bible study and headed down to Microdel Suites, a hotel near the Baltimore airport. However, we still had to be up at 4:00 a.m. to catch a 5:00 a.m. shuttle. We arrived at our hotel in Tucson around 3:00 p.m. It is beautiful but has expensive restaurants. After spending $100 between my and Mike's burger breakfast and drinks, we decided to have our meals at either Denny's or a cheaper mom-and-pop-type restaurant for the rest of the week. We toured the entire hotel, made note of the amenities, and then watched a movie in our room tonight.

On Saturday, we went out for a pancake breakfast and shopped at a Quilt Basket. I decided to start quilting crib quilts for my grandbabies (no, that never happened). On Sunday, we visited Desert Vineyard Church. God is anointing and working through Pastor Rick. Turns out he knows Pastor Sam. On Monday, we drove to Saquaro Park, and I hiked over a mile…getting ready for my first day back to work on Monday. Then I read by the pool, while Mike took another hike. At times, it was chilly enough, I had to cover up with a towel.

On Tuesday, we went to the Arizona Diamondback's spring training game. They lost. On Wednesday, we toured the observatory on Kitt Peak and visited another nearby park. Thursday, we went to the Tucson State Park. Friday was travel day back home. I feel rested.

As my body healed of its surgical cuttings, I wanted to also heal the parts of myself that led to my divorces in the first place. Repeating of old unhealthy patterns was not an option. But I knew I couldn't come through the other side without God's help. Understanding our remarriages can never include the D-word, Mike and I vowed issues would be talked out, and counseling would be sought after if need be. An abdominal scar, still visible, reminds me to never again compromise my true self and attempt to live up to the expectations of others.

Many years later, my hero was found in Ruth Graham, Billy's wife. During a tour of the Billy Graham Library, I listened intently to a partial-televised interview. When questioned if she ever contemplated divorce, Ruth quipped, "Divorce, never. Murder? Many times!"

Just as Dr. Northrup, I began

> to heal the unfinished business of my past…At midlife I, like thousands of others, have had to give up my fantasies of how I thought my life would be. I had to face, head on, the old adage about how hard it is to lose what you never really had. It means giving up all your illusions, and it is very difficult. But for me the issue was larger than where, and with whom, I would grow old. It was a warning, coming from deep within my spirit that said, 'Grow…or die.' Those were my choices. I chose to grow.

She also gave me great insight about my cousin Jill's hard life and the link to breast cancer:

> Your emotions are your inner guidance system. They alone will let you know whether you are living in an environment of biochemical health or in an environment of biochemical distress. Understanding how your thoughts and your emotions affect every single hormone and cell in your body, and knowing how to change them in a way that is health-enhancing, gives

you access to the most powerful and empowering health-creating secret on earth.

Natural foods, supplements, herbs, meditation, acupuncture, and so on are all powerful tools for building and protecting your health. But regardless of what supplements you take and what kind of exercise you do, when all is said and done it is your attitude, your beliefs, and your daily thought patterns that have the most profound effect on your health…Attitudes and beliefs also influence how well your food is digested and how effective your exercise is. You have, within you, the power to create a life of joy, abundance, and health, or you have the same ability to create a life filled with stress, fatigue, and disease. With very few exceptions, the choice is yours.

It has now been scientifically documented that specific patterns of emotional vulnerability affect specific organs or systems of the body… like all diseases, cancer has an emotional component as well as a physical one. Many women with breast cancer have a tendency to hide their emotions behind a stoic face…those who had allowed themselves to experience their grief fully when they confronted devastating losses were three times less likely to suffer from breast cancer than those who hid their emotions behind a brave face or submerged their grief in various forms of activity…not allowing ourselves to grieve uses up vital energy, depriving us of the resources we need to heal. At times of loss we must go through the painful and difficult process that I refer to as radical surrender…to God…we must allow this power to heal our lives, and this can happen only through the full experiencing our grief…

With a great deal of courage and a determination to put into practice lessons learned, my inner healing began too. Just as an annoying chin hair needs constant attention of plucking, any hint of disrespect toward Mike is dealt with. Sweeping resentments under the rug are counterproductive. Realistically, a spouse is 2 percent irritant and 98 percent spouse and lover. Communicate and fill in any sap-draining holes from your marriage. Scars tell stories; my abdominal scar is always present as a reminder that a wholesome relationship is well worth the hard work and all the efforts put into it.

One night during Mike's and my early courtship, Steph asked me, "Why should I let this other new man of yours in my life? How do I know you are not going to just walk away again?" Trying to convince her otherwise, that night had to sound lame to her ears. To explain to Steph some voice from my inner soul was confirming that this relationship would work, and I was going to trust it, probably wasn't too assuring. All Mike and I could do over time was to prove that this time our three-stranded cord would not be broken.

Another title for this chapter could be "Consequences of Divorces." As the Martin family of nine children married and had their own children, eventually my parents' home was no longer large enough to support a family gathering at Christmas time. Since Mervin and my sister-in-law Linda did not believe in birth control, they had twelve children!

Our gatherings were held in a local fire hall. Over time, as we each were finding ourselves, the twenty-something smart-mouthed siblings held verbal attacks and gave opinions, not sounding much different than when we were youngsters. Belonging is inherent and apparent in nature. However, members in a group are not necessarily like-minded. Even though families are not close-knit, they do share histories. This was obvious of the Martins. Loud discussions and arguments around the dinner table arose to the point that Daddy finally put his foot down. "Enough is enough. No more talking about religion and politics at our family get-togethers," he sternly said.

Marlin and Mervin's families attended their last scheduled summer picnic down at Mom and Daddy's "park." Lenora's family drove down from Williamsport to join in. The twenty-plus grandchildren ran around, rode bicycles and trikes, scuffed knees to their heart's content, in between eating Grandpa's mouth-watering chicken BBQ. The next day, Mom received a call from Mervin. He said that he was choosing to no longer attend the Martin family gatherings. "The clothes that Lenora is wearing on her little girls are immodest. I am not going to have my sons around that," he elaborated. "We were forced to look the other way when Lenora and Leanne got divorced and started bringing new husbands around. But the sleeveless tops, or should I call them small snippets of material called blouses, has made my decision final."

Mom called Lenora immediately. "Lenora, I can't remember what your girls were wearing yesterday. Whatever it was, it is the final straw. Mervin and probably Marlin will be calling as well. Said they won't be coming around anymore for our get-togethers. They don't agree with you girls' divorces and the way you dress your girls."

Lenora's smoke probably came through the phone line. "For Pete's sake. My girls are five and seven years old. Does he think his boys are never going to see little girls on the street wearing tank tops?" she blurted out. That summer picnic was the last time we all gathered together as a family, until Daddy's funeral years later.

My personal experience of being the reason Marlin needed to place a phone call occurred when I helped plan Mom's eightieth surprise birthday party. Lenora, by then, had married Jack, and I had married Mike. Children and grandchildren traveled from several states to attend. Only those nieces and nephews of Mom's who lived in a foreign country were unable to attend the celebration. I booked the nursing home's chapel to hold the party for over one hundred family members. A professional photographer, Bob, was scheduled to snap photos of the special occasion.

After birthday cake was served, Bob started planning his photo shoots. Some were of Mother only with great-grandkids flanked around her. Some were of her and her grandchildren. Then Bob took photos of Mom and her nine children, which followed by a photo of Mom and her children and their spouses. Over twenty shots filled his camera by the time he was finished, as it was most difficult to get grandchildren ranging from twenty-three to six months all smiling and with eyes open.

The next Monday night, Marlin called me on the phone. "Leanne, you know how I have a slight hearing problem. Well, I never heard correctly when Bob asked for all nine of us kids and our spouses to report to the front of the room. I can't be in the same photo with Lenora's and your husband." Say what? Is this where I jiggle the phone "hello, hello?" I surely have not heard what I just heard!

I began tapping my toes. "I don't see how that is possible," I commented, thin-lipped.

Marlin obviously was ready for any pushback. "Oh yes. Bob can airbrush both Mervin and me out of the picture. It'll be easy, as I know we are standing in the back row at the end. Let me explain. If your husband was standing along the highway with a flat tire, I would be happy to help him change his tire. But, Leanne, I was a witness at your wedding, where you promised 'till death do we part.' Because you are remarried, you're living in sin, as long as John is alive. That's just what I believe, and that's how you were raised to believe too."

I first blew out some smoke. Okay, air, and responded, "I am not going to waste your or my time. Obviously, anything I say is not going to change your mind, and anything you say is not going to change mine. I truly don't understand why divorce cannot be repented from. You make it the unpardonable sin, and it is *not*! I am not going to call Bob about airbrushing anybody out of our family photos. These pictures belong to Mom, and she has the final say. Good-bye." Shaking, I hung up the phone.

Poor Mike could not wrap his head around the summed-up conversation. "But he'd change my tire, huh?" He shook his head in disbelief. Turns out Mom did not have her two sons airbrushed out of the photo. But she did have to promise she would never display on her photo wall the one taken of her children with their spouses. Its home, instead, ended up in a photo album kept in a drawer.

I can count on one hand the times I ran into either Marlin or Mervin over the last twelve years. Sometimes, their family was just leaving, as my family was arriving to visit with my parents. The wedding announcements stopped arriving in my mailbox once nieces and nephews realized I would not attend a wedding when the invitation was only addressed to just me and did not include my husband. Mom was the catalyst who would report on my two conservative brothers and their families to the rest of my brothers and sisters, such as who had a baby, moved, or who was getting married.

Much later, as we gathered around Mom's deathbed, the playing field was leveled. Religious opinions and differences were kept at the door. Our mutual ground was a love for Mother and seeing to it she died in peace knowing all nine of us could be in the same room day in and day out. Daddy too had to be looking down and seeing his quiver-full behaving like, well, his reared family.

Families have built-in legacies. But I've never heard of the term "hysterectomy legacy." Dr. Northrup also spoke about this topic in her book. Unfortunately, both of my divorced daughters, though for varying reasons, have had hysterectomies. My prayer is that my grandgirls intercept the legacy of two generations of women and carry on nuggets of inherited women wisdom. My prayer is they will live fulfilling lives, knowing the only one true God, and have one true love of their lives. By the grace of God.

Thought of the Day

Grace once fathomed by sinners, now became saints because grace changes everything.

Chapter 51

Steph and Eric's Journey

Continue in the grace and blessing of God.

—Acts 13:43

Parents are hopeful that their children, as they are experiencing and growing in their world and become their own person, will be true to their own values, be aligned to their goals, and emboldened to their spirit. I had always said Steph was fairly easy to raise. She had common sense, no noticeable bad habits (okay, okay, she obviously had Mom snowed about a few), and considered her church youth group friends as important as her school classmates. I can only remember two times when we hit our last nerve with each other. When she was about fourteen, she back talked one too many times. I did not hesitate to slap her across the face. Not used to me behaving in this manner, she was as shocked as I was; she knew she definitely crossed over an unspoken line. The time when I was a witch of a mother was when she was almost sixteen and begged for me to drive her somewhere. I told her she was not allowed to go that night, and I had no intention of driving her anywhere. Steph ran upstairs, slammed shut her bedroom door, and yelled, "Fine, then I'll drive myself in my Mustang!"

The most repeated arguments held between us were over her unkempt room (remember, I cannot stand clutter). I made my bed every morning, hung up clothes, put dirty laundry in the hamper, and kept things in their place. Entering Steph's room and wading through piles of clothing strewn all over the floor or on her chair or at the bottom of her unmade bed, finding empty soda cans or candy wrappers caused a rise in my blood pressure. I never forced my children to do their own laundry, but I figured they could at least put it in their designated laundry basket for me on laundry day. But no. Steph's room led me to guessing what was dirty and what was clean. Thus, many a day after school or before she walked out the door for her planned activity, I begged her to please clean up her room first. But to no avail. After about three weeks, my arteries could no longer stand the elevated pressure. I cleaned up her room, dusted, and vacuumed it. My reason, I told Steph was, "Since I am paying for fire insurance in this home, I need to prevent raising the risk."

Report card time was not always a happy occasion for Steph. In tenth grade, she had two Ds: English college prep and Spanish III. How to punish? Cut back on boyfriend time and remove her phone (this was long before cell phones) from her bedroom. Instead of twice on weeknights, she was only allowed to see Steve one night, and it must include him helping her study. "If he really cares for you, Steph, he will be willing to do it," I told her.

One journal entry reads: "Why does a mother bother to make rules? I make them and believe all the kids understand them. But I am asked to constantly make exceptions. Steve showed up tonight. Steph quickly told me he is here because she is giving up a weekend night. But lo and behold, the weekend is here and Steph wants to see Steve after all, forgetting about her end of the bargain. I will allow it, but only if I can inform Steve of the house rules myself, since apparently Steph can't seem to communicate them herself very well." Her rules were may see boyfriend one time on a school night, 10:00 p.m. curfew; Friday and Saturday night, midnight curfew; Sunday night, 10:00 p.m. curfew. Certainly seemed more than fair to me.

Steph was blessed to attend three high school proms, starting in tenth grade. Each time, dresses and jewelry were selected with care. It was hard to believe my daughter, whom I had to fight about brushing her hair at twelve years old, now stood in front of me looking gorgeous. The young lady, who fought over her wanting to wear her brother's sweatshirts to school, looked beautiful proudly showing off her gown and wrist corsage.

Because Jeff worked for a car dealer and had an interest in cars, it wasn't long before he found a 1966 wrecked blue Mustang. At the time, Steph was only fourteen years old, but he knew it would take a long time for him to fix it up, working on it only evenings and weekends. She could not have been more excited about her future car. As one side of the garage was overcome by this fixer upper, the wrecked model over time took on the look of a drivable one. In the meantime, we stressed with Steph how important it was no one else beside her was ever allowed to drive her Mustang. She agreed.

Shortly after Steph's sixteenth birthday, she received her driver's permit. My journal entry reads: "Stay off the sidewalk! Steph got her permit…and lost it already. Don't teenage girls carry purses anymore? She is going to have to start; she will need one on hand at all times that holds her permit, emergency gas, or phone booth money, both house and car keys, etc." A few days later, I wrote: "Steph received her permit on Saturday, and by Wednesday, her nickname is Speedy. After Jeff's lecture of the possible serious consequences, a $200 fine, an increase in insurance rates, and her permit would be revoked, Steph slowed down."

I lectured Steph on the importance of always locking both car doors when driving alone. Rumors were spreading among teenagers at that time that if an oncoming driver flashed his high beams, you might be followed, pulled over, and who knows what else could happen. They, you know, they are looking for beautiful blonde virgins to kidnap (sounded a lot like my mom's generation white slavery folklore?). Nonetheless, many prayers went heavenward when Steph drove to and from school, work, and all her weekend teenager activities. Who wouldn't notice this beautiful blonde sitting behind the wheel of the bright blue 1966 Mustang?

As soon as she was able and felt confident, Steph took her driver's test driving her Mustang. But she did not pass. Being embarrassed and less confident, Steph postponed retaking her test for months. Finally, one Saturday morning in January, I convinced her not to tell any of her friends that she planned on taking her test and just do it that very day. She agreed and passed. As most excited teenagers who can now drive with a true license, Steph planned for her and her boyfriend, Steve, to double date that evening with her friend, who lived in Lebanon County. Sunday morning, Jeff noticed the cool-looking Mustang was not parked in its usual spot in front of the house; yet Steph was obviously home.

Jeff entered the kitchen and asked me if I knew how Steph got home last night? "I hope she didn't wreck it or anything," he added. After I got Steph awake, I asked her to come down to the kitchen as Jeff and I were wondering where the Mustang was. Her first weekend driving, and she perhaps had a wreck already? Yikes!

"Steph, is there a serious reason why the Mustang isn't parked out front?" I asked her as I sipped my coffee. After a big sigh, she started explaining the events of the past twelve hours. "Yes, I wrecked the Mustang…but it could be worse." Jeff left out a geezz.

Steph started rubbing the back of her neck. "It doesn't look like you're hurt. Are you?" I asked her.

"Just a little. Here's what happened," she started. Jeff sat down at the head of the table as Steph stood in front of the refrigerator. "I drove up to Karlene's house, and around eight o'clock, it started snowing and sleeting. The roads were slippery, and I lost control of the car." Tears started welling up.

Of course, we were glad she wasn't hurt. Both Jeff and I asked her questions attempting to get more clarity about what did she do to try to prevent the accident. I saw it as a moment to teach a new driver how to handle an out-of-control vehicle. Steph couldn't answer our questions. Then it clicked with me. She wasn't driving, was she? She slid down the refrigerator door and started to cry. Steph explained to us when she saw it was snowing and the roads were slippery, she asked Steve to drive home. While he was driving, he lost control. The car spun around, hitting a guardrail, sideswiped a tree, and landed in a ditch.

Jeff was annoyed. However, I was okay with her decision. Why wouldn't she rationalize a driver with experience in driving in snow be the one to get behind the wheel? She recognized her limits. I told her she did the right thing in spite of going against our wishes. Jeff, saddened, shook his head. He simply saw more hours stretched out in front of him spending time with Mr. Garage. But first things first: Jeff and another buddy had to have the Mustang towed back home. He was shocked when he saw the extent of the damage done to all four sides of the car.

Steph was treated for whiplash for several weeks. She wore a neck brace and got relief from muscle therapy. Steve promised to pay for the damages; he paid for the replaced parts. Eventually, the blonde driver was behind the wheel of her Mustang and had no other issues with her car until she traded it in for a 1975 Capri. Learning to drive a stick shift was truly a new adventure, but her boyfriend was more than willing to teach her to become an expert. Eventually, Steph figured out her cool Mustang with its V-8 engine and rear-wheel drive doesn't work well driving on snowy roads during Pennsylvania winters.

Steph's after-school jobs started with working at the famous local Boehringer's Drive In. As most neighborhood kids do, once they have their fill of scooping their last french fry and ice cream cone, they move on to other jobs to keep some jingle in their pockets. To my surprise, Steph applied and was hired part-time at her uncle's grocery store. Why surprised? Because she had to wear a uniform: a beige skirt that fell below the knee. Not having anything like it in her wardrobe, we visited Goodwill and returned with a handful of appropriate skirts. Seeing her leave the house with her so-unlike-Steph-attire, I could only shake my head and smile. Rather her than me!

Steph, unlike her brother, could not decide which major or college was best suited to help meet her future goals. She decided to take a year off pursuing college and start working. One day, she received a flyer in the mail about attending Consolidated School of Business. Several certificates were being offered. Becoming a travel consultant appealed to Steph. Before long, she was signed up and started her daily trek to York to attend the eleven-month course. Turns out the cost of her schooling was the exact amount of my student loan (I paid each semester mostly in full), which was needed for my three years of college. Yikes!

For both of my daughters, their education to pursue their careers before becoming a mommy was not cheap. Wouldn't you think the hourly rate would be a little higher than barely above minimum wage when it was required to obtain a degree or certificate? I believe it is so sad when education is barely affordable and is necessary to start the first rung of a career ladder and yet pays so little. In their experience, there was hardly any monies left to pay back loans. So Steph saw an opportunity to take on an enjoyable part-time job to start paying back her loans. She was hired by Holiday Inn as a hostess. To pull in new customers, the Inn held country line dances on Thursday nights. Along with other coworkers, Steph became a teacher of the country line dances.

Whether it was due to the strain of her boyfriend having to drive down into another county or because he was older than her, Steph and Steve eventually broke up. She soon had her heart beating faster over a guy, who also came from Mennonite roots, from a local church youth group. Unfortunately, the relationship never really took off the ground. Thus, it wasn't long before she started dating Neil, a roommate of a friend. At first, Neil seemed to be a good match for Steph. However, as their relationship turned over into the fourth calendar year, I began to see obvious differences between him and Steph, which could have serious consequences if they would choose to marry someday. It was taking much more energy to fuel this relationship. Hoping to bring on an absolution that appeared to be Steph's idea, I began pointing out some areas of concern. One day, I read an article in *Good Housekeeping* magazine about a compatibility quiz for couples. I pointed out the article to Steph and said, "Just curious. Why don't you take this quiz and see how you score, okay?" She agreed to take it. Absolution came within a few weeks. Neil was no longer frequenting our living room on Steph's date nights.

For a few months, Steph concentrated on her job, training, and time spent with girlfriends. Through Darrin's buddy, Davis, Steph met her new love, Eric. Muscular, short (like Steph), and handsome, Eric pursued Steph and set aflame a new desire in her. Within six weeks of dating, Eric proposed! Ask me if she and Eric took the compatibility quiz. Ah, no.

Mother and daughter at the same time were falling in love with the new men in their lives. As written about earlier, I was not a very good role model for my young adult daughter. Choosing to live in sin, I watched Steph date, stay overnight at Eric's apartment, and then attend a church event singing praise-and-worship songs with hands lifted high. Been there, done that! Her mother was basically living the same double life: go to church, yes, which is important, but we kept Christians at arm's length because neither one wanted to have our sinful lifestyles pointed out to us. The Holy Spirit was muted.

Mike and I gradually learned to know who Eric was and what made him tick. What was it? Work. Much to my dismay, we soon noticed Eric arrived late to any family get-togethers. I learned to plan on making a plate of hot food for Eric and giving it to him around eight o'clock or so. Better late than never. We learned Eric worked seven days a week. He had a great sense of humor, similar to Darrin, and he felt comfortable around our dinner table. His parents were divorced, and he had one sister, who became a fast friend of Steph's. Eric shared a love for country music, like Steph, but not the love of her Lord and the importance of attending church. Eric attended church twice a year: Easter and Christmas Eve.

Before I knew it, Steph and I were planning their wedding. Traveling around the area attempting to find the perfect reception hall, I realized how much a workaholic Eric really was. Steph informed me their wedding needed to be held on a Sunday, not the typical Saturday because Eric won't take off. Plus, their honeymoon needed to end Thursday night because he needed to be at work on Friday morning. Say what?

But Eric loved my daughter, and their wedding day brought on beautiful weather for a beautiful bride. Wearing something new, borrowed and blue, she walked down the aisle on her father's arm anticipating the most hopeful future any bride would dream of. Eric and

Steph spent a honeymoon in Cancun, Mexico, at a huge discount thanks to her travel agent career.

Kept hidden from her mother for quite some time, Steph disclosed one day that Eric brought a huge amount of debt into their marriage. Having both common and money sense, Steph devised a budget to enable them to get out of debt within five years. She wanted them to be debt-free before having their first child. She handed Eric a twenty-dollar bill and told him that was his spending money for the week. What was it spent on? Cigarettes and soda. For several years, Steph paid down huge debt amounts, but it was not long when she noticed Eric did not see eye-to-eye on spending and saving money. It was like sweeping water—useless.

My journal entry on December 2005 reads: "I am shocked! Steph revealed they are still $5,000 in debt and are short consistently every month by $700–800! God told her to cut up their charge cards and trust Him, as she is relying on it and not Him. Eric and Steph held a long conversation about it. She feels this is all part of his submission to God and the importance of tithing. Steph told Eric he needs to pray about it and come up with a plan on how to change this financial situation because they can't continue to keep living like this. Eric was excited and commented, 'Great. I'm finally going to hear from God.' Steph is both excited and nervous. Where will this lead? Will they end up getting another credit card when they run out of faith? Will Eric commit to the Lord, even if that means he needs to quit his job, sell their house, and go to Bible school or the mission field? Will Eric's boss give him a day off? Father, we commit this situation to you. In reverence and awaiting yet another surprise...."

Since God woos His children, Steph started building her faith, attended church regularly, and grew in her faith by believing God's promises. To write about her journey would entail writing an entirely separate book! Having a soft, tender heart has led Steph to needy friends who need her much more than she needs them. She gave wise counsel, was loyal and dependable, and had a great listening ear. Steph broadened her base of friendships. Eventually, child number one, Kiersten, and two years later, child number two, Christian, were born, completing the family to a total of four. Eric started having off on Tuesdays after the arrival of his baby daughter.

Just as a neglected fixer-upper slowly deteriorates, marriages can start to crumble as well. Many times, it occurs due to lack of attention, or in my daughter Steph's case, true ignorance. She was supporting her workaholic husband, busy raising their two children, managing the bills and a household, while holding down a part-time job. All the while, a hidden bubbling volcano was just about to blow. Eric, her husband, was living a life of total frustration and discontentment, apparently. The conversation about this volcano one night had me about to fall off the kitchen barstool!

During one of my visits back up to Pennsylvania, Steph asked if I could take some time out of my schedule of catching up with my girlfriends to meet with her and Eric after the kids went to bed. Of course. I had an unsettled feeling as I entered their kitchen. I was instructed to sit down, listen, and not ask questions until they would tell me I could. Well, I could not have predicted in a hundred years the conversation I was about to be engaged in, once I was allowed to speak, of course.

Long story short, Eric looked at me intently but spoke somewhat angrily about how he had fallen out of love with Steph in about the third year of their marriage. He wanted to apologize to me for his not being able to love her as she deserved to be loved. Shocked, looking to Steph for confirmation, I was reminded to just listen. What ensued for twenty minutes made me sad, hurt, angry, disappointed, and downright ticked that my beautiful daughter's family, my precious grandchildren, Kiersten and Christian, would need to bear such a burden. I did not want this apple to fall from any tree.

I arrived back at Darrin's house to sleep and realized it was too late to text or call Mike. My mind raced a mile a minute and my friend, Pillow, failed me by not granting me the luxury of falling to sleep as soon as my head hit it. I had a date with Tylenol PM. I put myself in Steph's shoes, and having experienced these crossroads myself, I prayed and cried and then cried and prayed some more. In spite of my bedpartner Tylenol PM, I did awake in the middle of the night. It was then I decided I was going to get up and be back at Steph's house the minute I knew Eric had left for work. It was time for our mother-daughter talk.

Steph informed me she did indeed sleep okay. "Remember, Mom, I have had two weeks to digest this information. But wait to you hear how awesome God has been. You wouldn't believe what transpired for me the last few hours since you left last night," she said while getting dressed for work. Steph proceeded to tell me because Eric was so wound up last night, he realized he would have trouble falling asleep. So he decided to take a drive to calm down. Steph was lying in their lonely bed and started talking to God. "I am sure Eric left so he can call his girlfriend. How long must I put up with his shenanigans?" During a half-asleep-half-awake state, the Lord showed her Eric had simply driven down the street about one-half mile to the King's Market parking lot. He was sleeping in his truck. "Go to sleep, my daughter." And Steph did.

The next morning around six o'clock, Eric returned and started getting ready for work. Since Steph already knew of his whereabouts, she had no reason to ask Eric; so, she didn't. I guess Eric was surprised Steph had not inquired where he spent the night last night. "I just went up to King's." Steph answered, "I know. God told me," and walked out the door to walk the dog. Close your mouth, Eric.

Repeated patterns of Eric coming home from work—ah, from wherever, I should say—any hour of day or night continued for about two weeks. Steph's pastor, who had been frequently updated on the turmoil, smartly advised Steph one day. "Steph, you need to kick Eric out of your bed and onto the sofa. He is not going to disrespect you and the kids by being on the phone for hours talking to his girlfriend while sitting in his pickup truck in your driveway. You tell him he must move out. Until he finds an apartment, his bed is on the couch." Agreeing and having a blessing of one whose opinion matters greatly, Steph did just that.

A few weeks later, I opened up a lengthy e-mail from Steph, which was sent to about twenty family and friends entitled "A Day in the Life of Steph." I read it while tears streamed down my face. I forwarded it to close friends of mine and my prayer warriors, who were privy to Steph's nightmare. I wrote, "I am honored to be her mother. I am speechless right now."

By the time you are finished reading this excerpt, you'll be convinced Steph should be the author of her own book. It follows:

> So you all have been on this crazy journey with me. I give you full permission to push back, call anything out that does not sound right, and correct me in any way. They say it is wise to have good counsel, so that is what I'm doing. Many of you are used to how I feel God talks to me and about my visions. This was yet another one.
>
> I awoke at 4:19 a.m. because someone texted me. It said, "Text me if you want to have a good time. Wanna see me naked?" Seriously! Did Eric use my phone or did someone sell my number? I hate my life! But then, I was wide awake. So I prayed for, I assume, the woman and asked God to surround her with loving people who could show her she does not have to be that person (May I add: Take that Satan! What you meant for evil, my daughter turned it around into something good.)
>
> I sat up and said, "God, talk to me." But in true style, I started talking. Last night, after Eric hung out with Rich (someone included in the e-mail list), he said he had to be honest with me and tell me that most everything he shared with me the last two weeks was really exaggerated. Let's call it for what it really is: he lied! He lied, so it looked worse than what it really is, and so I'd be so mad and hurt I would just kick him out. So how much is a lie and what part is the truth? Then God gave me clarity.

MY LAST LAST NAME IS GRACE

I saw a big chess game, and Eric was very precise on how he designed all his different masks for each of the game pieces. His masks were so he could manipulate each piece, the many different people in his life. It was all for his own selfish reasons but also because he was lost. But then, it got the best of him. He got exhausted and did not remember which mask represented the real him and did not get the reaction he wanted when he wore what he thought was his real mask. He got mad and put all the blame on everyone for making him wear the masks.

The one game piece in his game he could not manipulate very well was me. He resented me the most because I wasn't playing nice and didn't like his many masks. He did everything thinkable and unthinkable to make me play the game his way, and because of God's protection, it never worked. Eric stands on the fact that he knew he should have left me at the altar. He was going to marry me for his own selfish reasons and knew he wasn't being fair to me but did it anyway. Three years in, I could not stay perfect or be his Jesus and he resented me for it. He realized the kind of husband I needed him to be and because of his own selfish reasons and some because I got good at showing him his shortcomings. He failed at being Jesus to me. The kids came along; he wanted them as much as I did. Then he had the affair.

Everything he's done the last eleven years to me and the kids was so that I'd hate him as much as he hated himself, and then I'd leave or have an affair. Little does he realize he's not bigger than God. God showed me that our marriage was not a mistake, though I wanted God to say otherwise. Eric thinks he just caved and married me despite himself. But that's a lie! We got married because God is in control. He has always been in control. The more I fought God to walk away and want to hate Eric, the more God poured out unconditional love for Eric, and I would get back in and fight for our marriage.

Then, God showed me why. I have cussed God out for feeling forced to love and stay with someone who did not love me back. Read Romans 12—the whole chapter is my life. My cousin, Kim, said something that echoed as truth to me. She said, "Loving Eric was 'heaping fiery coals on his head.' God showed me what that meant. He showed me how he used my love to conquer evil with good."

Part two of this e-mail was entitled "God is Going to Avenge Me!" (Hold on tightly, here we go.)

If Christian was endlessly punching Kiersten in the face till she was covered in blood, both her eyes were swollen shut, and every bone in her face was broken—pretty much what Eric did to me emotionally—she would trust that Eric would deal with Christian with harsh discipline while still loving him as his son. Kiersten would know her dad was going to handle it but still feel bad for Christian for having to be punished so harshly because that is who she is. I then saw me looking at Eric dead in the face and said, "How long did you think you would get away with treating the King of kings and Lord of lord's precious daughter like that? Do you realize who you're messing with?' I've dreamt about seeking revenge, but

God did one better. He started avenging me by pouring out His unconditional love through me to Eric. That love was breaking him. I was killing him with kindness. Eric is filled with self-loathing, unworthiness, as well as selfishness and pride. The more I loved him, the more he hated who he was and who he had become. I've screwed up many times and walked in my flesh and wanted him to feel every bit of the pain he made me feel.

But God would bring it back around at different times in our marriage.

Next thing I know, I saw a courtroom. We all heard the analogy of God being the righteous judge, and Jesus takes the punishment we all deserve. This was playing out with Eric. It was God showing me that Eric is saved from God's wrath. The only reason he isn't damned to hell is because of his salvation. Eric is relieved to know he's one of God's sons. Then God points to Eric and says, "Come here, son." Eric walks slowly to the judge's stand, as God stands up and meets up with him. God looks down at him and says, "You and me, son, need to have a little chat." God puts his arms of love around Eric's shoulders and walks him into His chambers. Eric's head is hung low in shame, but he knows he's loved, so he walks in. The door closes. This represents Eric leaving me and the kids. The door to God's chambers has *I Am* across the top. All over the door were all His names: Creator, Judge, Counselor, Son of Man, Prince of Peace, Mighty One and so many more names that represent the Trinity. Some of the names represent God for who He is, some Jesus, and some the Holy Spirit. But all of them described the three-in-one.

I started talking to Jesus at different times during the trial and asking questions. But Jesus wouldn't answer "Objection, you're speculating," and then He'd smile at me. Then we would both laugh because we know how I am. But when the door closed behind Eric, Jesus was standing beside me. He simply said, "We have work to do." The reason Eric has to leave me and the kids is not only because of the choices he's made, but also to protect me from not having to watch Eric get to the lowest of low, as God unleashes his discipline over Eric. It's gonna be swift, loving, and fierce! He's gonna tear down the strongholds, all his idols, his godlike complex, pride, and selfishness and destroy the very identity he has owned all of his life and build him back up to how God sees him and designed him to be.

I smiled as Jesus walked me out of the courtroom. It was only then I saw all the spectators. There were a few rows of prayer warriors and intercessors. Rows and rows of family and friends cheering me on, embracing me, and yelling, "You go, girl. We're here for you!" But what was most shocking was the front few rows were filled with lukewarm Christians, confused, hurt and lost Christians, and many non-Christians. They assumed Eric got hauled off to jail to be punished, and some even thought he had been taken to the mental ward. But all were watching, and I saw why they were there because when Eric comes out, they will be the first he runs to and tells them all that happened to him; their lives will be changed forever.

Then I am whisked away to a dark, dry barren land filled with thorn bushes, steep scary mountains, deep dark valleys…just an ugly, ugly place; Jesus was leading the way. Sometimes He would walk ahead of me, sometimes beside me. There was no path to follow really. Sometimes I would stumble, got cut up by the thorn bushes, but never stopping. One day, Jesus stopped. He turned me around; I noticed what once was barren and dark was now smooth, straight, and beautiful with lush green trees and a golden street. Off in the distance, I saw a crowd coming, people on crutches, broken, angry, beat-up, and confused. Jesus told me to go to them. Some saw me as the way they feel about themselves. They could relate to me because they too have been hurt. Some saw me the way they see their victims. I talked with rapists, murderers, and adulterers and could show them how they made their victims feel. Then I was able to speak into their lives and show them how God sees them. I would take their hand and lead them down the road and said, "There is Someone I want you to meet. His name is Jesus." At the end of the road, Jesus was standing there with His arms of love and forgiveness wide open; they run to Him. I would turn my back and do the same thing with the next person.

God showed me Romans 12 isn't just something I needed to do as a Christian—it's my life, my calling, and my legacy. I cried tears of joy this morning because I have true understanding of my purpose. My DNA, my fingerprint from God, is living out and paving the way to be Romans 12. Those that call themselves an enemy of God will become His sons and daughters because through my crazy life, He has equipped me to be Romans

> 12. I do not know where Eric is in this journey. But when Eric leaves this house, his story and my story will just have begun.
> To be continued…

I am so proud to be the mother of this beautiful person inside and out!

One of Eric's coworkers, Phil, came to Steph's spring yard sale. He proceeded to tell Steph how she had "little idea of who your husband truly is." Phil told Steph facts about how Eric truly spent after-work hours when he should have gone home to his family. Of course, once Phil learned about Eric's unfaithfulness to Steph, he quit his job and no longer worked for Eric's company. By the end of that summer, Phil asked Steph to go for a motorcycle ride. (Turns out, Steph fulfilled a great caregiving need for Phil, when his daughter later on, suffered a severe head injury from a car accident. However, as the daughter recovered from her injuries, Steph realized their relationship was unraveling.)

Would I still be able to say, "God is good," if my daughter's bloodwork indicated Eric had passed on an STD and her results were "positive?" Would I be able to forgive Eric? Only with God's grace could I ever come close to doing that. However, our Heavenly Father blessed her with a clean, "negative" lab results.

Eventually, Steph reviewed literature on divorces and blended families with her two children. Counselling appointments were made to understand hurtful decisions of hurting parents. I was so proud the day I learned how Steph informed the kids she wanted to start blending families with Phil's family. She said, "What are the three things that need to happen that I told you must occur before you meet the man I plan to date?" Together, Kiersten and Christian answered, "He must love Jesus more than he loves you. Pastor Joe has to approve of him, and he has to be a great dad to his own children."

Christian had the easier time adjusting to Mom's boyfriend; however, Kiersten, after much hard work of processing in her mind that Phil was *not* the cause of their parent's divorce, opened her heart beyond a crack. On Steph's and Eric's anniversary that first year, Steph had totally forgotten about it. The date stood out for Steph, not because of remembering her own anniversary date, but Pastor Joe and his wife's anniversary was on the same date. Her text to me that day read:

> "One year ago today I was devastated, broken and destroyed. Today, I'm walking in forgiveness and couldn't be happier. I recognize the road of healing I've been walking on and how far I have come. God amazes me! I was reminded again how you were there for me and still are, and I just want to thank you a thousand times over for your love and support shown to me. I'm disappointed for my kids, but I know God will restore their hearts as well. God's showing us that we are valued. He *does* in fact redeem and restore. We have a long road ahead of us; but, God is leading the way and showing us where we are weak, He is strong. Thank you again. Love you"

However, as God designed, after much prayer, Steph ended the relationship. With wisdom and discernment, she concluded that Phil needed Steph to be his savior…and she surely cannot! She concluded:

"Mom, it didn't matter how much I loved him or how much Phil loved me. Nothing changed! Only God's love changes people. Someday, I know he'll get it. I hate that I've hurt him; but, I need to move on. In fact, I'm going to buy a cheap wedding band and say I'm married to Jesus," she chuckled. Steph recognized it was time to fully concentrate on her children's needs.

About a month ago, Steph was the recipient of a blind date. Her friend, Anita, hooked her up with her husband's best friend, Nick, who had a huge God encounter (that lasted five months) after his wife walked out. At first, they both resisted…but unbounded love won out!

"Mom, he's my forever. I first fell in love with his heart and how God designed him. His outside is just a bonus. Nick's amazing. He's my match. He owns my heart and can be trusted with it. Nick brings out the best in me." During my last visit to Pennsylvania, I met and approve of the man who stole my daughter's heart…one last and final time! A state trooper, Nick has become a hero in my grandson's, Christian's, eyes. Kiersten is relishing, too, in Nick's love and attention, not only shown to her, but recognizes her mother so deserves to be adored.

Promising to be an open book, Nick beamed whenever he glanced my daughter's way. He boldly confessed to me, "She's like a re-modeled, powerful '67 Mustang priceless possession; the best part is 'under the hood' one cannot see. She makes me melt! Steph brings out my very best…loves me, prays for me, encourages me, and adores my three kids. When we are together alone, I feel like we are the only people on this earth. No more rear-view mirror. Just a big, beautiful, clear windshield in front of us."

Building on their God-centered solid, best-friend foundation, the happy couple has grown leaps and bounds in a few weeks more than Steph and Phil ever did in one year. On April 7, Steph emailed me the following: "God has recently shown me: 'Look where you were two years ago and you thought your world was falling apart. I was already making beauty from ashes from that event.' I told Nick my anniversary date and the date of Eric's infidelity means nothing now. We cried happy tears together. Yesterday was a God-mind-blowing day for us. I just wanted to share this with you because I love you. Thanks for your prayers and supporting us."

No rubbing a lamp to conjure up a genie ever can be desired if you truly plug into your one true Source. Steph's wishes, desires and dreams are God-centered. I am so proud how Steph ("crowned one") has lived a life of grace and has become a much better example to her family than her Mom ever did. Steph, Kiersten, and Christian can eagerly stand on their tiptoes and gaze through the window of their future, anticipating any fork in the road will be an eventual, sure and straight path marked…God's grace.

MY LAST LAST NAME IS GRACE

Thought of the Day

Grace...transforms a life when one touches the hem of His garment. A life that truly encounters Jesus Christ is a transformed life.

Chapter 52

Rochelle and Carl's Journey

> When I said, "My foot is slipping," your love, Oh, Lord, supported me. When anxiety was great within me, your consolation brought joy to my soul.
>
> —Psalms 94:18–19

ROCHELLE'S CHILDHOOD MEMORIES INCLUDE MUCH heartbreak, sadness, and actually being scared of her brother. After all, having her earliest memory be having her brother pull her arm out of joint affected her. Fast forward many years, there were times they enjoyed sitting on the sofa watching an after-school TV program and laughing at the humorous show. Next minute, Darrin would yell at her and tell her to leave the room and go somewhere else. Being the only girl around Darrin and his neighborhood buddies for hours at a time did not help Rochelle either. Where was the mother? She was working or attending college courses and oblivious to what all went on in her household. Steph was an advocate for Rochelle at times, but she did not have the solution Rochelle desperately needed. She was constantly walking on pins and needles around Darrin.

Rochelle was in middle school when Darrin decided to join the Marine Corps. Having gotten her education from war movies on TV or history class, she was terrified for him. Even though they weren't close and barely spoke to one another, she did not want him to join. Then she got an idea. Recently, she had seen a movie about a girl dealing with anorexia. Already dealing with poor body image, she reasoned, "Maybe if I get sick, Darrin won't go." It could be a win-win. So her starvation diet began. Rochelle did not brag about it, but neither did she hide it very well. Thus, after about one week of noticing her not eating lunches at school, her friends told the guidance counselor. But her friend Denise called me before the guidance counselor did.

"Hi, I hate to have to call you. But I don't know what else to do. I don't think I have much of a choice. You know how you give Rochelle lunch money every week? Well, she has not been spending it on lunches. She is not in fact eating at all. I am really worried about her. Do you agree with me she is losing weight and is too thin?" Denise asked. I thanked her for calling me and caring enough to place a phone call to me about Rochelle. I told her I would get a handle on this situation; I assured her over and over again she's done the right thing. Totally shocked and sickened, I knew time was of the essence. My niece had been an anorexic, and I was aware of the danger of this potential deadly trap. Learning to be a nurse, I knew more than most the spiraling trap a teenage girl could be caught in about her self-image, which could lead to devastating results.

By the time Rochelle came home from school, I had a game plan. I got Rochelle's attention and prefaced my conversation by asking, "Do you know what truly good friends do for each other who care for one another? They call their mothers if they see they are on a path of destruction." That got her attention.

Puzzled as to what possible motive Rochelle had for not eating, I asked her point-blank: *why?* Of course—a boy! She explained about liking someone who no longer liked her, and she was hurt (later on, the *real* reason came to light). I knew when I worked the three-to-eleven shift, I would not be available to supervise her meal intake. For the next few minutes, I proceeded to tell Rochelle of my plan: "(1) you *will* buy lunch; in fact, you will write down every day what you ate for lunch for me; (2) every Monday morning, you will report to the school nurse, who will weigh you weekly (which meant I would be placing a phone call shortly to the school nurse); (3) you *will* step on the scale for me every Monday night, and we'll keep a log of the results, and (4) you will thank Denise for being an awesome friend and calling your mother."

Having no choice but to agree, Rochelle told me her starvation diet wasn't truly because of a boyfriend. Rather, she was scared for Darrin and didn't want him joining the marines. Later, Rochelle was sitting on top of the stairs when she overheard me explain everything to Steph and Darrin. Then, adding more fuel to the flame, Darrin's remark: "She's such an idiot. I can't wait to get out of here" devastated her.

Unbeknownst to Rochelle, Darrin's joining the marines was the turning point for the relationship for both of them. The first letter that Darrin sent home from boot camp saddened her. Darrin sounded scared and depressed. The second letter was worse than the first one. Each day the letters arrived in the mail, Rochelle slept in his bed that night and prayed he would just get out of there.

In her words:

> On boot camp graduation day, Darrin looked so much thinner and weaker than the eighteen-year-old muscular soccer player that left home. As soon as the ceremony ended and parents and family were allowed to greet their marine, I ran up to him. He hugged me for the first time ever! To my surprise, it wasn't a blow-off hug but truly a sincere one. Our relationship changed from that point on. Darrin no longer hated me, and I no longer feared him.

Rochelle's after-school job was to work for the local fast-food restaurant within a mile of our home. As with any of these situations, parents have no idea if coworkers will become good or bad influences. One New Year's Eve, Rochelle asked permission to attend an after-work party. She assured me, her friend that I knew and approved of was allowed to go. So I granted permission. Hearing nothing, I believed the evening had been uneventful for her.

After the New Year's Eve party, Rochelle began battling the demon of that night. As annoying as a toothache, the memory was too close to the surface and reared its ugly head too many unexpected times during school, church activities, and whenever. Like everything else, she kept it to herself. One day, tired and weary from losing the battle of forgetting about the memory, Rochelle took one of her Girl Scout mugs, went downstairs to Jeff's bar, and poured some booze into the mug. Out the door to school she went while sipping on her "coffee."

About a month later, I received a shocking phone call at work from Rochelle's high school principal. She was asking me to report to school immediately as an incident occurred that morning involving Rochelle. "What happened?" I asked, mouth gaping. Assuring me that it was serious, and the results will include Rochelle being suspended for a few days, the principal wanted to tell me in person about the event. "The reason you need to come in now is I want you to hear firsthand what Rochelle told me earlier today. You need to hear it from your daughter, not me."

Announcing to my boss why I needed to leave, I drove to Rochelle's high school. The entire five-mile drive had my head spinning. Was she taking drugs? Did she steal something? Did she cheat on a test? I could not begin to fathom what possible choice Rochelle had made in such a big erroneous way. I entered the principal's office, saw Rochelle sitting in a chair, and walked over to give her a big hug. Giving us privacy, the principal left the room.

Rochelle then proceeded to try to explain what did happen the night of the New Year's Eve work party. No, the coworkers were okay and behaved (doesn't underage drinking mean misbehaving?). But a cousin of one of the coworkers came to the house where the party was held. Long story short, at one point, Rochelle went up to the second-floor bathroom. Upon her return trip down the stairs, Ed, the uninvited guest, who was drunk, came up the stairs, proceeded to push Rochelle into one of the bedrooms, and threw her down on the bed. Squirming and yelling, Rochelle attempted to get out from under his tight grip on her. Rochelle too had drunk too much and had little fight in her. Ed was having a hard time unbuckling Rochelle's bib overalls. Due to the loud music, no one heard Rochelle yelling. She did come to at one point and realized she was being sexually assaulted. Somehow, by God's great providence, Rochelle escaped, told her friend she was leaving, and headed home. She was shaken to her core! The assault that occurred was bad enough, but thank God, nothing worse occurred.

Rochelle's same concerned friend, after repeatedly smelling booze on her breath, reported to the principal about the "coffee" brought to school and was hidden in Rochelle's locker. When the principal had Rochelle brought into her office, she learned at that time the sexual assault was the cause for her drinking. Thus, the phone call was placed to me. Having a zero tolerance for drinking alcohol, the principal, though acknowledging the difficult, sad, ineffective purposes for why Rochelle was bringing alcohol to school, she was suspended for one week. There was a small blurb about the incident in the local newspaper.

Rochelle had to report to the local magistrate's office for her sentencing. Being informed as to the cause and effect of Rochelle's decision and being somewhat empathic, the magistrate's sentence was attend four teen AA classes and return for an evaluation. After fulfilling the sentencing, Rochelle once again faced the magistrate. Realizing she was not a typical teenager dealing with true alcoholism and one who did not warrant any further lessons, the magistrate basically scolded her and said that she needed to promise that she would never see Rochelle's face in front of her ever again! Rochelle promised.

Another personal abusive incident occurred in Rochelle's life when she was thirteen years old. The poor girl had another life blow that she had to deal with, which will go unnamed. But she kept it all inside and told no one right away. Later on, when I did find out about the incident, I became her best advocate, as any mother should be, and acted quickly. The New Year's year occurrence, the fourth serious, sad event most likely had Rochelle thinking, as the song lyrics say, "So, wake me up when it's all over." Thankfully,

MY LAST LAST NAME IS GRACE

Rochelle experienced something that has carried her for life. Here is her story:

> I was sixteen years old and was coming out of a bad time in my life. A life of bad choices, drinking secretly, and self-loathing, due to trauma in my life, led to my attending teen AA classes. They showed me *I do not belong* with these types of people.
>
> My mother moved her new boyfriend into our apartment that we had only spent a few weeks in. I was frustrated, upset, and felt like, once again, I could not control my life. While being torn between being the "good girl" I appeared to be and being the miserable my-life-sucks girl in the inside, I had a Visitor that I took for granted way too much at the time. But I can appreciate it now.
>
> In the middle of the night, an extremely bright light filled my bedroom. I woke up, but I could not open my eyes. I kept yelling out, "I can't open my eyes." After about the third time, I heard a voice tell me, "I am watching over you." Right away, I felt extreme peace, and just like that, darkness filled my room. Scanning around the dark room, I was trying to figure out what had just happened. Then I saw an awful monsterlike figure standing outside my bedroom window. But just as soon as I was about to thank Jesus for his visit and being there for me, my focus left Him and went straight to the enemy with a that-figures! attitude.
>
> Of course, the enemy is always there to steal my peace, a feeling I know all too well. Looking back as an adult, I get frustrated with the sixteen-

year-old girl who did not change her life right then. I had seen the light literally, heard from God Himself, and yet I still could not focus on the good but only on the bad. I also find it amazing that the enemy may have been outside my window, but only Jesus could come inside and be by my side! That is what I held on to as a baby Christian, when I was still trying to figure out this whole Christian thing. Yes, the enemy is real, but only Jesus is Almighty!

Isn't God's love amazing? He proves over and over to His children that He does indeed hold them in His righteous right hand. He made His presence known to my feeling-helpless daughter, whose heart was heavy and burdened.

In spite of my hoping, Rochelle did not have great influential neighborhood girlfriends when our family moved into our new home, when I was in nursing school. As she commented recently, when she was the same age as her daughter, Hope, she had been involved in things that today make her skin crawl. She was involved in soccer in high school and, thank God, had better, influential neighborhood girlfriends when we moved into our School Court apartment.

Rochelle fell in love with a cute guy who lived in town named Kenny. Living close, they spent hours together sometimes in group dates and sometimes alone. Kenny fit in quite well with our family. We all grew to love him as well. On occasion, we had opportunity to visit with Kenny's parents, but we did not have much in common with them. Not surprisingly, Kenny asked Rochelle to marry him. She said yes and bought a license plate as a souvenir from Ocean City with beautiful scenery and their combined initials. No wedding date had been set, but we went wedding gown shopping. Rochelle selected the most beautiful sleeveless wedding dress. She looked so lovely in it! We bought it and hung it in her closet waiting for the big day.

One weekend, Rochelle came home from spending the weekend at the shore and announced she and Kenny broke up. "Mom,

I just don't feel as though I love him enough as I should love a husband. He is like a brother or friend to me." Proud that she recognized this serious matter early on, I was glad she broke it off to prevent any divorce down the road. But the next family gathering without Kenny just did not feel the same without him. The wedding gown was moved to a different closet.

Rochelle had no desire to climb any career ladder. Her lofty goal was to be a mother and housewife. Until then, she recognized she needed to get an education to get a decent-paying job. She graduated from Reading Area Community College with a degree in child development. Before long, she was hired by a local day care center as a classroom assistant; the job helped her in raising her own children later on. Children who attended were from all walks of life. I was thrilled that she didn't have too far to drive to work during all types of weather.

One of Rochelle's students named Mindy was a daughter of parents who both took turns picking her up at day care. Thus, it wasn't long before I heard Rochelle discuss this couple's cute daughter and how Mindy was fast becoming one of her favorite students. One Friday night, she told me she was going to be babysitting for Mindy that night. Puzzled, I asked her if that was not against the policy of the day care. Rochelle assured me that she had become friends of both parents, and she was simply doing them a favor so they could have a date night and discuss their crumbling marriage. Shortly after that, I noticed Rochelle received an e-mail from the dad. Again, I questioned her. "Why would one of the dads of your students have your personal e-mail address?" She answered, "They were having marriage problems," and she was "counseling" both husband and wife, attempting to have them see both sides. In summary, I later heard myself saying to my friends when asked, "How did Rochelle meet Carl?" I would sadly answer, "He simply flirted and flirted with her until he got into her (dare I say) panties!"

Carl was ten years older than Rochelle. I didn't mind that she was dating a man who already had a child, but it soon became obvious Carl had some financial problems. If her family can see this, why can't

Rochelle? On their first date, Carl took Rochelle to a local ball game and bought her a drink and a hot dog. I thought nothing of it until I realized no date ever consisted of his taking her out to a nice restaurant of wining and dining her. They did not do fun things together as a couple, like taking walks, sightseeing, or go on road trips. Extra money to properly woo and date Rochelle just was not available.

On Rochelle's birthday on December 21, 2002, I journaled:

> Today Rochelle turns twenty-two. Wow! What a young lady. To celebrate her birthday, we all gathered together. It was the first time Carl and Mindy were in our home. At first, Carl seemed nervous but said he was just tired. We played some card games, and we all seemed comfortable together. Taylor and Mindy played great together also.

Eventually, Carl, filled with nervous energy, instead of playing games or cards, started bringing work payroll sheets with him on the weekends. He explained it was one of his supervisory duties for his job; he worked for a local business that designed countertops. It was during this time, Mike started a new habit of taking long walks Saturday mornings. Why? Seeming comfortable was disappearing for Carl. Plus, Mike had no desire to be in the same room with a guy who was watching trash on TV Saturday mornings. Having little in common, Mike and Carl were civil to each other, but there was an obvious disconnect.

After a short while, Carl divorced his wife using Rochelle's money. He picked an apartment only blocks away from both our home and his daughter and ex-wife's home. Rochelle stayed over most weekends in his apartment. After Rochelle's choice of boy-next-door-type in Kenny, her choice of Carl was confusing to all of us. Of course, Rochelle would be a great stepmom to Mindy, but that was the only positive thing I could see. Our Bible study group started praying mightily for her to see the light before it was too late. Then, one night, she disclosed that she and Carl broke up as he was too controlling. Thrilled our prayers were being answered, I encouraged her to forget about Carl and move on. I told Rochelle I was thrilled that she was noticing the negatives about him. But the breakup did not last long. After wooing her back into his arms, Carl was once again back into our lives and warming Rochelle's heart.

More unsettling concerns came to light when I heard about Carl's being pushy and forceful at times. But Rochelle figured she could soften him once he learned she was totally different from his first wife. Then, one Saturday morning, Rochelle called me hysterical. She had planned a weekend down at the beach with a girlfriend. But Carl didn't want her to go. He was hanging onto the car door, not allowing it to shut in order for her to drive over to her friend's house. Mike was quickly alerted to drive over to Carl's apartment and intervene. Obviously, Carl allowed Rochelle's car door to close, as Mike pulled up, and she drove off. Staying on the phone with her, I could hear the confrontation and yelling that occurred between the two men. It is only by the grace of God Mike walked away without punching the guy. As he got back in his car, Mike yelled some more and told him to forget about Rochelle and leave her alone.

Before I hung up with Rochelle, I told her to have a safe trip down to the beach, and I would see her back home Sunday night. She said she was breaking it off with Carl, and she will indeed plan on sleeping in her own bedroom upon her return. Sunday midnight came; Rochelle still was not home. She had not answered my phone calls. I called some friends of hers, who informed me, yes, the girls returned from the beach, and Rochelle's car was parked at Carl's apartment. No! He wooed her once again with all his sweet talk. Within an hour, we spoke, and I heard from Rochelle, "We talked things out. I'm staying here." Just as her mother earlier, Rochelle did not want to hear what she should have listened to.

Within a few months, Carl was promoted at work and was asked to move to a neighboring county to be a plant supervisor in another facility. Thus, Rochelle and Carl became engaged before shacking up together and moving out of town. But Carl needed to keep his every-other-weekend visitation with Mindy. Twice a month,

Carl and Rochelle stayed overnight in our home. Those weekends consisted of menu planning for me and what agreed-upon activities could be shared during their visits.

Rochelle got a job working for a day care and later on as a part-time church secretary. Having good money sense, Rochelle was the obvious choice to take over managing the household finances and budgeting. She soon found out, however, since Carl earned the bigger paycheck, he thought he should get the final say on how to spend their money, even if it made no sense to Rochelle or she disagreed. For example, bills were piling up, but he decided to purchase a Jet Ski. What do you need in addition to a Jet Ski? A method for hauling it. Rochelle's paid-off car was traded in for a small SUV (attached with car payments) that had a hitch to pull a trailer (more payments) so the Jet Ski could be hauled to the nearby lake. Bless her heart, she attempted to stay within a grocery budget, but she had a hard time, as Carl would spend the money on nonessential items.

Another serious money drainer on their stretched household budget was his love of bowling. He had high aspirations of becoming a professional bowler. In order to pursue such a lofty goal, one needs to spend money traveling weekends to various bowling tournaments. He needed to get his name out there to be known as an aspiring bowler. Tournaments have entrance fees with no guarantee of a cash prize win. Unfortunately, the fees were faithfully paid, but little winning cash was returned to Carl's wallet. Eventually, his dream died, and he started driving down reality road.

My journal entries during this time were sprinkled with frustration, heartache, and eventually, rejoicing. At one point, I asked my friends to bombard Rochelle with cards sent to her work address to encourage her. Late February 2003, during my hysterectomy recuperation, a phone call from Rochelle stressed me out. She called to ask me, since we were leaving for our vacation Friday morning, may she, Carl, and Mindy stay at our house the coming weekend? Apparently, Mindy's mom did not want Mindy staying at Carl's mom's house because she was a heavy smoker; she did not want Mindy around all that smoke.

First, trying to please, I asked "Yes, but why can't you all hang out at Carl's mom's house throughout the day, but then stay overnight at Steph's or your dad's house?" Feeling uncomfortable with my answer without consulting Mike, I put the phone down and asked Mike his thoughts. He said, "No, I don't like the guy. I don't trust the guy, and I certainly don't want him in my house when I'm not here." I told Rochelle, "No, sorry." She started crying, said hurtful things, got angry, and started swearing. I handed the phone back over to Mike. He said, "Don't be angry at your mother." Someone hung up the phone on somebody. Rochelle called back and said, "Fine, if that's how Mike feels about Carl, he's not invited to the wedding." I said, "Fine!" and hung up. Boy, I'm supposed to be recuperating.

For four days, the e-mails and phone calls went back and forth. "On my dime, Rochelle wanted to blast me," Mike commented. It wasn't long until I recognized this was a spiritual battle, and Satan was trying to sow discord in this family. Earlier, a friend sent me an appropriately timed e-mail stressing Satan's wiles. I forwarded it on to Rochelle. Only then did she soften and said, "God will have to fight my battles." Great! But what does that mean for her?

Steph was a big help in trying to intervene and remain a neutral party. God revealed a solution to me. As it ended up, I invited the family over for dinner Saturday night so we could once and for all discuss the matter openly and pray about everything. Long story short, Rochelle was asking me to accept her husband. Because Mike was not a stepdad who openly displayed affection, she had a hard time accepting my husband also. Does not Carl understand Mike paid for some of the wedding expenses and honeymoon? But Mike doesn't deserve to attend the wedding? I'm supposed to attend, be happy for them, and expect my husband to pay for stuff, but not be in attendance?

Then another unexpected event occurred that only added more fuel to the already rising-higher bonfire. Rochelle and Carl's premarriage counselor mailed me a five-page questionnaire about their upcoming marriage. I was very blunt about my feelings about not believing this was the husband whom God had planned for my beautiful daughter. Too many reasons to explain here. But for starters, the fact that Rochelle had to give Carl $1400 out of her savings account so he could file for a divorce from his wife—but the clincher, wait for it, wait for it—at the counselor's insistence "to close up loose ends with your first wife, Carl, you need to file for bankruptcy before mixing banking accounts with Rochelle." Thus, Rochelle emptied out her savings account to pay for Carl's bankruptcy. Downright pathetic! This proof of his sad financial picture only worsened as time went on—the worse is yet to come.

My answers must not have remained confidential, I learned later. I had encouraged their counselor to talk to both of them about how Mike has become the scapegoat and for her to explain that concept to them. I have shed many tears; I felt pulled between my husband and my daughter. My heart ached for the consequences of my own choices. But I trusted the Lord to work it all out, and I began to have peace about it all. Steph, after praying, envisioned it being a happy wedding day for Rochelle. Mike, after praying, sensed there will be no wedding. Then I feared the answer to how is God going to do that? Does something happen to Rochelle? Before I panicked again, I felt God reminding me to let go and let God. Our Bible study group prayed consistently for Rochelle and Carl. There were so many people praying about this situation. I know my Lord has the answer.

God is so good and faithful. The solution came to me through wisdom from above. Little did I know it would come on the day of Rochelle's surprise March bridal shower. Though not really surprised, Rochelle had fifteen people attend her shower, and she received practical gifts for their home. I found out Lorna, my sister, who was a pastor and frequently led premarriage counseling for couples, was planning on attending Rochelle's shower. Thus, I invited Lorna to extend her stay for our long-overdue family discussion. I informed Carl and Rochelle of my plans; they brought along another couple, I guess, for their support. Rochelle and Carl believed they were simply spending the weekend at our home, and it would include a visit from Aunt Lorna.

After the shower ended, we all gathered in our family room, and I started the discussion. I began by trying to explain to Carl why we felt he needed to come and talk to us a long time ago. We needed more time to build trust before he gave Rochelle an engagement ring. Lorna was a big help with this subject. Later, each one of us had an opportunity to express their thoughts. Mike and Rochelle both got a chance to clear the air. About one and a half hours later, we all held hands. Mike purposefully grabbed Rochelle's hand. I started praying when Mike suddenly reached over and gave both Carl and Rochelle a hug. All four of us were crying!

Since we didn't approve of Carl as Rochelle's choice of a husband, Mike and I were adamant we were not paying for most of her wedding. We asked varying friends of their opinion about whether or not we were doing the correct thing and were assured we were. Having her wedding gown already purchased was a plus. I suggested that Rochelle not tell Carl it was a dress purchased for another wedding. But she ended up telling him, and he had no problem with her wearing the gown, since she had not actually worn it.

One weekend, Rochelle and I went to a bridal shop where I purchased several items, such as the cake top, knife, her garter, champagne glasses, and such like. Mike and I paid a week at the Pocono for their honeymoon using our time-share. The reception was to be held in the church's fellowship hall, which was a huge money saver. Though her dad paid for most of the reception, we did assist by paying for the simple, but lovely, table centerpieces.

On April 12, 2003, Rochelle and Carl, assigning cute niece, Taylor, as their flower girl, said their vows to each other. She looked stunning in her gorgeous gown! Of course, Mike attended it with me. Want to know the biggest surprise? Mindy, at age seven, cried hysterically, getting everyone's attention, during their bride and groom dance. "No, Daddy, No!" That's a first! I hoped the marriage counselor finally had her eyes opened to the entire situation on Rochelle's special day. But even if she did, it was a little too late. Carl couldn't calm Mindy down. Only after Rochelle threatened to send Mindy home early with another relative, who was in the process of leaving, did she calm down. Poor Rochelle!

Rochelle's homemade, personalized thank-you note was read by me several weeks later:

> Thank you, Mom and Mike, for helping with our wedding costs. I know it wasn't easy having to support something you don't believe in. But believe us when we tell you that our love is real. Trust in God that he put us together for a reason, even if you don't understand. Mom, we have always been really close, and I know that will never change. I hope I have the same relationship with my kids that I have with you. I just know eventually you both will see Carl as a wonderful person. Thank you for understanding and sharing this day with us. Love, Rochelle and Carl.

The every-other-weekend visits continued in our home with the bride and groom and Mindy. The pattern of Carl completing payroll paperwork and Mike taking his Saturday morning walks continued. Rochelle's plan was to work full-time at her day care until she became pregnant, which occurred within a year of their marriage. She did her best to be the smart money manager. Then, not helping their dire situation, it wasn't long until Rochelle experienced something I never experienced from an employer: her paychecks would bounce, not just once or twice, but three times. Yikes! By the third time, she threatened to call the state regulation board on them. Finally, someone got their act together, and paychecks could be trusted.

On September 19, 2004, I journaled:

> Wow! God has been so gracious and merciful! By now, we are all a happy family of fourteen including Carl, Mindy, and baby Hope…the earlier journal entries seem like a blur….Yes, God

answers prayers. In His wisdom, if Carl needs to be a part of our family, and that helps in getting him saved, I'm honored.

Family members attended Hope's baby dedication at their church. It was comforting knowing that, at least most Sundays, Carl and Rochelle were attending church faithfully. Carl spoke about his being pleased with God and all of his blessings in their lives to the small congregation that morning. He would send our family glowing e-mails stuffed with pride. One would never have suspected the sad conversations between husband and wife behind closed doors. Starting during dating days even, Carl thought nothing of demeaning Rochelle by talking about other women to his friends in front of her. He made comments about how beautiful a waitress was or how nice of a butt she had. Once, he pointed out to a neighbor which window was the bedroom of their neighbor lady. But, without proof, Rochelle fell into denial. Infidelity did cross her mind, but the thought fled out as quickly as it fled in.

By Thanksgiving 2005, Rochelle and Carl's financial situation was becoming dire. Carl's ignorant, impulsive purchases had caused them to have more month at the end of their spent paycheck way too frequently. But a man's gotta do what a man's gotta do. For Carl, his devious mind conjured up a method of making extra cash. He lined up side jobs using his employer's stolen countertops, charged $150 for installation, and pocketed the money. In spite of telling Rochelle the money was being turned in to his boss, she now knows better.

One day, Rochelle called me. "Mom, I was pumping gas in my car when a stranger walked up to me and told me that all four tires of the car are unsafe. He said they were too bald, and he would be concerned if any of his family members were driving around on such unsafe tires that could blow at any moment. I don't have the money to pay for tires." Yikes! Her trips back home are over one hundred miles round-trip each time. Thank you, Mr. Stranger, for speaking up.

Sensing the desperate situation, I told her I would pay for four new tires. But it would be paid directly to the tire supplier. I needed peace of mind for Rochelle's road trips back home, as sometimes Carl did not always accompany them if he attended a bowling tournament. Later, I had to ask Mike for forgiveness for not consulting him first (we had a rule between us, the maximum amount on a purchase without consulting the spouse was $100).

As spiraling water going down a drain, their financial situation was spiraling out of control. Rochelle's good credit was going down the drain. One fall weekend, when Rochelle was pregnant with Talon, we all enjoyed Darrin and Heather's purchase made at their church's Raffle Auction. It was a weekend at a cozy cabin in the Pocono's roomy enough for our family of fourteen. We all made plans to meet for dinner at a restaurant en route to the cabin. Arriving at the restaurant, Rochelle literally dug through the ashtray and around the car for at least a dollar's worth of change to buy Hope chicken nuggets. Steph and I both noticed that Carl did not purchase a meal for himself. But I had no reason to think more about it. "I'm going to just drink the ice tea that is out in the car. I'm not hungry." Rochelle and Hope shared a meal. Steph kindly shared some of her food with Rochelle, leaving more for Hope to be able to eat.

By Saturday afternoon, Steph asked me to come into one of the cabin bedrooms. Rochelle was sitting on the bed looking distraught. Long story short, Rochelle disclosed that they barely could afford the gas it took to make the trip. Plus, they were also short in cash to pay for their dinner last night (she had purchased her share of the groceries for her meal items for the weekend). She confessed she doubted they had enough gas to make it home. My heart broke for her and my granddaughter. How many other times were Rochelle and Hope hungry? Of course, the entire time, Rochelle stressed that Carl can in no way, shape, or form realize that she has opened up truthfully about their dire financial situation to me and Steph. With deep frustration, I came up with a plan; Mike, who agreed, and I would fill each of the children's gas tanks for their trip back home, so Carl would not suspect anything.

At the end of Mike's and my discussion about Rochelle's family's plight, we decided to give Rochelle $1,000 for her December birthday present and again $1,000 for her Christmas present. Mike could only shake his head as he could not fathom such selfish spending on Jet Ski trips and bowling leagues when a pregnant wife fears where her next meal is coming from before each payday. We spent time informing her which bills to pay and again were confident she would make sure it was spent on all necessities, such as heating fuel. However, even though Mike agreed heating fuel was important, he was unhappy about how we kept throwing money and feeding Carl's big hole that he keeps digging for himself. I stressed with Rochelle that we could not keep bailing her out. Without Mike's knowledge, I told Rochelle, "The next time I give you money is to help you and your kids move into an apartment and away from Carl."

Because Rochelle was so scared Carl overheard us discuss their money situation, we had to sneak conversations while in the bathroom or in the empty kitchen. I could tell, Rochelle had a real fear Carl would find out and get really upset with her. Each time I watched their car disappear out of our development, I could only pray for Rochelle and Hope's angels of protection to work overtime. I wish I could have been in the car to be assured Carl had not sensed how Rochelle divulged to her mother about their sad financial situation. With a heavy heart and tears running down my cheeks, I prayed to my heavenly Father to please bring an answer speedily. This was way over my head!

Surprisingly, the next day, Carl called us to say thanks for the $1,000 birthday present we planned to give to Rochelle in December and another $1000 for her Christmas present. He said he really appreciated it and wanted us to know the money would help them to buy a house. Hmmm, buy a house? Right, buddy! At first, when I heard the phone rang, I was so afraid it would be Rochelle calling to tell us how upset she was. Perhaps, Carl had overheard our financial discussion on Thanksgiving? But, I guess, the tide had changed.

Carl's frustrations were not stuffed in his fists that landed on Rochelle, but his emotional abuse was just as painful. Totally disrespecting Rochelle, Carl would sign her name to credit card offers to open new accounts. They routinely spent more money than they earned in spite of Rochelle's common sense about finances; Carl would not listen to her suggestions. At the same time, Rochelle was realizing Carl's methods of making extra money coincided with stealing from his employer. Totally at her wit's end, Rochelle had sought out counseling privately for her crumbling marriage.

As any mother can relate to, the more your emotions are heightened due to stress in an unhappy marriage, the tougher it is to keep them at bay and not take it out on the kids. Thank God, Steph was a great sounding board for her. One early January day, Rochelle called Steph and asked if she and the kids could come down, as she was "getting so depressed, and I do not want to take it out on the kids." She decided she would stay with Carl until their income tax refund arrived so she could assure the money went to pay bills. As most friends do, Rochelle confided in one of her friends about their crumbling marriage. The "friend" betrayed Rochelle and told Carl the things she shared in confidence. Needless to say, Carl and Rochelle got in a huge (and their final) fight.

Since Talon was less than two years old, Rochelle, once separated, struggled with the thought of young Talon and Hope staying at their dad's house every other weekend. Talon had not spent one night alone without his mother ever. Earlier that week, Rochelle had attended her MOPS (Mothers of Preschool) class at her local church. The guest speaker's topic was about abuse. The speaker handed out a picture of a wheel that had various forms of abuse on each spoke. Rochelle checked off all areas but two on the wheel. After the session, she walked up to the guest speaker and showed her her wheel. Wisely, she advised Rochelle to make plans to remove herself and her children out of the hostile environment immediately.

Her final confirmation came in the form of Carl's night out with the guys. A good friend of Rochelle's happened to be in the same restaurant where Carl was having dinner with another woman. She telephoned Rochelle immediately. Upon his return back home and being confronted, Carl told Rochelle that she was just a friend; in fact, she is a lesbian. Rochelle put her escape plan in action immediately.

I was informed about Rochelle's wise decision when I came home from my Bible study. Mike asked, "Are you able to give your work short notice on calling off tomorrow? Your daughter wants you to go up with a moving van and pick her and the kids up." Yes! I'll be more than happy to pay for an apartment, and Mike wholeheartedly agrees.

Getting caught up to date by Steph, I found out about the huge fight and worried that Rochelle would not be safe for one more night; it seemed Carl's temper had worsened severely. Due to guilt? I called Rochelle, and she said she would call 911 if she felt she was in any danger during her last night of sleeping under his roof. Obviously, many prayers went heavenward that night on behalf of Rochelle, Hope, and Talon. Steph adjusted her schedule also. As soon as the moving van business opened, we rented a U-Haul truck. Mike drove the truck, while Steph followed in her van, which was used to haul items Rochelle did not want packed in the moving van.

Rochelle was so relieved to see and have us, her support team, around her. Carl had gone to work just as he had usually done; he suspected nothing. But just in case he would decide to stop by their house during his lunch hour, we wanted to be packed and on our way to Lancaster County. A phone call was made to the local Denver Storage Company to rent a storage unit. The plan was for Rochelle and her two children to move in with Mike and me until she found an apartment.

By 1:00 p.m., the U-Haul was loaded with selected items Rochelle believed she would need. Just as with her mother's moving out, Rochelle knew she had one opportunity to take what she needed this time around. On the way home, Carl called Rochelle. She handed the phone directly over to Hope. "Yep, Daddy, we all moved out. No, Mommy doesn't want to talk to you right now." After Hope finished the conversation with her dad, Rochelle hung up the phone. Carl tried calling Rochelle five more times then finally stopped calling since she hadn't answered the phone.

Two things occurred that put some stress on my marriage. Mike had wanted me to call John and ask if he would contribute some money toward getting Rochelle an apartment or grocery money until Domestic Relations would be consistent with routine child support payments. I tried to explain, daughter or not, John did not believe in divorce and would not give her money to move out from her husband. Secondly, Mike, who is a neat freak and likes things in order around the house, had to adjust to three people, including two youngsters having toys around, extra dishes in the sink, and simply more clutter. I was in my glory. Our household needed some shaking up besides the same two people rattling around in it. As with typical blended households, we came up with a few house rules, and Mike began to relax. Ten days later, Rochelle, Hope, and Talon moved out and into their apartment, which was a duplex along Main Street in the same town we had lived in earlier. All three of my kids and six grandkids were finally within four miles of our home!

The next summer, our family vacationed at Williamsburg. Introduced by her older sister, Rochelle met Duane, the love of her life. Steph drove her kids and Rochelle and her two kids down in her van. Steph's friend, Duane, was often calling to chitchat with her during their long drive. Duane and his son, Alex, were vacationing in Maine. At one point, Steph, who was busy driving, asked Rochelle to talk to Duane, whom she met recently at an event with Steph. So she did. She knew Duane was divorced and also ten years older than her. By the end of that week's summer vacation, Duane and Rochelle spent many hours on the phone. A friendship formed—and soon true love. Duane also was raised Mennonite and had left to attend a different church. A firm foundation of both having Mennonite beliefs in their background was beneficial.

By the last day of our vacation, Rochelle said she and Duane were planning on going out to dinner the following weekend. "Mom, we are going to put all our crap on the table…crap about our exes and all that stuff. If we think we can deal with each other's crap, we are going to start dating." Wow! That is the exact opposite of what Dr. Phil advises divorcees when starting to date.

Over candlelight dinner, the couple poured out their heart and soul and left nothing hidden. Duane's divorce was no fault of his own, as his wife decided she liked the same sex better. Rochelle admitted to marrying the wrong guy and was now paying the price. She was on the path of growing in the Lord, being an awesome mom to her two children, and rebuilding her credit score. Through Steph, Duane was aware that our family was close and an important part of her life.

Having the same weekend without children led to spending many hours together learning to know each other and confirming how realistic a future together could be. Unlike me, Rochelle did it correctly. She waited to introduce her children to Duane until she felt they could handle it. Duane protected Alex, also, from his dating until he felt it was the right timing. Eventually, it was obvious the family blended well. I was vacationing in Disney World the day my cell phone rang. Rochelle excitedly told me that she was engaged. She had walked into his house the prior evening and discovered both Alex and Duane on their knees, saying in unison, "Rochelle, will you marry us?" How thoughtful is that? You go, Duane!

After a two-week engagement, they got married with all three kids acting as their bridal party in a nearby county in a cute white chapel Rochelle noticed sometime earlier. She tucked away the thought of it being a great place to get married in some time. Today was the day! Atypical, all five "honeymooned" together in North Carolina during our summer vacation. Rochelle and Duane labeled it honeymoon when they celebrated their third anniversary alone in Punta Cana.

Someday, Rochelle will explain to her children when they would be old enough to comprehend her choices. She would have them grasp the decision to leave their father was not meant as a cruel self-indulgence geared to make them unhappy. Rather, it was a necessary act of love for an improved life for them. Both she and her children now taste morsels of the food of angels, with Duane as a wonderful husband and stepdad. Duane is a wonderful spiritual head of their home and recognizes potential conflicts; he allows Rochelle to discipline her own children. In sharp contrast, Duane has great money sense and fully entrusts Rochelle with the family checkbook. He became a sanctuary for her; she can lean in and trust him completely.

Today, Duane and Rochelle attend the Worship Center, a source for her too of learning about God's grace. In summary, the Lord gave her a fresh understanding of Himself. She has been through a lot, but she indeed proved she is a rock.

A cherished Mother's Day card from Rochelle to me reads:

> Thanks, Mom, for caring and praying…I know you used to pray for me…how much, I have no clue. But I turned out okay, I think, thanks to the Lord and you. And even though I'm all grown up, I'm very much aware that you still try to keep me safe with tender loving prayer. Happy Mother's Day. Love, Rochelle.

Thought of the Day

Grace renews us to live in the fullness of Jesus Christ now as we envision paradise before us.

Chapter 53

Semper Fi Power Wash Inc.

You then, my son, be strong in the grace that is in Christ Jesus.
—2 Timothy 2:1

UNLIKE HIS SISTER WHO ALWAYS had a boyfriend, Darrin could have cared less about having a girlfriend. Of course, as with any new kid coming into a different school, he had several seventh-grade girls glance his way. I answered the phone only once when a girl was calling for Darrin; it was simply to invite him to someone's birthday party. To my delight, a group of Darrin's friends, made up of about six guys and four girls, by high school started hanging out together after school and on weekends. They were nicknamed the Koffee Kult and could be seen frequenting the local truck stop having coffee and eating meals together. Only two of the group members made up an actual dating couple. The remaining group members became close friends. Heather, Darrin's future wife, was part of the Koffee Kult. Thus, Darrin had many opportunities to hang out with her, learned to know her well, and came to understand what made Heather tick.

Darrin invited Heather to be his date for their senior prom. What a lovely couple they made posing for pictures, standing around my sparkling-clean, maroon-colored Ford Probe. More pictures were taken of the Koffee Kult members on our front porch and lawn. I encouraged Darrin to give Heather a kiss at the end of the evening because I could tell she was smitten by him, whether he realized it or not. Later, I asked him, "Did you kiss Heather?" "No, Mom. We are just friends," he answered. "You disappointed her, I'm sure," I said.

Reaching the great milestone, Darrin, Heather, and his Cocalico classmates participated in their graduation ceremonies on a beautiful June summer evening. New roads were waiting to be forged. Heather's wise parents suggested an alternative to the typical senior class trip. They were willing to book a beach house large enough for the Koffee Kult gang in the Outer Banks after graduation. Thus, Darrin's share of expenses was paid by us as his graduation present. What great memories were made that week! Darrin's heart was softening toward Heather; unfortunately, Darrin's attention must have been a little too late. Heather decided to go back to dating a previous boyfriend. By week's end, they realized each member of the Koffee Kult would soon be spreading out in different parts of the country as they started college, joined the armed forces, or began new employment in the fall.

Darrin headed off to Parris Island for boot camp, finished his training there, as written about earlier, and was assigned additional training for his military occupational specialty (MOS) in Meridian, Mississippi. While stationed there, he received training to become an aviation operations specialist. Over Christmas holiday, Darrin came home for two months and worked for the local recruiting office as a recruiter assistant. During this time, Darrin and Heather became a dating couple, and eventually their love blossomed. New Year's Eve (or should I say, early morning hours of New Year's Day), I heard Darrin's knock on my bedroom door. "Mom, are you awake?" "I am now," I answered. He walked over to my side of the bed and knelt down. "I kissed her, Mom. I kissed Heather tonight," he excitedly said. "Good! In her mind, it has been long overdue," I commented, laughing.

One weekend, several privates drove over to New Orleans for Mardi Gras. Whoa! What an experience for this nineteen-year-old country boy. Having a girlfriend back home waiting for him, I hope, had kept him behaving somewhat. For the return trip back to Mississippi, Darrin needed to fly out of Atlanta airport. Due to a severe snowstorm, his flight was canceled. While Darrin, using his duffel bag as a pillow, was catching up on some missed *zzzzz*'s on an airport bench, a local TV crew videoed this oblivious marine snoozing. It was broadcasted, I learned, during the news in the Atlanta area.

The romance blossomed from a school classmate to a fiancé over the next two years. Though he was not supposed to drive the distance to Pennsylvania on the weekends, Darrin broke the rules. His '96 silver Mitsubishi racked up high mileage, and his checkbook lessened in dollar amounts paying for speeding tickets. I realized driving home was illegal and against the rules, but young people in love are motivated to drive hundreds of miles on a Friday night after work and return late on a Sunday night. Love trumps rules.

One weekend the following summer, Heather and Darrin both came to see me at my job. *Hmm, this is a nice surprise!* Assuming Darrin was simply stopping by to see me at work before heading back to Jacksonville, I took a brief time to hug him good-bye. Darrin asked if we could go into a more private setting. "Mom, I have asked Heather to marry me. We're getting married next February," he said excitedly. Proudly displaying her sparkling ring, Heather was grinning from ear to ear. "But, Darrin, you know how I feel about being married too young. I always said you kids have to wait until you are thirty, remember? Can't you wait until you are at least discharged from the marines?" Knowing I was joking about his waiting until he was thirty to marry, he convinced me he was so lonely and wanted Heather down there with him to finish out his remaining two years. Besides, the driving back and forth was not wise. In fact, he sold his more-expensive Mitsubishi and traded it in for a cheaper car payment on a Honda Civic, as advised by his staff sergeant.

The months flew by, and in his absence, Heather planned a beautiful wedding. Her parents seemed down-to-earth and taught Heather how to be a hard worker. In February, Darrin and Heather exchanged married vows (lasting twenty years and counting). Darrin was deployed by September for his six-month float onboard an aircraft carrier in the Mediterranean as part of the Twenty-Fourth

Marine Expedition Unit in the Atlantic Theater. During their six-month separation, Heather chose to move back to Pennsylvania temporarily. She missed Darrin so much. Her Christmas gift that year from both sets of parents was to pay for her flight to Italy to visit Darrin, which she so appreciated. Their seven days together ended much too abruptly.

Exciting opportunities opened up for this young marine. He hit various ports in Greece, Egypt, Israel, Italy, Romania, and Spain. Some of Darrin's productive downtime on the float was spent studying for a bachelor's of science degree in business management. It is a toss-up whether or not more bad habits were picked up by this young Lancaster County boy than good ones. Smoking, playing poker for money, and swearing became a way of life. Let's just say, what happened on the float, stayed on the float, and it is good Mom does not know it all! Only someone serving their country can understand the anxiety of living on an aircraft carrier for six months near enemy waters. At one point, near the end of their deployment, due to Saddam Hussein not cooperating with weapon inspections, his unit was afraid they would need to extend their deployment. As God would have it, they were relieved of their duties on schedule. Darrin had an uneventful excursion, and his six months passed by quickly; he was soon back on American soil, reunited with his wife, and on to his next assignment.

While living in New River near Jacksonville, North Carolina, Heather attended college to earn a degree to become a paralegal. Our first granddaughter, Taylor, was born during their last leg of serving the Marine Corps. After Darrin's four years of serving in the marines ended, he moved his wife and baby daughter back into Lancaster County. The next step was to find a job to support his family. At first, Darrin was hired by a local car dealer as a bookkeeper and, later on, by an insurance company as an information technology (IT) assistant; neither job worked out for him. Darrin felt his promised on-the-job training never materialized. Frustrated also about not finding his niche he enjoyed in his new civilian life, he gave his two-week notice.

MY LAST LAST NAME IS GRACE

Knowing his brother-in-law, Eric, was a manager for a power wash company in a nearby county, Darrin decided to work for him. After all, he needed a full-time job *now!* Within months of being employed, a desire had begun to stir in his heart. Observing the operations of this power wash company, Darrin decided he should be able to start his own business in Lancaster County. How difficult can it be? Using the knowledge he learned while working toward his bachelor's degree, Darrin started putting his dream on paper and devised an awesome business plan. He spent quite some time discussing his goals with his marine buddy, Dwight. The two of them decided to start a business together, with Darrin having slightly more control in the overall partnership.

One night at twenty-two years of age, Darrin stopped by our home to inform Mike and me of his starting a power wash company. After hearing about his lofty goals, I commented he reminded me of his uncle, who owned a huge grocery store and smorgasbord. "You might as well work for yourself and be your own boss," I told him. After spending hours devising a business plan, Darrin made an appointment and presented it enthusiastically to the local bank loan officer. "I have never seen such an impressive business plan from a twenty-two-year-old," the loan officer commented to Darrin.

After signing the loan, Darrin read manuals on power washing companies and attended seminars to learn about his competition. He and Dwight came up with a company name and logo: Semper Fi Power Wash. A bulldog, the Marine Corps mascot, holding a pressure washer wand (instead of a gun) was painted on the side of the white company vans. Day one of business for Semper Fi Power Wash began and continued for over fifteen years before he sold it to another relative. In fact, today, another business has branched off from Darrin's business and continues to support about a dozen families. Darrin's focus was mainly servicing restaurant's kitchen exhaust systems to satisfy state regulations on fire safety. Crews were established to service several states. It wasn't long before Darrin saw the need for devising a cleaning system for kitchen exhaust filters. His inquisitive mind aided him in solving the problem. He designed his own soaking tank and filter wash room system.

Semper Fi has given employment to both his sisters and other relatives. I tease Steph and Rochelle "it must be great to go to work in sweatshirts and to be able to work for your brother's business." Most times, they agree. As with all small businesses, the growing pains of being in business with a partner, learning the ropes, choosing a trustworthy, affordable accountant, and growing into a profitable business kept Darrin focused. Unlike his workaholic brother-in-law, Darrin's crews' work schedule was Monday night through Thursday night. Friday could be devoted to improve his golf swing.

By July 2003, a second daughter, Madison Grace, was born into the Weaver household. Taylor became the proud big sister and, to this day, is a great role model for her. After moving twice before landing in their new, lovely big home, the Weaver's address always remained in the Cocalico School District, my childhood one. Eventually, two family pets joined the bustling household also.

Being a visionary, Darrin knew it was wise to finish his bachelor's degree; thus, Albright College was chosen as the institution to do just that. With great relief, Darrin finished his last course for his final credits by December 2007. Realizing Darrin now had his degree, a prerequisite, one of his high school friends encouraged him to consider officer candidate school (OCS), as he had done, to become an officer. With Heather's blessing, he started his officer training and excelled in both physical fitness and leadership. Once again, his wife, two daughters, and other family members were honored to be part of yet another graduation for Darrin when he graduated September 2012 as a second lieutenant of the US Army. After eighteen months, in March of 2014, he became a first lieutenant while working for the 131st Transportation Company in Williamstown, Pennsylvania.

Darrin devoted one weekend a month to the Army National Guard and two weeks every summer on training assignments. The most nerve-racking for me, since his float deployment, was when I learned Darrin would be driving a semitractor trailer as part of an army convoy from Wyoming to Philadelphia area. After the briefest tractor trailer training in history, he and a convoy commander, without incident, drove over 1,800 miles. I was so glad when he had arrived safely back home.

To meet his goals, Darrin realized a captain-type job is required to move up his career ladder. By January 2016, he was assigned as commander of headquarters company, 728th Combat Service Support Battalion. Today, Darrin is employed by a contracting command within the Department of the Navy, which purchases supplies for our navy's submarines. His goal at the end of twenty years of serving Uncle Sam is to be commissioned Major Darrin Weaver and to become a contract officer.

The best hope I have of which one of my three children will most likely move down to the South is Darrin and Heather. She has always loved the beach and remembers the difference between North Carolina and Pennsylvania winters. An expected goal is to move back down in the South when Madison is sent off to college. May returning back to the South bring them full circle from where their journey began, give them more exciting experiences, a true sense of accomplishment, and ongoing happiness for the two members of the Koffee Kult.

Today, the Semper Fi white vans with the picture of a bulldog holding a pressure washer wand no longer cruise along highways. The sixteen-year-old mapped out his life and is now plodding along happily married, raising two beautiful daughters, and is moving up through the ranks from Marine Corps recruit to, hopefully, major with the Army National Guard.

Thought of the Day

Grace is needed in special ways for every calling; some require extra grace.

Chapter 54

"Dearest Daddy"

The Spirit helps us in our weakness. We do not know what we ought to pray for, but the Spirit himself intercedes for us with groans that words cannot express. And He who searches our hearts knows the mind of the Spirit, because the Spirit intercedes for the saints in accordance with God's will.

—Romans 8:26–27

Parents' 45th anniversary picture

THE FOLLOWING IS A LETTER that I wrote to Daddy on January 30, 2001, and inserted it inside a card. He was battling the last stages of multiple myeloma. Because I was a daughter he was so unhappy with about with all my choices, I wanted to write down my feelings and thoughts that had to be said. He passed away on March 10, 2001.

> Dearest Daddy,
>
> I wanted to send you a card, but it was kind of tough finding one that says, "So the Doctor Gave Up on You." So here is one that I thought conveyed what I wanted to say—to accept what you cannot change and know that God loves us, every one, very dearly.
>
> Since I'm an RN and work in a nursing home and am around death and dying, I thought you might wonder about this process. Just because you are prepared to die and are ready to meet your Maker doesn't mean that you might not have some questions. After all, folks that have gone on before cannot come back and tell us about it. It doesn't mean that you can't feel frightened or don't want to be alone (if I am way off base here and you don't have questions, I apologize).
>
> As you already were told by Dr. Kane, you most likely will die in your sleep. The medical term is an "unresponsive state." Dying is not all that much, unlike birthing. I believe just as the baby in the womb stops wiggling and settles into the birth position and prepares for some work ahead of him/her, passing over onto the Other Side is similar. The tired, weak body stops all its "wiggling," tired body parts take a rest, and unlike a birth, the hard work is over, except for the heart beating and lungs expanding. Lesser important functions stop working up to par. Similar to varying births, the process is in stages and goes

more smoothly for some more than others with individually varying lengths of time in each stage.

Most importantly, to be kept pain-free is the key. Death need not be a painful experience. I know that this is hospice's plan as well, and I will personally see to it that *is* followed through for you. Of the many deaths I have witnessed, most were peaceful and smooth. I am sure not one would want the choice of coming back (if I could ask them) once they have seen those many angels lined up at the pearly gates. Once you see Grandma and Grandpa Martin and Grandma and Grandpa Fisher and Jill (now I'm crying) and Lee (who drowned), and Mom's, Lenora's, and my miscarriaged souls (among many unmentioned others already in heaven), you will probably feel sorry for those of us left behind. That's how awesome I picture this sacred time!

To stand at a resident's bedside when they take their last breath is truly an inspirational moment. I cannot help but be in awe imagining what is occurring for that person. Reverently realizing how God has designed the cycle of life, I am touched that He has given me the gift and opportunity to work in a nursing home (little did I know when I took the nursing oath eight years ago that this is where God would place me). I also take this opportunity to pray. It usually is an emotional time just trying to picture myself meeting my Lord and Savior face-to-face too. I imagine meeting my best friend with my arms outstretched and with a big smile on my face, watching Him waving me into His home at this last leg of life.

MY LAST LAST NAME IS GRACE

Praise God, we can know of an assured salvation! How difficult to picture someone on their deathbed without that hope! Since it is emotional for me when my residents die, I am trying to anticipate how much more emotional it will be with a loved one like you, Daddy. As the scriptures promise, we can know that we *will* see our loved ones again. It is with that hope, promise, and faith that your family, Mom and all us kids, will be ever so reverently singing hymns, possibly, as we gather around your deathbed. It is with this same hope and promise, rest assured, that we will help Mom, comfort her, and attend to her needs (of course, all the while speaking highly of you). You *know* how much Mom adores you. Until it is her turn to reunite with you, we will take good care of her; no worries there.

Death is a time for reflection, and I have so many good memories to reflect on. Another dream I have, once we are all in heaven and our hardworking days are over, is one where we will sit around and talk about happy times. As I reflect on my childhood and my adulthood, there were happy times, and there were sad times. Luckily, there were more happy times than sad times. I thank God for the Christian home and values in which you and Mom raised us. That is a priceless eternal gift! There are so many good memories of weekends at the mountains with that huge cabin gang…the trip to Bushkill Falls…weekly Hinkletown visits to the country store for ice cream…your taking me ice-skating at Nancy's house while you went fox hunting with her dad.

You taught me how to tithe and how to be a hard worker (I'm one of a few employees who has called off work only twice in eight years)...how to turn off the power before you put gas in a lawn mower (remember when I did that?)...you taught me that men are to respect their wives, so much so that you hired *two* maids for Mom following childbirth...one maid to personally take care of her needs, and the other maid to look after the remaining little ones...Why do you think I had such high expectations for my husband?...and then was hurt deeply when I thought he wasn't measuring up as to what I saw a model husband should be? (but that requires another letter for another time).

You taught me having devotions are important (I can still hear Mom reading the Bible to you through your closed bedroom door each night)...you taught me that you dare make decisions or choices separately from your parents (Oh, I will never forget sitting behind a horse's butt in Grandma and Grandpa Martin's buggy when I was about six years old)....you taught us that we did *not* gossip and to have the preacher for lunch...you taught me that feeling sexy is something fun...a natural expression and not something to be tabooed...you taught me that fathers get up in the dark and go to work and many times come home in the dark...you taught me that certain foods are only for Daddy's lunch ("you kids keep your hands off")...you taught me that not every extended family member is of our choosing, but you go with the flow...you taught me to appreciate reading, as you enjoyed your *PA Game News*, the newspaper, etc....you taught me it is okay to settle for average...it doesn't have to be the best, but you should not settle for the cheapest....save up the cash then buy it.

You taught me going to church other than Sunday mornings is important...you taught me to appreciate 5th Avenue candy bars...you taught me in some things, it is okay to spoil your husband shamelessly...you taught me that a daddy is the head of a home, and you can feel safe when he is home...this is just a sampling...it would take pages to list them all....Oh, yes, thank you, thank you, for allowing me to be the first kid to graduate!

Being your daughter, you gave me the gift of...a sense of humor...the love of music of various kinds (I can still see you walking through the house singing with your hands waving in the air like a chorister)...you gave me the gift of a smart mind...you two gave me the gift of having high self-esteem...the gift to know who I am and am to be proud of it...the gift of so-so good looks...(Mike likes my legs...I say..."look at my seventy-plus-year-old mother's legs")...the gift of confidence....gift of competition...isn't that what makes a good Haas or checkers game?...the gift of trying something, and if it doesn't work....move on....(I remember how you tried the supervisory position, but you did not like it and weren't too proud to say so)...the gift of appreciating a hard-earned dollar...the gift of independence for your wife (I remember very well all the times Mom made independent decisions apart from you)...the gift of having a trusting husband, who turned over his paycheck to a trustworthy wife, who treated it with respect and its hard-earned efforts...the gift of knowing that there may be times in your spiritual walk when you figuratively may wrestle with the angel of Jacob and cry out as he has done; but you are not letting go until you are blessed and satisfied…again…this is just a sampling.

So thank you from the bottom of my heart, Mom and Daddy, for what you have done for each one of your children. How can I not close without repeating that saying…which says it all…"There are Martins…and then there are those that wish they were Martins"…for all that that could possibly mean…I thank you.

I know one thing though that Martin's are *not*…is a touchy, "feely" family. But I wanted to share with you two of my feelings and hope you can appreciate how proud I am to be your daughter (more tears flowing). I know that there were times that you were ashamed of me, were hurt deeply by my choices, and, Daddy, you probably wanted to take me over your knee! But you must know that, just as on your own journey of life, sometimes you made wrong choices, you have had to reap what you sow, or needed the opportunity to start fresh.

Parents are to raise their children to become a free butterfly…to be able to stand on their own two feet…and no two persons' journey is the same. Life is lessons, and some of us have to learn some things the hard way. But God's fresh and new promises are always around the next bend in the road. God can make lemonade, when lemons are in front of His children. It is Satan that fills the mental institutions of many religious people who are depressed and insane because they cannot get beyond the lesson in front of them…they don't see that refreshing, offered cup of lemonade God is handing to them. I praise God every day that He is a God of forgiveness of second, third, fourth, fifth…beyond seventy-seven times seven…just as the sun arises and sets every morning and every night, His mercy is fresh and new and everlasting!

Well, I need to reach for the tissues again and blow my nose. I love you very much and will miss you when you're gone. Here's to your experience of going on first to the Other Side, and in the meantime, being one of my angels of protection…as you also will be to Mom as well.

Peace,
Leanne

Not one word was ever mentioned about my letter from either Mom or Daddy. I do realize that they were coping with a grave situation for six weeks. It was *not* about *me*.

Thought of the Day

Grace is falling back to sleep when howling winds, severe storms, and pounding rains are surrounding me. Have you heard the story about the little girl who asked the porter, "Is my daddy on deck? Good, I can sleep now." We can also rest in our Father's arms. He's got this.

Chapter 55

Daddy's Death

When I saw him, I fell at his feet as though dead. Then he placed his right hand on me and said: "Do not be afraid. I am the First and the Last. I am the Living One; I was dead, and behold I am alive for ever and ever! And I hold the keys of death and Hades.
—Revelation 1:17–18

I WAS AWARE DADDY HAD written down his funeral arrangements in advance and scripture verses for the officiating ministers. But I was not aware of its contents. During a time of grieving for Daddy at his funeral, while sitting in the same church I attended and was forced to listen to many scoldings about proper dress code, expected behaviors, holy living, and hell-and-brimstone sermons, I once again had to hear from the same pulpit about the sins of divorce. Seriously, Daddy? Your final scolding to me needs to be during your funeral service?

As tears streamed down my face, the only consolation I had was being confident Daddy—by now had a full understanding of God's grace. Daddy was walking the streets of gold and holding the hand of the Man who stilled the water. He knows he was wrong. God's grace *does* trump all my sins!

During Daddy's illness, he and mother had plenty of time to write down his wishes for both his upcoming funeral and graveside services. To make it easier for the ministers, Daddy had written down his choice of ministers, the hymn selections, and scripture verses to be read. Excerpts are listed below (with interesting tidbits highlighted, which made me smile):

> Preach to the living…life is short…Isaiah 40:6–8, James 4:13–16…assurance of salvation…John 3:16…Romans 10:9…Blessed is a cheerful giver…2 Corinthians 9:7…Malachi 3:7–12…no escape…John 5:28–29…1 Thessalonians 5:2–8…Revelations 20:11–15…Romans 14:11–13…Remember the Sabbath Day…Exodus 20:8–10…read "Abide With Me" hymnal page 441…sing hymnal 496…graveside scripture: John 14:1–6…(for the mortician): request white shirt, dark pants, no suit coat (*coat is not needed to sleep*), no tent if not raining, congregational singing only, no music at viewing, no flowers…" (In my mother's handwriting): "…I want them to kneel for prayer for those who can…*no pallbearers wearing neckties…not to "paint" me up to look like a live person…no wig if I lose my hair…*"
>
> Concerns (for sermon content): the drift (meaning falling away) I saw over the last fifty years…also for the unsaved, *divorced and remarried.* PS: I was not a perfect father. Where you see I done good, do the same. Where you see I have failed, do better(signed).

Sermon content, as listed above, was obviously the most important topics on Daddy's mind. This was his last chance to have them shared with his family. What topics would I choose if I were to do the same for my family and officiating minister?

Daddy died March 10, 2001, approximately 8:45 p.m., with all nine of his quiver-full of kids and Mom by his side. Helping me to deal with Daddy's death, I started journaling my experience three days before his death. His story begins: Daddy was diagnosed with multiple myeloma, November 1996, when he showed signs and symptoms of something being seriously wrong: dizziness, messed-up equilibrium, falling down, chest and rib cage pain, and "tingling going up my legs." As explained on WebMD, multiple myeloma is a cancer that affects plasma cells, a kind of white blood cell found in the soft inside of your bones, called marrow. Plasma cells are part of your body's immune system. They make antibodies help fight off infections. There is no cure for multiple myeloma, but treatment can often help you feel better and live longer. With this type of cancer, your plasma cells multiply and grow out of control. They crowd out healthy cells, including red and white blood cells and those that keep bones strong. Over time, plasma cells spill out of your bone marrow and travel to other parts of your body, which can damage your organs....You may not notice any symptoms until the cancer is advanced, meaning it has spread inside your body." (http://www.webmd.com/cancer/multiple-myeloma-symptoms-causes-treatment#1).

While doing my own research, I learned that this type of bone marrow cancer appears in people employed in poor environmental situations, such as a stone quarry, where Daddy worked for over thirty years.

Daddy had a bad cough earlier that fall; he blamed his chest and rib cage pain from coughing too much. He decided to make an appointment to see his primary physician, who sent him home with an order for an antibiotic for his "ear infection" (an X-ray had shown he had in fact broken some ribs from coughing). On Saturday, while in the garage, Daddy started experiencing equilibrium problems and had fallen down, but he had not told Mom. That night, Daddy realized something was very wrong when he could not get out of bed; he called Doug. About 10:00 p.m., after retrieving his messages, Doug went to check on him. Speaking in Pennsylvania Dutch, Daddy told Doug something was very wrong with his legs, and he could not get out of bed.

An ambulance was summoned via 911. The ambulance crew's assessment revealed something was very seriously wrong and transported Daddy to Ephrata Hospital. The emergency room (ER) physician conducted a neurological assessment using a pin. Doug watched the doctor prick Daddy, starting at both his feet and legs, moving up to his calves, above his knees, and onto his abdomen. Only at the level of his chest did Daddy respond "Ouch!" to the pinprick. The ER physician informed Mom and Doug indeed this was a grave situation. Recognizing his assessment results were beyond the expertise of the Ephrata Hospital staff, the ER physician recommended Daddy be transported onto Lancaster General Hospital's trauma unit, which was about twenty minutes away.

I will never forget receiving the shocking phone call at work from Jeff that Sunday morning informing me Daddy was "a paraplegic and at Lancaster General Hospital facing emergency surgery!" What? My healthy, hardly-ever-sick Daddy is now a paraplegic? What is causing that? My stomach lurched as I hurried out the door.

Most of my siblings traveled from various counties of Pennsylvania and reached Lancaster General Hospital by midday. We were all anxiously awaiting the surgeon's report. We took turns assuring Mom to be hopeful and optimistic for a good outcome. We learned an MRI revealed Daddy had five multiple myeloma spots throughout his body: forehead, ribs, both legs, and his spinal cord. His ribs were the primary site. The secondary site was his spinal cord, where a tumor had encapsulated around it. As the tumor was growing, it was paralyzing him from his feet up. That was exactly what Daddy expressed to Mom and Doug earlier when he could not get out of bed and realized something was horribly wrong. He said, "I can feel tingling going up my legs."

After several hours of anxiously waiting for Daddy's emergency surgery outcome, we were finally updated by the neurosurgeon, Dr. Lambeck. Then the "both good and bad news" update landed on us. Dr. Lambeck reported he was able to remove most of the spinal cord tumor. The neurosurgeon believed Daddy would benefit greatly from physical therapy. Then the bad news: "I cannot promise he will ever walk again," Dr. Lambeck commented as he looked down at the floor for a few seconds. He went on to explain the remainder of the tumor would be treated with chemo and radiation. Only Doug had one question for clarification: we were too numb to put the scrambled thoughts running through our minds into a sentence.

Daddy spent a few weeks in the intensive care unit and was discharged to a rehab floor of Bethany Village, a local nursing home. My parents' choice, Fairfield Homes, the local conservative Mennonite nursing home, did not have any nursing beds available when he was discharged from the hospital. Rehab included teaching Daddy on how to use a slide board for transfers from his bed to a wheelchair, and wheelchair to commode, etc. Daddy learned whenever you are immobile, patients are susceptible to getting bedsores on your coccyx or buttocks; Daddy did end up having to be treated for a coccyx bedsore, which meant pain control was needed for him.

The siblings took turns driving Mom to Bethany Village to visit Daddy. We watched him be a brave patient and observed how he kept a positive attitude, expecting a full recovery (and being discharged back home to Mom). Sometime later, Daddy was discharged from Bethany Village and was admitted to the rehab unit at Fairfield Homes, which was closer for Mom, and she could drive herself to visit.

Because of my nursing experience, I knew what to ask and checked to see if the doctor's orders were being followed. Was he wearing prescribed compression hose to improve circulation? If they were not applied when he was dressed that morning, I went to the nursing station. As Daddy's advocate, I insisted the nurse's aide apply them.

By February, it was decided the homestead was no longer feasible as a living arrangement for Mom and Daddy. Plans were initiated to sell their five-bedroom house. The five acres demanded much lawn work. My brothers started helping them find a new home. As Sovereign God planned, a cottage became available for them at Fairfield Homes. Their two-bedroom cottage was considered independent living and gave them access to emergency round-the-clock nursing staff. There was no maintenance or lawn upkeep. Plus, a nursing bed in the skilled unit was promised to them if the need ever arose. Close-by neighbors were a bonus.

MY LAST LAST NAME IS GRACE

In February 1997, I was going through my divorce. I felt bad having to update Daddy, while he was a patient at Fairfield Homes and not feeling well. He felt it was his duty to chew me out, his right as my father. I respectfully listened to his scolding me. Then I made it very clear to him I was not planning on listening to him preach to me every time I came to see him. He stopped scolding me temporarily. We changed the subject and ended up having a nice visit together.

Within three months, Daddy was happy to be discharged from the nursing unit and returned home, even though he was confined to a wheelchair and was not able to walk. He was proud of his accomplishment; he knew how to safely transfer with Mom's assistance and the use of the transfer board from bed to chair or chair to toilet.

The next step was for all nine of his children, including spouses, to work hard and prepare the house and the two-car garage for the planned public sale. I've always said we might not have spent the Christmas holiday celebrating as an entire family. But, we pulled together and did what needed to be done in behalf of our parents when the need arose.

The workday was the first time, since Lenora and I divorced and remarried, that all eighteen of us were together. The women were assigned by Mom to go through items and boxes in the house, including the two storage rooms and basement. The men were assigned to clean out the garage and shed. The women had the best end of that deal.

An auctioneer was contracted, and we selected a date for the public sale and auction. Two family heirlooms were passed onto my oldest brother and sister, which were the antique family Bible for Junior, and Mom's grandmother's quilt for Lenora. About the remaining items, Daddy simply announced, "If you want it, buy it at the auction." (Years earlier, Mom had handed out some family heirlooms of glassware to each of the children.) I guess Daddy realized due to his large family that was the simplest, best way to divvy out items and lessen any squabbles. But it was a little embarrassing for us to be bidding on an item we wanted. If a neighbor or distant cousin saw a family member was bidding, most times they stopped competing, and we were able to purchase the desired item as the highest bidder. The items I purchased at the public sale were Mom's handmade wall-hanging quilt, which had a doll pictured on it, my wooden doll cradle I played with as a child, and two of Mom's dolls from her doll collection.

The public sale notice reads:

> One-owner custom-built one-and-a-half story Holland stone house with first-floor kitchen with dishwasher and disposal, dining or family room, large living room, three bedrooms, full bath, and sewing room; second floor has two bedrooms and large storage area (future rooms); basement has large 15' x 34' recreation or family room with provision for wood/coal stove and full bath. Stoker coal hot water baseboard heat, two-car detached Holland stone garage and 16' x 20' storage shed building with electricity; on lot well and septic system; Rural 5-acre M/L tract of land with over 522' frontage and borders Muddy Creek; well-kept pond, large mature shade trees, grape arbor, raspberry patch and fruit trees. NOTE: extremely well-built house with over 2500 SF finished area on first floor only. Plaster walls, spacious rooms, full basement, mostly finished with walk-in outside entrance...Items to be sold include: 250 doll collection, furniture, appliances, linens, dishes and collectibles, lawn and garden items.

Over one thousand people attended my parent's public sale. The home built by Mr. and Mrs. Right, with much love and attention to detail, was sold for over $252,000!

From the spring of 1997 to the winter of 2000, Daddy's progress was a miracle. James 5:14 reads, "Is any sick among you? Let him call for the elders of the church and let them pray over him, anointing him with oil in the name of the Lord" (KJV). A faithful Bible reader, Daddy, expecting a miracle, did request to be anointed with oil following the Lancaster Conference ordinances. He had radiation, as ordered by his oncologist, Dr. Kane, and chemotherapy in pill form—a winning combination for Daddy.

Unfortunately, a side effect of chemo is suppression of your immune system. Fortunately, Daddy did not have visible hair loss, nor did he become terribly sick. He did become severely anemic and had low platelet, red and white blood cell counts.

Over time, Daddy progressed from being wheelchair-bound and using a transfer board, to standing with a use of a walker; from walking with the use of a walker, to walking only with the use of a cane. Though he sustained a permanent limp, he was too proud to walk using his cane most of the time. Sometimes he did not use any ambulatory aide. Dr. Lambeck would be so proud.

Because of his diagnosis and inability to walk, Daddy lost his driver's license. Thus, my parents sold one of their vehicles. Later on, Daddy ended up reapplying for his driver's license and passing his driver's test and bought another pickup truck. We praise God, he was able to become independent once again and continued his favorite hobbies. During the 2000 hunting season, he might not have trekked through the woods as he preferred, but Daddy was able to hunt (after granted a special permit) sitting on a lawn chair in his pickup truck bed. It was the last photograph Doug took of him.

Mom and Daddy's cottage became a cozy home with lots of visitors, including family and friends. There were regularly planned nights of playing cards, checkers, or marbles. They were also invited to attend many activities held by Fairfield. We did not have to worry about them being lonely or not being around people with their new lifestyle change.

Even though I was the daughter who lived the closest to Mom and Daddy, I was probably the child who visited them the least. Who needs to be blasted about "you are going to hell" or "you are living in sin" whenever you visit them? Sometimes during my visit with my parents, Daddy scolded me in front of his company. How embarrassing! Mom was put in the middle. She believed somewhat like Daddy on the matter of divorce and remarriage; but she never thought it should be embarrassing for me. One time, she scolded Daddy, "You are worse than a minister. Even he lets them alone after a while." Go, Mom!

By October 2000, Daddy had a follow-up CT scan to check on his prognosis at the same affected sites on his ribs and spinal cord. His blood work showed his platelets, red and white blood cells were too low. Daddy started driving into Lancaster to Dr. Kane's office, so her nurse could administer a medication via an injection to help produce and stimulate growth of these much-needed blood components. As he fatigued, Daddy had to be driven by Doug to his doctor's appointments every few weeks.

In December, during one of Daddy's assessments, Dr. Kane took one look at him and sent him right over to the Lancaster General Hospital (LGH) ER. He was jaundiced and severely anemic. Of course, he drove himself. He had an abdominal CT to rule out any medication side effects, which can cause liver problems. Daddy received a blood transfusion for his anemia. He was sent home and continued to receive his weekly injections. Several more follow-up CBCs (complete blood counts) showed he was still anemic and required many more transfusions. By this time, Daddy still participated in playing checkers, marbles, and cards with his many visitors but spent more time resting in his recliner.

At the end of January, Dr. Kane recommended hospice care for Daddy. When Mike and I visited my parents, I spent some time explaining to them how to keep Daddy healthy through the winter with his weakened immune system. He could not afford to get pneumonia. Daddy understood why I was stressing the importance of his staying away from large crowds and to wash their hands frequently. He did listen and heeded my advice.

Mom and Daddy were beginning to feel overwhelmed with Daddy's prognosis and diagnoses. Dr. Kane recommended a family member accompany them to their first hospice appointment.

Granddaughter Dawn, who was an RN, followed Dr. Kane's advice and cheerfully took her grandparents to the doctor's office. Lenora also came down and took them to doctor appointments as well. My brother Matt suggested Daddy drink a natural rose tea and a mineral drink. "Why not let them have hope?" he reasoned.

Mike and I were planning on visiting Mom and Daddy on March 4. The weather forecast was predicting a snowstorm, but it ended up to be nothing. Mike drove me to work for my scheduled shift. I sensed Daddy's end was near and encouraged my children to visit. Steph and Darrin visited their grandparents (Rochelle did not). Daddy, appreciative of his grandchildren's visits, talked very little and relaxed in his recliner all evening. At that time, he was not using oxygen full-time, but his lack of energy limited his card-playing.

Daddy received a blood transfusion every four days. A week later, he requested another one due to his fatigue. Dr. Kane approved one more transfusion. Mom, though she seldom drove into Lancaster, braved it and did so. Daddy was too weak to get out of the car. The nurse had to walk out to Daddy's car and draw his blood for his cross-and-match specimen. As soon as Daddy got home, he vomited. By the next day, he was too weak to even care about getting a transfusion, which we were warned would happen.

Junior called Lenora to update her on Daddy's condition. She felt the need to drive down so that Mom would not be alone in caring for Daddy. Mom left a message on my answering machine while I was at work. I noticed she sounded down. When I checked in with Mom, she said Daddy was only taking a few bites of food and drinking small sips of water. She said he was now using a walker to get to the bathroom and bedroom, and he had oxygen hooked up to him.

When I phoned Mom again around 9:00 p.m., on Thursday night, March 8, Mom answered the phone sounding pretty excited. No wonder! She thought I was the Fairfield Homes' nurse calling back because Mom had pulled the bathroom emergency cord. Daddy had fallen down while walking back to his bedroom. I prepared Mom to hear from the nurse that his ambulatory days of being able to walk from chair to bed or bed to wheelchair might need to end. Due to his fatigue, Daddy needed to simply stand and pivot during transfers.

Lenora arrived at our parent's home. She commented that later when she entered their home, Daddy called out, "Who's there?" Mom asked, "Is that you, Lenora?" She could tell Daddy was relieved Mom had a partner in caregiving. Mom could care for Daddy while living, but it was difficult for her to care for him while dying.

On my scheduled weekday off from work, I babysat our granddaughter, Taylor. Thankfully, I had Friday off. Taylor and I spent the day at Mom and Daddy's house. Taylor was so good; she could sense Great-grandpa was sick and often stood in the doorway and watched. She was content to play by herself and did not need much attention (I am sure having Great-grandma's set of unfamiliar toys to play with helped her be content).

When I first saw Daddy Friday morning, he was lying on his right side in a half-made bed with a folded old tablecloth (I phoned the hospice nurse ASAP for proper bed pads) underneath him in case of any potential incontinence. Lenora said he had not changed his position all night. He moaned with each breath and made some jerking movements but aroused easily. Mom was offering him sips of ginger ale. I noticed his hands shook as he attempted to hold the glass. It was not long before Daddy vomited the ginger ale back up. Lenora offered him his liquid pain med, Oxyfast, every four hours, except during the night. While I set out some lunch, Lenora went to pick up another prescription of Oxyfast at Yoder's Pharmacy. (I had stopped earlier at Spring Glen and picked up some soups and salads for a no-fuss meal.)

During lunch, the salesman who sold the rose tea drink Matt suggested called. He informed Mom he thought it a good idea to have a doctor come to the house to review Daddy's history and make further natural remedy recommendations. Lenora and I both wanted Mom to be hopeful but, at the same time, convinced Mom it would be a waste of money. In my experience, Daddy was not going to live through the weekend. But how do I tell Mom that? Mom wanted to confer with Matt. However, first, she did walk back into Daddy's bedroom and discussed the situation with him. Daddy agreed he was too sick and too tired to drink it. We convinced him his body probably could not tolerate it, either, since he was already vomiting up ginger ale.

On Friday, during times of caregiving, Mom, Lenora, and I made priceless memories. We laughed at times, which was so therapeutic. One time, Mom was washing Daddy's buttocks. Lenora and I were holding up a pink blanket blocking any view because we knew Daddy was so modest. By the time Mom finished changing his Pamper (as she called it), we realized Mom had the oxygen tubing fastened inside Daddy's brief. We had to roll Daddy back into position again. We joked how he probably wanted to say his familiar phrase, "*Ach du lieber*" or "Well!" Since his brief was a size large and much too big (Daddy's weight had dropped below 139 pounds), I decided it would be easier to simply slip the oxygen cannula off his face, pull it through his brief rather than repeat the steps: reposition him, open up his brief again, hold up the blanket, etc. All finished, we repositioned Daddy onto his left side. Mom said he did not like to lie on his left side in bed; he never complained. Too sick, I guess.

The hospice social worker visited Daddy and ordered a hospital bed with an alternating air mattress and an overbed table. I had requested mouth swabs, smaller-sized briefs, and waterproof bed pads (the hospice nurse had to bring those items).

Daddy kept his sense of humor until the end. When the maintenance men came to move Daddy's bed over to make room for the hospital bed, he joked about their fee. Once, when Lenora asked Daddy if she can get him anything, he answered, "$100,000." One time, the phone rang, and Lenora jokingly said, "It's President Bush calling…no, it's Bill Clinton." Daddy looked at me and commented, "Well, your sister voted for him." Caring for him in this manner, I (the divorced black sheep) was in essence saying, "I forgive you, Daddy. I am doing all this for you out of love."

Daddy slept most of the time but was easily arousable. Not certain if he was breathing one time, I performed a nursing procedure called a sternal rub to arouse Daddy. I startled him out of a deep sleep, but he made no comment about my disturbing him.

I left to go home to put Taylor down for her afternoon nap. As I was leaving, Lorna arrived from Virginia. It seemed Mom was more than happy to step aside and let the girls take over Daddy's caregiving. I did not sleep too well Friday night. At one point, I almost got up at 4:00 a.m. and thought about heading over to Mom and Daddy's house. I was afraid I would disturb them if I did. Turns out, I learned later Lorna and Lenora were up throughout the night giving Daddy his medicine. Between the noisy oxygen concentrator and Daddy's breathing sounds, Lorna and Lenora did not get much sleep, as they took turns sleeping in Daddy's room and the spare bedroom.

Since it was my weekend to work, Saturday morning I called into work and reported I would be late in arriving, as I wanted to stop off at my parents' house and check in on my dad first. Mom answered the door. She was just getting ready to step into the shower. I noticed Daddy was lying on his back and seemed to have more labored breathing. Lenora had spoken to the hospice nurse and was told to increase his dosage of Oxyfast. When I went to arouse Daddy, his eyes could not focus; he mumbled something. I teased him and said, "Mom is expecting you to join her in the shower."

I counted Daddy's respiratory rate several times: thirty to forty per minute. I felt his respirations were too labored for as frequently as Lenora said she had given Daddy his Oxyfast. He had two sips of ginger ale and lifted his head for us as when we were shaving him. Mom said he sort of kissed her at one point, but that was the extent of any responsiveness from him. I left around 7:30 a.m. and told Lenora to call me if there were any changes. We planned for all nine of us, including our spouses, to be at Daddy's bedside by 4:00 p.m. to sing hymns. Phone calls were placed to the remaining siblings.

I called at 9:30 a.m. and again at noon from the nursing station to check in with Lenora. Every time an outside line on my desk phone lit up and rang, I was concerned I was about to hear bad news. Indeed, at 2:30 p.m., Lenora called and said she does not think Daddy would last until 4:00 p.m. I left work and hurried over to

Mom and Dad's house. When I arrived, Marlin and Erla were already there. Eventually, Junior and Verna, Elvin and Linda, Sharon and Doug, and Matt and Renee arrived. Poor Doug and Sharon were in the middle of moving to another home that Saturday! Mervin and Linda, who lived the farthest away, arrived around 6:00 p.m. We all believed Daddy would not die until we all gathered at bedside. In between blowing our noses and crying, we sang hymns. Marlin read some scriptures. We took turns standing by the bed or hugging Mother. She cried some but soon regained her composure—she had some strength. It could not have played out any differently than what it did. God was merciful! At one point, Junior started reading from the book of Joel about the "damage from the locust and how we can start from anywhere…it is never too late." Junior had a difficult time finishing reading the scripture aloud.

The next few hours were filled with my frustration of being both nurse and daughter. After all this time of being on routine Oxyfast, I did not think Daddy should have had such labored breathing. His pulse was 120! It was difficult to watch him breathe so hard (using his abdominal muscles and all). I called the hospice nurse. She suggested we increase the Oxyfast dose again and start giving Daddy crushed Ativan (an antianxiety med). I suggested we switch to the drug Roxanol. She commented, "We don't always have success with Roxanol. Let's try this combo first."

Doug had a real hard time watching Daddy suffer. He also could not figure out how Daddy could possibly have the energy to labor so hard to breathe. The hospice staff informed me, "At 5:00 p.m., we are going to send out a new nurse coming on duty, a fresh pair of eyes." They asked me to hold off on administering Daddy's meds until the RN arrived. What a joke!

The newly assigned fresh-pair-of-eyes hospice RN arrived and began her assessment. Because two Ativan had been given earlier to Daddy, his heart rate came down to ninety and later, eighty-two. The RN pulled back Daddy's bedcovers looking for signs and symptoms of cyanosis (a bluish discoloration of the skin resulting from poor circulation or inadequate oxygenation of the blood). At one point, she pointed to some marks and asked Mom, "Are these some insect bite marks?" She never tried to arouse him or check on how alert Daddy was. The RN inquired of Mom what time was his regular bedtime. She recommended we give Daddy two Ativan later to help him get through the night. She advised if he appeared to be drowsier to cut back on his meds. We were to start giving the Oxyfast less often and the Ativan every four hours. She determined his oxygen concentrator was broken and requested another one be delivered. I commented, "Don't bother." Her conclusion: Daddy was having "nonlabored breathing, a respiratory rate of twenty, he's comfortable, and in a deep sleep." She left.

Lenora was almost as frustrated as I was and realized too that changing medications and ordering another refill of Oxyfast was a joke. (I found out later, Linda had also called her daughter, Cyndy, who was a respiratory therapist, and asked for her opinion on the med management.) I asked the family if they did not agree with me if the RN's assessment was incomplete and useless. After explaining my own experience with dying patients and the use of Roxanol, my family agreed I could call the doctor and get my own Roxanol order as I had wanted (it ended up not being necessary).

I explained to my family when Daddy's breathing slows down and his respiratory rate keeps dropping, death is imminent. We agreed Daddy would not want to linger without quality of life. Around 8:15 p.m., I could not very easily feel a pulse in his right wrist. Daddy's breathing changed. His eyes began to open and roll back into his head. I alerted Mike and the spouses, who were sitting out in the living room, and told them to gather around Daddy's bed, as his condition had changed gravely.

Again, we started to sing hymns and prayed Daddy would experience a "quick" death, as he did not want to linger. At one point, Mom asked we stop singing as she wanted to be able to hear him take his last breath. I lay across the bed exhausted and had such a headache. I reached out and rubbed Mom's shoulder. Daddy's respiratory rate slowed down to eight a minute, then four, then two. Then a breath seemed to be his last one. Someone said, "That's it." Mom started to cry. I said, "No, let me count them for one full minute." After forty-five seconds, Daddy took another breath. Again, we thought it was his last breath. But again, after forty-five seconds, Daddy took another one. Then there was no more. Someone said, "We love you, Daddy." Lenora said, "Bye, Daddy." Matt said something about seeing him soon in heaven, and it would not be too long until he did so.

Mom reached over and kissed him and cried, putting her head on his chest—an image I will never forget! She was thrilled he did not linger long nor suffer. Lenora commented, "You could see his spirit leaving him with his last breath." Someone closed Daddy's eyes, and I asked to have someone turn off the oxygen concentrator and remove the tubing from his nose. I called the hospice RN, who in turn called the mortician.

Mom requested we clean Daddy up before the mortician arrived. So everyone left the room. Lenora and I assisted Mom in doing so and putting on a clean pair of pajamas. Again, Lenora and I were holding up towels while Mom washed Daddy, giving him the respect he deserved, even in his death. We laughed, bringing much relief after an unforgettable day.

Mike had been absolutely positively wonderful during this entire event. After Daddy's death, e-mails and cards poured in from understanding friends. My friend Pat, who was aware of my black sheep status, reminded me before Daddy's viewing to "stand tall, be strong, look past any judging faces, and to remember the verse in Isaiah 26:3: 'You will keep in perfect peace him whose mind is steadfast, because he trusts in you.'" I stood tall and felt peace enveloped me.

While dressing for his viewing, I pictured Daddy walking around in heaven, as I witnessed him do many times in the evening after work, singing one of his favorite hymns. He pretended to be the church chorister and waved his hand in the air, as though leading the congregation in song. Now, experiencing in heaven what he sang about, Daddy can sing the words to "In the Sweet By and By" (Sandford F. Bennett Faith Publishing House, Evening Light Songs, 1949):

BEATY MILLER

There's a land that is fairer than day,
And by faith we can see it afar;
For the Father waits over the way
To prepare us a dwelling place there.

Refrain: In the sweet by and by
We shall meet on that beautiful shore
In the sweet by and by
We shall meet on that beautiful shore

We shall sing on that beautiful shore
The melodious songs of the blessed;
And our spirits shall sorrow no more,
Not a sigh for the blessing of rest.

To our bountiful Father above,
We will offer our tribute of praise
For the glorious gift of His love
And the blessings that hallow our days.

Other favorite hymns of Daddy were "When the Roll Is Called Up Yonder" and "I'll Fly Away." Whenever I hear them, I always think of Daddy. The lyrics to "I'll Fly Away" bring comfort, knowing he is on God's celestial shore. They were:

(Refrain:) "I'll fly away, oh glory, I'll fly away
When I die, hallelujah by and by, I'll fly away.
Some bright morning when this life is over, I'll fly away
To a land on God's celestial shore, I'll fly away
When the shadow of this life have gone, I'll fly away
Like a bird from these prison walls, I'll fly away
(Refrain)
Oh how glad and happy when we meet, I'll fly away
No more cold shackles on my feet, I'll fly away
(Refrain)

MY LAST LAST NAME IS GRACE

>Just a few more weary days and then, I'll fly away
>To a land where joy will never end, I'll fly away.
>(Refrain)

Several times a year, Daddy took our family to a local fire hall to listen to bluegrass bands of which several of his hunting buddies played instruments. Harmonizing, the group belted out the song "Where the Soul of Man Never Dies" (Audrey and Hank Williams *Health and Happiness Show*), while playing their banjo, guitar, fiddle, or mandolin. The lyrics are:

>To Canaan's land I'm on my way
>Where the soul of man never dies
>My darkest night will turn to day
>Where the soul of man never dies
>
>Dear friends there'll be no sad farewell
>There'll be no tear-dimmed eyes
>Where all is peace and joy and love
>And the soul of man never dies
>
>A rose is blooming there for me
>Where the soul of man never dies
>And I will spend eternity
>Where the soul of man never dies
>
>I'm on my way to that fair land
>Where the soul of man never dies
>Where there will be no parting hand
>And the soul of man never dies

I will never forget the night of Daddy's viewing. Martindale Church was packed full with family members, neighbors, former neighbors and coworkers, church members, and friends. In an organized fashion, people who wanted to view Daddy's body were seated in the pews and then directed one row at a time to greet the family members and Mom. There were nineteen of us: me and my eight siblings, including our spouses, plus Mom, standing in a line from oldest to youngest in front of the church. A chair was available for Mom to sit down, if she so chose.

It was tiring to stand for over four hours starting at 5:30 p.m. to 10:00 p.m. accepting condolences. I have never shaken so many hands in my life! I spoke with many relatives I had not seen in a long time. However, we were so grateful to have such a huge turnout. We were told later some people who were lined up outside the church were turned away at 10:00 p.m. and asked to return the following morning if they wanted to view Daddy's body. All total, there were over a thousand people who attended either Daddy's viewing or funeral. We were all reminded how Daddy impacted the lives of many people.

On the morning of Daddy's funeral, Mom and all of us gathered around Daddy's open casket for one last time. I thought Daddy looked great and had just enough "paint" to not look alive but in a natural sleep. You would be pleased, Daddy.

My large family filled up the front quarter of the church. Following Daddy's instructions (mostly), the officiating minister began the funeral service as spoken about earlier in this chapter. I found out later the officiating minister, not surprisingly, used his discretion and did *not* mention specifically divorce and remarriage in the funeral sermon. He presented it as an overall concern for the church members in general and the need for all to be ready to meet their Maker (not exactly as Daddy had written down earlier).

I loved the poem that Daddy chose for his memorial pamphlet:

Safely Home

I am home in heaven, dear ones;
Oh, so happy and so bright!
There is perfect joy and beauty
In this everlasting light.

MY LAST LAST NAME IS GRACE

> All the pain and grief is over,
> Every restless tossing passed;
> I am now at peace forever,
> Safely home in heaven at last.
> There is work still waiting for you
> So you must not idly stand;
> Do it now, while life remaineth—
> You shall rest in God's own land.
> When that work is all completed,
> He will gently call you Home,
> Oh, the rapture of that meeting,
> Oh, the joy to see you come.

Lorna and I walked with Mom to the graveside. Finally, I felt Mom had released some of her grief. She grieved tremendously, but when you love much, you grieve much.

Mom wanted each one of us children to have a picture of Daddy lying in the casket. In my cedar chest among memorabilia is Daddy's picture as I last saw him. I can truly say I never heard of anyone doing this. But in Mom's eyes, Daddy was always special!

Excerpts from Daddy's memorial obituary, March 10, 2001:

> Aaron W. Martin, 77, of 32 Nolt Drive, Ephrata, died Saturday at home after a brief illness. Martin was a quarry worker for Ivan M. Martin Inc. for 35 years. He also owned and operated a stone-hauling business, retiring in 1988. He was a member of Martindale Mennonite Church, where he was a Sunday school teacher. Martin volunteered at Christian Aid Ministries and was an avid hunter. He was married 58 years in October to Elizabeth Fisher Martin...

A few weeks later, Mom sent me a thank-you note—a refreshing one to read from her. It read:

Thanks, Leanne, for all you done for me and Dad during his illness and death. It was nice you all could be in his presence when he passed away so peacefully. I miss him. He had nothing left here. He is enjoying the bliss of heaven. My love and prayers, Mom.

Thought of the Day

Grace is understanding all doubts and uncertainties will one day end with certainty and assurance.

Chapter 56

Unconditional Love from Grandchildren

And may you live to see your children's children.
—Psalm 126:6

Back row, from left to right: Darrin and Mike
Center row Heather, Author, Steph, Rochelle holding Talon
Front row: Christian, Taylor, Hope, Madison and Kiersten

I LOOKED AT GRANDMA AND asked her, "What are *you* doing here?" She did not answer me. Again, while my tears streamed down both cheeks, I vented, "Why were you such a lousy grandmother? Why didn't you have a good relationship with me? I am so jealous of the grandmother-grandchild relationships I see among my nursing home residents. Why didn't you show me love? Why couldn't you be a nurturing grandmother to me?"

She did not answer me. Grandma got up, moved to the bus seat closest to me, and patted it inviting me to sit down beside her. I did. I looked at her and commented, "You know, I am going to be a grandmother soon, and I am going to be the best nana there ever was. I cannot wait to love, teach, share, and spend time nurturing my grandbaby. Maybe I flubbed up with some things with my own kids. But this is a time to redeem myself." The mind exercise ended, and we were asked to open our eyes.

Let me start from the beginning: In March 1999, Mike and I attended a seminar and workshop given by various New Age authors (yes, I have repented). One speech was on the healing of America. One of the workshop selections we chose was titled "God and Angels Unaware." Unfortunately, there was a misprint on the schedule. So we had to select a different workshop. The main focus of the presenter's speech was how we all have both extremes inside of us: selfishness and selflessness, arrogance and humbleness, for example. I learned when people rub us the wrong way, it is actually being mirrored back to us what we do not like about ourselves. She invited us to pretend we were wearing a vest filled with hundreds of buttons. Some people's behavior simply bounces off you. It does not bother you. Some people's behaviors push your buttons and zing. If you are a prick, turn that personality trait into something positive. My examples I was reminded of while being a prick aided in getting my way to have the repairman come at a convenient time for me. Or having a pricky personality at times allowed me to have the staff respond to what work needed to be done on the nursing unit. It is not always a bad thing.

Next, the instructor asked the attendees to participate in a mind exercise. We were to close our eyes and listen to her instructions as follows: "Picture in your mind a quiet warm candle-lit room with soft music playing in the background. Imagine an elevator in the room along one wall. Walk toward the elevator and push the button to go down to the seventh floor of your subconscious mind. Get off and walk over to the yellow bus parked nearby and get on the bus. After getting on, decide which side of the bus you want to sit on. Notice the beautiful view of palm trees and beaches around you visible through the bus window. Look around you and decide who is already sitting on the bus waiting for you. Let them speak to you and let them name themselves. For example, if you have a weight problem, see 'Fat Fanny' and have a dialogue with her, or 'Aggressive Alice,' or 'Arrogant Andrea,' and so forth."

Well, my mind did *not* do that at all. Totally unexpected, I looked around the bus and envisioned two people sitting in the back row. One was my dead Grandma Fisher, who was sitting on one side of the bus. On the opposite side sat my dead cousin Jill, who died at thirty-two years of age.

Oblivious to others around me, I started crying. In my mind, I did not sit down but continued to stand in the aisle about four seats away from them. I turned toward Jill first and said, "Jill, life treated you so unfairly. You died much too young with breast cancer leaving two young children behind. All you wanted was to be loved by a father. Instead, your Mennonite foster father gets you pregnant at fourteen years old. You gave up your baby for adoption and experienced pain that I cannot even imagine. Then you met your husband, Gary. You waited until you were engaged to tell him about your giving birth and of your situation. It spoke volumes to me when I learned Gary showed you unconditional love. He was such a sweetheart to you through all of that." But Jill did not comment back. Then it was Grandma's turn in my mind exercise (as described above), where I emphatically said I plan on being the best nana ever.

I opened my eyes and wiped away the tears. Mike was also finished with his mind exercise. We left the conference feeling refreshed. Over dinner, I learned Mike's mind exercise took him back to his kindergarten days. However, he shed no tears but sensed an evil power has been allowed to evade his life. The little boy sitting on his bus was the first person to have made fun of him for stuttering. Not realizing his imperfect speech until his classmate made fun of him, Mike wrestled with his "angel of Jacob" as a kindergartener during his mind exercise. Kids can be so cruel! He concluded, every time he lets his weakness rule, he is not allowing God to be his strength. In fact, someone, impressed with how he overcame this imperfection, has advised him to write a book on how he has conquered childhood stuttering. How-to lessons are valuable and need to be passed onto others.

Finally married and able to be labeled *Nana and Grandpa*, we welcomed our first grandchild, Taylor Nicole. My chance to be the best nana ever was paved before me. On the day of her birth, I resumed journaling:

May 22, 1999

Today at approximately 12:20 p.m., Taylor Nicole Weaver (only two days late) graced this world with her beautiful presence. After nine months of praying for you, Taylor, God has so richly honored our prayers, and you are beautifully, perfectly created.

I wish so badly I could have been there for your birth, but it worked out for Grandma Wellman to be present instead. But we plan to visit ASAP. Grandpa and Nana will drive down Memorial Day weekend when you will be seven days old. This will give Mommy and Daddy bonding time with you and a chance for him to be a proud daddy—and boy, is he ever!

Today is such a busy day for Nana. We had a yard sale in the morning, a wedding to attend in the afternoon, and Aunt Rochelle's prom. What a surprise when we arrived home and Aunt Rochelle told us about your birth. We didn't expect you to be born until later on that evening. Aunt Rochelle was so tickled to be the one to receive the phone call from your parents and not Nana. Of course, I could not wait to arrive home and call your parents. Both Grandma Wellman and Mommy could not stop raving about how sweet and precious you are. I could only imagine what I believed "a good mixture between Darrin and Heather" would look like.

Only journal entries for that remaining month include: "Grandpa and Nana drove all evening, after work, to arrive in North Carolina, so we would not have far to go in the morning until we will see you."

Memorial Day Weekend, 1999

Wow...the first time I saw you, I thought you are so much more beautiful than I had imagined! You were sleeping so peacefully in your bassinet in the living room. You were lying on your belly and looked so tiny, as I noticed you had dark hair like your nana. I was just in awe as I disturbed you and picked you up. I wanted to cry, but I was too busy just looking you over and over, realizing that your grandma and mommy were so right. You are the most precious little one I had ever seen! Just perfect! You have ten little petite fingers and ten toes, a cute little nose, and across your eyes, I think, you look like your daddy. You look a lot like your Daddy's baby pictures. But you also look like your beautiful mommy too. I cuddled you and kissed you over and over. No one else got much of a chance to hold you. I snuggled with you, whispered to you for hours. Of course, I had to hand you over to Mommy sometimes to be nursed. Apparently, you need some practice time to get that right. Mommy said you were too lazy to nurse very long that first week. Now you cough sometimes and decide that takes enough of your energy and want to go back to sleep instead of nursing.

Saturday was your first outing. Mommy was ready to get out of the house too. So we decided to go to a craft and pottery store. Your daddy pushed your stroller for the first time. Unfortunately, I heard your first serious cry when Mommy accidentally closed the stroller buckle and pinched some of your little skin. You cried out a little yelp—but that was it. What a trouper you are. Your mommy felt so badly. She kissed your first "ouchie" away. In the craft store, Daddy bought you your first "spoiling" gift: a spoontique collectible. It was a blue crystal dolphin. He said it was your week-old gift.

Saturday night, we all went to a seafood restaurant for dinner and sat on the deck…your first dining out experience. The next morning, your mommy said you did not sleep too well overnight. You weren't fussy, but you wanted to be awake at 3:00 a.m. So Mommy asked Nana to try to keep you awake longer Sunday night.

Sunday morning, I had the privilege to give you a bath. While lying on your belly, you tried to lift up your head…so cute! You did fuss while I was finishing your bath, but you soon stopped and took the pleasure all in. We picked up your birth photos at the store. I also bought my first scrapbook to arrange your pictures. Your daddy had the great idea of packing a picnic dinner and going to a nearby marina. It was a little windy, but you slept most of the time, allowing us to play a game of scrabble. Later, I tried to prevent you from going into a deep sleep, but I could not keep you awake. I had so much fun playing with your cheeks, kissing you, and trying to arouse you.

It was so difficult to kiss you good-bye, knowing it would be five weeks until I will see you again. I could have cried, but instead, I held you and told you that I'll be praying for you. There is no other grandbaby loved more in this whole world than you, Taylor Nicole. I'm so looking forward to spending time with you, exploring the world together, praying with you, and teaching you so many things. Nanas have lots of experiences under their belts, and it's our job to "teach those behind us" our lessons learned.

You are so lucky to have Aunts Katie, Steph, and Rochelle to spoil you. Not many children can say they have four sets of grandparents. (Well, maybe there are way too many of you…one of those lessons learned by me worth passing on.)

I miss you so very much and can't wait to see you in four weeks to see your precious face and hold you again. Of course, I realize I will have to share you with your aunts. I'll keep phoning to hear how you are growing until I see you. I decided to take one of your baby pictures and put it in a heart-shaped pin to wear it every day on my nursing uniform for the next month until I see you.

By July 4 weekend, Darrin had finished his commitment to Uncle Sam and the marines. He and Heather were so ready to move back to Denver, Pennsylvania. Realizing that Darrin could have moved his family to any other place in the country, I was selfishly thrilled they chose to move back to Lancaster County. Yes, they both wanted to be around family and friends, as they raised their child. Mike and I, Rochelle, and one of Darrin's friends, Dwight, drove down to help them pack up their home and help move them into their Reamstown second-floor Main Street apartment. Journal entries of this event follow:

>Grandpa and Nana drove down to North Carolina to help pack up the house and bring you all home now that your Daddy's stint with the Marine Corps is finished. Of course, Aunt Rochelle had to be the first one to rush through the front door to see you…she was so anxious. You were nursing, but Mommy took a break so Aunt Rochelle could hold you. She was so excited and in awe too and could have cried. Of course, somehow, I got Rochelle to hand you over so Nana could kiss you and tell you how much she missed you.
>
>We all worked hard to load up everything onto the moving truck, clean the apartment, and shampoo the carpets. Your daddy made reservations at a Japanese restaurant for dinner as a thank-you for helping them. During dinner, I laid you on your belly across my lap and legs; you are so content.
>
>That night, we all stayed in a hotel and headed out for Pennsylvania in the morning. Your Mommy and Aunts Rochelle and Katie decided to leave after your 5:30 a.m. feeding, thinking that you would need several stops to nurse on the road trip back home. But Mommy reported later that you did great, and she only needed to stop twice…no different than for anybody else in the car.

> When we arrived at your apartment in Reamstown, many people were there to greet you, especially Aunt Steph. Boy, she was so happy to see you! Your other grandparents and aunt also were there to meet you.

Journal entries continued with bragging about my first grandchild and how we spent bonding time. If, for some reason, we did not get a chance to visit with Heather, Darrin, and Taylor during the week, they would stop by every Sunday. Our blue-striped hammock that was attached to the deck became a cozy place to cuddle. (Each grandkid has had many pictures taken of them against this backdrop.) My sporadic journal entries listed all the firsts: first roll-over, first laugh out loud, first step at Nana's, etc.

The first time that month when I babysat for Heather so she could have a girls' night out, Darrin reported to Heather later that Nana had Taylor covered up too much to the point of her sweating. Nana believes babies need to be covered when they sleep. My parents came to Heather's twenty-second birthday celebration at our house. Great-grandma called Taylor a "cute little button."

My friend, Roz, loaned me a car seat, playpen, a stroller, and lots of clothing, so I could babysit for Heather one day a week when she returned to work as a paralegal. Since I worked every other weekend, I had off one day a week. So I babysat Taylor on my day off lessening Heather's child care bill to only four days a week. I jokingly said later, babysitting kept me out of the stores; we saved a sum of money, and God only knows how much.

Having signed up to join the Marine Corps in eleventh grade, Darrin had not been baptized by our pastor before he left for Parris Island. So he promised me he would get baptized by the marine chaplain. Well, for whatever reason, that never happened. Thus, Darrin got baptized and became a church member of Heather's Lutheran church on the same day that Taylor was christened on July 19, 1999. Aunts Steph, Rochelle, and Katie were joint godparents, so they proudly stood in front of the church and gathered around the baptismal.

Of course, a journal entry included the Winnie-the-Pooh first birthday theme. A huge party was thrown so the spoiling could continue among four grandparents, other family, and friends. Taylor's first Christmas was also special, as every grandparent is aware. Later on, the Christmas wrapping paper was just as much fun for Taylor as the more expensive toy that was wrapped inside it.

During my years of babysitting Taylor, Rochelle was attending Reading Area Community College earning her degree for childcare development. So she was home many times in the morning when Heather dropped off Taylor. One memorable morning, Taylor was wearing a pair of white sunglasses that came with a cute outfit that was a birthday present. Wearing her sunglasses, Taylor, carried by me, and I went into Aunt Rochelle's bedroom to wake her up. Peeping out of the covers, Aunt Rochelle burst out laughing hysterically at the cute, adorable niece who was peering down at her wearing her white sunglasses. What memories!

Favorite toys were selected from Nana's toy box, lids from the bottom stove-drawer stash, and books from the bookshelf, which were read to her over and over again. As Taylor, along with her curiosity, grew, Nana's house had to become childproof. We all had to become safety-conscious, which led to the purchasing of outlet plugs, cabinet locks, and stairstep gates. My dust-collector knickknacks were named "Nana's pretties" and were moved to higher ground, where possible. Never leaving her out of our sight took intentional living and awareness, as Taylor perfected walking at ten and one-half months. A once-thrilled purchase of a glass round coffee table became a potential cause of injury. So it was covered with an afghan whenever young toddlers stopped by. (Thank God, no broken or chipped teeth occurred from their hitting their mouths on this table by the time all six of our grandkids were raised.)

By the time grandbaby number two, Kiersten Hailey, came along, Taylor had at least four photo albums filled with pictures and the second scrapbook started by Nana. Reading novels took a back seat during those years of designing scrapbooks (a time when this craft was popular and economical). With limited creative abilities, I did the best job I could with the resources I had and the amount of money and time I chose to spend on each page. Today, each grandchild enjoys glancing through their scrapbook pages, lovingly put together by Nana, and walking down memory lane.

Knowing that Steph's pregnancy was the reason Mike and I were not to be moving out of state, I jumped in again wholeheartedly to share this first-time excitement with my daughter. The baby shower was held, the nursery was established, and countdown to her labor day began. But one problem. This laboring mommy was petrified of needles. I knew my job as an assistant labor coach would be more than to encourage her. Distractions during needle pricks or talking her through the administration of an epidural would be my job.

As typical of first-time births, Steph labored for more than a few hours. She passed time soaking in a whirlpool tub, walking the halls, and visualizing her precious miracle lying in her arms and nuzzled up at her breast. Of course, just when Dad decided to leave the room for a soda and snack, the urgency of delivery was imminent. I was honored to be allowed in the delivery room, along with Eric in this private moment. Eight pounds and six ounces of perfection graced this world as one of God's most awesome miracles—Kiersten Hailey.

Nana's camera was kept busy from seconds after Kiersten's birth throughout her hospital stay. Grandparents and aunts and uncles felt they needed Nana to hand over the bundle at times so they could gaze into the chubby face. Mommy took her from me to nurse, and I reluctantly handed Kiersten over.

So the second grandchild's scrapbook was started. Cousin Taylor and Kiersten became great friends and playmates. *Ad nauseum* in my dictionary means Nana's bragging on her family.

A roses-in-December moment came when Heather announced she was pregnant again. Expecting grandbaby number three to be the first grandson or nephew, we were all thrilled. After all, the only son most likely would have a son to pass on the family name. I could not have been more proud when Heather, along with her mother, invited me to also be in the labor room.

In God's providence, awesome Madison Grace was born around 7:30 a.m. on July 14. I barely made it in the labor room before she blessed us with her presence. Tears flowed as my heart expanded to include grandbaby number 3. No one batted an eye about Darrin having two beautiful daughters. Their family was complete. Over time, it became very apparent God knew exactly what He was doing in designing Darrin to be the father of two girls. At times, two fighting siblings in the Weaver household had to remind Darrin of his sister. When the estrogen is flowing, he takes it all in stride and makes room for the women-of-the-house emotions to wax and wane. Heather recently said it best on Darrin's fortieth birthday:

> Happy fortieth birthday to my husband, my best friend for over half our lives, the person who calms me when I am stressed, cheers me up when I am down, stands by my side through thick and thin, puts up with my OCD, and who very calmly handles a house of three (sometimes moody) women and never complains. Although I am not that far behind, I'm glad you get to achieve the status of middle-aged before me (even though our girls have been calling us middle-aged for the last five years - LOL)! Looking forward to truly celebrating our birthdays with the girls in forty days! Love you babe!

One of my favorite pictures of Madison and Taylor reveals Madison's kind nature. After Taylor got a boo-boo, Madison, as a toddler, simply reached out and attempted to comfort and simply hold her as Taylor cried. Ahhhhh. Taylor has been a great role model for her younger cousins and sisters. How can you put a price on that? Between both Taylor and Madison's gymnastic, cheerleading, and soccer trophies, they can fill an entire wall.

Early on, for Nana and Grandpa, it was understood summer vacations were geared around family time, playing cards, taking walks, going out for dinner, eating ice cream, and making memories while soaking up the sun. Nana was busy spoiling three stunning grandgirls. We looked for every opportunity to celebrate birthdays and holidays simply to spend time together. I started a tradition of including Mom, after Daddy died, in our family get-togethers as Mom always loved the cuddly baby stage too. Mother's Day teas and Christmas angel breakfasts at the Worship Center became a must-do calendar item. Oh, the memories!

Being close sisters, Steph and Rochelle were both pregnant in 2004. Steph was due in March and Rochelle in May. They were proud to pose for a picture, pulling up their maternity tops and showing off their big bellies, grinning from ear to ear.

Again, Steph invited me and added Eric's mom to be in the labor and delivery room with her. What an honor! Having a fear of needles but wanting to limit how painful labor could be, she opted again for an epidural. Thus, she had moments where she was trying to sleep in between contractions. After several hours of labor, our heaven-sent present came into this world at 11:57 p.m. on March 15. Weighing nine pounds and twenty inches long, Christian Jayden Shunk, our first grandson, wailed and alerted his environment, "I've arrived!" Camera-ready, I was prepared to take a picture of our perfect, newest grandbaby (using discretion of course), which occurred when the doctor was wiping off the baby. Not a single dry eye among the nanas and parents when the bundle was placed in mommy's arms.

I took time off from work to keep Kiersten for Steph during her convalescence. Of course, we could not wait to take her into the hospital to show off her new little brother. She was more interested in her Etch A Sketch than who occupied the bassinet next to mommy's hospital bed. Discharged from the hospital, Steph and Christian, a "little one to Him belongs," headed home to continue an awesome bonding that continues today and began the work of blending this little bundle of joy into their family of (now) four.

I kept Kiersten overnight at our home, but I would go over to Steph's house to clean, do laundry, and make dinner. On the following day after Steph's hospital discharge, I took a picture of Kiersten and Steph sitting side by side on the sofa, which I still cherish. Tears were streaming down Steph's face while answering Kiersten, "But, honey, you can't sit on Mommy's lap right now because Mommy's feeding the baby." Not buying it, Kiersten kept sobbing and begging to be held. Though I could not help it, my giggling while taking the picture was not appreciated by Steph.

I was thrilled how often on weekends Steph would visit and bring Kiersten and Christian over to spend time with Nana. Steph would gladly hand the two children over into my care while she slept or watched TV on Saturday or Sunday afternoons. Sometimes she would have me babysit then went out to visit friends or go grocery shopping. Needing the break from parenting, as Eric wasn't able to help on weekends with his work schedule, Steph had her reprieve, and Nana got her grandbaby fix. Each grandchild has their own scrapbook filled with Nana's and Grandpa's pictures taken over the years. Isn't it amazing how hearts keep expanding to include the love of many?

Christian and Kiersten are a great duo too. Your size did not always mean you were winning a battle. Their household walls echoed with some yelling matches—but eventually into fits of laughter, automatically bringing calm into a heated discussion. Christian is smart and hopes to be an engineer someday. Putting ideas on paper to seeing an end product keeps him busy for hours.

As with any of my grandkids, Christian learned the hard way the difference of having a neighbor boy as being a good or bad influence. Lying one too many times, Christian's punishment one day was to have his dad shave off his envious hair. Character building isn't always fun, but he learned it is painfully necessary. Steph does an awesome job of applying scripture to everyday situations. She taught them God, our Creator, and the Holy Spirit are living inside us to help us be good and make right decisions.

Rochelle and Carl wasted no time in getting pregnant after they married. Hope was born the following spring. *My baby is having a baby!* The ultrasound showed the little peanut was going to be a girl. With another reason to celebrate, we gathered for Rochelle's baby shower, which was all things pink and pastel.

Rochelle's three pages of typed notes explained Hope's birth. Her story started by describing Rochelle's energy surge when she helped friends prep their house for painting. Two days later, cramping could no longer be ignored, and Rochelle believed she was in early labor. Her midwife wisely advised Carl to take her out to dinner and "go walk the mall" to keep the contractions moving. In fact, Rochelle was motivated to keep her labor progressing. Why? She wanted to have her baby on Kiersten's birthday—which happened!

After a possible threat from the midwife that Rochelle might be sent home if she did not move off three centimeters dilated, she changed her prayer: "Please, God, do not let me be sent home. I am so ready to have this baby. In the name of Jesus, my contractions will pick up, and I will dilate." God answered her prayer. Her next examination revealed she had moved up to four centimeters dilated. Carl called to inform me that Rochelle will be admitted to the hospital, and I should start my trek, about two hours' drive away.

At 10:45 p.m., while I was en route, the doctor stated he wanted to break her water. Carl thought, *No, not yet. Not until Mom Miller gets here. I'm not sure I can do this on my own.* Rochelle took a hot shower and allowed the water to stream over her belly, which was helpful. Her pain was increasing, and finally, Carl talked her into accepting an epidural. Just as her sister, she too had a fear of needles. But with Carl holding her hand, she braved the "relaxing" injection.

I arrived around twelve midnight. Carl was relieved. "Thank God, you got here safely and on time." After the doctor broke Rochelle's water, I thought too much time had passed before a follow-up internal exam was done. Carl asked the nurse to check, but she declined due to the fear of causing an infection. I understood that. However, Rochelle seemed to be getting very uncomfortable.

Believing her to be in her transition (the final stage), I asked the nurse to please check her. After all, this was not my first rodeo.

An exam revealed she was at nine centimeters, and she was told to slightly push. After eighteen minutes of, "Am I doing okay?" and "Why won't this baby come?" Rochelle finished her laboring and presented Hope Elizabeth (named after my mother) to this world. Another sacred moment occurred, but this time for my daughter.

Hope was just beautiful. She had a thick head of dark hair. The first time I bathed her in my kitchen sink, I thought about the note I had recently read and placed in her scrapbook titled "Beautiful Hands":

> Angry at being old, a grandmother bathed her new granddaughter in the kitchen sink. She coveted the glowing skin, envied all the wonderful years that stretched before this magical spark of herself. In washing the tiny hand the grandmother noticed its miraculous construction… beautiful miniature, perfect nails, even the little wrinkle on the tops of the fingers. She studied her own hand beside her granddaughter's hand and, in a moment of clarity, realized that both hands were the same. The only difference was time. Each was perfect in its time…each served its function in its time. And the grandmother realized that her own hand was beautiful too, only different. (Author unknown)

I smiled the day Hope visited me, and I noticed the saying on her onesie. It read, "My fingers may be small, but I can still wrap Nana around them."

When Hope was eleven months old, I kept her overnight for the first time. Rochelle handed me some notes on how to take care of her. I read,

MY LAST LAST NAME IS GRACE

Friday night: She might get sleepy around eight or nine. She rubs her eyes and gets fussy. Just lay her down with her pacifier and shut the door

Saturday morning: When she wakes, you can change her diaper and get her dressed. She eats 2/3 cup of cereal with 3 small spoonsful of applesauce and 1/4 cup of juice and 3/4 cup of water in her sippy cup.

Nap time will probably be in three or four hours after she wakes up in the morning. She usually eats after her nap. Give her 1/2 jar of veggies and 1 and 1/2 jar of fruit. She is not used to stage 3 yet. She might not eat it. Just give her fruit and snack and veggie bites. If she still doesn't seem to eat, tear up pieces of bread and sneak in food bites.

And the clincher. Wait…wait for it…

PS: Please comfort her while she struggles and cries when she poops.

Too much!
Loving motherhood and fulfilling her dream, Rochelle wanted one more child. Thus, she was soon pregnant with Talon. After his ultrasound revealed the proper equipment for a boy, she e-mailed, "I had a feeling that God was having me follow right into my sister's footsteps, starting with our daughters sharing the same birthday."

The doctor advised Rochelle to stop traveling to our home mid-February as he believed she was going to have a February baby. As with Hope's labor, she was encouraged to walk the mall to keep labor progressing. Steph and I dropped off Kiersten and Christian at Heather's house, and we headed to the hospital. All four of us walked the halls back and forth while Steph logged contraction times and lengths. Tears flowed while the nurse inserted an IV in Rochelle's arm. After her "relaxing" med, Rochelle commented, "My body feels sooooo good." *Good, keep thinking that. You'll soon be working hard.*

By 9:30 p.m., she felt the urge to push. After two small pushes, the nurses noticed a crowning head. One nurse scurried out of the room for the doctor, who was next door finishing up with another delivery. Eight more pushes and minutes later, baby Talon delighted this world with his inquisitive presence. An eight-pound-three-ounce bouncing boy screamed and expanded his lungs, demanding attention.

To this day, active Talon seeks one's attention if you are sharing the same space in a room. He prefers not to have to sit still for long periods. His muscles were used to swing a bat in T-ball, graduating to baseball, and later on, soccer. Presently, Talon's pursuit of swinging a hockey stick, following in his stepbrother Alex's footsteps on the ice, and slamming the black puck into the net fills up his attention span and energy.

His sister Hope is the most awesome older sister any younger brother could wish for. Their connection is astounding to observe, and Nana grants them an A- for sibling-rivalry shenanigans. Being short for his age, Talon's nickname given by mommy, *little man*, has always been appropriate. At a young age, Talon started putting his hands in his pockets while standing around idle, appearing to be older than he was, in spite of his height.

Step-grandson, cousin, and nephew, Alex blended into our family when his dad started dating Rochelle. We have been blessed and grateful to be able to say we have seven grandchildren. Yes, learning how to play with four girl cousins led to many, "Be careful, Alex. You're too rough," or "Take it easy, buddy." Alex is a great role model in showing his younger cousins and stepfamily that to have a love for a sport takes time and dedication. Look out, Hershey Bears!

Of course, unconditional love cannot only be penned by grandparents. But to be a grandparent—while nurturing, encouraging, supporting, teaching, and influencing someone who has a part of me inside them—is a relationship that builds an oh so necessary foundation. Their successful development depends on it. Just as with Mike, I wouldn't think of ever falling out of love with them. To teach them to count by counting each stair step, to have them learn Sunday school songs while driving in Nana's car, to observe nature as we walked to the horse's meadow down at the end of our development, to be touchy-feely and hug and express *I love you* often built a solid-rock one.

Grandpa shared the love of hiking in the woods, astronomy and constellations, and the hobby of collecting state quarters. Bedtime prayers are as important as the air that we breathe. Every birthday or Christmas present from Nana and Grandpa included activity, sticker, and storybooks (including Bibles) to expand their knowledge base and, hopefully, the love of reading. My grandchildren recognize Solid Gold Oldies used in popular movies or current commercials because they heard them first blaring from Nana's car radio at times.

Unlike my childhood, celebrating birthdays was a big deal. Christmas was a time to spoil them. I was never one to purchase gifts all year long every time we were out and about. However, Christmas gift giving and selecting the perfect gift *did* occur all year long. After Christmas, sales would start my shopping for the following year. The guest-room closet and under-the-bed space held the gifts until needed.

Having and following traditions also brings importance and security into family legacies. I would read the Christmas story from the Bible to the gathered-around grandchildren. In the meantime, Rochelle would be the one to pile the presents at each family member's assigned seat. Tradition is, from youngest to oldest, we watch each present being opened. Each family poses in front of the fireplace for the annual Christmas family photo by the end of the day.

By the time our grandchildren ranged in the ages of nine to two, I realized we would be missing out on some great memories on the funny things kids say if I didn't resume journaling again. My first entry was in 2008 on Rochelle's twenty-eighth birthday, when she was separated from Carl. I wrote about a cute comment made by Hope when she was four years old:

Mike and I took Rochelle and Steph and their kids out to lunch at Isaac's after church to celebrate Rochelle's birthday. One of her gifts was a great pair of sexy shoe boots. As Rochelle was opening up her present and pulling them out of the shoebox, I commented that these could be "dating" shoes. Hope piped up, "Daddy is the only one dating in *this* family."

A journaled, cute saying by Talon was:

While babysitting Talon, I was having a difficult time buckling his car seat in my car. After several attempts, I started getting frustrated. Sensing this, he said, "Get *hon* to do it." I laughed and laughed. Of course, he reasoned I would call out for "hon" to get Mike's attention and not "grandpa," as he would have done.

Another observation of Talon's:

Since Rochelle was waitressing at Charlie Brown's restaurant in the evenings, I babysat Hope and Talon several nights a month. I was holding Talon on my lap; Hope was sitting beside me and holding the one end of the book. While reading the story to them, Talon looked up at me and said "Nana, do this." He licked his fingers and then turned the page of the book for me. Later on, when I told Rochelle about Talon's comment, she said that he had said the same thing to her. Earlier in a similar setting, while reading a story, Talon said, "No, Mommy. Do what Nana does." It took her awhile to figure out she was to lick her finger before turning the page.

My brother Marlin experienced a sad tragedy. One day, while driving to work, I heard a news broadcaster mention a tragic farming accident in Lancaster County. A nine-year-old third-grade boy was killed. Not recognizing the name of the deceased nor realizing it was a relative, I simply prayed for the grieving family. Mom called me that night and informed me it was my niece's son, Timothy Earl. My heart broke. I could not fathom the pain this family was enduring. Details worth sharing began to be passed among the funeral attendees. I learned that Marlin and my sister-in-law Erla were visiting their son in Guatemala when they received the news about the death of their grandson. That night, Marlin was restless and had difficulty sleeping. He got up in the middle of the night and went out into his son's kitchen. Suddenly he had a vision of daddy standing in the doorway, smiling, and he seemed to be saying, "Everything is going to be okay." When his mother heard about Marlin's comforting vision, she commented how amazed she was that daddy showed up in Guatemala!

That night, I journaled, "Wow. Thank you, God. Daddy, Jack, cousin Jill, and now Timothy Earl are all together in heaven. Your Word promises that your followers will have prophetic visions and dream dreams."

The insert of Timothy Earl Stover's memorial explains,

> Taken from us by a Tender Loving Shepherd to His pastures above:
> Anthony (16) and Curtis (12) were assigned to pick up rocks in a field on our place after school Monday, May 8, 2006. Earl (9) was always an energetic, lively young boy, though nearly the same size as Curtis and desired to do what the other boys were doing whenever possible. Having received permission from Mother to help pick up rocks, he was very diligent and helpful.
> The boys were using a skid loader to transport the rocks from the field. Anthony was

operating the skid loader having operated farm equipment frequently the last several years and especially since our move to Marietta the end of January.

While traveling from one place to another in the field with one-half load of rocks, Curtis and Earl were riding in the loader bucket. Suddenly, the rear wheel of the loader on the side Earl was sitting dropped into a hole. This jerked the loader into the air and Earl flipped over the back of the bucket and apparently landed with his head between the front wheel and the bucket. His head was crushed badly causing extensive injuries. There was a massive loss of blood from the back of the head and a scrape on his forehead.

Emergency personnel were called and they arrived promptly. After working on Earl in the ambulance, he was flown to Hershey Medical Center. The trauma team there was not able to resuscitate him and he was pronounced dead there.

We appreciate the prayers and presence of each and desire your continued prayers for our family.

The Timothy Stover Family

The reverse side of the memorial listed a poem written by his sister Karen Stover, age fourteen and a half in grade 9:

> We feel so sad and lonely,
> Our brother now is gone.
> Why did God take him only?
> Why couldn't we go along?
> But we must see that it's God's will

MY LAST LAST NAME IS GRACE

> To let a person die.
> Because God wants them with him
> In heav'n, our home on high.
> It happened all so quickly;
> We never knew it would.
> But God alone allowed it;
> So we must think it good.
> So many things were then his last;
> It seemed it couldn't be true.
> But God is right beside us,
> And He will help us through.
> He now is very happy
> Up in that home so high;
> And we will go to see him
> Up yonder by and by.
> So may we all be watching;
> For God to come someday,
> We never know when that will be;
> It may be night or day.

I mean no disrespect to the Stover family, but I want to blame the destroyer, not God, for Timothy Earl's death. With the mindset believing God is behind tragedies, deaths, and many misfortunes marches in the reality that at the end of one's such a life, they would arrive at the pearly gates bloody and full of battle scars. In fact, Satan is the enemy and wants burden-laden Christians not to become victorious and true warriors crossing the finish line and winning the race. Don't blame God for things that are not His doing.

One of the spiritual lessons I have learned throughout the years is how I need to place each of my family members in the palm of my hand, open it up, and turn them all over to Him. Hard to fathom, but He loves them even more than I do! My job is to pray for them, their future spouses, and that they walk under His guidance and Light.

I could not be prouder of each one of them—souls of gentle spirits and personality to boot. Last Christmas, I asked them to write a description about each cousin. Each grandchild's name was written at the bottom. "Write your answer on the notebook paper, fold down the answer, and pass it to your neighbor." Here are the results in order of age:

Taylor – Dreams big, funny, talented, indecisive, beautiful, creative and artistic, sweet and awesome, a good role model, ambitious, to be the next Taylor Swift, and is attending Temple University this fall

Alex – (his name means "helper of man"). A goofball, funny, handsome, dedicated to hockey, loves to hug, a ladies' man, determined, strangely energetic, competitive, and strong; goal to be on US Olympic ice hockey team?

Kiersten – Creative, beautiful, a tender spirit, compassionate, bubbly, pretty, and contemplative, has contagious laugh, uncertain of career but has a desire to help others

Madison – Witty, energetic, follower and respecter of her sister, great sense of humor, athletic, competitive, adorably funny, loves her dogs, uncertain what she wants to be, but she truly will be happy and fulfilled in it

Christian – Smart, inventive, energetic, independent, artistic, creative, serious, handsome, neat dresser, deep analytical thinker, naturally talented athlete, book smart, funny, and plans to be an engineer

Hope – Stylish, loves clothes, likes to be in charge, adorable, girly, strong leader, determined, caring and thoughtful, and plans to be a chef or a teacher

Talon – Outdoorsy type, goofy, crazy and fun, giggling jokester, athletic, loving, handsome, wants to be a farmer

I concluded about my seven grandchildren:

MY LAST LAST NAME IS GRACE

*L*avished attention on
*O*verabundance of acceptance
*V*aluable and priceless
*E*xtremely proud of each one

One day, when Kiersten was about twelve years old, I read a note from her that said,

Dear Nana,
Thanks for being everywhere. You're awesome. I'm very glad and thankful.

Love you,
Kiersten

After reading such notes, I stood ten feet tall.

Having been raised without TV, I feel stupid sometimes. Don't ask me Lone Ranger's horse's name because I am not sure—Toto? What were some differences between *The Munsters* and *The Addams Family*? Don't know. Don't ask me my favorite character in *The Addams Family* either. I know the Jetsons mode of travel was a flying spaceship. Was their house futuristic also? Did Gomer Pyle have an antagonist? Even though I did watch some Saturday-morning cartoons and the show *Flipper* on occasion, my grandkids have a better chance of answering a trivia question more correctly than I do.

One funny memory I have of the proof of TV-less little Mennonite children having the wool pulled over their eyes occurred when I worked at Four Seasons Produce. One of our truck drivers, Isaac, walked between my and Allen's desk, the other salesmen who handled telephone produce orders.

Isaac stopped at Allen's desk. "I have a message from Chef Pete from the Greystone Country Club. Are you Elmer Fudd?" Philadelphia-raised Allen all but choked on his soda. I quickly ended my phone conversation so I could laugh aloud (I *did* recognize that name). Allen's face was priceless when he realized that Isaac had no clue Chef Pete was being funny (Allen and Chef Pete had a great telephone relationship during the times of getting his produce orders from him several times a week). I get it, Isaac. Don't feel bad.

Even though some '60s TV shows were televised again later in the '70s, I was busy raising a family, and TV viewing was limited on weeknights and watched mostly Friday through Sunday nights. The exact opposite, Mike had done not much more than watch TV in the '60s and '70s. In fact, he became a "Trekkie," from the love of Star Trek from the very beginning. While we were e-mailing back and forth early in our "cyber-dating" days, Mike impressed me the first time he typed this sentence to me: "to boldly go where no one has gone before." He 'fessed up it was not his original thought but, in fact, from the popular *Star Trek* series once he realized I had no idea what he was talking about.

Mike jokes today and says, "We'll make a great team playing trivia. I'll do well on TV shows, history, and geography. You'll do great answering biblical, medical, and golden-oldie questions."

During the peak of our household income, Mike and I decided to purchase a small double-wide trailer in a beach community near Ocean City, Maryland, in 2004. Each of our incomes paid for one of our two mortgages. Choosing to rent it out also aided in making the mortgage payment. Since family is important to us, we planned on spending our family vacations in it. Carl and Rochelle, excited for us, were with us the day we signed on the dotted line of our purchase. Our family memories began to include spending weekends in our beach house and exploring Assateague Island.

As infants outgrew makeshift cribs in the corner of the beach-house living room, the community pool abounded with giggles and laughs of toddlers. As our family grew to twelve people requiring sleeping quarters, it was necessary that a second beach house be rented in the same community for our weekly summer vacation. Thus, Darrin and Heather did so.

Some grandchildren have great memories of our Assateague days; others can only review photos in their scrapbook. It soon became obvious the almost-four-hour trip down to our beach house on Friday nights was too laborious. Mike feared we would soon need to start spending monies on repairs or a new roof. A storm did cause our one tree to fall over and required our sawing it in small logs in order to be placed in the trash receptacle. In other words, I would look forward upon our arrival to spending time with family on the beach, going out to dinner, biking, and serving simple meals. Mike was concerned he would spend his time *away* from family fixing repairs, pulling weeds, and making sure our property presentable. Eventually, the eight-hour round trip no longer looked too appealing, especially when there was room for only one of my three children's families to share a beach weekend, not all of us.

With great reluctance, Mike finally convinced me to put our beach house on the market. Taking a loss, we signed off on our final second-home property. Our Friday-night tradition of having ice cream at the beach slowly faded. About this same time, our car was requiring a huge repair bill. I encouraged Mike that now was the time to take some money from the sale of the beach house, trade in our car, and to purchase his favorite vehicle—a Jeep. So he did.

As grace and forgiveness are basic to the Lord's nature, unconditional love and acceptance are basic to my grandchildren's nature. Lucky me! As they grew older and wiser, I dreaded the day, while attending a family member's birthday party, that my grandchildren would figure out that three of the men in the room were or is Nana's husband. Not only will my past choices and behavior be revealed, but clarity could come at a cost of tainting their view of their beloved nana. May these pages bring understanding and my lessons learned. My prayer is that they will be happily married to only one faithful partner.

Thought of the Day

Grace was traded for my past sins. I have no past. It is now called *grace*.

Chapter 57

What the Locusts Have Destroyed Has Been Redeemed

> I will repay you the years the locusts have eaten—the great locust and the young locust…you will have plenty to eat, until you are full, and you will praise the name of the Lord your God, who has worked wonders for you.
> —Joel 2:25–26

ONE MOTHER'S DAY, AFTER OUR last grandbaby Talon was born, Steph called me on the phone. "Mom, did you read the *Gazette* yet?"

"No," I answered. "I don't usually skim through it."

"Well, today you must. Check it out and call me back," Steph directed.

Because she had me curious, I did not hesitate to stop what I was doing, locate the small local newspaper, and find the section devoted to mothers. Under a recent family photo of all fifteen of us, I read the following:

> Mom and Nana:
> Do you know how much you're truly loved and appreciated? Despite all the times we tease you about who is your favorite, we know each of us has a special place in your heart. No mat-

ter what choices we've made, you stood by us. It wasn't until we became parents that we fully understood all the sacrifices you've made. Now we can see, not only have you been our mother, but also a teacher, nurse, chef, a listening ear, a woman of strength, courage, and wisdom, as well as our friend. Your love has no boundaries and it's grown to overflow onto your grandchildren. How they love their Nana! They wonder what will happen next: a sleepover, a fun day of crafts and games, maybe a day at the park, or better yet, a vacation at the beach. When Nana's around, the parents don't exist and we wouldn't want it any other way. So thank you for your unconditional love, your creative ways of making wonderful memories, and your countless hours of prayers. None of us would be who we are without them. We love you!

No mother was prouder than thinking about my adult children together compiling this newspaper article. What is my zenith? What is my bed of roses? What is more precious as the biggest diamond anywhere? What I just read made me feel ten feet high! My first response was to (figuratively) fall on my knees and express praises to my Lord. I soared on angel's wings the rest of the day. I was still smiling when my head hit the pillow. Thank you, God, for restoring what the locusts have destroyed. Thank you for redeeming me. May all fifteen of us continue to have blessed, redeemed days.

Praying became comforting for me. I begged God to take a huge eraser and remove all scars and pains from my children's memories. Sometime ago, Billy Graham made the statement he believed people probably forgot about him. He was quickly assured that, that indeed was *not* the case. In my case, I wished people *could* forget about some of my past.

As only He can do, God was asked to make my children and grandchildren stronger, better, and more mature in spite of their mother and nana. I have enough faith for the entire family and believe my grandkids are wiser, more responsible, and will *not* make stupid choices as their nana had.

Hints of God answering my prayers continued to come in the form of a letter or card. Following is the Mother's Day letter from Steph, right before her June wedding. It reads,

> Dear Mom,
>
> Okay, I know this isn't much, but it's better than any "thing" I could get you to clutter up your big house. This Mother's Day probably has more meaning than all the others. I now have to go out and actually use all the thousands of things that you have taught me over the years and prove to you that just because I refused to clean my room doesn't mean I can't clean a house. Just so you know, all those lectures have paid off. You may be amazed, but don't hold your breath. Anyway, despite all the times I swore I'd hate you forever for spanking me, or not letting me stay out pass my curfew, or whatever major catastrophe didn't go my way, you've been loved more than you will ever know. You've made some decisions I didn't agree with, but look at all the things I've done that weren't exactly the best choices in life either. And that's another thing. You knew when to let go and let me make my own decisions, no matter how stupid they were, knowing that I'd learn from them. At least you'd hope so. Well, here we are four weeks before the wedding, and now I have to use all that you have taught me (the good along with the bad) to start my new life

and eventually my own family. I guess when I have my first Mother's Day, you'll get a card that has some comment about the first time I heard myself scream at the little brat and realized I sound like you. YIKES! But for now, I'll stick to thanking you for all your tough love. Boy, is that an understatement! I love you, Mom, for everything you have done through the years and all through this wedding stuff. I have enough of Dad's gentle heart and your tough spirit to make it through whatever life wants to throw my way. Thank you for being so understanding, loving, helpful, and demanding. None of us would be the awesome kids we are if it weren't for all of that. (Well, Darrin and Rochelle are the exceptions, but we won't go there.) Anyway, I hope you have a great day despite your work schedule and know that we are thinking of you.

I LOVE YOU, MOM,
Steph

Mother's Day was within a few weeks after Kiersten's birth. Thus, Steph had mailed me a precious card. The card was a personal expressions Hallmark card, which had words by LeeAnn Ahern on the front. LeeAnn's printed words were as follows:

> Mom, no one sees me like you do—you see me with eyes that have known me for all of my days. No one understands me like you do—we're alike in more ways than we even know. No one empathizes like you do—when I hurt, it affects you deeply, and when I'm up, you're happier than you'd be for yourself. No one loves me like you do—there's something about a mother's love that is unlike any other…(and inside the following is

printed)…and that is why no one could appreciate you and love you more than I do.

On the inside Steph wrote:

Mom,

This card is small and simple, but it holds the BIGGEST thank you! They say a child never appreciates a parent until THEY become one, and man, is that so true! I went through so many emotions over the years. Love, then hate, then love, then anger, and love again. I may not understand everything, but I do understand your love for your children. And I especially understand your new love for God. I've seen the change in you over the past few years. Those who knew you when I was a child would have to also agree with me and see you're an even more spiritual woman. The "Christian Mom" that I saw as a child doesn't even come close to the godly grandmother I see today! And I thank God for that all the time. You knew the reason I was hesitant to have you in the delivery room with Eric and I, but I knew later, without a doubt, that I—I mean *we*—needed you there. Kim said it would be awesome, and she was right! To have you a part of Kiersten's life from her first breath of air was truly a blessing. You were just so helpful to me through my long labor and, what seemed forever, my recovery. But I can't possibly tell you how awesome you make me feel when you do things with Kiersten…even though we have different ideas. You say, "You tell me what you want to do, you're the mother!" Even though you may know what's best, you let me just be, Mom. I love you for that! Thank you for always showing up at just the right time…for always calling at the right time. I love watching you with her. I'd like to think you were the same with me at her age. What a shocker. Our little angel just woke up for her long nap, crying, of course. She's STARVING! But, thanks, Mom, I love you so much.

From Steph

Thank you, Father, for redeeming what the locusts have destroyed.

The Mother's Day following Christian's birth, Steph designed her own card, which I cherish. A beautiful calm ocean scene was printed on the front, and she typed "Happy Mother's Day." The inside cover was Proverbs 31:29–31:

> Many women do noble things,
> But you surpass them all.
> Charm is deceptive, and beauty is
> Fleeting, but a woman who fears the
> Lord is to be praised.
> Give her the reward she has earned,
> And let her works bring her praise at
> The city gate.

On the opposite page, she typed,

> Mom,
> There's so much more I wish I could do to show you how much I appreciate all you do for us. It goes without saying that you are the best Nana EVER. You've blessed them in every way a Nana could, and for that we are very thankful. There's not a day that goes by that I don't thank God for our relationship. I can always count on

your listening ear, your words of encouragement, your never-ending love, and all your mother prayers. Thank you for always going the extra mile, and mostly I thank you for your friendship. I pray every day God will give me the opportunity to bless you double what you have given to us, and I know He will.

All my love on this special Mother's Day,
(signed) Steph, Eric, Kiersten, and Christian

Then one day, for no special reason, I opened up an e-mail from Steph and read,

Hi, Mom,

I just got done talking with someone who once again reminded me about something...I really appreciate and value our friendship! You weren't trying to be my BFF when I was a kid... you were doing your job just being a mother. And you've heard me say it before I never truly appreciated you until I became a mother. But to hear other people's stories about their relationship, or lack thereof, with their moms...it just breaks my heart. They were robbed of something beautiful. So without being a complete sap...thank you for being my mom, the best Nana in the world to my kids and my friend.

Love you and have a great day!

Steph

After Talon's birth, I spent some time with Hope and Rochelle. Rochelle e-mailed me a thank-you note. On top, it said, "With You— the Sun Always Shines," pictured next to a sun and clouds. It read,

MY LAST LAST NAME IS GRACE

Just a little thank-you note! I could not have gotten through my long labor, painful delivery, or my first couple of days home without your help. You are such a wonderful mother and an even better Nana. Thank you for the cleaning, buying groceries, having playtime with my kids, and your love and support. This note just can't express my gratitude enough. Just know that it was appreciated! We love you! Your baby and her babies, Love, Rochelle

Let's all together say, "Ahh."

What relationship needs to be also cherished? The one between a daughter-in-law and mother-in-law. God blessed our family when Heather came into our lives. Heather is such a hard worker and so compatible with Darrin. She chose a career as a paralegal, which enabled her family to enjoy some extras in life. Darrin and Heather together get an A for truly loving each other as best friends and lovers *and making their marriage last*! Heather has always made me feel so special when I would read her cards given on various occasions. She has a gift of selecting just the right card with a message that I felt was truly sincere and not just a "flowery" one meant to flatter. Her Gibson Mother's Day card reads,

>You're a Wonderful Mother and Grandmother:
>With loving thoughts and memories
>Of the wonderful mother
>You've always been…
>With heartfelt gratitude
>For the special grandmother
>You are…
>With warm wishes for you
>To enjoy your day

And remember
How very much you're loved.
Happy Mother's Day
(signed) Love, Darrin, Heather, Taylor and Madison

My sister Lenora experienced healing somewhat from our mother. One morning, Lenora received a phone call from Mom, who was crying, a rare event.

"Lenora, I didn't sleep too well last night. I had a dream, and in it, I could tell that you are very upset with me," Mom's voice began to quiver. "I should have been in attendance at your husband, Jack's, funeral. I was wrong for not doing that. Will you please forgive me?"

After catching her breath, Lenora commented, "Yes, Mom. *You* of all people know what it is like to lose your husband. I was hurt that you were not there for me. It would have meant more to me than you'll ever know. But yes, I forgive you."

Lenora finished her phone call with Mom and returned to her tedious chore. What? She spent an entire year unemployed so she could work on designing a daily calendar. Eventually, handed over as a gift to her four children and several grandchildren, the 365 pages are filled with scripture, inspirational thoughts, and reminders how God has restored decades of heartache on various levels. She too finally rode on a path of a truly happy marriage and could pass on many nuggets of wisdom to her loved ones and precious, intimate moments from having a close relationship with the true Lover of her soul.

Ann Spangler, one of my favorite authors, says in her book *Praying the Names of Jesus* (Zondervan, 2006, p. 243),

> No wonder Jesus liked to hang out around sinners. There are no other kinds of people to associate with…Jesus can do little for the strong and the self-righteous who don't even know they are lost. It's the poor, the weak, the addicted, the troubled, and the fractured people—those who

have an inkling of how off course their lives have become who are often the most responsive to grace. This principle applies even after our conversion. Jesus seeks to bless the people who admit their need, not the ones who act as though they know it all and have it all. Blessed are the poor in spirit, the meek, those who hunger and thirst. Blessed are the empty, not the full.

Pray today for the grace to know how much you still need Jesus. Ask him for the grace to see beyond your wants to the things you really need—more compassion and less harsh judgment, more generosity and less fear, more patience and less irritability, more faith and less doubt. Pray that Jesus will enable you to move beyond the kind of selfish praying we all do so that you can pray in a way that reflects his heart, letting whatever moves him move you. Then pray for the privilege of joining him as he seeks and saves those who are lost.

Thought of the Day

Grace is being a conduit of His love and grace. Be present with others through all their seasons. Keep Christ busy.

Chapter 58

Our First Mission Trip to Mexico

Dear friends, we are children of God, and what we will be has not yet been made known. But we know that when He appears, we shall be like Him, for we shall see Him as He is.
—1 John 2:3

SOME CHRISTIANS BELIEVE GOD WILL pave their path like a neatly wrapped present: perfect corners and matching folds. Last time I checked, my wrapped packages have imperfect, mismatched ends. Sometimes I have way too much excess paper causing folds to be somewhat bunched. As God does similarly, I needed to "snip off" the excess and watch God leave a perfectly wrapped, Holy Spirit–inspired life. Choosing to go on a mission trip instead of a second vacation in 2005 was wise and necessary. I learned how missionaries rely on prayer far more than I could ever imagine.

Fearing for our safety if we went elsewhere, Mike and I decided to sign up for a Mexico mission trip with someone we felt could be trusted. The answer: our friend and fellow church members Henry and Diane Fisher, executive director of Dunamis Connections. Like Pastor Sam, Henry was also raised Amish in Lancaster County. As a thirty-year-old, Henry was called by God out of the car-salesman business, and instead the love for unsaved people of third-world countries bubbled up inside him.

Under the influence of Dr. Myles Munroe and Pastor Sam, Henry started Dunamis Connections. Today, DC's website reads,

> Dunamis Connection empowers individuals to reach their potential through connecting resources. Through strategic team building exercises, individuals and teams are strengthened, as they serve developing countries. We build in three different ways on each trip. This is seen in how we: build individuals, build teams and build nations. We partner with various nonprofits and churches as well as any type of corporate entity (i.e. business, construction, medical, education, etc.).

Every nurse learns about Maslow's hierarchy of needs: physiological, safety, and love and belonging rest on the bottom first three rungs of the ladder. Driving through impoverished Mexican countryside and sharing meals and fellowship around a scantily set table opened my eyes to one avenue of true peace and contentment. Whistling and humming was heard as the pastor's wife cooked to serve us a simple meal of enchiladas and refried beans. Unhurried, relaxed movements were plentiful in this culture.

Our Mexican hosts had their safety needs met in a roof over their head, in spite of it being a plain gray square building with a thatched roof, no fancy curtains at the window or flowerpots on the windowsills. Love abounded among family members as strong as the pull of an ocean tide. Need to use the facilities? Use the cement slab in the shape of a toilet!

By the time our mission trip concluded, I realized they had the wealth of kings.

One Sunday morning in September, Henry spoke for a few minutes about the need to take a group with him to distribute goody bags to impoverished families of Mexico. We learned the goody bags were eighteen-inch square cloth bags with a drawstring that a ninety-plus-year-old Amish lady had sewn. Many people's various donations allowed three hundred plus bags to be filled with school supplies, small toys, coloring books, and candy. Two Mexican pastor friends of Henry's were overseeing the distribution of the goody bags. Henry planned that some of the time would be spent driving to the country schools to the excited, expectant students. However, at the end of the ten-day trip, Henry scheduled enough free time to feel like we were on vacation. Plus, the cost was reasonable. I looked over at Mike and whispered, "This is the one." He agreed.

On Saturday, December 3, twenty-four of us, including Adrian, our Spanish interpreter, gathered at the Worship Center parking lot to be bussed to Harrisburg Airport for our flight to San Antonio, Texas. Henry rented two passengers and one cargo van. The cargo van held our entire luggage and the goody bags. Our first time of intense prayer was to get through both the border and a checkpoint. The goody bags could not be discovered (a cargo van full of traveling tourists' luggage looked innocent). Pastor DelToro had a church member assist us, but God was the Navigator. We stayed at Nuevo Laredo's Hilton Garden, an awesome, gorgeous motel, and probably the last nice one for some time.

On Sunday, after a great breakfast, we headed to Matehuala, the location of Pastor DelToro's church. We pulled up to a cement-block building that had a broken sidewalk, so we had to step carefully. Pastor DelToro greeted the Americans warmly (in front of his 125-member congregation). After one hymn, Henry slowly preached the sermon, allowing Adrian to translate. It was a sermon about how Jesus came as a baby, grew up to be a little boy, and never reached the age of an old man because He was crucified. "He can give you a gift that keeps on giving," Henry preached.

At that point, Henry selected certain people out of the audience and specifically prayed for them. The Lord revealed what their needs were. Then Henry asked for Pastor DelToro and his family to come forward. Some of us gathered around the DelToro family while Henry prayed specific prayers over them. I stood next to the pastor's wife and held her hand and softly prayed over her in English, knowing she could not understand a word I was saying. Tears flowed down her cheeks, a universal sign of feeling the touch of God. I felt so warm all over as we prayed for the pastor and his family. Henry asked the congregation to be generous and held a special offering, not for the church's budget but to bless their pastor. Thank You, Jesus, for Your presence.

We drove to a little restaurant for a bedtime snack before heading back to our hotel, and that was only the second day!

Monday morning after breakfast, we all assisted repacking the three vans with the goody bags that earlier were emptied out of various people's luggage. We drove to another pastor's father's house. He was to be our tour guide to the location of all the schools' students who would receive the bags. We made six different stops between one o'clock and five o'clock. Some schools held forty to fifty students; others held around sixty to seventy. Teachers also received their own goody bag.

We drove to an area, and then our tour guide would make people aware of our purpose. How? Using a town crier! He made an announcement, and the people started gathering around our vans. What an unforgettable sight! Some mothers brought babies on their hips or toddlers less than two years of age. Some children acted shy; some said, "Thank you;" others, "Gracias." Regardless of their ages, it seemed all the children knew how to use the drawstring and was thrilled to rummage through the bag for their goodies. Candy was the first preference to devour. It matched many of my childhood Christmas mornings.

We took the tour guide home and headed to dinner. Over coffee, we lingered and learned to know more about our fellow traveling companions. Again, we repacked the van with more goody bags to repeat the excursion tomorrow.

Tuesday morning, after the best cup of coffee on this trip thus far, we left to pick up our tour guide. Today the count of the five different schools ranged from 20 to 109 students. I would never tire of seeing the excitement of children dumping their bag's contents and watching their friends rummage through their gifts. Using the items found in their bags, the children played jumping jacks and jump rope.

We went to the pastor's house for a late lunch, where his wife served us tortillas, beans, and rice. What activity occurs after a meal? We took turns using their toilet: a two-foot-high toilet-shaped concrete toilet seat in a lean-to with no lid or tissue paper, which sat at the edge of their vegetable garden. Do I want to know what is used for fertilizer?

Back at the hotel, we changed our clothes to go shopping in downtown Matehuala. At one of the best restaurants in town, I selected goat as my entree for the first time—not too bad.

On Wednesday morning, I had a difficult time rising. I guess because I drank coffee too late, I did not sleep well. After breakfast, we traveled the Mexican countryside to three more schools. I made a new friend, Irlanda, who was in second grade at the last school we handed out goody bags. As I handed her the bag, her beautiful dark-brown eyes opened up to the size of marbles. As we raced around the schoolyard together and played ball (using one of her gifts) tag, Irlanda was talking in Spanish a mile a minute, which, of course, I could not understand. She was so cute and chubby with really thick dark hair. We just clicked. Before long, it was time for me to leave. I handed her some pesos. Through Adrian, our interpreter, I told Irlanda I would be writing her letters as a pen pal and would faithfully pray for her. It was so sad to leave her. Mike snapped several pictures of me and my new friend.

Later on, I did send my new Spanish friend, Irlanda, letters via a Spanish Internet program several times. Once, I even included an American postage stamp for her to write back and an American one-dollar bill. One day, I opened my mail and found a letter from Irlanda. Tears welled up as I read her brief note about her school and family. I said a prayer as I refolded the letter. But that was the last time I heard from her. Henry said my mail was probably intercepted, and items of any worth were probably removed before Irlanda ever received them.

The pastor's family made us lunch again. We could relax a bit before heading out at four o'clock for a church service. The Lord taught me another lesson: I was amazed how people walked barefoot for miles to our special midweek church service. Would Americans do that? Henry said he wasn't sure what he was supposed to preach about that night. So he asked if Mike and I would go up front and say a few words using Adrian as the interpreter. Say what? No prep time? I guess I can talk about what I'm learning in the book I'm currently reading, *Waking the Dead* by John Eldredge? The only advice Henry gave as he looked at us and smiled was, "Don't forget, you need to take breaks after phrases for Adrian to interpret." Mike and I did not have very much time to plan our part of the service. By the time Henry and Diane prayed over Mike and I, we felt more confident.

Pastor DelToro opened the service with the congregation singing two hymns. Then he read from the Twenty-Third Psalm. Pastor DelToro looked over at me; I walked to the front of the room and looked into the faces of about forty people staring back at me. There was no podium. I held a small tablet of notes in my hand.

I explained I felt led to say something about what I learned from the book I was reading on this trip: Man is to be made whole, feel safe and secure, and have an abundant life all for God's glory. But the enemy doesn't want us to experience that. I spoke briefly on how I was taught to tithe and how the amount does not matter. Our tenth is different for each one of us. Then I gave my partial testimony of how I fell away from God for a time, how God drew me near to Him—He never went anywhere.

I acknowledged that I sat under awesome teachings about grace that helped to heal me. I testified about the Sunday morning on how I gazed with my spiritual eyes upon the cross. When I looked into my loving Savior's eyes, I knew and realized He was sincere when He called me by my married last names. I heard, "I love you, Leanne Ann Martin, Weaver, Krall, and Miller!" By now, my tears were flowing, and I noticed my girlfriends were wiping their eyes too. I was grateful for the necessary pauses allowing Adrian to translate. I then reread the Twenty-Third Psalm and emphasized how the verses were talking about wholeness, safety, or abundance.

Mike felt led to talk about trusting God. He invited people to come forth to the altar so he could pray for healing for them.

That's trusting God all right! About five ladies and one man did so. Mike and I and a few others from our group laid hands on them and prayed for God's healing. Mike encouraged them to expect the healing so that the whole village will know of His glory. Another bonus would be realizing they would never be the same. By the time we were leaving, through Adrian, one lady thanked Mike for praying for her as she was healed of her left foot pain.

That night, Henry proposed that the pastor was allowing anybody from our group to sleep on the floor of the church that was located in the middle of a field. About one fourth of the group, including Mike, took Henry up on his offer. We learned later it rained sometime during the night. It was an answer to prayer, as they needed the rain desperately because it hadn't rained in over a year! I believe these Mexicans were praying for trusting God in a way that we Americans had no idea.

As my head hit the pillow that night, I was in awe about my new friend, Irlanda, and how dozens of Mexicans walked to a midweek church service to hear Americans lead their service. Henry joked about his "new ministry" team in Mike and me.

The following morning, those who slept on the church floor had a chance to shower before heading to de Catorce, a quaint town where the movie *The Mexican* (starring Julia Roberts and Brad Pitt) was filmed. It was necessary to drive through a one-way almost-two-mile-long tunnel. We shopped in the markets. The road out of town was steep and narrow, unlike any road I ever traveled on. Walt, our van driver, couldn't get our packed-full van up the steep hill. We were a little frightened until someone reminded us, "Where's the trust we learned about?" Henry ended up driving us up the steep hill by keeping the pedal to the medal until we reached the top.

Our hotel was very quaint with a small fireplace in the corner that did not quite heat the room. The uncarpeted floors were much too cold, but of course, we knew we didn't dare complain. During our dinner table conversation, I asked the question, "What do you fear the most?" which led to good, intimate discussions. Mike answered, "I fear that I will die alone." Hmmm…

The next day on Friday, we did a little more shopping at the markets. Then we loaded up our vans for our trek back over the border and into San Antonio. I finished reading my one book and started the second one titled *Surprise Me, God*. At one point, the song "How Great Thou Art" came across the van's radio. Intently listening to the words, I was so touched. My tears ran in devotion to my Lord as I anticipated a more intimate encounter between Him and me. When having these mountaintop experiences, I fear I'll bump into heaven. As I reviewed my last week, I drew strength from the Mexican believers' life-filled contentment and attitude of humility and gratitude. Nothing is meaningless in life.

As expected, we had no issue with crossing back into the United States's border, but it was quite unnerving though for all twenty-four of us to pass through customs. We were hoping to spend some time strolling the River Walk. But, instead, around 1:00 a.m., our tired bodies crawled into our Day's Inn bed—much too fatigued to enjoy the River Walk.

Saturday, December 10, started out for me with a great cup of coffee and a delightful American breakfast of bland (nonspicy Mexican) food of bacon, eggs, and toast. Mike and I, along with most of the group, enjoyed shopping along the River Walk. Finally, we headed to the airport for our flight home.

I was so glad to be sleeping in my own bed and hugging Mr. Pillow. As I was falling asleep, I pondered on the "bookends" of my life: my birth into a Mennonite family as God designed it and reaching the pearly gates. In between, God placed people in my path, like Dr. Myles Munroe, Henry Fisher, Pastor DelToro, and Irlanda, someone who could easily look like a relative of mine. It is only by God's providence He planted her in Mexico, and I was planted in Lancaster County, Pennsylvania. As He created each one of us with our personalities, talents, and giftings, God wants us to shine our light in our world of influence, whether that is teaching students in the backcountry of Mexico, being a town crier, or supervising a nursing team.

On this journey, between my "bookends," sometimes my actions stank up my life, just as the dead mouse that died in between the kitchen walls in the farmhouse stank up my house for weeks. For both a "rich" American and a poor Mexican farmer, we all have settled for the world's cheap glory of tinsel at times. How pathetic for us when we settle for tinsel; how matchless it is up against God's glory of everlasting brilliance: faith, truth, and everlasting life.

Thought of the Day

Today is a day of grace. But I understand that Jesus is coming soon. Thus, daily I need to live expectantly.

Chapter 59

A Vacation That Changed Our Lives

We know that in all things God works for the good of those who love him, who have been called according to His purpose.
—Romans 8:28

LONG BEFORE RETIREMENT AGE, I wrote in my journal on January 1, 2008: "Give Mike a job he enjoys, my three kids to have an awesome walk with You, and a retirement relocation that is very obviously a blessed one. Help me to walk closer and closer to You, amen."

In 2010, I climbed into the bathtub and slithered down into the piling bubbles. I played our dinner table conversation over and over again in my mind. Mike reiterated once more how he could not stand his job. "Hate is a strong word, so I won't use it. I'll use its cousin: *extremely detest*," he commented without smiling. As we ate our pasta meal together, Mike spoke about his day and how his female boss slammed the door when he and another coworker were reamed out in her office. "The office politics are getting to her head, and she is making poor leadership decisions. As Larry joked, we all take turns being her scapegoat. She doesn't have a clue how to run an IT department." If I behaved as badly and unprofessional as his boss, I'd be written up!

By the time we were loading the dishwasher together and wiping down the stove and counters, it was decided that Mike would start looking for another job. Hesitating before speaking and weighing his words, Mike asked me, "Any reason why it can't be in Arizona?" He pleaded with his eyes.

Looking down and curling up one upper lip, I responded, "I know you can't fathom having a beloved and fulfilling job, such as mine. I want that for you as well. Sure, go for it. You can always say no," I pointed out as I started the dishwasher.

As the soothing hot water poured into my bathtub, my tears began to mingle with the bubbles. I couldn't even put a prayer together except beseech, "God…Jesus…Oh, my Lord…" After a few minutes, I looked heavenward, sat up, pounded my fists on the tub's edge, and hissed through clenched teeth, "*Fine. I'll move! But you will bless my faithfulness!*"

My salty tears ran until I could taste them no more; my gulping ended as one deep breath. As the bath water cooled, my attitude simmered down as well. *Lord, please guide our steps. Thy will be done, not my will. If Mike's new job takes us to Arizona, help my kids and grandkids to understand.*

The following Friday night, we all gathered in our dining room to celebrate both Darrin and Eric's birthdays. Our home was abuzz with grandchildren putting on skits for the adult's entertainment, some pounding on the portable piano, which sounded like "racket" (good word, Daddy) from a grandchild's unskilled fingers, and table conversation abounded around Steph and Eric's recent successful hunting trip when they both bagged a buck.

As I curled under the blankets that night, I fought back tears. *Lord, I can't do it. I can't move away. My family needs me. I would miss my grandbabies so much. You know I want to be a submissive wife and honor Mike and his wishes as the head of our home.* But moving way out to Arizona cannot be an option. By the time Mr. Sandman arrived, I had a plan.

The following day, I called our church's counseling center and made an appointment to meet with the head counselor, Mr. Johnston. During our dinner table conversation that evening, I invited Mike to attend the session, scheduled for next Thursday. "You don't have to. I'll go myself. The purpose is to sort out my issues about your applying for jobs out of Pennsylvania. But I'd love it if you would go with me," I pointed out. Mike was actually surprised about my need to sort things out with a counselor. It didn't require deep introspection in his mind, but mothers are wired so different than fathers, especially stepdads.

After filling out a three-page questionnaire on our intent and purposes for the counseling session, Mike and I sat across from Mr. Johnston. After hearing a nutshell-version of my dilemma and Mike's job frustrations, Mr. Johnston leaned back in his soft leather chair. "I see my wife and I driving across the country in our new RV. We'll stop off at all the national state parks and cross into Alaska and Canada. Perhaps, we'll spend a summer on Puget Sound. Definitely a winter or two in Yuma, Arizona." He then leaned front and placed both elbows on his desk and looked directly at Mike.

"But guess what. It's only a dream. I'd never be able to get my wife on such a trip, at least not until the last grandchild graduates from college." He chuckled. With a big sigh, he asked Mike, "So tell me again. What good reason do you have to take this awesome mother and grandmother away from her children and grandchildren?" Dr. Johnston glanced my way and smiled.

Mike looked at me and immediately concluded, "I guess I don't have any." I reached out and grabbed his hand and gave it a big squeeze. His words hung in the air unchallenged and true. His conclusion for me was as refreshing as a shower must be to the homeless.

As the hinges to Mr. Johnston's office door closed only one time for the Millers, the hinges of the future door we opened and walked through was oiled by God's perfect timing. No pounding on a bathtub was necessary.

Mike's remaining employment was entrenched with more detested days and, eventually, a layoff during the 2010 recession. During his four-month unemployment, Mike volunteered some hours at the Prince Street Rescue Mission in Lancaster. Meeting homeless heroine-addicted men, who barely survived day by day, was an eye opener. It was one thing for Mike to hear me say, after a complaint about his workday, "The resident I have that has MS would love to trade places with you." It was another to rub shoulders with men he was never sure he would ever see again because they didn't survive the demons of the night literally and figuratively. As belief in Santa Claus diminishes and fades, reality took its toll. If he could have seen the ashes of their broken lives, Mike's eyes would have seen piles of psychosis, alcoholism, drug abuse, haunting prison memories, and heartbreak. Most men sat through the required church services at the mission, and some even answered the altar call. They met Jesus for the first time.

By year-end, Mike was employed by a bank located in Lancaster several blocks from the Rescue Mission. Even though his annual salary was $20,000 less, at least he was employed. He never held a job before that required he drive into the city and pay for parking in a parking garage.

On the second week of Mike's job, I was driving to work and listening to the local news in between praise-and-worship songs. The news broadcaster announced there was a shutdown at the bank where Mike was employed, as well as all the businesses, on an entire block. Police were on the scene searching for a gunman in the Prince Street parking garage. I believe Prince Street parking garage connects to the bank's second floor where Mike works. The timing of Mike parking his Jeep and walking into work would be about the exact same time. God, please keep my honey safe. I couldn't arrive at my work fast enough that morning. My fingers nervously dialed his work number. Only when I heard Mike's voice could I stop holding my breath. Thank you, Lord!

The conversation that night around our dinner table meal of soup and salad was about the gunman. From reading the newspaper article at the gas station checkout line, when he stopped to get gas, Mike learned the man was one of the poor souls he ministered to during his volunteer days at the mission. According to the article, he robbed a pawnshop to get his hands on a gun and set it up, so the police would need to kill him. Grabbing a gun while having three policemen point their guns at you was definitely granting a death wish. The tortuous soul can finally sleep in the arms of Jesus.

With a new job, Mike's spirits soared, and his energy increased. Yesterday was gone, and tomorrow was full of promises. However, within three months of hiring, Mike's nice boss quit and moved to the Philadelphia area. Over the next three years, three more bosses were assigned to spearhead IT and new banking software. Mike learned from his last boss the only difference between a meltdown and a breakdown is your age. Our dinner conversations were once again about his job dissatisfaction and unfulfillment.

That spring, our church's small group completed a financial course. A personal questionnaire challenged each one of us about how fulfilling were our current jobs. Out of the seven men in the room, Mike and another friend didn't hesitate to raise their hands during the discussion about job dissatisfaction. They would accept another job in a heartbeat if an appealing job offer dropped in their lap. However, neither was seeking at the moment.

"I would love to make less money and work for a Christian organization. To be doing something that changes people's lives would be awesome," Mike stressed, closing his one fist and talking with his hands. I don't see a question on this form asking, "Want to make less money?"

Typical for us, every winter, Mike and I loved to plan a vacation somewhere warmer than Pennsylvania winters. We have cruised on both Western and Eastern Caribbean tours, to Bermuda, Jamaica, and Mexico, besides our Arizona, San Diego, and Palm Springs trips. One day during an Internet search, an ad for The Cove: Billy Graham Training Center in Asheville, North Carolina caught my eye. After more in-depth searching, I printed out material to attend a seminar at the Cove in March to review with Mike as our potential vacation.

Our dinner conversation that night was exciting as we discussed our trip. I made the Cove hotel reservations and completed seminar registrations for their scheduled guest speaker for March. The seminar was called Five Days with the Master. Happy with the topic, Mike and I both requested time off. I booked a cozy cabin in the mountains of North Carolina for three days prior to the seminar.

My Acura was packed, and we headed out with job responsibilities a distant memory. Well, perhaps for Mike. My personal care wing was expecting the second-half of our state survey on Monday, which I would be missing. Many check-in phone calls from the road were finally behind me. The state surveyors left, and I was thrilled with the survey results of only two minor citations. Now I can forget about work and have a good time with my honey and Master.

Our cozy cabin was a great place to unwind and supplied great rest and recreation. By Tuesday, we were checked into the impressive Cove. Looking around the beautiful hotel room, I noticed we had no TV in our room. Several books from the Billy Graham Evangelistic Association (BGEA) were lying on the nightstand and marked "free." By the time our vacation had ended, I finished reading one of the books.

The Cove's hospitality, surroundings, and purpose, as described in the brochure, were met beyond our expectations. Mike commented on the beautiful natural wood, which graced the interior. The lobby was simple yet gorgeous. The meals were great, and the surrounding wooded area was a recipe for a relaxing atmosphere as we rocked away on old-fashioned rocking chairs on the long stone patio, which ran the entire length of the hotel. We had enough downtime to meet other people in our break-out sessions (a group e-mail ensued for months between the women I met at the Cove).

During our drive back home, I scanned through some more of the free material we were given at our departure. I noticed a reference to a website about job opportunities at the Billy Graham Evangelistic Association in Charlotte, North Carolina. "Why don't you check out this website? They might be hiring computer programmers," I innocently commented. "I was really impressed about this entire association, weren't you?" Mike agreed and said, "You do know applying for a job in Charlotte could be life-changing."

"Yeah, but applying for one and getting one are two different things," I answered. "You can always say no."

Unbeknownst to me, Mike faithfully checked the Billy Graham Evangelistic Association (BGEA)'s website weekly for job opportunities in his field. His present job was making him so unhappy, but he felt trapped. I even began to talk negative about the company too for the first time when Mike was not allowed to take a vacation to attend our beach family week because of the implementation of the bank's new software.

Six months later, in September, one night, Mike called out from the living room, where the computer was located. "Hmm, BGEA has a posting for the perfect job for me. What do you want me to do?" he inquired. I had totally forgotten about Mike's possibility of checking the BGEA website all that time. But unhappy people are motivated. "Sure, apply. No sense putting the cart before the horse, though. See what happens," I nonchalantly answered.

Mike decided he wanted to pray about it some more. We spent a get-away weekend with friends in the Pennsylvania mountains. Loving to get up early and walk in nature, Mike took a hike by himself. Later, the four of us enjoyed a hearty down-home-cooking breakfast at the local diner. Mike announced while sipping his hot tea, "God and I had a talk today. I sense in my spirit I am to apply. This job is mine." Our friends were one of the couples who also took the financial course with us and knew about Mike's recent job histories. Their encouragement was priceless.

"Well, if God 'told' you to apply, then who am I to stop you?" I commented. Upon our return back home and after he unpacked his suitcase, Mike logged onto BGEA's website. Within half an hour, a completed online resume and his application went through cyberspace. My life was about to be forever changed!

Within one week, Mike received an e-mail about setting up a telephone interview with the human resource director, the first step of employment once an application is considered. Mike needed to go to work late that Friday morning to hold the telephone interview. It was scheduled on my day off. Even though Mike had taken the call in the privacy of our library, I could hear his muffled interview answers from time to time. Wow. I would never be allowed to ask such questions in an interview.

Later, he excitedly explained the first half was strictly about his personal information. "I had to give them my testimony, share how

I witness to people, and the reason behind our possible relocation. I guess the director was fishing for how sincere I was in doing that. He asked which church do we attend, how, and where I was baptized. He asked questions too about my family."

"I guess they want to make sure they aren't hiring any riffraff," I commented as I dusted the furniture. Mike took a swig of his ice tea and stared at me. "Are you sure you want me to pursue this? The next step is to complete an online personality test of sorts. I can stop here if you want me to." I stopped dusting and looked at him and sighed, "For the past week, I have done a lot of praying on my drive back and forth to work. No radio has been turned on. During my jogging, each slap of my foot was a prayer for guidance for us. I am going with one word, *peace*. So far, I have peace about every step of this journey. When I don't, you'll be the first to know."

With the biggest smile I haven't seen in a long time, Mike walked toward me and gave me a hug and a kiss before heading into work. "I know. I know. I don't understand it either. I was calm and collected during the whole interview. The second half was about my computer programing experience. That was easy to talk about."

The next month dragged on. Mike checked his e-mail box or phone messages daily for a word from BGEA. Nothing! Being impatient, Mike sent an e-mail inquiring if he was still in the running as a possibility. He was told by the HR director that he was. They were also holding on-site interviews among current employees.

The following Sunday morning, someone with the gift of prophecy had a prophetic word for the congregation (I only ever heard this occur once before at the Worship Center). It follows:

> I want you to know that what concerns you really does concern Me. I am always listening. There is nothing that you do, nothing that you say, no problem that you face, no bill that comes in the mail, no difficulty in relationships, no hidden thing, no sin that you try to cover up… there is absolutely nothing that I'm not aware of

all the time. Before you begin to feel ashamed, know in your heart that I love you. Period. What concerns you concerns Me. So let's start talking more about it. Let's get down to the heart of the matter. Don't try to impress Me. Just come as you are and tell Me what's on your mind. And then give Me a chance to speak, to reveal My will to you, to show you the awesome picture that I have for each of you. It differs because each of you is different. I have given you different personalities, different gifts, and different callings. So don't compare yourselves among yourselves or measure yourselves by yourselves.

As I told you in My Word, those not having any understanding, come and let us reason together. I wrote to you in Isaiah, "Though your sins be as scarlet, they'll be as white as snow." I can remove everything. I can change things. I can make something from nothing, just as I did when I healed the crippled man who was lowered down through the roof. I recreated cells in his body for him to walk. I can do that and more in your life. Don't limit me. Stop limiting me. I remind you again…I love you just the way you are, but I love you too much to leave you that way. My Kingdom is about change. I want to change your life, and I want to change other people through you. Just start letting Me be all that I want to be whenever you need for Me to be it.

I looked over at Mike with big eyes and mouthed, "Wow." He reached over and grabbed my hand and gave it a confident squeeze.

The following week, Mike received a thanks-but-no-thanks letter in the mail. The minute I saw his drooped shoulders and slack expression, I knew he received bad news about the job. "You said you sensed in your spirit God told you this job is yours. That means whoever they are hiring is *not* going to work out. Just wait and see," I pointed out as he handed me the letter. The previous Sunday's prophetic word was allowing me to open myself up to the wide spectrum of God's ways and future prospects. In Him, our future was secure.

But it is difficult to face reality. The dream of a blue-ribbon panel for Mike's company's leadership team was fading. Mike was swamped with the bank's software changeover, and it kept his mind busy at work, even into the weekend, at times. By the end of December, Mike was forced to take off three days or he would lose his vacation time. I don't ever take off around the holidays, so it was a little disheartening to know he missed a summer vacation, but he would be off when nobody else was.

One night, I woke up and had difficulty falling back to sleep. Prayers for our future were sent heavenward many times during those moments. At one point, I opened my eyes in the dark bedroom. I got it! Mike has three days to remodel our kitchen. It's time to remove the outdated kitchen grape wallpaper, paint the walls, and lay new flooring in the kitchen and laundry room. His three days off will not be wasted.

Mike did just that. With the assistance of a professional, our finished, remodeled kitchen looked great with tan walls and new vinyl flooring. Little did we know, within six weeks our house would be on the market. The next step of this God-is-in-control story was that my mother was moved in early January from her independent home into the personal care wing. My large family held a surprise ninetieth birthday celebration for Mom. For me, that meant she was well taken care of, and less responsibility was placed on me as the daughter who lived the closest to Mom.

The second week of January, Mike received a phone call from the BGEA's HR director. "Are you and your wife still interested in relocating to the Charlotte area?" Mike stood up quickly and almost knocked over his office chair. "Yes, yes. But I received a letter from you saying the position was filled." By the time, Mike hung up the phone; he had an on-site interview scheduled for the following week.

He felt so giddy. That night's dinner table conversation was about God's perfect timing. "I told you this job was yours," I said. "Peace is still ruling. Mom is moved, and I no longer have to worry about taking her grocery shopping. Wow."

In His matchless amazing grace, God sent appropriate praise-and-worship songs through the radio airwaves on my drive to work that week. DC Talk's "My Will" and Ben Cantelon's "Guardian" blared out: "It's my will, and I'm not moving 'cause if it's your will, then nothing can shake me" and "Where you go I'll go…Show me the way…Every step I take…Be now my guide…"

My heart swelled as I listened to Kari Jobe's "I am Not Alone": "You will go before me, You will never leave me…I am not alone…" or Hillsong United's "Oceans (Where Feet May Fail)": "The great unknown where feet may fail…Your grace abounds in deepest waters…Your Sovereign hand will be my guide…"

The warmth in the car I felt that morning had little to do with my car heater. My Lord's attention to details in this journey was beyond astonishing. I literally reached over while driving and pretended to hold My Savior's hand. I envisioned Him to be sitting in the passenger seat (to have Him as my traveling companion and to speak to Him out loud was not unusual). *Yes, leaving my family and babies behind is only going to be possible if You direct every step because I'm not moving unless You do.* This story could only play out the way it was. It was *my* fault we most likely were moving. It was *my* idea for Mike to apply for the job after our Cove weekend. I swear I heard Jesus chuckle!

If my tears were bottled, they would be enough to wipe my windshield clean. The most difficult part was making sure it didn't look like I was crying before I walked into my office. I couldn't take a chance of having coworkers ask about my tears without lying.

Mike informed the HR director (who never revealed why he received his no-thanks letter) he would research for the best flight from Harrisburg to Charlotte. To save BGEA money, he decided to have one layover in Atlanta and not book a straight flight. Everything was set for Mike's interview the following Wednesday. However, due to a bad ice storm in Atlanta, his flight was cancelled Wednesday morning. Harrisburg Airport remained open, but Atlanta Airport was closed? How often does that happen? Mike was rescheduled for a direct flight into Charlotte. However, he missed the informal lunch interview with his coworkers and barely made it on time for his one o'clock interview with the HR director. Interviews with two tiers of bosses were scheduled for two o'clock.

All I could do was pray and wait. By the time I heard from Mike, when he returned back to Harrisburg Airport, I was as anxious as one waiting for pregnancy test results. "Yes, I have a good feeling about all the interviews. But I couldn't quite read the one boss. I don't know what to think." By the time he crawled into bed at 10:00 p.m. (his day started at 3:00 a.m.), he was exhausted. I heard more negatives than positives. You got this, God. I'm leaning and trusting on You.

The next morning, as our typical routine, I climbed into my bath barely awake, as Mike shaved at the sink. He was talking a mile a minute, waving his arms using grand gestures. "I know last night I sounded negative. But I'm excited. The interview went well. So we'll see." He turned and looked at me while moving his shaver around on his face. I had my eyes closed and my head leaned back in the tub trying to get awake and absorb all this information. "I know you're only half awake. You know me. I'm not a night person. I was so tired last night. It is morning now, and I'm wide awake." When he heard no comment from me, he smiled and said, "Enjoy your bath. We'll talk tonight."

The dinner conversation that night over steak and baked potatoes was about the logistics of a new job and our possible relocation. If Mike was offered the job by bedtime, we concluded:

* Our winter vacation would be looking for an apartment for Mike in the Charlotte area.
* We'll contact my niece, a realtor, and put our house on the market.
* I would stay behind in Pennsylvania until the house was sold.

* I would give my employer my thirty-day notice only after we got an offer on the house.
* Mike would drive the Jeep down to the Carolinas loaded with clothing and necessities.
* I will plan on driving back to Pennsylvania every quarter to see my family and friends, as long as I so choose.

Most importantly, we determined we would not discuss any of this with my family until the for-sale sign was placed in our front lawn. We also figured it would be wise to rent a house or apartment for a year in the Carolinas, giving us time to check out several neighborhoods.

Within the week, Mike received the much-anticipated phone call with the news: "Congratulations! Pending a drug test and signing our Covenant Agreement, you are hired as our Technical Analyst in our Information Systems Department. Your new-hire packet is in the mail." Know what other great news the good Lord implemented? The starting salary was over two thousand dollars more than his present salary! Mike was uncertain how to answer the question on "expected salary" in the application. He didn't want to put down an amount that was too high and cause his application to be placed in file 13 (the trash can). So he dropped the amount by ten thousand dollars of his current salary. This is the guy who wants to make less money.

The fat packet of paperwork arrived, was reviewed, and signed. The drug test was scheduled and passed, of course. Mike was told his starting date was March 10. We took a week's vacation to check out the Charlotte area. No man was happier when he handed in his two-week's notice.

However, first, we needed to update our family on our move. At the time, our grandchildren ranged between eight and sixteen years old, a busy time of sports and cheerleading for them. It would be much easier to see them less often, as they were filling their lives with their own schedule of busyness. Nana and Grandpa's time became quality time, not necessarily quantity time.

None of my three children were totally shocked when Mike and I presented our news. We were gathered around the dinner table while the grandchildren were playing outside. Keeping a straight face, I presented our news as a guessing game. "Pick one: we won the lottery (Rochelle gasped), Grandma is dating (Darrin snickered), or we are moving to South Carolina (Steph slowly nodded her head). Who wants to go first?" I asked as I pinched my lips to prevent from laughing. I looked across the table at Mike who was beaming and thinking *my crazy Leanne*. Rochelle called out, "C…moving!" Darrin looked at Mike and implied, "I know Mom wasn't planning on quitting her job any time soon. Where will you be working? Tell us your story." Steph interjected, laughing, "Mom, don't you have to play the lottery to actually win it?"

By the time the evening was over, my children were all on board and truly understood God's hand in our moving. Throughout the evening, each grandchild came into the kitchen for a drink or for various other reasons. Each one was enlightened on our plans to move. Kiersten teared up and came over and gave Mike and me both a big hug. Before she could comment, I quickly said, "Don't worry. Nana will be coming back to see you often. I promise." Each family member received an extra big hug from me as they left; grandkids were squeezed long and hard. They understood no one was to know just yet (eventually, our pastor and other church members learned about our relocation since Mike used our pastor as a reference). The entire evening seemed so surreal. I could only imagine the thoughts that went through my kids' and grandchildren's heads as they fell to sleep that night.

Just as our country started on faith, prayer, and a dedication to Jesus Christ, our new journey needed to be full of dribbling down of the same.

MY LAST LAST NAME IS GRACE

Thought of the Day

Grace is realizing God is the source of true joy, a constant, pervasive inner sense of well-being. When you're not looking, it will find you.

Chapter 60

It Is Only Stuff

Do not store up for yourselves treasures on earth, where moth and rust destroy, and where thieves break in and steal. But store up for yourselves treasures in heaven, where moth and rust do not destroy, and where thieves do not break in and steal.
—Matthew 6:19–20

DURING THE INTERVIEW, MIKE HAD inquired as to what area is the best one to relocate into. He was told Fort Mill or Rock Hill in South Carolina, right across the state line, was the answer. An Internet search revealed there was an efficiency close to Mike's work that was a possibility for his future living quarters. All that was needed was his signature on the application upon his touring the small hotel suite. Thus, checking out this hotel was our first stop after leaving the airport, as it was located very close to BGEA. Unfortunately, the hotel was booked full thanks to a popular basketball game. The hotel manager assured us we could see the suite on Sunday night. As we were leaving the hotel lobby, I pointed out to Mike it had a strong smell of cigarette smoke. Smoking must be allowed on the premises, and Mike would not be happy with that. He agreed the efficiency-possibility door was slamming shut.

During our week's vacation, we held several appointments with three different realtors to check out housing. One bed-and-breakfast manager suggested we drive through the development her in-laws lived in, as she felt it was perfect for us, since other middle-aged and older couples resided there. One homeowner told us to investigate the Heritage International Ministries Hotel (the old PTL building) as a place for Mike to reside until my move south. Since we were in need of lodging for the evening, it made perfect sense to kill two birds with one stone: book a room, tour the hotel, and inquire about renting a long-term suite for him.

In the spirit of all things falling into place, Mike signed a lease for a long-term rental of six months at a very reasonable cost compared to the efficiency he almost booked but cancelled. I was thrilled this hotel was Christian-based and felt it deserved to be a recipient of Mike's monthly lodging bill. I realized too, while Mike was at work during my extended weekend visits, I would feel safe. Another bonus, Rick Joyner held his MorningStar Fellowship Church services behind the huge lobby. There was mail delivery, a small grocery store, soda machine, bookstore, café, and plenty of other long-term residents with whom Mike could converse. The atmosphere was Spirit-filled, and the Christian music that played over the loudspeaker was a constant reminder of our awesome God.

It was an easy trip to BGEA; Mike drove directly up Route 77. Several restaurants were located near his hotel, including a grocery store, to feed his diet ice tea addiction. Mike's favorite part was the hotel grounds, which had a walking path circling a large lake, and the easy accessibility to several hiking trails, which snaked through a nearby forest. Frequent noisy jets, either arriving or departing from the Charlotte Airport, flew overhead, while he walked around the lake, reminding him *You are no longer in Kansas.*

We left the bed-and-breakfast and took the manager's advice to check out Whispering Pines development. We drove up and down Pleasure Road several times. We could not find any sign indicating Whispering Pines. On the third try, I noticed a developer's sign to my right. I read it aloud: "Six lots left for 55+ development for Meadowbrook starting at $180,000."

Mike turned the wheel of the rental car. From that point on, I retold the story as "God took over the wheel and pointed our car to the right and directly past a gorgeous one-floor model." By the time we pulled out of Meadowbrook two hours later, Mike and I signed the dotted line purchasing a Canterbury-style condo. The sales secretary informed us the builder planned to put a shovel in the ground early May; we could plan on moving into our new home early September. Our partnership in our endeavors to secure our promising future in South Carolina and Mike's new job began. Never in a million years did we expect to be buying a home without first selling our home in Pennsylvania. But God got this!

On this trip, we activated the love for Southern sweet ice tea, fattening hush puppies, and Zaxby's chicken. Just as great Southern cooking was feeding our bodies, our last stop on our vacation nurtured our soul. We toured the Billy Graham Library in Charlotte before heading back home. Spending over two hours in the library and bookstore, we were respectfully silent and held little conversation. As we walked toward our car, I commented, "Wow. I felt like I was walking on holy ground." Mike asked, "Who am I to be working for such a saint?" Our drive to dinner that night was full of being in awe of God's guidance thus far.

Upon our arrival back home, Mike had ten days to assist me in going through the entire house and determine which of his items were to be packed or sent to the auction to be sold. We signed the paperwork with my niece to put the house on the market and scheduled the first open house. Mike rummaged through his clothes and determined if he was packing it for his immediate use, storing for next winter, or giving it to Goodwill. His biggest project was clearing out the attic and making a decision on the contents' future home also. Commonplace for most people, the attic was full of unmissed items: ski boots and poles, his childhood toy tractor, unused Christmas yard ornaments, and box of books from his college days.

My early-morning wide-awake moments were populated with many details such a move entails. Clarity came with the idea of calling the auctioneer near Mom's nursing home. I scheduled a pickup date to gather and load all unwanted items to be sold at an auction.

After several prayers, tears of good-byes and watching Mike's Jeep go out of sight on March 7, I was kept busy handling every item practically in my house. Think about that chore! I bought bright pink adhesive tape and labeled some boxes "SC" (packed for the moving van). Other boxes were marked "A" for auction. Some items were boxed up for Goodwill. Just as Mom had done, I did separate my Princess House items and my purse and teapot collections and divvied it all among my four grandgirls to start their own hope chest (temporarily in a sturdy egg-packaging box).

I simply contemplated, as I went through the storage room, two bookcases, three clothe closets, as well as kitchen cabinets, and boxes of holiday decorations: "Would I buy this again? Do I want to see this in my new home?" Mike's simple response was, "Don't forget. It's called downsizing." One day, the auction truck was backed into our driveway. Two hefty Mennonite farmer boys with flexing muscles jumped out. In slightly under an hour, they loaded a truck full of items of boxes and furniture for the auction, which was held ten days later.

The day the check came in the mail from the auctioneer was exciting. As I scanned the sold-items list, I was surprised in two ways: some items didn't go for much (meaning, cheap, as my mom would say), and other items brought more than what I would have expected. For example, a used loveseat we had purchased six years earlier cost $99 but sold for $310. "One person's junk is another person's treasure" was clearly evident. The total auction proceeds of my not-wanted items paid for several months of hotel rent for Mike.

As God had planned, Mike and I were separated for six months. Our new home construction did not start early May, but rather in August, which meant we moved in in December. We planned on one of us traveling over all holidays. I flew down Memorial Day weekend. At that time, we together selected the details for our home, such as lighting and bathroom fixtures, flooring, carpeting, our kitchen cabinet design, etc. Mike flew to Pennsylvania over July 4. Our reunions were bittersweet. But knowing Mike was finally so content and thrilled with his new job was satisfying. For Mike missing me while staying in a hotel was the roughest part.

I kept busy earning a paycheck to purchase some new furniture and having my home always have a show-ready appearance for potential buyers to stop by with a realtor. Keeping my mouth shut at work, while busy packing and traveling to North Carolina, was my roughest part. Every family birthday party had me sadly thinking, *I won't be here to celebrate next year.*

Six months of having our house on the market led to no offers. During our nightly one-hour phone conversation, Mike and I discussed some options. "We are apart long enough. Let's just pick a date when you are going to give your thirty-day notice at work and a moving day to move South. Obviously, we'll put our stuff in storage. It will simply mean we will need two moves to move into Meadowbrook."

So that is what I did. I shocked my boss, Joyce, when I updated her on our plans. Just as I had, she assumed I was working until my retirement. "As you know, this is difficult for me to move away from my family. But as I say, only God and Billy are worth moving for." Joyce was surprised how I was able not to let the cat out of the bag during months of secretive planning. My last day at work was scheduled for July 30, after thirteen years of employment. Mike flew home to help load up our moving van and assist driving my Acura, which eventually was filled with items unsuitable for a moving van, to Rock Hill.

A game I'll call Do you Trust Me? was happening behind the scenes. Jesus was orchestrating circumstances in which someone was the answer to our prayers. Or I was the answer to their prayers. Since we had no offer on our three-bedroom, colonial-style house, it occurred to me early one morning to check into a lease-to-own contract. I concluded finding someone to rent our home while accruing some down monies toward principle was a possible solution. Thus, in walked Lori Anderson (my previous student nurse when I had my hysterectomy) and her family to solve that problem. They are the ones who deserve our home. They love everything about it: the school district, my garden bathtub, almost-an-acre yard on a corner lot, and having Christian neighbors.

Then the Lord surprised me with yet another phone call. The physical therapist at work was looking for a temporary home to move into until their new home was finished. She knew I was moving, and our house would be sitting empty; yet, it needed to continue to be show-ready for any prospective buyers, including a mowed lawn, which her hubby could do. Having just come through that experience themselves, she understood the house needed to remain tidy at all times and be asked to leave the premises for a few minutes. What do you charge for something like this? I decided on the exact amount the hotel was charging Mike per day; she was thrilled by the cheap-living, six-week arrangement for her family. It was a win-win for both. Plus, the amount she paid me covered our storage unit bill.

As though God wasn't finished with surprises, we had one more. Thanks to being basically healthy, except for my one major surgery, I only called off work two times in over thirteen years. Unlike Mike's previous employer, any unused paid-time-off was reimbursed to me. Guess what? The amount of my second paycheck was the exact amount it cost to rent the moving van!

Our family and friends were so wonderful and supportive. Many hands make light work when it comes to helping someone move. Steph and Kiersten filled her van with fragile items and followed us down to South Carolina. Darrin offered his big muscles for loading heavy items on the moving van and assisted with oversight as to how best pack it. Every inch was needed. Our friends helped me clean the home before closing the door behind us one final time. Along with Darrin, our friend did a great job in getting all desired items in the moving van, except a patio table, which simply was just not going to fit in anywhere (our renters got good use out of it). Darrin joked with Duane, "You could pull the moving van out for a bit, then slam on the brakes. That will shift some things around and might give us a few more inches." We all held our breaths as Darrin grabbed the moving van's door handle, and the door was able to close.

Duane, our son-in-law, offered to drive the moving van to our storage unit. Rochelle accompanied him. Plus, she wanted to be included in being able to picture our new southern location. Our thanks were paying for a one-way ticket home for both, plus any expenses. Duane and Rochelle got an early morning start and headed down the turnpike with all of our items. I commented later, "You can't think too hard and long about how does everything you own fit in the back of one van?" Mike curtly answered, "For you, one word: downsized."

Steph and Kiersten followed my Acura in her van packed full of "Nana's pretties." They planned on staying in our family suite, which had four beds (Duane and Rochelle had their own hotel room). Once they learned his wife would now be joining him in their hotel until our home was finished being built, the Heritage staff provided a double room and only charged us $100 more. The suite was simply two hotel rooms when the room divider was opened. The extra two beds became another "closet" for me. We each had our own bathroom and closet. A small dining room table and chairs, a desk and two-end tables with lamps, and a TV in an armoire finished off our room furnishings. Mike had purchased earlier a microwave and small refrigerator. It was a perfect temporary arrangement. Of course, I didn't mind eating Healthy Choice dinners or going out to eat other times. After all, I was used to not cooking for the last six months.

Our move-in weekend into the hotel flew by much too quickly. It took me two days to sort through the clothing and items that were emptied from the two cars that filled our hotel suite. I sent a picture of our cluttered, messy hotel room to my friend Roz. Misunderstanding the picture, she asked me, "Wow. Did someone rob you?"

Before I knew it, it was time for Steph, Kiersten, Duane, and Rochelle to head back to Pennsylvania. Help me keep it together, Lord! On the morning they were leaving, Kiersten handed me an envelope and informed me to not read it until they were on the road. Of course, this nana was much too curious to wait. While Kiersten was busy packing her suitcase, I read the letter. As though my emotions weren't already maxed out, I had to pretend I had not read the letter and remain cool. Her letter said:

> Dear Nana and Gramps,
>
> I hope you guys are going to be happy down in South Carolina together. Gramps, I wish you to be happy with your new job and is glad Nana is with you again. I hope you will enjoy your SORTA new life. Nana, I hope you can find something to do down there while Gramps is at work for the day. I wish you guys good luck in your again SORTA new life together. We will miss you both and will miss your loyal support at concerts, parties, cookouts, and all those other things. I will be the one missing you both SOOO DEEPLY more than anyone else in our family or your friends. Hopefully, you will be comfortable with your new house, new job, new state, and new friends. WHY DID YOU HAVE TO MOVE TO A DIFFERENT STATE? THAT'S JUST CRUEL ON SOOO MANY LEVELS!
>
> On the bright side, I hope you both live in a beautiful house, or is going to, and Gramps has a work that fits him just fine, and you like your amazing state. But is it still as amazing as Pennsylvania? Anyway, it will be different with both of you gone. It will be very lonely without you guys. But I can't wait till we see each other again after twelve weeks or three months. But I am sooo lucky to have family members that have an important job and live in a gorgeous state! I am happy for you both!
>
> I wish and hope we will still do the tea parties, birthday parties, hangouts and just have a grand time at your house when we come over too. I can't wait till we go to the beach with all

of us again. But you guys are lucky that you only have to drive about three hours while we have to drive like five and more (I don't know the right number how many hours it will take us to get there. I am guessing).

I am going to miss you guys sooooooooooooo very much!

Love with all my heart,
Kiersten

The tracks of my tears were again pouring down and the too familiar salty taste nipped my lips. Kiersten got three big hugs, one for each month, until I would see them all again at Thanksgiving and Christmas. Rounds of thanks, best wishes, good lucks, and good-bye hugs spread among us. Lord, I need you to give them understanding. Please be the hole filler for Kiersten and all my babies.

I'll never forget the first Monday morning waking up and not having to get dressed for work. A big yahoo! left my lips as I threw up both arms. I would be dancing in the vibration of life in a different manner. Reality surely had not hit me entirely. In God's providence, my plans on working part-time as an RN fell flat. My heart's desire was to be hired in some healthcare field realm as a staff scheduler, receptionist, or office assistant.

Instead, that fall, God strategically had me planted to reside in Heritage International Ministries (HIM). Why? The huge upper conference room of the hotel was a preparation area for Samaritans' Purse's (an outreach of BGEA) Operation Christmas Child. I spent hours in between Bible study packing shoeboxes for children that would be shipped overseas. In addition, MorningStar Ministries had a cute boutique along the hotel's main street selling used clothing and items. All proceeds went toward purchasing items for the shoeboxes. It took care of two needs of mine: perusing the boutique and finding a "must-have" clothing on occasion or assisting with managing a boutique (just as in my own shop earlier).

When I did finally complete an application to have my RN license transferred, the Nursing Board of South Carolina would not accept my PA CEUs even though I had almost double the amount necessary. My early retirement life became like the name of the popular body wash: endless weekend. God slammed that door shut, and I'm okay with it all.

Upon his move down in March, Mike diligently prayed and shopped around for a home church for us. After observing several church services, God led him to North Rock Hill Church, a miniature Worship Center. We both felt so at home. Mike joined a men's Bible study and volunteered as part of the worship team to do the graphics (putting pictures and scriptures tied in with the sermon on the auditorium screen). Fellow church members and his Bible study group were a godsend in helping us with our moving, not just once, but twice.

Every Sunday morning after church, we drove over to our new home construction site to check on the progression. How exciting to first see a cement slab, walls, then drywall, bathroom tubs and showers, and kitchen cabinets be installed. Finally, flooring and all other details were finished, and moving day was set for December 10. Merry Christmas to us!

Yes, as with most moving and new home construction projects, I could write an entire chapter on mistakes, challenges, and grievances. We were missing a bathroom door, interior painting was unsatisfactory, the tub and shower were reversed, and our foyer hardwood floor needed replacement because a worker forgot to close the door on a night it rained. Furniture was delivered (on the third try) with a twelve-inch slice on the back of my sofa. Ten days after moving, we had no water because the construction crew accidentally hit the main waterline. But through it all, I realized I needed to be a Christian example to the construction foreman and his crew, the developers, and other griping fed-up neighbors. Our developer assured me, "I promise you, Mrs. Miller. At the end, it will all be to your satisfaction." It was—mostly.

Remember all the realtors we met with before purchasing our home (coincidentally, a realtor wasn't necessary in our case)? Well, the realtor associated with Meadowbrook gave us a check for $2,000. Even though she wasn't needed to close the deal on our new home, in order to get paid, she needed Mike and me to sign her contract earlier that spring. Mike signed it prior to leaving for South Carolina and said, "Do what you want. Here's my signature." Once she sensed my hesitation, she promised us $2,000 toward extras on the house if we would both sign it. After all, she wanted to get paid by the developer. I figured she would forget her promise nine months later. Nope, the Lord wouldn't let her forget. Oh, happy day, when I reached in my mailbox that day!

Perhaps having just lived through watching all your remaining possessions being packed into a moving van, I came to realize *it's just stuff*. Even my awesome southern home with its sunroom, big windows, and delightful floor plan I so love will someday all burn.

Thought of the Day

Grace is realizing God is not just the God of the universe. He is the God of me. I have so many reasons, besides His trumped-up love, to celebrate Jesus.

Chapter 61

Bald Eagles Flying Overhead

But those who hope in the Lord will renew their strength.
They will soar on wings like eagles; they will run and
not grow weary, they will walk and not be faint.
—Isaiah 40:31

Author (back row center) with her mother and two sisters

I WALKED INTO MOM'S HOSPITAL room one Saturday morning. She was so pale and frail as she looked up at me and weakly commented,

"It's about time you get here." Leaning down to kiss her forehead, I chuckled. My sister Lorna, who had arrived at her bedside a few minutes before me, cautioned Mom. She did not think that Mom's first words out of her mouth should be to scold me. But it did not faze me one bit.

A few weeks earlier in January 2016, I received an e-mail that my Uncle Theodore, Mom's eighty-eight-year-old brother, was hospitalized for pneumonia and was not expected to live through his diagnosis. Several of my brothers and sisters drove Mom three times to visit with Uncle Theodore in the hospital. A devoted niece, Jane, did not want him to die alone and stayed overnight to be by his side on his last night here on earth. After Uncle Theodore expired, my brother, Doug, who has power of attorney for Mom, told her that Uncle Theodore had passed away. Mom commented, "Well, now that's over with." (Mom held a special bank account for her brother's funeral and burial expenses, which indirectly, Doug was handling.) Did Mom's comment mean that she could not pass on until her younger brother, Theodore, had done so?

January 10 was Theodore's birthday, and January 12 was my mom's birthday. My family held a ninety-second birthday party for Mom in her personal care home's activity room on Sunday. Since I had just been in Pennsylvania for our family Christmas celebration, I chose not to drive back up to celebrate Mom's birthday. My cousin, not realizing our family was holding a small birthday party for her aunt, brought Uncle Theodore over to visit my mom. Lorna took a picture of both Uncle Theodore and my mom sitting side by side. Little did we know that within weeks, we would be burying both Uncle Theodore and our mother!

While dealing with a bad cold, I drove up to Pennsylvania to attend Uncle Theodore's funeral. I made plans to stay at my son, Darrin's, home to be with my granddaughters, Taylor and Madison, and their two dogs. I am always delighted to see my kids and grandkids. I prayed I would not spread my cold. Turns out Uncle Theodore's funeral timing coincided with Darrin and Heather's scheduled winter vacation and anniversary celebration in Jamaica. My staying overnight in their home meant the girls were not staying alone during their parents' trip. Plus, I made memories I'll always cherish.

Being one of the nurses in the family and one of those who felt most comfortable handling Mom's equipment, I frequently volunteered to pick up Mom at her home for family events. That meant I needed to load one or two portable oxygen tanks, an oxygen concentrator at times, and her walker in my car. Thus, on February 8, I planned on being the sibling to pick up Mom, and we headed to Mohler Church of the Brethren for Uncle Theodore's service. During the viewing, Mom, attached to her oxygen concentrator, sat beside his coffin. Although looking thin and frail, she enjoyed shaking hands with nieces and nephews, other family members, or acquaintances she had not spoken to for some time. Later, Cyndy, a niece, who was a respiratory therapist, commented that Grandma seemed to be wheezing more.

Following a great funeral service for Uncle Theodore, I, along with the funeral director's assistance, helped Mother, her concentrator and walker get back in my car. Having handled quite a few of my family members' funeral services over the years (Daddy, grandparents, aunts and uncles, cousin, etc.), the funeral director commented to me that he hoped he would not see my family members again for some time. He was surprised how frail and thin my mother looked since the last time he had seen her. I commented, "God only knows, but Mother at ninety-two has outlived all her siblings." Little did I know I would be seeing the funeral director in a few short weeks!

Since it was a cold breezy February day, Mom had decided not to attend the burial service of Uncle Theodore. Instead, we headed back to her home. Once again, Mom's personal care home's activity room held a gathering for our family and friends to share in the meal after the funeral and burial service. For some family members, they did not realize this would be the last time they would be visiting with Aunt Elizabeth.

The following Sunday, Mom was too tired to walk to the dining room for both her breakfast and lunch meals and told the staff she was just "too pooped". At supper, the staff pushed her in her wheelchair to the dining room and thought perhaps she was grieving the death of her brother. By Monday, during my check-in phone call, the staff reported to me that Mom was "back to normal" and coming out of her room for meals. Her oxygen blood levels started dropping on Wednesday to a dangerous level of 80 percent. Fearing Mom had aspirated, the staff called 911. Thus, my mother was transferred to Ephrata Hospital on Wednesday. Diagnosed with pneumonia, high levels of potassium due to kidney failure, and ongoing congestive heart failure, Mom was admitted to the hospital.

As God's providence would have it, my niece Dawn (the same niece who took her RN state boards at the same time I had) was the RN case manager for Mom's unit. Between conversations with Dawn, Cyndy, Lorna, and Doug, I was updated frequently on Mom's condition. By Thursday night, when I heard that Mom seemed to have improved kidney functioning levels, but her congestive heart failure levels were worsening, I planned a road trip to Pennsylvania. Mom confirmed my decision to do so. During a Friday morning phone conversation, when she sounded weaker, I asked her if she wanted me to come. She answered, "Of course, I want you to come." By 2:00 p.m., with Mike's blessing, I started out on yet another trek to Pennsylvania with appropriate funeral attire packed, just in case. Thus, it was on that particular Saturday morning, when I walked into Mom's hospital room and heard her say to me, "It's about time you get here."

Lorna and I prepared Mom for her hospital transfer to the skilled nursing wing of Fairfield Nursing Home. An ambulance was scheduled to do the transfer by 11:00 a.m. I provided morning care for Mom by helping her brush her teeth and assisted her in getting dressed. Lorna combed Mom's hair into the Mennonite-style bun and applied her head covering. While Mom was waiting for the transfer ambulance, Lorna and I drove over to Mom's personal care room and gathered a few familiar items. We displayed Daddy's photos and other comforting knickknacks. We wanted to make her skilled nursing room feel more like home before her arrival.

Over the next week, I acted as Mom's caregiver and made many special memories with her that will always be cherished. She was scheduled to have a male caregiver, and the most important task in her eyes that I could do for her was assist her to the bathroom and give her p.m. care. It was a pleasure to change out oxygen tubing, wheel her down to the dining room for meals or an activity, and tour the nursing home wing. We sat together in the living room and watched the parakeets or looked at magazines, or I read the newspaper to her. Sometimes we watched the *Waltons* DVD together. I helped her select her clothing and prayed with her before I left for the evening—all chores I was honored to do for my mom. Once, after she had toured the nursing unit and conversed with some former neighbors, I wheeled Mom back to her room.

"Leanne, what am I doing here? I want to go home. This floor is for old sick people," she pointed out. It brought a smile to my siblings' faces when I told them about Mom's comment.

Warm fuzzy moments occurred between us when I would tell her, with tears running down my cheeks, I was so glad I could be there and help to take care of her. Unlike with Daddy, I expressed my love to Mom often during this time. "I love you. I'm honored to do this for you, Mom." Hearing her respond many times during that week, "I love you too, Leanne" was priceless.

"Thank you, Leanne, for all you are doing for me," Mom repeatedly told me. Her warm hands were comforting, and her words were sincere. After all, this was the mother who wrote me plenty of "scolding" letters decades ago because I was a divorcee. The daughter, who was at one time a source of embarrassment, was now a source of a helping hand and a giver of peaceful rest.

In between caregiving, I wrote the following:

My Hands

Remember: if you ever need a helping hand, you will find one at the end of each of your arms. As you grow older, you will discover that you have two hands, one for helping yourself and the other for helping another" (Author unknown).

BEATY MILLER

I should have bought stock in hand lotion from the time I was a teenager. By my age now, I'm sure I would have a great return for my money. Though I have small hands, the wrist check indicates I have a medium-bone body structure. You'll never find natural long fingernails for any length of time on my hands. Whenever I do discover a nail or two of perfect length, it shortly thereafter has split, cracked, or become ragged, requiring a clipping. Because I spent too many summers of my youth sunbathing with coconut oil, my body and hands now reveal spots, which I call sunspots, not age spots. To be dishonest about my age, which I've been known to jokingly do, the truth be told by the appearance of my hands. If I continue to joke about my age, I should be hiding my hands behind my back.

Though they have weathered and aged much to my dismay, my hands have served me well over several decades. From when I was a baby grasping my mom's thumbs, holding a bottle or playing patty-cake, my chubby hands were always moving. During examinations of your baby, did you know that pediatricians simply observe for healthy activity of feet and hand movements?

As soon as I was able to repeat my mom's bedtime prayers, my hands were closed to say the prayer, "Now I lay me down to sleep…" My hands accepted Sunday school tickets, a hard-earned free Bible for verse memorization, and completed many a Sunday school lesson.

My right-hand dominance allowed for learning how to tie shoes, swing a bat, hold many playing cards in one hand, and do household chores. Imagine not having two hands! How would one complete homework, get dressed, hug, bake, cook, and tend to a garden?

As a teenager, my hands allowed for driving a car, holding hands of boyfriends, learning how to type, do shorthand, work in a factory, and finally, grasping for my high school diploma from the superintendent's hand.

As a wife and mother of three children, hands were priceless to nurture them through life. Did I mention hands were needed to wipe snotty noses, remove tears, nurse boo-boos, and swat bottoms when the child got unruly? As Ruth Graham said, "You raise children on your knees (with hands clasped in prayer)."

Unfortunately, these hands have signed divorce papers, church membership resignation papers because of my divorce, and custody battle papers. Proudly, these hands have signed RN licenses, grandchildren cards, new church membership paperwork, a final marriage certificate, and paychecks that allowed me to be a generous person. Needing hands to raise a question in a classroom, I've used them to clarify communication how-to in a Dale Carnegie course.

Requiring not only hands but a brain, I've had a career as a secretary, two-room parochial school teacher, office manager, RN serving the geriatric population, and finally as a personal care home administrator. But His hands have always clasped mine and guided me through my journey.

As a volunteer, these hands served as a candy striper, a Red Cross RN volunteer, led women's Bible study for over ten years, aided in housing two different teenagers looking for a Christian's home to act as a halfway house, and cooked meals for families in need requiring hospitality as part of my church's outreach program. More recently, my hands served me well while volunteering at the Manor Street homeless shelter. May our hands never tire to serve others!

Today, I look at my somewhat wrinkled hands on my lap and say, "Yikes! These hands are my mother's hands." When and how did that happen?

I had plenty of time to contemplate how each one of us had our own special or not-so-special bonding with Mom. Mom was not stupid about the sibling rivalry that went on among her children. Not having much in common and using words like *competitive, hurtful or humiliating* depicted some childhood memories. Siblings continued to push each other's buttons without knowing why of the reasons behind it. Mom settled for "it is what it is" and, regrettably, accepted it as the normal state of affairs for her family.

I remembered how Mom, after Daddy's funeral, wisely said to Marlin and Mervin: "If we can all be together for Daddy's death, we surely can be together while I'm still alive." Unfortunately, that did not regularly occur. It was only during Mom's dying days that her conflicting family rallied together and put their focus on Mother.

On Sunday, I knew many family members and friends would be visiting Mom. I left to spend some time with girlfriends and family. This allowed other siblings to make their special memories during alone time with Mom. Starting Monday morning and the rest of the weekday mornings, I drove over to spend most of my day and evenings with Mom that week. Mom's nurse practitioner examined her on Monday and reported to me during our phone conversation, "Mom seemed good, but you know how it is with CHF." We discussed finishing out Mom's current supply of medications but not reordering any unnecessary meds unless they would provide comfort for her, such as pain medications.

My brother Elvin told me on Sunday during his visit, "Mother asked me to call Matt and have him come to visit her." She also named other siblings who lived out of state. He followed Mom's instructions and called Matt our brother. To follow through on her request, Matt and Renee did drive up from South Boson, Virginia, and visited with Mom on Tuesday. Visitors would say Mom vacillated between periods of being very sleepy and too tired for conversation, to times of cracking jokes.

Doug, as power of attorney, by the following Wednesday needed to make a decision about selecting either hospice services and beginning comfort care versus participating in physical therapy sessions. I paid close attention to Mom's physical condition and relied on the nursing team. I told Doug that I felt Mom would make the decision easy for him, and she did. By Wednesday, she barely had enough strength to hold her own spoon and could not sit on the side of the bed for any length of time. Just as with Daddy, comfort became Mom's plan of care. We all pitched in and emptied Mom's personal care room. It was sad closing the door on her last address. We simply prayed that she would not linger in the nursing wing because we all knew she did not want to be there.

Killing two birds with one stone, some girlfriends of mine would meet me at the nursing home's café to give us catch-up time, which I so appreciated. During the times Mom napped, I sat on the rocking chair across the room and read a book at times. I reminisced as I gazed at the warm family photo blanket Lorna had given Mom earlier for Christmas. Some memories had me cringe; others brought on a smile.

I can recall only one time when I literally yelled at my mom over the phone and hung up on her. It was during a time when I was married to Jeff and was considered a black sheep and not very close to my family. During our conversation, while I was at work, I started getting upset with her. So I had transferred the call to the office's private conference room. Long story short, Mom began to question me about a conversation she heard several weeks earlier. She inquired if it was indeed true about the rumor that Jeff was abusive to me. I was so shocked that my mother would wait weeks before double-checking that her daughter was okay. Turns out when she clarified the rumor, I realized she was mixing Jeff up with my remarried niece's husband, who was abusive.

"Mom, if I *ever* heard my daughter's husband…I don't care how far apart we were…was beating her up, I would be on her doorstep so fast, he wouldn't know what hit him," I verbalized loudly as my body tensed up. "You talk to me about nontrivial matters for five minutes and wait to say, 'Oh, by the way, I heard Jeff hits you.' I'm hanging up before I say something I regret…Oh, but wait…learn how to spell my daughter's name correctly…after all she is twelve. It's S-T-E-P-H-A-N-I-E!" *Slam!*

Of course, that night, I had to call her and apologize for my behavior. I guess it was my turn to be the culprit for the quote she often repeated when we were growing up: "When they are little, they traipse all over your lap. When they are older, they traipse all over your heart."

During the time I was far from God and my parents, it was difficult for me to select the most appropriate Mother's Day or birthday card for Mom. If they were too mushy about being a best friend or one who did lifelong nurturing, I rejected it, and it remained in the card rack. A more general card about "thoughts sent your way today" or "make it special; you deserve it" was just about all the warm fuzzies it contained on the final selection.

How did my mother end up in the personal care wing? In her late eighties, she was wise enough to announce she was no longer going to be driving her car and no longer needed a driver's license. I came to visit her one day after work, and she said to me, "I almost fell asleep driving the few miles home from church yesterday with my three friends in the car. I'm selling my car. Doug knows to start asking family members who would like to purchase the Buick." Wow! How many power of attorneys and families would love to hear *that* conclusion from an elderly parent? Mom made that way too easy. *Yes, Daddy, I know you are looking out for Mom.*

Since I was the daughter who lived the closest to her, I would take Mom grocery-shopping at times. One Saturday, we both bought sausage, which was on sale. Lorna would frequently visit with Mom on Monday, her day off. Lorna walked in this particular Monday morning and got a whiff of something that had burned. Upon questioning her, Lorna learned Mom burned the sausage she was cooking on the stove last Saturday for supper. Wow. *That must have been some smoke if I can still smell it days later.*

Mom did not want to discuss it with Lorna. She did find out Mom put the sausage on the stove and lay down on the sofa to "close my eyes." The smoke alarm sounded. But the ringing of the phone from the nursing supervisor woke her up. Needless to say, it was the final straw. Doug held that "had-to-happen conversation" with Mom, and she understood. After over a decade of living alone as a widow, it was time to move out of her home.

Mom was willing to be transferred out of independent living and into the personal care wing. The first available room was a recently remodeled deluxe suite with an awesome view over Lancaster County farmland. Her guest book was signed by many friends, neighbors, and family members. Watching selected DVDs (*The Waltons* or *Little House on the Prairie*) filled her days in between scheduled activities.

Each time I would visit, I opened up the guest book to see who had visited her since my last visit. Cards and letters from out-of-town granddaughters arrived in her mailbox. One day, Lorna called me to report on the latest quote of Mom's.

"Leanne, you know how Mom always says that no one in her big family comes to visit her?" she asked. "Mom said it again today as I was leaving. I responded, 'But, Mom, you didn't go to visit Grandpa and Grandma Martin very often'."

"Yes, but we should have," Mom concluded.

As I sat in Mom's presence, I pondered about what it will be like for our previous neighbor and Mom's reuniting in heaven. In the late 1960's, the man's wife had asked Mom to stop by. Her husband was actively dying and agreed to visit with my mom to make things right between him and God. Mom gladly did so and said the Sinner's Prayer with him.

Mom was the cornerstone and diligently prayed for her large family. We all knew Mom, Grandma, Great-grandma prayed for her family without ceasing and had a phone line into heaven. She loved passing on answers to prayer. One day, during my visit, she reported on an event that occurred to my nephew, Loren, Matt's son. Loren and about one dozen youth had signed up for a mission trip to Guatemala. One evening, while walking down a city street, Loren and three boys felt someone shove himself in between Loren and the boy beside him. The intruder knocked Loren down and started dragging him into an alley. Suddenly, the youth saw angels surrounding Loren. The criminal quickly dropped Loren's arm and stepped back in fright. He turned around and ran down into the dark alley. Wow! What an awesome miracle-working God!

By the weekend, I faced the problem of staying for another week with Mom or returning home. I made the decision to leave Friday morning, knowing other family members were planning to spend their weekend in Mom's room. Each sibling could make their own special memories with their dear mother, just as I had done. Mom did not seem to have one foot in heaven and strolling toward Daddy just yet. So I packed up and headed home.

Making the decision to leave that morning and return back home was a difficult one to make. Mom was in a stable declining state. I realized she could pass to the Other Side, and I would miss the opportunity to watch her take her last breath. However, she had eight other children who could do that for her. Most likely, Mike and I would be returning to Pennsylvania within the week. The black funeral dress will be taking another road trip.

As I drove down the Pennsylvania turnpike, my mind was filled with gleanings of insight I had recently experienced during my nine days of being by Mom's side. My mind was going a mile a minute faster than the wheels were turning.

"Leanne, is that young man my nurse for tonight? If so, I want you to put me to bed." Gleaning number 1: opinions don't die but are taken to the grave with you.

"Leanne, get my covering and pin it on my head, please, before Mervin and Marlin get here." Gleaning number 2: showing respect for her two more conservative sons continued.

In spite of feeling weak, one can be gracious to your doctor, nurses, caregivers, and be a star patient. Gleaning number 3: who says getting older gives you the right to be a grouch?

Earlier, my siblings and I reviewed Mom's written-down wishes for her funeral service. We had her new blue dress and Sunday head covering ready for her to be buried in. The six pallbearers' names were listed, making that job easy. My son, Darrin, was one of them, which made me so proud. Doug explained, while reviewing the list, that Mom chose names of grandsons with whom she spent the most time. Unlike Daddy's service, we were allowed to display flowers and pallbearers were allowed to wear neckties. My parents honored tithing by writing in their will that Martindale Church and Christian Aide Ministries will split a tenth of their estate.

After my Acura crossed over the Virginia line, I decided it was time to place a check-in phone call to Mom's room. My brother Marlin softly answered the phone. "Hey, Marlin, any updates on Mom?" I heard a long pause. I gasped, "Oh no, did Mom pass on?" I questioned him.

"No, she's still with us. Here, she wants to talk to you." I could hear Mom weakly ask if that was me on the phone. "Hi, Leanne," she weakly said. I proceeded to tell her that I was just sitting here driving and thinking about the great memories we shared recently. "I love you, Mom. Mike and I will be back up soon." My voice quivered.

I heard a rustling sound. Then Marlin got back on the phone. "Leanne, Elvin is going to call you right back on his cell from the hallway."

Within minutes, my cell phone rang. Elvin then clued me in to why Marlin was hesitating when I called into Mom's room. "Both Marlin and I were on each side of Mom's bed and were holding her hand. Right before you called, Mom looked up toward the ceiling and asked if we see the angel? She asked us if we were all ready for this." I sucked in my breath.

"I assured her, yes, Mother, go on home to Daddy. Marlin said that we were all ready for this," Elvin explained. "Mom then got glassy eyed and seemed to be staring at something. Just then, the phone rang, disturbing the peace." Elvin laughed and said, "So, Leanne, it is your fault Mother is still with us and not with Daddy." Unbelievable! After that, I called only Lorna or Doug's cell phone and no longer called into Mom's room "disturbing the peace."

Throughout Sunday, I placed several phone calls for updates. I informed Lorna that I wanted to be on the cell phone, dialed in, and listening when the family was gathering around Mom's bed and singing hymns. Mom's taking one step into heaven occurred Monday night. Six of her nine children and spouses were present to sing her through the glory gates and into Daddy's arms once again. Listening long distance through my cell phone, I heard my family sing about three hymns. Then I heard Lorna say, "She's gone." Standing on both feet inside heaven had not taken very long before Mom walked across the Other Side and greeted her Master. Home at last! I called my children and informed them Grandma had died. Darrin was reminded to dig his suit out of the back of his closet.

All siblings made travel plans and rummaged through personal possessions about Mom to put on display at her memorial service. My brother Doug was relieved of his power of attorney duties and was more than happy to hand over the reins to his two older siblings, Junior and Elvin, Mom's executors. Martindale Mennonite Church's Sunday school class planned for two delicious meals for our big family: 160 people!

Over eight hundred people attended either Mom's memorial service or funeral. We joked that the number could not possibly reach over thousand in attendance, as it was with Daddy, because Mom outlived many friends and Sunday school members. Several nieces and nephews, in behalf of the rest, expressed their devotion and shared thoughts about their Grandma during the service. Several of my brothers read heartfelt, tear-jerking thoughts. Lorna read off Mom's life sketch. A few excerpts follow:

MY LAST LAST NAME IS GRACE

Elizabeth enjoyed many interests and hobbies throughout her life. In the mid-1950s, she began making quilts, and this craft became a lifelong pleasure and pastime for her. By the time she moved from her cottage at Fairfield Homes in January of 2014, she had pieced approximately 140 quilt tops and, in the latter years, quilted many of them by herself. She made numerous quilts for each of her nine children, created a quilt for each of her 39 grandchildren and designated an unquilted pieced quilt top to the oldest great-grandchild in each of her children's families. She donated quilts to the MCC Relief Sale, Lancaster Mennonite School auction and gave a quilt to other families who experienced a loss.

In the 1980s, she began collecting dolls and had a collection of over 200 dolls by the time of their household sale in 1997. She loved raising vegetables and some fruits in her gardens and each year canned and froze a lot of food to feed her large family. She also enjoyed growing several kinds of flowers in her many flowerbeds and took a special interest in growing her own saffron. She modeled daily Bible reading and prayer at nighttime before going to bed and taught her children to do the same.

Elizabeth was preceded in death by her husband, Aaron W. Martin; her parents; her brothers and one sister...she had 9 children and 38 grandchildren, 137 great-grandchildren and 6 great-great-grandchildren.

It was a cold balmy March day when we walked to the canopy and Mom's gravesite for the final service. Photographs were taken of different siblings shoveling ground over Mom's casket before the mortician took over.

Linda my sister-in-law remarked, "Look. There is an eagle flying overhead." I looked up and saw a white-headed bald eagle flying toward us over the latent countryside. It seemed to circle back and then head toward us once again. Admiring it, I thought of the symbolism of this. It's Daddy saying: I got Mom now. Thanks for taking care of her. *Wait. Is that a second eagle flying overhead?*

Sure enough, a second eagle began forming circles in the sky. Sometimes they would be facing each other, and other times not. Then, together, they both flew off into the horizon. As I watched their wings flapping, I pictured it as both Mom and Daddy waving good-bye and saying "see you later." Bye, Mom and Daddy. We'll all see you soon.

During the ride home, Mike and I shared what the eagle's presence meant. We have driven hours to go eagle sighting. Moving down south, we seek our wildlife preserves where eagles are most likely to nest. I can probably count on two hands the total amount of times I have seen an eagle out in the wild. How fascinating during an unexpected time one shows up!

My nephew Darvin wrote his thoughts in his genealogy on his grandma. I love this. It follows:

> My cousins and I were pallbearers and helped carry the casket from the church service into the cemetery. Here we also held a small portion of the service by the graveside. After we lowered Grandma's body into the ground, we gathered outside the tent so that it could be removed in order for us to begin filling the grave.
>
> Someone called out pointing to a bald eagle in the eastern sky. The sky was clear and bright.
>
> The sun was shining boldly on the eagle, so we could clearly observe its white head from a great distance. We all watched this eagle in

amazement, as it flew closer and closer to where we were standing. As though it was curious of our presence, the eagle flew directly overhead and then circled above us. More than a hundred people were present to witness this experience. I watched for well over a minute, until my head grew tired from looking up. The eagle eventually flew on, and we again approached the grave, now with the tent removed. We then took our shovels and began to fill in her grave and then walked back to the church for a meal. Over the next few days, I pondered over the connection between the eagle and Grandma's death and wrote these details down so they would be remembered.

Our human story, regardless of time, culture, or context has always invoked a sense of mystery in regards to death. Connections are important, and here something special and significant occurred right at the same time as the sacred moment of burial. Our family ties to a strong religious tradition require us to explain these mysterious events in spiritual terms. A standard interpretation involves the eagle as a symbol of God's blessing, a symbol of Grandma's spirit ascending onward to heaven. While I have peace in the truth of this explanation, I think the event carries a special significance beyond the standard interpretation. Such a dramatic sign doesn't necessarily happen to every person who shares God's blessing.

In 2013, I had tested Grandma's DNA with her approval and found that her genetics includes a small Native American component. The size confirms the Native contribution is from about 200 years before Grandma was born—straight within the time and place when our recently arrived European ancestors were living side-by-side with Native Americans.

I want to hold the eagle event open-handed, as a mystery, recalling the story for those who knew Grandma but were not present to witness this, and for her great-grandchildren and great-great-grandchildren, yet to arrive in the future. I think this event somehow honors and confirms the small Native American component of her heritage, perhaps God's confirmation to what has been discovered. Native people would traditionally explain the event by understanding that Grandma transformed into the eagle as a testimony to her strength and courage. The small portion of Grandma's own Native ancestry back in early colonial times and before would have explained the eagle's presence in that way. While I personally am not completely comfortable with an overtly animistic explanation, I still want to hold this experience in a way that honors Grandma along with the characteristics of the eagle, as a sign to us from God. Grandma will from now on be associated with eagles—because we encountered the unexpected. I find that to be an awesome blessing and think our early ancestors would have found the association equally remarkable, as we did that day. From this time forward, every time I see a bald eagle, I will be reminded of Grandma. That is a tremendous gift for which I give thanks.

When the time came to empty Mom's cottage, she held a family meeting and formulated a method of disposing her furniture, lamps, cookware, and all other household items. Mom was smart in how she did it. All nine of the siblings' names were put in a dish. First name called got the first selection of their choice: Rainbow vacuum cleaner, expensive mattress set, extension table and chairs, patio furniture, and so forth. I noticed Daddy's cane propped up against the wall. I leaned over and joked to Mike, "My luck. I'll be the last name called kid number nine, and I'll be stuck with Daddy's cane." He chuckled.

First name was selected. "Mervin," Mom called out. He walked over and picked up Daddy's cane. Mike and I looked at each other and burst out laughing. Wow! The remaining smaller items were laid out on the bedroom and living room floor for grandchildren to select their desired items. Whatever was left over, which was only a few items, was bagged up and given to Goodwill. I smile today when I see Great-grandma's Avon bottle of perfume sitting on my granddaughter's dresser.

I was fortunate enough to be able to select my parent's homemade wooden table with ten extension boards and four wooden chairs and a dry sink. I see through the eyes of faith all ten boards being used to extend the table for my future family of thirty, including great-grandchildren.

Turns out I found some of my Southern friends had no idea what I was talking about when I mentioned I inherited Mom's dry sink. A dry sink is a piece of furniture common in homes before the invention of indoor plumbing. It is easy to picture its purpose in my grandparent's home. Styles vary, but generally, it consists of a cabinet with a slightly recessed top made to hold a basin and pitcher for water. Often used in kitchens, bedrooms, or on porches, the lip around the top of the dry sink was made to contain any overflow of water, along with the items being washed or other toiletries, if it was in a bedroom. The cabinet was a convenient place to keep supplies out of sight. Towels, scrub brushes, and soap could all be tucked away, yet readily available.

With the advent of indoor plumbing, the functionality of the dry sink was no longer necessary. However, the look of a dry sink is still very popular in home decorating. Because it is not hooked up to any plumbing, the dry sink can be used anywhere as decoration.

Mom's dry sink was not an antique, nor did it have the recessed decorative water basin. It provided a little extra storage space for her behind the doors of the cabinet area, which is how I use it.

    I grieve as one with hope and comfort. I have so many memories I can look back on. I do not want to dwell on the negative ones but concentrate on my path of faith pointed heavenward. I have a great future to look forward to when Mom and Daddy and all of my eight siblings will gather around the supper table. Daddy will be at the head of the table, and Mom, at the other end, smiling at their large brood renaming us kids "Grace."

Thought of the Day

    Grace upon grace upon grace, grace on top of grace, and grace's zenith is displayed by Christ hanging on the cross. I, Leanne, put Him there!

Chapter 62

Touching the Hem of His Garment

> Remember the former things, those of long ago; I am God, and there is no other; I am God, and there is none like me. I make known the end from the beginning, from ancient times, what is still to come. I say: My purpose will stand, and I will do all that I please, what I have said, that will I bring about; what I have planned, that will I do.
> —Isaiah 46:9–12

To realize one day that I might not have consecrated myself to Him is daunting. I hoped just because my spiritual temperature waxed and waned did not mean God vacillated toward me. One memorable night, God showed up exquisitely. My family took a road trip to visit Lorna and Ray in Kansas. A countryside of mass wheat and cornfields abounded. I have never seen such huge wheat harvesters working the acres of waving grains. While driving on straight roads, I thought how one could truly give simple directions: "Go straight three miles. Turn at the second mailbox on the left." From a bird's-eye-view, houses, nestled in between large ranches, had to look like a Monopoly hotel piece in comparison. Because towns were located miles apart, a quick run to a grocery store was probably unheard-of.

After a great meal, where we played catch-up, Lorna and I headed outside to sit on her porch. As our conversation droned on, the stars slowly started peeping through the expanse of the sky. The silence in the peaceful countryside was calming. Not having any man-made lights to distort our view, the diamond-like sparkling stars spread across the canvas of heaven and shone brightly. I have not ever before or since seen such a stunning natural phenomenon—such a gift! It was as though the stars were kissing the hem of heaven. I felt so small in comparison.

Years later, I "touched the hem of His garment."

One Sunday, the church bulletin included an invitation for women to attend an all-day seminar about the Person of the Holy Spirit. Intrigued, I signed up. That Saturday's session made a huge impact in my life. Refreshing teaching flooded over me. Just as a hurricane is full of power and might and can flatten trees into toothpicks, true teachings of His Word carry power and might flattening Satan's wiles, making effectual change.

The lessons I learned while sitting under full-gospel teaching were:

> In the beginning, creation was God's idea. He is the Engineer. Jesus agreed to the plan and said, "I love it! I'll do My part." The Holy Spirt said, "I'll help You carry it out. I'll be the oil and the wind to assist the created ones to love us back." I understood God's gift of grace was needed to become more alive and to truly love without abandonment. It was time I started to live under the umbrella of "I'm capable and valuable as much as God says I am."
>
> When the Good Shepherd is trusted and seen as my source of "no want," this stupid, dumb sheep was willing to follow Him anywhere. It was logical to expect to be anointed daily with oil to handle aggravations and annoyances. I sought "surely goodness and mercy." I needed to wake up and live under the calm assurance of His management of my affairs. I wanted to desire Him

and have a ravenous hunger for learning more
about my Engineer, Lover, and Oil.

The days of pew-warming were over. It was time I got off my duff and pursue a totally consecrated life.

After a short but much-needed lunch break (my mind was as full as a soaked-up sponge), the leader resumed part 2 of her session: individual prayer. She recognized her audience was hopefully seeking the Holy Spirit's help to live out the truths that we learned. I wanted my half-filled glass to be overflowing; my dirty, cloudy contacts (vision) to become clearer; and the voice of condemnation inside needed to be quieted so the Wind of Truth could blow through me. The leader asked, "Who wants to have us lay our hands on you and pray over you?" I was one of the first to move to the front row to be nearer the chair, which was positioned in the center (I later dubbed "the hot seat").

Wow! What an experience! I knew what is like to have a most sacred moment when my beautiful daughter was first laid in my arms. I knew what it was like to feel water dripping off my head in baptism that felt like a flood of peace. I can tell you about the contentment that engulfed me after Mike and I repented of our sins before our wedding day.

But nothing compared to the powerful moment of feeling my Lord's blanket of love wrapped around me that day. His love poured over me like a fifty-gallon barrel of liquid warm oil. Soothing tears gushed forth. I lifted my head heavenward and barely felt any hands touching me. It was a private moment between me and my "I Am." I have little recollection of what was actually prayed over me. If a panacea can be described, this was it, or an earthly, heavenly hosted moment, or when Spirit and daughter became one. The oil of warmth and love was more comforting than the thick cushy bed of intimacy I experienced in the luxurious Parisian hotel.

After I got up from my seat to allow others to be prayed over, I had difficulty listening to what was being prayed about for the other women in the room. I joked earlier how Janie and I did not need an airline to fly us back home from our Dallas trip years earlier. We were simply riding on our own "fuel of excitement." Today, I was riding above the clouds and touching the hem of His garment, and I was never letting go! My "bleeding issue" of bad choices, selfish decisions, and having my own way needed to end. Yes, bad decisions make great stories, but the remainder of my days needed to be written on a clean page. I recognized nothing in this world had the answer to my deepest longing. If there was, I would have put in my hope in it. We can't be selfless until we invite the One who made myself to daily guide me. I needed raw, tangible faith in all matters, knowing God got this. My Redeemer lifted the weight of a piano off me.

As I climbed in my car that day, "Unchained Melody" (a favorite golden oldie) started playing on the radio (I would move back and forth between the praise-and-worship music radio station and an oldies' station). With tears of joy coursing down my cheeks, I sang along loudly, transferring the love from Mike to the love of my Savior:

> My Love…I've hungered for Your touch…Time can do so much…are You still mine?…I need Your love…Godspeed Your love to me…lonely rivers flow to the sea…to the open arms of the sea…lonely rivers sigh, wait for me…I'll be coming home, wait for me…And time goes by so slowly…Godspeed Your love to me.

As the Righteous Brothers and I together belted out their top hit song, my fervor was unequal to the urgency of a quarterback. I wanted to desire Him and have a ravenous hunger for learning more about my True Shepherd. I was a willing vessel under new management.

Many times, after that experience, I listened and sang along with the radio with a different slant. Loving golden oldies, my naturally bent mind went to makeshift, applicable titles and lyrics, such as:

Stop (living selfishly) in the name of love
I'm leaving it all up to YOU,
Help me build a bridge over troubled waters,
You're my brown-eyed girl,
Let it (deep desire for You) burn, burn, burn, the ring of fire
The tracks of my (repentant) tears
I'm a believer
I want to hold Your hand
I can't stop loving You
It's now or never
I heard it through the Vine
Build me up
For your love
A change is gon' come...just like the river, I've been a-runnin' ever since
I can't explain
River deep, mountain high love
You'll still love me tomorrow
Reach out, I'll be there"

Within the month, I received a phone call from Judy, the woman in charge of our church's women's Bible studies. She was asking me to consider being a table facilitator for the WOW (Women of the Word) Bible study on Monday evenings. *Do you realize, Judy, I was required to give up my monthly book club at the JOY bookstore for WOW and almost didn't sign up? Now, you want me to be more than a participant?*

Judy went on to explain after reviewing her list of signed-up women, she had no clue whom to ask to be her last table facilitator. Thus, in desperation, she showed the list to our associate pastor, Amos. "Leanne. Ask her. She's the one," he pointed out.

Well, as only our Sovereign God can do, my journey of spiritual growth stretched before me. I tremendously enjoyed studying the Word through several series of Holy-Spirit-inspired-Bible teachers.

Within three years, I was asked to replace Judy and be the evening WOW section leader. For over ten years, forty to sixty women soaked up Jesus Christ's promises and became adorned as His beloved. We anchored down "I know that I know that I know" and stood on His Word during our ebbs and flows of our lives. Women looking for peace, friendships, and a lifeline of hope were cemented together, as we opened our Bibles and learned about the "I am the resurrection and the life." He took dry bones and breathed new life in them, healed us of ovarian and breast cancers, spurred one woman to publish her autobiography, put back together marriages, and prodigal children walked back home.

Another mountaintop experience occurred when I attended a ladies' seminar at Janie's church. The timing of the session was within months of my move south. I assisted Janie in serving an appetizing breakfast to over two hundred women one Saturday. After cleanup, we sat in on the session titled "I Surrender." My heart quickened to teachings that if you want a change in your life, if you want forgiveness and peace and joy that you've never known before, God demands total surrender. He becomes the Lord and the ruler of your life.

The speaker taught from Romans 12:1–2, and snippets from a Billy Graham sermon:

> The 12th chapter of Romans says: "I beseech you therefore, brethren, by the mercies of God, that you present your bodies a living sacrifice, holy, acceptable to God, which is your reasonable service. And do not be conformed to this world, but be transformed by the renewing of your mind, that you may prove what is that good and acceptable and perfect will of God" (verses 1, 2)…It says be transformed; be changed. That's what we need today. Among young and old alike, we need a change—a spiritual change, a moral change. God calls on all of us to make a total

surrender to His Son Jesus Christ…You're surrendering all the time.

God said, "I know the plans I have for you, … plans to prosper you and not to harm you, plans to give you hope and a future" (Jeremiah 29:11, NIV). That's what God says. He's not here to condemn you. He's here to bless you and love you and take you into His arms and say, "I forgive you. I'll change your life. And when you die, you will go to Heaven." That's what God is saying, if you will surrender totally and completely. But you can't hold anything back.

"That you may prove what is that good and acceptable and perfect will of God" jumped out at me like never before. In our time of private meditation, I pondered what that meant for me in my life:

* The "good" will was getting married at barely nineteen and following my parent's cultural traditions.
* The "acceptable" will was repenting of my sin of divorces and marrying Mike.
* The "perfect" will was living out of my remaining days in the center of my Lord's will as never before. I was submitting to my Potter's hands, as He molded me into what He wanted me to be. Perfection will come when I'm wearing my crown of righteousness in heaven.

We also dissected a wisdom nugget of Oswald Chambers from Mark 10:18:

> Peter began to say to Him, "See, we have left all and followed You."
> Our Lord replies to this statement of Peter by saying that "this surrender is for My sake and the gospel's" (10:29). It was not for the purpose

of what the disciples themselves would get out of it. Beware of surrender that is motivated by personal benefits that may result. For example, "I'm going to give myself to God because I want to be delivered from sin, because I want to be made holy." Being delivered from sin and being made holy are the result of being right with God, but surrender resulting from this kind of thinking is certainly not the true nature of Christianity. Our motive for surrender should not be for any personal gain at all. We have become so self-centered that we go to God only for something from Him, and not for God Himself. It is like saying, "No, Lord, I don't want you; I want myself. But I do want You to clean me and fill me with Your Holy Spirit. I want to be on display in Your showcase so I can say, 'This is what God has done for me.'" Gaining heaven, being delivered from sin, and being made useful to God are things that should never even be a consideration in real surrender. Genuine total surrender is a personal sovereign preference for Jesus Christ Himself.

Where does Jesus Christ figure in when we have a concern about our natural relationships? Most of us will desert Him with this excuse—"Yes, Lord, I heard you call me, but my family needs me and I have my own interests. I just can't go any further" (see Luke 9:57-62). "Then," Jesus says, "you 'cannot be My disciple" (see Luke 14:26-33).

True surrender will always go beyond natural devotion. If we will only give up, God will surrender Himself to embrace all those around us and will meet their needs, which were created

> by our surrender. Beware of stopping anywhere short of total surrender to God. Most of us have only a vision of what this really means, but have never truly experienced it.

Now that's a totally consecrated mature Christian! Again, when asked to walk to the front to the altar for prayer, flocks of desperate women willingly sought after a hopeful God to help us fully surrender. I was willing to surrender my will, my career, and my future to whatever the Lord wanted from me. My spirit connected with the Holy Spirit, and I felt indescribable lava of love pour over me once more. I envisioned Jesus collecting in bottles my happy tears of surrender. Someday, I will pour my collected tears over His feet, all the while praising Him for His goodness and mercy have surely followed me all the days of my life.

The summer Mike and I were separated after his job transfer, my friend Val asked me to attend her church one Saturday evening. My anticipation for my unknown future stretched before me. Yes, I knew I was moving to South Carolina. However, there were many unknowns about the details how I would spend my time serving Him and if, and where, I would be employed. Val's husband was on a mission trip to Guatemala and was hoping to have her move down and minister by his side. Both of us were facing huge crossroads in our lives.

The Holy Spirit was palpable in the room that evening. Val and I both blocked out whatever was going on around us. We believed and trusted with resounding "Yes, Lord, Yes, Lord." We were assured, as anointed hands prayed over us and confirmed God's leading. As my tears ran like the Niagara Falls, each one was glistening with hope and a promise. Though I had only little clues how God was directing Mike and me, I knew I could put my trust in Him.

In 2012, I submitted a devotional entry for another "God Stories" volume. Within two years, little did I know what God would ask of me to surrender, submit to, and show as one proof of consecration. I wrote:

Love the Lord your God with all your heart, all your soul, all your strength, and all your mind. And love your neighbor as yourself. (Luke 10:27, NLT)

Being employed for over eighteen years in long-term care, I have been taught and expected to embrace best practices in this industry. Having many beneficial consequences, creating resident-centered-care is one evidence of accomplishing these goals. Regulatory agencies and advocates want to make nursing homes and personal care facilities a great place to live and work. However, the required annual unannounced surveys by the Department of Health can be quite stressful. This almost-a-week-long survey is one method of assuring quality initiatives are being followed and our own policies are in place. If not, deficiencies are cited, which may include monetary fees, if serious enough, with an expected plan of correction. The surveyor's exit interview to announce the score results is a time of great stress and nervousness.

I believe that, simply put, the best practices of scripture is to love the Lord with all my might, soul, and strength and to love my neighbor as I love myself. Pursuing and embracing this best practice every day of the year to assure my heart is Christ-centered will benefit me beyond anything I dare, think, or image. Perhaps every January should be assessment time and an honest evaluation of my love acts toward my Lord and neighbor. As I heard Sheila Walsh say on a TV program lately, "It is the Shepherd's job to lead the sheep home. It is the sheep's job to have a tender heart toward the Shepherd." I love that!

MY LAST LAST NAME IS GRACE

>Lord, please continue to guide me on my path that leads straight into your everlasting arms of love.

Similar to the importance of both sodium and potassium's role in our bodies, it is important I understand I'm a reservoir of God's grace and a giver of grace to people I rub shoulders with. Romans 8 tells us, just as His grace casts out fear, we are called to extend the same. Imagine how our world would be if we all understood this principle!

One Lancaster County community of believers who did this was the Amish of the West Nickle Mines tragedy. Mike and I were on a Bermuda cruise during this event. While getting dressed for dinner, I tuned in to the one available TV channel.

"Hon, come here," I gasped. "I think the news broadcaster said something about a shooting in Lancaster County." I could not believe what my eyes were seeing. The screen showed several distraught Amish women facing away from the camera, looking over a schoolyard fence. I turned up the volume.

"Charles Roberts, a milk truck driver serving the community of his victims, walked into the Nickel Mines one-room Amish school house earlier this morning…what is described as a mass massacre…"

I sat on the bed, stunned. A sour taste welled up inside me. Any appetite for dinner was gone. By the time we did retire for the night, we watched more of the news about this sickening, heart-wrenching event. After we arrived home, I later learned a disturbed father of two children walked into the Amish one-room schoolhouse, October 2, 2006. In a little over thirty minutes, eighteen rounds of the killer's pistol took the lives of five Amish girls, ranging in ages seven to twelve, and injured five more innocent victims; a final shot took the perpetrator's own life.

God's grace was extended that day in a myriad of ways:

* A visiting mother had the opportunity to escape and run to a nearby farm to get help; four other women, either pregnant or carrying infants, were allowed to exit.

* One first-grade Amish girl did not understand the English command to "stay here and do not move"; she only understood Pennsylvania Dutch. She escaped in spite of the threat of being shot and followed her brother out of the building.
* The boys, who were asked to assist with unloading the killer's pickup truck, had no idea the items they were unloading were planned to abuse the little Amish girls and barricade the front door; all boys were allowed to leave.
* Little girls lined up at the chalkboard, thankfully, were not abused as planned before being murdered.
* The quick response of police officers and emergency personnel thwarted, most likely, more victims because the killer committed suicide.
* The wife of the killer did not hesitate to call 911 as soon as she read her husband's suicide note; he had phoned her and admitted to his ill-intentions and how distraught he had been since their first child, born nine years earlier, died within minutes of her birth.
* A first responder needed a healing of the mind from the grotesque images of blood, body parts, and glass that were splattered throughout the classroom, affecting every desk and chair.

Within the week, West Nickel Mines was put on the map and had gotten the attention of world-wide mainstream media. The Worship Center held a memorial service where Michael W. Smith sang the song he wrote about one of the victims, Rosanna. As our hearts were broken, we could only rely on the One who binds up all our wounds.

The world sat back in awe as news reporters shared about the message of forgiveness the Amish displayed within hours and throughout the horrid ordeal. An Amish neighbor comforted Robert's widow; another Amish man, for almost an hour, simply held the killer's father as he wept bitterly. Mrs. Roberts wrote an open letter thanking her Amish community for their acts of kindness, forgiveness, grace, and mercy. She knew healing could only come for her, her children, and the affected Amish families by looking upon the face of the One who understands incomprehensible pain.

Because of the extreme nature of the tragedy, the Amish did allow for a fund to be set up at a local bank to benefit the Amish families and the Robert's family. By 2007, 4.3 million dollars poured into the fund! The Grace-Giver directed the Amish leadership to plow down the schoolhouse within the week. A new school appropriately named New Hope today stands proudly in a field several miles away. Daily scripture readings can be heard within its walls and sustain them over and over and over again.

Sometimes a gift comes wrapped in a barbwired box.

Thought of the Day

Grace is realizing some days I can only pray: Spirit of the Living God, fall afresh on me, melt me, mold me, fill me, and use me. I'm Yours.

Chapter 63

The Best, Mature Me Dancing with Jesus

> And God is able to make all grace abound to you,
> so that in all things at all times, having all that you
> need, you will abound in every good work.
> —2 Corinthians 9:8

HAVE YOU HEARD ABOUT THE mom who asked her son before he headed back to college to empty his bedroom trash can? He forgot. Within a few days, he received a "care package" from good ole' Mom. Oops. What he discovered inside, when he excitedly opened the box, was the stinky forgotten trash from his room! Aren't you glad God doesn't mail us reminders of what things we should have done and didn't do? He doesn't throw away His promises, either, as easily as I have thrown away my marriage vows. God not only knows how to pack the good things in my life in between my "bookends" (from birth to deathbed), He uses His Word to gently nudge me toward character-building and living out the fruit of the Spirit. Why? To become Christlike.

Just as the care-package recipient thought his mom's sense of humor was noteworthy and passed on a picture of the package contents via social media, God is not surprised by any one of my slipups, either. However, He does expect me to repent, turn away from any stinky defilement, and demonstrate His goodness all of my remaining days.

A popular praise-and-worship song by MercyMe is titled "Dear Younger Me" and is packed full of insight. The song encourages one to pretend "if I knew then what I know now," would not we live and think differently? For my eulogy, I put a twist on the song title and would name it "Meeting the Best, Mature Me."

Once I have lived out all my days to my final "bookend," I envision holiest *me*. My prayer is to meet *me* in my purest form, the best me, full of maxed-out, faith-filled days, and my relying on the Holy Spirt occurred moment by moment. Every time, my fleshly responses were so closely related to His responses, others could not tell where my thoughts ended and His began.

The highest self-actualization form (actually making it about self-centeredness and selfishness) of me, I was taught in nursing school, will not even come close to me, as a thick mature, old oak tree. The strengthening source of the tree would be so grounded by such a knotted, intertwined root system of our embrace. The Lord's arms and mine would be difficult to entangle. If a gardener would be called to cut and separate the root system, it would be impossible to do so without maiming the Creator's arm along with mine.

Mature me will have the thickness of an oak tree compiled by circling rings of righteous living. Grace-filled days weaved around and around and built a thick foundation. No one intentionally was able to hug the tree and expected to have their fingertips touch. This mature tree was so fat with fulfillment and love for the Father and others placed in my path, one never expected to reach around it completely. From my attractive, inspired life, others are wooed by the Father too to hug the oak tree from the other side. When your and His fingertips touched, you would never be the same either.

In order to become fat, the tree roots absorbed soil nutrients and transported them upward to their trunk, branches, and leaves. When dying leaves and needles of sin fell, they decayed to become organic matter in the soil, which I named "lessons learned." Organic matter also stored and released nutrients that were then sucked up by plant and tree roots. These nutrients were essential in perpetuating a healthy forest, a group of growing neighboring trees. The forest made up the body of Christ and was designed to provide oxygen, air, and sunlight to the dependent inhabitants. Just as a forest was full of touching trees, we together, assigned and commanded to making disciples, could nourish thirsty souls. No fungus of the enemy could destroy the mature forest either.

The leaves mysteriously fulfilled their purpose by invisibly drinking from the Living Water supply, yet obvious results remained. Chloroform colored the leaves in due season for the benefit of others. No one noticed the boring, plain important branch, which supplied the nutrients to the leaf. Yet, if that had not occurred, no eyes would have been able to gaze upon the stunning leaves, the results of the Source's nourishment. At times, the tree poked energy and fuel to bring about beautiful red, yellow, or burnt orange-colored leaves. When I looked back on my life's journey, at times my "leaves" were facing down toward the ground in reverent worship. Other times, the "leaves" stretched heavenward in anticipation and gratitude for the gift of grace and a life packed full of many blessings.

Every step of the oak tree's process from a healthy acorn (a twinkle in my daddy's eye) to the old oak tree planted by the still (meaning, no resistant tides) waters, which flowed toward heaven's door were planted with purpose. I could be confident my steps were ordered by You.

Eventually, my smiling, translucent dying face will reveal a peace that passes all understanding, tresses of my hair will have washed away regretful tears, as I washed the feet of Jesus in devotion, and my arms will be outstretched to start the dance with my loving Savior. I want to be a miraculous old oak tree who demonstrated what sounds like an impossibility.

The Amplified version of 1 John 2:20–27 speaks about the unction of the Holy Spirt. Unction is the highest experience of anointing through the Holy Spirit. Unction has proven to keep and teach me about all things, as I remained in Him. That is what will help my final "bookend" stand up.

Please, dear God, I want to willingly stop resisting and lean into the rhythm of your slow-dancing footsteps. I plan to listen and anticipate the Shepherd's voice every time I open Your Word. I want to accomplish all Your plans and live out Your divine purposes for me while you grant me breath. Using the spiritual gifts you gave me, I pledge to follow You all the days of my life and anticipate Your whisper, "Well done, my good and faithful servant. Enter into the joy of your Lord."

"Know where the wealthiest place on earth is? The answer: a graveyard! It is wealthy because it is full of books never written, paintings never painted, music never played, businesses never opened, ideas never manifested, and the place where someone's visions and plans died and were never executed—a graveyard, a generational thief is full of potential untapped power and purposes never fulfilled, but buried." This is only one of the nuggets of insight I received sitting under the teaching of Dr. Myles Munroe, who was a guest speaker at the Worship Center. Reading his books about the Holy Spirit and how to maximize your potential have been priceless. I could not take notes fast enough. Below, are some snippets of his teachings: "Pray and believe for knowledge, wisdom, and understanding. Thoughts are your closest friend. Your spirit can only receive what comes through your thought life. Hunger and thirsting after God pleases Him. Nothing is yours until you understand it. God will only tell you what you want to know. Whatever you invest in, you succeed."

Living in Bermuda and experiencing an earthly kingdom differently than me, Dr. Munroe opened my eyes to some clarity about the purpose of the Holy Spirit. He taught me:

> We are a spirit to extend Christ's kingdom. The divine goal of God is to extend His heavenly kingdom. His vision was to establish a colony on earth. The goal was to manifest the glory of heaven on earth. Whatever happens in the kingdom shows up in the colony. A king requires a domain. The first kingdom existed prior to the creation of the physical earth. The first kingdom's mandate or mission statement was to have

> dominion and rule. What is a kingdom? It is a sovereign governing influence over His territory impacting it with His personal will, purpose, and intent, establishing a community of citizens reflecting the nation. God made Adam to make earth like heaven.
>
> The goal of colonization is to transform and make the colony just like the Kingdom. My kingdom is not of this world. The Lord's Prayer includes a phrase about establishing a prototype of the original country in another territory. The role of the governor is to establish the king of kings in the territory. The King decided to send the Holy Spirit back to the governless-earth. The Father/King and the Kingdom came back to earth while the Holy Spirit remained hidden. The Calvary Act was needed to clean the body. The culture thrives on the fruit of the spirit. You cannot lose what you never had. Until you receive what you lost, you are still searching.

Dr. Munroe spoke about the Holy Spirit and compared it to his Bermudan way of life. Kings of kingdoms do not directly extend their influence in the colony. The most important person in a kingdom-colony is the governor: "When he was present, we did not need the king in Bermuda. How do you destroy a kingdom? Destroy the governor (the Holy Spirit). The Bible is full of the King's decrees. You destroy the Holy Spirit when you become your own governor."

Dr. Myles Munroe's book, *The Most Important Person on Earth* (Whitaker House, 2007) reminded me I will continue to be a victim of my own corrupt nature.

> That is why the Creator's design for humankind's life on earth requires that human beings be filled with the very Spirit of the Creator himself—the

> Holy Spirit—the Governor of heaven. As individuals, each of us needs the Governor for true life, purpose, and effectiveness. The breath of the Spirit that originally ignited life in the first human being did so in three distinct ways: (1) in the invisible spirit of man, made in the image of God; (2) in the soul of man—the total human consciousness of mind, will, and emotions; and (3) in the physical body of man, the living vessel housing his spirit and soul. While our King communicates with us individually, it is not his intention that the citizens of his kingdom live in isolation. His plan is a community of kings and priests who will reign on earth. The Governor is the key of life for all of humanity.

To understand God created me as a triune body of spirit, soul, and body gives me the potential to be governed by its physical capabilities. My spirit relates to God (pick up the spirit world), my soul relates to the mental realm (intelligence), and my body relates to the physical environment (to pick up earth). The key to knowing my true potential is recognizing God as my Source. The reason we maximize our potential is so we do not settle for mediocrity, and it can influence others in the kingdom of God.

> Learning to tap the hidden wealth of your potential is the greatest task and the most pressing need of your life because if you do not discover how to expose and use this treasure, you will die with it. This wealth, which is the all-surpassing power of God within you, is never given to be buried. God wants you to release all He gave you for the benefit of others and the blessing of your own life. (Dr. Munroe)

An aha moment was found when reading Hebrews 12:15 about how one can "miss the grace of God" (it could be a chapter title for this book). If I am living out under my self-sufficiency, I am independent from God and not God-dependent. If I miss or fall from grace, I rely on self-performance, and I am my own source and not focused on God as my Source. When I depend on my own strengths for successes and self-efforts, I am basically self-centered.

The scriptures will allow grace to guide me. Amos 9:13–14 reads grace will flow as new wine dripping from the mountains and flowing downhill, and as it flows (Joel 2:9), my heart is intensely satisfied, one who doesn't deserve it. He put a change in me that only He can get credit for. Just as my mother's quilts were patches of Daddy's worn-out shirts and my and my sister's dresses and supplied another extended purpose, painful experiences should be passed on to instill wisdom.

Bottom line, He needs to be the center, and I need to move myself off center. How do I know when I'm the center? When someone offends or insults me, and when I'm more self-conscious than God-conscious. I can do nothing without Him! He needs to be in the center. I need to look up as I walk in His footsteps, not gaze down on my own two feet but look up, look ahead, and follow Him. My feet will follow without making it all about me. One time, I noticed an armed forces gentleman wearing a T-shirt that read, "Pain is weakness leaving my body." My T-shirt would read, "Me is toppling and leaving my body."

As Andrew Wommack says, "The only sin that is going to send people to hell is the singular sin of rejecting Jesus as their personal Savior." A large majority of conservative Mennonites believe they can only hope they will enter heaven. They do not have the full assurance that "by grace you have been saved" (Ephesians 2:4). Hoping you have done enough, done it right, and done it with God and noticing it all makes me exhausted to even think about before I even get started!

Andrew Wommack wrote,

> James 1 is saying that when you come into tribulation, rejoice. But, not because God brought

it. You must resist the tribulation knowing that it is from the devil, but it's an opportunity to put your faith to work. As you work your faith, you'll get experience, and experience will give you hope. You'll be stronger and better because you stood against, resisted, and fought the devil. But if you just sit there, roll over, and let these problems dominate your thinking, "well, it must be God's will," you aren't going to be better or stronger. You'll be destroyed by these tribulations. (*Living in the Balance of Grace and Faith*, Harrison House, 2009)

Charles Stanley wrote about Hebrews 12:10:

The Lord is committed to transforming each of us according to His special plan for our lives. Even His correction is an expression of His loving favor. When we falter or fail, we can rest assured that His amazing grace hems us in and always offers us redemption. Grace is a sphere where we live the Christian life. Internalize this truth…it is the most powerful, life-changing force in the world. What's your response to this miracle?

If you truly grasp this truth, you will never be the same. No, grace is not one of the fruit of the Spirit, nor is it just a mealtime prayer or a name given to a newborn baby girl.

He also said grace is like having a criminal judge tell me that he will take my punishment, serve my time for the crime I committed, and allow me to go scot-free. Unheard of, right? But that is exactly what Christ did. Not to accept this free gift is as ignorant as the guy in a recent news clip: he was carrying a gun case while walking across the campus of a local college. The campus security policeman opened the case and found it full of books. Duh! Whatever was he thinking?

Hurricane Matthew was displaying its fury while I was writing this book. Just as Hurricane Matthew left swaths of damage in its path, my life choices marched in devastation as well. Starting in Haiti in early October, moving through the Caribbean, and spreading up the southeastern coast through the Carolinas, Hurricane Matthew was the focus of the Weather Channel long before actual landfall. As sure as an oncoming train, meteorologists, the experts, were forecasting, predicting, and advising innocent people of Matthew's path. Advanced technology allowed for weather experts to track Hurricane Matthew and the placement of the actual eye of the storm.

Not liking the results, announcers gave repeated pleas to prepare, evacuate, and heed warnings to aid businesses and innocent people, whose only fault was having their address located in the predicted path of the hurricane. The experts' knowledge, past experiences, and training made them confident in both what their brains told them, plus what their eyes could see on radar maps. Sometimes weather forecasts predictions are incorrect or less severe than predicted—always a good thing. Regardless, prayers were sent heavenward, asking for God to cause the storm to remain offshore and turn toward the ocean.

Compared to unpredictable Hurricane Matthew, which some aspects were unknown, my future is known. It is set and secure. I know Christ's position is to make me righteous. As Philippians 3:12–19 tells us, Paul was encouraging the church of Philippi to have the winning mentality realizing their (and our) victory is secure. However, we still must press on to completion in Christ.

Our fill-in pastor, the first Sunday in October during Hurricane Matthew, preached on this text. He reminded us that to "press on" means to vigorously pursue with the desire of obtaining. Because we live in the flesh, we daily fight the sinful nature. However, our goal should be to reach maturity in Christ. Any more than a dead person whose life ended due to the hurricane can help himself, neither can spiritually dead people help themselves outside the completed work of Christ. How is this mystery achieved? Christ, in His love and mercy, pursues you. He wooed me, drew me onto Himself, and now He enables me to achieve maturity and obtain completion in the work of Christ. He wants to do the same for you.

Paul's teaching brings assurance to me if I follow it. I need to completely forget what is behind me: my failures, regrets, moments of pain, and sins. They are all covered under the blood. To "press on" vigorously is an ongoing action verb. A long-distance runner strains toward the finish line; so shall we strain toward the end goal, keeping our eyes on our prize: eternity with Christ Jesus.

Don't neglect the work of Christ or cheapen grace. He handled my past and secured my future. The pastor said dead works and spiritually dead people cause complacency and apathy. Dead works get me nowhere. Earthly-minded ones are far from Christ and on the path of destruction. Their gods satisfy and bring them temporal pleasure in the here and now. Their life is bent on material things. Our job is to repent of our sins and hold true to what we have obtained in our righteous position in Christ. Be eternally minded, not earthly, materially minded. I know who I am in Christ. With the Holy Spirit's help, I am able to press on. Paul asked his followers to imitate him, but not because he was perfect. He wanted them to imitate his pursuit in their trajectory with their "straining" force as they vigorously pursued. Leave your past where it belongs: at the foot of the cross.

We were challenged, "What if what occurred to hundreds of people in Hurricane Matthew's destructive path occurred to you? What if you lost your family, your possessions, your bank account, your health—if all sources of joy were stripped from you? What do you have left? Do you have enough? Would you have what is most important? Do you have Christ? Do you know my Jesus? Yes, if you have Christ, you have all you need! I have a twofold citizenship: American and heaven. I need to live today in lieu of tomorrow, my eternity in heaven.

Our pastor questioned the congregation, does your path include steward gifts of family, friends, opportunities to give? God uses things and people to make us more Christ like. My job is to help others "strain" toward the heavenly prize. Live God glorified every single moment of each and every day. Be dependent on the Lord, and He will guide your steps. As Philippians 1:6 reminds us, it is *His* responsibility to finish the good work that has begun in us. I see more weight is put on my Lord rather than me in this verse. Hallelujah!

During a recent women's conference at church, my pen scurried across the page to take many notes: We all have our treacherous paths this side of heaven. One wise one has said that there are three kinds of people in this world: (1) either you are coming out of a trial (hopefully, not crushed by it), (2) fearful about heading into one (not enjoying life in abundance in your anxious state), or (3) heading into one just around the corner (anticipating you will survive and not be totally crippled by it).

One conference speaker spoke about her treacherous path of her "the valley of weeping" from Psalm 84:5. This scripture is talking about the Jewish pilgrimage to the temple of the Lord and the need to pass through Bacca, which means "valley of weeping." Don't play the comparison game. We all have our specific view from the seat of Christ, just as we have a slightly different view from a football stadium, planetarium, or theater to view center stage. But they all point to Christ.

Our anointed speaker spoke about her tragedy of losing her firstborn to SIDS (sudden infant death syndrome). The Lord birthed in her that the most healing method was in letting go and opening up her hands loosely. Her pain was a doorway into a deeper relationship with God. She found comfort in realizing not one person ever gets lost in the valley of weeping. If Zion is in our sight, an overflowing cup helps in going from strength to strength because God shows up. Our guest speaker reminded us we need not live in the camp of what-if. That is not what God would want.

Rick Joyner wrote,

> The path of life is usually between extremes, and it takes great faith, wisdom, and above all, staying close to the Lord to stay on the path… in the greatest darkness we can find the greatest grace, but it is not a grace that overlooks

our sin. Rather it exposes and extracts the sin, and then the sin nature, from our life. Jesus had seemingly unlimited grace for sinners, but little for the prideful and self-righteous. We are not better than those who did these evil things if we are the recipients of more grace. It is all about grace. It is all about Christ...there is nothing on earth more valuable than the grace and favor of God, and He has made it abundantly available to any who seeks it.

My choice to divorce was following my self-centeredness. I stopped participating in women's Bible studies. I asked the wrong questions of my friends and did not think to ask them to help me be accountable. Someone should have smacked me upside the head (I know, I know. My mom was trying)! It is not about pulling up my bootstraps and making them a little tighter. Walking through life depending on my own abilities, personality, and fruitless living needed to stop. The difference now is I have a reliance on God and not faith in myself only and self-esteem (yes, a healthy place to make decisions). However, my throwing out a lasso and see what gets roped in days are over. I want to steamroll through life with my best-is-yet-to-come God. Problems send me to my knees in prayer, and I want to serve Him with reckless abandonment. Problems force me to literally crawl into my Father's lap and feel His comforting arms and gentle touch.

"I Need You Every Hour" is not just a cozy title to a hymn. It is my motto. Just as a ship is not manufactured to sit in a harbor or an airplane to sit in a hangar, my walk of holiness needs to be a daily striving and leaning on Him. What makes living out faith a verb? Making faith a present action by always seeing the unseen as reality. As the truths of faith and grace washed over me, I learned a church doctrine will not save me. The church will not save me. The blood of Christ has saved me, bought me for an expensive price, and His promises are to be held high.

An ex-Mennonite blogger wrote,

> The war against sin is the same, regardless of our "heritage." If we are not engaged in fighting sin, mortifying the deeds of the flesh, and guarding our souls like Hebrews warns up to do, we are no better off as Mennonites or any other denomination…it is easy to find security in our heritage, rather than repenting of our sin, and placing our hope completely in the finished work of Christ on the Cross.

Just as I attempted to walk in Daddy's same footsteps as a five-year-old little girl in the soft soil of our cornfield, my family should see deep ruts of correct choices finally. Hebrews 12:13–17 speaks about the road of sanctification and a path of holiness. A challenge and litmus test for any believer is maturity. Is my path rutted so deep that my family, following behind me, can easily tread on my same path or "wheel tracks"? Yes, there will be occasion to misstep and make a dusty, incorrect footprint that I am not proud of. But mostly, a path that leads home is full of grace and follows peace. What a privilege we have to follow Him! We do not have to wonder why not, beg, or convince God to spill His will over earth. We are commanded in the Lord's Prayer to pray, "Thy kingdom come, thy will be done."

My hunger for His Word is my spiritual temperature gauge. Just as important as breakfast fuels my body, wearing Gospel-viewed glasses helps me walk in steps that are planted and sure. Travel advisory ahead. Life is rough; tough times will come! However, there is nothing I can do to keep me from Him. As a dirty pig wallows in the mud of the pigpen (and loves having company when rolling about), a stumbling Christian needs to stop wallowing, get up, repent, and take another faith-filled step. When grace impacts a life, one does not want to continue sinning. Just as a heavily seasoned steak permeates with herbs, the Word needs to permeate my life. There were plenty of times I was waiting on God, but mostly God was waiting on me.

There is a reason what surrounds the heavenly throne is described to be like crystal (Revelation 4:10). I picture a large pond of it surrounding the throne, which could carry lots of weight. Think your problem is too "weighty" for God? Think again. As we turn over problems and concern to Him, His gifts of comfort, protection, and grace are dropped over us like snowflakes in a snowstorm, flashes of lights in a storm, and sunbeams on a hot summer day.

Daily look for his gifts of grace. Several years ago, I read a book titled *Surprise Me, God* by Terri Easu. He challenged believers to do a thirty-day experiment and look for God's surprises. I took on the challenge. How inspiring to read my journal at that time. Some entries on God's faithfulness of His daily surprises ranged from a simple, gorgeous sunset to a coworker's uplifting comment to me, "I have never seen so many miracles around here at work since you started here."

Being sensitive to relatives and friends who continue to live in legalism and under many church regulations of dos and don'ts, I am grateful I was awakened from legalism and piety. For some, there is no hope or a way of escape as a works-mentality tradition has seeped into their core. This way of life is all they know in how to live as a Christian.

I so appreciate God directing my path to sit under the teaching of Rhema Bible College–trained Pastor Sam of the Worship Center. Pastor Sam taught Mike and me there is not one thing, not one iota, God expected for me to do that would earn me more of His favor or grant me more grace. Living under my previous religious background of works mentality, I believed when I was following the church's ordinances that God smiled the broadest smile over me. I fell into the trap of linking God's responses to my performances. It was similar to my childhood hopscotch game: messed up, one foot in hell; repented, both feet in heaven—oops, removed my head covering, both feet in hell. Carrying the burden of trying to move God's hand in my corner every day and carrying the suitcase full of shameful actions for a time was stealing my peace and eventually killed my walk with God.

But by sitting under Pastor Sam's biblical foundational teaching on the balance of faith and grace, I absorbed God's truth like a sponge. As my inner well was being filled up and refreshed with Living Water, the tears flowed every Sunday for an entire year! Singing many praise-and-worship songs about my Father's love, I had a "heart transplant" stitched by my Lord's hand that was a secure, permanent surgery. Realizing there were no little or big sins, I relished in the thought my heavenly Father *desired* a relationship with me. Not accepting His complete work on the cross by faith can only cheapen grace. He was not to be looked upon as a slave driver waiting to push me off the hopscotch block to punish me. Nor was I to compare Him to my somewhat emotionally distant earthly father.

How refreshing to understand that the stepping stones on my earthly path are marked *grace*, *faith*, *salvation*, and *trust*. The results of my search on how to live a holy life as a believer in Christ's full redemptive work brought full understanding. Providing grace is God's part. Believing in God's plan of salvation is my part. No works or "no thing" can change that. But it is only by God's grace that I can even attempt to walk a path of holiness. Believing that all my past sins, today's sins, and all of tomorrow's sins are covered under Jesus's blood is priceless. Hallelujah! Read that sentence again, dear reader! When have you last heard that freeing message preached from your pulpit?

By God's grace and mercy, you do not have to live in bondage and feel enslaved. But if grace, as seasoned throughout my legacy, has sparked a hunger or an interest in the possibility that some amazing grace is indeed needed to give you some freedom, please pray about it. With an open mind, study scriptures on grace. Read Charles R. Swindoll's book titled *Grace Awakening* (Word Publishing, 1996) and other inspired authors who understand that grace needs to become your "last name."

My stepping-stone path, labeled with grace and mercy, is headed toward my heavenly gates. But it is running beside my neighbor's path as well. Just as our vertical relationship with our heavenly Father is based on being saved through faith, a gift of God, our horizontal relationships, as we rub shoulders with each other, must be seasoned with offering grace to others. We are commanded to love one another. Many times, I can only do that with God's grace! Acts 13:43 commands us to "continue in the grace," making that an action on my part. Simply making progress on our walk of holiness is a tribute to God's grace.

What one focuses on is most important. D-day proved this point very clearly. There were a portion of soldiers that focused on the storm and ended up seasick. The group planted on the gangplank only focused on the obstacle (the enemy) they faced. However, those soldiers who focused on ground cover experienced the victory. We have an "I Am, in Me, you are, we together can, it is done" religion.

Being raised Mennonite, I was not taught how to dance. I have no memory of standing on top of Daddy's shoes, as in typical of fathers when teaching their daughters how to dance for when they are a future bride. Wedding receptions I attended did not give opportunity to practice my dance steps either as a youngster or teenager. Also, I was not allowed to attend my middle-school dances, or later on my high-school prom.

In my midthirties, when I no longer attended a Mennonite church, I would venture out to nightclubs or attend a high school reunion where I was given the opportunity to dance. Though I enjoyed listening to music and could feel the beat of it, I always felt I was not a very good dancer. I wanted to perfect both slow and fast dancing while spending many a night with girlfriends at the Jukebox, but I did not achieve that goal. One night, I was asked to slow dance for the second time. I felt uncomfortable slow dancing with my partner. Shoes would hit each other, and I'm sure toes of his were stepped on. Don't even think about dipping me!

However, the Word tells me my Father is preparing a heavenly place for me (John 14:2). Also in scripture, I read five different crowns are promised to overcomers:

> The incorruptible crown (1 Corinthians 9:24–27)
> The crown of rejoicing (1 Thessalonians 2:19–20)

The crown of life (James 1:12, Revelation 2:10)
The crown of righteousness (2 Timothy 4:8)
The crown of glory (1 Peter 5:24)

So when the woes of this world weigh me down or when my heart is burdened, I daydream of heaven. I picture a mansion designed by Him with me in mind. Certainly bigger than any house I ever lived in here on earth, my heavenly mansion in my dream will have a huge foyer. What will the foyer be used for? Just like a bride with her Bridegroom, we will be dancing perfectly to heavenly worship music. With a crown of glory sparkling much brighter than Queen Elizabeth's jewels ever did, I will feel elegant, confident, and very comfortable as a dancing bride.

Not knowing what it was like to dance on my father's toes, I know His agape love will complete me. My heavenly Father's love and grace brings comfort and reassurance to me. Now when He reaches out for my hand to lead me around the dance floor, I will feel whole, forgiven, and loved unconditionally! When Jesus and I dance together, He will be calling me by my promised new name (Revelation 2:17). At the end of our dance, He will be worthy and deserves for me to lay my crown at His feet. He will be praised for evermore!

Does the evil of this Satan-owned world make you weary? Are you tired of facing one more day of battling the demons within you? Are you fed up with your failures in your daily life? Feeling like you're always losing, never winning, and not growing into a mature Christian?

Just breathe, daughter, and step on to the dance floor. Your Partner right now is lovingly smiling at you and holding out His hand. Grasp it tightly and let His supreme love engulf you today. Together, you will be an overcomer. Come quickly, Lord Jesus! Your dance partner is waiting.

You understand now, dear reader, why my title for this book is so appropriate. What a journey I have been on sharing my heart and soul with you! Hopefully, you noticed how my story is sprinkled with

MY LAST LAST NAME IS GRACE

God's grace throughout its pages. It is only because of His grace I was even able to muddle through it all and type my last sentence. Tears will flow freely as I hear Him call me by my last, last name, "Grace, you are home!"

"Such Amazing Grace"

God designed it I be born in rich America on Pennsylvania soil
Not the daughter of a Mexican farmer, or town crier
But into a Mennonite family, whose large garden took many hours of toil,
...such amazing grace.

Grandparents' decisions over mode of transportation: car or horse?
Cemented the path for my Dad to drive his family around in a Ford
But plenty of cousins passed me and waved from their buggy, of course.
...by the grace of God, go I.

Public school teachers, who influenced me, could read "Look upon the hills from whence comes my help"
While Sunday school leaders rewarded my memorization efforts with Bibles,
Pulpits abounded with hell and brimstone sermons causing my repentant heart to melt
...by His amazing grace.

Friends wore pigtails like me and had no bad Daddies; we spent our childhood playing in hay mows and meadows

While our neighbors were watching on their TV, the "Jetsons" or "The Adams Family,"
My innocent naive mind and stature grew, albeit a short one, making Daddies our heroes,
…such amazing grace.

A family of nine fulfilled the quiver-full for my parents, who taught us all to tithes and work hard,
We were middle class, average in looks, brains, and endeavors,
The "dys" in dysfunction was spilt out only in a thimble-full and not a size too large,
…such amazing grace.

My parents' combined gene pool included gumption, spunk, and a willingness to forge ahead
Being the first to graduate, I taught in a two-room parochial school
Before becoming a mommy of three and embracing motherhood instead
…such amazing grace.

Then anger and dark clouds arose out of my ashes of two divorces, and I turned away from God on high
To be a "black sheep, stupid and crazy," were applied labels
My parents looked elsewhere, scolded, and left me to sink in my own muck and mire
…but amazing grace found me.

Since marriages didn't fulfill me, perhaps nursing school will, so as a 40-year old, I began to attend

MY LAST LAST NAME IS GRACE

Hard work, making new friendships and eventually holding a degree in my hand,
My life purpose was temporarily found in caring for residents and helped my broken heart to mend
…such amazing grace.

Nothing like grandchildren, to give and receive unconditional love, a healing balm of sorts
Husband number three came along in the nick of time to save me from myself
One church hurt me, but another one healed me, as I sang about a Heavenly chorus
…about God's amazing grace.

By now seven grandchildren fill my quiver and they each have personality to boot,
No one is a druggie, had a face on a milk carton, or visited Saint Jude.
My heart expanded to love as the number grew and no Nana is more proud of her brood,
…such amazing grace.

What is this amazing grace that I surely don't deserve, whether rich or poor, black or white from arms opened wide?
A gift bestowed on all once we opened the cracked door and answered His persistent knock from the other side
A path that leads to fulfillment, peace, understanding and aha moments
…called amazing grace.

How do I want to be remembered? What is left to accomplish? What message is still hidden inside?

BEATY MILLER

A pearl necklace remains unpurchased in the jewelry store unable to be passed down,
But the unseen pearls of wisdom I surely earned must be dusted off and not laid aside,
…nuggets of amazing grace.

Sometimes my pearl necklace breaks and I go scrambling to pick them up, restring, and reapply,
One spells Love, another Faith, Eternity, Joy; once again each touches the other
The measure of grace is boundless, limitless, and poured out from on High.
….do you know His amazing grace?

Sixty plus years and counting, my pearls of wisdom are about to be traded in,
The day is coming when the eleven-membered Martin clan will sit at the Lord's Supper
In exchange for believing in my Lord's promises, He'll take my pearls of experiences
And trade them for a crown of Righteousness.
…and give me a new name: My Last Last Name is Grace

About the Author

BEATY MILLER BROKE THE MENNONITE tradition and continued her education past eighth grade and graduated high school from Cocalico High School. Beaty began her career as a secretary with the Mennonite Central Committee in Akron, Pennsylvania. At nineteen years of age, she accepted the position to teach at a parochial school in Lebanon County. Later, as a single mom, she resumed a full-time job as a secretary for Four Seasons Produce in Denver. After a promotion to the office manager, Miller started classes at Reading Area Community College and earned an Associate Degree of Applied Sciences to become a registered nurse.

Upon graduation, she began a twenty-year geriatrics career with long-term care in nursing homes, ending as a Personal Care Home Administrator in Pennsylvania. Her desire to help others became a reality, and she flourished in confidence and life purpose. Beaty was praying to find a godly man as a husband, and she found that person in Mike Miller. Their search for a more fulfilling life and work led Mike to accept a position with Billy Graham Evangelistic Association, and they relocated to the beautiful Southern town of Rock Hill, South Carolina, a suburb of Charlotte, North Carolina.

Beaty and Mike are currently active members of the congregation of North Rock Hill Church. Beaty spends her days when she is not writing and creating speaking platforms with her Waterfalls of Grace ministry in various Bible study groups within her church, neighborhood, and community. She volunteers with a nearby retirement community's programs and hones her writing skills in creative writing classes. Visits with her children and their families are frequent and wonderful times. Beaty looks forward to her speaking engagements with churches, community organizations, and women's groups so that she can share her story of the gifts of God's grace throughout her life. She hopes to inspire others to seek to heal from their life storms and to recognize and celebrate the gifts of God's grace in their own lives. Grace continues to pour out onto Beaty's life in wondrous ways.

Log onto Waterfallsofgrace.org to contact Beaty Miller to book speaking engagements or as method to contact author and to view more pictures of her Mennonite heritage, etc.